AMERICAN DREAMS

LOST AND FOUND

AMERICAN DREAMS

LOST AND FOUND

STUDS TERKEL

THE NEW PRESS
New York

LIBRARY OF CONGRESS CATALOGING-IN-PUBLICATION DATA
Terkel, Louis.
American dreams: lost and found.
1. United States Biography. 2. Interviews. 3. National characteristics, American.
I. Title.
CT220.T42 920'.073 80-7703
ISBN 1-56584-545-5

Published in the United States by The New Press, New York
Distributed by W. W. Norton & Company, Inc., New York

The New Press was established in 1990 as a not-for-profit alternative to the large, commercial publishing houses currently dominating the book publishing industry. The New Press
operates in the public interest rather than for private gain, and is committed to publishing,
in innovative ways, works of educational, cultural, and community value that are often
deemed insufficiently profitable.

www.thenewpress.com

Design by Susan Mitchell
Printed in the United States of America

9 8 7 6 5 4 3 2 1

To Nelson Algren

Amazing grace, how sweet thy sound
That saved a wretch like me
I once was lost, but now am found
Was blind but now I see.

—An American hymn

All people dream: but not equally.
Those who dream by night
in the dusty recesses of their minds
wake in the day to find that it was vanity.
But the dreamers of the day
are dangerous people,
for they may act their dream with open eyes
to make it possible.

—T. E. Lawrence

CONTENTS

i x

CONTENTS

Fantasia

True Believer

Arriving: Then

Generations: First and Second

Arriving: Now

Going and Coming

x

CONTENTS

Stirrings in the Neighborhood

BOOK TWO

Visions

Winning

Gathering and Letting Go

Mother & Son

Politics

CONTENTS

Touching Thirty

The Woods

The Train

ACKNOWLEDGMENTS
AND APOLOGIES

I am especially grateful to my editor, André Schiffrin. His soft-spoken encouragement during recurring moments of self-doubt are evident in these pages. His associates Ursula Bender and Tom Engelhardt, as the project was nearing its end, came through with patently helpful suggestions. My thanks to Donna Bass, for her bright-eyed look at this mountain of copy, and to Connie Allentuck, for listening to my long-distance digressions.

For the fifth time around, Cathy Zmuda transcribed hundreds of thousands of words—in this instance, a cool million, I suspect—onto pages that sprang to life. As the pressure grew, there was gallant assistance by Valentine Regan, Dru Cass, Florence McNaughton, and Kathy Cowan.

My colleagues at radio station WFMT, notably Ray Nordstrand, Norman Pellegrini, Lois Baum, and Jim Unrath, were once again remarkably cooperative during my prolonged leaves of absence. As usual, I gave them a hard time. Theirs was a patience that passeth understanding, as was my wife's, who, for the millionth time, heard it all.

Finally, a salute to my extraordinarily selfless scouts: Sandy McCall, who drove me hundreds of miles over southern California cement; Tony Judge, who drove me through New England country, wholly unfamiliar; John Platt and Elizabeth Furse, who drove me toward the timberlands of the Northwest; Gary Voghtman, who drove me from the bluegrass country to eastern Kentucky; Otho Day and Henry Osborne, who drove me from Tougaloo College, across expressways and dirt roads, to a Mississippi farm; Ed McConville, who guided me through the Carolinas; Bill and Dorothy Ojala, who were my hosts and cicerones in northern Minnesota; and Mary Cygan, who led me to a Chicago neighborhood I didn't know as well as I thought I did.

To those friends, acquaintances, and wayfaring strangers who so generously offered me tips and God knows how much time they spent on the telephone calling others: "I know someone who knows someone who knows exactly the person you're looking for . . .": Randy Harvey, Eloise Jones, Sid Blumenthal, Bella Stumbo, Jerry Ward, Bennett Snyder, Norman Ross, Elma Griesel, Pat Powers, Ellen Frank, Carey McWilliams, Ann Banks, Bill McClory, Judith Wax, Vivian Cadbury, Gerry Temaner, Barbara Burton, Moe Foner, Bill Newman, James Graham, Jack Scott, Esther Ohr, Dick Simpson, Paul Terkel, Pastora Cafferty, Bill Spraggins, Quentin Young, Ron Schiffman, Deedee Halkin, Pat Lyons, Beatrice Neiburger, Chuck Gardenier, George Ballis, Will D. Campbell, Myles Horton, Barbara Knuckles, Henry de Zutter, Don Klimovich, and Marvin Miller.

It is no hyperbole to suggest that this book is a result of a collective intelligence and curiosity.

Not included in this book are about two hundred people whom I visited. Each, I discovered, was a singular person, imaginative in his/her own way. Each graciously offered me time, in many instances discommoding himself/herself. Each was generous in recounting a personal life and reflecting on a public dream. Their noninclusion is due to others covering a similar terrain and to my zig-zagging without compass through uncharted country. As a sportscaster would put it, mine were judgment calls. To these two hundred, my apologies and profound gratitude. In a deeper sense, they are in these pages.

—Studs Terkel
Chicago
February 1980

INTRODUCTION

At the end of the most extraordinary period of transformation in human affairs, old landmarks have disappeared, new ones are not yet recognized as such, and intellectual navigation across the suddenly estranged landscapes of human society becomes unusually puzzling for everybody.

—Eric Hobsbawm

For the nine-year-old boy, in 1921, traveling on that day coach from New York to Chicago, it was simple. And exhilarating. Though he wasn't the proper British butler Ruggles, whose mind was boggled by images of a Wild West and equally wild Indians in multifeathered headgear, the boy envisioned a midwest that, too, was frontier country.

It was a twenty-four-hour journey, clickety-clacketing through the outskirts of large and middle-sized Pennsylvania cities, through the main streets of small Ohio towns, of sudden appearances in the aisles of hawkers bawling out their wares, of steaming hot coffee and homemade sandwiches, of local newspapers called *The Globe, The Sun, The Star, The Planet.* Yes, *The Herald,* too, for something terribly exciting was being heralded. It was a momentous adventure, uniquely American. Out there was more: a reservoir of untapped power and new astonishments.

"One of my earliest memories was a trip across the country with my grandfather." A Chicago physician reflects in 1979. He is the grandson of the late General Robert E. Wood, who was, at the glowing time, chairman of the board of Sears, Roebuck and Company. *"We were sitting in the engineer's cab. It was the Great Northern. We were going through the mountains. The steam engine was a huge one. I remember thinking how big the country was and how powerful the engine. And being with someone as powerful and confident as my grandfather. It was about 1940. I was seven and optimistic."*

The sprawl of the Chicago stockyards, whose smells on a summer night, with a stiff breeze blowing from the south, overwhelmed the boy. It was not at all unpleasant to him, for there was a sense of things happening, of propitious times ahead. The condition of those who had actually worked in *The Jungle*, revealed some fifteen years earlier by Upton Sinclair, had caused something of a stir, but time, benign neglect, and editorial silences had deliquesced public indignation.

Warren Gamaliel Harding, handsome, silver-haired, genial, was our president. Hollywood couldn't have done better. He was a cross between Francis X. Bushman and Theodore Roberts. Normalcy was on the wing, and the goose hung high. 1923. Came the first political scandal in the boy's memory: Teapot Dome. It was, the teachers told him, an aberration. Corruption was not endemic to the American scene. Bad apples in every barrel. And our barrels, praise God, have been a fruitful lot.

It was another story the boy heard in the lobby of his mother's hotel. The guests were boomer firemen, journeymen carpenters, and ex-Wobblies, as well as assorted scissorbills* and loyal company men. The cards were stacked, groused the former, between rounds of solitaire, hearts, and cribbage. If you don't like it, go to Russia, retorted the others. Inevitably, the wild political arguments became highly personal, fueled as most were by bootleg whiskey.

"The early part of the century was an exciting period in the life of the United States." The ninety-five-year-old economist taps his memory. *"Almost every community had a channel of expression: city clubs, trade union central bodies, forums, Cooper Union. Speakers would go from state to state, town to town, get ten dollars here, fifty dollars there. There were thousands who would come to hear Gene Debs, myself, Clarence Darrow, crowds, crowds, filling Madison Square Garden."*

---

* A scissorbill was the pejorative ascribed to the workingman who was pro-boss and anti-foreigner. A turn-of-the-century piece of doggerel was perversely dedicated to him.

> You're working for an Englishman
> You room with a French Canuck
> You board in a Swedish home
> Where a Dutchman cooks your chuck.
> You buy your clothes from a German Jew
> You buy your shoes from a Russian Pole
> You place your hopes on a dago Pope
> To save your Irish soul.

Ed Sprague and Big Ole were the two most eloquent and hot-tempered lobby performers. The others, usually full of piss and vinegar, were unusually subdued when these two had the floor. Ed was much for words, though little for food. He dined on graveyard stew, bread broken up in a bowl of hot milk. He had no teeth: they had been knocked out by vigilantes in Seattle during the general strike of 1919. In no way did it interfere with his polemics, bellowed through snuff-stained gums. It was mortal combat between himself and the devil: big business. The boy was reminded of Billy Sunday, exorcising *the* devil: "I'll stomp him, I'll punch him, I'll bite him and, by God, when my teeth are all gone, I'll *gum* him back to hell!"

Big Ole was Ed's *bête noire*, closest at hand. He defended John D. Rockefeller, J. P. Morgan, Henry Ford, and gloried in Teddy Roosevelt's credo of soft words and the big stick. He was Ed's equal in decibel power. They were wrestling, not so much for the hearts and minds of the others as for the pure hell of it. Theirs was the American yawp. Every man a king. Every man a Demosthenes. It was a fouling, gouging, no-holds-barred match: Hackenschmidt versus Frank Gotch. Along with the others, the boy was enthralled, for it was, behind the wild expletives and runaway metaphors, power they were "discussing." Of the potent few and the impotent many.

"If you listen to any president of the United States," says Nicholas Von Hoffman, " 'power' is a word he never discusses. Senators never use that word either. It gets people thinking. Who knows where your thinking might take you? If you don't talk about power, it's like not lifting the hood of the automobile. You don't know how the damn thing works."

Ed Sprague and Big Ole had three things in common. Each was singularly skilled with his hands, a craftsman. Each visited Gladys on Sunday mornings. She ran a crib along Orleans Street. It was Ed's defiance of God and Ole's show of reverence, one of the weisenheimers put it. Gladys was fond of both; she favored lively men. She favored quiet men too. Gladys was an egalitarian, and a true entrepreneur. Each wrote letters to the editor with the regularity of a railroad timepiece. When, in the course of human events, the name of one or the other would appear on the editorial page, it was an occasion for celebration. Let the record show that Ole Hanson's name appeared more often than Ed Sprague's.

One of the more sober and scholarly guests at the hotel turned

the boy on to E. Haldeman-Julius Blue Books. They were small paperbacks, encompassing the writings of all the world's wise men—and
an occasional wise woman—from the Year One. Published in Girard,
Kansas, twenty such books would come to you in return for one buck
plus postage. An especially fat one would go for a dime. Aristotle,
Voltaire, Fabre on the life of the mason bee, a nickel apiece. All of
Shakespeare's tragedies, a dime. Not a bad buy. These booklets, fit-
ting neatly in the hip pocket, became his Dr. Eliot's Five-Foot Shelf.

It was his first acquaintance with the writings of Tom Paine. In
school, he had been taught the troublemaker's words about times that
try men's souls, but not his words that challenged men's minds. "As
America was the only spot in the political world where the principles
of human reformation could begin, so also was it the best in the natural
world. The scene which that country presents to the spectator has something in it which generates and enlarges great ideas. He sees his species,
not with the inhuman eye of a natural enemy, but as kindred. . . ."

*In the woods of northwest Oregon, the embattled logger neglects the
breakfast the waitress has laid out before him. His thoughts are elsewhere, and his fervor. "The forest to me is an awesome and beautiful
place. The young loggers were not here to see what was there before.
If you've never known something, it's difficult to appreciate what's
been lost. What happened to all that majestic timber? I believe that
only by being in the presence of beauty and great things in the world
about us can man eventually get the goddamn hatred of wanting to
kill each other out of his system. The beauty is going."*

*The traveling singer from Idaho no longer experiences the ances-
tral pull toward her hometown. "Boise hardly exists for me any more.
All the things I remember with pleasure have been torn down and
replaced by bullshit. . . . Downtown Boise, all covered, is like a cattle
chute for customers. It used to be like a little cup of trees. Just trees
and this river. Old, old houses and a sense of community. None of
that's there any more. It's all gone."*

In the mid sixties, while journeying through the farm states on the
prowl for depression storytellers, I came upon Marcus, Iowa, along
the South Dakota border. Population: 1,263. At the supermart, the
three people I encountered were unaware of the man I was seeking;

his father had founded the town. The checker at the counter, seemingly at home, thought "the name's familiar, but I just can't place it." For her, too, it was an estranged landscape.

A few days later, in the town of Le Mars, I was walking toward a hamburger joint. It was at night. It may have been on the outskirts of town; as I recall, there was no sidewalk. A patrol car slowed down beside me. The two policemen were curious, that's all. Nobody else was walking.

"We began pretty well here in America, didn't we?" Jessie Binford, Jane Addams's old colleague, asked herself rhetorically, as she, in 1963, returned to her hometown, Marshalltown. Her father had founded it. "When you think of all the promise in this country . . . I don't see how you could have found much greater promise. Or a greater beginning. Yet the commonest thing I feel in this town is fear of the unknown, of the stranger. Fear, fear. We should have the intelligence and courage to see the many changes that come into the world and will always come. But what are the intrinsic values we should not give up? That's the great challenge that faces us all."

The twenties, the time of the boy's train ride, were neither the best of times nor the worst, though innocence, like booze, brings forth its morning-after hangover. A better world was acomin', the boy felt. How could it miss? There was so much of it, so many frontiers. And what, with so much inequity, so much room for improvement.

With Bob LaFollette and George Norris, senators of independent mind, ringing the bell in the night—a warning of power in fewer and fewer hands—Americans, aware of sharp truths and even sharper dangers, would respond. With the certitude of a twelve-year-old, and the roaring eloquence of the hotel guests remembered, the boy was never more certain. What he did not quite understand was that infinitely lesser men were awarded much more attention, much more printer's ink. In later years, the clones of Coolidge, expertly machine-tooled and media-hyped, have done, and are doing, equally well. Ed Sprague's thunder still rolls in the boy's ear: "Who owns these things? Who makes scrambled eggs of our brains? In their stately mansions, they rob us of our stately minds."

Cannot Hannah Arendt's "banality of evil" be subject to transposition: the evil of banality? In 1792, Paine observed: "The mighty objects he beholds act upon the mind by enlarging it, and he partakes of the greatness he contemplates." In 1972, the less fraudulent of our two presidential candidates, on winning the California primary, beamed over all three networks: "I can't believe I won the whole thing." Thus did an Alka-Seltzer commercial enrich our political vocabulary.

Vox populi? Is that all there is to the American Dream, as celebrated in thousands of sixty-second, thirty-second, and ten-second spots each day on all channels? A mercantile language, debased, and nothing else? Is there no other language, no other dream?

"Some people may think it's childish of me, a poor white, to have faith in the deep yearnings of my people," says a woman from the South. "They're much like the people of Mexico. If a person in their midst is identified as a poet or he can draw or play an instrument, this person has stature." (Remember the surge of pride in Pa Joad's voice as Connie picked up the guitar and sang? "That's my son-in-law.")

"It's amazing, even in the backwoods of Alabama, there's a classic tucked away in some country school. It's funny, poetry has a way of molding people. There's a buried beauty—(suddenly) Gray's Elegy *changed my life. Who knows who's buried, who could have been what? The men in power should get all the poetry out of schools, anything that touches on real beauty. It's dangerous."*

The ninety-year-old Pole who came here in 1896 and worked his livelong life in the mills still hungers. "I used to attend lectures at Hull House. The things that bothered me were so many things I couldn't understand. There was a professor from the university lecturing on relativity, Einstein. The worst of it was I didn't understand half the words he used. I never understood relativity. I guess I got too old and too tired."

Kuume is the Finnish word for fever. It was the American fever. They came early in this century and at the turn. All to the land, by nature and industry blessed. To make it, of course, and to escape, as well, the razor's edge and, in remarkably many instances, the Old Country draft. Their mothers didn't raise their boys to be soldiers, either. The manner in which they came varied with geography and circumstance. In all cases, it was hard travelin'.

A wooden ship across the North Sea, "with sugarloaf waves, so the boat would rock, where you just crawled into bunks," to Liverpool, the *Lucania*, and on to America. Another: from Italy, by way of Marseilles, "all by myself," on the *Sardinia*, hence to El Dorado, which turned out to be a Massachusetts textile mill. A third: from an Eastern European *shtetl*, "ten of us," by wagon to Warsaw, by train to Hamburg, by train to Liverpool, and five weeks on a freighter to the land of milk and honey. For most, it was *mal de mer* most of the way. For all, it was *kuume* all the way.

When in 1903—or was it '04?—my mother and father came to the United States from the Old Country, their dream was not unique. Steady work and schooling for the boys, who were born during the following decade. He was a tailor, a quiet man. She was a seamstress, nimble of finger and mind. He was easy, seeking no more than his due. She was feverish, seeking something more. Though skilled in her craft, her spirit was the entrepreneur's. Out there, somewhere, was the brass ring. This was, after all, America.

When my father became ill and was unable to work, she made the big move. Out west, to Chicago. She had a tip: a men's hotel up for sale. 1921. It was hard work, but she toughed it out. She was an *hôtelière*, in business for herself. She was May Robson, Apple Annie, making it. These were no apples she was selling; she was a woman of property. They were pretty good years, the twenties. But something went wrong in '29, something she hadn't counted on. The men she admired, the strong, the powerful ones, the tycoons (she envisioned herself as a small-time Hetty Green), goofed up somewhere. Kerplunk went her American Dream.

Most of her tight-fisted savings were lost with the collapse of Samuel Insull's empire. It was a particularly bitter blow for her. He was the industrialist she had most admired, her Chicago titan. She had previously out-jousted a neighborhood banker. R. L. Chisholm insisted on the soundness of his institution, named, by some ironic God, The Reliance State Bank. Despite his oath on his mother's grave and his expressed admiration for *my* mother's thrift, she withdrew her several thousand. His bank closed the following day. Yet the utilities magnate took her, a fact for which she forgave neither him nor herself.*

The visit to R. L. Chisholm on that day of reckoning was a memorable one. At my mother's insistence, I accompanied her to the bank. Often, I had strolled there to the deposit window. Now came the time of the big withdrawal. The banker, a dead ringer for Edward Arnold, was astonished and deeply hurt. He had been, after all, her friend, her advisor, the keeper of her flame. Didn't she trust him? Of course she

---

* *Hard Times: An Oral History of the Great Depression* (New York: Pantheon Books, 1970).

did; her reservations, though, outweighed her trust. It was an epiphanic moment for me as I, embarrassedly, observed the two. The conversation, which had begun with firm handshakes all around, easy talk, a joke or two, and a semblance of graciousness, ended on a somewhat less friendly note. Both, the banker and my mother, were diminished. Something beyond the reach of either one had defeated both. Neither had the power over his own life worth a damn.

My mother's gods had failed her; and she, who had always believed in making it, secretly felt that she, too, had failed. Though the following years didn't treat her too unkindly, her fires were banked. Her dreams darkened. She died a bitter, cantankerous old woman, who almost, though never quite, caught the brass ring.

Failure was as unforgivable then as it is now. Perhaps that's why so many of the young were never told about the depression; were, as one indignant girl put it, "denied our own history."

The young mechanic, driving me through the bluegrass country to eastern Kentucky, lets it out, the family skeleton. His father, a fast-talking salesman, was Willy Loman. "I always identified with Willy's son Biff. My father's staying with me and my wife. My brothers' wives don't want him around. They come right out and say so. I think he represents the horror of failure. Both my oldest brothers and my father were steeped one hundred percent in the idea of strength and supremacy, machismo and success."

During the Christmas bombings of North Vietnam, the St. Louis cabbie, weaving his way through traffic, was offering six-o'clock commentary.

"We gotta do it. We have no choice."

"Why?"

"We can't be a pitiful, helpless giant. We gotta show 'em we're number one."

"Are you number one?"

A pause. "I'm number nothin'." He recounts a litany of personal troubles, grievances, and disasters. His wife left him; his daughter is a roundheel; his boy is hooked on heroin; he loathes his job. For that matter, he's not so crazy about himself. Wearied by this turn of conversation, he addresses the rear-view mirror: "Did you hear Bob Hope last night? He said . . ."

Forfeiting their own life experience, their native intelligence, their personal pride, they allow more celebrated surrogates, whose imaginations may be no larger than theirs, to think for them, to speak for them, to *be* for them in the name of the greater good. Conditioned toward being "nobody," they look toward "somebody" for the answer. It is not what the American town meeting was all about.

Yet, something's happening, as yet unrecorded on the social seismograph. There are signs, unmistakable, of an astonishing increase in the airing of grievances: of private wrongs and public rights. The heralds are from all sorts of precincts: a family farmer, a blue-collar wife, a whistle-blowing executive. In unexpected quarters, those, hitherto quiescent, are finding voice. A long-buried American tradition may be springing back to life. In a society and time with changes so stunning and landscapes so suddenly estranged, the last communiqués are not yet in. The eighties may differ from the seventies by a quantum jump.

The capacity for change is beyond the measure of any statistician or pollster. Among those I've encountered in the making of this book are: an ex-Klan leader who won his state's human relations award; the toughest girl on the block who became an extraordinary social worker; the uneducated Appalachian woman who became the poetic voice of her community; the blue-collar housewife who, after mothering nine, says: "I don't like the word 'dream.' I don't even want to specify it as American. What I'm beginning to understand is there's a human possibility. That's where all the excitement is. If you can be part of that, you're aware and alive. It's not a dream, it's possible. It's everyday stuff."

There are nascent stirrings in the neighborhood and in the field, articulated by non-celebrated people who bespeak the dreams of their fellows. It may be catching. Unfortunately, it is not covered on the six o'clock news.

In *The Uses of the Past*, Herbert Muller writes: "In the incessant din of the mediocre, mean and fraudulent activities of a commercial mass society, we are apt to forget the genuine idealism of democracy, of the long painful struggle for liberty and equality. . . . The modern world is as revolutionary as everybody says it is. Because the paradoxes of our age are so violent, men have been violently oversimplifying them. If we want to save our world, we might better try to keep and use our heads."

In this book are a hundred American voices, captured by hunch, circumstance, and a rough idea. There is no pretense at statistical "truth," nor consensus. There is, in the manner of a jazz work, an attempt, of theme and improvisation, to recount dreams, lost and found, and a recognition of possibility.

PROLOGUE

MISS U. S. A.

EMMA KNIGHT *

Miss U.S.A., 1973. She is twenty-nine.

I wince when I'm called a former beauty queen or Miss U.S.A. I keep thinking they're talking about someone else. There are certain images that come to mind when people talk about beauty queens. It's mostly what's known as t and a, tits and ass. No talent. For many girls who enter the contest, it's part of the American Dream. It was never mine.

You used to sit around the TV and watch Miss America and it was exciting, we thought, glamorous. Fun, we thought. But by the time I was eight or nine, I didn't feel comfortable. Soon I'm hitting my adolescence, like fourteen, but I'm not doing any dating and I'm feeling awkward and ugly. I'm much taller than most of the people in my class. I don't feel I can compete the way I see girls competing for guys. I was very much of a loner. I felt intimidated by the amount of competition females were supposed to go through with each other. I didn't like being told by *Seventeen* magazine: Subvert your interests if you have a crush on a guy, get interested in what he's interested in. If you play cards, be sure not to beat him. I was very bad at these social games.

After I went to the University of Colorado for three and a half years, I had it. This was 1968 through '71. I came home for the summer. An agent met me and wanted me to audition for commercials, modeling, acting jobs. Okay. I started auditioning and winning some.

I did things actors do when they're starting out. You pass out literature at conventions, you do print ads, you pound the pavements, you send out your resumés. I had come to a model agency one cold day, and an agent came out and said: "I want you to enter a beauty contest." I said: "No, uh-uh, never, never, never. I'll lose, how humiliating." She said: "I want some girls to represent the agency, might do

* See copyright page.

you good." So I filled out the application blank: hobbies, measurements, blah, blah, blah. I got a letter: "Congratulations. You have been accepted as an entrant into the Miss Illinois-Universe contest." Now what do I do? I'm stuck.

You have to have a sponsor. Or you're gonna have to pay several hundred dollars. So I called up the lady who was running it. Terribly sorry, I can't do this. I don't have the money. She calls back a couple of days later: "We found you a sponsor, it's a lumber company."

It was in Decatur. There were sixty-some contestants from all over the place. I went as a lumberjack: blue jeans, hiking boots, a flannel shirt, a pair of suspenders, and carrying an axe. You come out first in your costume and you introduce yourself and say your astrological sign or whatever it is they want you to say. You're wearing a banner that has the sponsor's name on it. Then you come out and do your pirouettes in your one-piece bathing suit, and the judges look at you a lot. Then you come out in your evening gown and pirouette around for a while. That's the first night.

The second night, they're gonna pick fifteen people. In between, you had judges' interviews. For three minutes, they ask you anything they want. Can you answer questions? How do you handle yourself? Your poise, personality, blah, blah, blah. They're called personality judges.

I thought: This will soon be over, get on a plane tomorrow, and no one will be the wiser. Except that my name got called as one of the fifteen. You have to go through the whole thing all over again.

I'm thinking: I don't have a prayer. I'd come to feel a certain kind of distance, except that they called my name. I was the winner, Miss Illinois. All I could do was laugh. I'm twenty-two, standing up there in a borrowed evening gown, thinking: What am I doing here? This is like Tom Sawyer becomes an altar boy.

I was considered old for a beauty queen, which is a little horrifying when you're twenty-two. That's very much part of the beauty queen syndrome: the young, untouched, unthinking human being.

I had to go to this room and sign the Miss Illinois-Universe contract right away. Miss Universe, Incorporated, is the full name of the company. It's owned by Kayser-Roth, Incorporated, which was bought out by Gulf & Western. Big business.

I'm sitting there with my glass of champagne and I'm reading over this contract. They said: "Oh, you don't have to read it." And I said: "I never sign anything that I don't read." They're all waiting to take pictures, and I'm sitting there reading this long document. So I signed it and the phone rang and the guy was from a Chicago paper and said: "Tell me, is it Miss or Ms.?" I said: "It's Ms." He said: "You're kidding." I said: "No, I'm not." He wrote an article the next day saying something like it finally happened: a beauty queen, a feminist. I thought I was a feminist before I was a beauty queen, why should I stop now?

Then I got into the publicity and training and interviews. It was a throwback to another time where crossed ankles and white gloves and teacups were present. I was taught how to walk around with a book on my head, how to sit daintily, how to pose in a bathing suit, and how to frizz my hair. They wanted curly hair, which I hate.

One day the trainer asked me to shake hands. I shook hands. She said: "That's wrong. When you shake hands with a man, you always shake hands ring up." I said: "Like the pope? Where my hand is up, like he's gonna kiss it?" Right. I thought: Holy mackerel! It was a very long February and March and April and May.

I won the Miss U.S.A. pageant. I started to laugh. They tell me I'm the only beauty queen in history that didn't cry when she won. It was on network television. I said to myself: "You're kidding." Bob Barker, the host, said: "No, I'm not kidding." I didn't know what else to say at that moment. In the press releases, they call it the great American Dream. There she is, Miss America, your ideal. Well, not my ideal, kid.

The minute you're crowned, you become their property and subject to whatever they tell you. They wake you up at seven o'clock next morning and make you put on a negligee and serve you breakfast in bed, so that all the New York papers can come in and take your picture sitting in bed, while you're absolutely bleary-eyed from the night before. They put on the Kayser-Roth negligee, hand you the tray, you take three bites. The photographers leave, you whip off the negligee, they take the breakfast away, and that's it. I never did get any breakfast that day. (Laughs.)

You immediately start making personal appearances. The Jaycees or the chamber of commerce says: "I want to book Miss U.S.A. for our Christmas Day parade." They pay, whatever it is, seven hundred fifty dollars a day, first-class air fare, round trip, expenses, so forth. If the United Fund calls and wants me to give a five-minute pitch on queens at a luncheon, they still have to pay a fee. Doesn't matter that it's a charity. It's one hundred percent to Miss Universe, Incorporated. You get your salary. That's your prize money for the year. I got fifteen thousand dollars, which is all taxed in New York. Maybe

3

out of a check of three thousand dollars, I'd get fifteen hundred dollars.

From the day I won Miss U.S.A. to the day I left for Universe, almost two months, I got a day and a half off. I made about two hundred fifty appearances that year. Maybe three hundred. Parades, shopping centers, and things. Snip ribbons. What else do you do at a shopping center? Model clothes. The nice thing I got to do was public speaking. They said: "You want a ghost writer?" I said: "Hell, no, I know how to talk." I wrote my own speeches. They don't trust girls to go out and talk because most of them can't.

One of the big execs from General Motors asked me to do a speech in Washington, D. C., on the consumer and the energy crisis. It was the fiftieth anniversary of the National Management Association. The White House, for some reason, sent me some stuff on it. I read it over, it was nonsense. So I stood up and said: "The reason we have an energy crisis is because we are, industrially and personally, pigs. We have a short-term view of the resources available to us; and unless we wake up to what we're doing to our air and our water, we'll have a dearth, not just a crisis." Oh, they weren't real pleased. (Laughs.)

What I resent most is that a lot of people didn't expect me to live this version of the American Dream for myself. I was supposed to live it their way.

When it came out in a newspaper interview that I said Nixon should resign, that he was a crook, oh dear, the fur flew. They got very upset until I got an invitation to the White House. They wanted to shut me up. The Miss Universe corporation had been trying to establish some sort of liaison with the White House for several years. I make anti-Nixon speeches and get this invitation.

I figured they're either gonna take me down to the basement and beat me up with a rubber hose or they're gonna offer me a cabinet post. They had a list of fifteen or so people I was supposed to meet. I've never seen such a bunch of people with raw nerve endings. I was dying to bring a tape recorder but thought if you mention the word "Sony" in the Nixon White House, you're in trouble. They'd have cardiac arrest. But I'm gonna bring along a pad and paper. They were patronizing. And when one of 'em got me in his office and talked about all the journalists and television people being liberals, I brought up blacklisting, *Red Channels*, and the TV industry. He changed the subject.

Miss Universe took place in Athens, Greece. The junta was still in power. I saw a heck of a lot of jeeps and troops and machine guns.

The Americans were supposed to keep a low profile. I had never been a great fan of the Greek junta, but I knew darn well I was gonna have to keep my mouth shut. I was still representing the United States, for better or for worse. Miss Philippines won. I ran second.

At the end of the year, you're run absolutely ragged. That final evening, they usually have several queens from past years come back. Before they crown the new Miss U.S.A., the current one is supposed to take what they call the farewell walk. They call over the PA: Time for the old queen's walk. I'm now twenty-three and I'm an old queen. And they have this idiot farewell speech playing over the airwaves as the old queen takes the walk. And you're sitting on the throne for about thirty seconds, then you come down and they announce the name of the new one and you put the crown on her head. And then you're out.

As the new one is crowned, the reporters and photographers rush on the stage. I've seen photographers shove the girl who has just given her reign up thirty seconds before, shove her physically. I was gone by that time. I had jumped off the stage in my evening gown. It is very difficult for girls who are terrified of this ending. All of a sudden (snaps fingers), you're out. Nobody gives a damn about the old one.

Miss U.S.A. and remnants thereof is the crown stored in the attic in my parents' home. I don't even know where the banners are. It wasn't me the fans of Miss U.S.A. thought was pretty. What they think is pretty is the banner and crown. If I could put the banner and crown on that lamp, I swear to God ten men would come in and ask it for a date. I'll think about committing an axe murder if I'm not called anything but a former beauty queen. I can't stand it any more.

Several times during my year as what's-her-face I had seen the movie *The Sting*. There's a gesture the characters use which means the con is on: they rub their nose. In my last fleeting moments as Miss U.S.A., as they were playing that silly farewell speech and I walked down the aisle and stood by the throne, I looked right into the camera and rubbed my finger across my nose. The next day, the pageant people spent all their time telling people that I hadn't done it. I spent the time telling them that, of course, I had. I simply meant: the con is on. (Laughs.)

Miss U.S.A. is in the same graveyard that Emma Knight the twelve-year-old is. Where the sixteen-year-old is. All the past selves. There comes a time when you have to bury those selves because you've grown into another one. You don't keep exhuming the corpses.

If I could sit down with every young girl in America for the next

5

fifty years, I could tell them what I liked about the pageant, I could tell them what I hated. It wouldn't make any difference. There're always gonna be girls who want to enter the beauty pageant. That's the fantasy: the American Dream.

THE STREAM

LEONEL I. CASTILLO

Former director of the United States Immigration and Naturalization Service (INS).

"My father's father came from Mexico to Victoria, Texas, in 1880. He paid a toston, *a half-dollar. That automatically made him a U.S. citizen. In the early years of the century, he was fighting for the right to bury Mexicans in the same grounds as Anglos. There was no place to bury Mexicans. He finally got a piece of land from some German Lutherans. It was deeded to our family and the Mexican community in perpetuity. My grandfather and his friends cleared the land for the first funerals. We've kept the records since 1898. We have many, many people buried there."*

New immigrants are trying all over again to integrate themselves into the system. They have the same hunger. On any given day, there are about three million throughout the world who are applying to come to the United States and share the American Dream. The same battles. I still read old newspaper clips: 1886. Housemaid wanted. We'll accept any person, any color, any nationality, any religion, except Irish. (Laughs.) Rough ads: No Irish need apply.

Most of the undocumented here without papers, without legal permission, think they're gonna go back home in six months. Relatively few go back. Some old Italians are going back to *pensionares,* and some old Eastern Europeans are going back home. But, by and large, immigrants, old and new, stay. They don't feel they know anyone in the old village. Their children don't speak Polish or Italian or Greek. Their children are used to air conditioning, McDonald's.

The Vietnamese boat people express it as well as anyone. They don't know if they're gonna land, if the boat's gonna sink. They don't know what's gonna happen to 'em, but they've a hunch they might make it to the U.S. as the "freedom place."

There is the plain hard fact of hunger. In order to eat, a person will endure tremendous hardship. Mexican people who come here usually are not the most destitute. Someone who's too poor can't afford the trip. You've got to buy *coyotes*. A *coyote* is a smuggler of people. He's also called a *pollero*. *Pollo* is chicken. He's the one who guides chickens through the border.

Sometimes the whole family saves up and gives the bright young man or the bright young woman the family savings. It even goes in hock for a year or two. They pin all their hopes on this one kid, put him on a bus, let him go a thousand miles. He doesn't speak a word of English. He's only seventeen, eighteen years old, but he's gonna save that family. A lot rides on that kid who's a busboy in some hotel.

We've had some as young as eleven who have come a thousand miles. You have this young kid, all his family savings, everything is on him. There are a lot of songs and stories about mother and child, the son leaving who may never return. We end up deporting him. It's heartrending.

He's the bright kid in the family. The slow one might not make it, might get killed. The one who's sickly can't make the trip. He couldn't walk through the desert. He's not gonna be too old, too young, too destitute, or too slow. He's the brightest and the best.

He's gonna be the first hook, the first pioneer coming into an alien society, the United States. He might be here in Chicago. He works as a busboy all night long. They pay him minimum or less, and work him hard. He'll never complain. He might even thank his boss. He'll say as little as possible because he doesn't want anyone to know what his status is. He will often live in his apartment, except for the time he goes to work or to church or to a dance. He will stay in and watch TV. If he makes a hundred a week, he will manage to send back twenty-five. All over the country, if you go to a Western Union office on the weekend, you'll find a lot of people there sending money orders. In a southwest office, like Dallas, Western Union will tell you seventy-five percent of their business is money orders to Mexico.

After the kid learns a bit, because he's healthy and young and energetic, he'll probably get another job as a busboy. He'll work at another place as soon as the shift is over. He'll try to work his way up to be a waiter. He'll work incredible hours. He doesn't care about union scale, he doesn't care about conditions, about humiliations. He accepts all this as his fate.

He's burning underneath with this energy and ambition. He outworks the U.S. busboys and eventually becomes the waiter. Where he can maneuver, he tries to become the owner and gives a lot of competition to the locals. Restaurant owners tell me, if they have a choice, they'll always hire foreign nationals first. They're so eager and grateful. There's a little greed here, too. (Laughs.) They pay 'em so little.

We've got horrible cases of exploitation. In San Diego and in Arizona, we discovered people who live in holes in the ground, live under trees, no sanitation, no housing, nothing. A lot of them live in chicken coops.

They suffer from *coyotes*, too, who exploit them and sometimes beat 'em. *Coyotes* advertise. If the immigrant arrives in San Diego, the word is very quick: where to go and who's looking. He'll even be approached. If he's got a lot of money, the *coyote* will manage to bring him from Tijuana all the way to Chicago and guarantee him a job. He'll get all the papers: Social Security, birth certificate, driver's license. The *coyote* reads the papers and finds which U.S. citizens have died and gets copies of all their vital statistics. In effect, the immigrant carries the identity of a dead person.

Often the employer says he doesn't know anything about it. He plays hands off. He makes his bucks hiring cheap labor. The *coyote* makes his off the workers.

Coyotes come from the border with these pickup trucks full of people. They may put twenty in a truck. They bring 'em in all sorts of bad weather, when they're less likely to be stoppped. They might be going twenty, twenty-eight hours, with one or two pit stops. They don't let the people out. There's no urinal, no bathroom. They sit or they stand there in this little cramped space for the whole trip.

A truck broke down outside Chicago. It was a snowstorm. The driver left. People were frostbitten, lost their toes. In Laredo, the truck was in an accident. Everybody ran off because the police were coming. The truck caught fire. No one remembered the two fellows in the trunk. It was locked and no keys. Of course, they burned to death. The border patrol found thirty-three people dying in the deserts of Arizona. They were saved at the last minute and deported. I'll bet you a dollar every one of them, as soon as they are well enough, will try again.

At least a quarter of a million apprehensions were made last year. If we apprehend them at the border, we turn 'em around and ask them to depart voluntarily. They turn around and go back to Mexico. A few hours later, they try again. In El Paso, we deported one fellow six times in one day. There's a restaurant in Hollywood run by a fellow we deported thirty-seven times. We've deported some people more than a hundred times. They always want to come back. There's a job and there's desperation.

In World War Two, we recruited Mexicans to work here. As soon as the war ended and our young men came back, we deported them. In 1954, the deportation problem was so big that the general in charge of immigration ordered Operation Wetback. That one year, we had a million apprehensions. It was similar to what we did during the depression. We rounded everybody up, put 'em on buses, and sent them back to Mexico. Sometimes they were people who merely looked Mexican. The violations of civil liberties were terrible.

Half the people here without papers are not Mexicans. They're from all over the world. They came legally, with papers, as tourists ten years ago. They're much harder to deal with. We're discussing a program that would allow people to have permanent residence, who have been here seven years or more, have not broken any laws, have paid taxes and not been on welfare. You can't be here and become a public charge. All too often, the public gets the impression that all immigrants are on welfare. It's the exact opposite. Very few go on welfare.

A lot of people who are humanitarian, who believe they should be hospitable toward the stranger, are very restrictive when it comes to their jobs. (Laughs.) We've had protests from *mariachis* and soccer players. The *mariachis* are upset because the Mexicans were coming in and playing for less. The manager of soccer teams would rather hire the foreign nationals because often they're better players.

We get people coming in from Haiti, the poorest country in the western hemisphere. They come over by boat and land in Florida. The Floridians raised hell about this. I've even had Cuban-Americans tell me that Haitians were going to destroy their culture. There's a weird pecking order now.

We make three thousand apprehensions at the border every weekend. It's just a little fourteen-mile stretch. Our border patrol knows this little fellow comin' across is hungry. He just wants to work. They know he's no security threat. They say: "It's my job." Many of them come to have a great deal of respect for the people they're deporting. What do you think of a person you deport three, four times, who just keeps coming back? You would never want to get in the same ring with that person.

9

I'm torn. I saw it in the Peace Corps, when I was in the Philippines. A mother offered you her infant. You're just a twenty-one-year-old kid and she says: "Take my child, take him with you to the States." When you see this multiplied by thousands, it tears you up.

It's clear to me that the undocumented, even more than the immigrant, is a contributor to our society and to our standard of living. It's one of the few groups that has no parasites. They walk the tightrope and try not to fall off. If you're a citizen and you fall, we have a net that catches you: welfare, food stamps, unemployment, social services. If you're undocumented and fall off that tightrope, you can't go to any of the agencies because you may end up bein' deported. He can't draw welfare, he can't use public services. He's not gonna call a policeman even when he's beat up. If he's in a street fight and somebody whips him bad, assaults him, robs him, rapes her, there's no complaint. In Baltimore, an employer raped two girls. The person who complained wouldn't give us the names of the victims because she was afraid we'd deport 'em. We end up in this country with enormous abuse against four million people.

The only thing that helps me is remembering the history of this country. We've always managed, despite our worst, unbelievably nativist actions to rejuvenate ourselves, to bring in new people. Every new group comes in believing more firmly in the American Dream than the one that came a few years before. Every new group is scared of being in the welfare line or in the unemployment office. They go to night school, they learn about America. We'd be lost without them.

The old dream is still dreamt. The old neighborhood Ma-Pa stores are still around. They are not Italian or Jewish or Eastern European any more. Ma and Pa are now Korean, Vietnamese, Iraqi, Jordanian, Latin American. They live in the store. They work seven days a week. Their kids are doing well in school. They're making it. Sound familiar?

Near our office in Los Angeles is a little café with a sign: KOSHER BURRITOS. (Laughs.) A *burrito* is a Mexican tortilla with meat inside. Most of the customers are black. The owner is Korean. (Laughs.) The banker, I imagine, is WASP. (Laughs.) This is what's happening in the United States today. It is not a melting pot, but in one way or another, there is a melding of cultures.

I see all kinds of new immigrants starting out all over again, trying to work their way into the system. They're going through new battles, yet they're old battles. They want to share in the American Dream. The stream never ends.

BOOK ONE

One's Self I sing, a simple separate person,
Yet utter the word Democratic, the word En-Masse.

—Walt Whitman

The individual has become more conscious than ever of his dependence upon society. He does not experience this dependence as a positive asset, but rather as a threat to his natural rights. All human beings, whatever their position in society, are suffering from this process of deterioration. Unknowingly prisoners of their own egotism, they feel insecure, lonely, and deprived of the naïve, simple, and unsophisticated enjoyment of life. Man can find meaning in life, short and perilous as it is, only through devoting himself to society.

—Albert Einstein

ONWARD AND UPWARD

T H E   B O S S

W A L L A C E   R A S M U S S E N

It is 7:00 A.M. *A frosty winter morning. The executive offices of Beatrice Foods in Chicago. The long corridors are empty; you walk through as in an Ingmar Bergman dream sequence. You enter a large room; seated at the end of a long table, alone, is the chief executive officer of the corporation. He glances at his pocket watch. There is coffee for himself and his visitor. Big-boned and heavy-set, with calloused hands, he has the appearance of the archetypal elderly workingman in Sunday clothes. He is bluff and genial. He is a winner of the Horatio Alger Award.*

I'm just a country boy. Born in Nebraska and came up right through the Great Depression. I'm convinced it will repeat itself when it's time, and probably it'll be good for the country. It will be hard on people who never experienced doing without, but it's amazing what you can get along without. You don't have it, so you begin to spend more time with your family. There's a way in history, a way in nature, of always bringing people back down to earth.

Some people are more aggressive than others. People are always protecting their turf. That's a natural instinct. The bull elk on the mountainside, when he bugles, he doesn't bugle to other bulls. He bugles to them: Stay away from my harem. The male does not fight to be fighting; he fights to protect his territory. You could always tell the survivors because they were always in there punchin'. Takes a lot to get them upset. They would swing with whatever comes along. To me, that's a survivor.

Somebody asked me: Did you ever dream of being in the job you're in? I say no. My only ambition in life was to be just a little bit better off the next day than I was the day before. And to learn a little more than I did the day before. I was always reading. As a child, I read every *Popular Mechanics* magazine I could get ahold of. Even in school, they would bring me things to fix.

In those days, each farmer helped the other farmers. At twelve, I hitched the team and hauled bundles of hay and pitched them into the thrashing machine. I upset a load of bundles by turning too sharply. I went across the ditch. Do you think those farmers would help me? Let's see if he could do it by himself. It was a good lesson because I never upset another one.

I learned the traits of human beings. You can learn from nature why people do what they do. I'm talking about wildlife. I spent my entire life doing some hunting, out of necessity for food on the table. You learn that animals and people have the same habits today that they had two thousand years ago.

I never wanted to be a loser. I always wanted to be the first one off the airplane. I have a theory that when you walk through a crowd in the airport—I don't care how crowded it is—if you look fifty feet ahead, people will separate. Don't look straight at the person, and people will make room for you. Years ago, I took my wife to Tulsa. I was ready to get on the airplane when the fellow said: "Don't you have your wife with you?" I said: "Oh, my gosh, yes." I forgot her. (Laughs.) People would say they saw me on the street and I didn't say hello. I was thinking about something else. It isn't my nature to be friendly.

I think hardship is necessary for life to be good, for you to enjoy it. If you don't know hardship, you don't know when you have it good. Today, the father and mother don't want their children to go through the same hardships. I don't look at it that way. I have two children. One is forty and one is thirty-six. I can still say, "This is what you do," and that's what they do. I'm a firm believer that they had to know things weren't always that easy. There's a price you pay for everything.

People are now so used to being given something for nothing. They think it's for nothing, but there's a price. Loss of their pride, loss of their ability to take care of themselves. It's like caging animals. I don't care how wild the animal was, if you cage him long enough, he forgets how to take care of himself. The same is true about human beings. Like a lion that's forgotten how to take care of himself, they will kill others, the slow ones because they can't catch the fast ones. That's why you have crime today in the element not employed. They don't know how to take care of themselves other than to take away from those that have. A recession or a revolution will bring it back into balance. It's happened throughout history. That's one thing I know out of reading history.

It comes down to—who's gonna be the survivor? It will test the strength of a lot of people. It will be every community for itself. You cannot stand still. You grow or die.

When I left home, I went to California. I had odd jobs delivering handbills. Oh, did I learn a lesson! I couldn't figure out why some of them would deliver a thousand in a couple of hours when it took me all day. I followed one and saw he was putting most of them down the storm drain. I went to the fellow I was working for and asked how come he was allowing him to put them down the storm drain. I put mine all out, I'm wearin' out my shoe leather. For ten cents a day. I could buy a bucket of grapes for ten cents, that was enough to eat. He says: "We expect that." I said: "It's not right." He said: "We're not gonna pay you any more." So I quit the job. You had to be brave to quit jobs that paid ten cents a day. (Laughs.) I think he was rippin' people off. California was then known as the place to do unto others before they do unto you.

I worked three months on an alfalfa ranch at ten dollars a month, room and board. All you'd get was black-eyed peas for breakfast, for dinner, and for supper. The milk was always sour. They gave me a letter that they owed me twenty dollars to take to the owner of the ranch, and he'd pay me. Dumb me, I gave him the letter and I never got my twenty dollars. That was a lesson to me. Trust everybody with reservations.

I came back to Nebraska and helped shuck corn. We sold it at ten cents a bushel and burned the rest of it. Then I got a job putting cedar chests together. I never told anybody I couldn't do anything. The company failed, so I got a job cutting out jigsaw puzzles. I got ten cents for each one.

I was reading about people who were successful and how they did it. How they got ahead. That was basically all my reading. I made up my mind that if I ever got with a big company, I'd never leave. My mother's brother was an engineer at Beatrice in Lincoln. I got a job there. I was nineteen. I started pulling ice out of a tank. You pull up 400-pound cans with an electric hoist. There was always a challenge: How much could I pull? The maximum was a hundred tons. I always wanted to go over that. The engineer would come in and say: "Slow down." (Laughs.)

I kept all the equipment up myself. I didn't want anybody fooling with it. The chief engineer recognized I had mechanical ability. He

1 5

said: "Do you think you could handle maintenance in the creamery?" I said: "Sure." (Laughs.) I knew what a creamery looked like. I'd walked through it a couple of times, but that's all. I'd never seen any pasteurizing equipment in my life. But it didn't take me long to learn. I never doubted that anything I intended to do, I could do.

In six months I went to the chief engineer and said: "I don't have enough to do." He said the other man worked at it full-time. I said: "I don't care. You gotta get me something else to do." I wanted to keep busy. So I went to the dairy side, where they bottle milk. I learned a lot from the fellow there, a fine machinist and refrigeration man. Anybody who had information, I would soak it up like a sponge.

It got so, I took care of all the maintenance in the dairy and cream- ery. I went to him again and said: "I'm running out of something to do." He said: "Why don't you go over to the ice cream plant?" Soon I was taking care of all three. It wasn't enough of a challenge, so I got a job at night, taking care of the air conditioning of a hotel. I also did home wiring. I would require only two, three hours of sleep.

Beatrice offered me the job as chief engineer of the plant in Vin- cennes, Indiana. It was the largest milk plant in the country. I was twenty-two. The people who were working there were in their forties and fifties, some of them in their sixties. I thought maybe there might be some resentment because of my age. I tried to be tolerant of peo- ple's weaknesses, knowing I'd get the maximum amount of work out of them if I treated them with respect.

The man whose place I was supposed to take wasn't capable of handling the job. He was a genius with equipment, but a tinkerer. Say you had a body on the table and it's bleeding to death. The doctor would say: "What kind of car accident was he in?" This fellow would always make an analysis. Consequently, he had four or five people standing around doing nothing. My theory was: Let's get it fixed, then we'll analyze why it broke down.

I finally told the management he's gotta go. That was the first time I knowingly practiced brinkmanship. I needed that job like you need shoes in cold weather. I knew they needed me worse than I needed them. I stayed in my room for two weeks. They called me and said: "He's gone, come on back." From then on, we got the plant in shape.

I worked out of the Chicago office drawing layouts. I had no ex- perience in this. I bought books, started reading, and got the equip- ment. I told the engineers we have today that I could tear a piece of refrigeration equipment down with a suit on and never get greasy.

They don't ever tear them down themselves. If you're going to direct people, you must have knowledge of the job. If somebody comes in and says this is so, I know immediately whether that person is telling me a fact. Facts in your hands before you make the decision, that's part of the survivor.

Another lesson I pass on: Whenever you're going to work for somebody, make sure that you make him successful. Otherwise, you must jump over him. Now, I've had to jump over . . . (He trails off.)

I always considered that as part of life. This is our world. If we're going to keep it a strong society, you have to have strong leaders. You can't have what we have in Washington today.

He refers, wryly, to a profile of himself in Forbes *magazine. "The only thing they said unfair is this last sentence: 'That is a tough and determined man. Even though he's pushing sixty-five, he doesn't allow anybody to do to Wallace Rasmussen what he has done to others.'"*

It can appear to be ruthless at the time that you do it. When someone is not producing in a corporation, or even in a family, and he doesn't recognize he's holding up the works, someone has to make that decision for him. If you're going to be successful, you can't let any person stand in the way. The company is a hundred thousand people and fifty thousand shareholders. We have a moral responsibility to at least a hundred fifty thousand individuals. Multiply a hundred fifty by three and a half, which is the population of the average family, and you got half a million people. We have a responsibility to those who trust us.

You are respected by a hundred thousand employees. Are you feared, too?

(A long, long pause) You'd rather not say that it was fear, but you have it. You can't help it. Some of it may be awe. Ninety-nine percent of it has to be respect. You have all three. I make it a habit of talking to the most junior person in the office. I find out more from him than I do from the senior officers. (Laughs.) Senior officers try to cover up their mistakes. Poor little junior down here doesn't know he's making mistakes, so I find out more.

When the company was 4.3 billion dollars, I wasn't chairman, I wasn't president, I wasn't executive vice-president. I was a senior vice-president and I had three-fourths of the company as my load. This goes back to '68, '67.

I became president and chief executive officer on July 1, 1976. In those two years, we have grown from 5.2 billion to 7.4 billion. No, no, you absolutely cannot stop your growth. You must increase enough to keep people interested in investing in your company.

There's many people asking: When are you going to retire? I made a comment when I took the job, I would go out when I had eight billion. Now I say I'll go when it's ten.

POSTSCRIPT: *He was retired in 1979 as chief executive officer of Beatrice Foods. The company had reached 7.8 billion dollars.*

GAYLORD FREEMAN

◇————————————————————————————————————◇

It is a morning in 1975.

He is chairman of the board of the First National Bank of Chicago. It is his last year; he has chosen his successor. His tie bears the bank's insignia: the name and the coin. "I got one of our boys to design it. I have never worn any other tie on a business day. I wear this as an indication to the troops that I'm thinkin' about the bank."

It is an expansive office, with objets d'art here and in the anteroom. Adjacent is his private dining room. On the fifty-seventh floor is a huge dining room where, this noon, his successor will host a luncheon for the ambassador of Japan; among the several hundred guests will be the city's leading industrialists and Mayor Richard Daley.

I came in in '34 and go out in '75. That's more than forty-one years. Do I feel withdrawal symptoms? (Chuckles softly.) A friend was telling me of her father, Edward Ryerson.* After his retirement, nobody invited him to lunch. He had to find somebody who didn't have a damn thing to do. I've already sensed it. As soon as we designated Bob as our successor, it was inevitable that people say: "Gale Freeman, he's a nice guy, but Bob's the fella we should be talking to."

I find now that every couple of weeks, I have a free luncheon en-

---

* Chairman of the board of directors of Inland Steel Company during the thirties and forties, and a leading civic figure

gagement. It tickles me. I find it amusing. It doesn't upset me. I kind of laugh at myself because when I retire, where will I have lunch? I've had a magnificent dining room. I'll go to a club. I've belonged to the Midday Club for over thirty years, and I've never had lunch there. Now I'll have places to go to.

I won't be in demand. I'll be seeking company rather than being sought. If you're happy, that's all right. I'm very lucky. I've achieved everything I hoped to achieve. I'm not rich, but I'll be comfortable. I don't aspire to anything more. I don't feel short-circuited or let down. I'm graduating from business with a good report card. Already I feel less competitive. Let somebody else have the credit. I don't have to fight for that any more.

It can be very pleasing if it doesn't come too late. I remember a friend of mine who was a very tough man in business. When he was retiring, he said: "There's nobody in town that really likes me. From now on, I'm going to lead my life to be liked." It was too late. Attitudes were set, his habits were so ingrained, he couldn't make the change. He died an unhappy man, with great tension between himself and the children. The trick is (laughs) to put all that competitiveness into your life when it's necessary but to moderate it with a degree of love and modesty.

My good friend Milton Friedman* says the worst thing is for businessmen to feel responsible to society. He says that's a lot of baloney and it's contrary to the businessman's assignment. It's an arrogance he should not have. I don't accept that, though I greatly admire Milton.

Is this a Christian thought? No, we hope we'll be in business for years. There's nothing sacred about a profit-oriented society. There's no guarantee in the Bible or the Constitution that you can have private property. If we're going to continue to have these opportunities, it's only because this is acceptable to a high enough proportion of our people that they don't change the laws to prevent it.

I work hard. I try to be here about a quarter of seven. I work until five-thirty or six. I haven't played bridge in thirty years. I haven't played golf in twenty years. I like work better than golf. I don't like the artificial camaraderie of the locker room, havin' four, five drinks and goin' home a little plastered and havin' to take a long nap so it ruins the whole goddamn day.

Which would you rather be doing: traveling through Europe and calling on the ministers of finance and heads of state, or playing

* Professor of economics, University of Chicago

bridge with people who haven't had a new thought in twenty years? This is going to be the problem of retirement. No intellectual stimulation.

Three years later. It is a morning in 1978.
We are seated in a smaller office on another floor. There are no objets d'art around.

I don't feel I've sacrificed anything. As a younger man, I sacrificed closeness with my children. But in our mature life, it isn't a sacrifice. We have two grandsons, eighteen and sixteen, who've been with us the past few days. Very idealistic.

I run into the businessman in the board room or the locker room, and by God, he's for the American Way one hundred percent. Anybody that deviates from that is a goddamn Communist. I say to him: "What do you mean by 'the American Way'?" "Well, everybody knows that." I say: "What were the concepts that led to the creation of our country?" He's ill at ease, he doesn't want to talk about it because (a) he's never given it much thought; and (b) he's not sure he can defend a system that permits as wide a variety of income as we have. So he wants to avoid it.

My feeling's always been that no system is perfect. But ours has done more, not only for the rich, but for the poor, than any other system. Let's not be embarrassed about it; let's understand it more. I wouldn't have pursued this as much if I didn't have doubts.

I think our nation has grown old, and very rapidly. We've lost a lot of the Dream. We're like people my age, whose world narrows. A young man comes out of school and he's interested in everything. Then he gets a job, and his world narrows a bit. He marries. Job, home, family. And it narrows a bit more. Finally, he gets older. Through with his job, his family gone away, his ultimate concern is his bowel movement every morning. Our country is going through a great deal of that now.

This January, I sat down in the afternoon and read a novel. That's the first one I read since I got out of school in 1934. I never felt I could waste a minute. It was cheating. I felt I had a terrible duty to the bank and a duty to society. It took a hell of a lot of my time. People are silly. I'm not as good as I was. I'm not as physically strong. I'm not as mentally sharp. I have a hell of a time with names. So I don't feel the same duty I had when I was a more efficient machine.

Machine?

(Laughs softly.) I know. I shouldn't have said that.

It's worse if you've been top dog. It's harder to retire than if you never were the boss. (Suddenly sharp) Business is so goddamn competitive! The head of a business is really competing with everybody all the time, not only with his competitors. You're competing with your friends in other businesses, your dearest friends. It influences your life tremendously. And not necessarily in a good way. (Laughs.) It tends to make business friendships not quite friendships.

The guy who's been intensely competitive all his life and then—click!—he's retired, it's hard for him to joyously admire the success of his associates, his friends. He can't help feeling it's a little at his expense. Of course, it isn't. He's not in that league any more. This is a hard thing for many men to take.

I've been retired a year and a half now. I wrote some poems about it.

Our names are as they were. We look the same. Our wives are just as kind. In fact, more thoughtful. But we don't feel the same, not quite. The young men do not stand, we never felt they should. Our old friends smile, but turn a moment sooner to the younger man. And that is fair. We're just as good friends as we were, but not quite so important any more. Not so important. No. But wiser?

S. B. FULLER

Outside, the elevated trains frequently rattle by; trucks rumble, cars whiz. It is a busy thoroughfare in Chicago's black ghetto. Inside, an oblong hallway leads toward the inner office. There is an air of subdued order as a few young women work behind the counter. Two small children are amusing themselves.

He sits behind his desk. His stern, bespectacled face evokes the portrait of a no-nonsense high school principal. (He had cut short our first conversation: "You have been drinking." I had had one Scotch and soda during lunch. This is our second encounter.)

He is seventy-three.

When I was nine years old in Monroe, Louisiana, I started sellin' Cloverine salve. I wanted to become a man. When I became a man, I wanted to produce somethin' similar to what I was sellin'. Today that's what I'm doin'.

My family were sharecroppers. When I was ten, they leased some land, bought a mule, and were farmin' themselves. When I was fifteen, we moved to Memphis. My father left home. Two years after, my mother died and left seven children. When she lay dyin', she asked me to take care of the children. I was seventeen. I worked and sold and was able to take care of those kids. Five years after that, we found my father in Chicago. He remarried and his wife came back to Memphis lookin' for the younger children. They wasn't her natural children, but she brought them back with her.

I only received a sixth-grade education, but my mother told me before she passed: "The good white people give themselves nine months schooling each year. They give you three." We received only three months' schooling each year out on the farm. She said: "It's not that they are unfair, but they believe you can learn as much in three months as they can learn in nine. Whatever you do, son, don't disappoint the good white folks."

I had learned that reading people was ruling people. I started buyin' books to educate myself. I was readin' everything I could get my hands on. When you know you don't know, you gotta read. I didn't just read for entertainment. I was seeking understanding. I found in America in 1912, there were 4,043 millionaires. Only eighty-nine had high school educations. Some didn't finish grammar school. So I found myself in good company. This was the greatest motivation I ever received, when I knew there were these white men in America who made good without formal education.

I left Memphis to come north where there was more people to sell to. I hitchhiked in Chicago and arrived on the twelfth of May, 1928. By this time, I got married and had five children. I got a job in a coal yard. I sent back for my family. The owner seemed to like me and said he was gonna help me educate my children. I told him I didn't want security from anybody, so I quit the job.

After that, I started sellin' burial insurance door to door. A magazine was printin' the names of people that were getting fifteen thousand dollars and over. The president of the Metropolitan Life Insurance Company was getting fifty thousand dollars a year in 1934. The president of Lever Brothers, a soap company, was earning $485,000. I quit sellin' insurance and started sellin' soap.

I took twenty-five dollars and bought me some soap and started sellin' it from door to door. That was in the depression, 1935. Your disadvantage can always be your advantage. Because people was out of work, it wasn't hard to recruit people to do any kind of work. The thing that discouraged people out sellin', they thought people didn't have any money. But soap was sellin' for ten cents a cake, and it was hard to find people that didn't have a dime.

I didn't count the hours. I sold as long as people would let me in their homes. They'd say they didn't have money. I would take the order, bring it back when they gonna have the money. Repetition is the mother of knowledge. I learned by sellin'. You had to rouse people's curiosity. You had to convince them what you were sayin' was true. Once they were convinced, they wanted what you were sellin'.

I studied a little psychology because I knew that all this had to do with a man bein' master of his own fate. The captain of his own soul. I knew what will affect me will affect other people. I always believed that I wasn't exceptional. I was an ordinary person. All people are ordinary. I learned that all men are created equal. The rich boy has money but no initiative. The poor boy has no money but initiative. Initiative will get the money. This is the thing every kid should be told when he first comes to America. The greatest advantage in the world is to be born in America. Only in America, you're free to eat if you can find something to eat and free to starve if you don't. In America, they won't let you starve, but you'd be better off starving than go on relief. You may not be physically dead on relief, but you are spiritually.

Today, I could use in our organization a hundred thousand young people, doin' what I was doin' when I was young; sellin'. The reason we have so many people unemployed is because we don t have enough salesmen. There's no problem makin' merchandise, it's sellin' it. Door-to-door sellin' gives anybody the opportunity. Some of the things door-to-door sellin' made possible: vacuum cleaners, percolators, carpets. You name it, it was sold door to door.

What is hurting youth today is pacifiers. Dope. Nature gave you energy, and you're not supposed to relax that energy. You're supposed to use that energy to make the world a better place to live because you are here. I know that nature never made a nobody. Everybody was born with some kind of talent.

In 1935, with twenty-five dollars, I started buyin' my merchandise from Boyer National Laboratories. They were reluctant about creditin' me, so I told 'em I was gonna buy the company out. Twelve years later in 1947, I bought Boyer out. I promised I was going to fire the credit manager, who failed to let me have credit, but he was gone. I retained all the employees. I still own Boyer's.

By 1939, I'd organized the Chicago Chamber of Commerce. Black businesses. We had a slogan: For economic emancipation, trade with your own. Out from that came several minority businesspeople. I trained a lot of young men who have succeeded.*

In 1965, I bought a department store. I wanted to start my people thinkin' about retail sellin' in our own community. People that was receiving relief, I was the first gave them credit. Today all the major department stores are lettin' them have credit.

I had thirteen corporations operatin' at one time: box factory, newspaper,** farms, and what not. I wanted to teach people how to do business for themselves, but they wasn't ready. It cost me a fortune. I had an asset of eight million dollars and a liability of three million, a cash flow of ten million, but I could not get credit from the established white sources.

The banks denied me credit because they'd never known a black man being engaged in a department store. They had never known a black man to own theaters. I owned a whole block. The financial institutions feared that because it was new. This is one thing I've always tried to make people understand. Plato said: Let him that cannot reason depend on instinct. Reason come from observation. If you remember something, you can reason. These bankers had nothing in their storehouse of memory where they'd known a black man to make good in the field I was engaged in. For that reason, they feared.

I decided to go to my own people. The government investigators found out that we didn't go about it in the right way, so we had to drop that. It caused the downfall of my whole empire. By 1968, we were in bankruptcy. It's been very hard because I was then sixty-five years old. Everybody's told me I was too old to get started again. But I'm on my way back, using the same method I used when I started with twenty-five dollars. I never had doubts. The only people with doubts was the government and people who had never known anything like this to happen.

When they threw me in bankruptcy, they wanted to wipe out all my

---

* Among his disciples are John H. Johnson of Johnson Publications; George E. Johnson of Johnson Products; and Rich Maguire of Seaway Furniture Company.
** The *Pittsburgh Courier*, one of the most influential black newspapers in the country

debts. I wouldn't agree to that. I wanted to come out of bankruptcy paying off my debts one hundred percent. Because I technically violated a law that I didn't know anything about, I was indicted. And when I told the court I would pay back all the people I borrowed from, they thought that couldn't happen because I was too old. They gave me probation for five years. Probation was over with about a year ago. I was somewhat handicapped because I couldn't travel unless I told them where I was going. About a year from now, I will have all my debts paid off. I never have been bitter. I always knew that whatever people were doing to you was because of fear, not understanding.

I employ white people. The human race is the only race I know. I employ all people coming to me, seeking work. I accept them on their merit.

We sell to everybody. H. A. Hair Arranger, we still have that. During the civil rights movement, back in the sixties, the White Citizens Council found out. They hurt me in door-to-door sellin' and put us out of business. They can't hurt me today.

Didn't the civil rights movement affect the sale of some of your cosmetics—for instance, hair straighteners, with the oncoming of Afro styles?

It not only hurt our business, it hurt black business as a whole. The biggest industry black folks had at the time were the barber and beauty trade. When the Afro style come, blacks stopped going to the barbershop and beauty parlor. They're just beginnin' to come back, but they're still not groomin' themselves the way they used to. The thing that hurt Fuller Products is that the people who should sell can get on relief.

You got to convince them the government is not their brother's keeper. The New Deal of Franklin Roosevelt hurt us. He was a rich man's son. All he received was given to him. So he thinks it's right to give. He didn't understand, when you give people, you hurt them. We had soup lines and the depression because men lost confidence in themselves. President Hoover told the American people that prosperity was around the corner. But you had to go around the corner to get it. They didn't want to go around the corner, so they elected Mr. Roosevelt.

Welfare kills a man's spirit. It may give his body the vitamins that make him big and fat, and he may be happy. But he doesn't have the spirit of initiative. A dog you feed will not hunt. If you want a dog that hunts, you have to let him get hungry. If you want a man to search, man needs to face the recesses of life. You're free to eat if you can pay for your food, and you're free to starve if you don't get the equivalent to pay for it.

It's contrary to the law of nature for man to stand still. He either marches forward or the eternal march will force him back. This the Negro has failed to understand. He believes that the lack of integration has kept him back. This is not true. The lack of initiative is responsible. In 1953, the Negro's income was fifty-seven percent that of the white man. In 1962, it was only fifty-three percent. The main reason is the Negro's lack of understanding our capitalistic system. Competition.

He spend over three billion dollars yearly for automobiles alone. Yet he don't realize the world of opportunity in his own community. How many Negro automobile dealers are there in America today? Every evening, the substantial citizen that leaves that community and goes home to another community, that's leaving the Negro community impoverished and the wealth derived from there in retail sales transferred to the other one.

Dr. Martin Luther King thought civil rights legislation gonna solve the black man's dilemma. I knew better. I talked with Dr. King when we boycott the Montgomery bus line. I told him the thing we need to do is go down there and buy the bus line. Then we ride where we choose because it's our bus line. He didn't want that.

They had to sell the bus line because they were in trouble. The biggest folk that were riding the bus were black folk, and they were boycottin' it. They wasn't nobody ridin' it. They were ready to sell.

Ignorance is the root of misfortune. Gandhi was highly educated from Oxford. Dr. King had his Ph.D. Andrew Carnegie came here, an immigrant, without any formal education, and died worth three hundred million dollars. There's a difference between ignorance and illiteracy. You can be an illiterate man and not be ignorant, and you can be ignorant and not illiterate.

My mother, she was born a slave, she knew that and she pointed it out to me. "You are my first-born and I want to tell you the truth." She told me that white people feared black folks because they didn't understand them. She wanted her first-born to make a place in this

1,

world for himself and to help everybody else. "They are not going to have a mother like you have, and you owe them a debt. You will know something they don't know."

JIM VRETTOS

It is a supermart on Chicago's North Side. There is affluence to the east, whence come most of the regulars. There is young people's traffic to the north and south. We're in the heart of New Town, the busiest corner. To the west are the working and lower middle classes. They shop elsewhere.

He is in his office on the second floor, above the store. He wears an old-time celluloid visor and is bent over his desk, looking over his books. He is forty-nine.

The year is 1975.

It's the self-satisfaction more than anything else. Sometimes I'll sit back in that office downstairs and look down the aisles. I see five cash registers goin'. I see buggies goin' up and down the aisle. I say: "God-damn it! It's workin'! It's workin'!" (Laughs.) Probably my greatest pleasure is sittin' back there in that office and watching these five cash registers goin', seein' people and carts and merchandise movin' off the shelf. That's music.

About two weeks ago, one of the registers broke down. (Laughs.) I got so mad, I felt like throwin' things. With all these cash registers goin', it's like all the weights are taken off. Everything is beautiful. (Laughs.)

I'd like to have about three supermarkets now. Not for some chain to absorb me, no. I feel the government has got to start setting up some standards so the small-business person isn't swallowed up. 'Cause he's the only one who can keep these big guys in line. What the hell, look at the automotive industry. There's three or four of 'em. Those bastards sit down together once every year and decide how much they're gonna raise their prices.

If a chain tried to buy me out, I'd tell 'em to go to hell. Even a terrific deal. I don't like the idea of somebody else calling the shots. You're better off if you can stay on your own two feet and not depend on these conglomerates or any of the b.s. they give you about how big they're gonna make you. I don't think money is the whole reward. It's the satisfaction of knowing you've *done* it. (Laughs.)

A return visit, three years later. It is 1978.

(Laughs.) When I was a real young kid, I was thinking how great it would be to be at the top. I wanted to be the boss. (Laughs.) When you go to the movies, you see this guy with a big cigar in his mouth and his feet up on the desk, and he was callin' all the shots. You'd think: Gee, it's great. You want to be on top, so you have life easy. (Laughs.) Now I'm on top, and I work harder than I ever did. Sometimes when I get angry I say: "Goddamn it! The next business I go into, it's gonna be a one-man business and the hell with everybody." (Laughs.)

I need a new challenge to get the wheels movin'. That's the American Dream, really makin' things work. That's what I really get a kick out of. Once I see it workin', all I want to do is watch it to see it continue.

My wife works here, too. Our business becomes not only our family life but our social life. Some families say, "Oh, gee, let's go out on a picnic," and they have it in the park. That doesn't interest me. The movies don't interest me. The great American city, whatever the hell they call it, doesn't interest me.* That stuff doesn't grab me. This is what I delight in.

You've got to make money if you want to continue on. That's the name of the game. If you don't show results on the bottom line, no bank'll touch ya. It's not like a social agency, where you can go out and ask for contributions. (Laughs.)

We just bought a condominium, across the street from the store. When I was a kid, we lived above the restaurant. We were high-class Greeks: we lived above it, not behind it. (Laughs.)

I would have liked to see my son be a professsional person in the sense of being a C.P.A., a lawyer, maybe a doctor, a dentist. I was wrong. I think I was being a little bit selfish and snobbish. There are some people who I know, they're so goddamn overeducated that they're really sick. Educated idiots, I call 'em. I think education's very important, but I'm talking about like some of these Harvard graduates. They're so educated, they're dumb. (Laughs.) They've sold us a couple of leaders who weren't what they were cracked up to be. We're hard workers, but we're not dumbbells.

* Great America, the amusement park

DAN O'BRIEN

◇————————————————————————————————————◇

He is married and has six children. A large man, he speaks slowly,
deliberately, as though his reflections were achingly offered.
His is a rueful smile. He is fifty-seven.

Our society has reserved success for the young. The others . . . (He
trails off.)

My father was a man who loved to live. He was a tremendously
successful real estate man when he was young. He invested his money
in options on real estate, lost it all during the depression, and came
back as the president of a brewery. And as a politician. He was thirty-
nine when he died. He had no insurance. I was eighteen at the time.

The Irish measure of a person's success is by the kind of wake he
has. For two nights and three days, the stairs of our house was
crowded with people. My mother, who hadn't worked since she was
married, bullied her way into a political job. At the wake, the politicians said: "Rose, there's plenty of time to talk about it later." She
said: "We're gonna talk about it now." And she did.

Both of us worked, and I was going to school at the same time. We
conducted the family as though we were husband and wife. She once
said of me: "Dan was never young. He was an old man from the time
I remember him." My wife often said that my mother and me
sounded like two businessmen.

I was working to a point of exhaustion, and I was going to law
school in the evenings. When World War Two broke out, I was
twenty-one. I volunteered just to get my year over with. I was in four
years and ten months.

In the army I met very important people for the first time in my
life. I was an infantry officer and was selected as the aide to the new
commanding general in Sicily. At our table were Omar Bradley,
Eisenhower, Patton. I had missions to General Montgomery.

One of the most miserable days I ever spent was D-day. We took off
on a small skiff in the English Channel. It was one of the roughest
days anyone had ever known. I was really sick. In spite of it, I never
forgot the magnificent sight, the air black with planes.

I was wounded that day. I was one of the five to survive my O.C.S.
class of a hundred or so. I still think I have the ability to survive

hardship and bounce back. When I came back, I attended management school and learned everything about industrial plants.

I became vice-president of a company doing twenty-five million dollars a year. I was promised the presidency and left when the promise was not fulfilled, according to my nervous schedule. Went to another company as president and got caught in a merger.

I joined a company that had lost a million dollars the year before I came and made a million dollars' profit at the end of my second year. I performed miracles for them in many ways.

They had one of the toughest unions in the country. It took seven months of negotiations, and I talked their representatives into a settlement. The president of the union said: "You've done a job on us, but we can't take this to our workers." I said: "Let me do it." I heard the union members talking in the hall—my office was close-by. They were yelling, tough guys: second-, third-generation Irish, Poles, Italians. The kind of people I was raised with. I got on the podium and told them stories. I had them laughing and then explained this package. I made a tape of the speech. As I left, I was applauded and the package was unanimously approved. Oh, I had all kinds of praise. It was a historic negotiation. Everybody was listening to the tapes. I was riding very high. One of my grandiose dreams was of moving along. I wondered if I wasn't a bit too good for this company. I was looking for something larger to tackle.

(A long pause) One of the great tragedies of American business life is what happens to talented executives who dedicate their lives to the company, who are successful and part of a system that is so bad. I didn't take the company from a million-dollar loss to a million-dollar profit without hurting a lot of people. One of the things I had to do was reduce the administrative personnel by thirty-five percent. These were people with twenty, twenty-five years of service. You do to others, and then it's done unto you. I've been part of it having to happen to other men. I've identified with the baseball manager who's taken a team to the World Series. He didn't win it, and on the whim of someone who's disappointed, he's discharged.

Although I considered it one of the most brutal and bloody jobs I've ever undertaken in my life, it went off smoothly. The company functioned better than it had prior to the bloodletting.

I wanted to celebrate this marvelous result and took some of my key executives to a private club for dinner. I said: "Let's make it a Friday night, it's more convenient for everybody. We'll eat our fish and bear it." The story in the big office was that I wanted to know what religion these men and their wives were. That's how it began.

(A very long pause) I have a daughter who is epileptic and has to be chauffeured to her private school. It's Catholic. In the car, she always had little holy pictures and sayings. I pulled into a parking space that is sometimes used by one of the sales executives, though I didn't know it. He went to the chairman of the board and said: "Some religious nut has my space." I said: "I'm afraid I'm the religious nut you're talking about." Sometime later, the chairman said: "Dan, how would you like to have drinks and dinner with me tonight? I said: "I can't, I'm going on a religious retreat." I had no idea . . .

One morning, I found my own resignation on my desk. Absolutely no reason was given. I didn't know what to think. I thought it must be some terrible misunderstanding. I got into my car and drove at a very high speed. I couldn't reach anybody. All the directors had taken off. They were intentionally out of town. I couldn't reach anyone for three months. Was this the end of my career?

I left immediately. That was part of the deal. They used the same formula I had used. You do to others, and then it's done unto you. I've been part of it happening to other men. Now I was hoisted by my own petard. When I terminated the others, it was with a check of twenty-five thousand dollars or eighteen thousand dollars, an offer to help, and good references. Not in my own case.

There was a breach in my references. I had become what executive searchers call a "controversial figure." It means you have left for an unknown reason, there's something about you. Perhaps you're a troublemaker or a deviate. It's something no one discusses. It reduces your market value greatly.

I don't recall anger. It wasn't anything like: I'd like to punch this guy out, or if I had a gun I'd shoot him. I was desolate, frustrated. I felt alone. I didn't want to go home and tell my wife what happened because I didn't know what happened. I had my picture in the financial pages of *The Wall Street Journal* three times and suddenly this happened.

You begin to wonder about this capitalism you preached, the profit motive. I used to tell young executives the name of the game is profit. You wonder whose game it really is. I can understand that someone who isn't producing should be gently reduced to a level where he can perform well, and someone who is performing well should be allowed to rise. I played the game that I had been taught.

At this point in my life, I feel deflated. I'm trying to earn enough money to pay for the things I like to do. I'd give anything for an exciting challenge, probably an arm. It's hard. A neighbor, an accountant for a large company, tried to interest them in my coming in and managing it. I was all excited. He called and said: "You're too old."

Our profit system, the one we all live by, is presented as a fun game for young people training to be managers. If you can reduce the time it takes to do something, you increase the profit. Growth and investors' happiness are based on this. You can expand your facilities . . . that's why America is the land of the *plenty*. I'm so *proud* of the system. It's a wonderful thing that so much has been created, that we all have television sets and cars and pollution and everything. There's no place like it.

But what the hell is capitalism? Look what it's done to one of its greatest proponents. It's knocked me right on the head, and I'm crawling around on the street, trying to breathe.

There's a great line from the movie *Save the Tiger*. Jack Lemmon says to this highly skilled craftsman: "What are you really looking for? What's your objective in life?" The guy looks at him innocently and says: "Another season." Right now, I'm just looking for another season. I just wanna know things are gonna be all right for a little while ahead.

I've got a lot of strength I can draw on out of my own family. My oldest daughter is tremendously successful and has a tremendously successful husband. My two sons, who are out in the business world, have had good luck with their companies. I have a daughter who is the movie-star type, brighter than hell and has straight A's in college. Opportunities are just great for these young people—the younger, the better.

They like me, but they're beginning to wonder what the hell's happening. When they were growing up, I was president of a company and everybody was talking about me. Now, what the hell's happened to the old guy? And I was so concerned about how they'd fit into this confused world that I seemed to be leaving. (Laughs.) Yeah, let's have another season.

BILL VEECK

◇──────────────────────────────────────◇

He's nursing a beer at a table in the Bards Room, a casual restaurant-saloon under the stands of Comiskey Park, serving freeloaders, among journalists, friends, friends of friends, and an occasional wayfaring stranger.

He is president of the Chicago White Sox. He is sixty-four.

For the most part, we're losers. We're losers in a country where winning means you're great, you're beautiful, you're moral. If you don't make a lot of money, you're a loser. The bigness, the machines, the establishment, imbue us with the idea that unless you make a lot of money, you're nothing. Happiness has nothing to do with it. I'm challenging that, and I'm having fun doing it.

We have a lousy team out in the field right now, but they're singing in the stands. We have just about the worst ball club and the oldest park in the country. We have an exploding scoreboard in Comiskey Park. At first, they declared it illegal, immoral, fattening, terrible, too bush. (Laughs.) Funny how you pick things up. It came from reading Saroyan's play *The Time of Your Life*. All took place in a saloon. There's a pinball machine and the fella, he goes up to the bartender and he wants more nickels. He plays and plays, no luck; and just before the final curtain, he hits a winner. The bells rang and the flag went up and it played "Dixie" and all sorts of extravagant things. That's what happens on our exploding scoreboard. Saroyan was sayin' something: You keep tryin' and tryin', and finally you do hit a winner. You hope, you dream, the guy's gonna hit a homer. Suddenly he hits it. The rockets go off, the bombs burst in air. (Laughs.) The loser has his day.

There is in all of us a competitive spirit, but winning has become life and death. We lose sight that it's only a *game*. It's a delightful game that is occasionally played by skillful men. Phil Wrigley once said that all you need is a winning club. It's a damning comment. We all like winners, but winning without joy isn't worth the candle. I hate to lose, but it's not the end of the world. Tomorrow may be better. (Laughs.) I'm the guy at that pinball machine waiting for all those rockets to explode.

I guess that's one of the reasons I was thrown out of organized baseball. I'd like to say I withdrew gracefully. They agreed to let the St. Louis Browns move to Baltimore if I withdrew. It was '53 when they terminated me. When I came back to the Sox thirteen years later, I was not welcomed with open arms. I didn't show proper respect.

I've reached the conclusion that I'm an anachronism. My wife and I have created a couple of other anachronisms: our sons. I'll settle for that.

POSTSCRIPT: *In 1954, I ran into Eddie Gaedel. He was a midget, three feet seven, who worked as a messenger. In 1951, Veeck had hired him as a ballplayer, as a member of the St. Louis Browns, for one turn at bat. "He got on base," Veeck recalls. "He had a foot-and-a-half strike zone. If I had any courage, I might have signed eight midgets, and we might have won a game in '51."*

Gaedel, wistful, rueful, remembered: "I batted a thousand that year. One time at bat. I get on base. I'm disappointed in Mr. Veeck. I sure thought he'd use me again. But," he smiled beatifically, "I'll never forget that day as long as I live. The fans went wild. I still think I can do it." It was his one glory moment.

THE HIRED GUN, THE TRAVELIN' LADY, THE WANDERIN' KID, AND THE INDIAN

JAY SLABAUGH, 48

I sometimes think of myself as a hired gun. I come into a company and correct the problem, then go on to another company. I've been president of two corporations, twice at Rock of Ages, and executive vice-president of two others. The hired gun goes off to wherever he has to do whatever he has to do. You have to go where it is.

He's president of Rock of Ages, a stone quarry and manufacturing company. Barre, Vermont. "In memorials, we've done some very big things." On the walls of his office: a panoramic view of San Francisco and an autographed portrait of Ronald Reagan. "I was on his personal staff when he was governor. He is a fantastic person."

I was born and raised in a small cow-desert-oil town halfway between Los Angeles and San Francisco. My father was a farmer. He preferred to be called a rancher. We had about three hundred acres, which isn't much land out there.

My grandfather was something very special. He became quite powerful and helped start a poor guy from Georgia, J. G. Boswell. He taught my grandfather how to drink and party. My grandfather couldn't handle the alcohol, and finally J. G. Boswell had it all. Now J. G. Boswell is one of the biggest farming corporations in the country. J. G. II, Jimmy Boswell, sits on the board of General Electric. My grandfather wound up with nothing. If you grab something and can't hold it, is it somebody else's fault?

Because there wasn't money to have help, we learned what the world was like very early. It was an advantage that kids don't have now. When I was twelve and the men went off to war, I got a job driving a tractor. I did this for twelve hours a day, six days a week— and hated it. I decided right then that I wouldn't live like this. The kids can't do that now. Before they realize how tough and grubby the world is, they're thirty years old and it's too late to change.

I spent some time in management consulting with Price Waterhouse. I went with Wallworth Valve Company who, after a year or so, sent me to St. Louis. My wife is ready to go to just about any place in the country I have to go.

I left there to go back to consulting in San Francisco. An old friend, executive vice-president of Wallworth, wanted me to look at this little company down in Dallas. I thought I'd sell him a consulting engagement. He thought he'd buy me to run the company. He did that. I went down and ran this company, and it grew very quickly. He left because of internal company politics. Very soon, I left. That was the Delta Pea, Inc. We had that stock up to fifteen dollars a share. After we left, it went back down to two. I went to International Heating in Utica, New York. That thing went up seven times the first year and doubled again the second year.

How do I do it? I listen a lot. People in the company know what has to be done. If it means taking out certain people, they'll tell you to take them out. They won't tell you directly, but if you listen and hear, people tell you. Sometimes there are people who have to be replaced, but this is a last resort.

Sometimes they might say: "Don't fire this guy because you'll make the people mad." If there is a guy who's goofing off, everybody knows he's goofing off; and if you fire him, they say: "Why the hell didn't you do that a long time ago?" They all respect you more. They say: "Hey, the guy now recognizes that I'm performing because he's taking out the people who don't."

If the guy who doesn't do anything gets as much as the guy who does, nobody does anything. You can motivate them with other techniques, but if you really have to get tough, threaten to fire them. There's nothing to me in the world as rewarding as making people do things they don't believe they could do. You've made 'em bigger in their own eyes. Bigger in their family's eyes. Bigger in the community's eyes. Nobody will ever do them a favor that great, but they'll hate you for the rest of their life because of the pressure you had put on them. Yet that is very rewarding to me.

I've had long discussions with some of the top people in motivation. One said that when he was in the military, he carried a gun. He never drew it, but the gun was there. He said: "I never deliberately put fear in people, but I had the gun."

I identify with the company, not the place. I've always felt a bit of an outsider. I feel you should be an outsider to be objective. You can make more rational decisions. When you get emotionally involved in anything, you make a mess of it. The whole world knows about what messes you make when you get emotionally involved with a woman. To the degree that you get emotionally involved with your kids, you don't handle them well. If you're completely objective about them— what's best for the kid?—you do what's right. But if you're too emotional, if it's love, you might baby the kid too much. You can't avoid getting emotion into everything, but to the degree that you can be cool and rational about it, you're gonna do it better.

What benefits the company benefits everybody in it, everybody in the company, all the customers, all the suppliers, the government, and God. (Laughs.)

The first year I was at Rock of Ages, the after-tax income increased two hundred fifty percent and sales increased twenty-five percent. Then I left to go to Whitney Blake and American Flexible Conduit. When I came back, Rock of Ages had gone down to a no-profit, perhaps even a loss. This last year, our annual report shows a profit of nearly two million dollars.

I haven't always been a success. I was fired by Nortek, Inc., the parent company of Rock of Ages. We're a wholly owned subsidiary of a conglomerate. They wanted more than I could give them at the time, though I felt I had been successful.

It's necessary that people want more than there is for continual growth. The executive vice-president of Nortek bought Whitney Blake. It was a bad acquisition: a wire and cable company. That was in 1975. There wasn't a wire and cable company in the industry that was making money. I had gone down there to put that thing in shape for him, not really knowing the problems of the industry. Copper prices were down to the fifty-cent level. When the prices are down, the wire and cable industry is a disaster. Nortek didn't understand this. We had been at a loss when I got there, and we came back to break even. The parent company felt it should be making significant amounts of money. There just wasn't any way. The executive who bought it against the wishes of the president of Nortek couldn't admit his mistake, so the president said: "We'll do something to correct it." He did. I was fired. I felt it was unfair. The year after I left, the company lost almost two million dollars.

Do you remember your feelings when you were fired?

(Pause) I remember my feelings, but I don't like to talk about them.

I got a call from Nortek asking me to come back to Rock of Ages. They said: "We made a mistake." Nortek is an aggressively managed conglomerate. Its sales are just slightly under a hundred million.

You must be aggressive. I've always had the feeling that if you don't go up, you go down. Nothing ever stays the same. You get better and bigger, or you go the other way.

My feeling is everybody in business is against you. Everybody in the world is against you. Your people are against you because they want more money for less hours than you can afford to pay them. Your suppliers are against you because they want more money for the product than you can afford to give them. Your customers are against you because they want your product for less money than you can afford to sell it. The city is against you because they want to tax you more. The federal government is against you because they want to control you more. The parent company is against you because they want to take more cash out of your operation and don't want to put the cash investment into it. When anybody gets in the way of your being a vital, growing force in the economy, they're hurting themselves and everybody around them.

Let's face it. If we don't grow and get more profit, there isn't more money for raises, there aren't promotions for people. If you don't grow, you don't buy more products from your suppliers. You don't have new machines, so you don't give more and better products to your customers. There's not more income for the government to tax. I can make a case of hurting God because there isn't more money for the collection plate. (Laughs.)

The American Dream is to be better off than you are. How much money is "enough money"? "Enough money" is always a little bit more than you have. There's never enough of anything. This is why people go on. If there was enough, everybody would stop. You always go for the brass ring that's always out there about a hundred yards farther. It's like a mirage in the desert: it always stays about a hundred yards ahead of you.

If I had more, if the company had more, I could accomplish much more. I could do more good for the economy. You must go for more —for faster, for better. If you're not getting better and faster, you're getting worse.

(Reflectively) Growth—better—faster. I guess that's my one big vice. I feel a very heavy sense of compulsion, a sense of urgency. When I get in a car, I also feel it. I drive much too fast. I'm always moving.

ROSALIE SORRELLS

There's a terrible mobility in this society. It's too easy to run away from things. I do that too. The ease with which you can shift your ground makes the ground fall away from under you all the time. The sense of being someplace goes faster every year.

She is a traveling folk singer.

I think of the town I grew up in—Boise, Idaho—of my family and how they got there, and my own sense of place. I love the feeling of the country that you find in writers like Thomas Wolfe.

My grandparents were an adventurous kind of people. My grandfather was a preacher, wanted to live with the Indians, so he became a missionary to the Crow and the Sioux. He went to Montana. He crossed the Bad Lands all by himself. 1900. He's sort of mysterious to me except through the stories that my grandmother and my mother and father told me about him.

My father was born in Montana. They lived in tents and lodges. My father was one of four sons. My grandmother was a real good photographer. My mother still has some of those photographs. There's pictures of their first trek, this great long trek, with pack horses all strung out across the hill. They all went out on horseback.

They went on river trips. They didn't meet any hostile Indians. Everything they had to do with them was religious. Just the business of living in that time and place was dangerous, having babies in the wilderness and all those things. The trip took seven or eight years.

My grandfather became the pastor of a church in Hailey, Idaho. He used to snowshoe from Hailey up to Ketchum and preach a sermon in the church there. They turned that church into a bar years later. I sang there. The Espresso House.

My mother's father was a wild-eyed adventurer. I think his wife was scared of him. (Laughs.) I didn't get along with her for a long time. She was real southern. She didn't like blacks and she didn't like Japanese people. She didn't like anybody she didn't know for a hundred years. (Laughs.) But I remember my grandfather better than anyone I ever met. He died when I was nine. He was in the Spanish-American War, he went to Alaska in the Gold Rush, and he did labor organizing up in Seattle. He talked to me incessantly. He taught me all the soliloquies from *Hamlet* when I was a little bitty girl. He'd say the words are like music and I will come to understand them. He used to swear at the horses in Shakespearean language. I remember him so well 'cause he always treated me like I could do anything. He let me drive the hay wagon with a four-horse team when I was this tiny little girl. And didn't ever behave like I shouldn't be up in that tree where I was. (Laughs.)

I always thought of my father, until the day he died, as a young man. He was very handsome, had a little mustache and a light slender body. He was very alive, and I think of him with a lot of pleasure. He liked words, too. He loved Balzac and Rabelais. He turned me on to those things. He liked to play games with words and loved to tell stories always.

After I got married, I took up folk singing as a hobby. I collected old songs. So I'm not thinking of myself as a singer so much as someone who repeats old songs that they heard. I began to write, and I had this big repertoire of folk songs from Utah and Idaho that nobody else knew. I got invited to Newport in 1966. I'd never been east of Denver. When I drove into New York City at seven o'clock in the morning, it was like goin' to Mars. There was that skyline. I just flipped. I nearly had a heart attack, I was so excited. (Laughs.) We came into town—my brother was with me, and a couple of friends—it was too early to wake anybody up. We came to a bar. It was open at eight o'clock in the morning. Never saw a place that was open at eight o'clock in the morning. We had a bottle of champagne to celebrate the fact that we had finally arrived in New York City, and we went to the top of the Empire State Building. (Laughs.) Everyone always told me I'd hate it in New York because it was cold and awful and mean. I just loved it, every second of it. And I still do. (Laughs.) I'm a city junkie. I'd like to find cut what makes each place so particular.

Boise hardly exists for me any more. All the things I remember with pleasure have been torn down and been replaced by bullshit. They want to make a mall of it. Downtown Boise, all covered, is like a cattle chute for customers, my mother says. All just for selling and consuming. I remember all those wonderful things that just aren't there any more. Boise is a corruption of "le bois." Trees. It used to be like a little cup of trees. A river runs right through the middle. You could hardly see more than two or three buildings. The statehouse and Hotel Boise. Just trees and this river. Oh, corridors of green. Trees so old and big that came together and made little corridors. It was against the law to shoot a squirrel, and the place was just all full of little brown squirrels. Old, old houses and a sense of community. None of that's there any more. They've cut down the trees, they tore down the old buildings. It's a real consumer town. What I remember with any pleasure is gone.

I was always a misfit, so I didn't have nice memories of, say, going to school. I didn't relate well to the kids 'cause I could read faster than they did. I was in third grade, and they had these reading tests, and I had very high scores. I didn't think I was that much smarter than anyone else. It's just that I read since I was a little bitty kid. You weren't supposed to be smart when you were a girl in 1949 in Boise, Idaho. You weren't supposed to let anybody know you knew anything. (Laughs.)

One day I got out of school, there were four or five big girls out there, fifth and sixth graders. They dragged me into the alley and knocked me down and told me I had to crawl home. They told me I shouldn't get such good scores any more. Like some kind of kid Mafia.

(Laughs.) They're poking me with sticks. I lost my temper. I just became completely enraged, and I hurt a couple of 'em pretty bad. I hit one of 'em in the Adam's apple, and she had to stay out of school for a week. I kicked another in the groin, and she couldn't walk. And I ran home. I remember I threw up for about half an hour after I had gone into this terrible rage. I still think about it. I have not got used to the idea that somebody could do something like that to another person because that person was winning. Their sense was that I was winning. My sense was I wasn't competing.

I'm not trying to beat anybody out. I do what I do. It seems awful to me that anybody bases their whole life on winning. I always loved that song where Malvina Reynolds says:

> *I don't mind wearing raggedy britches*
> *Because them that succeeds are sons of bitches.*
> *I don't mind failing in this world.*

There's another line:

> *I'll stay down here with the raggedy crew*
> *If gettin' up there means steppin' on you.*

I never thought of myself as being really poor because we had a house. We didn't have any money at all. But I think of myself as privileged because we had so many books and a place to live. My brother is ten years younger than I am. I was the only kid for a long time. I didn't know how to make friends.

My husband's family was so different from mine, and he was so different from me. When I met him he was in rebellion against his middle-class WASP family. Their values seemed to rest in the possession of things.

His family was very rich. They always had plenty. They never suffered during the depression. The men in my family were disasters of the depression. They never learned how to make money and be successful. I always thought of my dad as a success because he was a wonderful man. When I was in high school and he was drinking a lot, it hung me up. But my memories of him are all delightful because he seemed so particular, like no one else.

When he died, I remember this asshole (laughs)—excuse me— from the funeral home. My brother and I didn't want my mother to have to deal with it. First, he gives us a line about how cheap we are because we don't buy an expensive coffin. We were gonna have a cremation anyhow and take Dad's ashes up and put them at the cabin

41

where he always lived. This guy: "What florist you want us to call?" I said: "We're gonna bring some pine boughs and dried weeds from the cabins." (Laughs.) He said: "Well, what organist do you want me to call?" "I'm gonna sing for my father." And he says: "Well," (clears throat), "one of our services is to write the obituary. Tell me something about Walter." I said: "Well, we called him Walt." (Laughs.) I'm looking at him and I can't think of anything. He said: "What was his religion?" I said: "Well, he wasn't very religious." He says: "Hmmm. What did he do for a living?" I said: "He hadn't worked for a long time." He says: "He was retired?" I thought: Well, I'm not going to say anything. Then he says: "What fraternal organizations did he belong to?" I'm looking at him and I'm thinking: My father could walk for two blocks on his hands. He used to do that all the time, just walk along on his hands. People would come by and he would say good morning as though that were just the regular way to be walking along.

He used to jump over a card table from a standing jump every year on his birthday. I think he was fifty-six when he missed. (Laughs.) He had this piece of land. He built this beautiful house. He cut every tree. He made every brick. It looks like it grew out of the ground. And he went hunting all the time. He loved to walk through the woods making up dirty limericks. He knew the name of every bird and every flower. He hated the AMA and the assholes like this guy I'm talking to. (Laughs.) So I didn't say any of that to him. I just said: "I can't think of anything to tell you about my father that you want to hear." (Laughs.) So he just wrote something and put it in the paper. How do you describe a man like that? He just wasn't like anybody else in the world.

Since 1966 I've been on my own. I've been so lucky in the friends that have come to me. People who've put me up across the country. I consider myself to be incredibly successful. I don't have any money, but I'm respected by those whose respect I crave. I'm given love by my audiences, and I make enough money to get along. I'd like it to be a little easier, but I do want my way.

I can't live with despair. I don't want to live with the notion that it's all downhill from here. I don't believe that. I don't have a sense of despair because I'm alive. When I'm dead, I don't expect to have a sense of anything. (Laughs.)

I look at my children and I could develop a sense of despair. My oldest son committed suicide. He went to some trouble to make me understand that that was not directed at me. But I can't figure out why I couldn't impart to him this sense of delight in being alive.

I look at a lot of these other children and I feel sorry for them. They get bored. I don't remember ever being bored. They're not curious. They practice alienation as if it was a thing to do. I think there's a giant conspiracy on the part of—who? ITT or them?—the rich, the powerful, the manipulators, to make us all the same. Make sure that we watch a lot of television. Make sure that we all have credit cards and cars and houses that are all kind of sleazy. We're so afraid we'll lose 'em that we'll do anything they want us to do to keep those things. I think that sense of values that measures a person's worth by how much they have is perpetrated by those rich and powerful people. To me, the most valuable people are the ones who kick and scream and won't go there. Who insist on being mavericks. Who refuse to go in that direction.

I have no intention of going under. I will play my drum my way.

ANN BANKS

The way you know an army brat is when you ask them: "Where are you from?" A normal question. There's a silence. I've trained myself to say Florida. That's where my family's from and where I was born. But I didn't grow up there and I don't really feel from there. Usually, there's just a silence. You're gathering your energy to say: "Well, nowhere really."

A journalist, she is working on a book concerning army wives.

I was sheltered from growing up, on those army posts. You had to go through a sentry gate to get in. I lived on this little protected island in the middle of America. It was sort of an enchanted princess atmosphere. The one thing that struck me is that all these army posts look alike. That's probably very carefully orchestrated. Even in the middle of the desert in Oklahoma, the residential section is green. Grass, very carefully trimmed, and shade trees. It's a beautiful way to grow up—in a way. It's like a vast playground. It's a very safe place and the kids can run wild. I think very early I knew this wasn't real America.

You go to schools on army posts, too, so your world is self-contained. When you go off the army posts, there are commercial strips of bars and tattoo parlors and used-car joints. So you go from this extremely ordered environment to a total honky-tonk chaos.

When you're an army brat, it means your entire environment is conditioned by much more than what your father does for a living. You grow up in a total institution. I always thought of it as being like a circus child, there are many second- and third-generation military families. Every need is taken care of and you're not expected to ever leave. If you're a woman, you're an army wife in training. If you're a man, you're expected to go to West Point.

My father, who had a lot of interest in my marrying an army officer (laughs), would have been totally appalled if I had said I want to make the army my life, I want to join the women's army corps. I think he would have fainted. (Laughs.) He had a certain image of the WACs' being not what he wanted his daughter to be.

My father would say to us: "You're going to visit your cousins. Poor them. They have to live in one place all their lives. Doesn't that sound boring? We've gotten to live all over. We've had a lot of different experiences. Doesn't that sound more interesting?" We'd say: "It sure does." And we really felt it. Obviously, he felt a little guilty about schlepping us all over all the time. The odd thing was, until I went to college, I had no idea that anybody could have thought differently.

My father was at the embassy in Bonn, and I went to a boarding school for military and embassy kids in Frankfort. The first week, I met this guy who had grown up in one place, Miami, all his life "How many times did you move?" he said. "I moved fourteen, fifteen times," I told him. "Oh, poor you," he said. I said: "Poor *you*, that had to live in one place all your life." (Laughs.)

You grow up a certain way. You never realize other people grow up different. I had this epiphany about five years ago. I was in California, driving down Highway One, which bisects Fort Ord. Sometimes you hear something and it's intensely familiar before you quite understand what it is. You're overwhelmed with emotion before you know what it is. I heard this sound. It was reassuring, like a lullaby. Then I realized what it was. It was artillery practice. It was the distant sound of these guns, booming.

The first song I was taught was the artillery song: *Over hill, over dale*. There were the flag ceremonies. Very compelling. They'd play taps at five o'clock every afternoon. Wherever you're going on the post, you have to stop your car and stand facing the flag. How you knew where it was, I don't know, but everybody did it.

When I was six, we lived in Carlisle Barracks, Pennsylvania, and then we moved to Fort Sill, Oklahoma. It was a city surrounded by walls. I think the army tries to make it seem like a small town. You have the commissary, you have the movie theater, you have the bowling alley. You have stables, you have a swimming pool, you have lots of swimming pools. Nobody can drive fast. If you drive over fifteen miles an hour, they send you to jail. You have the houses. The lieutenant colonels' houses are all alike. The colonels' houses are all alike. Your grass has to be mowed a certain way or you'd get a letter from the quartermaster corps. At this point, I was beginning to understand there were other ways of living. I was learning to read.

I was in fourth grade when my father went to Korea. My mother decided that we'd live on Anna Maria Island, off the coast of Sarasota. I felt this was my one chance to see what real American life was like. I watched everything. This one family, with six kids, lived right down the street. I thought: Boy, I've got myself a typical American family. I was a little ten-year-old anthropologist. The mother was trying to get the kids into growing avocados or taking care of the goldfish. She'd try to interest me in the constructive projects, too, and I used to think: My project is watching you. (Laughs.)

I thought Anna Maria Island was typical America. What's funny is the place was so bizarre. (Laughs.) It was the kind of odd conglomeration of people who end up in some warm climate, drifters and runaways. A lot of alcoholics there. It was a place where every sort of drifter and ne'er-do-well, you'd tilt the country and they'd all float to California or float to Florida, all the ones who weren't attached. I loved the place. They had these little ticky-tacky houses right on the ocean. Whenever there'd be a storm, there'd be sandbagging parties. I remember sneaking out and watching them. There they were, all night in a howling storm, getting drunker and drunker. What was funny about it was that I was convinced this was the real heart of the country.

I remember reading a *Saturday Evening Post* or a *Life* that year. There was a corporate ad for Bell Telephone. It was a charcoal drawing of a soldier. It said something about husbands, fathers, brothers, boyfriends, who might be killed at any moment, blah, blah, blah. It never crossed my mind that my father might be killed. That never, never occurred to me. I thought: What are they doing, telling me this? I'm not supposed to know. Nobody told me that before. It's a very protective environment for kids, very idyllic.

There were problems, as part of a total institution. If you were an adolescent and got into trouble as adolescents do, there'd be a file on you, and your father's career would be affected. Certain demerits.

When we were in Germany at the embassy, my sister told me of a club some kids belonged to, the Mercedes Club. The way to get in was to break the silver star off the car. Mercedes has this hood ornament. It was their daredevil exploit, a typical delinquent act. When it was found out, whole families were sent home.

When I was sixteen, two things happened. I was doing a term paper on the Hungarian revolution. I used the American Embassy library and I read the U.N. transcripts. About the American role: the Voice of America and Radio Free Europe giving the Hungarian rebels false hope. I knew some Hungarian refugees. I interviewed one. I thought: This is an outrage.

The other thing. I was in Livorno, northern Italy. I went dancing with these two Italian men one Saturday night. I was sixteen, just completely the belle. We were frolicking around the town. It was, by this time, eleven-thirty or twelve o'clock at night. We walked by this little tiny cubicle. It was a shoe repair stand. There was a young man, extremely handsome, pounding these shoes. He looked so full of energy and vitality, and yet he looked so angry. It looked like the anger of everyone in the world who was at the bottom that he was pounding out into these shoes. I had just been on top of the world, we'd been drinking champagne and dancing. I was just so caught up by this sight. The world was beautiful. Then I saw this man hammering these shoes. I still remember it. It's like a photograph.

It still took me a long time to become aware. At Fort Bragg, I'm a lifeguard at the officers' club swimming pool. I'm nineteen. It's in the early sixties. People were being trained to go to Vietnam as advisors. I remember one young man finishing something called HALO school. That's an acronym for high altitude, low opening. You jump out of an airplane at a very high altitude, you free fall, then you open. He was learning jungle survival skills. Then he was sent to a language school to learn Burmese. It didn't take much to figure out the plans for him to parachute into the jungles of Burma. The feeling I had was these men who got to lord it over others, just because they jumped out of airplanes, were macho. My only weapon was to make fun of it. I've tried to trace back my feelings about American imperialism. It was no one thing. A lot of people who were army brats ended up being against the war.

There's a man I went to high school with. He was an army brat. Brilliant, incredibly egotistical, and abrasive. He was in the class at West Point that was like *the* Vietnam class. He had graduated and was a Rhodes scholar, a brilliant lunatic. He was killed in Vietnam. He had written his own obituary for *The New York Times* Op-Ed page. He felt the war was totally justified and didn't want anybody making political capital out of his death. I felt on reading it: That goddamn Alex, grandstanding again, just the way he always did. (Laughs.) Yet the moral authority of a person who's written something which he knows will be published only posthumously was indisputable. He was talking about the life I'd known, the life of an army brat. I thought: Unfair, unfair advantage. (Laughs.) My reaction was really bizarre. He's making unfair points 'cause he had to go and get himself killed.

The funny thing is that I feel I'm very American even though I spent seven years of my young life out of the country. Though I'm opposed to what we do politically around the world, I'm emotionally and culturally very American. I like jazz, country and folk music, and open roads and the desert and space.

The military tries to promote a sense of community and a sense of shared purpose above and beyond one's individual family. It's a terrifically pleasing life in a certain way. I think it's a deadly life for the wives. There are all these traditions and all this protocol. Yet there's a kind of ceremonial quality to the life that is satisfying to the children.

But, I think, the shared purpose is a spurious one, an evil one. I want no part of it.

VINE DELORIA

As soon as we began to travel faster in this country, the importance of place got lost. I can get in an airplane in the desert, and in three hours get off in the Great Lakes. I didn't really travel. I wasn't aware of anything happening.

A bleak, rainy morning at O'Hare International Airport, Chicago.

He is a Sioux Indian, en route from Tucson to Washington, D.C. His most celebrated book is Custer Died for Your Sins. *He teaches political science at the University of Arizona. He is forty-five.*

Our conversation is occasionally interrupted by an elderly waitress of salty tongue, who constantly refills our coffee cups. She has been casually eavesdropping. "American Dream? Come on, you guys." She recounts, between her self-appointed rounds, a tale of her being cheated of thousands by a crooked lawyer. "American Dream? Are you kiddin'?"

I know a lot of Indian stories about places in America. St. Anthony Falls was once a holy shrine of the Sioux Indians. You go there, and you're filled with wonderment: What did it look like when we had it? What did it really look like before television and fast cars and jet airplanes?

I often think of the Donner party. 1846. Caught in the pass, they ended up as cannibals, eating each other. I remember following the same route, going by it in my Olds 98 on the salt flats. The interstate highway, from Denver to Cheyenne. I covered those salt flats in about forty-five minutes. In the pioneer days, you had to cross those salt flats in thirty-six hours. If you wasted any more time, you'd arrive at the Sierra Nevadas at a dangerous time of the year. It took the Donners six days. I went past those flats at seventy-five miles an hour, just zap! Knowing all kinds of people died there. You begin to raise questions about the white–Indian conflict.

None of these tribes saw enough whites at any one time to ever regard them as dangerous. If you have a tribe of five hundred sitting on a hillside and a wagon train of two hundred people goes by, that's no threat to you. You hear a lot of stories, traditional ones, that the Indians were afraid of the whites because they thought they were crazy. You read the tremendous sacrifices the pioneers made to get across the Great Plains. You think of your own people who sat on the hillside, who knew every creek and rock for a thousand miles around. They're looking down at these people, who are terrified because they're in tall grass. Neither side understands the other. Perhaps the Donner party might have been saved had they been friends of the Indians, had they not been frightened of these "enemies" who knew the terrain. You have to take a new look at what you thought America was before you can figure out where it's going.

I grew up on the Pine Ridge reservation in South Dakota. It was about thirty-five miles from Wounded Knee. The town was about four blocks long and three blocks wide, off Main Street. It was really only about two blocks of buildings. I remember before they put the pavement in. The roads were just cow pastures. When it rained, you were there for a couple of days. Very few whites lived there.

I went to grade school, half white and half mixed-blood Indians. They taught us Rudyard Kipling's world view. It was a simplistic theory that societies marched toward industry and that science was doing good for us. We're all Americans and none of us is ever disloyal. The United States has never been on the wrong side of anything. The government has never lied to the people. The FBI is there to help you, and if you see anything suspicious, call them. There was a heavy overtone of the old British colonial attitude. Nothing about the slaves. Minority history just didn't exist. The world somehow is the garden of the white people, and everybody else kind of fits in someplace. And it's not demeaning to fit in, 'cause that's the way God wants it. You're not being put down. Western civilization's finding a place for you.

It was glossed-over history that Americans used to recite on Memorial Day in the twenties and thirties. I remember going as a six-year-old kid to these roundups, where the old cowboys and all the old chiefs would gather. After a big barbecue, some broken down tenor would sing "Old Faithful" and "Wagon Wheels," and everybody would cry. They'd moan about the frontier being closed and they'd beat the drum. It takes you a long time to realize these things aren't real.

My father was an Episcopal missionary on the reservation. His father was too. I suppose our family was one of the first to move from the old ways to the white man's ways. It was a weird situation, schizophrenic. My family had been religious leaders before they'd become Christians. The old Indian religion. I was not just a minister's son. Mine was a long family tradition of medicine men. People came to my father for all sorts of things. He knew all kinds of medicine songs and stories.

He held on to the two cultures without much conflict until the late sixties. The civil rights movement turned him off. The church put tremendous pressure on the Indians to integrate. He said: "We don't have to. We can be what we are without getting into the melting pot." There are thousands of Indian Christians who looked upon Christianity in the old Indian way. The message of Jesus wasn't all that big. But a lot of the Indians were turned off and ended up with no religion. My father just gave up on Christianity.

Maybe my generation is the last one that was affected by Indian values. I'm forty-five. Now I see people, about eight years younger, going to a meeting and starting to dominate things right away. When I was five and six, older relatives shushed me up at meetings because no one should talk unless the oldest person talks. People of my age still feel these social constraints. If you move eight years down, you find people who've grown up in postwar brashness. The hustler. The further down you move, the worse it gets. The younger people have taken the rat race as the real thing. It's a thing in their heads. In my generation, it was a thing in the heart.

The young Indian as well as the young white has no sense of history whatsoever. I think the Second World War did it. History, for a long time, was dominated by Europe. The United States came out of World War Two as the great power. All of a sudden, we had responsibility. Our history had always been parochial. We were separated by oceans, we didn't know where we were. The anti-Communist paranoia took over: nobody's ever gonna conquer this country, by God. If we're destroyed, it will be self-destruction.

An old Sioux chief, Standing Bear, once said that the white man came to this continent afraid from the very beginning. Afraid of animals and nature and earth. This fear projected itself onto the land and the animals. They became frightened of the whites. When the whites would move in, the animals would move out. I had always thought that was a clever Indian saying until I re-read de Tocqueville last year. He says: You have ten thousand Indians living in an area with animals all around. You get two or three settlers there, and the animals and Indians leave.

You have to ask yourself: What kind of people were these that came here? They must have been absolutely frantic to set down roots. It was more than subduing the land. I mean, that's a hell of a toll to pay for the right to live on a piece of land.

Maybe the American Dream is in the past, understanding who you are instead of looking to the future: What are you going to be? 'Cause we've kind of reached the future. I'm not just talking about nostalgia. I'm talking about finding familiar guideposts. Maybe this is a period of reflection.

Last February, there was a meeting of some medicine men and some Jesuits. One of the medicine men stood up and said the whole problem with America is that everybody tries to be young. He said: "All you guys in the Indian community, you've got to start acting your age. You're all trying to stay young, so there are no wise old men any more. If you're grandfathers, you better start acting like grandfathers. If you're fathers, you better start acting like fathers. Don't act like white men. You can't ever do that."

I think there will emerge a group of people, not a large percentage, who will somehow find a way to live meaningful lives. For the vast majority, it will be increased drudgery, with emotions sapped by institutional confines. A grayness. A lot of people are fighting back.

Somewhere, America stalled in perpetual adolescence. But I don't really despair. You can't despair that you have to grow up.

FANTASIA

JILL ROBINSON

She is the daughter of a former Hollywood film producer.

Growing up in Hollywood was the only reality I knew. The closest I ever came to feeling glamorous was from my mother's maid, a woman named Dorothy, who used to call me Glamour. She was black. In those days, she was called colored. When I would see my mother—or my mother's secretary, 'cause there was a hierarchy—interviewing maids or cooks, I'd think of maids and cooks represented in the movies.

I used not to like to go to school. I'd go to work with my father. I'd like to be with him because power didn't seem like work. He had four or five secretaries, and they were always pretty. I thought: How wonderful to have pretty secretaries. I used to think they'd be doing musical numbers. I could imagine them tapping along with his mail. I never saw it real.

To me, a studio head was a man who controlled everyone's lives. It was like being the principal. It was someone you were scared of, someone who knew everything, knew what you were thinking, knew where you were going, knew when you were driving on the studio lot at eighty miles an hour, knew that you had not been on the set in time. The scoldings the stars got. There was a paternalism. It was feudal. It was an archaic system designed to keep us playing: Let's pretend, let's make believe.

First of all, you invented someone, someone's image of someone. Then you'd infantilize them, keep them at a level of consciousness, so they'd be convinced that this is indeed who they are. They had doctors at the studios: "Oh, you're just fine, honey. Take this and you'll be just fine." These stars, who influenced our dreams, had no more to do with their own lives than fairies had, or elves.

I remember playing with my brother and sister. We would play Let's Make a Movie the way other kids would play cowboys and Indians. We'd cry, we'd laugh. We'd do whatever the characters did. We had elaborate costumes and sets. We drowned our dolls and all the things one does. The difference was, if we didn't get it right, we'd play it again until we liked it. We even incorporated into our child play the idea of the dailies and the rushes. The repeats of film scenes to get the right angle. If the princess gets killed in a scene, she gets killed again and again and again. It's okay. She gets to live again. No one ever dies. There's no growing up. This was reality to us.

I had a feeling that out there, there were very poor people who didn't have enough to eat. But they wore wonderfully colored rags and did musical numbers up and down the streets together. My mother did not like us to go into what was called the servants' wing of the house.

My mother was of upper-class Jewish immigrants. They lost everything in the depression. My father tried to do everything he could to revive my mother's idea of what life had been like for her father in the court of the czar. Whether her father was ever actually in the court is irrelevant. My father tried to make it classy for her. It never was good enough, never could be. She couldn't be a Boston Brahmin.

Russian-Jewish immigrants came from the *shtetls* and ghettos out to Hollywood: this combination jungle-tropical paradise crossed with a nomadic desert. In this magical place that had no relationship to any reality they had ever seen before in their lives, or that anyone else had ever seen, they decided to create their idea of an eastern aristocracy. I'm talking about the kind of homes they would never be invited to. It was, of course, overdone. It was also the baronial mansions of the dukes' homes that their parents could never have gotten into. Goldwyn, Selznick, Zukor, Lasky, Warner. Hollywood—the American Dream—is a Jewish idea.

In a sense, it's a Jewish revenge on America. It combines the Puritan ethic—there's no sex, no ultimate satisfaction—with baroque magnificence. The happy ending was the invention of Russian Jews, designed to drive Americans crazy.

It was a marvelous idea. What could make them crazy but to throw back at them their small towns? Look how happy it is here. Compare the real small towns with the small town on the MGM back lot. There's no resemblance.

The street is Elm Street. It's so green, so bright, of lawns and trees. It's a town somewhere in the center of America. It's got the white fence and the big porch around the house. And it's got three and four generations. They're turn-of-the-century people before they learned how to yell at each other. It's the boy and girl running into each other's arms. And everybody else is singing. It's everybody sitting down to dinner and looking at each other, and everyone looks just wonderful. No one is sick. No one's mad at anyone else. It's all so simple. It's all exactly what I say it is.

Aunt Mary is a little looney and lives with us because she loves us. It's not that she's crazy and gonna wind up killing one of us one of these days. Or that she's drunk. It's simply that she'd rather live with us and take care of us. The father would be Lewis Stone. He'd have a little bit of a temper now and then. The mother is definitely Spring Byington. She's daffy, but she's never deaf. She hears everything you say and she listens. And she hugs you and her hug is soft and sweet-smelling. The daughter is Judy Garland when she believed in Aunt Em. The boy is Robert Walker before he realized he was gonna drink himself to death. And love and marriage would be innocence and tenderness. And no sex.

The dream to me was to be blond, tall, and able to disappear. I loved movies about boys running away to sea. I wanted to be the laconic, cool, tall, Aryan male. Precisely the opposite of the angry, anxious, sort of mottle-haired Jewish girl.

I wanted to be this guy who could walk away from any situation that got a little rough. Who could walk away from responsibility. The American Dream, the idea of the happy ending, is an avoidance of responsibility and commitment. If something ends happily, you don't have to worry about it tomorrow.

The idea of the movie star, the perfect-looking woman or man who has breakfast at a glass table on a terrace where there are no mosquitoes. No one ever went to the bathroom in movies. I grew up assuming that movie stars did not. I thought it was terrible to be a regular human being. Movie stars did not look awful, ever. They never threw up. They never got really sick, except in a wonderful way where they'd get a little sweaty, get sort of a gloss on the face, and then die. They didn't shrivel up or shrink away. They didn't have acne. The woman didn't have menstrual cramps. Sex, when I ran across it, in no way resembled anything I had ever seen in the movies. I didn't know how to respond.

I think the reason we're so crazy sexually in America is that all our responses are acting. We don't know how to feel. We know how it looked in the movies. We know that in the movies it's inconceivable that the bad guy will win. Therefore we don't get terribly involved in any cause. The good guy's gonna win anyway. It's a marvelous political weapon.

The Hollywood phenomenon of the forties—the Second World War—was distinct from the Vietnam War. War was fine. Sure there were bad things, but there were musicals. Comedies about soldiers. The dream was to marry someone in uniform. I believed every bit of it. I saw how the movies were made and still I believed it.

I remember seeing a carpenter in front of the house and telling my father he looked like Roy Rogers and that he ought to test him. He did. The guy couldn't act. We were always testing everyone, always seeing what raw material they would be. I'd sit in class pretending to be an executive. I'd be sitting there figuring out who could this kid play, who could that one play. I used to look at Robert Redford in class and imagine he would be a movie star. In fourth grade. You always looked at humans as property. It affected all our lives.

I hated the idea that I was bright. There was a collision between bright and pretty and seductive. I wanted to be one of those girls the guys just wanted to do one thing to. I wanted to be one of those blond jobs. That's what they used to call them—jobs. A tall job. A slim job. Somebody you could work on.

I wanted to be Rhonda Fleming or Lana Turner. I refused to see what the inside of their lives was like. They didn't see it either. It was carefully kept from them. My God, look at the life. Getting up at five-thirty in the morning before your brain has begun to function, getting rolled out in a limousine, and having people work on your body and your face. Remember, they were very young people when they came out here. Imagine having all your waking life arranged all the time. They became machines. No wonder the sensitive ones went insane or killed themselves.

The studio had the power. The studio would hire the fan club. The head of the club was on the star's payroll. The star was usually not even aware of where the money was going, to whom, for what. The whole thing was manufactured. Fame is manufactured. Stardom is manufactured. After all these years, it still comes as a surprise to me.

The rest of the country for me consisted of the Sherry-Netherlands Hotel, which I assumed my father owned because of the name—I thought they spelled it wrong*—and the Pump Room.** We would take the Super Chief. You would have a drawing room and two bedrooms all the way across the country. You would get to Chicago, and all the luggage would be transferred to the Ambassador East Hotel, where you would spend the night. You would have lunch with the gossip columnist. The first booth to the right. Perish the thought you weren't invited for lunch because you would know power had eluded you. Then you would get on the Twentieth Century, which I thought Zanuck owned.*** I couldn't understand why my father would take that train.

I assumed Hollywood owned everything. It never occurred to me that there was any other business. Everything was designed to sustain in the motion-picture business. Hollywood people played at being businessmen. They weren't. The people who really handled the money were the stockholders in the East. They'd come out like crows. We were scared to death of them. The Hollywood children instinctively knew the East meant trouble.

When they'd come out, you'd have more formal dinners. Everyone would be on the alert. Extra help was hired. They came in with hats and dark suits, chalk pinstripe suits. They were a different sort. You couldn't seduce these guys to smile. They were tough. There was a fear of the East, a fear that our toy would be taken away.

During the McCarthy days, some of the children we used to play with were suddenly not around. There was this silence, there was an absence. Actually, I don't even remember missing some of the kids. I do remember a sense of resentment from them later. I never knew exactly what it was. I had gone to parties with them. As kids, we weren't aware of each other as individuals. We were more aware of each other's parents.

We knew our playmates' parents' screen credits. The kids were interesting or uninteresting depending upon who their parents were. You wanted to get in good with this kid because it might be good for businesss. One would be asked when one came home: Did they know who you were? Favorite words, hateful words. Do they know who you are? It was defined entirely by who your father is.

When I was playing canasta with the daughter of someone more powerful than my father, I had the feeling she'd better win. It just

---

* Dore Schary is her father. He was head of Metro-Goldwyn-Mayer at the time.
** For many years, the dining room of a Chicago hotel frequented by celebrities
*** Chief of a competing movie company at the time

felt better to lose because her father held the strings. Winning games didn't mean that much to me. I was really a company kid. Hollywood was really the old mill town. We weren't told to behave this way by our parents. We just picked it up from the movies. Kids in the movies were pretty servile and knew which side of their bread was buttered.

When I was young, I thought the best movie I ever saw was *An American in Paris*. Maybe almost as good as *Wizard of Oz* and *Gone with the Wind*. If real life couldn't be applied to either of these two movies, it didn't exist. Everything about character, everything about dreams, everything about what really happened to you, was in those. There was nothing else you needed to know about life. They were the primary myth makers, these two films.

When my parents sold the house, all I could think of was Scarlett. When I went to sell dresses in Saks and got out my book of receipts, there was one little fist that shot up and I said: "As God is my witness, I'll never be poor again." And I really thought: If Scarlett can do it, I can do it. I wanted all my life to have the guts of Rhett and say to the men who drove me crazy: "Frankly, my dear, I don't give a damn."

The thing that affected me most doesn't exist any more. It's easy to forget how gorgeous and unreal that land was. Oz was not designed by art directors. Oz was just a copy of how it looked when you came from the East and first saw California. If you compare Dorothy's first vision of Oz, when she walks out that morning, it is exactly how I feel whenever I come home to California after I've been out East. There's nothing like the color. Can you imagine what it must have been for those people coming out there? Technicolor is a copy of what was actually California. My God, in such a land, how dare you not be happy? It's just not there any more. What was real to me and magical had nothing to do with the movies and more to do with the land. The whole thing has been computerized, wrecked.

The rest of the country was sepia-toned, like Kansas. My idea of the rest of the country came from the movies. The colleges were always seas of bright green and brick buildings with ivy and cheerleaders. And football teams. That's what you saw in the movies. I think the movies caused more trouble to the children who grew up in Hollywood, who never saw the rest of the country, than they did to the people outside. The movies were my textbooks for everything else in the world. When it wasn't, I altered it.

If I saw a college, I would see only cheerleaders or blonds. If I saw New York City, I would want to go to the slums I'd seen in the movies, where the tough kids played. If I went to Chicago, I'd want to see the brawling factories and the gangsters.

My illusions disappeared when I began to be a writer and had to look at the reality. I never learned it from psychiatrists. The American Dream is really money. When it finally sunk in that I was going to have to support two children, it was terrifying.

I remember lying in my bed in this beautiful castle house in the hills. All through the windows were these bowers of jacaranda trees with purple flowers, and the sun was shining. My husband called and said President Kennedy had been shot and killed. My image came from *Tale of Two Cities*. I thought: They're gonna tear the place apart.

Who is "they"?

They, the country, the people. The people I saw in newsreels, *March of Time* movies, where there'd be crowd scenes. I never thought of people as individuals, but just those crowd scenes. The extras. They're gonna get goddamn mad, the extras, and they're gonna tear the fucking place apart. It was all movies.

They made a movie of Kennedy being shot. And they kept playing it over and over again on television. I kept watching it like every other American, hoping this time the ending would be different. Why did we watch it day after day after day, if not to see that maybe the ending was going to be different? Maybe they'll do the movie right this time. But they couldn't retake it.

It just couldn't happen to these people, these extras. They had already taken their punishment. In the movies there was always fish thrown to the cats, the extras, who were the preview audience. I'd see them lurking outside the theater. There was a jeopardy clause in the censor's code: you couldn't have a child really hurt. I thought there ought to be a clause: you can't really have the president killed. It's too upsetting to the extras. They're not gonna tolerate it.

Out of the corner of my eye, I knew there were people watching who seemed smarter than we were. These would be the writers, who were cynical. They didn't believe it was all gonna work out all right. They didn't believe all movies were wonderful. I sensed this coming. I think the snake in the Garden of Eden was my growing awareness. The reality was always there. I chose not to see it. The thing that terrified me most was my own intelligence and power of observation.

The more I saw, the more I tried not to see. So I drank too much and took as many drugs as I could so as not to see.

Couldn't bear it, the reality. Couldn't bear to feel my father was wrong. Couldn't bear the idea that it was not the best of all possible worlds. Couldn't bear the idea that there was a living to be made. That punishment does not always come to those that deserve it. That good people die in the end.

The triumph of the small man was another wonderful Hollywood myth, very popular in the mid forties. Once that dream went, once that illusion went, we all began to suspect what was really going on. Once we became conscious, that was the snake. It was the awareness of the power, awareness that war was not a parade, awareness of reality. This is what killed the old movies. It was the consciousness of the extras, and I became one of the extras.

I think we're all skidding away, we're destroying. California is just a little bit of it. The more bleak I become, the more—I live in Connecticut, okay? I read somewhere Connecticut has the highest incidence of intestinal cancer in the world. I think that's because we eat ourselves alive there. We're filled with despair, and it just rots us away. Where I live looks exactly like the MGM back-lot idea of a small New England town. There's no pressure in Connecticut, it's all okay. Nobody is working much, there aren't many jobs, a lot of businesses are failing. But it looks so sweet. It looks endearing. During the blizzard, you would have thought that Currier and Ives came in there. That several people I know lost everything they own in that goddamn endearing blizzard, nobody really thinks about that. It looks like the American Dream.

Okay, we found Connecticut, and it doesn't work either. They go out to retirement homes in California, and they still get sick. And they worry about earthquakes. We always knew there'd be an earthquake. I loved the people who were trying to make it happen in the sixties. They were down there, on the Andreas Fault, with chisels and hammers, a whole group of fanatics, trying to saw it off. They needed the ending to make the earthquake happen. They predicted it and, fearful that it would not come true, they actually went up there. They really believed that God needed help. I say He's never needed help with that. Even my God is a movie god. He really runs the studio. Into the ground, as my grandmother would have said.

The Hollywood dream has driven us crazy, but no more than any other mythology. Religious orders that govern whole states and decide what they should believe. Greek and Roman gods and goddesses.

Catholicism. Hollywood is just another draft, a more polished version.

What else are we gonna live by if not dreams? We need to believe in something. What would really drive us crazy is to believe this reality we run into every day is all there is. If I don't believe there's that happy ending out there—that will-you-marry-me in the sky—I can't keep working today. That's true, I think, for all of us.

JOAN CRAWFORD

It is 1963. She is in Chicago during a nationwide tour on behalf of Pepsi-Cola; she is a member of the board of directors. Outside the door of her hotel suite sits a young police officer. You check with him before entering.

The motion-picture business taught me everything. My education came out of that, actually. I didn't know half the words I had to speak sometimes. I would live with a dictionary. I have five in my office in New York and in my home. I have Webster's and I have the French-English and the English-German. I have every known type. I use them quite often, believe me. (Laughs.) Never be satisfied with what you have. Always grow, grow, grow, grow. Seeds grow, plants grow, ferns grow. Our nourishment and water come from people who like us, who put out their hand and say: "Gee, it's nice to see you. What are you thinking about?" That's our sunshine.

I never had an image of myself. I was always struggling too hard. I've been working since I was nine years of age. We were very, very poor. We lived in back of a laundry. My mother did the washing and ironing, and I helped. I slept on a pallet on the floor. We had no bathtub. After my mother finished doing the laundry, I'd scour the washtub, heat the water on the stove, and take my bath. Between the ages of nine and thirteen, I cleaned a fourteen-room house and cooked six meals a day for thirty children at a private school in Kansas City. It was rough. I didn't go beyond sixth grade, but I think people grow in wisdom, beauty, stature, and spirituality.

I had so much competition. In working eighteen, twenty hours a day, you never get time to think of yourself. Live for today and this minute. There's a wonderful saying a very great woman said to me: "The minute you say 'now I'd like to do this,' the word 'now' is gone."

I think the world is more of a jungle today than it was in the golden days. We had healthy competition then. It wasn't vicious. Louis B. Mayer, one of the great, great men of the world, raised most of us at Metro. Metro-Goldwyn-Mayer, when Mr. Mayer had it, was the great studio of all Hollywood from 1926 on, when I went there. I've seen the disintegration and deterioration of the industry. Judy Garland wouldn't move without asking this man's advice. I never walked into this man's office unless I had a real problem. I stated it briefly, didn't bellyache. This is why I have such a wonderful relationship with all the people in Hollywood.

When I visited Africa on Pepsi-Cola business, I didn't think anybody in Mozambique would know me. At seven o'clock in the morning, there were ten thousand people at the airport. In Léopoldville, the same thing. There were about twenty thousand people at the Johannesburg airport. Even the natives were there with flowers, with their arms outstretched. You just say: "Thank you, God, thank you very much." I get tears in my eyes. Isn't that awful? I'm so touched.

It gives you a responsibility to be to them whatever they want you to be. It's quite a responsibility, dear friend. You get on your mettle, you get a little taller, you stand on your toes. You try to be everything they want you to be. It's such a wonderment to try and become that for them. You're never allowed to become lazy, I tell you. (Laughs.)

What do YOU *want to be?*

What people want me to be. I love people. When I'm home at night, I take off my shoes, take off my makeup, knit, and look at television. Those are my few precious moments.

A local gossip columnist had referred to her expensive jewelry. Did this have anything to do with the police officer on guard?

No, I don't travel with real jewelry any more. Everything is in the vault in New York, thank you, with all the robberies. What I have here is costume jewelry. This is a smaller suite than I'm accustomed to. Across the hall are my suitcases, ready to pack. Also, my hats, bags, shoes.

Across the corridor, the police officer opens a door. Another suite of rooms. On the couch and coffee table are small mountains of hats.

Thirty-three. About thirty-six matching bags and gloves to match my costumes. (She opens the closet doors.) Traveling outfits. I change five times a day, doing ten cities. You never know what the weather is, so I have to be prepared.

Honestly, I have no personal life. It is a lonely life. I'm so grateful to my children. I hope that I fulfill their lives as much as they are fulfilling mine. Oh, yes, I'm always me, Joan Crawford.

(At the door) God bless.

SHARON FOX

She is one of Chicago's most assiduous collectors of autographs. She earns her daily bread as a messenger at the Board of Trade.

"It's very prestigious to work there, even if you're a messenger, 'cause it's the largest commodity house in the world. There are a lot of rich people who work there, and it's respected. Not everybody can get a job there. You have to know somebody. Not everybody can walk through the door. So when I do, I feel kind of proud, even though I'm just a messenger.

"My father and mother are both retired. My father just worked in a factory. My mother worked years ago for Pepsodent Tooth Company. They're just laborers." (She pauses, then softly) "I shouldn't put it down."

She carries an impressively thick leather-bound book of signatures and photographs; there are scrawled phrases: "Best wishes" and "God bless" are among the most frequent.

I'm just one of millions. A hundred years from now, I'll be just a name on a gravestone and that will be it, I won't be in libraries or records or movies that they watch on TV. It's kind of nice to stand out in a crowd and be remembered rather than being just a face in the crowd.

Someone famous, they're important. That's why you want to see them and get their autograph. It means that you may never see them again, but you've shared a few minutes. We're rather quiet, dull people, and anything that has a little shine to it is exciting.

I met Prince Charles, and he kissed me for my birthday. He's important and he's also famous. When he came to the Board of Trade, everything just stopped. We were told not to even approach him, but it got so crowded, it was his idea to just come out and shake hands.

I happened to be there. He shook my hand and I said: "Today's my birthday." Which it was, it's no lie. I said: "Can I have a kiss?" He thought about it for a second and he said: "Why not?" He kissed me on the cheek, and I kissed him. Everybody at the Board saw it. I don't think my feet were on the ground.

I may never see him again and never have that opportunity, and he may be king of England some day. I wish I could get to know him. He seemed like he could be nice. It was just a few minutes between us, and there we were . . . I wrote him a letter and sent him a picture that I had taken. I said, "It's not every girl who can be kissed by a prince," and I wanted to thank him.

That keeps me happy. I'm not happy all the time at the Board of Trade, so I have this side project, which keeps me going: meeting celebrated people and getting autographs. (She opens her book of treasures.) Barbra Streisand, Presley, a lot of people in here. There's Sylvester Stallone, there is Jack Nicholson and Louise Fletcher. There's Jack Ford. The son of the president.

More pages of the book are turned; familiar faces appear and all manner of signatures. Let us now praise famous men: Tony Bennett. Yul Brynner. George Burns. Buster Crabbe.

I've grown up with these people, watching them on TV. I never had many friends, so it was a substitute. I decided to go one step further and meet these people instead of admiring them from afar. My mother has an autographed picture of Jean Harlow. So maybe it's in the genes somewhere. (Laughs.)

I live at home. I never liked hanging out on street corners or going to parties. I don't drink or smoke. We're a churchgoing family, Baptist. My parents are all I've got, and I'm all they've got. They never had any hobbies. They have no real outside interest, outside of me. They want to see me happy, and they're interested in what I'm doing. Whatever I do reflects on them. They're like living through me. This is one country where you can do anything, and they prove it every day.

Are you familiar with Brenda Starr? I can identify with her. She's glamorous, not what I am. She's got this great love in her life, Basil St. John, which I don't have yet. She goes on all these exciting capers. (Laughs.) Dale Messick, the lady who draws her, drew me into Brenda's wedding a couple of years ago. She hardly knew me. I took pictures of her and looked her up. She said: "Brenda's getting married. Would you like to be at the wedding?" I said: "Sure." So she drew me while I was at her office. I would have to point out to people it was me 'cause there's an awful lot of people in the strip.

I keep up by following the gossip columns: Kup, Gold, Maggie Daly.* I know them and they know me. Kup has mentioned me once or twice. So has Aaron. So has Maggie. In my own little group, I became a celebrity. People I work with and the brokers at the Board of Trade, even though they make more money than I do, respect me more because I got my name in the paper.

I put out my magazine on Elvis Presley. It was after he died. It cost almost my whole bank account, but I wanted to do it. I put in the article "He Touched My Life." It was one of Presley's hymns I played all the time. People wanted *my* autograph. They asked me to sign the article that I didn't even write. My pastor asked me to sign the article. My pastor! (Laughs.) He was impressed that I get around and meet people, 'cause I look like a wallflower. They don't think I have it in me. They put it in the church bulletin, too.

My parents have everything they worked for. They have a house, they go to church. Whatever dreams they have now are through me. They can say: "My daughter got her name in the paper." Not every mother can say that. "Here's my daughter with Elvis Presley."

Her magazine lies open on the table. There are photographs of Elvis Presley. There is writing. She reads: " 'Elvis was a gift from God. How else could you explain the sudden rise from humble beginning to becoming a national star? It would be best if we remembered his religious songs. He was, after all, a being with human frailties. Thank you, Elvis, for touching my life. Love, Sharon Fox.' " (She adds softly) "Adios, I'll see you again."
Do you believe in the hereafter?

Yes. Because there has to be more to it than autographs. (Laughs.) There's just so many people and so many planets, and this is only one little step. If I can leave something behind creative, that I've done, maybe I'll be important to somebody.

* Three Chicago columnists who chronicle the comings and goings of the celebrated

What would happen if you lost your autograph book?

There are worse things that could happen. *C'est la vie.*

CAREY EDWARDS, 25

Bearded, skinny, freckled, red-headed.

My mother came from a poor family. When she was growin' up, she always wanted to be an actress. She took tap-dancing lessons. We all did a little bit of show business. My older brother was on the cover of *Liberty* magazine. It was during the war, had something to do with being bandaged up. Ansel Adams took pictures of him and my sister. I became a model when I was three. Modeling clothes and stuff for catalogs, billboards, and magazines. A freckle-faced little red-headed kid.

He shows me a photograph of himself at ten. He bears a startling resemblance to Wesley Barry, the All-American country-boy hero of silent films.

I did about a hundred TV commercials. My younger brother and I were the "Look, Mom, no cavities" kids. We each did three Crest commercials. They showed 'em a lot and were much quoted. (Laughs.) Of course, they don't do that any more. Now they say: "Look, I only got one or two cavities." The announcer comes in and says: "Even Colgate or whatever cannot guarantee you'll get only two cavities per checkup."

My brother and I were flown to New York, along with my mother, to do a Crest commercial live. Just this one-minute commercial. They interviewed us. I had three cavities at the time. I told the director that. He said: "Just go ahead and say you don't have any." In other words, lie to these millions of people who were watching and believing everything you say. I did what he said, and it really left a deep impression with me, about the power of the media and how it's abused.

I had to do it because it was my job. I didn't feel quite right about it. It's different when they give you a script and you're playing a part, a character, but they were interviewing me. They were saying: Here's Carey Edwards.

They were interviewing us with our mother. They asked her: "Do you always use Crest?" "Yes." Even though sometimes we used Colgate or Ipana. The whole thing rubbed me the wrong way.

I didn't want to get out of the business. It was a very enjoyable way to grow up. I remember the TV shows better than the commercials. I did a lot of westerns. I was very good at learning my lines. I was on *The Virginian* three times, once in a major role.

When I was twelve, I decided to get out of it. I wanted to be a normal teenager. Growing up as a child actor has certain disadvantages. We went on interviews after school, four, sometimes five times a week. We were in an adult world. We were workers. At first, I liked it very much. I got a lot of attention. It was like being a grownup. We had to go up to these producers and directors by ourselves and convince them we were right for the part. We'd introduce ourselves, shake hands, selling ourselves . . .

They were interviewing other freckle-faced red-headed kids. They'd ask me what I had done, credits and stuff like that. They'd rarely ask what your interests were. I'd have to read a script, which I was pretty good at. It all seemed perfectly normal and natural to me, because I'd started so young. I didn't have any inhibitions.

Television affected my life not only just by being on it but by watching. It was like an electronic parent. I spent a lot of time with it, and I learned a lot from it. You pick up things about what's going on in the world. It helped me get involved in what I'm doing. My brother and I used to sit around making up new lyrics to TV commercials, the jingles and all that. It was a fairly new medium, and I grew up with it. It came like right after the Milton Berle era. Being born and raised in Hollywood, it was all around us anyway.

I could still get back into show business if I really wanted to. If I had the chance to do the types Dustin Hoffman does—but I did not enjoy doing TV commercials. When I was eighteen, I went to a meeting of the Screen Actors Guild, I gave a short talk in favor of truth in advertising. The president pounded his gavel. He didn't like what I was saying. Since then, I've seen him on Bank of America commercials. (Laughs.)

I guess I'm still looking for the American Dream. To me, it's people having control over their lives. I feel like I have a hell of a lot of control over my own life, but I know that's not true for a lot of people. The real dream to me—I don't know whether it's a fantasy—is the attitude you see in the movies of the thirties and forties. Where people don't even have to lock their doors, you know all the neighbors and the milkman, friendly. That's not the way it is in the seventies at all. Maybe the image I have is just a Hollywood image and is not real after all.

We observe the photograph once more: Carey Edwards at ten: freckles.

I was on the Hennessey show with Jackie Cooper. (Wistfully, softly) After the show was over, he bought me an ice cream cone for each hand. A chocolate one and a vanilla one. He raised me up on his shoulders, and the crew all gave me three cheers. He'd been a child star himself, so I guess he knew how it felt. It was a small triumph.

Oh, I've had my moments of glory. (Laughs.)

TED TURNER

◇————————————————————————◇

He owns the Atlanta Braves, a baseball team; the Atlanta Hawks, a basketball team; the Atlanta Chiefs, a soccer team; Channel 17, a television station; and is a celebrated yachtsman.

Though his day may be somewhat planned, there is an improvised, jazz-like, high-spirited tempo to it. Our conversation came about accidentally, suddenly, whimsically. A phone call, a request, his response: "Whatcha doin' now?" "Nothin'." "Hop over."

There was a silly little thing that inspired me when I first saw *Gone with the Wind*. I've always been kind of a romantic. I featured myself as maybe a modern-day Rhett Butler. I thought he was a dashing figure. Everybody should see themselves as a dashing figure. Don't you see yourself as a dashing figure? He came to Atlanta. So did I. So I got a little mustache and everything. I was one of the first people to grow one, when I was twenty-five. Nobody had 'em fifteen years ago. I'll be forty next week. Looks like I've made it, if I don't crash tomorrow on my trip to Alabama.

I always wanted to win. I didn't win at that many things. I eventually found sailing and business. It's not the actual winning. Something's over, it's done with. It's *trying* to win. Whether it's the World

Series or a boat race, getting there is half the fun. Then I think about what I'm going to do next.

I'd say I'm from the upper middle class, but I don't like to use the word "class." In certain ways, my father was real low class. He was a wild man. He used to drink a lot and got in barroom fights. He was one of those rugged individualists. He was fifteen, sixteen when the depression hit.

My grandfather lost everything in the depression. It took him the rest of his life to pay off his debts. He didn't declare personal bankruptcy. He washed out with debts of forty thousand dollars, which was a lot of money in '31. It would be like three, four hundred thousand today. It took him another twenty years to pay it all off. He paid off every penny before he passed away.

My father had to drop out of college and go to work, but that didn't bother him. He went into business for himself, outdoor advertising. Small, but it got pretty big before he passed away.

My father was bitter about the fact that they were dirt poor. He decided, when he was about seventeen, that he was going to be a millionaire when he was thirty. He didn't accomplish it until he was fifty. When he achieved his dream, he was dead by his own hand, two years later. He told me, when I was twenty-four: "Don't ever set your goal. Don't let your dream be something you can accomplish in your lifetime."

If I made one mistake—I wanted to be a millionaire so bad that I missed out on a lot by doing it. Set your goal so high that you can never reach it, so you'll always have something to look forward to when you get old.

I would like to have lived a whole bunch of lives. I would like to have gone to West Point or Annapolis and had a military career, I would like to have been a fireman, I would like to have been a state trooper, I would like to have been an explorer, I would like to have been a concert pianist, an Ernest Hemingway, an F. Scott Fitzgerald, a movie star, a big league ballplayer, Joe Namath. (He pauses to catch his breath.) I like it all. (As he resumes, the tempo builds.) I would like to have been a fighter pilot, a mountain climber, go to the Olympics and run the marathon, a general on a white horse. (His guest's laughter appears to encourage him.) A sea captain, back in the days of sailing ships, sailed with Horatio Nelson. I would like to have gone with Captain Cook to find the Spice Islands, with Columbus, with Sir Francis Drake. I would like to have been a pilot, a privateer, a knight in shining armor, gone on the Crusades. Wouldn't you? I'd like to have gone looking for Dr. Livingston, right? In the heart of darkest Africa. I would like to have discovered the headwaters of the Nile and the Amazon River.

(Philosophically) When I lay my baseball bat in the rack for the final game, I'd like to have people look back and just gasp at what I did in my lifetime. In my time, I think maybe I can do it. When Columbus sailed, discovering the New World was the thing to do. The territories have been pretty well discovered. I'm blazing a new frontier. I'm a pioneer in this satellite technology. I'm building a fourth network. It won't be as big as CBS or ABC or NBC, but it's gonna be big.

I would like to think I'm a very humble person because of the things I haven't done. I consider my limited ability, but I'm proud of myself because I got the most out of it. I worked really hard in school, and the most I could get was ninety-five percent. I never was valedictorian. I couldn't make the football team, I couldn't make the baseball team, I couldn't make the track team. That's kinda how I got into sailing.

I've won the America's Cup. It's considered the Holy Grail of yachting. I've won the yachtsman of the year award three times. No one else has ever won it that many times. It's like the most valuable player award.

Our attention is turned toward the plaques on the wall. "You've been a cover boy of Time, *I see." "No, not* Time. *That's* Sports Illustrated. *Burt Lance knocked me off* Time. *There's all sorts of ways of becomin' a cover boy."*

I want to win the World Series. I want to set up a dynasty in baseball. I want to win the NBA Championship and set up a dynasty in basketball. I'm running so fast, I'm gonna burn myself out. So I'm taking up photography. I'm gonna become a wildlife and nature photographer. Hey, that's not competitive, is it?

Money is nothing. In America, anybody can be a billionaire, if they put their mind to it. Look at Ray Kroc, started McDonald's when he was fifty. Between fifty and seventy he made, I don't know, a billion or two. Seven years ago, I was almost broke. Today, I'm well-off. On paper. It could all go tomorrow. I've been broke before. Easy come, easy go. You never know whether a depression's coming. Money is something you can lose real easy.

Being something big to yourself, that's important. Being a star. Everybody's a star in the movie of their life. It was a pretty big deal when I had lunch with Muhammad Ali and Henry Aaron at the same time. Not many people have done that. Everybody wants to have lunch with a star, but if they could have both at the same time, wow.

JOHN FIELDING

A professor of American history at the University of Kentucky. A few days before this conversation, he had been denied tenure. "I'll be thirty-three next Monday. Happy birthday to me."

I remember growing up in a small Texas town, with all the red dirt, sandstorms, and cotton farmers, the isolation, the whole bit. Post, Texas. There wasn't a whole lot to do, other than play baseball, go to school, and watch the cowboys. Except, perhaps, movies and listening to Baptist preachers. If you've seen *The Last Picture Show*, you've seen my town.

You were given a sense that every American had a personal mission: the idea of personal destiny. Texas, in the fifties, was a special state: it was the growingest, the biggest.

The images you'd get on the movie screen in the fifties were different from what you get today. There were no Dustin Hoffmans, no Robert Redfords. There were none of these antiheroes. The heroes were not confused. They knew what they had to do. Randolph Scott, remember him?

You walk into the movies, you sit down, the lights go down, and suddenly you're in this fantasy world where the guy comes riding up on his horse. It's very real to an eight-year-old, young and blubbering. He lives his fantasies out in that dark theater, eating that popcorn, drinking that cherry Coke. Randolph Scott would come riding up and always save something, the man on the shining white horse. The ladies would look up to him, the townfolk, always muddled and confused, had no idea what to do until this one guy'd come along.

Fundamentalist religion is very big out there, and getting bigger. You have to do things and do them right, and if you don't, you're gonna suffer terrible consequences. If you do them right, you're gonna enter Emerald City. You'll be Dorothy and Toto running down the yellow brick road to Oz. Doing something important was always the big thing. It's hard to live this out in a little red-dirt Texas town. All the movies are set in Los Angeles or New York or Chicago or someplace like that.

All my friends had the same kind of feelings. You had to be number one on the baseball team, you had to be the best in class. When we got older, we had to have the best hot rod. A lot of it was success. That was the recurrent theme. You can't buy anything cheap.

I think there's more to the American Dream than that. I don't find a great many people happy with just a big income. I think they want something more. For the most bitter people I've met, it ends up being that bank account. For some of the others, the seekers, it becomes a sense of self-worth. For me, it became that sort of thing: patriotism. This idea that we're important to ourselves as individuals and collectively as a nation. There's a lot of that running around in Texas. It took on a kind of mindless chauvinism, as I look back on it.

For my generation, it took on an added dimension with the civil rights movement and with folk music as the expression. We'd see Peter, Paul and Mary, we'd see Bob Dylan up there, crooning away about missions. It gave you a warm, inspirational feeling.

"My father worked as a traveling salesman for International Harvester during the recession and spent most of his weeks on the road. He didn't have a big expense account, but it was enough. He had no place to spend it because he'd go to such great cities as Haskell, Laredo, Tahoka, and other such exciting urban centers.

"My mother would sit at home, taking care of the kids. I was the youngest of three boys. My oldest brother was married when I was eight. He's always been a distant figure. He's a very successful insurance salesman, working on an early death. In the meantime, he's making sixty, seventy thousand a year.

"My second brother was artistic, a musician. He made culture respectable for me, a hard thing to do in Post, Texas. One of my first memories is of this huge bookcase my brother built, filled with probably six hundred volumes, most of which we got from the Book-of-the-Month Club. I was the brightest kid in class, and also athletic. I had the best of both worlds. It was a happy childhood.

"We always had a new car every year, because my father sold Pontiacs as a sideline. He owned a farm implement store, sold tractors, pickups, trucks. He was good at his game, worked hard, and made money. For about ten years he was riding at the top of the wave—'47 to '57 were expanding years, particularly for farmers. About 1956, the

weather turned very bad. They had a three-year drought and, on top of that, the recession. It wiped him out.

"He was fifty years old in 1960 and did a courageous thing. He moved to a city about forty miles north, Lubbock, and started all over again. Just about starved. He became an insurance salesman. Lubbock's about 275,000, a huge place. And I got a chance to go to a good high school."

That was a very special time, 1960 to 1964, okay? They still talk about my graduating class of '64. It was scholastically one of the best. We were caught up in politics, music, struggle, mission. We all wore button-down madras shirts, 1¼-inch leather belts, white Levis, and black loafers. We were stamped out of a mold, but it was a pretty good one because it went beyond self.

In September of '63, a friend of mine was standing in the cafeteria line with a Yale catalog. I said: "Only diplomats' kids and the very rich can get into Yale." He said: "No, no, no, they got this thing called geographical distribution, with token Texans and Idaho people, to give it spice. Why don't you apply? You're smart enough." Yale intimidated me, but when a Columbia representative came along with a spiel, I thought: Hell, why not? Goddamn it, I'll never know unless I give it a try. March of '64, I got in.

My parents were scared. I was the first kid they'd ever known to get into an Ivy League school. And they were proud, man. Scared and proud. September 18, 1964, we all three rolled into New York. My mother, my father, and me. Drove all the way in. I was gonna take the bus, but my dad said: "I'm gonna take you, that's it."

It was a clear day, kind of hazy. We pulled over there into College Walk, and I looked at the library, a massive structure. It's got this frieze work: Homer, Herodotus, Plato, Demosthenes, and on and on and on. I thought this is it: I've arrived. Big city, big culture, I made it. That's where my life broke in two.

I was impressed, scared, intimidated, and really excited. It was more than just being an Ivy Leaguer. I'd have to go to Harvard or Princeton to really have that feeling. I was in New York! I had made the big jump. My roommate and I hit the subway, we went downtown. We were looking for the Empire State Building, we had to find that thing.

'64 to '68 was when Vietnam set in. The bombing started when I was a freshman at the time. I thought it'd be a quick war. I said: "Okay, just go ahead and bomb 'em." It was part of this whole patriotism: bringing democracy to the whole world. It was exactly what Kennedy was telling us in his inaugural speech. I believed that crap.

For the first year, I was for it. It kept going on and on. All the horror stories started coming out. I began to think: This isn't what we're fighting for.

I remember a dramatic scene. I was Paul on the road to Damascus. In April '67, I had to do an art paper on two Monets. I was walking toward the museum along Fifth Avenue, thirty blocks, because there was a victory parade. I saw this guy in a convertible with three little kids dressed up in Uncle Sam costumes. On the side of the car was a sign: *Bomb 'em back into the Stone Age.* I thought: Do these kids know what death is about?

I kept walking, and there was a long-haired kid, near the bleachers, being assailed by this guy. The guy was yelling from the top of the bleachers: "You guys ought to be eliminated. In a democracy like this, you're not fit." I stopped and thought: If this is what Vietnam is doing to us, it's time it was over. I was antiwar from that day on.

"The next year, when the marine recruiters came on the Columbia campus, the SDS didn't want them there. I said: "If they want to come on the campus, it's their right. This is a pluralistic society." When SDS took over one of the buildings and the riots began, I was caught in the middle.

"During the next six weeks, arguing days and nights with people who had wildly differing ideas, I learned more than I had in three and one half years. I was also 1-A at the time. I got out of it medically. I wasn't going anyway, but it was fortunate I got out the easy way, without going to jail or Canada."

During the summer of '68, I drove a taxicab. Again, I learned something about people. They're not really committed pro and con on issues. If they are, it's because they don't really know what other way to go. They're scared. They agreed Vietnam was a mess. They all had a sense that it would make or break the American Dream. For some, winning was as bad as losing. For others, we had to win, because if we didn't, we'd be the lesser for it. If the nation was demeaned, you personally were demeaned. They didn't know what the hell to do. There was such a void. Randolph Scott had not ridden up on the white horse. He wasn't there to save the struggling community.

What about the American promise and me? I'd come out of a small Texas town. I'd gone to one of the best colleges in the country and done well. Now I was accepted into another, Johns Hopkins. There I learned that success is a two-edged sword. There's a cost. It never dawned on the college student and it never dawned on the kid, sitting there in the dark movie house, watching Randolph Scott.

You start out in the Texas town, with the Protestant ethic that you've got to work hard and do well; and if you succeed, God will pat you on the back and send you into heaven. It was the same thing at school.

The universities are corporations first, educational institutions second. Education is what they market. They're also in a prestige race. Boeing wants the biggest jet. Universities want the most prestigious faculty. They do this through the tenure system. They give you six years, and then they review you. If you've taught well and done your committee work well and published the right things in the right places, they pat you on the head again and hand you this lifetime contract. Nirvana. The golden dream.

There are three buttons. I pushed all three. I taught well, I was reasonably liked by my colleagues, and I've published. I had more than fulfilled everything, right? Wrong.

The variable I hadn't counted on was the prestige race. The universities are committed to building up their faculty by hiring superstars. They're like the Yankees buying their ball club. They end up by firing untenured professors or denying them tenure. All of a sudden, what was acceptable a few years ago is no longer so.

I was recommended for tenure by the faculty, overwhelmingly. But the administration decided there was no room for another assistant professor in the history department. So I'm in my final year now.

This came as a total shock. I had no idea I was doing the wrong thing, nobody ever told me. They can change the rules at will. The administration has the power, the faculty doesn't. The faculty's ass is on the line, too.

They thought they ran their own department. Now they realize that they don't. I'm taking it hardest because I'm out of a job, with very little chance of getting another.

I'm almost middle-aged, but I feel like a kid. When I was eleven years old, Elvis made his first record. I kept wondering: What's gonna happen to poor old Elvis when he turns thirty? When the Beatles and Bob Dylan turned thirty, we kept thinking: What's gonna happen to them?

There are a whole lot of us over thirty: artists, failed historians, philosophers, mathematicians, overqualified and underemployed.

Unemployed humanists. What's gonna happen ten years from now when they start turning gray? What's gonna happen when the bitterness sets in? They'll be unemployed, but will they be humanists?

I discovered in the hardest way possible that I had let other people tell me what my values were. I was not Randolph Scott. I was the blithering town mayor who didn't know what he had to do, even though I thought of myself as Randolph Scott. What ever happened to Randolph Scott? (Laughs.)

TRUE BELIEVER

MATT MATEJKOWSKI

Large, powerfully built, iron-gray haired, he is a man in a hurry. He immediately opens his bulging brief case. It is full of paperbacks.

"I'm fifty-four years old. I'm a patent attorney on my own. Live in a small city in Connecticut."

Right now, I'm in Chicago trying to promote a paperback novel, which I've authored, edited, you name it, I did it. Found the printer. I'm here to distribute and sell it.

It really came to me, oh, about six months ago, after a lot of work on this book. I said to myself: Matt, what the hell is it all about? I said: Do you have a place in all this? I said: In the United States system, there's one key for all of us: competition.

I worked for Johns-Manville for twelve years. Somewhere along the line, you lose an election, on the corporate level. It's either him or me. It turned out it was me. You shouldn't feel bitter just because you get caught in a power play. This is the American system. As you go on, there's always gonna be one, two, three guys'll lose out. No question about it.

About a year or so, I'm writing out résumés and getting nothing back. I'm over fifty, fifty-one, something like that. It's just a stone wall.

Okay, I'm gonna write something. I said to myself: I admire *The Sun Also Rises*, and I think Dickey's *Deliverance* is just a masterpiece.

I said: All novel writing is twenty-five percent what you yourself have seen, envisioned, and seventy-five percent is kielbasa. It's stuffing, comes from your head.

That was roughly three years ago. I signed up for unemployment for about a year. The rest of it came from savings. We were being depleted. No new car, no new this, we started scrimpin'. About a year ago, the novel was finished. I said: Let's move somewhere near New York.

The novel's called *By Raz—1937*. It's about a twelve-year-old Picasso-like Huck Finn growing up in New England in 1937. I went to New York and knocked on doors of publishing houses. It's virtually impossible for people like myself to get something published. Nobody would buy it.

The paperback, that's where the spirit of the novel is. That's where the mass market is. The average person buying a hardcover novel is either quite rich, doesn't care about money, or is a darn fool. 'Cause you could get the same thing for a dollar ninety-five. Remember, I tried the hardcover publishers. I went through all the telephone directories.

There are a lot of publishing people in my area, around New Haven, Stamford. I latched onto a couple who were vice-presidents, and I knocked on their door. I caught one at the right time. It was a Saturday morning, and he was out mowing the lawn. He invited me in and I told him I would love some professional criticism of the book. Oh, God, I was the last person in the world he wanted to see. He said: "Okay, come back in a week and I'll give you my analysis of it." So I came back and he said: "I'm gonna be honest with you. I got to page sixty-five. It's lousy, it stinks." Gee, he starts giving me a lecture about Hemingway. I says: "My God, what the hell has Hemingway got to do with this day and age?" The competition is in the paperback novel.

I decided: Okay, Matthew, you're such a wise son of a b., go out on your own. I have a particular product. Who is your competition? Cookbooks is not your competition. Technical stuff is not your competition. Biographies of famous people, that's not your competition. You're not gonna stop people that are famous from writing their autobiographies. Your competition is novels.

I gave myself about a year and a half. I went to the local drugstore at K-Mart and said: "What's the going price for paperbacks?" I came out with a dollar ninety-five as my selling price.

I remembered reading about a printing house in Chicago. So I drove there. Bingo! I hit the jackpot. They talked price of a printing of twenty-five thousand at around thirty-five cents. And subsequent blocks of a hundred thousand, you're talking seventeen cents. I knew I was in the ball park. Your search for a printer is over.

I went to Chicago, door-to-door knocking.

I had my foot in the door with each of the critical men. The paperback buyers listened to my story. I think most of them disbelieved it, but they said: "We'll give you a chance." In Carson-Pirie they got the book on display right in front of the cash register. Marshall Field has got the downtown store, eye level. That's the way it stands now. I've broken the back of distribution.

Now I'm on promotion. I had prepared six or seven letters for the paperback reviewers of the dailies. I drop by the offices and say here's my book and here's a cover letter. Could I have a review?

Just before I left for Chicago, I was reading some little thing about Puccini. He worked on this opera—I don't even know what it is—and he said: "Okay, I will defend it. I'm ready to go on the stage and throw rocks at the gallery. This is what I produced." I said, like Puccini, I'm presenting to the audience and I'm ready to defend myself. I'm ready to go on the stage and throw rocks at the gallery.

Okay, I gotta go one more step. One of the main characters in my story is Ivan, a wonderful horseman. Hey, hey, hey, wait a minute now. One of the things that struck me was this darn Polish-joke phase. I said: Okay, you cannot be a Polish joke. I went through ten paperbacks. I was considering *The Godfather* at the time the movie was out. They paid Marlon Brando one million dollars. Why'd they pay Brando so much? I said: Hey, hey, hey, Matt, you got it. Brando gave *The Godfather* stature. No one was going to laugh at *The Godfather*. Why? Because no one laughs at Brando. Okay, supposing my book is good, but how do you defend it from becoming a Polish joke? I said: Hey, hey, Rembrandt. I remember seeing *The Polish Rider* by Rembrandt in the Frick Museum. Okay, that was it, the cover.

I looked at the title, it's a plus. I looked at the cover, a painting, come on, that's a plus. Okay, you've got a marketing base, that's a plus. You've got a great city, that's a plus. I've traveled all over Chicago on the surface lines system. I haven't used one taxicab. I lugged these books with me. I said all you have to do is get off your ass. You've got plus, plus, plus. I think we're gonna have it made. I am saying that, nationally, this is gonna sell between five and ten million copies.

Now, there's another thing I made an analysis of. The money is not in publishing. The money is in the movies. The screenplay has already been written. I wrote it. It's seventy, eighty percent there. I have my doubts, but I try not to show 'em.

I took an old wedding picture of my folks and I enlarged it. I put it up on the wall, and occasionally I'll look up there and I'll say: "Ma and Pa, that's you and me." My education was bought with the non-education of my brothers and sisters. I was the youngest. I am the result of a lot of stuff that comes from them.

You can go way back to Alexander, the Greeks, and there's no country since the beginning of time like America. Sometimes you gotta shake your ass a little bit to see it, but dammit, the diamond is there. Whether *I* succeed or not, the opportunity is there. Well, maybe I should have been a better writer, a better this or that, but I tried my best and that was it. Maybe someone better than myself—my son or your son—will gain from my experience.

O CANAAN LAND

ARRIVING: THEN

ANDY JOHNSON, 81

The poorest, the most miserable came here because they had no future over there. To them, the streets of America were paved in gold. They had what the Finns called *kuume*, the American fever.

Aurora, Minnesota, about thirty miles from Eveleth. Population, approximately 2500. It is iron ore country.

We're at the home of Bill Ojala. His wife, Dorothy, serves us all blueberry pie, homemade. Anton Antilla, ninety-one, who had worked in the mines all his American life, is here too.

Andy Johnson, craggy-faced, appears younger than his years. "I came to the seventy-fifth anniversary of Aurora this summer to see if I could find any of my old pals. I couldn't find a one. The place we lived in, when we came in 1906, it's where that big hole is now in the ground."

I was born in Finland and came here in 1906. My father was the son of a tenant farmer. Rocky soil. He didn't see any future in it. The Russo-Japanese War came along. He was going to be drafted in the army, so he beat it out of there as fast as he could.

My father was a typical Christian and conservative when he came here and for a long time after. In our bedroom, we had a picture of Christ on one wall and Czar Nicholas II on the other. I remember something about the revolution of 1905 in Russia and Finland. The assassination of the governor general of Finland, appointed by the czar. Our neighbors had rifles with fixed bayonets. I didn't understand what it was about, but I could sense a tension. I remember how they were jabbing this bayonet into the ground, trying it out.

We started off on a wooden ship. It was built of rough oak timbers.

No paint on 'em, no nothin'. It had a mast in case they ran out of steam. (Laughs.) They had a bull pen, one big room for most of 'em. The women and children had smaller quarters, where you just crawled into bunks. The North Sea is always stormy. You get those sugarloaf-type waves, so the boat would rock. They got sick, all those people in one big room vomiting. Mother took salt fish from home. When we started getting seasick, you'd cut a slice of that fish and eat it.

We went across England by train, then from Liverpool to New York City. It was a Cunard liner, *Lucania*. That was a big boat. When we came to New York harbor, everybody got out on deck to see the Statue of Liberty. My mother picked me up and held me so I could see it. There was a doctor at Ellis Island, and he took a spoon and shoved it in my eye, along with the others, to see if we had any illness. Those that had were returned.

We rode on a train for days on end. We came through some beautiful country. Lotta times, I thought we should stop here, we shouldn't go any further. (Laughs.) We came to New York Mills, Minnesota, a Finnish community. My father was working on the railroad there. He came two years before. We met him, and it was kind of emotional. Coming to America was like being transferred from one century to another. The change was so great.

They bought a bunch of bananas, which I hadn't seen before. I ate too many of 'em and I got sick. I swore off bananas. I didn't eat one for at least ten years. (Laughs.)

I saw the first black man in my life on the platform at the Union Station in Duluth. I couldn't figure out why his face was black. I thought he didn't wash it or something. It didn't dawn on me at that time that people were different. I remember at my grandfather's place reading about Africa and the missionaries. The only literature we had was the Bible and a missionary magazine. In this magazine there was a picture of black people tied together by their hands, one to the other with chains, and there was a big husky white man with a horsewhip. I didn't like the looks of that picture. I asked my aunt: "Why are those people chained?" She said they're slaves, but she didn't explain much further.

As soon as we got settled, my folks bought a Bible. They didn't bring it from the Old Country like a lotta other people did. So I started to read the Bible and learned to read Finnish. I got interested in it, but the stories were so wild and frightening to me.

When I was about thirteen, I got in contact with lumberjacks who had different ideas from my father's. I began to think about things, and my father did the same. He began to read the Finnish paper *Tyomies*. It was left-wing. When somebody first brought it to him, he took a stick from the wood box and carried the paper with that stick and put it in the stove. Soon after World War One started, he was reading it himself, and his views began to change.

Father got a job at the Miller mine. He'd come directly home with his mining clothes. Mother didn't like it at all. She didn't like the surroundings, the strange people. Most of the timber had been cut and everything was a mess. Iron ore on the roads, instead of gravel. When it rained, the stuff would splatter all over.

Father quit his job and got a job at Mohawk mine. I was supposed to start school, but something happened. He either got fired or quit, and he went to Adriatic mine. At the Adriatic, you had Slovenians and Italians and Finns. They all spoke a strange language, they couldn't understand each other. The company liked it that way. Some houses were company-owned, some privately. When we first came here, they were about six feet high, made out of poles stuck in the ground and boxboards nailed to the posts, and tarpaper over that. I don't think they had any floor.

The following summer they built a school, and my sister and I started. Learning English was a little difficult, although when you start playing with other kids, you'd be surprised how fast you learn. I never finished seventh grade because the snow melted too soon. I went to school altogether less than five winters.

There was the booms and the busts, we'd go from one to the other. About 1912, things began to slow down. By 1914, they were pretty bad, until World War One started. We moved out to the country, got a homestead. The government was still giving free land. So we moved out there in the wilderness.

Father got a job in the logging camp as a blacksmith. Mother did some laundry for the bosses. That helped us a lot that winter. When the big logging camps came in, they brought the railroads. My father had been a miner, a carpenter, a farmer, a common laborer. When a person moves so many times from one year, from one job to another, there's reasons for it. He wasn't happy with what he was faced with. When he began reading these papers and talking to people about capitalism and exploitation, he began to see and change his mind.

I didn't pay much attention to politics until I was in the neighborhood of thirty. When things got tough in the thirties, I began to express my views. I had a good job then, working for the county.

Every morning, the boss'd pick out certain guys and give 'em a day's work. The guys that didn't get any work would pass under my window, so we got to talking. Well, they started pointing the finger at me that I was a Communist.

The county commissioner called me into the office and warned me about talkin' the way I talk. I had my independence, except that it made my livelihood a little more difficult. That's the way it's been up to this day, and I don't think it'll change. When you're once fired for your political views, you're automatically blackballed with the mining companies, even if you never worked for a mining company. The superintendent of the mine was the mayor at one time.

Your American Dream? You got a terrible-looking hole down in the ground where we used to live once. It's filled with water, and the wealth is taken out of the land. I don't know what it's good for. On the other hand, people live in nice houses, they're painted well. There's jobs for those that have jobs, and there are a lot of people on welfare in this county.

I see a wonderful future for humanity, or the end of it.

If we continue this present trend, we're gonna go straight to hell, we're gonna blow ourselves right off this earth, or we'll poison ourselves off. It's up to the people. What bothers me is that they're not concerned. I don't know how to approach 'em. For forty-five years I've written a letter to the newspaper. I've tried to get one every month to at least one paper. That's the only thing I'm able to do.

VERNON JARRETT

He is a columnist for the Chicago Tribune.

I grew up in Paris, Tennessee. People in small towns considered nowhere identified with somewhere. So we were thirty miles from Murray, Kentucky, sixty miles from Paducah, a hundred twenty miles from Memphis, a hundred ten miles from Nashville, forty miles from Clarksville. We were on the L & N Railroad.

Louisville and Nashville used to come down from Chicago. It would be about two city blocks from my house. We were always train-conscious. We used to listen for the train, set your clock by it. You'd say: "Panama's late today. Number 619 is late." The engineer would blow his whistle, the people would listen, the dogs would howl.

Country people used to go walking on Sunday afternoons. They go down to the depot to see who's comin' in and who's leavin'. Or just to see the train comin' in. The trains always symbolized mobility. Somebody goin' somewhere, somebody leavin'. We were always aware there was another place outside of this. Somewhere. That you *could* go somewhere.

When I was a little kid, we used to play a game called swinging, with a car tire and a tree. One would push and one would be the conductor. You'd call off the cities: Paducah. St. Louis. Evansville. Somebody'd say: "I think I'm gonna get off here." And somebody'd say: "Naw, I'm gonna wait." And then everybody would say: "Chicago! Forty-seventh Street!" Listen to a lot of the old blues songs: "How Long, Baby, Has That Evenin' Train Been Gone?" "Going to Chicago." "Trouble in Mind."

Some of the pictures stand out in my mind right now. People chopping cotton. I used to wander around in the woods, workin' on a sweet-potato patch. When they'd hear the train coming, you'd see 'em standing there, with their hoes or their forks. Like, we'll pay our respects now, the train is comin' by. You'd see that look on their faces, that longing look. You might see folks in bandanas, overalls, older women, young people. They'd all stop in the middle of what they were doin' and they'd wave at the train, waving at anonymous people and maybe anonymous dreams.

In some parts of Mississippi it was a little rough because you had to sneak away. I learned from people who lived on the plantations, where you still had peonage, there was always that train. If push came to shove, you could go. If you lived in those little delta towns, the train was the symbol of where you could go to reclaim yourself as a man or become a woman.

We called ourselves a part of that Illinois Central. The tracks that began somewhere in Louisiana went all the way to Chicago. Chicago even has a different pronunciation. *Chi*cago. These trains were always gonna take you somewhere. They used to have excursions, too. Where you could at least say you'd been there, to the Promised Land. Weekend excursions even to St. Louis. St. Louis was one of those places we black folks called Negro Heavens. There was a movie made once that we stood in line to see when I was a kid in grammar school called *Harlem Heaven*. Bill Bojangles Robinson, the first time I ever saw him. They played it in our high school. It was farmed out and sold to schools and churches. You got to see Harlem. You'd even settle for Detroit. People in Alabama went to "Detroit City." They heard about those jobs with Henry Ford. Of course, for us in Mississippi, Alabama, parts of Georgia, Arkansas, Chicago was our heaven. Understand?

The *Chicago Defender* was our newspaper. You'd grab your newspaperman to see what was going on, black life in big cities. You were always there even if you never moved. Believe it or not, Cairo, Illinois, was one of those places they would brag about. (Laughs.)

We're talkin' about the thirties. We had a world of dreamers. Black people were some of the most creative people in the world, because you had to substitute dreams of what you thought might be the real world of one day. "In the Sweet Bye and Bye" was one of the favorite church songs. "I'm Gonna Lay My Burden Down" and "When the Saints Come Marchin' In." There was a mobility. What kind of crown you gonna wear? My grandmother, an ex-slave, used to talk about the number of stars that are gonna be in her crown when she went to the Promised Land.

I knew many ex-slaves who lived there. My grandmother used to sit around and tell us these stories. She'd mix fiction in with 'em, but some of 'em were true. About her life as a little slave girl. She remembers when General Grant came down to La Grange, Tennessee, and set up the army of the Tennessee. She heard the cannons. She used to tell us stories about how they used to trick Old Marsey. She was what they called a house nigger.

My grandfather on my dad's side was what you'd call a field nigger. These two old-timers used to meet in our home in the winter months, when our parents thought they were too old to live alone on the farm. They used to sit there and tell these stories over and over. She used to tell the ones about when they heard how the Union army was coming down to free the slaves. They would put on this big act. They would go in and tell Old Marsey how sorry they were and that if the Yankees came in, they weren't gonna give them their hams and this and that. And they'd go in the backyard and crack up laughing.

She was a little girl when slavery was ended. Dad's father was a runaway slave. He couldn't read and write. He heard that the Union army was freein' people and he cut out. He didn't even know what state he came from.

Some Sundays in church when they started singin' those old hymns, those people would start laughing and answering each other from across the room. We kids couldn't understand what on earth they were laughing about. I remember one of us got up enough guts to ask what was so funny. They'd say: "We're not really laughin', you youngsters would never understand it." They were really laughing about the fact that they had survived: Here we are sitting up here, free. These are our kids here with us. I've got a home, and my daughter is a schoolteacher. That's what I used to hear my grandmother say.

The thing I remember about these folks was the immense dignity and pride in the way they walked. They walked like straight sticks. They made us stand like that. This always slays me, that all of us had to stand erect. They would go around asking you: "Boy, aren't you gonna be somebody when you grow up?" They'd always say: "I'm never gonna live to see it."

Let me tell you about the day my brother got his master's degree from Fisk University. My dad didn't like any fooling around in church or when one of the great black speakers came to town. There were circuits of people who went around just to inspire you, to tell you about Africa, the sleeping giant. He didn't like anybody talking while somebody was making a speech. Or laughing or snickering. I think of all the kids my dad used to whip for talking when he was principal of the school. In the Fisk University chapel, he was talking to me all through the graduation speech by Dr. Alain Locke, one of the great black scholars.

My mother kept shushing my father. He just kept talking. She said: "Stop talking, people will think we're country and don't know better." He kept talking. I looked up, and tears were running down his face. He told me that in 1893, when he ran away from home "to make somethin' of himself," he helped construct that building where my brother was getting his degree. He leaned over to me and said: "These seats look like the same old iron seats I helped screw into this floor. I used to sneak back in here after the other workers had gone and sleep at night. I never thought I'd live to see the day my son would get a master's degree in this building." You know the funny thing? He was almost laughing, as I used to see the ex-slaves do. It was a celebration of that fact that "I am here, I exist, and there's still some hope." This is one of the real miracles of these people.

My dad used to tell me, when he was close to seventy-nine, that he didn't think any white man ever called him "mister" over four or five times in his whole life. My mother had been called "girl" and "nigger" and "auntie." She was a strikingly good-looking woman.

My dad didn't want to come to Chicago. He figured his thing was in the South. My parents were schoolteachers. My mother and dad put together a hundred and ten years in classroom teaching. They were old-time crusading schoolteachers, mother and father. My dad was known as a school builder.

The school was the size of an average city apartment. They had about two or three other teachers. They were making about twenty-five dollars a month. The kids, believe it or not, learned advanced mathematics. (Laughs.) This is crazy, isn't it? I learned Chaucer's *Canterbury Tales* when I was in the ninth grade. I can almost do it now, in Old English. We had oratorical contests all the time. There was a premium being able to speak well, enunciate clearly. I've lost some of that in the city.

That school to me was one of the most fascinating things I'd ever seen. A frame building. We had outhouses and no running water. They had a hydrant out in the backyard.

I was five years old. I was playing like I was Robert S. Abbott. He was the publisher of the *Chicago Defender*. There were some little towns where it wasn't permitted to land. It was considered inflammatory, encouraging black people to go north. The dream centered around the North.

In 1879 was a great exodus. It was two years after the Tilden-Hayes Compromise. People were leaving the South en masse. They were called the exodusters. Some of 'em were kidnapped and brought back to Mississippi and Alabama.

I came to Chicago when I was at Great Lakes during World War Two. That's why I joined the navy, just to see Chicago. When I came in, the only blacks were mess stewards. But I'd rather be a mess steward and live around Chicago than be in the army around Louisiana.

I heard about Chicago all my life. Some of the stories were fabricated. You'd hear folks say: "I didn't know I was black until I looked in the mirror." You go up there, you wouldn't believe it. They got a congressman named Oscar De Priest, they got blacks in government, black lawyers, black policemen.

It meant a great place where everybody's treated equal. You could be what you wanted to be. You didn't have to have white people abusing you. And they wouldn't call your mother "girl" or your father "boy." The whole works. Where you could become somebody. That's the stuff we were steeped in as little children. During Negro History Week, people would tell us about the Harlem Renaissance. We had to recite Langston Hughes's poems and Claude McKay's. You used to have to stand up and sing "Lift Every Voice." You sing about your day as if it were a reality. I never felt despair.

Some of the poorest people I knew in the South never really felt outright despair. This optimism was based on the fact that some of the older folks, the cooks, the houseboys, the chauffeurs, and even some of the field hands, felt that racism was such a ridiculous thing, they just figured it couldn't last. Black people figured that one day God was gonna rise up and do some damage to the white people. God was "gonna mess the white folks up one of these days for the way they treatin' us." You know what was there, too? The feeling that if you just stick this out, don't commit suicide, don't let it get the best of you, you're gonna win.

When there was despair, you took it out in the church. You'd see it in funerals. Black people have really clung to a genuine love for each other. That's why a funeral said so much. You can't let this person die as though it was nothing happening. A great loss had been suffered. I learned to cry at all funerals, and I didn't know who was dead. I had been inculcated with the idea that something very valuable has passed. I was a little boy. I'd sit there and just cry along with the rest of 'em.

Someone has gone. You'd hear people say: He could have been this or she could have been this if she just had a chance. Sometimes one of the older sisters would lean over and kiss her buddy good-bye. When my father died, my mother went to the funeral home. Before they had the casket ready, she just sat there and patted his hands. She said: "These hands have done a whole lot . . ."

The mortician across the street was a personal friend of ours. I hadn't seen him for years. A lot of folks didn't understand when I hopped on a plane and flew to Paducah just to say good-bye to him. I came back to Chicago just to meet my deadline. But I had to go by there and see old Bob Woodson, eighty-seven years old. And look at him and remember my childhood. This is the man who embalmed my mother and father. There was no such thing as an anonymous person. This is something that's been lost in the big city.

Oh, I was the biggest dreamer. I'd listen to Duke Ellington. They made us turn off the radio at a certain hour, but we'd sneak in there and hear Duke from the Cotton Club in New York. We finally got a radio to hear Joe Louis fight Max Schmeling. We had a prayer meeting that night. That tells you how desperate we were. Joe Louis was the greatest figure in our lives up until Martin Luther King.

When I first came to Chicago in the forties, I rode the el and I read the newspapers. I would check out on what great name was gonna speak here. I'd go out there and if it was free, I would hang around and get a seat. And I'd walk these great streets. I would write back and say: "I went down South Parkway, can you imagine that?" Or "I stood at the corner of Forty-seventh and South Parkway Saturday night." You'd put that in a letter. Or: I saw so and so. They said if you stood on this corner long enough on Saturday night, you'd see somebody from back home. That's where all of us met and paraded.

We always had a feeling we were on the move, that things were happening. Every time the NAACP would win any kind of little victory, it was a great moment.

Up here you could just let your hair down. When I used to listen at night, it was not only to hear Duke Ellington from the Cotton Club. You also heard the man say: "Fatha Hines from the Grand Terrace in Chicago." It seemed as though from the noise in there the people were just free. White people and black people in there together.

What was it? Thirty-five years ago? My dreams have not expired entirely. There are moments when I waver between despair and hopelessness and flashes of inspiration. Years ago, when we were in trouble, we thought we could one day go north. Well, we are north now. We are at that Promised Land. The Promised Land has less hope now than it had when we were not in the Promised Land. We used to say: "We're being abused now, but one day we'll have the ballot. One of these days we're not gonna have presidents and governors who abuse us. One of these days the Ku Klux Klan is not gonna be around lynching us." All that has happened. But we didn't realize that there were some basic corrections that haven't yet been made.

How can you get out? My parents could say: "One day my children are gonna have it better if they could just get an education." The catch is I might get a good job, but the community I'm living in is going to be so overwhelmed by other people's poverty that I won't be able to enjoy it. Do you realize I'm enjoying more luxuries now than the white families for whom I used to work were able to enjoy? Yet I have less hope now for the vast majority of black people than I did when I first came here. I don't see solutions to the problems the way I did then. There simply aren't enough jobs to go around.

I see more antagonism now than I saw a few years ago. In the South it's different. Some remarkable changes have taken place. I'd never hoped to see a crowd in Mississippi cheering a black halfback. But the North is another story.

Whatever is happening to blacks is an extreme version of what's going to happen to whites. Remember when people identified dope only with black kids? Now, in God-fearin' white middle-class communities, they're worried about their children and narcotics. Remember when common-law living was for black people? Now it's in vogue among young whites.

The ghetto used to have something going for it. It had a beat, it had a certain rhythm, and it was all hope. I don't care how rough things were. They used to say: If you can't make it in Chicago, you can't make it anywhere. You may be down today, you're gonna be back up tomorrow.

You had the packing houses going, you had the steel mills going, you had secondary employment to help "get you over." There was the guy spreading hope every day, the policy-wheel man. Policy was considered a part of our culture before the mob took it over. Everybody played policy. You were always hearing about somebody who hit the day. Oh, so and so hit. Somebody you always heard about was hitting or making it big. (Laughs.)

Now it's a drag. There are thousands of people who have written off their lives. They're serving out a sentence as though there were some supreme judge who said: "You are sentenced to life imprisonment on earth and this your cell here." What do you do if you've got a life sentence? You play jailhouse politics. You hustle, you sell cigarettes, you browbeat other people, you abuse the other cell mates, you turn men into weaklings, and girls you overcome.

There are people who don't see themselves making it in this automated society. Not many white people can figure things out either. You look at television and you see people pushin' buttons sending people to the moon. You say: "Man, these are people so far ahead of me I don't have a chance." You see people using language and reading skills at which you're incompetent. You say: "Hell, it's too late. Maybe I coulda learned but I blew it." You write yourself off. Then you don't see jobs even though you may have learned these things.

A few of us are making it pretty good. This is one thing that frightens me. I think there are some people in high places who've decided this problem can't be solved. We're gonna do what we did in World War One: practice triage. We can salvage maybe one third that's making it. Maybe close to another third is capable of being salvaged. The only thing we can do for the other third is contain them. Keep them from inconveniencing us. We'll just keep them where they are. There are not enough jobs for them. We're not going to rearrange our society so that it's possible for them to have some of the benefits we enjoy. In a few years you may have black people who are doing all right, who may lose identity with those who are not doing so well.

Racism is keeping all the haves from getting together. (Laughs.) A few years ago, racism was used to keep black and white workers from getting together. Now it's keeping the upper strata from getting together.

When I got married, some years ago, there were no apartments available. My wife and I gladly lived in the building right across from the Robert Taylor Homes.* I bought a long rope. In case of fire, we'd climb down those nine flights. We didn't care. We knew everything was gonna be beautiful later on. What about people who say everything is not going to be beautiful because there are three generations of unemployed males in the family?

That's something we didn't experience down south. You could always grub out a living, doing something. Food was cheaper. There were odd jobs for you. You can't make it on odd jobs today. There are a lot of whites in this situation, too. They don't want to admit it. They want black people to bear the whole burden of the crusade against unemployment. There are twenty-six million Americans living below the poverty level. Only around eight million of these are black.

Would you live opposite the Robert Taylor Homes now?

No, I would be frightened. I don't think I could take it unless there were other people, middle-class like me, and we could get together and form some kind of protective association. I tried. I lived in Englewood. Englewood at the time I lived there was number three or four in crime in the country. I lived where the Blackstone Rangers and Disciples fought each other. Some of the property was middle-class, but it was really tough trying to rear children in that community. My neighbors used to walk their dogs at night and gather in the schoolyard. These were not cute little pets. They were dogs that would bite if you entered their homes. When I first moved there, I used to see black women get off the bus at night and off jitneys as late as two in the morning and walk three blocks home on a summer night. They used to walk with purses and shopping bags in the late forties and early fifties. They can't do that tonight.

In 1950 the black population of Chicago was 492,000. At this moment it's close to 1,500,000. A million more people. Most of them

---

* A public-housing project, all black, on Chicago's South Side. It's the largest in the world.

came here seeking employment, got stuck, and couldn't go back home because there was nothing there. Our government set up some rules which made it more profitable for a family to break up in order to get welfare. So the black male living in poverty today can't have the respect that black men had when I was a kid. You know the spiritual "Sometimes I Feel Like a Motherless Child"? Today, it's sometimes I feel like a fatherless child. That may be worse.

The other day a black mailman was describing a ghetto scene. The father was giving his son a lecture about staying away from a vicious street gang, to get him to stop threatening and robbing storekeepers. The kid said: "Who in the fuck do you think you are? You ain't shit. How in the hell are you gonna tell me what to do?" This man has no prestige with his own child.

I remember men in the South who were yard boys, never called mister, who were considered Uncle Toms. But their children looked up to them. At home, they represented somebody trying. The janitor in the school where my father was principal was chairman of the board of trustees of the church my dad attended. This will never happen again in our lifetime.

Old man Van Dyke, who worked the city streets, walked around with great poise. Shack Wilkins, who worked at the L & N Railroad, over at the shops, I remember how he kept his shoes shined. Wow. I still do this on Saturdays. I'm imitating Shack Wilkins. He used to buy expensive shoes, Thom McAns. We called them expensive. Boy! He kept them shining. He used to take us chestnut hunting.

On Sundays, they dressed immaculately. We kept our outhouse clean, as many other people did. You shovel out the fecund and put it in a deep post hole and you put lime over it.

When you come to a city like Chicago, you get lost in the crowd. You're just another name. If a kid uses the word "motherfucker," he can do it with impunity because this old lady walking down the street doesn't know him. She doesn't know his mother or his father. You can hear 'em: "Kiss my ass, motherfucker. Go to hell." All this stuff, when some older people are coming by. Sometimes, out of habit, I say: "Can't you respect the sisters, man?" Then they'll calm down.

I remember I was caught playing the dozens once. It's a game of insults that blacks play, where a bunch of kids get together and hit at what they consider your weakest point: your mother. You don't have much else to lose, really. "Motherfucker" is not a sweet little name. It means you're the lowest son of a bitch on earth. Mother was the one thing that was permanent in your life, even in slavery. Today, with these kids, it's no longer a game. It's a way of life.

If I'm feeling good and want to have my morale lowered, all I have to do is drive out Madison Street on a bright, beautiful day and look at the throngs of unemployed youngsters in their weird dress, trying to hang on to some individuality. Can't read or write, looking mean at each other. You see kids hanging around, hating themselves as much as they hate others. This is one thing that's contributed to the ease with which gangs kill each other. Another nigger ain't nothin'.

In Englewood, we had a little bay window. I had formed a cooperative. We tried to fix it up and eventually lost it. But it was a pretty good experiment. We weren't trying to leave the ghetto. We were gonna stay there. We were sitting there, watching TV. We had our windows up. There was a walkway alongside. I heard what appeared to be an explosion. I had one of these Mattel guns. Have you seen these toy guns? They're very realistic. This gun looked like a high-powered rifle. Someone had given it to my sons for Christmas. It gives you an indication of the kind of toys they're selling. (Laughs.) I grabbed this gun because I didn't know if somebody was trying to break in.

Here was an unarmed black kid sauntering in the gangway. He had evidently leaped up, hit a light bulb, and made it explode. I thought when he saw me coming down with a gun drawn—it looked like the real thing—he would have held up his hands and said: "Don't shoot, mister, I was just playing." He didn't do a thing but look at me out of the side of his head and say: "What are you excited about, motherfucker? Go ahead and shoot." He didn't give a damn. This kid went away into anonymity.

We have become anonymous. We got lost. When I was coming up, the so-called ghettos had a stability, would you believe it? People didn't move as much as they do today. Folk had a chance to know who was living down the street, who graduated, who got married. All the black people went to the same churches. All the college graduates came home for Christmas. You had to get up and make a little talk. Your folks wanted to show you off.

You had an inspiration to go to college. But now your inspiration is to become, maybe, a hell of a basketball player because you heard about Cazzie Russell makin' it with the pros. You might want to become an O. J. Simpson because you see him on television. You might want to become a big-time singer 'cause you know Curtis Mayfield lived near the el tracks. But if you can't cut these things, where is your inspiration coming from? A lot of things have contributed to the death of inspiration, outside of race. You got a lot of white people who can't live without an excess of alcohol to keep 'em going because they feel imprisoned, too.

The city is not heaven any more. It is more of a refuge. It is not a city of hope. The whites are victims, too. They have no power. Being white has not paid off for them, but it's the only thing they've got. We have to work out a strategy to give ordinary people power. We've been bullshitting ourselves. We always were every man for himself, while we talked idealism. There must be a new way of thinking.

THOMAS BOYLSTON ADAMS

He is seated in a swivel chair of worn leather. There is an old-fashioned rolltop desk. A grandfather's clock with elegant Roman numerals is going tick-tock.

"This office furniture belonged to my great-great-grandfather, John Quincy Adams, and dates from 1820. The rolltop desk belonged to his son, Charles Francis Adams, and so did the clock. This chair was first used by John Adams, my great-great-great-grandfather, at Number 1 Court Street, where he had his first law office before the American Revolution. The family moved to 50 State Street in the late nineteenth century."

We are in his office in Boston's newest commercial building: 60 State Street.

"In The Education of Henry Adams, *my granduncle points to the unceasing war between the Adamses and State Street. You and I are on that street. (Laughs.) We are on State Street, not of State Street. State Street is a state of mind, the establishment's. State Street, with its trusts and wills, is the symbol of property. The establishment has never been part of my family. We've always questioned the idea that a million dollars entitled you to a more sound opinion than ten dollars."*

My people were very poor farmers who came from the less prosperous parts of England. The original Adams set up a brewery down there in Quincy. He raised his own wheat, turned it into whiskey, and prospered in a very small way. They were all freeholders.

A freeholder does not pay rent for the land he tills. One of the reasons our people came here was because there was land and it was cheap. All through the colonial period, the rich men in England tried to buy up, or get by grants, large acreages of land. They found they couldn't farm them prosperously. They had to sell to the freeholders. That's the foundation of the New England idea.

In the early days, with the discovery of the Bible, people thought if they could only understand the Book, which was thought to be the will of God, they would be able to live perfect lives. It was an illusion. But the idea that prompted the Puritan migration was not an illusion.

John Robinson, the Puritan pastor, expressed it well. In his Farewell Sermon to the Pilgrims boarding the *Mayflower*, he said: "I urge you to study the Gospels. When you think you have the answer, go back and read some more. You'll find you don't have the answer. It is something perpetually illusive, and you must always search for it."

He had taken me for a brisk autumnal walk along Boston Common and adjacencies. We peered into the Pilgrim Church, a bare, empty room with wooden benches. "There was no hierarchy. People sat in the church as they came in. They were all equally open to hear and discuss the Gospels." We entered the King's Chapel. "This was Royalist and allied to the Church of England. The floor was divided into neat pews, some more expensive than others. Presumably, that was how you entered the Kingdom of Heaven: in due order, according to the size of your purse." (Laughs.)

At the statue of Samuel Adams, we rested. "I don't entirely approve of Cousin Sam. He was an interesting man, but I think he went to extremes. He was the firebrand of the American Revolution."

We entered the Atheneum: old books, gentle folk, peace and quiet. Yet, for some reason, I turned my head as though I expected Margaret Fuller to bump into me and whisper the latest about Hawthorne, Poe, Mazzini, and the lot of women in the nineteenth century. Once outside, the feeling instantly vanished with the smell of corned beef from the delicatessen nearby. Trucks rumbled by olden gravestones.

My family remained poor people for a long, long time. If the family ever amounted to anything, I think it's really because they remain poor to this day. The family money's never been put in trust. It's always been turned over from generation to generation to spend or use as you wanted. I'm not sorry that all the money I have was used to fight against the Vietnam War, leaving me a very poor man.* I would a lot rather have the recollection that we helped stop the war than have the money today.

My earliest memories are of Lincoln, Massachusetts, a simple country town about twenty miles from Boston, where I still live. I was one of five children. We were urged to read. We would get into long discussions and were, I suppose, rather argumentative. My father was a great reader, and he was always talking about what he read. The conversation at our suppper table was as good as you could have found anywhere.

I remember long winter nights, sitting in front of a blazing log fire on a high-back sofa, because you had to prevent the draft from blowing you into the fireplace. Every fall, we'd put up boards around the foundation of the house and fill them with autumn leaves. That was the only insulation we had. A good northwester would just whistle through the house. We would sit there, all of us, and do our homework, under oil lamps. It was the only warm room in the house. My bedroom was desperately cold. I can remember sitting at my table doing my homework and holding out my hands to the space heater to warm them so I could write. One of my aunts undertook to teach me French when I was five. She had lived in France with her uncle, Henry Adams. I remember the Armistice very well, the terrific excitement. One autumn night, my parents went to Boston to hear Clemenceau, the Tiger of France. This was a great subject of conversation.

Our conversation? The country was going to the dogs, it always has been. (Laughs.)

I think the country was in greater danger during the twenties than at any other time in my life. It seems as though America had realized the American Dream: more money every year for everybody. Within a few years, roughly from 1918 to 1924, everything utterly changed. Suddenly, everybody owned a motorcar. It seemed as though we were all liberated by Henry Ford. All we needed to do was make more automobiles and build bigger houses. Then we began to realize that along with all the Ford cars came dust, dirt, automobile crashes, and the inevitable problems of the assembly line.

J. P. Morgan and the financial wizards were the people we listened to. And Calvin Coolidge was president. It seemed as though it would

---

* In 1966, he ran for the U.S. Senate as an antiwar candidate. "It was, of course, a forlorn hope. Still, it was a terribly important effort, one that I'm most proud of."

go on forever and get better and better and better. Just about then, when I was in college, the depression hit.

I remember Boston Common on a summer morning in 1930. It looked as if snow had fallen during the night. The entire surface of the Common was covered with newspapers spread by people who'd spent the night there. Suddenly we realized that Owen Young and J. P. Morgan and all the geniuses did not have the answer. The machine had gone clunk. It was my first experience with the failure of an establishment.

I've never doubted the American Dream. If people will not believe in a utopia and stick to the job of thinking things through, we'll not find *the* answer but *an* answer. Only in diverse answers will we ever get better.

I cannot think of a greater disaster than Harvard becoming the arbiter of what happens to us. They have wonderful ideas and the world would be bankrupt without them, but there are other minds and other talents. Many ideas of Harvard have found their way into legislation, not all good. I think it would be an excellent idea if everybody in his lifetime were allowed to do something for a year or two, totally different from what he's done previously.

After the war, I was doing quite well in business, but I was becoming interested in early-American history. I ceased active work in business and dug deep into the study. Then, bango! Something's going wrong. Our country is using its force to repress us the way the British Empire did. We were the redcoats, and they were the Yankees. Because of my studies, it made me so damn mad. I found myself thrown headlong into the mess in '65 and '66. How it came about was curious.

I had been asked to dinner by a friend. Another guest was Walter Lippmann. As we were discussing the problems, Lippmann pointed his finger at me and said: "Why aren't you in politics? Nobody would dare call you a Communist." Walter Lippmann was a very wise man, but in that he was wrong. (Laughs.) When I ran for the U.S. Senate as an antiwar candidate, I was called a Communist very often. I was a fifth columnist. I was everything you could think of. I can't say I was angry. I was more amused, I think.

I still believe ideas will save the world. Disasters have come when people have stopped having ideas. You've simply got to go on renewing thoughts constantly. What is fundamental to us is the belief that there is a better way.

ANGELO ROCCO, 94

◈————————————————————————————————◈

He's a small man, animated, all business. His age is of no matter as he conducts a transaction over the phone. He is a building developer. All the houses on the block are his work and enterprise.

His office is in a lower-middle-class neighborhood in Lawrence, Massachusetts.

In 1902, I came to the United States. I came from a province, Caserta. It's between Rome and Naples. That's the cradle where the Roman Empire began. My grandmother was the name Portia. You know? Was the wife of Brutus, the one that killed Caesar. (Laughs.)

In 1900, I went to France, Lyon. I stay there two years. I work and went to school, and I learned French. I wanted to be somebody, you understand? I began to read history. I learned about the Roman Empire and to what good they did do. I felt we came from a pretty good race. We did contribute to the world, more than anybody else did. I'm proud for where I came from.

My aunt came over the United States and I followed. I came all alone, by myself. *Sardinia* was the name of the boat. I arrived here on December 13 when I was just eighteen years old. Happened to be my birthday. If I stay another month in Italy, I would be subject to the army. (Laughs.) I came over here with the expectation that there might be work. I wanted to be educated. I learned English fast, you understand? I bought a dictionary from Italian word to English, and English to Italian.

First of all I worked in Pawtucket, Rhode Island, in textile machinery. I became sort of a foreman, 'cause I could talk French. Mostly what I worked with was some Italian people and French. I had a very good job. I got about nine dollars a week. Then I got a job in Lawrence on account of my brother came over, got work there.

I made pretty good money, so I sent enough for my mother and one sister to come over.

Somebody came from Yorkville, New York. We worked there. I didn't like it. Then we went to Burlington, Vermont. We traveled on Lake Champlain. We arrive at nighttime, and we had to sleep on the floor because the furniture had not come. (Laughs.) I didn't like the people in Burlington, so we moved to Winooski, Vermont. I weaved on the woolen mill, different kind. I learned good.

Somebody looking for men in Skowhegan, Maine. Another woolen company. They lookin' for worsted weaver. I was first-class, so I became a full-fledged weaver. Then in 1908, when William Howard Taft was made president, I wanted to go to Woonsocket, where the weavers get more money. We felt with William Howard Taft that things were gonna be good. We feel that if the Republican wins, that be good. We went by train. On the way to Woonsocket, we stop over here in Lawrence. We met all our friends. They tell me to stay in Lawrence. So we decide to stay.

I say I gotta go to school. I want to even work and go to school. I want to be somebody, you know. They had a night school here. I was twenty-four years old at the time. The others, they were much younger than me. I was put in high school. I remember one of the books, Charlie Dickens, about Christmas carol and so on. The next year, I went to day high school.

I begin to study algebra and geometry. I had the idea to become a mechanic engineer. I learned all kind of book. We read a lot of history things. I studied Greek and Latin. Then the strike began, so I quit school, due to the strike.

I was the one who organized the strike. You know why it started? Franco-Belgians from the province of Lille became textile workers. They formed a club of the IWW. I became friendly with 'em. I could talk French better than now. (Laughs.) They encouraged me to form an Italian branch of the IWW. The idea was instead of havin' people organize in craft union, they organize 'em in industry. One big union. Spinners, weavers, wool sorters, loom fixers. They began to sow socialism.

Most of the Italian people were unorganized. They did most of the dirty work, you understand? For the Italian people to procure a better job, they had to break a strike. They broke a lot of strikes. So they'd get a better job, you understand? The Italian bunch had acquired the name of bein' a scab. (Laughs.) But I tell you, I'm proud of my ancestors and I'm proud of where I came from. Now this was the time arriving where the Italian people could redeem themselves and join the other workers in the strike. And they did.

You know why strike started? The legislature in Massachusetts passed a law that women and children should not work no more than fifty-four hours a week. They used to work fifty-six. Wages about ten cents an hour. That was twenty cents a week. The workers got the pay cut twenty cents less, you understand?

Before the strike began, I called a mass meeting. I sent a circular to the townspeople and the meeting was overflowed. The mule spinner, the wool sorter, are goin' out. All these Italian people were gonna go like one man to go on strike with the other. I was proud. The French workers, they all joined. So they all start out . . . (Laughs.) Lotta women, they work in the mill, they come out. The newspapers callin' her un-American foreigners, aliens. The real American was the one who put up a sweat shop, paid no wage at all, makin' big money. That's good American. We were un-American tryin' to make better conditions to live. You understand?

I was in high school. Okay, what do I do then? I come out of school, half past one. The first thing I do, I send a telegram to Joe Ettor. Italian man. He was an organizer for the IWW that I met the year before. I tell him to come to Lawrence, we got this strike.

He call a mass meeting of all the strikers, formed a committee for nationality. There were twenty-four nationalities, you understand? The French, the German, Franco-Belgian, Franco-Canadian, the Polish people, the Lithuanians, Armenians, Syrians, Lebanese, Spanish, Portuguese. We formed a general committee that send out a notice for help, all over the world. We formed a soup kitchen to feed the people. I used to buy all the food, beans, macaroni. I was the chairman.

Joe Ettor bring up another fellow from New York, Arturo Giovannitti. Before this, the IWW was notorious for breakin' the law. If you remember, before 1912, the Pettibone and Moyer in Idaho.* The mill owners tried to discredit this strike, these two leaders especially. If they could be arrested and kept away, the strike would be settled, you understand? The first thing they do, they tried to plant dynamite where these leaders meet at night, to accuse the IWW.

Mr. Wood, he build the mill for the American Woolen Company, conceived this act. He got a fellow named Peterman to procure the dynamite, and give it to John Bregeen, the undertaker and school committeeman, to plant the dynamite into Columbo, the printer, where we used to meet. Mr. Columbo wouldn't accept it. So he left the dynamite into Di Prado, the shoemaker, wrapped up in newspaper. "Fix my shoes, then I'll come and get it." Immediately after that, he notified the police: "Hurry up, go down there, arrest everybody, they're gonna blow up everything down here." The police pick

---

* In 1907, Big Bill Haywood, Charles Pettibone, and Charles Moyer, IWW leaders, were tried in Boise, Idaho, for the murder of Governor Frank Steunenberg. Clarence Darrow was their lawyer. They were acquitted. During the trial, President Theodore Roosevelt had denounced the defendants as murderers.

up the thing, they arrest Di Prado, but God intervened in this business. You know what happened? Bregeen wrap it up in a Boston newspaper, addressed to John Bregeen. (Laughs.) So they arrested John Bregeen, and then Wood gave up, too. That boomeranged, this idea. See what I mean?

Okay, the strike proceeds to go on, and the mill owners don't want to negotiate with the IWW. They conceived another idea. These two leaders spoke on the Common from a bandstand. The crowd all listened. One guy from Boston was planted in the crowd, a saboteur, name of Cataldo. What they planned to do is to get him to testify that the strike leader was inciting and a striker killed another striker. So what happened? When another meeting took place, one of the police officers killed a woman named Ann Lupizzo and accused Angelo Caruso, a striker. They arrested Ettor and Giovannitti and accused them of inciting to kill.

As a matter of my life, I do not like violence. I don't know if it's 'cause I'm a small fellow. (Laughs.) There was over two, three thousand picketing. I tried to cool off, that was my ambition. One of the strikers was picked up for carrying a revolver. He was arrested and brought into the mill. The crowd want to break in, to take him out. I conceived the idea that if we break in, somebody gonna get killed. I tell the people that the boy's gone, and they took him over the police station. We avoid violence.

Next, a friend of mine, a Franco-Belgian, was arrested during the strike. I go to the police station to give him a bond to get out. When the chief of police sees I was Rocco, he say: "Lock him up! Lock him up!" He locked me up. (Laughs.) He accused me of disturbing the peace. I try to keep the peace, and he accuse me of disturbing the peace. (Laughs.) We went to the district court. He fined me fifty dollars. I don't pay. I appeal to the Superior Court. I win.

The strike continued. So the mill owners get the idea to influence prominent Italian people and have them convince the strikers to accept a raise of five percent. We rejected that totally.

We went to see the chairman of the manufacturers' association. We got a settlement. It was $7.25 a week. People used to work for $4.40. The strike was over twenty cents, but they had to give us a lot more than twenty cents. (Laughs.) They had to give us fringe benefit, they had to give us insurance. If they give us the twenty cents, the strike wouldn't take place. We won much more. That was a betterment for the working people, a betterment for the town. They got more money comin' in. Matter of fact, the merchants give us a banquet. The Jewish people give us a lot of nice chicken soup. That's how I learned to like chicken soup.

Ettor and Giovannitti are still incarcerated. I was the one originally got them. It is my duty to see that they are caught out of the problem. We got a permit to parade in Lawrence to protest. For a Sunday, after dinner. Some anarchists from Lynn and Boston came over to participate in our parade. We did not invite them. They brought a sign: *No God, No Master*. At the head of this group was Carlo Tresca.* Some Lawrence people followed them. (Laughs.) The police formed a cordon of about twenty-five to stop the parade. When Tresca arrived at the police, he broke the cordon with his hand like this (indicates a parting of the waves). He pushed the police officer to one side and the parade went through. (Laughs.)

We got Father O'Reilly and formed another parade sometime later. The people who followed the other parade—*No God, No Master*—followed Father O'Reilly, too: *For God and Country*. (Laughs.)

Now comes September 1912, the trial of the two leaders. Cataldo testified that Ettor and Giovannitti made the remark to kill, and Caruso killed the woman. I testified that they did no such thing. They wanted to see that the people get together, to win, not to kill. The verdict was not guilty. We celebrated then. See, my mission was all done. (Laughs.)

I wanted to go back to school. I lost three months to take care of the strike. The school superintendent didn't want me because I was connected with the strike and I was a bad boy. (Laughs.) I got admitted just the same, you got me? I graduated from high school in 1912. I started to go to college. I had mathematics and English, and I read most of Shakespeare and Greek and Roman history. I learn all about Julius Caesar and Catalina and the speech of Cicero when he spoke to the senate. He make one sort of speech like Nixon: He spoke out of two sides of his mouth. (Laughs.)

I wanted to be a mechanic engineer, that why I studied a lot of mathematics. But when I studied the way the situation was, that we needed somebody to defend the Italian people, I says, I better be a lawyer. I went to Boston University Law School and I graduate good, almost cum laude, 'cause I love to study. I graduated and made it at

---

* Carlo Tresca, a celebrated IWW journalist and organizer. He subsequently took part in the Paterson strike of 1913, the Masabi iron-range strike of 1916, and the Sacco-Vanzetti case. He was one of the earliest anti-fascists, condemning Mussolini. He was assassinated in 1943.

the bar. I was a lawyer for twelve years. I represented all kind of nationality. I was the best lawyer in town.

I became a rich man. I was thirty-three years old. Then war number one broke out. I was not married. I could claim my mother because of dependence, but I didn't do it. I was not called for service, but I subscribed because I didn't like the idea of the kaiser: might is right. I don't believe in that.

After the war, I continued my law practice and I make good money. I had a good home, and all the bankers come in and drink wine with me. I married in 1922. My wife come from the same town I come from, I know the father.

I invested money in second mortgages. They buy a home, they need the money, I give it. I was worth about three hundred thousand dollars. In 1924, the administration cut the Italian immigration. They adopted the census of 1890, when there were not many Italian people. They gave the Italian people a black eyes, you understand? They screwed the Italian people. Sacco and Vanzetti, they crucify 'em because they were foreigners and anarchists. They electrocute 'em.

We did all we could to fight that idea. I wrote an article for the Italian newspaper *Il Progresso*. I said to discriminate against the Italian people after they had done all the dirty work and build up the United States, the railroads, and the good buildings—the ingratitude, incredible. That stupid guy, Calvin Coolidge, his advice to people: Everybody wear an old hat, wear an old pair of shoes, go back to the kerosene lamp.

I voted for Hoover in 1928. I was a conservative. I was a conservative in 1908, too, because I favor William Howard Taft. I changed my mind after that.

I continued until 1928. Then the depression came, and all these people owed me money and I couldn't get nothing. They left all the house back to me. Nobody could afford to pay me. I was tied up. I represent a Franco-Belgian fellow. He died, left an estate of fifteen hundred dollars. I use that money to pay the bill, and then I was unable to make good. I intended to pay. They put me in jail for two years. I was released with good time in fifteen months, but they disbar me. I lost my profession.

We had lost all the houses we had. Okay, all right, I don't worry. I didn't get sick. I took it. I said: "God wants it that way." What do I do? I manage to get along, to buy and sell land, make some money like that.

"At that time, I had two boys born—one, a chemist—and one daughter. That's the first thing I gotta take care of: the boy and the daughter and the chemist." He points toward a photograph. "That's my son, he went into the Korean War. I got another son that went into the second war. He fought in Saipan."

In '33, I made some pretty good money. I bought some stock. I lost the money. I couldn't make any comeback. In 1938, I got the idea to go into the lumber business with the little money we had. I see it don't pay to sell lumber, we're gonna make lumber. I was buildin' a good business and the war breaks. (Laughs.) They put us on tight.

We went through the war. I made a saw mill, and we made our business good. I became a builder. I built all the houses on this block from '56 on. I'm still selling and working. I'm not retired yet. (Laughs.) Only thing, I draw my Social Security.

For me, it's a good country. The system is all right. Most of the time. The people who run it are no good. Henry Cabot Lodge, John Foster Dulles, and people like that. Free enterprise, completely, is no good. The abuse, you understand? You have to have some control, or like halfway. Take Rockefeller. How's he become a billionaire? It's because he gotta steal from here, from there, someone. He hasn't produced in correspondent to that. What we call not a noble thing to do. You know the monologue from *Hamlet*? "Whether it is noble to endure the insolence of office the proud man contumely . . . " (Laughs.) I believe in Goethe, the German: "I'd rather suffer an injustice than create one." And another thing: I don't like Napoleon. He said: "I'd rather eat than be eaten."

I think it is more better to help than to be helped. I was born to help. It's Angel Gabriel, my name. To fight the devil. (Laughs.) See, that's my ancestor. (Laughs.) I keep that up, and I'm glad.

STANLEY CYGAN, 90

◇————————————————————————————◇

We're in the first-floor apartment of a neat two-flat building, reflective of this Slavic community in Chicago. It is a Sunday afternoon. He is seated in a deep easy chair; he had been casually following the pro football game on TV. He is a small man, slender, soft and gentle in manner. Wistfully, he apologizes for his difficulty in remembering details.

My father was a farmer in Poland. It was a hard life. So he came to America in 1893. He landed in McKeesport, Pennsylvania, worked in a steel mill. Three years later, he saved up enough money to send for my mother, my sister, and me. I was six. I remember the trip because I was sick all the way. (Laughs.)

There were not many Poles in McKeesport. There were mostly German and Irish. The jobs we had were the lowest paid. (Laughs.) The Poles began to come to us from our part of the country. They stayed with us until they got resettled. Then we had a Polish community. Our school, parochial, was up in the hills. Eight grades in two rooms. Besides the Polish reader, we had an English reader.

I used to take my father's dinner pail to work. That's how I knew what he was doing. All sweated up with his little cap on. He died when I was ten years old. Mother couldn't afford to keep us, so I was sent to a boys' orphanage in Polonia, Wisconsin. Polonia was like a farm village, mostly German Poles. We called them Kaszubik. I remember it was the Fourth of July when we were sent there. In bed, watching the fireworks from the window, I was cryin'. I spent a year there. They only kept you until you were eleven. They said: "You're old enough to earn your daily bread." (Laughs.)

My mother remarried and I came back to McKeesport. My stepfather was ailing. He worked in one of them steel mills, hard job. Doctors told him if he wants to live, he better go on a farm. He couldn't afford to go on a farm here. He had some land in the Old Country, only about an acre or two. So they decided to go back to Poland. I was then close to thirteen. I refused to go. I was always told, when I didn't want to eat something, in Poland, you'd pick the crumbs off the floor. (Laughs.) So, of course, they scared me. Here, you don't do that. They left me with an aunt.

I went in the steel mills when I was sixteen. I'm sorry I ever did.

The boys coming from Poland, my age, they all worked hard. My salary was three and a half dollars a week. Ten-hour days, twelve-hour nights, six days a week. The lowest paid job in the steel mill. All the better-paid jobs were either Irish or German. I got a better job there because they ran short of Englishmen and Irish and Germans. (Laughs.) My mother said the Poles were downgraded in McKeesport. "Go to Chicago." I came to East Chicago. That was 1909, hard times, no work. Finally, I got a job in a rolling mill. The boss would come out and pick the people he wanted. There were always twenty-five of us out there, waiting to get hired. He'd pick 'em out like that. I had an uncle that had pretty good standing with this foreman. That's why he picked me.

I did some hard work. During the day, they had two men working on it. In the evening, I was there alone. I couldn't keep up with the mill. I lost favor with the superintendent.

In 1913, '14, I went to this stove-repair company. I started for ten and a half dollars a week. I started out sweeping floors and ended up being in charge of the pattern department. Maybe half a million patterns. You wouldn't believe there were so many different stoves in the world.

I worked with them until they closed down the place. Forty-two years. The Dan Ryan Expressway was goin' through. They got half a million dollars for the place. We had to go. They gave me three months' wages. (Laughs.) I was lucky. I doubt if others really got that much. They got what they wanted: our muscle.

When I came to America, I wanted to have a real job. I wanted to be smart. I enrolled in school when I was twenty-nine. After a season, I got my eighth-grade papers. I enrolled in high school, a couple of hours a night. I had three children already, but I wanted to be smart.

I used to attend lectures at Hull House. The things that bothered me were so many things I couldn't understand. I figured after I get through school, I'll know more about things. I don't know. I guess I got too old.

I dreamt I was gonna be a chemist. I talked to a professor about it who was giving lectures. He told me it would take at least six years. He told me out of half a dozen of his schoolmates, there are only two that make a good living. I figured six years is too much.

There was a professor from the university lecturing on relativity. Einstein. You read about it, it just makes you curious. I'd spend an hour and a half there, listening to him. But the worst of it was I didn't understand half the words he used. I never did understand relativity. There's a lot of things I don't understand, that if I had more schooling I would.

DORA ROSENZWEIG, 94

◇————————————————————————————◇

It's a bungalow in Los Angeles, neat and tidy, in a green and pleasant section of the city.

Though she has occasional difficulty moving about, she lives by herself and likes it. Her daughter, the older of two married children, frequently visits her.

"I was one of fourteen children, the only child among adults. I was born in 1885, in Russia, a small Jewish ghetto near Pinsk, a shtetl. *Talk of America was in the air. My father had gone there. My two older sisters were growing up and needed a dowry, so he went there to save money. In the meantime, our house burnt down, so my mother decided we should all go to America."*

All I can remember is the whole town following the wagon, shouting farewell. We had to go to Warsaw to catch the train. We lived on the border. Everybody had a package, even feathers for the bedding. Candleholders made of brass, brass pots and pans, clothing. My mother made sacks and sacks of black bread toast to eat on the way.

In order for immigrants to go to America, they had to hire a travel agent. A rumor came that an agent had taken a family to the woods and robbed them of all their possessions. So my mother said: "What do we need an agent for?"

Warsaw was a big town. The wagon stopped in a courtyard, and I remember a peddler shouting his wares. A head popped out of a second-floor window. I never saw a second floor. I never saw stairways. I wondered: How did she get up there? In our house, we had a ladder to the attic. The next thing I remember, my mother went to the wall and turned something and water came out! I knew water comes from the well. How does water come from the wall?

At the border, just before entering Germany, a policeman comes up to the train and demands to see our passport. He tears it up, and they throw us off the train—in Russia. My mother realized because she didn't hire a travel agent, they retaliated. Deals were worked out. Bribes.

The mother and ten children out in the street. What to do? She took the children and put 'em on the railroad track. I remember sitting in the middle of the tracks, thinking that the next train that'll come will kill us. The people were touched and took us in. My mother came in, saying: "Give up your souls, children. I made a deal with a travel agent; if he kills us, we have nothing to lose."

My mother dressed me in my holiday clothes and she told me I shouldn't look left or right, but straight ahead. She'll come later. We had come to the border. I turned my head, and there was a gun pointing at me. The sentry. We came into Germany, two babies and me. We were in a house, the travel agent's. I saw an organ grinder with a monkey. I had never seen that. I remember the tune, "Miserere" from *Il Trovatore*. I love it still.

We were smuggled in. They had to take us piecemeal across the border. My brothers came in disguised as errand boys, carrying bread to Germany. All the others came in, but not my mother. Night fell, and my mother isn't there. Imagine the terror. We waited. Some people walked across the bridge, some forded the river. My mother was carried on the back of a smuggler.

I remember the trains. Next stop was Liverpool. Whenever a train guard came by, we were terror-stricken, thinking we'll be thrown off again. By the time we came to Liverpool, the boat had left. We were late. So we got on a freighter. We were five weeks on that boat. My brother and I were the only ones that didn't get seasick.

We arrived at the depot in Chicago. My father met us there. He brought us a basket of fruit. I remember biting into a banana. I didn't know you had to peel it. (Laughs.) My mother thought it was pork sausages. (Laughs.) She said I shouldn't eat it. My father said it's kosher.

We got an apartment near the railroad tracks, a saloon on the corner. Ten of us in four rooms. My mother had never seen a stove. In Russia, we had little brick ovens. The wonder of all wonders: an inside toilet.

In Chicago, 1891, the sidewalks were wooden, except for fancy streets. It was the greatest pleasure to walk under the sidewalk because once in a while you found a penny. Streets paved with wooden blocks was a blessing for the poor people. When you couldn't buy coal, you went at night and dug up the blocks.

I started school, kindergarten. The teacher said something to me and I didn't understand. She must have thought I was stupid. So she slapped me. Well, nobody slaps Dora. I played truant and didn't go back. Luckily, I got sick and didn't go to that semester at all. Playing among children, I learned English.

Evidently, I was fascinated by books. I couldn't read, but I saw the illustrations. I listened to the class and memorized what they read. In the first two years, I made five grades. By that time, I was nine, ten years old. I had some wonderful teachers.

I became very interested in reading. Before Jane Addams, whom I came to know and love, a group of young women started a settlement in the ghetto. My father jumped to the conclusion that they wanted to impose Christianity, proselytize. They'd lure the children by giving 'em candy, and they had a library and music, to get the children to

Americanize themselves. My father thought they were going to make gentiles out of us. I had to cross the street to avoid them. My girl-friends didn't have such pious fathers and went in there. I liked the candy, but what I liked best, they'd come out with books.

One day I defied my father, was welcomed, and got a book. By stealth I'd go there, and that was really the beginning of my Americanization. That's the first time I met gentile children.

When I was eleven, my father began to talk about me going to work as a seamstress. My mother was interested in my education. She was proud of my learning English and wanted me to be a schoolteacher. That was the heights. In Russia, a woman didn't amount to much. So there was trouble in the house. By the time I was twelve, I got so tired of the arguments that I got a job as a cigar maker. Rather than be a seamstress, which I hated, I'd make cigars like my brother.

It was a garret with a couple of benches. Boys, girls, and men were working. The confinement and the tobacco smell made me sick. The place was called a buckeye, the name for a sleazy shop, filthy, no air. TB was rampant at that time, cigar maker's disease. We had a foreman, Fritz. He could be as mean as the devil. There would be an underground signal: Fritz is coming. We stopped whatever we were doing and shut up. He'd come with a smile. He knew what was going on. But whenever anyone was known to have TB, he was the first to organize relief.

Cigar making gave me more leisure, and we were equal to the men, got the same money. I grew up to earn fifteen dollars a week. Many men didn't earn that. We're talking about '98. Spanish-American War. I remember shouting: "To hell with Spain, remember the *Maine*." (Laughs.)

I got into a group of older immigrants interested in social questions, and I began to go to lectures. I met my husband that way. I met people who were interested in the labor movement. Working conditions were terrible, even at the American Tobacco Company where I worked, tops. The toilets were on the same floor where four hundred people worked. Open. That's the beginning of my interest in the union, the Progressive Cigar Makers.

When I was sixteen, my mother died and I left home. I lived with strangers. No Jewish girl lived with strangers, no matter how miserable the house was. It was my key to freedom. They called me anarchist, they called me Bolshevik, but I never joined anything. I was always very curious and went through all the lessons I could get in order to learn what it's all about.

1 0 7

I heard about free love. It scared me. This was when I was about nineteen. It was in the air, this search for freedom. Two girls furnished a two-bedroom rear apartment and asked me to live with them. Whoever heard of three girls living together? This was 1905. You know what it is? Prostitution. The sister I moved away from prophesied that I'd have four bastards. Why she took four, I don't know. If ever there was a naïve, innocent set of three girls, you can't imagine.

I always felt I was the equal of any man. I could think like a man. I could step on the sidewalk without help. I didn't have to have a man to hold my arm or open the door. We'd go to the theater. I'd pay my own way. I like the young feminists today. (Laughs.)

Most of the cigar makers where I worked wanted a better life, they were looking for culture, going to lectures, going to night school. I was the only so-called American because I knew English. I had gone to sixth grade. There was something in the air that affected all of us.

The shop was almost a block long. It had two rooms, a small one and a large one. I preferred to work in the small room, which held about thirty or forty people. They elected me a reader. I used to roll fifty cigars an hour. That was my piecework limit. So if I read for an hour, they would donate the fifty cigars I missed. If I read for two hours, they'd give me a hundred. I'd sit on a chair and read while they worked. I read about current events, a book, or even a play. I would choose the books. Whoever heard of a twelve-year-old girl reading Flaubert's *Salammbô*? Whatever struck me, I'd read to the others. Tolstoi, anything.

Most of them were still young and rebellious. The difference between the hippies and the rebels of my time—we didn't have enough. We were always lacking something, even food. We wanted theater, we wanted concerts. Theater was cheap. I saw Mansfield from the most prosaic roles to Peer Gynt. I'll never forget this Peer Gynt. Ibsen's *Ghosts* was played on special matinees. The theater was crowded, mostly with immigrants. I saw Isadora Duncan dancing. We hungered for the better things of life.

There was a terrible depression in 1903, 1904. There were many strikes. The Haymarket Riot of when? ten, fifteen years before? had a profound effect on us. I knew Lucy Parsons.* In one strike, we saw

---

* The widow of Albert Parsons, one of the four who was hanged as a result of the Haymarket Riot trial in 1889. A fifth defendant killed himself in his cell. The three survivors were pardoned in 1893 by Governor John Peter Altgeld.

the police bring out the fire hoses and knock down peaceful marchers who were just protesting.

They used to come and raid the houses for literature. Oh, it happened all the time. I used to go to meetings, but I never joined. I was never active. My name was never signed to any petitions or anything because I was cautious. I was Americanized. (Laughs.)

My husband was a leader of his union, ILGWU. We couldn't get into the AF of L. Samuel Gompers, the head of it, was a maker of Spanish cigars, which means making the whole cigar from beginning to end. He didn't figure on the industrial revolution where you began to be a section worker, the assembly line. We were just rollers, and our bid wasn't accepted. I was in that fight, too.

We'd go to free lectures on Sundays. In the mornings, we'd walk to the Fine Arts Building to listen to a lecture on literature. Then we'd walk back home for lunch. A nickel was a nickel. After lunch, at two o'clock, we'd walk to Orchestra Hall: a lecture on education, on history. We'd walk back home. After our evening meal, we'd walk downtown to the Masonic Temple and hear poetry readings.

"I was twenty-one and my husband was twenty-four when we married. Jewish girls didn't go to work after they were married. My mother-in-law was scandalized. What will the neighbors say? I said: 'To hell with the neighbors.' I rebelled against religion, too. I was the hippie of my age." (Laughs.)

My husband hated his work and I hated mine. We wanted to get out of the shops, and I wanted a family. We liked the country life and decided to become farmers. We wanted to homestead. In the early 1900s, the railroads wanted settlers in the West, for freight. For thirty-two dollars, you could go from Chicago to the coast. By 1909, it was all: Go west, young man, go west. There was a railroad show at the Coliseum: farm products of the West. Watermelons that big. They told us of all the wonderful things we could get. Nobody told us there was little rainfall.

The Rosebud Indian Reservation in South Dakota was thrown open for settlers. They took it away from the Indians. They had a lottery. My husband won a ticket, but he didn't want to be separated from his friend Charlie. So they came back to Chicago. On the train they heard about oceans of land in Montana. Whoever comes gets the land. So they came to Scobey, Montana.

You choose your plot of prairie land—three hundred twenty acres—and you didn't stop to ask why. I remained in Chicago to augment our income, to earn my $15.75 a week: a ten-dollar gold piece, a five-dollar gold piece, a quarter, and a half-dollar. We had saved two thousand dollars, a lot of money.

He built a twelve-by-twenty shack. I joined him in August 1910. I got off the train, and there was my brown-complected husband, sunburned, with overalls and a red kerchief. Nobody told me there was only nine inches of rainfall a year (laughs) and that the country was subject to prairie fires. In August, there was no grass, it was just yellow. It was blazing hot. I thought: My God, I'm in the Sahara Desert.

I got on a prairie schooner. We started at twelve o'clock. At evening we stopped near a creek. I volunteered to take the horses to water for drink. I'd never been near a horse. Nobody told me there's cactus. It went through my shoe. There was no wood, no trees. He carried a little kindling, took out a rusty pan, and made some coffee. He spread out some blankets and said this is where we sleep tonight.

The air was so clear. I thought I could reach up and take a star. It was beautiful. Everything was new. It took two and a half days to make the trip to Scobey.

The neighbors were simply wonderful. The first morning, a horseman stops near the door, Mr. Larson from three miles away. "Simon, I want you to come for threshing." I said: "Can I come along?" He says: "Come, be our cook." I could make gefilte fish, challah, but cooking for twenty-five Montana farmers . . . (Laughs.)

He tells me the menu: potatoes and ham. I had never cooked it. I asked my husband: "Where are the potatoes?" He said: "You have to dig 'em up." (Laughs.) And bake biscuits, too. I had never baked biscuits. Mr. Larson said it was a wonderful meal. The next morning, a sixteen-year-old girl came by and taught me how to cook country-style, and I made my first pie.

Our salvation were the neighbors who lived two miles away. Pious Methodists. If not for them, I don't think we could have survived. Mrs. Watts was my mother, my counselor, my everything. When my husband had accidents, they'd come help us. She knew folk medicine. At threshing time, everybody helped.

My husband had to go back and forth for business. I was alone. We were talking about going farther west. Why? I was hungry for people. I was hungry for the family. I wanted my daughter to go to school. By that time, I had another child. The school was six miles away, and

I was terrified that my daughters would grow up illiterate. How do you send a little girl in Montana winters to school so far away? We wanted to sell, but there was no one to buy.

The war broke out, but we weren't in it yet. Canada was. One day, as I was doing my chores, two horsemen drove up. Fifteen minutes later, my husband came in and said we sold the farm. There's a Canadian who doesn't believe in the war. He was supposed to join the English army, so he decided to move to the United States. My husband named the first price that came into his head, sixteen thousand dollars. There were two hundred fifty acres under crops that woulda brought in probably sixteen thousand dollars. My husband was not a businessman. (Laughs.)

We came back to Chicago. For years, we ran a summer resort in Michigan, where I was a square peg in a round hole.

I span almost a century. When I look back upon it, the worst thing was sanitation. Babies died the second year of their lives, usually from poisoned milk. They called it summer complaint. There was smallpox, there was diphtheria, there was typhoid. These diseases have been wiped out. Although we eat poisoned food, we breathe bad air, we live longer than we did. Children don't die as frequently.

Life at that time was hard, hard, hard. Now it's much easier. When my mother found a washboard, she didn't know what to do with it. Now I have a washing machine.

We are enjoying creature comforts. Don't forget, I remember candlelight. When we first got gas, it was for special occasions. And the flickering flame didn't do as good as the kerosene lamp. Electricity didn't come in my time until we came to Montana. The phonograph came in my time. When I came to my father and asked for a penny because "there's a man on the corner who puts earphones on you and you hear music," I got a nice little slap: How can a box play music? I lived from that to TV to the man on the moon.

I have a childish theory about the lifelessness of the moon. Don't laugh. I think there were people on the moon who became so sophisticated that they began to do what we're doing. First, it was the gun. Then it was the bomb. Instead of killing piecemeal, it kills thousands. Hiroshima. Now they have the H-bomb, and they're talking about a neutron bomb. I believe the people on the moon found the ultra-ultraweapon to destroy life, and it became a burnt-out planet. A childish thought, maybe, but if we keep going like this . . . I don't worry about it. I won't be here. (Laughs.)

The American Dream is the same the whole world over. Some live for living, some live for eating. If you're interested, you're alive. They tell me I have young ideas, that I look young. It's because I'm interested in life, in current events, in people. I've had a circle of dear friends that I kept for years, until they died. I made new friends, new interests. I widened my horizons. I still want to know things.

I used to wonder: What are we here for? How did we come here? What must we do? I'm an old woman, and I have quite a few disabilities. But I'm very thankful that my marbles are still working. And my sense of humor.

GENERATIONS:
FIRST AND SECOND

NORMAN MACLEAN

Professor emeritus, University of Chicago

My father and mother were immigrants from Canada. My father was all Scotch and came from Nova Scotia, from a large family that was on poor land. His great belief was in all men being equal under God. That old Bobby Burns line: A man's a man for a' that and a' that. He was a Presbyterian minister, and it was very deep with him.

My father loved America so much that, although he had a rather heavy Scotch burr when he came to this country, by the time I was born, it was all gone. He regarded it as his American duty to get rid of it. He despised Scotch Presbyterian ministers who went heavy on their Scotch burr. He put a terrific commitment on me to be an American. I, the eldest son, was expected to complete the job.

He told me I had to learn the American language. He spoke beautifully, but he didn't have the American idioms. He kept me home until I was ten and a half to teach me. He taught me how to write American. No courses in show-and-tell and personality adjustment. (Laughs.) I was young and I thought I was tough and I knew it was beautiful and I was a little bit crazy but hadn't noticed it yet. You took those little pieces of American speech and listened carefully for 'em and you put them together. My American training went clear down into my language.

He was great on rhythm. He read us the Bible every morning. We got down on our knees by our chairs and we prayed. We had it twice a day, the great King James translation, after breakfast and after what we called supper.

Literature was important to him: the prose of Mark Twain, and the odd combination of Franklin Roosevelt and Wilson and Whitman. He knew it wasn't English. It was American. He couldn't get over the fact that Wilson was the son of a Presbyterian minister. He was the model for many generations of prose writers, including Roosevelt.

The family was the center of the universe and the center of America. I don't know if we have *an* American Dream. We have American Dreams. One of his biggest dreams was the dream of great education in this country and the necessity of every person to be educated.

I was the first person in his family not to make his living with his hands. "Maclean" means son of a carpenter. That's what my family had been. They were all carpenters. My father was the pride and joy of his sisters because he made his living without his hands. He was a marvelous carpenter himself. He and I, way back in 1921, made this log cabin out there that's still mine.

Working with hands is one of our deepest and most beautiful characteristics. I think the most beautiful parts of the human body are the hands of certain men and women. I can't keep my eyes off them. I was brought up to believe that hands were the instrument of the mind. Even doing simple things. I still look pretty good with an axe. My father was very stylish with any tool he worked with. Yeah, the fishing rod also. He was just beautiful, pick up a four-ounce rod and throw that line across the Blackfoot River. It was just something beautiful to behold.

Roughly, I've managed one way or another till now to continue a life that is half intellectual and half back in the woods. I kept my cabin out there, although my family died long ago. Now that I'm retired, I spend a third of my life out there. I stay as long as the weather permits me. October, until the elk season is over.

In the city I cultivate beauty of several kinds. In twenty minutes, I can be where there are beaver and deer. I go walking practically every afternoon. Three or four times a week, I go out into the country. I've learned another kind of beauty we didn't have. I think the industrial geometric beauty of Chicago is just beyond belief. To go up the Calumet River by boat and see all those big elevators and cranes and all the big stuff over that dirty river, this is just pure design. Cézanne couldn't find more beautiful geometrical patterns. If I had to name the number one most beautiful sight in the world, given my taste, I would say standing at night by the Planetarium, looking across the bay at the big Hancock and Sears buildings. No place more beautiful. You can't be provincial about beauty.

As I've grown older, I've tried to put together the dreams into my own life. My cabin is only sixteen miles from the glaciers. It snows every month out there. And there are the Gothic halls of the University of Chicago. If you know of a more beautiful city college in the world, architecturally, I'd like to know it. University of London, Oxford, they're just outhouses in comparison.

You have to be gifted with a long life to attain a dream and make it harmonious. I feel infinitely grateful in my old age that I've had in this country, within my family, the training needed to be the best that was in me. It's no great thing, but at seventy-five, I'm fulfilled. There aren't any big pieces in me that never got a chance to come out. They may say at the end of my life, I have no alibis. I have two children of my own, whom I admire and love and try not to annoy very much. I see my father going right on with my children. You've got to pass the ball along.

FLORENCE SCALA

In the late fifties, she, in actuality, led the fight against City Hall to save her old neighborhood on Chicago's near West Side. It was a multiethnic, multiracial community, where Jane Addams had established Hull House. It was one of the city's most alive areas. It is now a complex of institutions, expressways, of public-housing projects, and a few islands of old-timers, hanging on.

She and Jessie Binford, in her late eighties, a colleague of Jane Addams's, had fought to the last days of demolition. They had appealed to Hull House's board of directors, some of the city's most distinguished citizens, of old and respected families. "It was pouring rain, and we walked out of the room the way people walk out who feel defeat. I mean, we walked out trying to appear secure, but we didn't have much to say to each other. Miss Binford could hardly speak. Something was crushed inside her. The Chicago she knew had died."

I had a feeling that things would happen in my life that would be magical. I think everybody has that feeling. I thought I would grow up to be whatever it was I wanted to be. I was a dreamer. When I was in high school, I wanted to be a writer, a journalist. My dreams have not been fulfilled personally.

I was born in 1918. My first memory, as a small girl, was going to school and not being able to speak English, feeling panicky and running all the way home. I became ashamed of my mother. She was very emotional and used to make scenes. I didn't want her to take me to school any more.

I remember a crowded city street, and my father on the pressing iron and my mother sewing in the store, and all of us playing out on the street. I don't remember those days with loving nostalgia. The street was miserable. But I always felt way up in the summertime and late afternoon, and the sun shining and people coming home. It was always a magic time for me.

My parents worked very hard. You had to when you're running a small business like that, a tailor shop. They worked with their hands all the time. He did the pressing and the tailoring. My mother did the more simple things of repairing. Getting up very early in the morning, working late at night. He would do the pressing during the day, the sewing in the evening. He'd close the store about nine o'clock at night. We lived in back of the store, until my teens. Then we moved upstairs. My mother decided I should have a room for myself.

Oh, our neighborhood was a mess. At the same time, it was a wonder. There was a lot of anxiety because of the hooliganism. Our parents were worried because the kids might get involved and that it would touch their lives. My father was frightened during the trade union wars in the cleaning industry, which was dominated by hoodlums. For weeks, his business was closed down because they struck the plant and he had no place to send the clothes. Then he was a scab and took the clothes to another cleaning establishment. There were killings on the streets. We were used to seeing that. Among Italians, there were *padrones* who went to mediate the fights within the neighborhoods.

My father never participated in any of this. He was aloof, a loner. He was really an educated man by the standards of the time. He did a lot of reading. He loved opera. He would buy all the librettos. We still have our old Caruso records. The other thing he loved was astronomy. He knew how far the moon was from the earth, how far Venus was. He thought the trip to the moon was a waste of time, a waste of money, because, he said, there is nothing they discovered that he hadn't already known.

He had this one dream that he wanted to see Grand Canyon. He never saw it. He was so tired by the time he had time that he was afraid to take the trip. I never really got to talk to him. He was very shy and lonely.

Black people came to our store, left clothes. They were people who painted and did carpentry. They were craftsmen. Our parents had no animosity toward blacks. They—the immigrants—saw themselves as being in the same predicament, trying to make it in the city. I never remember any racial conflict when I was little. Later I saw it.

Today the community is very small, five or six square blocks. There's public housing, largely black. The medical center students and young people from advertising and TV, who see it as part of chic downtown. Some old Italian families are hanging on. It began to change as my generation was growing up. People my age wanted to be more like the people from other communities. They inaugurated a cotillion (laughs) where they had the young daughters being presented at a dance, emulating "society." They were sending their kids to Catholic schools. Our parents sent us to public schools. Friends of mine would prefer to meet their friends elsewhere than invite them into the neighborhood. That didn't happen in my case because I went to Hull House. I was growing up in a whole different atmosphere of pride.

I don't have regrets. I believe strongly—and I see signs of it today —that what we were trying to do and didn't succeed in doing had left its mark on the people there. They don't take things sitting down any more. They remember the struggle to save the neighborhood with a certain amount of sadness and a certain amount of respect.

I don't dream any more like I used to. I believed that in this country, we would have all we needed for the decent life. I don't see that any more. The self-interest of the individual—"I'm number one"—is contaminating much of our thinking today. It's happening with our institutions as well. They seem to be acting in their own self-interest.

The world doesn't seem definable any more. Even this city. I see it becoming more and more disoriented. I'm against bigness for its own sake. We walk down the street and don't even look at one another. We're strangers. It's a time that's hard to figure out.

It's a world I don't know. The world of the computer and the microwave oven. I'll never have one. (Laughs.) There are things alien to my understanding. Younger people growing up will find it easier to contend with, but I doubt it. They'll conform because it's the only way to go. Big Brother is there. I think they will become digits. I don't see myself as a digit, but I know I'm becoming one. It's necessary for me to have my Social Security number available or my driver's license, because I don't have credit cards. It's un-American. Anywhere I gotta pay cash. You see, I'm not a digit yet. (Laughs.)

I don't even know what the American Dream is any more. Maybe it's picking up some pieces I've left behind.

STELLA NOWICKI

She appeared in the documentary film Union Maids *as one of three elderly women who recalled their young womanhood, the thirties, and labor battles.*

You dream of growing up and leaving home. What are you going to do with yourself? With your life?

I came from a very poor family in Mattawan, Michigan. Believe it or not, I wanted to become a doctor. I became a doctor of piggies. We used to do butchering, and I helped dissect a hog. I used to kill the chickens. Anything went wrong with any of the animals, I was the doctor. I put the splints on broken legs. In high school, I was the nurse's aide. I could stand the blood and the gore. I saw how the body looked inside. I realize, gee, I really wanted to do something like that, be able to heal. I graduated from high school and didn't even have enough money to come to Chicago. So I figured maybe I could be a nurse, the second-best thing.

That was in 1933, the depression. To be a nurse, you had to have a fountain pen and pencil set, you had to have a watch with a second hand, and you had to have uniforms. You had to pay for 'em yourself. I didn't have any of that. So the next best thing was to get any job. The American Dream was something that was way up there in the clouds. The reality was here. What could I do? What could I get?

My mother and father were born in Yugoslavia. They didn't know each other until they got here. My father came here in '17, to escape military conscription. He was one of eight or nine kids. When he got to be a certain age, his father just kicked him out: "We don't have enough food. Go to America, the land of golden streets, where you can get jobs and make money and get rich."

I remember tragedies in mines. I remember the wailing sound that means there was an accident. I remember all of us running to the shaft of the mine. I remember the nightmares. Some people we knew died. I remember my father being laid off, and my mother had boarders to make ends meet, and gambling and bootlegging.

It was prohibition. My poor mother would work like hell, taking care of us kids, the bootlegging, the lodgers. These guys would be out there playing cards and ordering stuff, they'd get so drunk. (Laughs.) She used to take money out of the pot. (Laughs.) My mother had fifteen hundred dollars from the gambling and the bootlegging. That was down payment on the farm.

We were a self-sufficient farm. Then came the frost. The grapes went. So my father got a job in Kalamazoo, in a foundry, pig iron. He worked two jobs. He'd ride twelve miles, work all day in the foundry, come home, and work the farm at night.

We'd go to school, and the minute school's out, we'd be home in fifteen minutes and work on that farm. Hard labor, hard as any man worked. I finished high school fast. I was bright. I loved school. Our teachers were just wonderful. It was a whole different attitude, especially foreign-born kids, 'cause our parents said: "You're not gonna be no greenhorn, you're not gonna be dumb, you're gonna have a better life than I had." The way to do it was to get an education. When I finished high school, I hitchhiked to South Haven and caught a boat to Chicago.

I was seventeen when I came to this city. I could not believe it. Nothing prepared me for this tremendous, complex city with all sorts of nationalities and colors.

When I came to Chicago, I saw blacks living in hovels worse than whites. The people I lived with would talk to me about it. They'd tell me discrimination is a necessity for capitalism. I wasn't politically sophisticated at all, outside of my father talking socialism a little bit.

My father bought some books in Croatian. Later, when I got to read these books by Lenin and Gorky, I recognized the faces. My father had been teaching me Croatian out of these socialist books. He would tell me the only way you're gonna get ahead is sticking together with other working people.

In Chicago, I saw bread lines, people getting kicked out with their furniture, unemployed marches. It was the depression. When I couldn't get a job, I thought something was wrong with *me*. My friends said: "You're not gonna get a job unless you lie." I said I was a butcher and got a job in the stockyards.

Before that I was doing housework for some doctor and his family for four dollars a week. Washing shirts, ironing, cooking, and taking care of this spoiled brat. Only every other Sunday off, Thursday afternoon off. I sent half this money home. Can you imagine? I sent them two dollars. I had this feeling of responsibility that was imbued in us. When you grow up and you leave, you have to help the folks. I hated it so, every night I would cry, 'cause I'd be inside doing all the shit work.

The first job I got in the stockyards was cutting up meat. The government bought up the drought cattle, canned the stuff, and used it for people on relief. All this stuff would come in steamers, hot, they'd dump it and we cut off the rough stuff, the sinews and aged meat. We were standing next to each other, with a knife, steaming hot, no ventilation, just horrible work.

The stench and the heat were so bad that women used to pass out, faint. Here I was, this strong country girl, seventeen years old, a hundred fifty-eight pounds, rosy cheeks, would pick these women up and carry them down these steep stairs to the ladies' room. That's how strong I was. I felled trees on the farm with a great big crosscut saw, used to lift these logs. That's why I can't understand this bullshit when they talk about women'll have to be forced to do the work men do. Hell, we've been doing it all the time. (Laugh.)

We talked about machines having safety measures on them so people wouldn't get cut up, that we should have guards on our thumbs so we wouldn't get cut up when we sharpened knives. Lo and behold, this woman got her fingertips cut off on the goddamn sausage machine. I was there when it happened. Our group met that night, three of us women working in that department. The next morning we got out a leaflet. We hid them in our bosoms, and we'd give them out. We suggested that the women not work until there were safety guards.

They finally realized that their limbs were more important than the job. We had a stoppage. We got the safety guards. Now we got our leaflets saying: See what happens when you stick together? What if we had a union and we all stuck together? That's before the CIO was organized. This was in '33.

I joined the Young Communist League. It's important what the Communist party did. You can speak of disillusionments, but I'm talking' about *then*. It's been hidden because of the cold war, the fear, the FBI. We had meetings up in the attic. It was rough. If the neighbors knew there were meetings going on with Negroes and whites, they would suspect something and report us to the police. We were very careful. We would come through the back, through the alley, and we would have these meetings.

We would talk about conditions. We would have classes on industrial unionism, on the history of the American working class. We read about Debs. We read about the history of socialism elsewhere, about the Soviet Union. Here we had the richest country in the world, and we were hungry. At least people were not going hungry in the Soviet Union. It was a tremendous thing for me as a young idealistic person to see that there was a way out.

So I joined the party. I had a good time, too. People think of us as old dunderheads. I remember parties held at the John Reed Club to raise money for the *Yards Worker*, our local Communist paper. We'd get all the stockyards news, and writers would help polish it up a bit. We'd talk union. Every now and then, we'd have an article about socialism. We didn't hide it. We tried to talk in terms workers would understand, not highfalutin language, not polemics.

We could not talk on the job. You just stood there like a machine. They were watching you. The rule was you don't talk. There were ten people waiting for your job. When the boss wasn't looking, I'd whisper. The only place you could really talk was in the washroom during lunch hour or during the fifteen-minute break. You'd be running to have lunch, in a half-hour, all your personal chores, grabbing a quick bite, whispering.

One day the personnel director came into the washroom right after I had left and saw all those *Yards Workers* around. (Laughs.) The end of the day, they handed me an envelope with a pink slip: pick up your pay, you're fired. Nobody gave you a reason, they didn't have to. I had to go back to housework again.

At this time, the Young Communist League sent all sorts of young people to work in the stockyards, to help organize. They did this in steel, in coal mining, in railroads, in electrical—to project the whole idea of industrial unionism. So this young woman comes down the street and says: "I got this job as a secretary. I don't want to work in those damn stockyards. They stink and it's hard work." I says: "What name did you use?" She said: "Rose Walsh." She was Jewish but used another name. She says: "Take my card and go to Armour's." I got there and the assistant to the personnel head, who fired me, was there. She said start working tomorrow afternoon, one to seven.

My friend said: "Let's go to the beauty shop and get your hair hennaed." I'd been out of work a couple of weeks, so I'd gotten a suntan. They thinned my eyebrows. I was a country girl and wore little makeup. Now I put on rouge and fingernail polish and a beautiful sunback dress with stripes. I came right into work and nobody recognized me. (Laughs.) A different name, same job.

Guess what happens? I'm there about a week or so and up comes the floor lady. She was a Croatian girl. She pokes me and she says in Croatian: "Keep your mouth shut and do your work and everything will be fine." She tipped me off. Can you imagine? I have a feeling she was pro-union. It was a wonderful feeling.

There was so much excitement. The CIO. Then the McCarthy period. Times of despair and disillusionment. The Stalin revelations. I always believed in socialism, but this really shook me up. It was like a horrible dream you didn't want to believe. You had a commitment for these years, a total dedication.

I was really shattered. I could not believe what I read in the what we called the capitalist press about the Soviet Union. What they said was true. How do you square that? Then, Czechoslovakia and what happened there. I was not a person who understood all the theory, all the nuances. After all, how could I? I worked all day. I had faith in the people who knew theory. Now I began to question.

A friend's aunt came from Moscow to visit here. She was talking about how wonderful it was in the Soviet Union. I asked her one question: "Give me a typical day." When she got through describing what she did that day, I said: "That's socialism?" Suppose I could be an engineer, or this or that, yet I had to go through all this shit, waiting in line, one after another, to buy bread and to buy meat and to cook and share the kitchen with how many people? I'm sure it's an improvement over what it was, but not much for all these fifty years. In '55, I left the party.

I feel hopeful about today. The kids, particularly young women, raise all sorts of questions. With the women's movement, there's a whole new awakening. Oh yes, I feel very optimistic. I think pessimism is a product of inactivity.

Some of my contemporaries are pessimists because they've gotten too fat. They're earning quite a bit. They're concerned about others, but they're not really doing anything about it. They're just bitchin'. People who are involved have a positive approach to life. People who are not dead. One has to become involved in things outside themselves if they want to grow. Not to close your mind, to learn all the time. I don't care what anyone says about the young kids of the sixties. I've learned so goddamn much from them, it's fantastic.

I feel like that young girl again. (Laughs.)

LEON DUNCAN

He is a historian in New England.

I was born into the ruling class. I grew up with the expectations that all was right with the world and that I would have some share in running this world. There were minor improvements to be made here and there, but everything was going along pretty smoothly.

My father was an executive of a large agribusiness company with interests in various parts of the world. It was a multinational. He was head of what is now a subsidiary. He was a typical businessman.

I went with my father on a trip to Latin America, where, at that time, the principal interests of the company were sugar plantations. I had a chance to go out into the countryside. That was one of the first times I began to make the connection, began to realize these dark-skinned guys laboring away in 100-degree heat for their six shillings a day were, in some sense, paying for my college education and the other good things I enjoyed. Some pieces of the puzzle began to fall into place. I was acquiring a different world view, just finishing college at the time. 1960.

I'm sure a great deal to do with it was my experience at age eight, nine, ten of being the only kid in town who was driven to school in a limousine. I hated it. I finally made a deal with the driver of the limousine to meet me two blocks away from school when it let out so I wouldn't feel conspicuous. You always feel that anything that makes you stick out is horrible. That gave me a great aversion to all the trappings that went with wealth of any kind. I've never had any inclination toward yachts or limousines ever since.

My mother was Jewish, my father was WASP. It was my grandfather who had come over in the 1880s. I never heard much about the United States from them. We were a Europe-oriented family. I saw so much of the world by the time I was twenty that I've had little inclination to travel since, except in this country.

My father's country was his class, the New England well-to-do WASP's he grew up among. He had many relatives in England and Ireland, whom we'd visit on trips. Neither of my parents has much feeling for America per se. I grew up feeling not very American.

For the first eight years of my life, I never say anything beyond

Beacon Hill. That was the America I knew. When I visit Boston and walk around that neighborhood, I still feel the center of the world is right on this spot.

I went to Groton, a prep school in Massachusetts. The four years at Groton were crucial in my life. In a big city, you have schools full of working-class kids and middle-class teachers, who often feel alienated from the students. In boarding schools, it's the reverse. The students were all upper-class and the teachers were all middle-class, mostly people who had worked their way through college. It was a good deal to get to teach in a school like this. They worked hard for it.

They were good people. Many of them had an ill-disguised horror at the class of kids they were teaching. They would talk to guys like me about their reactions to the waste they saw. I remember one teacher telling me his horror at seeing one of the boys in the dormitory throwing a pair of pants in the garbage. They were new, had just come out of a box. The kid said: "I just wanted the coat from this suit." That clicked something in me. It let me know it's all right to feel what I'd been feeling about not liking waste, living more lavish than you really need to. It was the first time I really began to think about class.

Was it the Duke of Wellington who said Waterloo was won on the playing fields of Eton? In a lot of ways, I think these elite schools function as the first training ground for the ruling class. The board of trustees met in a bank. They never even bothered to come to the school, except once a year. It was all boys, of course, who graduated to become stockbrokers, bankers, that kind of thing.

My father's model was always the Rockefeller family. The first generation makes the wealth. The second consolidates it. The third goes into what I call paracapitalist activities: state government, foundation presidents. They don't need to concern themselves with the messy details of keeping all this money. They can spread out. My father has aspirations for me to become that third generation. He'd have liked it if I'd become a lawyer, become an apprentice to some rising young WASP politician, like Mayor Lindsay in the sixties. And then went into politics as assistant secretary of state or something like that.

The American Dream always has a greater force when you don't already have it. People who grew up without it are told if you can only work long enough and hard enough, you can get that pot of gold at the end of the rainbow. When you already have the pot of gold, the dream loses its force. You can't aspire after anything material if, in fact, you're trying to get rid of the material things, as I was with the limousine and other appurtenances. You need some alternative way of giving meaning to your life. This applies particularly at a time when all institutions were being questioned, as they were in the sixties.

When my father resigned himself to my being a writer, it was: Why don't you write for *The New York Times?* His was the dream patrician reformers have always dreamed. It was the strong tradition of this country around the turn of the century: the Teddy Roosevelt types, good government, clean it up, make the existing structure work the way it's supposed to work. Nice people. But that's not what inspired me. For me, it was the dream of changing the society.

I envy people whose political dream was passed on to them by their parents. A couple of my friends are referred to as "Red-diaper babies." The socialist vision that I feel, I've had to put together in bits and pieces by myself. It's not something I've known since early childhood. Ironically, it may be stronger when you put it together yourself. I know a lot of Red-diaper babies who've gone off and become corporate executives. (Laughs.) But still, I find myself envying those who grew up with a political dream, almost like a religion. If I could go back in time and be born again at any particular moment in American history, I would plant myself in the thirties.

RAFAEL ROSA

◆————————————————————————————◆

He's a bellhop at a small theatrical hotel in Manhattan. He is forever smiling, eager to please, and quick to talk. He is the second youngest of ten brothers. He is nineteen.

"My parents were born in Puerto Rico. They been here a good seventeen years. My father works right here in the hotel, a houseman. My parents at home speak Spanish. I was born here in New York City, so when I went to school, my Spanish started turnin' poor. I figured it this way: I might as well hang on to both languages. Now when a Spanish-speaking person comes up to me, I like stutter. I made it to second year at high school."

My American Dream is to be famous. Like a big boss at a big firm, sit back, relax, and just collect. Oh, I treat my employees nice, pay 'em real good, don't overwork 'em too much, not like most bosses, they fire you right away.

I really would like to have a chauffeur-driven limousine, have a bar one side, color TV on the other. The chicks, the girls, oh yeah. Instead of coming in at eight in the morning and leavin' at eight in the afternoon. Maybe I'll invent something one of these days and wind up a millionaire. As for now, I'd really like to be chief pilot at the air force.

As I ride my bike here in New York, I see all these elegant-looking people, fancy-dressed, riding around in a limousine, just looking all normal. I figured if they can do, why can't I? Why can't I just go out there and get myself driven around for a while? I haven't hit it big yet, but I'm still working on it.

As I started growing older, I figured it's a jungle out there, you better grab a vine. So I grabbed a vine, and here I landed. (Laughs.) It's really hard out there in the city; you can't get a job any more. I would just like to be on TV, a newsman or something.

My friends are always talkin' about havin' a nice sheen. That's a nice car or van, something set up real nice on the inside with foldaway beds and wall-to-wall carpeting and paneling, fat tires, mufflers sticking out on the side, and speeding. Usually, they get together on this highway and they would race each other at the flat. It's really incredible. I don't see how these guys can do that. Drag racing.

I wanted to be a taxi driver. I figured it would be an exciting job, just riding around all day. Plus I had that driving fever. Most of the time, I dream I can fly, be all the way up there on the top. But I don't see how, unless I invent something, eh? Anti-gravity belt or something like that. It would cost a lot of loot just to make one of those. I'm a bicycle mechanic now. I ride 'em on one wheel also, but I don't think that's gonna get me far. I'd really like to be a motorcycle driver and explore the world.

Most of the time, I'm usually out in the streets, lookin' around. Scope on the nice women who pass by. I like their wardrobes and the way they walk, the way they talk. I should really be a gift to all women. I don't know how I'm gonna do it, but it's gotta be done somehow. (Laughs.)

My brother works in the post office, makin' some all-right money. My other brother works in a factory, getting some good money as long as he can put in overtime. We're all in the same business, tryin' to move up, tryin' to see if we can get this "flat fixed" place or a grocery store. With the right location, we'll move up.

I would really like to invest in something *real big*, like in baby food. You can never run out of baby food. And cars. We'll never run out of cars as long as we don't run out of people. I could invest in tires. Where there's tires, there's automobiles. I guess I'm gonna have to hit it big.

People today are more like keepin' it to themselves. They don't let their emotions show. They're afraid to lose respect, cool. I'm open most of the time, I kinda like to turn off and on. I'm the kind of guy that gets along with everybody. I'm Puerto Rican and I got the complexion of a Negro, so I can fall to either side. I've been chased by whites a couple of times, but nothing special happens.

What's goin' on these days with all the violence, a person's gotta think twice of walking down the street. One time I got mugged in the South Bronx. Three guys jumped me as I was walking down this dark street. One guy stops me for a cigarette, and as I go to give him one, two guys grab me from behind. They just started beatin' on me and took all my money and left me on the floor and fled. I recovered, and now I think twice about it. Before I was mugged, I walked down any street. I'd rather walk around a dark street than go through it, no matter how much time it's gonna take me to get there. If people call ya, I just keep on walking if I don't know the person. I look back and just keep walking.

I suggest: Don't walk alone at night. Walk with a stick to protect yourself. Don't get too high because it slows down your reflexes. You gotta keep your head clear. They say: Never look back. In real life, you gotta look back.

ARRIVING: NOW

ARNOLD SCHWARZENEGGER

Call me Arnold.

I was born in a little Austrian town, outside Graz. It was a 300-year-old house.

When I was ten years old, I had the dream of being the best in the world in something. When I was fifteen, I had a dream that I wanted to be the best body builder in the world and the most muscular man.

It was not only a dream I dreamed at night. It was also a daydream. It was so much in my mind that I felt it had to become a reality. It took me five years of hard work. Five years later, I turned this dream into reality and became Mr. Universe, the best-built man in the world.

"Winning" is a very important word. There is one that achieves what he wanted to achieve and there are hundreds of thousands that failed. It singles you out: the winner.

I came out second three times, but that is not what I call losing. The bottom line for me was: Arnold has to be the winner. I have to win more often the Mr. Universe title than anybody else. I won it five times consecutively. I hold the record as Mr. Olympia, the top professional body-building championship. I won it six times. That's why I retired. There was nobody even close to me. Everybody gave up competing against me. That's what I call a winner.

When I was a small boy, my dream was not to be big physically, but big in a way that everybody listens to me when I talk, that I'm a very important person, that people recognize me and see me as something special. I had a big need for being singled out.

Also my dream was to end up in America. When I was ten years old, I dreamed of being an American. At the time I didn't know much about America, just that it was a wonderful country. I felt it was where I belonged. I didn't like being in a little country like Austria. I did everything possible to get out. I did so in 1968, when I was twenty-one years old.

If I would believe in life after death, I would say my before-life I was living in America. That's why I feel so good here. It is the country where you can turn your dream into reality. Other countries don't have those things. When I came over here to America, I felt I was in heaven. In America, we don't have an obstacle. Nobody's holding you back.

Number One in America pretty much takes care of the rest of the world. You kind of run through the rest of the world like nothing. I'm trying to make people in America aware that they should appreciate what they have here. You have the best tax advantages here and the best prices here and the best products here.

One of the things I always had was a business mind. When I was in high school, a majority of my classes were business classes. Economics and accounting and mathematics. When I came over here to this country, I really didn't speak English almost at all. I learned English and then started taking business courses, because that's what America is best known for: business. Turning one dollar into a million dollars in a short period of time. Also when you make money, how do you keep it?

That's one of the most important things when you have money in your hand, how can you keep it? Or make more out of it? Real estate is one of the best ways of doing that. I own apartment buildings, office buildings, and raw land. That's my love, real estate.

I have emotions. But what you do, you keep them cold or you store them away for a time. You must control your emotions, you must have command over yourself. Three, four months before a competition, I could not be interfered by other people's problems. This is sometimes called selfish. It's the only way you can be if you want to achieve something. Any emotional things inside me, I try to keep cold so it doesn't interfere with my training.

Many times things really touched me. I felt them and I felt sensitive about them. But I had to talk myself out of it. I had to suppress those feelings in order to go on. Sport is one of those activities where you really have to concentrate. You must pay attention a hundred percent to the particular thing you're doing. There must be nothing else on your mind. Emotions must not interfere. Otherwise, you're thinking about your girlfriend. You're in love, your positive energies get channeled into another direction rather than going into your weight room or making money.

You have to choose at a very early date what you want: a normal life or to achieve things you want to achieve. I never wanted to win a popularity contest in doing things the way people want me to do it. I went the road I thought was best for me. A few people thought I was cold, selfish. Later they found out that's not the case. After I achieve my goal, I can be Mr. Nice Guy. You know what I mean?

California is to me a dreamland. It is the absolute combination of everything I was always looking for. It has all the money in the world there, show business there, wonderful weather there, beautiful country, ocean is there. Snow skiing in the winter, you can go in the desert the same day. You have beautiful-looking people there. They all have a tan.

I believe very strongly in the philosophy of staying hungry. If you have a dream and it becomes a reality, don't stay satisfied with it too long. Make up a new dream and hunt after that one and turn it into reality. When you have that dream achieved, make up a new dream.

I am a strong believer in Western philosophy, the philosophy of success, of progress, of getting rich. The Eastern philosophy is passive, which I believe in maybe three percent of the times, and the ninety-seven percent is Western, conquering and going on. It's a beautiful philosophy, and America should keep it up.

KARLIS ENINS

◈—————————————————————————————— ————————◈

He is the head maintenance man of an office building in Chicago's Loop. He is Latvian and came to the United States in 1956. "After World War Two, the Russians came back in that part of Latvia. I left in January of '45."

My family always was farmers for years, so my mother and father didn't leave the country. That's how farmers are. They're old people. We know the Russians come back, so people went over, like to Sweden. But mostly to Germany, because the Germans didn't let you go to Sweden. You must get some fisher boats to go over. The front came closer, we just moved back, until the war was over. We went into the camp for foreign nationals.

Displaced persons camp?

Yeah, DP's, not a nice name. I was in a camp in Holstein in Germany. Maybe about twenty thousand people was there. I married there. I stayed in Germany till both my kids are born. In 1950 we came over here.

America was something like happy land someplace, far behind the mountains, overseas. We have few Latvians in America and they're talking. They always are so happy people. What we always get was: America was the best. Never said America is something bad. They are talking, of course, of gangsters and stealing. But America was something where everybody would like to be.

My wife, son, and daughter, we landed in New York. My wife said: "See, that's our dreamland." (Laughs.) And it was. You come over and you feel like you can smell the country coming. It's hard to say in words, but it's really beautiful to be here.

We have friends in Chicago. We stayed at their house for a couple of weeks. I got the first paycheck, and I got the apartment. We on our own. I was never unemployed, for not even an hour.

In twenty-one years, the thoughts have not changed. I'm very happy in America. Once in a while I get sad, like we have Vietnam. I always support the government. If the government decided we must stand for the principles and we send armies in, then that's it. Because we elected the government. You must obey your elected government. Otherwise, how could it be other ways? I really think our government do a good job. Something may be wrong, but nobody's perfect.

Lots of Americans, like some film stars, they're nice people but I know they are leftists. We don't like that. Some people are always against. They want something different. How can you give up freedom for something else? But there are people like that. I don't think we have these problems between Latvians.

I see the press sometimes harming the government, like secrets going out. Ellsberg's case was an example of that. The press thinks he's right. I think he's wrong myself. The guy selling some secrets and get money for that. I mean, how could a guy be right about that? Some guys fighting in Vietnam and dying at that time. Maybe I'm wrong, but it's my opinion.

In America we have problem now. The cities is taking all over for blacks. No question about that. Some people said if they take over the big cities, they will rule the country. I don't know, really. I don't like the way it goes. The white people are running out to the suburbs. Even they're buying homes they can't afford, and very deep in the debts.

I live in Chicago. I'm very happy. That's old neighborhood. All kind of nationalities there. Everybody meets on business. It's honest people. You leave in the backyard, nothing is stolen.

I have a two-flat. Upstairs are three Latvian people living there, three bachelors. It's friends of mine. I have a son. He live in Bensonville.* He's twenty-four. He went to college two years, married, and never went back to college. He works as a truck driver and doing pretty good. His wife is secretary in Loop. My daughter, she's married, too. She's a nurse. My son-in-law, he's auto mechanic. So they're doing pretty good. My wife works as a bookkeeper.

My dream would be to get around, see the country, maybe in a couple years. I said to my wife: "We're not planing, we're driving." Yellowstone Park and where the redwoods are, the big ones. Los Angeles. Smoky Mountains in Kentucky. There's really so much to see. New Mexico, Death Valley. See America first. I never seen that. That's my dream.

---

* A blue-collar suburb of Chicago

MIGUEL CORTEZ

◇————————————————————————————◇

He appears considerably younger than his age, forty-two; his complexion, light brown.

I was born in the first capital of Cuba, Baracoa. A small city, very nice, with a lot of fun. Everybody a relative, most of them. My mother is from Santiago de Cuba, and she is a doctor. My father was commercial. I am a student in Santiago: pedagogy, education.

All my life I am thinking to come to this country. For what I read in the magazines, and the movies. Elizabeth Taylor, Vivien Leigh, Olivia de Haviland, Clark Gable, yeah. I would have a beautiful castle in the United States. I will have a thousand servant. I will have five Rolls-Royces in my door. These kind of movies: beautiful house, beautiful dresses, money, car. Especial car. We thinking everybody has this kind of life. Had money, very friendly people, beautiful people. I have this kind of dream.

You read the American magazines, *Life, People*, you think this is the best country in the world. This is the more great. When we grow up, I never change my mind. Also, I have a cousin who come every year to the United States, to Miami. But my mother would never let me come. She say: "No, you need to know nothing from there. You stay here." She tell me that, for the racial problems.

In my family, I never have these kind of problems. We come in with a nice name. My grandfather was one of the most rich people in Baracoa, owner of bank, theater house, and other businesses. We are no really black. We had a white family, we have a black, we have a mix. Mulatto. No, I didn't find this problem. Also, causing my father was a politic. His cousin was educational minister before Castro.

I continue to work, a teacher in Santiago. When Castro coming, they sent me to small town to teach. I working there for one year. After this year, they make a transfer to me again to the north in Oriente. I becoming inspector of a school. I working hard at this time, because this year, '61, coming the learning campaign. Everybody start to read and write.

Castro put all the teachers in Cuba, everybody, to work on this campaign. Professional people, middle-class people, everybody to work to help the people who don't read or write. At this time, I was assistant for education in Oriente. Technic education. This means to make plans how to send how many people on these farms. It was a better job. But I no like the Communist system. My father never liked Castro. He killed my cousin. He say he was a member of the CIA in Cuba, something like that.

In '67, Castro say the people who want to leave Cuba, go ahead. I sign the paper. We waiting for a year, a year and a half, two years. I say: "Uh-uh, no more." I tried to come from Guantánamo, American base. I stay in a good friend of mine, a doctor. We left Guantánamo, we walked for boat. In the way, the policeman, the guard, they caught.

I was in jail for two years. For me, no was treated bad because I was teachin' in there. After two years, I come to the United States. '71.

Miami, Florida, oh, this was very nice. The first time I see the American flag, I see many cars in the parking lots and airplanes. This is my dream. I was very, very happy, a lot. Many friend come to see me in Casa Libertad, Liberty House, where all the Cubans stay until they find a place. After that, I go to New Jersey because I have a lot of friends there. At this time is when I see the reality of the United States.

I start to work in the Newark Airport. I start to clean floor, washing dishes. The third day I was a little upset. I say: "Okay, maybe very soon I change the job." Also, I no speak English. I don't change my mind about United States, but something is wrong with me.

This is no my dream. I not come to this country to clean floors. Not because I no like to do that, but in Cuba I don't need to do that. I thinking if this a big mistake for my part to come to the United States. I start to hate my job. For what reason I come, when I have a good job in Cuba? Also, I didn't have money. Five people live in this apartment and only one bedroom. (Sighs deeply.) I became very upset. But I need to see the reality of the United States, to look for a better job, to do something for myself.

I have telephone contact with a friend who live in Rockford, Illinois. One day he tell me: "Come to Rockford and you working here in the Chrysler Corporation." I start to work, I have a better job, more money. It's in the assembly line. Everything was a little change. I found apartment. I have more American friends. I say: "Well, I'm on my way, according to my dream." I was working two and a half years in Chrysler, but I continue to think in teaching. I move to Chicago because Chrysler give many layoff. In Chicago, I take many tests for the state job, and I qualify.

America is like Cuba before Castro. The rich people, the middle class, and the really low, with nothing. Poor people, welfare. It is a rich and powerful country. Sometime we have a stupid government, and the rich people or high-class people to govern the system.

If the policeman stop you on the street and he want to give ticket and you give him five or ten dollar, the ticket, they're out. Like Cuba before Castro.

Could you bribe a cop in Castro's Cuba?

No, because everybody a cop. (Laughs.)

When I was in Cuba, the American was the owner of the big sugar factory. We see the American, the tall men, very business, something like God. Before Castro, the businessman, they think they are superior person in the other country: I am American. I am Mr. Smith. People are supposed to (deferential tone): Oh, Mr. Smith. Because he's superior and he's American. In my family farm, we're having a sugar-cane factory. I see many Americans who are working with the administration. The farm worker: Oh, Mr. Smith—with head bow. But after, no.

Everything was changed. In Cuba, with Castro coming, the poor people put in positions. It was a stupid thing because many of them don't know what they doing. The prostitute was working in the bank, no longer a prostitute. The servant was working in different offices. Cows in the government.

When Castro take over the power, after a year, the rich people found something wrong with the country. They say uh-uh, they start to send money to the United States, and then after that they are coming, the high-class people coming. After that the middle-class professional family. They bring to the United States servants, but servants leave. If you work in factory in United States, you will make about three dollars for an hour. They go to factory. (Laughs.) The servants, they get in Cuba for twenty-five pesos a month.

I have professional people as friend here who no love the country. The people who are very, very happy and love more deeply this country are the people who come from the especialist low class, who was never working in his own country.

I having a very nice apartment, beautiful furniture, nice furnished. I stay home, listen to classic music, go to eat out dinner with a friend, travel. I love my job.

I have a problem with my idioms, but I love very, very deep the United States like I was lovin' Cuba before. I no think my life will change. I want to see my family and they want to see me. My mother now say: "You stay here." She's happy I stay here. I have not what I'm thinking the first time here, but now I am happy to be here. I want to remain here. I want to die here.

ANASTASIAS (ANDY) KOSTELIS

◇————————————————————————————————————◇

I always loves to be something important. I love to come to the States, just to be free, to be me. I'll tell you this: in my country, when I was fourteen years old, we had dictatorship, the junta, and that bothered me a lot They were saying we were free, but we weren't free. Even they were going through our pockets, through our books, through everything.

His cab picks me up in downtown Boston. He talks easily as we cut through heavy traffic. On the expressway, heading toward Lawrence, he flirts, expertly, with a pretty blond girl driving another car. As she turns off at the next exit, he smiles boyishly into the rear-view mirror. "I'm not gonna drive for couple of years, maybe for couple months. Bein' alone in the States, I live by myself."

I was born in Piraeus, port of Athens. My father is a priest. We have five brothers and sisters. My older brother became priest two years ago. My second brother is a lawyer. My older sister is accountant. The little one, my lovely, is model designer.

In Greece, I get into merchant marine academy, from which I graduate. I had highest mark. I work on ship as a radio operator. I change four different ships. I went to North Pole, like three cruises, and one cruise down to northwest Africa. I been up to the equator. Being radio operator was making great money, especially for my age. I was making twelve hundred dollars a month and I was only twenty years old. Even Onassis' son wouldn't make so much money. You know Onassis? (Laughs.)

I had abilities, so they offered me more money. In Greece, it's hard to find radio operator. Greek is one of the biggest merchant fleets in the world.

They send me for one trip on the ship *Stella K.* I picked it up from Kiel, Germany, to get some fish in Gloucester and back to Poland. I had to be radio operator and captain's second mate. We had real bad weather, it was February '76. I told the captain there were storms, icebergs were coming down south. We fell in a cyclone. Oh, God, I will never forget these times in my life. The wind was going a hundred fifty miles an hour. My radio was broken, I couldn't send the SOS. The emergency transmitter, big surprise, that didn't work, too. Everybody was looking at me like I was God. I was praying to God and St. Nicholas—St. Nicholas is the sailor's protector—I saying: "God, please, even if you don't like me, help the others. I'm just a unit here, please." After nine days in the storm, I throw all my clothes in the ocean. I thought we're gonna be at the bottom of the sea. Same day we wake up and the sea was so calm like oil, like a piece of glass. We were real happy. Took us nineteen days.

In the storm, I was taking drugs, like codeine, to keep my mind flying, to stay awake and live, not soft.

I was at Gloucester with two hundred dollars in my pocket and my ID and my immigration pass. I was so sick. They grabbed me and gave me deportation order. It's a long story.

Since I was a kid I tried to become an eagle. I loved to be high. I reached the height at the top of the mountain. Two and a half years ago, I fell in the storm and my wings were frozen. I couldn't fly. I was crying. I was praying night and day till the sun would come up. I was trying to find many ways to melt the snow from my wings so I could fly again. Finally, thank God, after so long a time and so many tries and so much money spent, my sun came up and the snow started melting. My wings start drying, maybe to fly again.

The United States is the only one country in the world where you can do anything you want as long as you don't bother anybody. You wanna be rich? You can be rich. You wanna work? You can work. You wanna study? You can study. You can do anything. You have chances.

Now the first thing I'll do, I'll try to become American citizen, even by going to the army reserves. I wanna have full rights in this country, hopefully. I'll die here. Before I reach that point, I wanna offer whatever I can. I have lots of ideas, but my mind is still flipping. It's a few days ago, I took out my alien's registration card. A month ago, I was still under deportation order. Now I'm a permanent resident of the United States. This life is too short, and America gives you a chance to do it.

Now I'm alone, right? Where can I go to meet people? Tell me. Nowhere. Only the disco. You go in a bar to get drunk. Everybody who was in bars, they're not that high-standing people, they're lower.

I used to hang around with some guys from Greece, right? I met them in a disco club. They would see the Greeks had a special spot. We could see everything. (Laughs,) No girls could go by without to know she's no gonna be picked up. (Laughs.) She knows that if she goes by, ninety percent she's gonna be picked up. (Laughs.) We're about ten guys. Outside, they had Eldorados, with Mark IV's, Mark V's, and everything. They had money. They had mostly restaurants, from their fathers. The American girls is so easy to pick up.

With American dances, I'm very good for a Greek. In Greece, we just tease the girls in the streets. Hey, how you doin', baby? And this and that. These guys, they didn't know how to begin a conversation, right? I start talkin'. I was tryin' to pick up much more girls as I could, just to have some extra for them.

We would change discotheques. We thought we would find better company, start meetin' more important people. Even if you're a doctor or a young lawyer, you see some guys actin' like they're everything, the head of the thing, they start talkin' with us.

We saw that movie again and again and again. *Saturday Night Fever.* Yeah, by John Travolta. I saw that movie about four times. A lotta people, they say this movie is exactly like you guys. But we didn't have shit boxes like they had in the movie. My friends, I could count five Eldorados, one Fleetwood, two Mark IV's, the cheapest car was about ten thousand dollars.

When I got back to the disco one night, the girl I was dancin' with was beautiful. She was an excellent dancer, too. So my friend says: "Come on, John Travolta, do it." To the girl I say: "Come on, baby, shake it but don't break it." I'll tell you this: it's the first time in my life I saw couples goin' away from the platform and left three couples. This is the first time in my life I saw people just standin' on the sides just to see how we're dancin'. I was just goin' out of my mind. I didn't know what I was doing. It was so great that night. They took me out. They spent I don't know how much money.

I was so happy that night, my head was stickin' up. After being frozen, being in a refrigerator for so long about my immigration case, I couldn't feel free. But that time, I felt momentarily happy. I felt like an eagle.

I never fought for second place, first place only. I felt that way since I was young. Some pictures I remember when I was fourteen. We were a whole group from Sunday school. I was always in the middle or at the top, center or front. How can I be happy if I didn't reach my destination?

My mind is a little tired. I work since I was about eleven years. I have experience of so many bad things, that's unusual for my age. I lost so many years, three years. That's why I have to start again. About twenty years old, I was makin' great money. My father was a priest for twenty-five years, and I was makin' more money than him. You know how I felt that time? I was in heaven. I felt like I was born rich. You know how a young guy feels, twenty years old, to have one thousand dollars in his pockets? The storm happened, yet here I am. I completed the twenty-fourth year of my life August, and I have to start again. I'm not eleven any more.

GOING AND COMING

JENNY BIRD

We decided to leave the country. The oldest boy, one of his teachers was talking in class that one of her sons had migrated to Australia and the Australian government paid money for his passage. We had been considering foreign countries, and they had to be English-speaking. This just sounded terrrific. I called the consulate and off we went. We just sold everything and went. This was 1970.

Miles and miles past other neon-lighted tributaries of Los Angeles is Silmar. We are in a complex of stucco palaces, ersatz Spanish. It is home to the lower middle class of this region.

She is forty-three. Her daughter, Laura, who later joins in the conversation, is twenty-one.

"*It's a lot of Mexican and black people live here. They're all working-class, closer to the poor side than the rich side. They don't bother me at all. My youngest daughter thinks it's a horrible place, so she won't live here. She's fifteen, she hates blacks. She ran away and is living with someone else.*

"*I have a boy that's eighteen. He lives in his own place with three other guys. They each have a big dog and a boa constrictor in the house, dirt bikes and jeeps. He works in a machine shop and just loves it. The oldest, he'll be twenty-three. He's been in the navy four years, out in the Pacific somewhere. He's beginning a computer repair business when he gets out of the navy."*

I just always wanted to be a wife and mother until I got to be one. (Laughs.) I found out it wasn't so great. My husband and I fought all the time, and we never had enough money. I decided I wanted to go to work. Staying home with four kids wasn't quite so wonderful as it was cracked up to be. I was a wife and a mother, but I wasn't any me. I was just looking for myself. I haven't found it yet. (Laughs.)

"I came from outside Detroit. My friends all seemed to have better clothes, more spending money. There were a lot who had less than I did, but I was only looking at the ones who had more. My father didn't hardly talk to us at all. He just went to work and came home and laid down on the couch and went to sleep and ate dinner and went out. I didn't know my father at all.

"My husband quit college when he got married. It didn't matter, he was flunking everything anyway. (Laughs.) He got a job in Ford's on the assembly line. He lasted half a day and quit. Finally, he got into quality control work. That's what he's in now."

We never had enough money. My husband hated his job, his life. He liked to blame it on the blacks and on his rotten boss and on the rotten police. It's everybody but himself. He started drinking. Things got worse and worse, and we fought more and more. My oldest boy was always in trouble with the police and school and family. We were just all of us generally unhappy.

I worked in the supermarket. I liked it real well. There's a violent atmosphere in Detroit. We had two armed guards in the grocery store all the time. Personally, I never had any problems, but you felt it all around you. If we had been a peaceful people, we would have felt other peaceful people, but because we were all unhappy, we only felt the unhappiness of other people. You're just seeing a reflection of yourself. So everything that we saw looked bad. We were fighting all the time. We just thought the whole country was like that. We never had any trouble with black people or white people. We only had trouble with ourselves.

To us, everything around was violence, was trouble. We wanted to start over, completely fresh, a different place, different people, different everything.

We both quit our jobs. We had a rummage sale and sold off most of our stuff and gave the rest to the Salvation Army. We booked passage to Australia on the *Oriana*. Two days before we were supposed to leave, we got a letter that there'd been a fire on the ship and it was delayed. By this time, our furniture was gone, our lease was up, and we had nowhere to go. We fixed up our car, we packed the tent and everything on top, and drove across the country to San Francisco. It was a fantastic trip, two weeks. When we wanted to stop, we stopped. We stayed four days in one place. No fights. Everyone was friendly and great. We were different people, traveling. First time we'd ever seen America.

We finally got on the ship. It took two weeks and two days. Somebody from the consulate met us there, and we were gonna go to Melbourne. There was a Ford plant, my husband was gonna get a job there. They took us out to a migrant hostel. That was real nice—

LAURA: (interjects) But the people weren't.

JENNY: They never had any Americans in the hostel before. Blacks aren't allowed there and Orientals. They just don't want 'em. There were a lot of southern Europeans, a lot of Mediterraneans that didn't speak English. They were very hostile to our children. They'd spit on 'em and call 'em names. Dirty, rich Americans. (Laughs.)

LAURA: There was a big mall, and we'd go over there shopping. Nobody else could afford to do that.

JENNY: They were poorer than we were.

LAURA: They made us look rich.

JENNY: He tried to get a job at Ford's and couldn't. He got on a train and went to Sydney. A couple of days later, he called and said he had a job. It was still cold. We were not used to not having central heating. A little kerosene heater.

I got a job in the supermarket. It was like a little corner grocery store. In Detroit, I would work on Sunday and earn fifty dollars for seven hours' work. Down there, I worked five and a half days for fifty-one dollars for the *week*. Down there, the grocery stores, they're dark and they're narrow and there's no heat and there's no air conditioning and there's no prices written on anything. You have to memorize everything. In the morning, they open the sliding doors, and there you are with all the wind blowing in and the cold and the damp and the rain. But they're getting American supermarkets down there.

After a couple of years, I realized things were not gonna get any better. There's no way we could earn enough money to come anywhere near the standard of living that we had left. Our clothes were just absolutely shabby. Our furniture, we sat on orange crates. (Laughs.)

LAURA: I just started saying I want to go back. My friends were on American wages because they were missionaries with the church. They'd visit America, they'd come back and tell me all about how it was so wonderful. I kept saying I want to go home.

You agree to stay there two years or else pay the money back. Two years were up, we started saving money to send Daddy back. We decided that this was for the birds. Even though they speak English, they don't speak the language.

JENNY: It's a wonderful course in American appreciation. You just don't realize what a great place this is, how much we take for granted here.

LAURA: You take into account everyone speaking the same dialect or knowing the brands in the supermarket. You don't appreciate your heater or your telephone or your television or your car. In Australia, at least half our friends didn't have a car. Of course, rapid transit is wonderful there. Where a train doesn't go, the bus does. I could go anywhere in Sydney and all the surrounding suburbs and back for fifteen cents in one day. But I'd rather be here with a central heater and just little things like a dryer. (Laughs.)

I think they're as material as we are. They all want to get a car and color TV. They all asked us about Disneyland.

JENNY: My husband eventually got a job in Los Angeles. He worked seven days a week, twelve, fourteen hours a day, drove fifty miles each way every day, earning money to send for us. The day before we left, his father died and left him an inheritance of twenty-five thousand dollars. We came back and bought a house.

The funny thing is, toward the end, I didn't even want to come back. I wanted to stay there. You see, the five months he was gone made me realize that I didn't want to be married any more. We weren't violent any more, but I wanted out. I says: "I want a divorce. I just can't hack this any more."

I just don't ever want to be married again. I love California as a single woman. You can earn enough to support yourself and not have to put up with some rotten guy just because you don't have enough money.

LAURA: I'm totally different from Mom. I want to get married. I want to have a family. That's very important to me. I became a Christian in Australia. That's where I found out about God. I'm a fundamentalist.

JENNY: I'm metaphysical. The book that turned me on to it was Edgar Cayce. I bought this little paperback at a garage sale: *Mystery Man, Man of Miracles*. I got so excited, I couldn't put the book down. I went to the library and got everything I could about metaphysics. I went to night school and took a speed-reading course. (Laughs.) That's when my life started changing.

LAURA: Being a fundamentalist, I don't worry about dying. Anyway, my brother's in the navy, and he said if L.A. got hit with a nuclear bomb, we wouldn't all be dead. There'd still be a lot of people around. We've been hit with so much science fiction and brainwashed into thinking that everybody's gonna die if the bomb falls. It's just not true. Anyway, if I die, I'll go to heaven, and it's fine with me.

Heaven's gonna be great. Peaceful, and there's not gonna be any loud noise. I'm just not into loud noise at all. I may be twenty-one years old and living in southern California, but loud parties—yech! There's not gonna be cigarette smoking and there's not gonna be people getting drunk. In your ear, turkey. I lived with that for sixteen years and that was plenty.

JENNY: My feeling isn't like here at all. I feel like we're in school here and you die and go on to the next school. You keep coming back over and over. Of course, I believe in reincarnation. I want to come back as a woman. Last time I was a man. My mother was an alcoholic and she was drunk the whole time she was carrying me, so I was drunk when I was born. I started drinking when I was eight years old and died from drinking when I was nineteen.

In most of the lives I've regressed to, I was a woman and had a husband similar to what I had this time. I only went into six or seven of these lives. I'd like to come back as an independent woman who has more ambition than I have. I've been looking for years for something and haven't found it. It's something inside, something spiritual that I need. If I find it anywhere, it'll be in America.

LAURA: Something she said to all us kids before we came back to America again: "It's not like going back. It won't be the same and it's nothing like it was in Detroit. This is home in America, but we're not back home again."

PEGGY TERRY

◆————————————————————————————————◆

She was born in western Kentucky, lived in Oklahoma, chopped cot-
ton in Texas, picked fruit in the Rio Grande Valley, cut wheat in
Kansas, worked in a defense plant in North Carolina, was a checker in
an Alabama supermart, a waitress in Chicago, and became a spokes-
woman for poor southern whites in the city's Uptown.
  She lives with her daughter, son-in-law, and grandchild on Chi-
cago's North Side. She visits her family in Paducah as often as she
can.

I don't remember dreams when I was a child. Our dream was to get
through the week until payday. That the food would last from one
week to the next. We were sharecroppers. We picked cotton for a
living. No one gave us any reason to dream. The grownups had no
dreams, so they couldn't pass anything on to their children that they
didn't have themselves.

My daughter wants to start saving to buy a house, a two-flat. Things
like that didn't happen in my childhood. We just got through the
week, and that was that.

My grandmother and grandfather were third-generation Irish.
They seemed awfully old, and all they thought about was picking
cotton from the time the sun came up in the morning until way late at
night, sometime after dark.

My father did a little bit of everything. Oil-field worker in Oklahoma, coal miner in Kentucky. He could handle anything that had to
do with dynamite or nitroglycerine. My dad was the wildest one in
the family. He didn't believe all the malarkey that was pounded into
him. He was the only one in the family that had any life, any get-up-
and-go.

They weren't hell-raising Irish. If any race was meant to be dreamers, I think it's the Irish. What makes me sad is that none of the Irish I
know had any dreams. There wasn't anybody to say: You can widen
your horizons by dreaming. I'm sure the Bible kept them down.
That's the only thing I ever saw them read.

My grandmother was a real wonderful person, so full of joy, but
she carried this terrible burden with her. They call this being under
conviction. You're under conviction when you feel you have done

terrible sins. She couldn't have sinned that bad—she was too poor. (Laughs.)

The church made them feel guilty. They're so burdened down, and it tells them they're nobody. Don't look for anything here on earth. The day you'll die, you're gonna get all these things you didn't get while you were living. It took me thirty years to fight my way out of that. I thought I was nothing.

Everyone we knew was hungry, but there wasn't any understanding of why it was. That's just the way it was. I didn't understand it myself until I started learning.

I went through sixth grade. I always liked to sing, but the only music we were taught were those pale, ghostly songs that had absolutely nothing to do with us rip-roarin' hillbillies who liked bluegrass, songs with life to 'em.

Anytime there's life in somebody, the church wants to pound it out by telling them they're worms, they're nothing. There was this beautiful girl in the church where we went. When she'd come to church, nobody'd talk to her because she was a dancer on the stage. She had been the lead singer in our choir. I was fascinated by her and always sat by her side. She was so beautiful and she liked kids and she had life like my dad. As I look back, everybody who had the least spark of life, who dared dream, was ostracized. It's a killer of dreams.

One of the things that keeps my class of people from having any vision is race hatred. I can remember when we were picking cotton, we could look over the field and see black people over there picking cotton. Those were niggers. They had nothing to do with me. Which is exactly what the owners of the plantations wanted. They really did a good job on us. You're so busy hating somebody else, you're not gonna realize how beautiful you are and how much you destroy all that's good in the world.

I'm not sure anybody can say this particular thing happened to me and suddenly I was different. When I saw Reverend King in Montgomery during the bus boycott, I was amazed. I never saw anybody, white or black, dressed as he was dressed. All white clothes. He came out of jail and about five or six white men jumped him. Suddenly something says to me: "Two on one is nigger fun." That's what they always said when they saw two white kids beatin' up on a black kid. When I saw 'em beatin' up on Reverend King, something clicked.

I remember one thing in Paducah. I was walking down the street at night, coming home from work. It was dark. It was in the black section. A carload of white boys went down the street real fast. They yelled: "Hey, nigger, how about a quarter piece?" At first, I felt dirty and angry that they thought I was a nigger. Then I thought: What must it be like for her?

I was a great big girl and I was calling myself an Anglo-Saxon. My mother said; "You're not an Anglo-Saxon, you're a Celt." So I had to find out what that was, because I didn't want to be black or Indian or God knows what. I wanted to be Anglo-Saxon. (Laughs.)

I married at fifteen. We went to Texas and worked our way up to Detroit and then back to Texas. I got pregnant. I remember mostly people that helped us, but you don't forget the others either. We happened to be in Joliet when I went into labor. I remember the sister telling me that unless we pay the bill, I wouldn't be able to leave there with my baby. I cried and I cried. I had made up my mind that even if I bled to death, I was gonna go down the fire escape with my baby in the middle of the night. My uncle and my husband solved this problem nicely. They came to the hospital drunk, and they threw us all out (Laughs.)

I worked my way up to Chicago from Montgomery. I came to Uptown, the port of entry for poor southerners. The West Side should be called the port of entry for southern blacks. It's like we come from a foreign country. Southerners are as lost and bewildered when they come to Chicago as anybody come from Germany or Italy or Poland. We look like other white people if we're dressed fairly nice. It's hard for them to understand that we lose our way on subways and we don't know about addresses. Down home, we say somebody lives down at the bend of the road or halfway down by the old maple tree. It doesn't work that way in Chicago.

There's no difference between southern whites and southern blacks in what sends us up here: lack of jobs. We get hungry and we get scared and we want a better way of life. There's where the dreams come in. I don't know a single southerner that would be up here, black or white. We'd all go home if there was work down there.

We were told that up north niggers run everything. One of the first things I noticed when I came to Chicago was that black women would be going north in the morning and white men would be coming south: maids going one way and young executives the other way. I never saw any black women unless they were somebody's maid.

I met this black woman, Emma Tiller, who was a friend of my second husband's. He was gonna bring her home for supper. I told him I was not gonna cook dinner for a nigger. He said: "If you don't want to treat my friends decent, I'm gonna stop treating yours decent. I put up with some pretty raw things from 'em." Some of my hillbilly friends would come there drunk and he got 'em out of jail a couple of times. I decided I'd better keep peace in the family. (Laughs.) I better straighten up a little bit.

She came to dinner. He went out in the hall and helped her off with her galoshes. I'll never forget that. I thought: My God, that's just terrible. As it rocked along, I got kind of used to her. Without realizing it, I started learning from her and saw how much alike we were. She told me when she first came to Chicago from Texas, she went to an employment office. All her life, she'd been led to believe that all white people could read and write. She ran into this girl who asked her to help fill out the employment form. Emma said she was dumbfounded. The girl couldn't read or write, and she was white. In my own family, there are people who can't read or write. This is one of the things started me listening to her. So when the 1963 March on Washington happened, I got on the train with Emma and went. I had figured out by then I had been led down the garden path. I had been lied to.

It never occurred to me to organize hillbillies. I was this great white and I quit kickin' blacks, but I didn't want nothin' to do with hillbillies. You don't go organize people just like you, people you want to get away from, for God's sake. I learned to let my feeling spill over to my own people. I tell you, when I started organizin' poor whites, I never knew I could care so much about southerners. It made me proud of myself, which I had never really been. 'Cause I carried all this load of guilt from childhood on that I was nothing but a worm.

I started out by just talking to groups of women. We'd talk about things that were hurting us. I never mentioned black people. Sooner or later, they would say: niggers this and niggers that. Niggers are getting all the welfare. The reason there isn't enough for us, niggers are gettin' it all. I wouldn't carry the battle to them. I'd wait until they could relate it to their own experience. They were really beaten down. Out of the coal mines, out of whatever poor southern whites make their living. Most of the men had black lung. We didn't have much luck with the men. We had the most success with the women.

One thing we got men and women together on was a playground for the kids. Uptown was a hillbilly ghetto. There wasn't any place for the kids to play on except the street. At least twice a month, a child was struck by a car. We held a mock election, worked the neighborhood for about a month. These people who couldn't care less about voting all came out and voted.

A crowd of women went to the park district officials. They told us that black people were tearin' up the city and they spent all their money pacifyin' them. Using that racism again. This very quiet little hillbilly woman, no bigger than a bar of soap after a hard day's work, she stood up, and she had her baby in her arms, she was so mad, she said: "What you're tellin' us is niggers are raisin' hell for their rights an' you give 'em all the money and there's none for us. If that's what it takes, us hillbillies can work you up a real good riot." (Laughs.) I'm sitting here, I mean, my God, if it was me up there blowin' my big mouth, I wouldn't think nothin' of it, but this little woman who never said nothin'.

Uptown was a different place after we were there. It must've struck Mayor Daley as dangerous because the very streets we had organized the best were the first ones they tore down for urban renewal. The city punched us out. A lot of our people had to leave. The best organized people, they're gone.

I think we just burned ourselves out. I was so tired, my language turned to rhetoric. I could talk to twenty different people, and if you'd tape it, I swear I would have said practically the same thing to all those people. That's not good. You have to back up and see where you've been, reassess where you're going.

It was worth the battle. Many of the people we organized are in other places doing things. One of the women, who was really a racist, she's in Georgia now. When they closed the dress factory she worked in, she and other white women joined with black women and bought the thing. Those women will never be the same. Once you've stood up, once you learn you're being kicked and by whom, you're never gonna let them kick you again without protesting.

I'm full of dreams. A million. My dreams are gigantic. When I saw the Japanese farmers on television fighting to stop that airport, I felt I was one of them. I said: "Right on!" I think of all the races of people, and I want to be friends with 'em. I wish they'd hurry up with Esperanto so I could learn it and we could talk with each other.

The reason I have so much hope, I know darn well if I could start out the ignoramus I was, not knowing anything, anybody is capable of finding out the same darn things I did. It's no big secret. It's just something that has to touch you and suddenly you realize what a big world there is. You just want to know about everything. I believe everybody's capable of the same thing.

POSTSCRIPT: *"One day, fire trucks were in our neighborhood. A fireman was yelling 'Hey, you!' to all of us. We weren't antagonistic to the firemen, they had done us no harm. But we said, 'Why are you saying "Hey, you"?' If they had a fire in Senator Percy's neighborhood and somebody was watching it, they'd have said sir or ma'am. I think everybody should be sir or ma'am."*

THREE

IN THE COUNTRY

STIRRINGS IN THE FIELD

HERSCHEL LIGON

*On a farm in Tennessee. It is on the outskirts of Mt. Juliet, fourteen
miles from Nashville. "I'm just an average farmer, livestock. Cows,
hogs, sheep."*

*He's a big-boned man, face furrowed by a hard acquaintance with
the hot sun. He's out of a John Steuart Curry painting.*

My great-great-grandfather served in the American Revolution. Fifth
generation here. These farms have never been owned by anybody but
my ancestors. Maybe I'm a screwball, but I guess I still have a bit of
that stuff my great-great-grandfather had when he came here. My father had a heck of a lot of determination to stay in this thing during
the depression, which was as bad a shape as anybody could get.

Only time I was off the farm was in construction and World War
Two. I led my company on Utah Beach, and we built the main line of
communications from Cherbourg, France, to Frankfort, Germany. I
coulda gone back to work for the telephone company or construction.
I was offered a full-time job in the Tennessee National Guard. But I
said no, I'm gonna farm. It's just bred in me to be a farmer. But I'll
guarantee, it's been rough.

I just love nature. I love to be with livestock. It's one heck of a
challenge in farmin'. I just loved to be with my father. He'd take me
to the barn when I couldn't even walk. I milked my first cow when I
was four years old.

My father always hoped that we could get to where we could do a
little better. (Laughs.) He just kept on strugglin' and kept on strug-

148

glin' . . . He kept three farms together and took care of his bedridden uncle while I was four years in the war. So I figured if he could do that, the least I could do is come back here and be here with him the rest of his life.

If we don't keep the family farm, big business is gonna take over agriculture. There's no tellin' what the consumer is gonna have to pay. Look what's happened to our electric bills after the oil companies got control of the coal supply. Same thing's gonna happen to our food when the big corporations get hold of farms like mine. That's one reason I'm so stubborn about the thing. I'm the only one in this entire area.

Everyone else works somewhere else. I know three who have degrees in dairying. They just didn't go to school to get degrees, they grew up milkin' cows. The economic situation forced 'em out. The only way I was able to do it is my wife has worked away from home and got the kids through college. I have done without, used worn-out equipment. I got a tractor I bought in 1945. That's the only way I've been able to stay here. Kept astrugglin'. Maybe we're gonna make it. I've been told I'm doomed, but I'm still here.

No question agribusiness is set to force us out. We are still producin' a little stuff where they can't completely control production. Just to give you an idea: five corporations control a third of the swine-breedin' business today. That's my major income, swine-breedin' stock. It's just a matter of time before they get it all. They've run so many of these farmers off the land.

Fact is, many people are most unhappy with us because we won't sell. The real estate people. They're in the saddle now. There are ninety-five real estate agents right in this county. We are now a couple of hundred acres, surrounded by subdivisions, all the way around.

I farmed with mules and horses for years. There is not a greater tone to me than the sound that comes from a doubletree when the mules are pullin' the plow. Doubletree fastens the mules to the plow. If you talk about love of land and nature, there's no better sound than listenin' to that tone and walkin' behind it. I've done it until just a couple of years ago, when the mules died. We buried these last two mules of ours up on the hill where the family graveyard is. It was kind of asingin' back and forth, a real attractive tone.

Autumn is my favorite season. My father used to say on those real bad days: "If we just got enough feed and roll the feed down for the cows and they'll get plenty to eat, why it gives you a good feelin'." You get back in the house, build a fire. There's nothin' better than if you've got the livestock all cared for. If the day's good enough, you can go bird huntin'. Now that's livin'.

America's in the worst shape it's been in since the Revolutionary War. We're in such bad shape, a strong leader like Hitler could come in and start a revolution. Somebody could get control just by movin' in. George Wallace flew my associate and me to and from his headquarters to help write the plank of his platform. When he was runnin' for president in '68. (Laughs.) It was real funny. He said: "Come on in and talk to me while I'm dressin'." I just mentioned our program and he called in his staff and said: "This fella's got the best thing I've heard of." He said: "I was reared on a farm and my mother had to sell it and go to work because we just couldn't make it." Lotta people liked George Wallace. He represented the average person.

"I'm strictly a rebel, period. (Laughs.) In the war, our company had all black troops and white officers. We had twenty-seven officers, only four of us from the South. I hadn't been there a month when some of these northerners said: 'How do you get along with these men, treatin' 'em like you do?' I says: 'I've been treatin' 'em like that all my life.' 'Oh, you don't treat 'em right.' A month after we got to England, all these other officers were a hundred percent more prejudiced to the race than I was. 'Cause they didn't know what to expect and I knew what to expect. I understood 'em.

"I was a firm disciplinarian. I have discipline in my livestock. To be a good livestock man, you've got to be as smart as they are. 'Cause if you're smart, you'll learn from 'em. Livestock know when they're doin' wrong and when they're doin' right, no question about that. They know which gate to go through and which gate not to go through. You can teach them that right quick. I work 'em over and they don't do it the next time. Livestock have a temperament just like people have. It runs in families. They inherit that temperament."

I milk a Jersey now every day. Right now, I'm gettin' up at four o'clock in the morning. I turn the sows out, let them eat, put them back, come in the house, and eat breakfast. If the ground is dry enough, we go to the field. Otherwise, we work fences, work buildin's. There's always a million things to do. To hear that rooster crow in the mornin', to hear the ducks quack and hear the turkeys, I just say: "That's America, period." (Laughs.) We've got everything on this farm but money, and I don't see any chance of getting' that. (Laughs.)

They'd give me a good price, but if you're not happy, what the heck's the use of takin' the money? My wife and I could go to Florida and live like a king and queen. But what's gonna be left for my children and grandchildren? If my great-great-grandfather hadn't stayed, would I be here now? I don't intend for 'em to run me out. (Laughs.)

There's nothin' better in the world than gettin' up before daylight and goin' and seein' the sun come up. Nothin' better than bein' in the field when the sun comes down, come in by the lights of the tractor every night. Maybe I'm a durn fool, but I like it.

I intend to be buried up here in the family graveyard, out on top of the hill here. Everybody's up there but my great-great-grandfather and great-great-grandmother, which were buried in Williamson graveyard. A child died and the snow was so deep, they couldn't get down to the Williamson graveyard, so they buried the child on the hill over here. From then on, all the Cloyds are buried in the family graveyard. I intend to be put there, too. No question about it bein' continuity. (Laughs.)

POSTSCRIPT: *As we're heading for the Nashville airport, we pass a Holiday Inn, a McDonald's, a Marriott, an Arby's. He muses: "You really get a thrill out of goin' to a restaurant in a rural town when it's owned by local people. Everybody comin' in for coffee, discussin' the situation. That gives a great feelin' that we still have somethin' of original America. You don't find many of 'em, but it sure is a great feelin' to find 'em."*

JESSIE DE LA CRUZ

◆————————————————————————◆

A one-family dwelling in Fresno. A small, well-kept garden is out front.

"When I was a child growing up as a migrant worker, we would move from place to place. In between, I'd see homes with beautiful gardens, flowers. I always looked at those flowers and said: 'If I could only have my own house and have a garden.' We couldn't as migrant workers. Now, as you walk onto my porch, everything you see is green. (Laughs.) I have a garden now."

She has six grown children; the youngest is twenty-one. She is active in National Land for People.

"The American Dream for me is owning a piece of land. Something you can call home, where you can stay in one place all the time, raise a

*decent family, build a community. Where you have a job all the time
and nobody's gonna fire you. My mother's dream was having a house,
but she got sick and died in 1930."*

She is fifty-nine.

I and my mother, we were living with my grandparents. My father
went back to Mexico. My earliest memory is this big flood in Ana-
heim. I could see lanterns just waving back and forth. And shouting.
Men and boys and even us smaller children would be out there getting mud and building a bank to keep the water from coming into
our house.

My happiest memories was when my grandfather had Sunday off.
He would pick us up, wrap us in blankets, and put us around this big
wood-burning stove, while he went out to the store. He'd come up
with oranges and apples and good things to eat, something we did not
very often have.

All the teachers were Anglos. They would have us say our name
and where we lived, who we were. I said: "Jessie Lopez, American."
She said; "No, you're Mexican." Throughout the years, teachers told
me the same thing. Now all of a sudden they want me to say I'm an
American. (Laughs.) I learned how to speak English and how to fight
back.

I think the longest time I went to school was two months in one
place. I attended, I think, about forty-five schools. When my parents
or my brothers didn't find any work, we wouldn't attend school because we weren't sure of staying there. So I missed a lot of school.

I was quiet in school. I was punished sometimes not only because I
was quiet but because I couldn't speak English, I couldn't defend
myself. That is why I said I have to learn how to speak English. When
I was a child at the dinner table, my older brother would say: "Jessie,
eat your food." Then they'd say, "What are you doing?" I'd say: "I'm
writing in the air." (Laughs.)

My children were picking crops, but we saw to it that they went to
school. Maybe one or two of the oldest would stay away from school
during cotton-picking time around December, so we could earn a
little more money to buy food or buy them a pair of shoes or a coat
that they needed. But we always wanted them to get an education.

I musta been almost eight when I started following the crops. Every
winter, up north. I was on the end of the row of prunes, taking care of
my younger brother and sister. They would help me fill up the cans

and put 'em in a box while the rest of the family was picking the whole row.

In labor camps, the houses were just clapboard. There were just nails with two-by-fours around it. The houses had two little windows and a front door. One room, about twelve by fifteen, was a living room, dining room, everything. That was home to us.

Eight or nine of us. We had blankets that we rolled up during the day to give us a little place to walk around doing the housework. There was only one bed, which was my grandmother's. A cot. The rest of us slept on the floor. Before that, we used to live in tents, patched tents. Before we had a tent, we used to live under a tree. That was very hard. This is one thing I hope nobody has to live through. During the winter, the water was just seeping under the ground. Your clothes were never dry.

My husband was born in Mexico. He came with his parents when he was two and a half years old. He was irrigating when he was twelve years old, doing a man's work. Twelve hours for a dollar twenty. Ten cents an hour. I met him in 1933. Our first year we stayed in the labor camps.

All farm workers I know, they're always talking: "If I had my own place, I'd know how to run it. I'd be there all the time. My kids would help me." This is one thing that all Chicano families talked about. We worked the land all our lives, so if we ever owned a piece of land, we knew that we could make it.

Mexicans have this thing about a close family, so they wanted to buy some land where they could raise a family. That's what my grandfather kept talkin' about, but his dream was never realized.

We followed the crops till around 1966. We went up north around the Sacramento area to pick prunes. We had a big truck, and we were able to take our refrigerator and my washing machine and beds and kitchen pots and pans and our clothing. It wasn't a hardship any more. We wanted our children to pick in the shade, under a tree, instead of picking out in the vines, where it's very hot. When I picked grapes, I could hardly stand it. I felt sorry for twelve-, thirteen-year-old kids. My husband said: "Let's go up north and pick prunes."

We stopped migrating when Cesar Chavez formed a union. We became members, and I was the first woman organizer. I organized people everywhere I went. When my husband and I started working under a signed contract, there was no need to migrate after that.

I knew how to organize. My husband and I talked to other families.

What if we could buy some land? We moved to Fresno and talked to a large group of families. And have meetings. Each of us would borrow, and what little savings we had, maybe a hundred dollars, we would go together and buy some land. We were talkin' about a community, two hundred families.

We made plans of how we'd set up our own little school for pre-school children and the older children could be taken into town to attend public school. I came up with the idea of having our own rest home for the elderly. The Chicano people who couldn't work any more and needed to be taken care of. A clinic was discussed too.

A committee was formed to talk to these big growers. We went in a group of five to this man's office. We hear his land was up. He had to sell because of the 1902 law.* Nobody ever told us about a law or anything. Where anyone that lived within the Westlands district, they used federally subsidized water. A big project was built. Before, all the irrigating was done by pumps. These farmers were pumping themselves dry. So they asked the government to build a big canal there. They got it. They had a lot of money, and congressmen were helping them.

To me, this law meant helping small farms. It was for small family farms. They had to live on the land. It was a hundred sixty for the wife. A hundred sixty for the husband. And a hundred sixty for two children, no more than two children. That was six hundred forty acres. Who needs more than that?

I told this grower we had families interested in buying some of his land. He didn't even let me go any further. He asked me if we had

* George Ballis, director of National Land for People: "The Reclamation Act of 1902 says that no owner may obtain more than a hundred sixty acres worth of federally subsidized water. Beneficiaries must live on the land. You may obtain water in excess if you sign a contract in which you agree to sell the land within ten years, in parcels of a hundred sixty acres or less. The irrigators pay seventeen percent of the project cost and taxpayers pay the rest, eighty-three percent. It's a welfare program. It's a real good deal.

"Some of the land holdings are fantastic. Southern Pacific owns 106,000 acres, which is a hundred seventy square miles. They got that land from the federal government a hundred years ago as a railroad land grant. It was based on the assumption that the railroad would sell the land to the settlers. It never happened.

"There are paper farmers. A guy would control twelve pieces of land, but there'd be a different name on each piece. He had his brothers-in-law and their wives, the owner of the bar where he drank, the bar owner's daughter, a real estate salesman, two of his construction workers, and even the cocktail waitress at the bar—each was allegedly an owner of a hundred sixty acres. There are thousands and thousands of acres passed on this way. So we started raising hell. We brought a lawsuit and won the case."

154

half a million dollars. (Laughs.) He was paying us seventy-five cents an hour, picking cotton and cantaloupes for him for nine, ten years. Before I worked for even less. And he asked if we had a half-million as a down payment.

They were selling old tractors, levelers, the cotton gin. They were selling it with the land. We weren't interested in any landing strip. He wanted to include that, but we didn't have any private airplane. We feel as farmers you don't have to own these great big huge machines to do the work. There's plenty of people to do it.

At our next meeting, we told them what the answer had been. They became discouraged. All of the families left except six. We heard about this man who had some land he wanted to get rid of because he needed tax money. We were able to buy forty acres at a very reasonable price.

Six families on forty acres. That first year we couldn't plant. It needed to be leveled. It didn't have a pump. We didn't have the water. The land had just been sitting there for years. That winter we started pulling those tumbleweeds out and piling them up. It rained very hard that year and we couldn't do it.

A friend of ours said: "I'll rent you six acres." We started farming those six acres. We were out there from morning till late, on our hands and knees, planting tomatoes. There was the risk of a cold wave coming and killing our plants. So we had to use hot caps.

One day we had finished planting and said: "Tomorrow we'll put the hot caps on." They're cap-shaped papers with wire. Around two or three o'clock I heard on the radio—I always carry a little portable —I heard the weather was gonna be twenty-three degrees. It was gonna kill our plants. I was scared. I ran back to the group and said: "Hey, it's gonna freeze tonight, we're gonna lose our plants." Right away we started putting the hot caps on.

We put dirt around it to hold it down. We had them by the thousands. It was very windy and very cold. We started out there on our hands and knees. I was crying. It was beautiful. I'm not calling it beautiful, my crying. But to have little children five, six years old helping us, because they knew how important it was to save those plants. The wind was very strong, it was just ripping those paper caps off of our hands, and you could see them rolling. (Laughs.) We ran out of caps. Okay, each of us got a hoe and started pulling dirt over our plants, very gently. We covered all of them. We came home, it was dark, cold, and wet.

The next morning we were all anxious to find out what had happened during the night. Oh, it was great to go out there and remove the dirt from those plants and watch 'em shoot straight up like anything. We saved every one of 'em. It took hard work to do it.

If it had been one of the big growers, what would have happened? The farmer would just go out there and look and see all the dead plants, and he'd say: "Oh, what the heck." He'd go home and forget about everything. He would get on his pickup, push a button, lift up a telephone, and call the nursery to bring over this certain amount of thousands of plants and call the workers to plant them over again. That's his way of farming.

When we own land and we're working it for ourselves, we're gonna save everything that we can. We're not about to waste anything or lose anything. We keep on working every day. There's no holidays. We're picking until, oh, November. That is work and income. That first year, we sorted our tomatoes and we took 'em to the shipper and we ended up making sixty-four thousand dollars. Six acres between six families.

Before we divided the money, we saw there was a problem. We had to have the right amount for each family. My husband and I were only two of us and my daughter. How could we compare the work of three to a family that had eight? So we said: "We're gonna divide these rows between us all." It worked out fine. There were no fights about who's doing more work, who's getting more money. When you sit down with a group of people and discuss how you're gonna do things, things will work out fine. The following year we were working our own forty acres.

When some other family needs help or when we need help, they'll come over and help us. My husband is a mechanic. Whenever something breaks in one of those tractors, he fixes it in exchange for services we'll need. We need a tractor, the neighbor comes over and does the work for us. This is how we share.

We're in very marginal land. We survive by hard work and sacrifices. We're out of the Westland district, where the government supplies the water. There's acres and acres of land that if you go out there you can see green from one end to the other, like a green ocean. No houses, nothing. Trees or just cotton and alfalfa. It's land that is irrigated with taxpayers' money.

These growers that have been using this water signed a contract that they would sell, within ten years, in small parcels. It's not happening. If the law has been enforced, we would be out there right now.

It's the very, very best land. I worked it there. You could grow anything: tomatoes, corn, cantaloupes, vegetables, bell peppers. But they just grow one or two crops because they just don't want to hire any people. They have big machines that do the picking. Instead of planting a few acres of one crop and a few acres of another, they just go to one crop. What they're looking at, when they see the land and the water, all they can see is dollar signs. They don't see human beings out there.

We're not thinking about getting a lot of land so we can take European trips and buy a new car a year. That's not what we're talking about. I never hope to own an airplane. Not those machines that are worth thousands of dollars. We don't need these things. Everybody managed before these things were invented. So why can't we?

These farmers aren't thinking about putting food on your table. They're thinking how much money they're gonna make per acre. They're putting a lot of chemicals and pesticides into the soil in order to have a bigger yield of crop. They call it—what?—progress? With their progress, they're gonna kill the whole planet. Even themselves. In the not too long.

They're thinking: Well, I'm alive. I'm gonna enjoy life. I'm gonna have millions of dollars. We're thinking about our future generation. My children, my grandchildren, my great-grandchildren. We want a place for them. We don't want them to end up with land that won't grow things.

There are some big companies, individuals, who own land not only in California but in Arizona, Mexico, all over. They don't even know anything about the land. They know nothing about farming. They don't even live on the farm.

A young couple owns thousands of head of cattle and land. And big steakhouses. They felt they weren't getting enough money, and they wanted to make more. They come out to the hearings and going out to the people, and they say we're trying to take their land away from them. We're not trying to take it away from them. They can still keep on farming enough land. Just sell the rest of it. They lease a lot of acreage from Southern Pacific. They call themselves family farmers. Sixteen thousand acres . . .

One senator said: "These are third-generation farmers with calluses on their hands." How can they have calluses when they never held a hoe in their hand? Maybe they do have calluses from a golf club (laughs) but not from a hoe handle. This one young woman who testified said: "I don't want to go back to stoop, to back-breaking labor." I can almost bet my life she's never done a day's work. She and her husband own the biggest feed lot in the world.

I've gone to Washington a few times. I've never been shy talking to these people. I feel comfortable talking to anyone because what I'm talking about is the truth. I believe in standing up for what I believe in.

I was given a shot in the arm by Cesar Chavez. (Laughs.) All of the things I always felt, like I wanted to say, I held back because of fear of losing a job, of being thought not a very good woman, or some kind of fear inside me that had been instilled in me by my grandmother, who always warned us whenever we did something, the police would come. Always being scared by a neighbor: I'm gonna call the police and take you to juvenile. We always heard these. So when Cesar Chavez started talking to us and sayin' women have to become involved, they have to speak, they're farm workers, too, then, I just, oh, had a good feeling. I said: "Boy, now!"

I kept learning. I kept writing everything down. So I said: "Here I come." (Laughs.) And everywhere I go I'll talk about the hopes we have of owning our own land. We haven't been the landowners, we've been the farmers. We've been farming the land for somebody else. Until this time, I was very quiet.

My husband attended meetings; I didn't. I always sat back. Until one time I told him I want to go. The first few meetings I went to, I just listened and listened. And then one time Cesar says: "Does anyone have anything to say?" I lifted my arm and I said: "The way I see it" and I started. And he said: "That's the kind of people I want, people that will talk. It's not my union, it's your union."

A big meeting here in Fresno, that was my first public appearance. I was nervous. I remember that hearing. It was on—what was it?—wages for women. It was at Fresno High. I knew I was going to speak. I kept thinking: What am I going to say? I started writing something. I have to make a note of what I'm going to say.

I looked around, and there were all these big growers. And these big businessmen that had stores out in the vacation areas up in the mountains. They were there because they were against raising wages for women. I heard my name and I got up there. My knees were shaking. (Laughs.) I got up before these microphones and I looked around and saw my notes. The only thing I said out of my notes was "Ladies and Gentlemen." I said: "My name is Jessie de la Cruz, and I'm here as a farm worker." And then I started.

I said: "We are forced to go out and work in the fields alongside our husbands, not through choice and not because we love to be out in the sun working so hard ten hours, but because of the need. Us women have to go out there and help support our families." And I said: "I have six children, my husband and I raised, and we never had to go on welfare." Oh, they applauded. Good for you. Oh, it was great that I never had to go on welfare. And I said: "These men here who are growers and businessmen and restaurant owners, if they pay higher wages, they could just close down the welfare doors." Oh, I felt in the pit of my stomach, right there in the pit of my stomach, pain. It was a hard ball right there. I forget what I was saying and my hands were behind me. And I hear somebody in our group say: "Go on, Jessie, tell 'em, tell 'em." And I said: "What I'm gonna tell you is not something I read. It's something that's engraved in my heart and in my brain because it's something that I've lived and many other farm workers' families have done the same." So I went on and on and on and on. (Laughs.) I was congratulated, but for about three or four days, there was a pain right here, a sore spot in my stomach. But I managed to tell 'em off. (Laughs.)

How can I write down how I felt when I was a little child and my grandmother used to cry with us 'cause she didn't have enough food to give us? Because my brother was going barefooted and he was cryin' because he wasn't used to going without shoes? How can I describe that? I can't describe when my little girl died because I didn't have money for a doctor. And never had any teaching on caring for sick babies. Living out in labor camps. How can I describe that? How can I put into writing when I'm testifying about things that are very deep inside? About seeing all these many people that have their little children killed in the fields through accidents? It's things that are a feeling you can't put into words.

Last year, right down this street, during the grape-picking season, I saw this family under a tree. The lady was cooking, and her living quarters were just blankets tied around trees. Last year, on Manning Avenue, this being 1977. And the owner that hired this family, there's a beautiful mansion. It's made out like Chinese-style. You see all the decorations and gardens. How can they see these people out there under the trees? They're human beings, they have babies. The babies were there, too.

I remember one time when I was a delegate to the Democratic Convention of 1972, a newspaperman said: "You're that radical. You're that Communist." (Laughs.) I laughed and said: "I don't know. They call me a radical and a troublemaker and all these, and I don't know what it takes to be a Communist, so how can I be a Communist?" (Laughs.)

When we were picketing, a Nisei* farmers' group was formed. And all these Japanese farmers came out to the picket line and called me all kinds of names. Four o'clock in the morning we'd be there. They have these big wire fences around the building. And they had all the people that were scabbing were drove inside that fence. And the Japanese farmers would be escorting the buses out with people who were gonna break our strike. And I'd tell them: "Hey, what does this wire fence remind you of?" I said: "I cried with your families when they were herded into cattle trucks and put in the fairgrounds behind barbed wire here in Fresno. So now you're doing the same thing to us, the farm workers, because we're standing up for what we believe in. You're doing the same thing that was done to you. How can you do it? That does not make you more American. America, the government, doesn't think of you as more American than me. You're still a Japanese and I'm still a Mexican." They bowed their heads down.

I remember, during the war, there were a lot of Japanese families who had small stores. I used to buy from them. I saw that day when these old Japanese ladies were crying. The few things they were allowed to take were tied up in white sheets and carried on their backs. They were herded into these cattle trucks. I saw that and I cried. Because I had a feeling: Are we gonna be next? They forgot that.

The Okies forgot, too. There's a radio annnnouncer here in Fresno. He always points out: "I was an Okie. I came out here and I made it. So why can't these Chicanos make it?" Oh, that just burned me up. I wish I could speak to him, not through the radio, but person to person.

I'm making it. It's hard work. But I'm not satisfied, not until I see a lot of farm workers settle on their own farms. Then I'll say it's happening.

Is America progressing toward the better? No, the country will never do anything for us. We're the ones that are gonna do it. We have to keep on struggling. I feel there's going to be a change. With us, there's a saying: *La esperanza muere al último.* Hope dies last. You can't lose hope. If you lose hope, that's losing everything.

The only thing that makes me sad is that this change didn't come about until I was old. I wish I was thirty, thirty-five right now, where I knew I'd have many more years. I'm the sort of person that will not

* First-generation American-born Japanese

sit back in a rocking chair when I get older and just feel sorry for myself. There always has to be something to do. There always is if you want to do it.

THEM

AKI AND JUN KUROSE

Seattle. They are a middle-aged Nisei couple. Both were born and raised in Seattle. They have four grown children.

They live in a middle-class neighborhood. The house is comfortable, rambling; the street is tree-lined.

JUN: *Caucasians always ask me: Did you always live in an integrated area? My answer is: Yes, I did. Half Japanese ghetto and half white prostitutes. We lived in the only area in Seattle that did not have paved roads. When the government project went up, the Japanese and the prostitutes were moved out.*

We bought this house sixteen years ago from a very liberal man, and it was a hassle. Even though restrictive covenants were illegal, they had a verbal agreement among homeowners not to let Japanese or blacks over this side of the hill.

AKI: *There was an actual paper. I saw it. It said: no blacks, no Jews, no Asians. They had to be white Anglo-Saxon.*

AKI: The American Dream? I think: for whites only. I didn't feel that way before World War Two. The school I went to was ninety-nine percent Asian. We were already segregated, but we didn't realize it because this was the accepted norm. When the war broke out, we found out what it was to be a minority. When Japan bombed Pearl Harbor, we were not part of American society any more. It was a shock.

The principal was always pounding away about Americanism, being loyal to your country, waving the red, white, and blue. Every morning we stood out in the hallway, gave the pledge of allegiance, and saluted the flag. At that time, I really had the feeling that America was my country. I was very proud to be an American.

JUN: I wasn't as naïve as she was. I played sports at high school, and when the team would have a party, usually us Asian boys were excluded. The only time they wanted us around was if they got in a scrap with somebody. Being raised in a ghetto, you had to learn to fight pretty darn good. We lived south of the Mason-Dixon line, the Caucasians lived north. (Laughs.)

AKI: My mother was an educator. She was one of the very few women that migrated to America who had a college education. She told me from the time I was small: "This is your country. Work hard. To get places, you'll have to do twice as much as the whites." *Shikataganai*—that's the way it is. It can't be helped.

JUN: I always wanted to be a physical ed instructor. I was doing fairly well in school, scholastically, until my junior year. That's when I talked to my coach, and he told me to forget it. So I forgot it, books and all. I just sat through.

I used to work in the salmon canneries. We're sent up there to Alaska in the steerage of boats, in the hole. We're packed just like sardines. The machine klunks out, and it's *us* that are fixin' it because the machinist doesn't know how to do it. They're makin' three, four times the money we are. They're eating steak, we're eating fish.

AKI: My dad was a porter at the railroad station, and my mother used to work in the restaurant, waiting on tables. When they got married in 1913, they came to America. My mother taught Japanese language until World War Two. Then we were thrown into the concentration camp. After stayin' there three or four years, she went to live in Chicago. She ended up her life working as a chambermaid in a hotel.

I was about fifteen the day Pearl Harbor was bombed. On the next day, Monday, when I went to school, the teacher immediately treated me as an enemy. She said: "You people bombed Pearl Harbor." Everything changed completely. Our friends looked upon us with suspicion. The idea that we were Americans was shattered.

JUN: On *that* Sunday, I was workin' at this gas station. An hour or two after I got there, the extra started comin' out. I says: "God-damn Hirohito." As bad as things were, I still loved my country. I figured: Dammit, one of these days I'm gonna make it. I was as mad as the next guy.

Within a week, I changed completely. I found out I'm not an American any more. We were being blamed for Pearl Harbor. I didn't even know where the hell Pearl Harbor was. (Laughs.)

AKI: You suddenly become someone without a country. We couldn't feel a closeness to Japan, a feeling of belonging. We were very much involved in our own community. Seattle was my world.

JUN: My dad served in the Coast Guard around 1910. Even at that, he wasn't accepted as a citizen. He was peddling fruits and vegetables in all-white areas. Quite a few name people were his customers. He was scared. He wouldn't go. I was workin' for this produce man, delivering at the University of Washington: lunchrooms, fraternities, dorms. My boss was scared. I said: "Aw, let's go." By then, I figured even if they kill me, by God, they're gonna have a fight on their hands. I wasn't gonna take it layin' down, because I didn't do anything wrong.

Even though we didn't have our constitutional rights, I thought the law would uphold us. As the months went by, I found out otherwise. Some of the students I ran into were pretty fair, but the cooks who worked at the university gave us a rough time. I figured they were just uneducated people. As time wore on, I saw everybody was that way.

They say we can't be trusted. I spent a little over a year in the concentration camp. Then I was in the army. Within another year, I had the highest security clearance in the United States. (Laughs.) I was put into the counterintelligence corps. From an untrusted guy, they sent me to the land of my ancestors to interrogate Japanese nationals. Still they say I can't be trusted. You face those kind of things, you wonder: Oh, what the hell.

My brother was an honor student at the University of Washington, with a master's in electrical engineering. He couldn't get a job at a time when the U.S. really needed engineers. 1940. We didn't even know there was gonna be a Pearl Harbor. He was offered a job by a company in Japan. The president of the university said: "Take it. You don't have a chance in this country." If he stayed here, he'd probably be down there selling vegetables, yelling: "Lettuce, five cents a head!" He went to Japan, to a good job. A couple of years later, someplace in the Philippines, he got killed by a bomb dropped by the U.S. Air Force.

At last they were gonna do us a favor and let us go into the army. I wanted to volunteer because all my friends did. My folks having lost one son already over there, I promised my mother I won't volunteer, but if I'm called I will go. Nine months later, I was called.

There were over ten thousand Japanese-American soldiers in Europe. There were six thousand in the Pacific. These guys had to really sneak to the front of the front. They'd go into caves, flush soldiers out. We were trusted enough to be sent into the Pacific to fight a lot of our ancestors.

AKI: Having served didn't make you a first-class citizen. These people came back in 1945 and weren't acceptable to the American Legion. My girlfriend lost her husband in the European theater. She was told: "Don't come down to the Legion hall. We don't accept Orientals." They were still in their uniforms, my brother one of them, and weren't served in many establishments. The drugstore on our corner would not serve "Japs," even in uniform. Finally, when they were told they must, they put ashes in the Coke. When we were given our release, there were signs: *No Japs allowed.*

Dave Beck* refused produce from Japanese-American farmers. My brother-in-law was a prisoner of war in Germany and was all shot up. He came back to produce row to see teamster signs: *Japs not wanted.*

JUN: Before we joined the army, they gave us all a loyalty test. Question number one: Will you drop all allegiance to the emperor and be loyal to the United States? Answer yes or no. If you said yes, it means you had allegiance to the emperor. I answered: No. I would not drop allegiance to the emperor because I never had any. I wrote a sentence. That master sergeant gave me hell. The other was: Will you volunteer? I wrote no. I will go if I'm drafted. He called me disloyal. I said: "Did you volunteer or were you drafted?" He said: "I was drafted." I said: "You and I are in the same boat." That stopped him right there. Most of the guys wrote yes, yes, yes, because they were scared. Some of the fellows who answered no were known as the no-no boys. They were ostracized by the Japanese community as disloyal. There's a group in Seattle called the Nisei Veterans Committee, they are so gung ho, they made it tough for anyone who didn't serve.

When I came back from overseas in the United States uniform, I was walking downtown, with ribbons and all, by God. A guy walks by, looks at me, and says: "You lousy Jap." This was after the war. I said: "Man, this is it." I'm pretty violent in my ways. I didn't fight because I had a girl with me. Doggone, if I was by myself, I woulda ended up in jail. By God, giving so much of your life to your country, you're not gonna take it. Being young, being hard-headed, being a man, there's certain things like honor.

AKI: That was the most impressive thing to me: all of a sudden

* Lived in Seattle and was, at the time, president of the International Brotherhood of Teamsters. He was subsequently sent to prison for racketeering and thereafter received a presidential pardon in 1975.

to see so much fear in adults, it was constant. My parents were trying to hide it from us as much as possible. As soon as Eseis* would get together, it was always: What's going to happen to us? The leaders of the community were immediately taken into camps, sent to Missoula, Montana.

The FBI was surveilling the house across the street. They come into our house and suddenly it wasn't our home any more. Here were these strangers taking it over. I remember one FBI that came, looking around for contrabands of war. Even the Japanese kimono became contraband. And Japanese children's books, readers. We went to Japanese school on Saturday to learn the language. This became an indication that we were disloyal.

Many people in my peer group would deny that they could even understand Japanese and were showing a hatred to Japan because they didn't want to be considered disloyal. Many people, to this day, deny they can understand Japanese. I'm sure I must have had those feelings, too, though I try to deny it myself now.

JUN: We didn't think citizens had to go to these camps until about two weeks before it happened. We were born and raised here. We had nothin' goin' for us in Japan. To them, we were foreigners. The only thing we had was a Japanese vase. (Laughs.)

AKI: First, they imposed a curfew on us. That really made us angry. We were afraid to discuss it openly among white people. We became very careful not to say anything. I was afraid as to how anything might be interpreted. It was almost paranoia. I was always feeling that I was suspect.

I thought the war was coming right into Seattle. The hysteria was so great. I saw the Eseis taken away. Rumors started that we also were going to be herded off. All of a sudden, the orders came. We were gone six months after the war started.

JUN: I was one of the first to go, in April 1942. They took it by districts. (To Aki) You came sometime in May.

It was the whole family. We were told to meet at a certain location at a certain time in the morning, with no more than we could carry in our hands.

AKI: Two pieces of luggage.

JUN: No contraband. No radios, scissors, razors. You couldn't even take a kitchen knife. Some people did, and it was confiscated. My dad used a straightedge to shave, and he got that confiscated.

* Japanese-born

AKI: The whole family was given one room. We were six.

JUN: My father just sold everything, the whole business. He got about twenty-five dollars for his truck. It musta been worth about three, four thousand dollars. Everything that was accumulated from 1913, '14, when he and my mother came to America, just went down the drain. We didn't even have to put an ad in the paper. People just came to the house. "You selling anything? How much do you want for this?" I said: "I should get at least a hundred dollars." "I'll give you fifteen dollars." They were lookin' down our throats. I wouldn't sell my piano, so I loaned it to the church.

Just at the point it was gettin' better for the immigrant family, because the children were bringin' in a little income, pooling our hard-earned pennies, buying furniture and this and that, we had to go. My dad had all his customers owin' him money. Some paid back, some didn't.

AKI: People were offering twenty-five cents for a table. A very nice deacon of one of the main churches downtown came over and said he was so sorry this was happening to us. He'd like to help us. If we gave him power of attorney, he'd take over everything. My father and mother were so grateful. All of a sudden we heard, in camp, that all our furniture, all our savings from the bank, were gone. He took everything. We had believed he was an honest man. We were so naïve.

JUN: We were first sent to the state fairgrounds.

Ramona Bennett, a Puyallup Indian who is present, interjects: "It was the place where we used to have pony races and games and weddings. It was our traditional, tribal campground. We invited white people to come visit and share our food. Now we can't even get a booth out there."

JUN: We were fenced in behind barbed wire. We were put in sheds made of tar paper. The rain came through the walls, and it was all mud.

AKI: My father became very ill. He had appendicitis, and because of the red tape you have to go through, his appendix was ruptured. But he survived.

They gave us burlap bags. We were told to stuff straw in them and they would be our mattressses. My sister who was very asthmatic became very ill because she was allergic to straw. She was finally allotted a GI mattress. But you had to prove you were ill.

JUN: Machine-gun towers were in the main parking lot. If you jump through the fence, man, you're dead. This is what gets me today. They say: "We did it for your protection." When you protect somebody, you don't aim a gun at the guy you're protecting.

AKI: The guns were not aimed outside but inside, at us.

JUN: People would drive around in their cars, calling us names. You'd feel just like an animal in the zoo.

AKI: Animal shelters were converted to shelters for some of us.

JUN: Pretty near half of us lived in horse stalls and former pigpens.

You'd read in the papers where Dave Beck said kill 'em. And Walter Lippmann, he was a bad one.* Westbrook Pegler, Walter Winchell, they were out for blood.

Franklin Roosevelt, to all white Americans, he was a great president. New Deal. As far as I'm concerned, he was a crud. Concentration camps. My spine is not gonna quiver at the thought of him.

AKI: Our guards were very young soldiers with machine guns. They were frightened themselves when they heard a noise outside our barbed wire. One night, there was a gunshot and we heard a moo. They had killed a cow. It was terrifying.

Some of the soldiers had never seen a Japanese person before. I remember a young boy from the South. He was very lonely and started talking. He was surprised that we talked English. He was frightened and upset by the whole thing. A decent kid.

JUN: Then we were sent to Idaho. We were in altogether a little over a year.

AKI: The barracks and mess halls were converted into classrooms. I graduated in camp. I don't know if this is something I dreamed up, but I really think it was true. Everything was so surreal. The assignment one teacher gave us was: "Write why you are proud to be an American." (Laughs softly.) We had to salute the flag every day and sing the national anthem.

JUN: Some of us were released earlier. That's when they started accepting Japanese-Americans into service. Anyway, it was costing the damn government too much money, so it was better to have us out workin'. I left first chance I got to grab any old job. They gave us railroad fare plus twenty-five dollars. I went to Chicago.

---

* "On February 12 and 14, 1942, two extremely influential columns by Walter Lippmann, based on talks with Earl Warren, then attorney general of California, tipped the scales of national opinion in favor of mass evacuation." Carey McWilliams, *The Education of Carey McWilliams* (New York: Simon & Schuster, 1979).

AKI: The American Friends Service Committee had a student relocation program. We had to find housing before we could be relocated. There were many calls for domestic jobs. Many people wanted maids. I went to Salt Lake City, where I was supposed to work for my room and board and attend school. But this lady's idea was for me to work all day and go to night school. I would say to her: "I came to attend school." She says: "Go at night. If you complain, I can always send you back to camp." My brother, who came home from his furlough in the army, said: "You don't have to take that." Another lady took me in.

Do you know that many who were in with us tried to justify the camps? When we were told to evacuate, the American Friends Service Committee said: "Don't go, we will help you." They almost became our enemies. Some of the Japanese were saying: "Stay out of this, you're making it rougher for us." If we'd listened to the Friends, we might have been able to avert much suffering. We went willingly, we really did.

JUN: Us Nisei were still too young and too naïve. Remember, all our community leaders were packed up within hours and sent far away to Montana. Most of us were still dependent on our parents for everything.

AKI: Many of the Nisei wanted to forget about all this. Why bring up the past? For a long time, they were blocking it out as unpleasant memories; also, they were afraid of being disloyal. They were real gung-ho Americans, waving the flag, never questioning the government.

JUN: I got into quite a few squabbles at Boeing, where I work as a machinist. During the fifties, before the civil rights movement, I'd kind of have to shut up for a while or I'd be out of a job. With my kids and all, if I'm not workin', I'm sunk. Since the sixties, now that my kids are all grown, the job doesn't mean that much to me any more. I go gung ho on tellin' 'em what it is.

They still say: "We did it for your protection." I said: "Protection, my eye. The machine gun wasn't facing your way, it was facing ours." I don't know why they want to justify the wrong so much. Thirty years later, they still justify it. Especially with all this redress stuff.* Hayakawa, look at him.** (Laughs.)

---

* A movement for redress of grievances has come into being on behalf of Japanese-Americans who were interned during the war years.

** Senator S. I. Hayakawa of California, who is opposed to redress, has described the internment camp experience as beneficial and educational to the inmates.

The younger kids who work in the shop are more educated than their parents were. When I first went to Boeing, the journeymen machinists had fourth- or fifth-grade educations. Everything they heard from the rabble-rousers, they believed. But the kids have had some college, and they have a better understanding.

AKI: He equates education with understanding. I don't. I'm a schoolteacher, and I'm still concerned about the attitude of my colleagues. There's a desegregation program going on right now in Seattle to make the schools more racially balanced. I was teaching in a school of black and Asian children. Being of a minority myself, I was sent out to one of the ritzier schools in the north end of town. I put up a fight. I didn't want to go. I enjoyed my job and was more comfortable where I was. I said: "I was educated to teach children, not certain kinds of children." It was kindergarten.

The principal said: "We don't have Asians out here." Before, the term was "Oriental." (Laughs.) She said: "The parents want to meet you." This was summertime 1976. They set up a date in the middle of August. I cut my vacation short. The principal was quite nervous about it. She drove me there.

It was a beautiful home on the lake. Two guards were flashing their lights so we'd find the house. I came on the scene at eight. Thirty parents had been there since seven. They had a meeting. They were out to test me. Where did you get your education? What degree do you have? What was your major? Where did you learn English? I played the game very well. I brought out Bruner and Piaget.

They didn't know what the hell you were talkin' about.

Neither did I. (Laughs.) But they didn't know it. These are all upper-middle-class white parents. They were very impresssed. (Laughs.) I happen not to like coffee. I prefer tea. They said: "Would you like coffee?" I said: "I don't drink coffee." One of the parents said: "Of course!" (Laughs.)

When these women saw some black children coming into the classroom with a Nisei teacher, they really freaked out. Phones were ringing like crazy in the school district, parents were walking in and out of my classroom, constantly questioning me about the curriculum. My first year was really hell on earth.

The faculty, I thought, would make me feel welcome. First, one teacher said to me: "Kurose. What kind of name is that?" I said: "It's my husband's name." "What is he?" "He's my husband." "Where are you from?" "Seattle." "No, where *were* you from?" "I was born in

Seattle." Finally, I said: "Are you trying to find out my ethnic background?" She said: "You really ought to be more careful." I asked why. She said: "The community still remembers this Japanese family that lived here. We were very nice to the family, but they stayed private. Their son joined the Japanese army and became an officer." I said: "I didn't know Japan sent a carrier over to pick up one person and put him in the Japanese army. I think you're referring to the Ishtane family that lived here. Their son was in the Japanese-American army. The U.S. Army did not allow Japanese boys to be in with regular white boys." She replied: "You really should be more careful."

I asked the librarian if they could put in some books about Japanese-American history. She said: "Why do you have to bring up the past?" I said: "It's part of history." She said: "You must remember, you people started the war." These are educated people.

JUN: At work, when I might disagree with a guy about politics, he'll tell me: "Why don't you go back where you came from?" I say: "I was born and raised here. If you don't like what I say, why don't *you* go back where you came from, Europe?" They're surprised. It's the first time they ever heard this.

(Mumbles) August 6, 1945 . . .

AKI: (Softly) The bombing of Hiroshima and Nagasaki. It was a shocking thing to the Japanese community. The Eseis were especially affected. Some of them tried to hide their grief because everybody was afraid to show any kind of feeling for the people of Japan. But you couldn't help feeling. It was just complete annihilation.

JUN: There's more immigrants from Hiroshima in America, percentage-wise, than any other part of Japan. Most of the people that came here were from agricultural families. Whether your brother's an enemy or not, you're gonna grieve. I think it was a racial thing. They had the bomb before Germany was defeated but didn't drop it there.

AKI: It was so unnecessary. And the bombing of Nagasaki, why? Why? I feel we have to remind the people over and over again what that kind of bomb can do. Now we're talking about something many times more powerful!

I think things are changing. The new generation, the Sanseis,* are saying: "How could you have kept so quiet? Why haven't you told us?" There are so many families that never discussed it. Their kids are

---

* Second-generation American-born Japanese

saying: "We're hearing about this from other people. How come?" The civil rights movement did a lot to bring this out for us. They took the lead, and it's easier for others to follow. Many Niseis and Sanseis got involved in the black movement, yet they were reluctant to discuss their own situation. It took a long time for them to come out.

JUN: For a long time, we lived with *shikataganai*—it can't be helped. Until many of us said: "What the hell do you mean, it can't be helped?" No more of this silence, hell, no.

GIRL OF THE GOLDEN WEST

RAMONA BENNETT

We're on the highway, heading from the Seattle airport to Tacoma.

"Do you know we're on a reservation at this moment? It was reserved forever for the members of my tribe. 'Forever' meant until some white people wanted it. I'm a member of the Puyallup tribe. It's called that by the whites because they couldn't pronounce our foreign name: Spalallapubsh. (Laughs.)

"We were a fishing people. We had camps all the way from McNeill's Island to Salmon Bay and clear up to Rodando. In 1854, agents of the United States government met with our people and did a treaty. They promised us they only needed land to farm. They assured us that our rights as commercial fishing people would not be disturbed. Because Indian people have always been generous, we agreed to share.

"Our tribes were consolidated onto this reservation, twenty-nine thousand acres. We lost eleven thousand in the survey, so we came down to eighteen thousand. We should have known, but we're a trusting people."

We were long-house people, matriarchal, where the whole extended family lived together. We didn't have real estate problems. There was lots of space for everybody, so we didn't have to stand our long houses on end and call them skyscrapers.

The white people decided we'd make good farmers, so they separated our long-house families into forty-, eighty-, and 160-acre tracts. If we didn't improve our land, we'd lose it. They really knew it wouldn't work, but it was a way of breaking up our society. Phil Lucas, who's a beautiful Indian folk singer, says the marriage between the non-Indians and the Indians was a perfect one. The Indian measures his success by his ability to share. The white man measures his importance by how much he can take. There couldn't have been two more perfect cultures to meet, with the white people taking everything and the Indians giving everything.

They then decided that because we couldn't read or write or speak English, we should all be assigned guardians. So the lawyers and judges and police and businessmen who came out with Milwaukee Railroad and Weyerhaeuser Lumber, all these good citizens were assigned their fair share of Indians to be guardians for. They sold the land to each other, kept the money for probate fees, and had the sheriffs come out and remove any Indians still living on this land. Those Indians unwilling to be removed were put on the railroad tracks and murdered. We became landless on our own reservations.

The kids were denied access to anything traditionally theirs. They had programs called Domestic Science, where little Indian girls were taught how to wash dishes for white people, cook meals for white people, mop floors for white people. If they were very, very smart, they were taught how to be beauticians and cut white people's hair, or to be waitresses and serve white people in restaurants, to be clerk typists, maybe, and type white people's ideas. All the boys went through a program called Agricultural Science, where they were taught how to plow white people's fields and take care of white people's cows and chickens and to care for the produce that was being raised on their own land, stolen by non-Indians. If these boys were very, very smart, they were taught to be unemployed welders or unemployed sheet-metal workers. People that do the hiring are whites, and they tend to be more comfortable with people who resemble them.

We are entering a complex of buildings. One stands out from among the others; it has the appearance of a stone fortress.

This is a jail for young Indian boys. It used to be a little Indian hospital. It was the only hospital for us in the whole region. That's Alaska, Montana, Idaho, Washington, and Oregon. The good white folks saw this new modern hospital going up and right away got mad. They started lobbying to get it away from us. About eighteen years ago, the government snatched it away.

I spent eight years as chairwoman of Puyallup Tribal Council, nonstop, working to reacquire the building. Right now, it's used by Washington State as a jail for children. It's called a juvenile diagnostic center. (She nods toward a young boy on the grounds.) You just saw an Indian child. Who the hell do you think gets locked up in this country? Children, minority and white. It's a system that is so goddamn sick that it abandons and locks up its children. Didn't you see the barbed wire? (Impatient with me) I mean, didn't you see the cyclone fence? See the bars on the windows over there?

We enter one of the smaller buildings across the road. It is noninstitutional in appearance and feeling. Small, delighted children are busy at their tasks or listening quietly to one of the young women teachers. A teacher says: "Most of our students and teachers are Indian. We concentrate on traditional crafts and arts and history. We teach respect for the visions of others. We honor elders for their wisdom. We prize good humor, especially when directed at oneself. All natural things are our brothers and sisters, and will teach us if we are aware and listen. We honor persons for what they've done for their people, not what they've done for themselves."

We demanded a school building to get our kids out of the public school system, where they were being failed. It was a struggle getting this school. I've learned from the whites how to grab and how to push. When the state would not return our hospital to us, we just pushed our way on this property and occupied it.

When you read about Indians or when you see them in movies, you see John Wayne theater. You see an Indian sneaking through the bushes to kill some innocent white. (She indicates people walking by, all of whom know her. On occasion, she chats with one or two.) You'd never think those two guys are fishermen and the guy that just walked by is an accountant. So is that gal. You don't think of Indians as professionals. You think of the stereotype that everyone needs to be afraid of.

In school, I learned the same lies you learned: that Columbus discovered America, that there were no survivors at Little Big Horn, that the first baby born west of the Mississipppi was born to Narcissa Whitman. All the same crap that you learned, I learned. Through those movies, I learned that an Irishman who stands up for his rights is a patriot, and an Indian who stands up for his rights is a savage. I learned that the pioneers made the West a fit place for decent folks to live. I learned that white people had to take land away from the Indian people because we didn't know how to use it. It wasn't plowed, logged, and paved. It wasn't strip-mined. It had to be taken from us because we had no environmental knowledge or concerns. We were just not destructive enough to be considered *really* civilized.

What happened is we had land the whites wanted. The government ordered the Indians to move. They were moved so many times, they might as well have had handles. There were always a few patriots who'd say: "For God's sake, we were born here, we buried our dead here. Leave us alone. My God, it's a federal promise. We got a contract. I'm not makin' my grandmother move, I'm not makin' my children move. Bullshit, I'm sick of this." They pick up arms and that would be an uprising. The cavalry rides in. Since we all look alike, they'd kill the first bunch of Indians they saw. This was just tradition. Every single one of those cavalry officers had one of those damn little flags and damn little Bibles. Oh, they were very, very religious. (Laughs.) They opened fire and did a genocide.

They always teach that the only survivor at Little Big Horn was that cavalry horse. Since then, I've realized there were many survivors of Little Big Horn. (Laughs.) They were Sioux and Cheyennes and therefore didn't count, apparently. You never see a roster with all of *their* names.

When I went to school, we learned history so we won't make the same mistakes. This is what I was told. I know damn good and well that if American children in school had learned that the beautiful Cheyenne women at Sand Creek put their shawls over their babies' faces so they wouldn't see the long knives, if the American schoolchildren learned that Indian mothers held their babies close to their bodies when the Gatling guns shot and killed three hundred, there would never have been a My Lai massacre. If the history teacher had really been truthful with American children, Calley would have given an order to totally noncooperating troops. There would have been no one to fight. There would have been a national conscience. The lie has made for an American nightmare, not dream.

When I was in first grade, really tiny, I played a small child in a school play. This was during World War Two. I was born in 1938. My mother was a little dark lady. Caucasians cannot tell people of color apart. To the average white, Chinese, Filipinos, Japanese, all look the same. When my mom came to the school grounds, a little boy named Charles made slanty eyes at her and called her ugly names. I didn't understand what he was saying, but I just jumped on him and started hitting him. He was a friend of mine, and he didn't know why I was doing it. Neither did I. When the play started, my clothes were all disheveled. I was confused, hurt, and really feeling bad. When I went on that stage and looked at all those faces, I realized for the first time my mother was a different color from the others and attracted attention. Her skin had always been rich and warm, while mine looked pale and cold. My father was white. It was such a shock that someone could hate my mother for being such a warm, beautiful woman. Much later I found out that Charles's father died in the Pacific and that his whole family was very uptight about the Japanese.

I think of Indian people who, at treaty time, offered to share with a few men from Boston. They never knew there'd be a Boeing Airplane Company or a Weyerhaeuser. They never knew there would be a statue in the harbor inviting wretched masses and that those masses would come like waves of the sea, thousands and thousands of people seeking freedom. Freedoms that those Indian people would never be afforded. With all those waves coming at us, we were just drowning in the American Dream.

The median lifespan for Indians is somewhere in the forties. That's deceptive because our infant mortality rate is four times higher than the national average. We have the magic age of nineteen, the age of drinking, violent deaths, and suicides. Our teenage suicide rate is thirty-four times higher than the national average.

Forty-five is another magic age for the Indian. That's the age of deaths from alcoholism. Our people have gone from the highest protein diet on the face of the earth—buffalo and salmon—to macaroni. If we're not alcoholics, we're popoholics. Ninety percent of us, eighteen and older, are alcoholics. It's a daily suicide: "I can't face my life, lack of future. I can't face the ugly attitudes toward me. I can't face the poverty. So I'll just drink this bottle of Ripple, and I'll kill my-self for a few hours. I'll kill some brain cells. Tomorrow, when I get sober, maybe things will be different. When I get sober and things are no different, I'll drink again. I'm not so hopeless that I'll kill myself." It's an optimistic form of suicide.

1 7 5

I once drank very heavily. A little seventeen-year-old girl, who I considered just a child, would just get in my face and give me hell. She would say: "Don't you care about yourself? Don't you realize you're killing an Indian? Why do you want to hurt yourself?" At that point I stopped, and I can't be around people who drink. Oh, I don't mind if you drink. I don't care what non-Indian people do to themselves. But I hate to see an Indian killing himself or herself. That Indian is waiting, marking time and wasting, decade after decade. The family is broken up.

They rush through our communities and gather our children. Thirty-five percent of our children have been removed from their families to boarding schools, foster homes, and institutions. A Shoshone or Sioux or Navajo woman lives in a house like mine. Substandard, no sanitation. No employment on the reservation. Inadequate education. The Mormons have a relocation—child-removal—program. Here's the routine:

A woman from the LDS* knocks on my door. I'm gracious and I invite her in because that's our way. She says: "Oh, look at all your pretty children. Oh, what a nice family. I see that your roof leaks and your house is a little cold and you don't have sanitation. By the looks of your kitchen, you don't have much food, and I notice you have very little furniture. You don't have running water and you have an outdoor toilet. And the nearest school is sixty miles away. Wouldn't you like your children to go and live in this nice house, where they'll have their own bedrooms, wonderful people who care about them, lots of money to buy food, indoor plumbing, posturepedic mattresses and Cannon sheets, and wonderful television sets, and well-landscaped yards? And a neighborhood school, so your children won't have to spend three hours a day on a bus?" And then she says: "If you reeeeeeally, reeeeeeally love your children, you wouldn't want them to live like this. You would want them to have all the good things they need." And that mother thinks: My God, I love my children and what a monster I am! How can I possibly keep them from this paradise?

"My mother grew up poor, like many Indians. She was taken away to boarding school, where they forbade the use of her language, her religion. But she kept her wits about her. She learned to look at things with a raised eyebrow. When she hears something that's funny, she

---

* Latter Day Saints

laughs out loud. She provided me with pride, humor, and strength: you don't snivel, you don't quit, you don't back off.

"She talks to graves, talks to plants, talks to rivers. Aside from knowing the traditional things, she was busy growing things, digging clams, smoking fish, sewing. She's an excellent seamstress. At the same time, she's politically and socially sharp.

"When I was a little girl, a couple of FBI agents came to the house. I was maybe four years old. World War Two had just broken out. In a secretive way, they said: 'We'd like to talk to you about security risks. Next-door is this German family, and on the other side these Italians. We want to know if you think they're loyal.' My maiden name was Church, a very British, acceptable name. She said that the Germans were third-generation and are Americans to the core, and the Italian family had already lost a son in the Pacific. Then she said: 'If you're looking for a security risk, I suggest you investigate me, because I don't see any reason for an Indian to be fighting for a government that has stolen lands from the Indian people.' She just shouted at them to get the hell off her porch. Gee, they just back-pedaled off and went." (Laughs.)

I met a bunch of Eskimos from Alaska that the Methodists got hold of. They call it the Methodist ethic. If you work, you're good, if you don't, you're bad. I don't impose that ethic on other people. These Eskimos are now so task-oriented, they're very, very hyper. They don't know how to relax. The Methodists got hold of their heads, and they lost what they had. They're in a mad dash all the time and don't know how to sit and cogitate.

My little six-year-old will go out, just sit and talk to one of those trees or observe the birds. He can be calm and comfortable doing that. He hasn't been through the same brainwash that the rest of us have.

There's a knowledge born in these little ones that ties back to the spirit world, to the Creator. Those little kids in school can tell you that the nations of fish are their brothers and sisters. They'll tell you that their life is no more important than the life of that animal or that tree or that flower. They're born knowing that. It's that our school doesn't beat it out of them.

History's important, what happened in the past is important. But I'm not satisfied with just talking about what happened in 1855 or what happened in 1903, during the murders, or 1961, when they seized our hospital. I want my children to have something good to say in 1990 about what happened in 1979. They're not gonna look in the mirror and see themselves as Indians with no future.

My little son shares the continent with 199,999,999 other folks. (Laughs.) If your government screws up and creates one more damned war, his little brown ass will get blown away, right along with all your people. All those colors (laughs) and all those attitudes. The bombs that come don't give a damn if he's got cute little braids, is a little brown boy, talks to cedar trees, and is a sweet little person.

I see the United States government as a little baby brat. If you say no, it throws something at you. If it sees something, it just grabs. Just drools all over and soils itself, and has to have others come in and clean it up. It's a 200-year-old kid. They gave us dual citizenship in 1924. How can a little teeny stupid 150-year-old government grant citizenship to a Yakima Indian who has been here for eight million years? To a Puyallup? What an insult! (Laughs.) How can a lying little trespasser that doesn't know how to act right grant anything to anybody? Why doesn't somebody get that kid in line? Eventually, some stranger will go over and grab that little kid and shake 'im up. I think the United States is just rapidly heading to be shaken around. Unfortunately, I'm living right here and I'm gonna get shaken around right along with the rest of us. (Laughs.) We're all in the same canoe.

SOWING ON THE MOUNTAIN

FLORENCE REESE

Come all you poor workers, good news to you I'll tell
How the good old union has come in here to dwell.
Which side are you on? Which side are you on?

Grandmotherly-appearing, much like the TV stereotype: gray-haired,
sweet-faced, glasses. She is seventy-nine.

I was born in Union City, Tennessee. Farmin' country. When I was writing songs, I was just small. I would write about anything that came to mind. After I got older, I began to write about the workers. I wanted to do something better than just frilly songs or little songs, so I began to write bigger songs, until I got up to write "Which Side Are You On?"

My father was a coal miner. He was killed in the mines, 1914. He was loadin' coal for fifteen cents a ton, and he was pushin' it on a wooden track about a hundred fifty feet. The coal operators didn't bury 'im and they didn't give my mother not one penny. Miners would get killed. Just almost every week, you'd see a man brought out. If he wasn't dead, he was crushed.

You could see the miners—I'd go sometimes at four o'clock in the morning—they had a little kerosene lamp that they put on their cap and it had a wick in it. Like fireflies, the mountains would be full of 'em agoin' to the mines. They'd go in there and maybe never come out. They didn't have safety nor anything. It was a real hard life to live, without a union. So in 1917, they got the union and miners together. They began to get better wages.

When they got the union—why, it was 1922—they come out on strike again. The guards and thugs started there after the miners, and the miners had to hide out in the woods. They'd get together and organize. They sent the National Guard in to put the men out, put their furniture out and everything.

Oh, my husband was a miner, too. He has black lung. He was organizin'. They would go from one mine to another to get the men to come out. The thugs'd come and ask him if he'd come back to work, and he said if they got a contract, he would. If they didn't, he wouldn't. And they started on him. They wanted to do away with him. So they arrested him and took him to Harlan jail. They took him out thar and they stopped. They thought if he'd try to run away, they'd shoot him. They wanted an excuse. So he wouldn't run. He just set there until they got ready to take him. They took him on to jail and kept him there with five more men on the concrete floor. One of the men went up there and tried to make bond for him, but they wouldn't let him. So the next day, they took him to Pineville jail.

And then he come home. But they still kept after him. John Henry Blair, he was with the coal operators. He was the high sheriff, and he would hire what he said was deputy sheriffs, but they was gun thugs, real gun thugs. They would search miners' houses, and if they had any guns, they'd take the guns. They'd take the miners off to jail.

So they come to our houses and they come in four or five carloads. They'd have two pistols, they'd have belts of cartridges, they'd have high-powered rifles. So they come up there, they searched our house, and they looked in everything in our house. They looked in suitcases, under the mattress, in the stove, in the chest. In a few days, they'd come back and say: "Well, we're back." I said: "What're you after?" They said: "We're lookin' for IWW papers." I didn't know what IWW was, and I asked the neighbors if they knew. And they said no. I said: "Well, it's time we're findin' out, then maybe they'd help us with the gun thugs." But we didn't find out. So we just stayed on.

They was on strike in 1930 and '31. I told the thugs that I'm not used to anything like this. They was a bunch of 'em, all in the house. I didn't know what to do because Sam was gone and most of the men was gone. So I thought: Well, I could write somethin', maybe. Maybe I could get it out. We didn't have any food. You could see little children with big stomachs. They'd eat anything they could get. The miners, you could see 'em kinda staggerin'.

So they put one miner in jail, George Taylor. His wife had pellagra. She'd stay with me and they'd say: "Florence, aren't you afraid you'll catch it?" I said: "No, that woman caught that pellagra at the table because she didn't have nothin' to eat." So she took her little twin daughters and went to see her husband in jail, and she saw John Henry Blair. He probably had a guilty conscience. He saw the condition the mother was in, and he gave the little girls a dime apiece. He told the daddy: "If you leave the state, I'll turn you out." He said: "I'll not do it. I want to stay here and help organize." But they made it so hard on his family that he left. It was gettin' worse and worse. I thought I *had* to do somethin'.

I had an old calendar there, and I jerked it off the wall. It was the only paper I had. I began to write "Which Side Are You On?" The longer I wrote, the faster I got. The words was just—to me, it was like somebody else, it wasn't me, it was comin' so fast. I was so hurt and worried and scared, too. So then I put the tone to an old hymn. I was a Baptist. The words I remember is (sings):

I'm gonna land on that shore
I'm gonna land on that shore
I'm gonna land on that shore
And be saved forever.

So I took that, it come from that—"Which Side Are You On?" (She sings:)

We're starting our good battle, we know we're sure to win
Because we've got the gun thugs alookin' very thin.
Which side are you on? Which side are you on?

I just got to eighth grade. There was no high school in the coal camp, so I went as far as I could go. I wanted to be a writer more than anything. But then I thought I couldn't be a writer. I didn't know enough. I thought: Well, if I get to go to college, I might become one. But I just forgot about that. Some of 'em says: "I'm glad you didn't go because if you had, you wouldn't a wrote the things that you've written now and you wouldn't be athinkin' like you did now. You'd want to go to higher fields and write different things." But I knew what I wanted to do. A lot of the miners had children like that. They wanted to do better for themselves, but they couldn't.

When I was little, four, five years old, my brothers and sisters, if we'd have anything, a cat or a dog or anything, why they told me we would have a funeral and they'd say: "You have to sing over it." I wouldn't know a song, but I'd make one up. From then on, they started callin' me preacher. (Laughs.)

My mother's father was an old Baptist preacher. She was a teacher. My father, though, he didn't get much schoolin'. He would just spell the words like they sounded. So my mother, she would be so sorry for him. He was a good man, a hard worker. He moved us to the country for a while, and he'd walk two mountains when he wanted to come home. Sometimes every two weeks, sometimes it'd be a month. We'd get a letter from him. She'd read it to us children and she'd say: "Poor Jim, poor Jim." She wanted him to know more, but it was too late.

So I married a miner myself. I had ten children. I've got seven now. Thirty-one grandchildren and eight great-grandchildren. And I'm happy to say not a one's ever crossed a picket line. (Laughs.) They know how we stand.

At Brookside, where they had the strike, the judges, they'd get after the men, so the women, they took over. The men didn't want 'em to. I went up there, and I told 'em to let 'em do it. When the scabs would come in, the women'd turn 'em back. They'd whip 'em with switches, they'd hit 'em with sticks, and they'd scratch their faces all to pieces. Some of the scabs got past 'em and got up on the mountain. The sheriff and the highway patrol, they drug 'em across there. When they come back, the women was waitin' on 'em. They wouldn't let 'em go home. The scabs said: "We gotta get home." The women said: "You got up there, now you're gonna stay there." One woman, she'd been to jail. I said: "Did you ever whip a scab?" This finger of hers had long nails, and she said: "See them nails? I dig them off on one of them scab's faces. I dug him all to pieces." And she did. They told us that Hitler said that women's duty was church, children, and kitchen. That's not true at all.

I would go to the store. I would see plenty of food, I would see clothes. Still I'd see the people that they didn't have it. I wondered why it was. I didn't know, nobody ever told me. We had to do all the work, the miners, but they didn't get the money for it. Somebody got the money while they done the work. They made ever'thing, but they didn't get it.

Before my father died, we didn't get a newspaper. You remember the *Titanic* when it sunk? I never knowed where he found out about the *Titanic*. Maybe someone told him. He said: "They put the poor below, they's the first that had to go." My father, he would read his Bible. When he'd come out of the mines, he'd always go to the stove and get that coffee pot, and he'd get him a cup of coffee, and he'd probably go out on the front porch. I remember he come in and he says: "There's some more of them rich sons of bitches gone to hell." And mother says: "Jim, not that kinda talk in front of these children." It frightened me. I didn't know what he meant by that.

I thought: Why would they put the poor to drown first? They'd be sure to go, and if anybody got out, the rich would get out. So I began to wonder. I kept thinkin' about that, and I tried to talk to Mother about it, but she wouldn't talk about it. I began to think about there was somethin' better, that there should be somethin' better for the workers. But I had nobody to explain it to me. I couldn't understand why it was.

Well, I'd see people aprayin' and offer their hands for work, and they didn't get it. And they'd say: "The Bible says the prayers of the righteous avail us much, prayers of the wicked avail us nothin'." But they's wicked, and their prayers would be answered. I couldn't understand that. I'd say: "Why if they're so wicked do they live so good and we have to live so poor?" I thought that the poor should have decent wages and decent homes to live in and good medical care. But we kept workin' and workin', and if all the workers would stick together, we'd have one big union and we'd have better times for all.

America's good and beautiful. They tell me we're the richest nation in the world. And the most Christian nation. I don't believe it. We may be rich, but we're not the most Christian nation. Or it wouldn't be as bad as it is. There's robbery, stealin', killin', and rape agoin' on all the time. People don't want to do that. It's forced on 'em. They put 'em in jail and it makes 'em worse. If I'm gonna steal a loaf of bread because I'm hungry, they're gonna put me in jail. But if a millionaire steals somethin' with a pencil, he would go up to the top, he's not put in jail. I don't think it should be that way.

They don't work, and the men goes out and works and they want to have a good home and take their children to the seashore and to the mountains and all them places and get 'em a good education. If my daddy'd a had his rights, he'd had a good education. And I coulda had one. Then we could write and things like that.

It's a beautiful country, and it could be made good for people. But they'll have to do it for themselves, just like the coal miners. If they let 'em break the United Mine Workers, it's just like a big dam breakin'. They'll do away with the automobile, the steel workers, the rubber workers, the textile, there'll be no unions. And they'll go back to work for fifty cents a day. I told 'em, I said: "Don't let your fellow men push that wagon to the top of the hill and you jump on and ride over. You help him push it up thar and you'll both ride over and get there quicker." (She sings:)

> *If you go to Harlan County, there is no neutral there.*
> *You'll either be a union man or a scab for J. H. Blair.*
> *Which side are you on? Which side are you on?*
>
> *They say they have to guard us to educate their child.*
> *Their children live in luxury, our children almost wild.*
> *Which side are you on? Which side are you on?*
>
> *Gentlemen, can you stand it? Oh, tell me, how you can.*
> *Will you be a gun thug or will you be a man?*
> *Which side are you on? Which side are you on?*

JOE BEGLEY

We're seated on the porch of the general store, Joe and Gaynell Begley, proprietors. Blackey, Kentucky. It is in the eastern part of the state. The Cumberlands, despite a heavy fog—or is it smog?—are impressive. We're not too far from the Virginia border.

Driving along a dirt road off Route 7, into what appeared to be a ghost town, we had asked an ambling, gaunt, Lincolnesque figure the whereabouts of Joe Begley. "You're talkin' to 'im," he replied.

He is sixty years old.

"Forty-five years ago, Blackey was an incorporated town. There were seven coal mines here, deep minin'. They had six passenger trains here a day. We had a bank, we had a drugstore, we had an ice plant, we had a hotel, we had two or three restaurants. Along about '19 and '27, they had a tremendous flood here that destroyed a lot of things. Immediately after that, the depression wiped some more out. It's been a battle ever since."

To me, the mountains here has been kind of a wild animal refuge for people. I don't think people know the history of Appalachia. They don't know much about the history of the country, as far as that goes. The school system has failed. It's been dead for a hundred years.

It took me fifty years to stand up and make an about-face and realize who I was and what I was doin'. What I was taught was a Mickey Mouse world, a make-believe thing. I knew nothing about a broad-form deed until fifteen years ago. I knew nothing about the Trail of Tears. Our schools tell us nothin' about this. I didn't get to go to school, so somewhere along the line I shoulda picked up on that.

My grandmother was a Cherokee Indian, and her family escaped the Trail of Tears. She could remember about her folks tellin' her about our federal soldiers amarchin' fifteen or twenty thousand Cherokee people outa here to North Carolina and Georgia, scatterin' 'em out. It's not in the textbooks, the massacres. She was part of the ones that refused to leave here. I feel I owe my grandmaw somethin'. I think I owe this environment somethin'. I don't approve of George Armstrong Custer and I don't approve of the way industry has dominated people here the last fifty years.

My grandmaw was tellin' me one thing, and my father was tellin' me another. I was taught that Indians was undesirable, that black people was undesirable, that poor people was undesirable. It took me fifty years to admit that I was wrong and go in another direction.

My father said: "We can't survive in this community if we don't learn to keep our mouth shut. Your grandmaw is old and she's atellin' you somethin' that she *thinks* happened." My father was scared. He needed a job, he had a family. That's what's wrong with this country: we're all runnin' scared.

My father was a well-liked man in the community. When I was a little boy, I saw him and five other men stand out like roses in a wheat field. They was helping poor people, they was tellin' 'em how to go to court, they was afurnishin' lawyers for 'em, they was afurnishin' 'em beans and 'taters. They was loadin' up wagons of groceries, sendin' it to the head of one of those hollers, to a poor man who couldn't help hisself. The church didn't go along with these men because occasionally they drank a little whiskey. Actually, they was castouts, but they was people really doin' somethin' in our community. My father had—what did they call it?—a split personality.

When I was small, environment was important to me. I missed school because I wanted to kick around in the mountains. I was watchin' the game. I was in the rivers and streams. I didn't have time to go to school because I could read a book in ten minutes and the teacher's talk was like a preacher's. I heard a hundred preachers, and they preach the same tune all the way. I've just not got the time to tolerate that. I wanna live thirty years, and every year I'm gonna try to live thirty years. Life is short as it is. I'd like to live a hundred fifty years. I wish everybody could live a hundred fifty years. My dreams was to meet all sorts of people. They had a story to tell. I wanted to see where they went and where I was gonna go.

"I was in the navy, a torpedo man. At that time, I thought blowin' up Japanese ships and killin' people was fine, and we were citationed for that. Thirty-five years later, I lay awake at night, I have nightmares. I've got my family raised, and they're in pretty good condition, nothin' to worry about financially. They've got homes and good jobs. But these other people here in the hollers that got no money and cold nights in the wintertime and freezin'. And I wake up with a temperature and salt water in my mouth, and I got to thinkin' about bein' in the navy and torpedoin' the hell out of people, and it's got me rattled some."

Actually, I'd like to been probably a lawyer. I'd like to know the law of the land, because all my life people were denied of their rights. That's still on my mind. We've got highly educated people, and I guess that's somethin' that I wanted to be. I wanted to be part of helpin' somebody else, one way or the other. I always had it since I was a little boy.

Where I really needed an education is when a highly skilled educated man is shootin' his mouth and knockin' me down with some goddamn big words that I don't understand and the skillful way that he does it I know nothin' about. That's the place that I would like to have an education, so I could knock him down.

The people here, they're livin' on the richest natural resources in the world, yet they get no part of it. Around a hundred years ago, industry from up north sent these land agents here, skillful lawyers, and got this land for twenty-five cents an acre. The people signed a contract known as a broad-form deed. It took everything they had away from 'em fifty or ninety years later. People here were never educated, didn't know how to read or write, and signed with an X. Industry bought the rights of what they called natural gas and timber. It didn't mention anything about strippers or bulldozers. The people knew nothin' of the modern methods of minin' coal, gas and oil, mica, limestone. It's all here. There's twelve precious metals here that big industry will come and get. Jewel Ridge, Blue Diamond, where'd these companies' names come from? The children and the grandchildren of these broad-form-deed recipients, they thought they owned the land. You know that song? "This Land Is Your Land?" There's a legal device that says it's not your land. As long as it's like that, it's gonna be trouble here. Ever since I was a little boy, my father taught me to buy something legal and honest. He said: "If you buy an acre of land, you own it hell deep and heaven high." No such thing with a broad-form deed.

They're just strip minin', auger minin', surface minin'. It's complete destruction of the hills. The strip miner just blasts the whole top off, and this all eventually comes into the streams and air, taking all the wildlife, destroyin' homes, runnin' people out. It's an ugly, indecent way to get coal. I call strip-mine operators sidewinders or rattlesnakes. They're destroyin' Appalachia. If we kill a rattlesnake, the law's in back of us. But these rattlesnakes got the law on their side.

Oh, it's a fast way of gettin' coal. You bet. In Reno, Nevada, there's a gamblin' joint, they have a silver slipper that's lit up by light bulbs and power-operated neon lights. From that one sign, enough power is generated to furnish power to 3,400 five-room houses to poor people. Not long ago, at Northhampton railroad yards, there were fifty-six 670-ton railroad cars of coal awaitin' at a dock to be loaded to go into Japan. This is what's buryin' the people of Appalachia.

Austin Miller, a friend seated on the porch, interjects: "Where I live, they have this big road goes about six hundred feet above it. They cut these big trees around the hill and all this dirt goes all over in the trees to hold it for a time, and when the trees rot out and the water gets behind it, why it's all slide down and cover your home up. That's on most all these strip-minin' jobs. Pretty soon, it's gonna rot out and cover everybody up.

"The companies just pull out and leave. They operate under so many different names, if you get in a lawsuit, you don't know who to start with."

People, when it's rainin', avoid livin' in their home. Emmett Sexton's already moved out. He told me he hasn't slept in his home for three weeks. The big slides were comin' in, and he didn't know but what they were gonna cover him up.

The operators used to avoid comin' near the highway where people can see what they're doin'. They know they were doin' wrong. But now there's such a demand for coal, they don't give a damn who sees it.

Some of our neighbors wanted to put in a laundromat and a car wash, to develop some jobs. We could do it in a way that wouldn't pollute the streams, buyin' the right kinda soaps. But our health officers here condemned it right off the bat. Yet they let these strip-minin' operators and the deep mines pour tremendous acid, pollutin' the streams.

A few of our neighbor boys were fishin' without a license, and the conservation officer got 'em. These boys are too poor to pay fines. I run into the game warden and I said: "Did you write any citations for the big minin' industry?" He dropped his head, grinned a little bit, and said: "I'm gonna tear all these up. Let's forget about it."

A young fella just got back from Vietnam, and his land was bein' destroyed by the strip miners. His lawyer said: "You ain't got a chance. All the court officials is in the coal business." He got all kinds of citations for killin' people he didn't even know, and he runs into this. He's gettin' a new education, and he's gettin' it the hard way. Lot of our young people is seein' it like this.

People here in Appalachia have been poor for a hundred thirty years. We have about ninety thousand people in these four counties that's under thirty-six hundred dollars a year. I'm talkin' about dirt-poor people. Many's on welfare and got black lung and emphysema.

Some of 'em can't hear. They're good people, honest people, and they have worked awful hard all their lives.

People come up and they say: "We've been beaten down so many times, what the hell's the use to stand up and fight now? We need to win some battles." We formed a Citizens League to Protect Surface Rights. There's little organizations like us all over the country with the same kind of complaint. And we beginnin' to win some battles.

I don't know if this thing in Appalachia can be settled without violence or not. I hope it can. I was taught to recognize the American flag, to pledge allegiance, to serve in the navy, and to do my part. But now, with the bulldozers, I just don't believe poor people is just gonna sit still and take it. A man can't run scared. If he does, he might as well end it right now.

We want to do it legally and politely. Then, if you can't get justice, there's other ways. I don't want violence. But people here got reason to be violent. I saw the deer go and I saw the beaver go and I saw the fish go and the game go and the streams go, and now I'm beginnin' to see the people go—when all this can happen in my sixty years, you wonder where is the end.

"We know what happened in Vietnam. We were fightin' people we didn't even know. I was in the navy in Tonkin Gulf thirty-five years ago, and Ho Chi Minh and all his people were our friends. The Japanese was our bitter enemies. My son fought in Vietnam the very same people that was a friend to me and against somethin' else. And here in these hills, the people really out to destroy us is backed by our government. I'm confused. I'm trying to determine the good from the bad."

I believe in law and order. I was a police officer for four years. I been a deputy sheriff for probably twenty-nine years. I put a lotta people in jail. Recently, I helped get some escapees. They called me and said: "We don't wanna be killed. We want you to come and get us. We know you won't beat us up, you won't treat us bad." I took 'em to jail. Some of the best friends I got is some of the people I've put in jail. I don't believe in blackjackin', I don't believe in pistol whippin'. I believe in tryin' to tell 'em just what they done and why they should not do it. To be decent with people, that's the main thing.

I been a jack-of-all-trades. I could shovel coal, I can lay track, I can pull a jack, I can pick and shovel, but that's not what I want to do. I wanna fix a motor, to understand what's wrong with it. If it works on a motor, it works on a man. Trouble is, we don't give a damn how it works. We know it works, but we don't know why it works. We got a Mickey Mouse educational system that doesn't teach us how things work, how the government works, who runs it.

People know somethin's missin'. During a lifetime, a man just runs over all these calamities. I hope that he can remember most of 'em. He tries to go back. I don't believe in goin' back. It's all out in front of me, they's no back. Let the dead stay dead, and let's move on. But this country is goin' over it so fast, they've got no time to realize the beauty of it and the miracle of why in the hell we're here in the first place.

The hills, to me, was somethin' God put here in the beginnin', and they been here, I imagine, for four million years. The streams were clear, the timber was green, there was all sorts of wildlife. They weren't put here to be torn all to hell by bulldozers, by greedy people.

You don't give up because a handful of people can win in this country. A handful of people in the beginnin' saved this country. They did the fightin' while three quarters of 'em, by God, watched it. You don't need an army, you don't need ten thousand people. You need a few people determined to win. I don't wanna win 'em all. I'm glad we lost some of 'em. If we'd a won 'em all, we'd a had nothin' to fight for. If you finish a buildin', it's done. You don't work no more. We don't want to finish the buildin', we don't want this land to end. We want it to go on and on and on and on. I want to live to be old, old, old, and watch it. I'm sixty years old, and I'm gonna live another sixty, and I'm gonna enjoy it like the first sixty years, and the last goddamn flicker of my life will be against somethin' and not for it. I'm gonna be challengin' all the way.

GAYNELL BEGLEY

Joe's wife.

She is behind the counter at the store. There is a steady stream of customers: small children, old people, husky young men off the road repair gang. The sales: a Coke, a bag of potato chips, a carton of milk, a loaf of bread. No Rolls-Royce salesman is any more solicitous of his patrons. She addresses each by name. There are constant soft, jocular exchanges. "A transaction here is not entirely economic. It's a matter of friendship and socializin' for a minute. That's as important to me as gettin' that quarter."

This is America to an awful lot of people who don't really realize it's bein' pulled out from under 'em. That's the only time I get scared. I'm not really pessimistic at all, but I do hate to see certain things go. I got a letter from my sister who lives in Eddyville, but it's got a Paducah postmark. It's such a small thing, but it just tears me up. It's typical of the thinkin' of big government. What does the Eddyville postmark mean to them? Or Blackey?

It's not the same kind of population I grew up with. Just about every house then had father, mother, and a group of children. Now about every third house is a widow whose children have gone to Ohio or Michigan to get a job. Most of 'em would like to come back if they could make a livin'. Our elementary school in Blackey covers the first eight grades. Seventy percent of the hundred twenty students are eligible for free lunches. That tells you somethin' about the town. It's just heartbreakin'.

We have a lot of sick people. The men who've worked so long in the mines have black lung or—this man who was just in here without hands. They were blown off in a dynamite cap accident. There's not the same spirit in the town. Well, of course, there's not the same spirit in me. My mother and daddy had a restaurant. We're talkin' about the middle twenties, before the crash. She made all the pies herself, oh Lord, the most fantastic pies. It was a real busy place. The coal mines were workin'. Then, it was the expectancy. Things were going to happen to me in the future. Now it's just an awful lot of lookin' backward.

I'm ashamed of my expectations because now I know a lotta things I didn't know then. Advice from older people I respected was: Hurry up, get educated, and get out. I really didn't do any deep thinkin' about myself, who I was, what I could be. I just didn't think I'd ever come back to eastern Kentucky. I marked it off my list. (Laughs.)

I went to Berea College and then to New England to work. I had no idea that to be a mountaineer, to be an Appalachian, to be a hillybilly, was somethin' a person would be remotely proud of. I was terribly ashamed of it and didn't want anybody to know when I left here. In Connecticut, '39 and '40, I would try to talk the way they talked to show everybody I'd risen above bein' a hillbilly. I'm well over it now. Joe took care of that. (Laughs.)

Oh, I was really proud of my family. But back in my head, I'd keep thinkin': Why did such fine people stay in such a place? They could have gone to the bluegrass country. I really would not like to have been a mountaineer. Then I met Joe and, boy, there was nothin' about him that he was ashamed of. That was really great.

My daddy's name, Caudill, is one of the commonest around here. That's 'cause they were early settlers, dating back to the American Revolution. George Washington paid off some of his soldiers with land grants instead of money. One of his young soldiers was a James Caudill from North Carolina. For his payment he received several hundred acres. This was called Virginia at the time. He came here just before the 1800s and settled about two miles up. He was my grandfather's grandfather, unless I've left out a "great" somewhere. (Laughs.) Oh yes, we've been here a long time.

The idea that our land was no longer ours first came to me when I was about sixteen or seventeen. I was wantin' desperately to go to college, but there was absolutely no money. Yet down the road was a girl who was gettin' ready to go to college, with trunks and trunks of clothes. Her parents owned the mine. But it was my grandpa's land. Somewhere in my mind was the idea that there was somethin' at odds here. You can't believe how many years it took me to get to the root of the problem: the broad-form deed. This absentee owner is the same as the few men who own America, really.

What really makes me mad is when people talk about the poor. I'm not real sure who they are talkin' about. To me, the people who come in here happen to be desperately poor. But they're Stella and Uncle Wash and Bob. They're individuals. Bein' poor is just one more part of 'em as people. I wish they weren't. But they're not somebody on paper, just a percentage to us.

My daddy was a really, really patriotic person. He so strongly believed that the government was good and the government will protect you. I once believed that, but I no longer do. I'm not patriotic the same way my daddy was. I don't have this terribly nationalistic feelin' at all. I just can't see the insanity of dividin' the world into countries. Not that I want everything to blend. I love the diversity: the different look and the different speech and the different people. But I just feel one-worldish. (Laughs.)

What is education? I don't know how you get it. I think when you're educated, you're able to view things realistically and see yourself as part of a community and that community as part of the world. There's somethin' inside you that propels you. It's not without, with an educated person. If he's answerable to himself, he's an educated man.

When I was a little girl, I loved to read. One of the series of books my mother bought me was *The Chinese Twins*. There were *The English Twins, The Scottish Twins*, a series of books. They were really real to me. Here were these children from all over the world, but they weren't all that different from me. That's the earliest I can remember of people bein' different but still all part of the family.

I like poetry awful well, and Edna St. Vincent Millay wrote one when she was about eighteen. She said:

All I could see from where I stood
Was three long mountains and a wood;
I turned and looked another way,
And saw three islands in a bay.

And then it goes on to say—oh, darn. (Laughs.)

A man was starving in Capri;
He moved his eyes and looked at me;

You know, she saw over the hills to the rest of the world. It just touched me early, early, early, and made me think I was kin.

THE DIPLOMA

HARTMAN TURNBOW

A farm near Tchula, Mississippi, some sixty miles out of Jackson. He and his wife are at the screened door, greeting us. He is an ebullient, powerfully built man whose appearance confounds the calendar. He is seventy-five, though he can pass for fifty. There is a singing tone to his speech.

On the wall are portraits of two of his daughters in their gradua-tion dresses. There are several plaques. One is "For dedication and leadership in the fight for human rights. Tchula Attendance Center, May 1978." Another is "For inspirational efforts in human rights. The Mason Delta, 1978." The third is a high school diploma, 1976.

I started workin' in the field when I was eight years old. Full day with the plow. I just got my schoolin' part-time. Now I got big enough to get it by myself at age seventy-one. If I hadn't known somethin', I couldn't a got by in a heap of places, but I did. (Laughs.)

My grandfather was a slave. His own master was his daddy. He got free, and his own daddy sold him the place he was a slave on. Then he died, and his wife, my grandmother, willed me the place. I still own some portion of it today. I lived with them till I growed up to be a man. I'm still able to work, but I'm plannin' on restin' up this year.

Now you take the difference 'tween the hills and this delta. The hill was where, right after the war, most of the Negroes bought their places. Most of them's old marsters sold them little homes. But in this here delta, they didn't sell 'em none. The delta was in plantations and they wanted the Negroes for labor. Each plantation had some forty to two hundred head of mules in the lot. They'd haul from twenty-five to a hundred head of sharecroppers on the place, Negro families. They all belonged to the boss. They didn't have nowheres else to go. They lived like that, year in and year out, till the late forties. Now here comest the breakin' up.

The plantations didn't break up, but there comest the doin' away with labor. Comest the tearin' down the sharecroppers' houses, the timber shacks. There's machinery now on the plantation, convertin' 'em from labor form to a machinery-ized form, and they didn't need the labor no more. Bosses just tol' 'em to move: "We don't need you no more." They would tear the shacks down, give 'em away, sell 'em for little. Folks would haul 'em to town and rebuilt 'em. Couple of families, three families would double up in 'em. It never did catch me 'cause my place was my grandmother willed me. I had a home. They couldn't pressure me.

A lot of 'em thought, at that point, they would get to slave the Negroes again. They thought the Negroes would be glad to work for two bits a day. Some of 'em tol' me that, the plantation bosses. It didn't work out like they had planned.

Only thing I can see what took care of the sharecroppers was welfare. God must have jumped in the mind of the big-shot leaders of the U.S.A., 'cause it never had been a welfare department in that town. You got too old to work, they'd send you to that poorhouse and just sit up there an' eat what they give you till you die.

When they tore all the labor away, why the labor comest to move into these little towns. Some of 'em had a few folks in the North, and they goin' north an' just goin' every which a way. Just anywhere they could get the stake or just a little bunk. Right at that point, the federal government commenced to feedin' 'em.

American Dream? (He laughs loud and long.) That ol' slave-time spirit still lives today. It's not dead. Just like when they unloaded the first shipload of slaves in Richmond, Virginia. That spirit among the whites is still alive today, that thought is still among 'em. There's a Ku Kluck Klan aspringin' back to life, no joke. You know the prediction they made? They said that in fifteen years, they're goin' to reslave the Negroes.

You take the white people here in the South. They is very shrewd people. They ain't learned too much of a lesson 'cause it ain't nothin' hard on 'em yet. What really need the lessson today is Negroes. They need a big lesson. All the Negroes need educatin' to what the whites got in mind to do. You take the young Negroes. I go back an' talk about in the days I come along, when I lived on the plantations, how the white man would take Negroes in the blacksmith shop or in the barn, and he would whup 'em with a strap just like you whup chilluns.

They whupped me on it once. I'd be lyin' if I said they didn't whup me. I was a boy 'bout sixteen years old. It was two of 'em, they jus' grabbed me by the head and snatched me down and put his pistol to the back of my neck and went to beatin' me with this strap.

The young one today, you tell 'em that, they say "maloney," ain't nothin' to it. You go tellin' 'em about the white man today who talks friendly, pats you on the back, no soon's he gets out of your hearance an' out of your sight, he benoogin'* with all his strength to get you with nothin'. The white man says the only way to handle a nigger is to get 'im with nothin'. I agree with 'im.

The onliest thing the Negro got out of the civil rights movement— all these here professional mens, black and white, lost their life, lost their homes, got broke, went to the penitentiary and that flusteration —there ain't but one thing the Negro gained. That was his votin' priv'lege. Most of 'em ain't got sense enough to use that.

Votin' rights don't amount to much. Now they got kangaroo courts all over Mississippi. Ain't no way under God's sun for a Negro to get involved with a white man and then go to court and win. Since the Ku Kluck Klan sprung back to life, they givin' the young Negroes long sentences when they send 'em to the penitentiary. Since I been a man, I never heard of as many young Negroes bein' in the penitentary as they got now.

* Maneuvering

194

Twenty years ago, a white man could kill a nigger any time he got ready. There wa'n't nothin' to it. The news didn't get outside the boundary lines of the county. Today, since the civil rights movement stirred up social equality, the white man's got a new eye. They let the Negro have nothin'. I didn't say it, the white folks said it: Put a nigger out of a job everywhere you can.

'Bout fifteen years ago in 'bout fourteen southern states, the Negroes owned twenty million acres of land. Now the Negroes own about three million acres of land. The Ku Kluck Klan says they're gonna buy that. An' you know how many Negroes is out of a job? It's gettin' worser.

I never got the feeling that I *really* wanted to be free till in '63. Till this civil rights movement started. Some folks up in Tennessee brought it down to Greenwood and then down in Holmes County. They run up on us here and asked about comin' down here teachin' us citizenship. Teachin' us to redish an' vote. We tol' 'em to come back, and we'd pray over it. They come back, and we told 'em yeah. We said we'll spend our money on it, we'll sell our cars on it, and we'll put our life on it. We like it. We think it's right.

Before that time, didn't no Negroes redish and didn't vote. The whites just got along theyselves, and they 'point whoever they wanted to be in office. I didn't think about it. I was just thinkin' about eatin' an' livin' an' gettin' an ol' piece of car. You work from sunup to sundown in the cotton. But at that time, I had done lef' the plantation. I was workin' for myself. I had seen there wasn't no future in workin' on a plantation. You could work fifty years, and you'd be just like you was when you started. I did want to have something at the end of life when I got too old to work.

So we went on an' studied citizenship in the churches. We'd have it twice a week, every Wednesday night and every Sunday. When we thought we knowed how to redish and vote, we went out and tried.

We went to Lexin'ton, the county seat. My wife didn't go, all mens went. There was about twenty of us. We got in our cars and went. We stopped before we got to the red light and pulled over to the side of the curb and we said: "Now, we're goin' to get out and we're goin' to walk in two's so they can't 'cuse us of blockin' the street." We say we goin' to walk a distance behind one another so they can't say we gangin' up. We did that.

We went on round to the south door of the courthouse, and we was met by Mr. Andrew Smith, the sheriff. No sooner was he seein' us, he asked us: "Where in the hell is you all goin'?" John Ball said: "We come to redish." He put one hand on his pistol and grabbed that billy club and drawed back. I stepped out of line. I told him: "Mr. Smith, we only come to redish." He woulda bust his hat on that one. He stopped an' said: "Well now, you all go round to the front door, to the north door of the courthouse, and huddle under that tree and don't keep no noise." We done that. We went round there and huddled under that tree and didn't keep no fuss. He got round there. He looked at us. He put one hand on his pistol. He put the other one on his club. He raised his voice: "All right now, who'll be the first? Twenty of us, lookin' one at the other. I said to myself: These niggers fixin' to run. So I just stepped out of line and I say: "Me, I'll be the first." He lowered his voice. He said: "All right, Turnbow, if you'll be the first, just go right downside the edge of the curb, go in the courthouse, the first door on the left, and do what you got to do."

I went in there and the lady's in there. Circus clerk wasn't in then. She said: "What do you want?" I said: "I want to redish to vote." She said: "Redish to *vote*?" I say: "Yes, ma'am, redish to vote." She said: "You'll have to wait till Mr. McClennan comes." I said: "May I have a seat and wait?" She said: "Yes, you may." I sit on a chair there till twelve. She says: "Lunchtime. I'm goin' to lunch." I say: "I'll be back after lunch." She says: "All right." 'Bout a quarter after one, I went back in there. Mr. McClennan was there. I walked in an' he said: "What can I do for you?" I say: "I want to redish to vote." He said: "Redish to *vote*?" I say: "Yes, sir, redish to vote." He just grabbed a book and just shoved it at me. Said: "Fill out that there." I read it and I understood it and I filled it out and shoved the book back and went on out. Another went in there and he redished. All that whole day they redished two of us.

Folks, white and colored, what knowed me well, some of 'em growed up with me, was climbin' up on cars, lookin' at me like I was somethin' out the zoo. Made a show. We went on home. After that, they wouldn't let nobody redish, givin' them that hard lit'acy tests. They sent a federal redish down an' put him in the post office. Everybody went down there and redishes and passed. That's how we got redished.

'Bout a week after that, a drove came in one night and they firebombed this room. They throwed a couple of fire bombs in that window and in the back bedroom and shot all in this room. (He points toward a hole in the wall.) See that hole there? That's a .45. (He points toward another hole.) There's one right through the edge of the bottom of that window.

We went to a meetin' that night, and somebody come here an' killed the dog or runned him off. We ain't seen 'im since. When we went to bed, 'bout one o'clock, it started. I was asleep.

Mrs. Turnbow interjects: "They went in the car and got all the registration books. We come out that room, me and the girl, she's fourteen, you couldn't see nothin' but smoke. He was gettin' his gun. We come on out and met these two white men. They stopped an' we stopped. When he come out, they shot at him an' he commenced shootin' at them.

"Then I went on with puttin' out the fire. Pulled the curtains down and put them out with water. I went in the back room and dragged the bed ticks outa there and come back here and poured water on the couches. I come totin' water 'cause I knew he was out there shootin'. I snapped the curtains down in the floor, all of 'em was burnin', and I run in the back room and drug all the bed clothes off the bed and sprankled water on."

I commenced shootin' at them. They commenced to runnin'.

That night, I called the Justice Department in Washington, D. C., and told 'em to send some FBI's to investigate the shootin' an' the burnin' and they did. 'Bout eight o'clock that morning, they were sittin' here, writin' up the story. After they got through writin' it up, sheriff he come back late that evening and arrests me and puts me in jail. Say I done it. Say I set the fire. Say no white man's been here. Said I shot the holes in the house. Say I fire-bombed both rooms.

I stayed in jail, and the FDP* bailed me out. They had a preliminary hearing here in Tchula and convicted me. They said I did it for publisky, to get on TV. The FBI's, they had a secretary, and she had one of the little old things you tap. That's all they did. They set the trial in Jackson, in the post office building in the federal court. Mr. John Doar from Washington, D. C., come and they done dropped the charges. They didn't have nothin' against me. That was the end of it. If it hadn't been for that, they'd agive me fifteen years in the Mississippi State Penitentiary.

Mrs. Turnbow interjects: "They came by here and shot in here again."

* Freedom Democratic party, formed by black Mississippians prior to the 1964 Democratic Convention

They rode along the road the next year and shot in the house several times. I called up the FBI from Jackson. Told 'em: "I'm just givin' you a chance to save somebody's life, 'cause if it happen again, I'm goin' to kill up a lot of folks. I got a wife an' a daughter, and I love my wife an' daughter jus' like you love yourn. I'm just black an' you white, but the same love you got your wife and daughter, I got for mine. You jus' go aroun' and find the evidence and then cover it up and don't even turn it in. I'm not askin' you to turn in nothin'. I'm just tellin' ya, if it happen again, I'm gonna kill till I get killed. It's up to you. That's all I got to tell you." It didn't happen no more. They knew exactly who done it.

That was fifteen years ago. All that shootin', all that killin', it ain't but one thing the Negroes got and that's just their votin' priv'lege. They ain't got nothin' else.

Mrs. Turnbow interjects: "They do hire colored people in the store, they hire them in the bank."

But they're fixin' to take that back. (Slightly irritated) I tell you things what's goin' on to happen a year ahead of time, and you just won't listen. Till it go to happenin'. Then I remind you. I keeps up.

The Negroes in the South done got to the height of their growthin'. They ain't gettin' further. The white folks all over the South done got together, and they said it ain't but one way to keep a Negro down. That's to get him with nothin'. If it wasn't for the welfare, two thirds of the Negroes would starve to death now.

Mr. Carthan, a young black man, an admirer of yours, is the mayor of Tchula.

He has all kinds of trouble. The white folks want him to just sit there in the mayor's seat and be a dummy. He won't do that, and they keep some kind of stuff goin' all the time. And Negroes is so crazy till the white folks just take 'em and make 'em fight against theyselves. If the Negroes ever goin' to make any progress and ever get out from under this here mess the white folks is puttin' 'em under, they goin' to have to get together, goin' to have to stay together, goin' to have to work together. One's troubles got to be the other's troubles. Negroes won't do that. The white folks is jus' makin' absolutely fools out of the Negroes. If the Negroes don't wake up and start to benoogin', the white folks is goin' to slave 'em. It's gettin' like it used to be. It ain't gettin' any better. They got counties in Mississippi where they don't even know the sunup. The Negroes are where they was twenty years ago.

Now you take Martin Luther King. The las' time I saw him, I was in Atlantic City, New Jersey, in the annual convention. Here was a young lady ask me what did I think of Reverend King's nonviolent plan. I tol' her: "I think Reverend King's nonviolent plan is one of the biggest bunches of maloney that ever was." He was sittin' here there, lookin' at me. They all laughed. And no sooner they get through laughin', she say: "How would you handle it if you was in his place?" I said: "I'd meet 'em with whatever they oppose with. If they oppose with a smile, I'd meet 'em with a smile. If they oppose with a gun, I'd meet 'em with a gun." Everybody in that meetin' got up an' shook my hand. I say: "If you don't stop, he goin' to die somewhere ahuddled up on the groun' akickin' in his blood like a horse. 'Cause all they want you to do is tuck your head, with no eyes up, and they'll kill you quick." Sure, they'd akilled me, my wife, and my daughter, and throwed us in the house an' let us burn up. It's just like I predicted to Martin Luther King in that meeting. They shot him in Tennessee, an' he died layin' down, kickin' in his blood.

I feel like God is jus' lettin' us hang here. I feel like if it wasn't for Him, it would be all over. There's a whole lot of points in the Bible. The Bible did say: If you dig a ditch for your brother, say, dig two, 'cause the first one is yours. Folk can get so sinful and so wicked an' turn from God so far till God lets those things happen to 'em to get their attention again. You take all those young Negroes everywhere that done forgot God. Every paper you pick up is full of killin', full of stealin', full of everythin' but goin' to church an' Sunday school. Why, God might jus' let the white folks slave 'em, beat 'em, long enough to get 'em back to their senses.

If Negroes would jus' get up and stan' together—but that's just an "if." They ain't goin' to get together an' stand up. In a little village town like Tchula, no sooner than they go to gettin' together than a white man comes to split 'em and start 'em to fightin', and they can't go nowhere. The white folks aroun' here, they all together. They on one accord.

They talkin' 'bout we makin' progress. We makin' dyin' progress. We makin' progress to dig our grave. That's the kind of progress we're makin'. My Lord in heaven, if I had another life to live and it was like this one, I wouldn't want it. In ten year from now, that the Negro don't be slaved, the good Lord'll be with 'em!

You know what kind of dream I'd like to see? The way I'd love to see America? I'd jus' love to see it that all folks could shake hands an' be brothers and forget they're different. Me and you jus' shake hands and be brothers. I live happy, treat you nice, and you treat me nice, and you forget I'm black and I forget you white. And just live. But it won't be.

How can we make it be?

(He laughs long and loud.) I don't know. I don't know when it's comin', but I won't be here to see it. It'll be a long way off. 'Fore time end, it ain't goin' to be no black folks and ain't goin' to be no white folks. It's just goin' to be just one race of peoples. That's the time everybody goin' to get total justice, but it won't be long then 'fore Jesus comes. That's what the Bible says. Everybody get plum satisfied an' contented, then he'll come. But I won't be here. It's goin' to be a rough mile an' a few days out, and I jus' feel sorry for the young folks.

The old ones, old marster had 'em trained to tell 'em what they do. To tell him what go on. So when they got free, that ol' tellinism was still in the Negroes, and they'll still do it. You'll find 'em all over the U.S.A. They'll tell the boss on other Negroes. All that kind of ism has got to die. They jus' got to keep a bein' born an' growin' up and dyin' till all that ol' ism goes.

C. P. ELLIS

We're in his office in Durham, North Carolina. He is the business manager of the International Union of Operating Engineers. On the wall is a plaque: "Certificate of Service, in recognition to C. P. Ellis, for your faithful service to the city in having served as a member of the Durham Human Relations Council. February 1977."

At one time, he had been president (exalted cyclops) of the Durham chapter of the Ku Klux Klan.

He is fifty-three years old.

My father worked in a textile mill in Durham. He died at forty-eight years old. It was probably from cotton dust. Back then, we never heard of brown lung. I was about seventeen years old and had a mother and sister depending on somebody to make a livin'. It was just barely enough insurance to cover his burial. I had to quit school and go to work. I was about eighth grade when I quit.

My father worked hard but never had enough money to buy decent clothes. When I went to school, I never seemed to have adequate clothes to wear. I always left school late afternoon with a sense of inferiority. The other kids had nice clothes, and I just had what Daddy could buy. I still got some of those inferiority feelin's now that I have to overcome once in a while.

I loved my father. He would go with me to ball games. We'd go fishin' together. I was really ashamed of the way he'd dress. He would take this money and give it to me instead of putting it on himself. I always had the feeling about somebody looking at him and makin' fun of him and makin' fun of me. I think it had to do somethin' with my life.

My father and I were very close, but we didn't talk about too many intimate things. He did have a drinking problem. During the week, he would work every day, but weekend he was ready to get plastered. I can understand when a guy looks at his paycheck and looks at his bills, and he's worked hard all the week, and his bills are larger than his paycheck. He'd done the best he could the entire week, and there seemed to be no hope. It's an illness thing. Finally you just say: "The heck with it. I'll just get drunk and forget it."

My father was out of work during the depression, and I remember going with him to the finance company uptown, and he was turned down. That's something that's always stuck.

My father never seemed to be happy. It was a constant struggle with him just like it was for me. It's very seldom I'd see him laugh. He was just tryin' to figure out what he could do from one day to the next.

After several years pumping gas at a service station, I got married. We had to have children. Four. One child was born blind and retarded, which was a real additional expense to us. He's never spoken a word. He doesn't know me when I go to see him. But I see him, I hug his neck. I talk to him, tell him I love him. I don't know whether he knows me or not, but I know he's well taken care of. All my life, I had work, never a day without work, worked all the overtime I could get and still could not survive financially. I began to say there's somethin' wrong with this country. I worked my butt off and just never seemed to break even.

I had some real great ideas about this great nation. (Laughs.) They say to abide by the law, go to church, do right and live for the Lord, and everything'll work out. But it didn't work out. It just kept gettin' worse and worse.

I was workin' a bread route. The highest I made one week was seventy-five dollars. The rent on our house was about twelve dollars a week. I will never forget: outside of this house was a 265-gallon oil drum, and I never did get enough money to fill up that oil drum. What I would do every night, I would run up to the store and buy five gallons of oil and climb up the ladder and pour it in that 265-gallon drum. I could hear that five gallons when it hits the bottom of that oil drum, splatters, and it sounds like it's nothin' in there. But it would keep the house warm for the night. Next day you'd have to do the same thing.

I left the bread route with fifty dollars in my pocket. I went to the bank and I borrowed four thousand dollars to buy the service station. I worked seven day a week, open and close, and finally had a heart attack. Just about two months before the last payments of that loan. My wife had done the best she could to keep it runnin'. Tryin' to come out of that hole, I just couldn't do it.

I really began to get bitter. I didn't know who to blame. I tried to find somebody. I began to blame it on black people. I had to hate somebody. Hatin' America is hard to do because you can't see it to hate it. You gotta have somethin' to look at to hate. (Laughs.) The natural person for me to hate would be black people, because my father before me was a member of the Klan. As far as he was concerned, it was the savior of the white people. It was the only organization in the world that would take care of the white people. So I began to admire the Klan.

I got active in the Klan while I was at the service station. Every Monday night, a group of men would come by and buy a Coca-Cola, go back to the car, take a few drinks, and come back and stand around talkin'. I couldn't help but wonder: Why are these dudes comin' out every Monday? They said they were with the Klan and have meetings close-by. Would I be interested? Boy, that was an opportunity I really looked forward to! To be part of somethin'. I joined the Klan, went from member to chaplain, from chaplain to vice-president, from vice-president to president. The title is exalted cyclops.

The first night I went with the fellas, they knocked on the door and gave the signal. They sent some robed Klansmen to talk to me and give me some instructions. I was led into a large meeting room, and this was the time of my life! It was thrilling. Here's a guy who's worked all his life and struggled all his life to be something, and here's the moment to be something. I will never forget it. Four robed Klansmen led me into the hall. The lights were dim, and the only thing you could see was an illuminated cross. I knelt before the cross. I had to make certain vows and promises. We promised to uphold the purity of the white race, fight communism, and protect white womanhood.

After I had taken my oath, there was loud applause goin' throughout the buildin', musta been at least four hundred people. For this one little ol' person. It was a thrilling moment for C. P. Ellis.

It disturbs me when people who do not really know what it's all about are so very critical of individual Klansmen. The majority of 'em are low-income whites, people who really don't have a part in something. They have been shut out as well as the blacks. Some are not very well educated either. Just like myself. We had a lot of support from doctors and lawyers and police officers.

Maybe they've had bitter experiences in this life and they had to hate somebody. So the natural person to hate would be the black person. He's beginnin' to come up, he's beginnin' to learn to read and start votin' and run for political office. Here are white people who are supposed to be superior to them, and we're shut out.

I can understand why people join extreme right-wing or left-wing groups. They're in the same boat I was. Shut out. Deep down inside, we want to be part of this great society. Nobody listens, so we join these groups.

At one time, I was state organizer of the National Rights party. I organized a youth group for the Klan. I felt we were getting old and our generation's gonna die. So I contacted certain kids in schools. They were havin' racial problems. On the first night, we had a hundred high school students. When they came in the door, we had "Dixie" playin'. These kids were just thrilled to death. I begin to hold weekly meetin's with 'em, teachin' the principles of the Klan. At that time, I believed Martin Luther King had Communist connections. I began to teach that Andy Young was affiliated with the Communist party.

I had a call one night from one of our kids. He was about twelve. He said: "I just been robbed downtown by two niggers." I'd had a couple of drinks and that really teed me off. I go downtown and couldn't find the kid. I got worried. I saw two young black people. I had the .32 revolver with me. I said: "Nigger, you seen a little young white boy up here? I just got a call from him and was told that some niggers robbed him of fifteen cents." I pulled my pistol out and put it right at his head. I said: "I've always wanted to kill a nigger and I think I'll make you the first one." I nearly scared the kid to death, and he struck off.

This was the time when the civil rights movement was really beginnin' to peak. The blacks were beginnin' to demonstrate and picket downtown stores. I never will forget some black lady I hated with a purple passion. Ann Atwater. Every time I'd go downtown, she'd be leadin' a boycott. How I hated—pardon the expression, I don't use it much now—how I just hated that black nigger. (Laughs.) Big, fat, heavy woman. She'd pull about eight demonstrations, and first thing you know they had two, three blacks at the checkout counter. Her and I have had some pretty close confrontations.

I felt very big, yeah. (Laughs.) We're more or less a secret organization. We didn't want anybody to know who we were, and I began to do some thinkin'. What am I hidin' for? I've never been convicted of anything in my life. I don't have any court record. What am I, C. P. Ellis, as a citizen and a member of the United Klansmen of America? Why can't I go to the city council meeting and say: "This is the way we feel about the matter? We don't want you to purchase mobile units to set in our schoolyards. We don't want niggers in our schools."

We began to come out in the open. We would go to the meetings, and the blacks would be there and we'd be there. It was a confrontation every time. I didn't hold back anything. We began to make some inroads with the city councilmen and county commissioners. They began to call us friend. Call us at night on the telephone: "C. P., glad you came to that meeting last night." They didn't want integration either, but they did it secretively, in order to get elected. They couldn't stand up openly and say it, but they were glad somebody was sayin' it. We visited some of the city leaders in their home and talk to 'em privately. It wasn't long before councilmen would call me up: "The blacks are comin' up tonight and makin' outrageous demands. How about some of you people showin' up and have a little balance?" I'd get on the telephone: "The niggers is comin' to the council meeting tonight. Persons in the city's called me and asked us to be there."

We'd load up our cars and we'd fill up half the council chambers, and the blacks the other half. During these times, I carried weapons to the meetings, outside my belt. We'd go there armed. We would wind up just hollerin' and fussin' at each other. What happened? As a result of our fightin' one another, the city council still had their way. They didn't want to give up control to the blacks nor the Klan. They were usin' us.

I began to realize this later down the road. One day I was walkin' downtown and a certain city council member saw me comin'. I expected him to shake my hand because he was talkin' to me at night on the telephone. I had been in his home and visited with him. He crossed the street. Oh shit, I began to think, somethin's wrong here. Most of 'em are merchants or maybe an attorney, an insurance agent, people like that. As long as they kept low-income whites and low-income blacks fightin', they're gonna maintain control.

I began to get that feeling after I was ignored in public. I thought: Bullshit, you're not gonna use me any more. That's when I began to do some real serious thinkin'.

The same thing is happening in this country today. People are being used by those in control, those who have all the wealth. I'm not espousing communism. We got the greatest system of government in the world. But those who have it simply don't want those who don't have it to have any part of it. Black and white. When it comes to money, the green, the other colors make no difference. (Laughs.)

I spent a lot of sleepless nights. I still didn't like blacks. I didn't want to associate with 'em. Blacks, Jews, or Catholics. My father said: "Don't have anything to do with 'em." I didn't until I met a black person and talked with him, eyeball to eyeball, and met a Jewish person and talked to him, eyeball to eyeball. I found out they're people just like me. They cried, they cussed, they prayed, they had desires. Just like myself. Thank God, I got to the point where I can look past labels. But at that time, my mind was closed.

I remember one Monday night Klan meeting. I said something was wrong. Our city fathers were using us. And I didn't like to be used. The reactions of the others was not too pleasant: "Let's just keep fightin' them niggers."

I'd go home at night and I'd have to wrestle with myself. I'd look at a black person walkin' down the street, and the guy'd have ragged shoes or his clothes would be worn. That began to do somethin' to me inside. I went through this for about six months. I felt I just had to get out of the Klan. But I wouldn't get out.

Then something happened. The state AFL-CIO received a grant from the Department of HEW, a $78,000 grant: how to solve racial problems in the school system. I got a telephone call from the president of the state AFL-CIO. "We'd like to get some people together from all walks of life." I said: "All walks of life? Who you talkin' about?" He said: "Blacks, whites, liberals, conservatives, Klansmen, NAACP people."

I said: "No way am I comin' with all those niggers. I'm not gonna be associated with those type of people." A White Citizens Council guy said: "Let's go up there and see what's goin' on. It's tax money bein' spent." I walk in the door, and there was a large number of blacks and white liberals. I knew most of 'em by face 'cause I seen 'em demonstratin' around town. Ann Atwater was there. (Laughs.) I just forced myself to go in and sit down.

The meeting was moderated by a great big black guy who was bushy-headed. (Laughs.) That turned me off. He acted very nice. He said: "I want you all to feel free to say anything you want to say." Some of the blacks stand up and say it's white racism. I took all I could take. I asked for the floor and I cut loose. I said: "No, sir, it's black racism. If we didn't have niggers in the schools, we wouldn't have the problems we got today."

I will never forget. Howard Clements, a black guy, stood up. He said: "I'm certainly glad C. P. Ellis come because he's the most honest man here tonight." I said: "What's that nigger tryin' to do?" (Laughs.) At the end of that meeting, some blacks tried to come up shake my hand, but I wouldn't do it. I walked off.

Second night, same group was there. I felt a little more easy because I got some things off my chest. The third night, after they elected all the committees, they want to elect a chairman. Howard Clements stood up and said: "I suggest we elect two co-chairpersons." Joe Beckton, executive director of the Human Relations Commission, just as black as he can be, he nominated me. There was a reaction from some blacks. Nooo. And, of all things, they nominated Ann Atwater, that big old fat black gal that I had just hated with a purple passion, as co-chairman. I thought to myself: Hey, ain't no way I can work with that gal. Finally, I agreed to accept it, 'cause at this point, I was tired of fightin', either for survival or against black people or against Jews or against Catholics.

A Klansman and a militant black woman, co-chairmen of the school committee. It was impossible. How could I work with her? But after about two or three days, it was in our hands. We had to make it a success. This give me another sense of belongin', a sense of pride.

This helped this inferiority feelin' I had. A man who has stood up publicly and said he despised black people, all of a sudden he was willin' to work with 'em. Here's a chance for a low-income white man to be somethin'. In spite of all my hatred for blacks and Jews and liberals, I accepted the job. Her and I began to reluctantly work together. (Laughs.) She had as many problems workin' with me as I had workin' with her.

One night, I called her: "Ann, you and I should have a lot of differences and we got 'em now. But there's somethin' laid out here before us, and if it's gonna be a success, you and I are gonna have to make it one. Can we lay aside some of these feelin's?" She said: "I'm willing if you are." I said: "Let's do it."

My old friends would call me at night: "C. P., what the hell is wrong with you? You're sellin' out the white race." This begin to make me have guilt feelin's. Am I doin' right? Am I doin' wrong? Here I am all of a sudden makin' an about-face and tryin' to deal with my feelin's, my heart. My mind was beginnin' to open up. I was beginnin' to see what was right and what was wrong. I don't want the kids to fight forever.

We were gonna go ten nights. By this time, I had went to work at Duke University, in maintenance. Makin' very little money. Terry Sanford give me this ten days off with pay. He was president of Duke at the time. He knew I was a Klansman and realized the importance of blacks and whites getting along.

I said: "If we're gonna make this thing a success, I've got to get to my kind of people." The low-income whites. We walked the streets of Durham, and we knocked on doors and invited people. Ann was goin' into the black community. They just wasn't respondin' to us when we made these house calls. Some of 'em were cussin' us out. "You're sellin' us out, Ellis, get out of my door. I don't want to talk to you." Ann was gettin' the same response from blacks: "What are you doin' messin' with that Klansman?"

One day, Ann and I went back to the school and we sat down. We began to talk and just reflect. Ann said: "My daughter came home cryin' every day. She said her teacher was makin' fun of me in front of the other kids." I said: "Boy, the same thing happened to my kid. White liberal teacher was makin' fun of Tim Ellis's father, the Klansman. In front of other peoples. He came home cryin'." At this point—(he pauses, swallows hard, stifles a sob)—I begin to see, here we are, two people from the far ends of the fence, havin' identical problems, except hers bein' black and me bein' white. From that moment on, I tell ya, that gal and I worked together good. I begin to love the girl, really. (He weeps.)

The amazing thing about it, her and I, up to that point, had cussed each other, bawled each other, we hated each other. Up to that point, we didn't know each other. We didn't know we had things in common.

We worked at it, with the people who came to these meetings. They talked about racism, sex education, about teachers not bein' qualified. After seven, eight nights of real intense discussion, these people, who'd never talked to each other before, all of a sudden came up with resolutions. It was really somethin', you had to be there to get the tone and feelin' of it.

At that point, I didn't like integration, but the law says you do this and I've got to do what the law says, okay? We said: "Let's take these resolutions to the school board." The most disheartening thing I've ever faced was the school system refused to implement any one of these resolutions. These were recommendations from the people who pay taxes and pay their salaries. (Laughs.)

I thought they were good answers. Some of 'em I didn't agree with, but I been in this thing from the beginning, and whatever comes of it, I'm gonna support it. Okay, since the school board refused, I decided I'd just run for the school board.

I spent eighty-five dollars on the campaign. The guy runnin' against me spent several thousand. I really had nobody on my side. The Klan turned against me. The low-income whites turned against me. The liberals didn't particularly like me. The blacks were suspicious of me. The blacks wanted to support me, but they couldn't muster up enough to support a Klansman on the school board. (Laughs.) But I made up my mind that what I was doin' was right, and I was gonna do it regardless what anybody said.

It bothered me when people would call and worry my wife. She's always supported me in anything I wanted to do. She was changing, and my boys were too. I got some of my youth corps kids involved. They still followed me.

I was invited to the Democratic women's social hour as a candidate. Didn't have but one suit to my name. Had it six, seven, eight years. I had it cleaned, put on the best shirt I had and a tie. Here were all this high-class wealthy candidates shakin' hands. I walked up to the mayor and stuck out my hand. He give me that handshake with that rag type of hand. He said: "C. P., I'm glad to see you." But I could tell by his handshake he was lyin' to me. This was botherin' me. I know I'm a low-income person. I know I'm not wealthy. I know they were sayin': "What's this little ol' dude runnin' for school board?" Yet they had to smile and make like they're glad to see me. I begin to spot some black people in that room. I automatically went to 'em and that was a firm handshake. They said: "I'm glad to see you, C. P." I knew they meant it—you can tell about a handshake.

Every place I appeared, I said I will listen to the voice of the people. I will not make a major decision until I first contacted all the organizations in the city. I got 4,640 votes. The guy beat me by two thousand. Not bad for eighty-five bucks and no constituency.

The whole world was openin' up, and I was learnin' new truths that I had never learned before. I was beginnin' to look at a black person, shake hands with him, and see him as a human bein'. I hadn't got rid of all this stuff. I've still got a little bit of it. But somethin' was happenin' to me.

It was almost like bein' born again. It was a new life. I didn't have these sleepless nights I used to have when I was active in the Klan and slippin' around at night. I could sleep at night and feel good about it. I'd rather live now than at any other time in history. It's a challenge.

Back at Duke, doin' maintenance, I'd pick up my tools, fix the commode, unstop the drains. But this got in my blood. Things weren't right in this country, and what we done in Durham needs to be told. I was so miserable at Duke, I could hardly stand it. I'd go to work every morning just hatin' to go.

My whole life had changed. I got an eighth-grade education, and I wanted to complete high school. Went to high school in the afternoons on a program called PEP—Past Employment Progress. I was about the only white in class, and the oldest. I begin to read about biology. I'd take my books home at night, 'cause I was determined to get through. Sure enough, I graduated. I got the diploma at home.

I come to work one mornin' and some guy says: "We need a union." At this time I wasn't pro-union. My daddy was anti-labor too. We're not gettin' paid much, we're havin ' to work seven days in a row. We're all starvin' to death. The next day, I meet the international representative of the Operating Engineers. He give me authorization cards. "Get these cards out and we'll have an election." There was eighty-eight for the union and seventeen no's. I was elected chief steward for the union.

Shortly after, a union man come down from Charlotte and says we need a full-time rep. We've got only two hundred people at the two plants here. It's just barely enough money comin' in to pay your salary. You'll have to get out and organize more people. I didn't know nothin' about organizin' unions, but I knew how to organize people, stir people up. (Laughs.) That's how I got to be business agent for the union.

When I began to organize, I began to see far deeper. I began to see people again bein' used. Blacks against whites. I say this without any hesitancy: management is vicious. There's two things they want to keep: all the money and all the say-so. They don't want these poor workin' folks to have none of that. I begin to see management fightin' me with everything they had. Hire antiunion law firms, badmouth unions. The people were makin' a dollar ninety-five an hour, barely able to get through weekends. I worked as a business rep for five years and was seein' all this.

Last year, I ran for business manager of the union. He's elected by the workers. The guy that ran against me was black, and our membership is seventy-five percent black. I thought: Claiborne, there's no way you can beat that black guy. People know your background. Even though you've made tremendous strides, those black people are not gonna vote for you. You know how much I beat him? Four to one. (Laughs.)

The company used my past against me. They put out letters with a picture of a robe and a cap: Would you vote for a Klansman? They wouldn't deal with the issues. I immediately called for a mass meeting. I met with the ladies at an electric component plant. I said: "Okay, this is Claiborne Ellis. This is where I come from. I want you to know right now, you black ladies here, I was at one time a member of the Klan. I want you to know, because they'll tell you about it."

I invited some of my old black friends. I said: "Brother Joe, Brother Howard, be honest now and tell these people how you feel about me." They done it. (Laughs.) Howard Clements kidded me a little bit. He said: "I don't know what I'm doin' here, supportin' an ex-Klansman." (Laughs.) He said: "I know what C. P. Ellis come from. I knew him when he was. I knew him as he grew, and growed with him. I'm tellin' you now: follow, follow this Klansman." (He pauses, swallows hard.) "Any questions?" "No," the black ladies said. "Let's get on with the meeting, we need Ellis." (He laughs and weeps.) Boy, black people sayin' that about me. I won one thirty-four to forty-one. Four to one.

It makes you feel good to go into a plant and butt heads with professional union busters. You see black people and white people join hands to defeat the racist issues they use against people. They're tryin' the same things with the Klan. It's still happenin' today. Can you imagine a guy who's got an adult high school diploma runnin' into professional college graduates who are union busters? I gotta compete with 'em. I work seven days a week, nights and on Saturday and Sunday. The salary's not that great, and if I didn't care, I'd quit. But I care and I can't quit. I got a taste of it. (Laughs.)

I tell people there's a tremendous possibility in this country to stop wars, the battles, the struggles, the fights between people. People say: "That's an impossible dream. You sound like Martin Luther King." An ex-Klansman who sounds like Martin Luther King. (Laughs.) I don't think it's an impossible dream. It's happened in my life. It's happened in other people's lives in America.

I don't know what's ahead of me. I have no desire to be a big union official. I want to be right out here in the field with the workers. I want to walk through their factory and shake hands with that man whose hands are dirty. I'm gonna do all that one little ol' man can do. I'm fifty-two years old, and I ain't got many years left, but I want to make the best of 'em.

When the news came over the radio that Martin Luther King was assassinated, I got on the telephone and begin to call other Klansmen. We just had a real party at the service station. Really rejoicin' 'cause that son of a bitch was dead. Our troubles are over with. They say the older you get, the harder it is for you to change. That's not necessarily true. Since I changed, I've set down and listened to tapes of Martin Luther King. I listen to it and tears come to my eyes 'cause I know what he's sayin' now. I know what's happenin'.

POSTSCRIPT: *The phone rings. A conversation.*

"This was a black guy who's director of Operation Breakthrough in Durham. I had called his office. I'm interested in employin' some young black person who's interested in learnin' the labor movement. I want somebody who's never had an opportunity, just like myself. Just so he can read and write, that's all."

IN THE CITY

◆————————————————————————————————◆
N E I G H B O R H O O D B O Y

B E N G R E E N
◆————————————————————————————————◆

New York City at 5:00 P.M. *Cabs are hard to get. I may miss my plane.*
On Fifty-eighth and Fifth, a cab pulls up. It is a casual conversation
about the times, the traffic, then what the hell one thing leads to
another.

(Laughs.) I don't know. I imagine making it, for a fella from a poor
background, is lifting himself to a level where he could do the things
he'd like to do. I'm a guy that was born on the Lower East Side.

My father was a rough guy, who I loved very much. He used to
hang around with these guys in the neighborhood, hoodlums. He was
a married man, but he'd been in a lot of trouble. He was a fighter, the
1918 150-pound AAU champion. He had a vicious temper. He looked
like Anthony Quinn.

He was very quick with his hands. It landed him in prison. He was
driving a milk truck, Jersey, a rainy night. He pulled in for gas and
went along on his way. The truck began to buck. He was a mechani-
cally minded man. He knew there was water in the gas. He drove back
and busted the man up somethin' terrible. It got him a year in Tren-
ton. My mother was pregnant with me. This is what I heard. He was a
physical man, who ran the Coney Island to Bronx marathon. He was
that type a guy. As I got older, I saw he had shortcomings. I was proud
of him because he was—we call it macho now. He liked women,
which I think is a trait of this family with men. He liked to gamble.

All he wanted to know, you went in school and didn't get a D in
conduct. You got a D in conduct, you got a shot in the head. My
father hit. He had hands like this.

His mother had an outside candy store. When he was fifteen, she
paid a man who had a milk and cheese route to hire my father. She
paid my father's salary, and this guy got the benefit of my father

workin' for nothin', heaven help her. That's how he got in the milk business.

I was eight when we moved to the Bronx. My parents wanted to get out just like the black wants to get out of the ghetto now. When a family went from the Lower East Side up to the Bronx, you half made it. Some of them that made it turned their backs on the ones in the ghetto. Like some blacks today.

My only aggravation with blacks comes in being beat for fares. It's happened about three or four times, and it always was black. I understand it could be a white person, but to me it was black. I see things that annoy me. Maybe I'm a victim. I was brought up in a white world. New York had a very small black population compared to what they have now. It's a whole new ballgame. I try and adjust. Sometimes I do.

I'm number two of five kids. My mother was a straight-laced woman. She's alive today, a very unhappy woman, bitter. She kept everybody at arm's length. She was suspicious of people and very complaining. That's a whole other story. (Laughs.)

I'll tell ya, as a man fifty-seven years old, my father and my mother weren't meant for each other. My father was an outgoing type of man. My mother, all she knew was her kids. Every time she moved, she made sure if she looked out of the window that she could see a school so she could see her kids go from the house to the school. After my father died, 1954, the kids were growing up, raising our own families. We'd call her occasionally, and she felt neglected.

She never said: "I want you to go to school." No one ever pushed me, goddamn it. I wish they had. I felt I could have made it in college. I had an artistic flair when I got out of high school. They said: "Would you like to go to drawing school?" That's what they called it. They didn't push me. Maybe I needed a boot in the behind.

They never stressed education. One book I remember. *Collier's* magazine gave out a giant edition of rotogravure pictures. It was a sepia color. This book had everything, about sports, movies, builders, architects, artists. I pored over this, and I enjoyed it. I always loved books. When my kids came along, goddamn it, there were books in the house.

My father never spoke to us. My older brother was his boy. Isn't that a funny thing? I never resented it. I love my older brother. Man, if something good happened to him, I loved it. He's the greatest guy in the world. He's dead now. They were considering him for vice-president of John Hancock when he died. He was a successful man.

He was the kind of guy, he had to be first. Tremendous competitor. A fair guy, a fabulous guy. He wanted to be top. Not for the money. He was an officer in the army. Navigator. Led his class in graduating. A take-charge guy. Somethin' that I wasn't. I live vicariously, first with my brother, now with my son. Which is no good. I sell myself short. I have a low opinion of myself.

My oldest brother, he wasn't interested in books. He didn't want to know how things began, he wanted (claps hands)—what's doin' now? He didn't care how a clock worked. He was just interested in what time it told. Me? My grandmother once said: "You had to see from where the feet grew." I had to examine things, I had to know. Still to this day. I'm a curious man about everything.

At this stage of the game, I'm beginning to add things up. Take score. I should have gotten more out of life. Yet I look around and see how well I produced (laughs), and I say maybe I can't take credit for that.

When you're a young fella, success is bein' a big-league ballplayer. Or a fireman or a policeman. Then it becomes makin' money. I think success is if you can walk up to a mirror, look at yourself, and say: Hey, I like you. (Laughs.) I don't know, I don't know, I don't know. I really don't know whether I like myself. I've done some crappy things, some good things. Basically, I would say I'm honest.

My son is a very liberal type a guy. He went to Washington with Martin Luther King in 1963. I talked a lot to my son. I read his books. He went to law school. That's after going to college, dropping out, getting drafted, going back, applying to Harvard Law, being turned down. He hitchhiked down to Santiago, Chile. He had aspirations of seeing Allende. He was told to leave when the junta got in. Oh, he was a young fella. As he got older, I see him goin' over a little bit, joining the establishment. He's assistant district attorney now. I must confess I liked him better when he was a rebel, when he said: "Fuck you, I want to do what I want to do." He was quite a kid.

When he was angry and he wrote somethin', man, it was terrific. It takes a little courage to stand up for an unpopular thing, right? And he did. As he got older, he was disillusioned a little bit with the blacks. What can I say? He'll be thirty-two in December.

I remember a picture when he was a young kid. He was sitting on a traffic stanchion, smokin' a cigarette, like he was challengin' the world. I tried to paint it once.

I like art. I love drawing. I used to do drawing for a lot of kids, even in the biology class. I never pursued it. That's the story of my life. I never kept after something.

The American Dream to me is to get educated. When you have knowledge, you've got a lot of things. You can walk through doors that are closed to people who have no knowledge. If you don't have knowledge, you can't converse. I always worshipped knowledge. It's like a factory that manufactures people, by magic.

You know what I did at the age of forty-six? I went to high school. I was in the beauty-parlor business. I had almost ten years as the owner. I hated it. I hated the image more than the business. It was effeminate. What people thought. This is another shortcoming of me. I'm very concerned about what people think. My older brother didn't give a damn what people think. He said: "Screw em, fuck 'em, I don't care." He'd do what he wanted to do. You don't mind if I use the expletive?

I had to get out of the business. I was making a living, but I didn't like it. I saw myself boxed in again. A fear I always have. I always have to have an out. I felt I was getting old and not accomplishing anything. So I went down to this testing service at NYU. It cost me a hundred and ten dollars. A battery of twenty-five tests over a period of three 8-hour days. I was interviewed by a psychologist. Everything was collated. This woman said I was an unhappy man, but you gotta go to art school. I should apply to Cooper Union. I said: "You're crazy." She said: "Don't say I'm crazy." In one test, she said, spatial visualization, I so outranked my peers they compared me with professionals, architects, and—who else?—interior designers. I took the test for Cooper Union and I was accepted. I was the oldest one there, forty-six, among young kids. I felt great. It was college! People looked at me a little different. In my lodge, Knights of Pythias, they made a big thing out of it. This old bastard's going to school. Oh, it's a great feeling. Suddenly they discovered I'm alive. I like a little recognition. It was a good ego trip.

I was able to sell the business. I got into the insurance field. I was always afraid of talk, would you believe it? I was a stammerer, a stutterer. I was afraid to extend myself for fear I would have to speak, so I pulled back. Apropos to this, I see my son, a beautiful speaker. When he was doing hearings in court, I'd sit there and think: Jesus Christ, he can talk. We all try to feel something successful is an extension of us. The one that's not, we try to put in the closet. (Laughs.)

I was gung ho. When I made my first sale, my youngest daughter made a little medal out of paper—The Champion.

I have two daughters. My oldest is a lesbian. It kills me, kills me. I can't accept that. I'm intelligent enough to see it, to tell the other guy to accept it, but I can't do it with my own. Would you believe that? I often say: "Gee, I wonder what my old man woulda said." It hurts me because that was the one child I always felt had a strong feeling for me. She's a fighter. She was a drug addict, who was carrying a 3.2 index in college. I'm supposed to be smart. I was stupid. I couldn't even recognize a drug addict. She got herself into Phoenix House. It straightened her out with the drugs. She's a teacher now. She's fully independent.

I made the president's club. (Laughs.) You have to sell a certain amount. I went down to Miami Beach, all expenses paid. I did this until I walked out on my marriage. December 1, 1971. I remember the day. It was Wednesday, and it was raining.

I had to be me. I was unhappy for many years. My wife was a bright woman. She was attractive. At the beginning it was sexual. But she would try and dominate me. I'd rebel. So I walked out. I didn't take anything but my clothes. I left whatever money was in the bank.

I took a furnished room. I liked it. She wanted me back. I said no. Then I got a bad break. I was in Jersey, about forty miles from New York. All of a sudden, I felt a pain. I had a perforated ulcer. I later learned it's twenty-five percent caused by tension. I spent twelve days in the hospital and made a remarkable recovery. So I went to the cab in '69. Now I drive regular.

At the beginning it killed me. I picked up a man one day, a professional cello player. He gets in with a Hungarian accent and says: "You're not a cab driver." I said: "What makes you think so?" The first words he says: "I know, I can look at you." I felt good.

I had a low feeling about cab drivers. I still do. I don't like to mention it, I put it in the closet. I tell people: "Don't tell 'em I'm a cab driver." I could hold my own with most people. At Cooper Union, I got three B's and one C. The C was in lettering. When I went into the insurance business, I worked nights, so I couldn't go to school.

I'm makin' a livin'. I'm probably makin' more now than I'd be makin' in insurance. But it's that image again. Why am I so concerned with image? Guys peddle, guys shovel horse shit. Why am I concerned with my image?

Today, teachers are in school just to earn money. I don't think they're interested in giving an extra ten minutes of their time unless they get overtime. Cops don't make arrests at certain hours because it means they'll be held there to make reports. They look away from accidents. I see this in the street.

I think authority means nothing now. I don't think it should be like Germany. But I think people should be looked up to. They go in front of a judge and tell him to go screw himself. Years ago, you said something to a copper, he'd whack you across the ass with a club. I mean, I got hit. I don't say a cop should walk around hitting people. It's okay to question, but some people hate authority for authority's sake.

I think there's a change coming over now. One time in the sixties, I thought we're going to get the real revolution. I wonder what happened to those people. I liked that time. Because I feel this country is too boxed in. If you're in a certain group, you got it made in this country. If you're not, you have to fight like hell to get into that group. If you're black or Spanish, it's twice as hard. I don't like "my country, love it or leave it."

I think the youth changed. They banged their heads against a wall and just got tired of banging it and it hurt. They say it's easier to join the establishment. Or maybe when young people get older, they have to get on with their lives, an' makin' speeches isn't going to put food on the table. Jobs are tougher today.

I wonder what would happen if everybody was equal. Really equal. Where no one has the advantage on the other. What would happen? Here we have a condition where people have an advantage, not because they earned it. They were fortunate enough to be born into the damn thing. Hey, what do you think that does to me when I pick up someone I know is loaded and see that this is a man that mentally couldn't shine my shoes? I say why? Something's wrong. This son of a bitch, he knows nothing. He can't even speak. What did I do wrong? It really bothers me. Then it wears off, and I continue on.

KEN JACKSON

◈————————————————————————————————◈

A bitter cold day in New York.

"I work with kids in prison. Excluding dynamite, nothin's gonna improve them to any great degree. Society will pay for prisons as long as we have 'em. We have to find a new wheel. There's a hell of a lot of people I met in jail, and if you told me they're comin' home, I want to know where they're comin' to and stay away from that neighborhood.

"The Fortune Society was a great part of my life. It came out of a need. It gave me something. It was the opportunity for me to ventilate the anger from my prison experience. Fortune tries to inform the public of the penalty they pay for prison. And it tries to help those who come out to get adjusted: jobs, education, things like that.

"When we started Fortune in the sixties, it became very stylish to be an ex-convict. Now it's stylish to be an American Indian with a glass eye. When you had an ex-con for dinner, it was always: 'As long as we have to do it, let's get the white guy.' I was the token white."

He is thirty-seven, dapper, sporting a thin mustache.

I come from a tribe. My parents in weather like this decided to have children. It was the only way to keep warm. I came from a broken home. Alcoholic father, working mother too proud to go on what was then called home relief. It's now called welfare. We keep changing names of things, but everything remains the same.

I didn't like school. I found it a terrible bore and didn't like learning through abuse. The Catholic brothers have their way of teaching. I got enough beatin's at home. So I stopped goin' to school when I entered fifth grade and never bothered goin' back again. Nobody really cared. The truant officers would show up every six months and take me off to court. The judge would threaten to put me away if I didn't return to school. I'd return for half an hour and wouldn't go back for another six months. We'd go through that whole megillah every six months.

I grew up in the Bedford-Stuyvesant area of Brooklyn, primarily black. We used to call it a slum, then it became a ghetto, now we call it the inner city. We keep changin' names. We didn't even have a sanitation department. There was no dirt to collect.

I was arrested the first time when I was nine. For stealin' fifty cents off a kid in the Brooklyn Botanical Gardens. We had moved from NYC to Brooklyn. We were gypsies. When the rent came due and nightfall came, we left.

I was destined for trouble long before the first arrest. I started usin' junk back in 1952, before it was stylish. Heroin. I was twelve. There were only three connections in Brooklyn at that time. Now there's a connection on every block. At that time, you had to search them out.

It was always competition. I went from competing in sports to competing in crime. I wanted to be the first Irish guy to head organized crime. I always wanted to be at the top of something. So I became the first dope fiend in the neighborhood. I grew up with the infamous Joey Gallo, guys like that. I figured, shit, I was way ahead of them. If they could surround themselves with guys to do things for them, well, I could do it, too.

I organized a burglary ring when I was thirteen. We stole over a million dollars. The oldest was seventeen. I was the ringleader. I got five other guys, and we picked different areas. We'd hit this area Monday, this area Tuesday, that area Wednesday. The following week we reversed it. We'd never go back the same way, so they'd never have a fix on us. We scheduled it around night ball games of the Dodgers. We knew Thursday was the maid's night out, therefore the Chinese restaurants were doin' a lot of business. We were robbing primarily Jewish areas. That's where the money was, and that's where we went.

After I was arrested, I went to the courtroom in the children's court and watched the sham called justice. I promised never to do it again. I also promised the cops, the night before, who were stealin' the stuff that I had stole and not gotten rid of, that I wouldn't tell the judge. They told the judge what a very nice boy I was. Their wife had a new diamond ring and a new mink coat. They had new rifles and booze. I had cellars full of the stuff.

When I was a kid, I didn't dislike myself. I disliked my lot in life. When I found out I was poor, I wanted to be Jewish. When I went to public school in a Jewish area the first day, after I got thrown out of Catholic school, it was a whole new world to me. Kids had books with covers on 'em. Not paper bags that they wrapped around 'em. They had nice clothes. It was an embarrassment because I didn't have the things they had. I didn't want to tell 'em my father was a wino. Their father was a lawyer or a judge or an accountant. I never had one of those kids to my house. I was ashamed. I thought: Jesus, Jewish is where it's at.

Then I rationalized that I was nothin' more than a twentieth-century Robin Hood. I was takin' care of all the poor people. I was very indignant that people thought I was a criminal. I didn't mind robbin' their parents. But there were a lot of guys from other neighborhoods that used to come in and beat these kids up. I didn't like that, so I more or less protected them. They were nice kids. I didn't know their families. I just knew they had somethin' that I wanted. And I stole it from them. I didn't discriminate. I stole it from strangers.

We had to fight for leadership. Once I beat my brother. He was three years older than me and like the head of the crowd. I looked upon my older brother as a model not to follow because he kept gettin' caught. I used some of the things he did without gettin' caught. I had long runs between arrests. He'd get arrested weekly. I could go six, eight months at a clip. Then I'd change the pattern. When I got busted for the burglary ring, I organized a car-theft ring.

Our thing was to get what we didn't have. We woulda never got into crime if we had not stepped out of the neighborhood we were in. We didn't know that people were other than what we were. We didn't know that poverty existed in our neighborhood because everybody was the same.

They talk about bussing. I was being bussed back in 1952. When I went to this other school, I found all this lavish stuff around here. So I started tellin' the guys: "Hey, wait a minute, there's another whole world out there." So we went to the outer limits, the other world, to get some of the gold that was out there. Oh God, we did everything. One time—I was about thirteen—we took off a joint for about eight thousand bucks, me and two of the guys. We took a cab over to the Algonquin Hotel. (Laughs.) The cab driver didn't want to take us to the city because his wife was expectin' a baby. So we gave the guy a $300-tip. We gave him a hundred apiece for the baby. He took our names and said if it was a boy, he'd name it after us.

We pissed the money away. We registered, got a room, and went over to Jack Dempsey's restaurant. We got a couple of hookers. They were good-lookin' heads. Hookers don't care if the money's right. I was accused of bein' forty when I was thirteen. I look the same today as I did then. I always had this face like this guy was hit with a train.

I'd come home, I'd give my mother five hundred or five thousand, and tell her I won it in a dice game. She thought I was the luckiest dice player in the world. She probably knew, but she didn't want to know. I was the head of the household, yeah. We went to Coney Island one time and spent fifteen thousand bucks in a day. We paid for everybody on the Cyclone for the whole day. Everybody who was on seemed to be havin' a good time, so we said whoever wants to stay, stay, and we paid. We went all over Coney Island payin'. We were tryin' to get everybody in on the party, total strangers. We spent it all. We had to steal bicycles to get home.

It was just: Let's have some fun, have a party. Everything was: Try and get away from the morbid life, goin' home fightin' rats and cockroaches. We'd walk in a joint, and if there were fifty people there, we took over the whole place. Everybody drank on us, and everybody ate on us.

My attitude changed when I got into junk. I don't care how much you steal, how much you make, if you get into junk, there's just not enough money to keep a habit goin'. I was stealin' to keep from bein' sick. The party was over. I wasn't goin' in any more gin mills or hotels. I was goin' to my connection. I was gettin' dope, goin' out stealin', goin' to my connection, gettin' dope, out stealin'. It was a vicious cycle. Then it was the arrests. Bein' sharp was gone, outwittin' cops was gone, 'cause it was a desperation kind of stealin'. Then it was off to jail. While in jail, I made a conscious decision that I wasn't gonna allow drugs to use me again. When I went away I was sixteen. When I came home I was just twenty.

When I went upstate, that's where the education came. I got two five-year sentences. I went up there to be rehabilitated. I grew up thinkin' Pat O'Brien ran the joint. He was a fatherly figure. Jimmy Cagney was every inmate. I thought you went to jail and talked tough. And Pat O'Brien came around and gave you cigarettes. And sometime later you left and became a priest. Or you stuck around and married the warden's daughter. I wrote Jimmy Cagney a letter and asked him if he'd try and help out gettin' rid of the myths that he created. I grew up with John Wayne winning every war. He planted flags on Iwo Jima, he won Bataan, we won everything. The guy never left Hollywood. (Laughs.) Oh, I discovered a lot up there. They should have ensured that I'd never get out again.

The rule of the prison: Whites and blacks don't speak. It's a microcosm of what's out here, with these blinds. Prison is based a lot on what society is based on. It's the horizontal kind of hostility where you keep each other going at each other so nobody's lookin' up at who the hell's runnin' the circus. We have a handful of people run this thing we're in. Okay, today we'll write about we're bein' ripped off by welfare cheats. So everybody's mad at welfare cheats. Tomorrow we're mad at thirteen-year-olds for muggin' eighty-year-olds. Then they're mad at somebody robbin' cab drivers. I can understand the fear of street crime, of violence. But I don't understand why there's not too much anger about the crimes of Richard Nixon. San Clemente became a prison for him. I heard for years about how prisons are country clubs. Boy, he made that a reality.

You can't tell a kid in one of these city jails that there's justice in this world. Kids aren't naïve. We give 'em that shit: Kids should be seen and not heard. They're gonna be heard from. Negatively. It's a hell of a legacy to give to a kid.

Upstate, they taught me to act like a jerk, talk tough. Dislike people who I didn't even know. Not to have an opinion. Follow the opinion of others. We were regimented into a system, and you took a piece of the property of it, you became the one with the opinion. I remember talkin' to tough guys, tellin' me of their big scores. You never stopped to think if this guy's so good at his work, what's he doin' here?

The longer you were there, the less likely you went to solitary, the more latitude you had. You became part of the institution without knowing you played this role. I spent ninety-three days in solitary, half-rations. No nothin', just a marble floor and you.

When I came out, I was angry. I remember I got on a train—one thing you'll find in prison is a great deal of respect. If somebody bumps into somebody, everybody's apologizin'. You hear more excuses there than you'll hear in the whole world. On the train, I was jammed in like a sardine, and the people were pushin' me back and forth. I was lookin' around for the prison guards to make sure they weren't too close so I could punch the guy in the mouth and kick his teeth out. I kept that anger for a long time.

Upstate, I learned a different approach to crime. I met the tough guys who see it as a business. It wasn't a fun business, it was a business. It was a means of survival. When I came out, I thought the only way I could survive is not to use drugs. So I got into a different kind of life. I worked for that nonexisting corporation: organized crime.

I met a more sophisticated criminal. I found out that stealing to take money and throw it away was ludicrous. Now I was learning the American value system, the Syndicate value system. What you were supposed to do is steal and get involved with the American Dream. You made big money, bought a home, and got away from the niggers. You bought the ranch house and you got the Cadillac. Or Lincoln. Depending on how much you could afford. What part of the Syndicate you were in dictated where you lived, how much you spent. Your kids went to good schools. Nobody knew your business. You kept the shades drawn. And you went only to the best joints. Syndicate-owned. This is where the jet set goes. So we gave the money back to the guys that gave it to us, who we worked for. It's a corporation. They're not licensed by the state of New York, but it's a buyer's market. Supply and demand. We supplied, and then we demanded they pay us. It's capitalism at its best.

When I came home, it was more muscle than anything else. I was always good with my hands. I had done a lot of boxing while I was away. I was first middleweight and then heavyweight champ of the joint. I was a collector for organized crime.

The machines. You go into these gin mills and see jukeboxes and shuffleboards and all that there. They're all organized-crime-owned. The percentage is fifty for the owner, fifty for organized crime. If the money wasn't there, I had to make sure it was. If a guy said, "I don't have the money," you were supposed to break his legs. That was the nature of the business.

I got sick of that. We went to a joint in Brooklyn. It was a small *bodega*, and the guy had an army of kids. They all lived in this little back room in the store. It was one of them ten-dollar-a-week joints. Me and my partner were there. The guy's machine was broken. You could tell nobody had broken into the joint, he had taken the machine off himself. So we were gonna put the money in and we just told him we're gonna send the guy in to fix the machine and make sure it don't happen again. But our boss showed up. He told us to whack the guy. I didn't want to hit the guy. His kids were there. So we took him in the back room, and I just told him to scream and fall down. And I put a hole in the wall. I came out and figured that's enough of this. My partner was a good guy. We talked it over and he said: "This isn't us. We gotta do something' else." So what we did first is we robbed our boss.

We had the book for all the stops. So we went around to all the stops and told the guys to give us ten percent of what was in the machine and keep the rest for themselves. And tell 'em we took it all. Then we called 'em up and told 'em that we had beat 'em for a couple hundred thousand dollars, and if he didn't like it, he could come and talk to us about it.

My partner got his brains blown out. When they were lookin' for me, I went down to the guy and told him if they're still lookin', the next time I come back they're not gonna have anybody givin' 'em orders to look. We struck a deal. Nobody would be lookin' for me, and I wouldn't be lookin' for him.

He woulda had to hire guys who worked with me, and I woulda got word. We worked together, we hung together. If he contracted for me, one of 'em woulda got to me and let me know, and I woulda went back and got him. And he knew it.

During the course of that period, I had went back to jail. I got locked up for a gun. I did a year on that one. This was in between workin' for these guys. I found out they were pretty much a slimy group, and I was just as slimy workin' for 'em.

But I had acquired a great taste for booze. When I came out, that's just what I did. For the next couple of years, I was drunk most of the time. I lived on the Bowery, lived in doorways, hallways. I found an escape, and I was gonna stay in it. I liked what I was doin'. I was goin' around in a trance. I didn't have to deal with reality out here. And then one day, I don't know why, I told my wife I'd stop drinkin'. I haven't had a drink in almost fifteen years.

I sobered up and I scrounged around, got this job, that job. I was a porter, I got fired. They found out I had a record. I was a doorman, I got fired. They found out I had a record. Then I went into the construction trade. They didn't care as long as you put in a day's work. Then I was a shape guy on the *Times*. You go down and you shape up and they pick ya if they need extras. I used to work for the mailers, the guys who put the Sunday paper together. I worked, oh Christ, any number of things. Outside of shape jobs or real garbage jobs, the record always showed up. You were always gone. I had got used to that. I knew that's the way it was.

I saved some money, borrowed some more, and I bought a restaurant business. I did fairly well. We were still in Bedford-Stuyvesant. When my kids started knowin' the names of drugs, I figured it's time to leave. We moved right into another area, predominantly white, where there was just as much drugs as there were in the area we had left. But nobody there knew me. So I became a pillar of the community.

I was involved in a lot of civic stuff. When it finally came out that I was an ex-con, everybody didn't know how to act. They had this maniac in their midst. Until they found out their kids were using drugs. Then they'd call me in the middle of the night to come over and do somethin' with their kids. And don't tell the neighbors. They ostracized me when they discovered I had the record, but when their kid's in trouble, they say: "We're gonna call this guy."

In the daylight, I'm an ex-con and I always will be. At night's when I get the calls. They don't know what to do. Should they come to me and maybe be seen comin' into the house? Or should I come to them and maybe be seen goin' into their house? It's very confusing for them. I tell 'em I'll wear a trench coat and put it over my head. I'm not interested in them. I'm interested in their kid. I don't want their kid goin' to jail.

They have higher standards for their dogs than they have for their kids. Dick Gregory once said if parents were told that their dog was going to be taken off to Vietnam they'd fight like hell. But when they were told their kids were gonna be taken off, they didn't fight at all. People are very concerned what the neighbors think. And the neighbors really don't think too much.

I been to other countries. I ain't givin' up on this one. I don't buy "love it or leave it." You can love it and stay here and try to do somethin' about what's wrong with it. I don't see the great American Dream.

America to me was the block I lived on. I was into one block and then I got into five blocks. Then I spread out and knew there were twenty blocks. Then I found out Brooklyn wasn't the only place in the world. I didn't have dreams, I had hopes. Hopes of someday being one of those people I always heard about. People who lived the good life. I wanted to be John Wayne, win all the wars. Maybe that's what the dream is: an illusion.

I'm not religious in the sense of being organized religious. But I know there's a God. This isn't the life I chose, it was chosen for me. I don't question why. I was supposed to be a crook. I was supposed to be a drug addict. I was supposed to have those experiences so I could have the experiences I have now. It wasn't something I chose. Anybody who chooses drug addiction or alcoholism or jail is crazy. Some scribes say we're made in the image of God. We may be made in the image, but we're certainly not carryin' out what God had in mind. I don't think this is what was meant to be. That's why I believe we're gonna get it right.

BILL LESKO

◇————————————————————————————————————◇

A Chicago police officer. He is thirty-one.

"I'm working toward a two-year degree. I might switch over, try to get something like business management. The Chicago Police Department is something like a big business. Has fourteen thousand people, a finance department, personnel, medical."

When you first put on the uniform, you think you're hot stuff. That wears off after a while. There's some excitement in the job—a policeman going out into the jaws of death—but it really doesn't happen that often. Most of the time you're just riding around in a car, and sometimes it gets pretty boring.

I work in a fairly busy district, about ninety-eight percent black. And poor. I have a steady partner. He's white too. When I first broke in, I was the only new recruit on the shift. So they spread me around. Every two weeks. Two of my training officers were black and two were white. I got along with all of 'em. You're either a good policeman or a bad policeman. Color doesn't enter into it too much.

Whites tend to hang with whites and blacks with blacks. Naturally, you go with your own kind. We're all friendly. But their good buddy is another black guy. There might be some hard feelings, especially now with the sergeant's test. You hear a lot about they have to take a certain amount of blacks even though they don't get the highest score. But out on the street, when the shit hits the fan and you call for help, everybody comes, black, white, it doesn't matter.

You'll get a call: man with a gun. The adrenaline starts pumpin' and you get kind of nervous and excited, but after you've gone on a hundred man-with-a-gun calls and there's no man with a gun, your guard drops. The hundred and first time a guy could be standin' there with a gun, so you have to force yourself to keep on your toes.

The times you find yourself in trouble are when you're writing a parking ticket or when you go on a call, domestic disturbance. It's always a volatile situation. A guy called us to his house to write a ticket for somebody blocking his driveway. When we pulled up to the place, he's standing in front of his house with a table leg in his hand ready to bash in the skull of the guy who had parked in his driveway, because the guy was tryin' to leave and had a baby with him. The next thing you know, you're rollin' around on the ground with this guy, get your pants ripped. We ended up lockin' him up. Then this guy complains, you got a CR, a complaint register. Then you have to go down to the office of professional standards and give a statement.

There are policemen on the job for a while who think they're all bad, anybody who lives in that area. I've found it's not always true. A couple of weeks ago, a black lady was drivin' down the street and she got a flat tire and she came up to us. It was dusk, about five or five-thirty. She wasn't anywhere near where she could get the tire fixed. She was an older woman in her mid fifties. We told her to sit in the car, and we changed her tire. She offered to give us a couple of bucks, but we wouldn't take it. She thanked us a lot and insisted on getting our names and star numbers. About a week later, we got a real nice letter from the superintendent. She wrote a long letter to our district commander thanking him and telling him how nice we were. It made you feel real good.

I don't think there's any policeman who really fears working out there. You find out it is not quite as bad as somebody who is not a policeman would think it is. I tell my relatives, and they're just shocked. They can't believe that I ride around in that district on days by myself. At night, you're with a partner.

A lot of times, I find myself going into buildings by myself. I stop to think a couple of years ago, if somebody told me I'd be walkin' into a run-down building in this neighborhood, I'd say they're crazy. You're riding around in that neighborhood more than you're riding around in your own. It really doesn't faze you.

People think it's a terrible place to work. If they got kicked out of a car on Sixty-third and Cottage,* they'd get ready to have a will drawn up. Sure, there's chances of getting your purse snatched, probably greater than walkin' around here. If you did it a hundred days in a row, sooner or later something would happen. But just because you get a flat tire on Sixty-third Street doesn't mean you're gonna get your throat slit.

I'm proud to tell people I'm a policeman. For other people, I don't know if it's a mixture of fear and respect or what, but you're not just a regular Joe, you're a policeman. I'm the first person in the family to be a policeman.

When I became a policeman, my mom was afraid and my dad was super proud. He tells everybody. They were a little bit nervous because everybody thinks a policeman is in gun fights every night. It just doesn't happen like that.

"Everybody in my family always worked, and they always looked down upon people that don't work.

"My dad's seventy-two years old. He's still working at U.S. Steel. He worked thirty-six years for Wisconsin Steel in the open hearth. They brought in oxygen furnaces and were gonna lay a lot of guys off. This was thirteen years ago. The guys who had enough time could draw a full pension or take a cut in pay and work the furnaces. My dad, who was fifty-nine, took his pension and went over to U.S. Steel. He mops floors, cleans up. He's working steady days and enjoying it. Altogether he's been in steel mills like fifty-one years.

"My mother always had some kind of little job ever since I can

* An intersection in Chicago's South Side black ghetto

remember. She worked in a laundry when I was a kid, throwing those big bags around. Now she just works two or three nights a week in a neighborhood clothing store, just to keep her hand in. She's seventy years old.

"If they sat back in the late twenties and early thirties, they'd never have dreamed of having as much as they have now. But they got it through hard work. All of the brothers and sisters live within four or five blocks of where my mom and dad live. It's kind of an old-fashioned type thing."

I think there is a macho thing about being a policeman. Last Sunday, I was driving with my wife and kids to visit her family. A guy was standing in front of his car cleaning his window. I said to my wife: "That guy looks like a policeman." He was in civilian clothes. When I got in front of his car, he had police stickers on his window. She was amazed. There's something you pick up. It's the way he stood, the way he looked. He had a real trim mustache and a haircut. I think they feel confident. I don't know if it's because they carry a gun. It might be. There was a guy in school who said he could always pick a man carrying a gun out of a crowd. It's the way he carries himself.

I have no reservations of working with a girl. A lot of times having her along has actually helped. They're so shocked to see this little five-foot-three-inch white girl standing there that a lot of times it actually diffuses the situation.

I was on a furlough last month, and there is a white girl working in a car by herself in an all-black neighborhood. She got a call to take a battery report, somebody got beat up. If there's a call like a domestic disturbance or a burglary in progress, they'll send a couple of cars, but for a service call it's just one car. So she goes up. It's one of those seedy little hotels that was turned into an apartment building, where each room is a separate apartment and everybody knows everybody else's business. She knocks on the door, a guy comes to the door: "Did somebody here call the police?" He said: "Yeah, my wife did. We got in a fight, she jumped on me, so I hit her." Mary, that's the cop, says: "Okay, if she comes back, tell her I was here." A girl comes running out the apartment down the hall. "I called the police!" All excited yelling and screaming that he hit her and all this stuff. People are opening their doors and looking. Mary says: "What do you want me to do?" She says: "I want to get my clothes out of there." So Mary says to the guy: "Are you gonna let her get her clothes?" "Yeah, yeah, I'll let her in." So Mary's got the situation all under control, no problems.

All of a sudden, there are nine policemen charging up the stairs, four plainclothesmen and five uniformed cops. Mary gets on the radio: "I don't know what's going on over here, but give a slowdown. There's a whole army of policemen coming up here." The dispatcher told her there were five calls from the building saying that a little white police girl is in trouble and you'd better send some help. (Laughs.) I guess they looked out the door and thought: Oh, Jesus, there's this little white girl here all by herself. These black people were indignant. The whole street was filled with squad cars. (Laughs.) The girl went in, got her clothes, and there was no problem at all.

I feel pretty content. As far as dreams go, I have a house, a wife, two kids. I have no trouble meeting my bills. I've got a nice car. I'm in a job where there's possibilities. It's important for me not to look ahead to your dead end.

What bothers me these days is the more you get, the more you want. When my parents were younger, they didn't think about havin' a car. They didn't have one till they were married twenty-five years. Now you get a car when you're eighteen years old, and you feel deprived if you don't have two of 'em. Hell, you were lucky if you had a radio. Now you got a radio in every room and a couple of TV sets, so you can watch two programs at the same time. I look for things to go back to a simpler type of existence. I hope it does. I like to talk to my mom and dad about the old times. They'd sit around evenings and have a good time, just talking.

ROGER TUTTRUP

The day is especially hot and muggy. A cat, playful, slithers onto his lap. Gently, he strokes it.

It is a third-floor flat in a working-class neighborhood on Chicago's North Side. It is adjacent to Uptown, a more depressed semi-transient area, where he and his wife had lived till recently.

He is fifty-five, stocky, crew-cut, gravel-voiced.

During the summer of 1968, he had worked with the subversive unit of the Chicago Police Department.

"When I worked, I enjoyed it. The only trouble is, there were

times when I was asked to do things. That's why the ulcers. I've been bleedin' inside. The police department . . . [he trails off.] In '68, the riots. I'm an observer. I'm a civilian workin' for the department."

I was on the planning staff. About half policemen, half civilians. Some of those guys hadn't seen the street in years. They went out and just wanted to bust heads. A guy came back braggin': "Boy, did I hit some people!" Some of the other guys felt like vomiting. The mayor didn't handle the thing right. I can't go with throwin' bricks and bags of shit and stuff like that. On that side, I'm with the policemen. On the other hand: Why the hell didn't we just give 'em the parks? Huh? They wouldn't hurt anything.

I still find it hard to blame the police. But they weren't trained for this. Shit, I was in one of those things in the Marine Corps. They taught you never hit anybody above the shoulders with a night stick.

One of the kids coulda been mine. I don't know, maybe he was down there. I thought for the most part, the kids were harmless.

"Did I ever tell you about my son? I said: 'I think it would be a good idea if you enlisted now, get your military over with, and then go to college.' You know what he told me? 'This isn't the same kind of war.' I paid his way to college anyway. The kid was old enough to make up his own mind."

In the Marine Corps, you could stand there all day long and let them call you pigs, and you just smile at 'em. You wouldn't make a move until anybody made a move. But some of these police wanted it. They wanted to beat up. Others were damn good. Only thing, they weren't trained to cope with that kind of stuff.

I went to the hospital four times in three years. One was a back deal, which you can't blame on them. Pneumonia you can't blame on them. But the other, ulcers, I don't know. I was more or less asked to sanction somethin' . . . (He trails off.)

I think I know why I got sick. I wanted to be on both sides at the same time. I thought what the police were doin' was right. I thought what most of the kids were doin' was right. It's kinda hard. You can't be on both sides at the same time.

I did quite a bit of work with the so-called Red Squad. We called it the subversive unit. It was a big joke. The guy who ran it, he kept every scrap of paper. Half the people he's got files on, what are they gonna do? You know who they put out on the job for surveillance and that stuff? Shit, cadets! Most amateurish operation from the word go. Good policemen are very quiet people. They don't say much.

I was seventeen when I joined the marines. I wanted to do somethin'. I was goin' to school, Oak Park High, okay?* I didn't get along with my family too good. I wanted to be a hero. Didn't work. I saw a little action. But I was no hero.

I learned discipline, that I should be able to conduct myself in a decent way. I shouldn't be a goof, though at times I have been. I think the Marine Corps did a hell of a lot for me. I was a smart-ass kid when I went in. In two and a half years, I changed real quick.

Marines mean to me tough people unafraid. You know why? They've got organization and discipline. They're the same kind of people as you and me, but their training teaches you gotta work together and obey. You know your goddamn life depends on the guy next-door to you. You get along, but you fight the system all the time.

In combat you gotta obey, but otherwise you tell 'em they're full of shit on certain rules. I got punished a few times. I'm an organization man and a malcontent at the same time.

When I got out of the Marine Corps, I said I will never take orders from anyone again. Guys above me? Fight 'em. That's the name of the game. It's no fun kickin' people around who can't fight back.

I was tryin' to organize the tenants where I lived in Uptown. It's a rotten place. It was about three-fourths black, an old white welfare lady, a few Appalachian types, some old and sick people. They were so afraid of the landlord, they wouldn't go along. They had no guts. It really hurt the hell outa me.

We actually enjoyed livin' there. We felt a hell of a lot safer there than in the middle-class neighborhood we moved from. When there are more people on the streets, there's gonna be less street crime. I remember during a super hot spell, I'd go to the air-conditioned tavern, get a couple of cold beers. I'm comin' back eleven-thirty, a lot of people sittin' out front, drinkin' beer, all colored. I sit down. The only white to ever drink with 'em is me. Some of 'em like me, some don't. It's that simple. I enjoyed the people.

But the landlords were slumlords. I woulda killed 'em for what they did to those people. They raped the building. The manager, the

* An old western middle-class suburb of Chicago, though changing in recent years

colored lady that lived downstairs, she was the last one to move. They condemned the building and she said there were rats all over the place. You know whose side she was on, don't ya? The landlord's.

During an earlier visit, while he was still living in Uptown, I saw mailboxes, nameless, all broken, with the exception of his, which had a lock. The bell wasn't working.

I tried to organize 'em, to say: "Don't pay the rents." I said: "I'll take the petitions to the city, to our congressman. I'll do any fuckin' thing you want." They said: "How do you know we're gonna win?" They had no spirit. You do what you think is right, for Chrissake. I don't give a shit for politicians or anybody else. The only kind of people that are gonna make the country work are the people that live in neighborhoods. I want to see my neighbors do as good as I do. I don't like to see cheap shit, lousy, scrawny, miserable assholes, those pimps, that go to Miami Beach every other week, livin' off a people that are on welfare.

I don't think our system is all bad. Right? I don't think it's wrong that some people have more than other people. What I object to is, there's no planning. I don't care how much money it takes. They should put every guy that wants to work, to work.

Right now, I'm doin' nothin', zero. I sit in my house, except for goin' out for my newspaper in the morning and occasionally to the store, to the library about once every two weeks, dependin' on how many books I took out, get a haircut every three weeks. Stop at the tavern once in a great while, but I'm gettin' priced out of them. I like Manhattans. Goddamn neighborhood tavern, they're over a dollar.

Appreciation of books I consider the greatest thing in the world. This set of Great Books here, I've read some of 'em but like most assholes, I only read what I like. I stay away from the sciences and read the other guys. In grade school, I could beat the shit out of anybody in spelling, including one of those original quiz kids. He's now a Jesuit priest, pretty high-class set. I coulda gone on that program, but I wouldn't do it. Why should I? I was always a hardhead.

I try not to hurt people. I'm pretty good at that, hurtin' people. Verbally. I've done it many times. I've a very vengeful guy. Somebody gives me a bad shot, they're gonna get it back. But I'm learnin' it don't work that way.

I wouldn't have a gun to save my life. I used to keep a baseball bat around here for protection. I gave it to the kids to play baseball with. I don't need that kind of protection. I'll depend on the people around here. You want to know somethin'? You can put a squad car on every block and it won't work if the people don't cooperate. I saw an ad about police dogs that got me fuckin' mad: how everybody needs one. I said: "Boy, won't that be the ultimate when everybody's got a dog for protection, not for friendship?" That's the day I'll move to Canada or Mexico or something.

But I won't have to move. I got all kinds of hope. 'Cause no matter what you think or whatever those stupid assholes on network television may think, it's those little fellows in the trenches that do the work, that make things work. That's why songs that Pete Seeger and Woody Guthrie sing make me cry. I know Seeger's a leftie, but I like his music. They sing about things the way they should be. I have lots of Woody Guthrie. "This Land Is Your Land," it should be the national anthem.

What I want in life is about half of what they got in China and about half of what we got here. Clean streets, everybody healthy, no fear of walkin' the streets or somebody screwin' you.

I hold one thing the key to raisin' the world: reading. 'Cause once everybody knows how to read, all these other problems will solve themselves. Shit, if everybody in the world could read books on agriculture, they wouldn't have to have smart asses from here tellin' 'em what to do. They could do it themselves. And that's what counts.

BOB LUCE

He is a promoter of wrestling matches in Chicago and environs.

"The people that come to wrestling matches: the common man, the average Joe. We have Chicanos, we have blacks, we have immigrants. They have a hero and somebody they dislike.

"The wrestler makes more money wrestling rough. There's more rough wrestlers than good-guy wrestlers."'

Every big kid thinks he's a wrestler. Many are called but few are chosen. There's only one Dick the Bruiser. He goes both ways. He's a big drawing card because people identify with him. When he's rough, he takes care of problems and they feel good. For many years, he was a bad guy. We call him a heel. What makes a great heel in wrestling?

Guts. When the Bruiser was bad, he was so rotten people didn't identify with him. As a good guy, he still maintains his roughness.

When they go in that ring, they're gonna do tough. They're gonna cheat, they're gonna get people upset, they're gonna get people out. They're going to make an easygoing guy in the audience so mad that when he comes out of the ring, you're gonna try to hit him. We've had guys hit in the head with a hammer. Bobby Heenan the Brain has been hit in the head by guys with ball-peen hammers.

You don't make money to start with. You take beatings and get hurt bad. We had two wrestlers by the name of the Dillinger Brothers, Jack and John. They wore motorcycle jackets: Hell's Angels. They made nothing but money. They became a big card in Chicago.

After a match in Milwaukee, the Dillingers went to a tavern. The bar was lined up with guys from the Outlaws gang. The leader says to the Dillingers: "Take off your colors." John took his jacket off and the guy says, "Fuck you," and another guy hit him in the back with a baseball bat. They beat him with chains, shot him in the leg seven times, and dropped him off in the alley to bleed to death. He had a great career in wrestling, and now he's a cripple for life. The guy hit him because he didn't like him, that's all.

In the early days, you could always tell the hero. He was a good-looking dude. But then came the time when people wanted the rough guy. The fans were seeing the Bruiser breaking guys up and pounding on them, breaking rules, grabbing chairs, baiting the crowd. One day, he wrestled the Terrible Turk. The fans hate them both. All of a sudden, they start cheering the Bruiser. They want him to beat the Turk. Suddenly, he's the new hero: rough and tough. The movies went along with this. Our hero is now the mugging guy who stands up for his rights, not sweet-looking. It happened about 1959, '60. Just at the time all the unrest and turmoil was starting.

Even with the riots going on in '68 and the marches, we were selling the Amphitheatre out. The night they hit Martin Luther King with a brick in Chicago, we had a lot of black people and a lot of whites. I had a black guy, Ernie Ladd, the ex-football player. He was the good guy. Mad Dog Vachon, a mean guy, a white, was the villain. The sergeant from the district came to me and said: "Make sure the white guy doesn't win." Mad Dog Vachon won. There's no way I talk to wrestlers before the match.

I thought it was decided beforehand who's going to win and who's going to lose?

(Deeply hurt) I'm surprised, really surprised, you should ask a question of that kind. It's very sad to even think about it. Whatever happens in the ring is up to the wrestlers themselves. It's up to the people.

I deal right off the top of the deck. I do not make arrangements with wrestlers. I do not do any of these things that the newspaper clique credits to a person like myself. I have a good family. It's a damaging thing. It just shatters my American Dream.

I did a hundred and two thousand dollars, I sold out the place, and the newspapers shun me. It isn't me they're hurting, it's all the people who enjoy wrestling. To them, it's the greatest thing since peanuts. Most of our fans are working-class, but I run two shows in Skokie also. It's upper-class Jewish people. We sell the place out. They root the same way they root in the Amphitheatre. Yet the papers crucify us. A certain elite has decided that wrestling does not belong as a respectable sport in this country. Is that the American Dream? I think it's a black day. The American Dream for me is splintered, a lost cause. There is no American Dream. It's a hype, an elusive nothing.

I'm part of a dying breed. My kind of guy is no more. I don't work with computers, I work with people. The new breed of promoters who do these rock shows never come to town. They send in the thing with Ticketron. There's no more like me. When I'm gone, it's the end of an era.

ED SADLOWSKI

◇————————————————————————————◇

We're at a one-family dwelling in South Chicago. The sights, sounds, and smells inform us we're in the valley of steel.

In 1976, as the youngest district director ever, he ran for the presidency of the United Steel Workers of America. He was defeated. He is now subdirector of the South Chicago district. He is married and has four children. He is thirty-nine.

All my life, I lived within a couple of miles of here. You could look out the window, and the steel mills were glaring at you. You could see, when the Bessemers would tap a heat, the skies light up in an orange glow. In the summertime, you'd lay on the back porch to get out of the heat and see the mills belching smoke . . .

My pa was my best pal. A lotta kids would go to the carnival with their dad. My old man would not only take me on the rides, but he'd show me the shill and how it worked. He'd show me how the guy would cut three-card monte, how the guy would cut the string. "I'll show you the ropes" was his expresssion.

When he was a punk kid, eighteen years old, he rode the rods. He played minor league baseball for maybe twelve years. Elmira, New York. Keokuk, Iowa. We'd go rousting 'round the town. We'd go the bleachers in Sox Park and hit a joint in Chinatown. He knows baseball better than any son of a gun I know. This guy'll tell you about Joe Jackson, Swede Risberg, that's 1919. He remembers when Ruth broke in with the Red Sox. He remembers when the Cubs played the west side park. He's the best billiard player in South Chicago.

When I got a little older, he started talkin' about social questions. I remember some of the rallies he'd take me to, union meetings. I can never remember my father speaking highly of the boss. I never remember my father having too much good to say about a businessman or a landlord. My father and me were very close.

My pa's not feelin' too well right now, but he still goes out at five-thirty in the morning to the plant gates. Handbillin' 'em at seventy-five years of age. Handbills about the union, about the community, political, social questions. He's been out there for forty goddamn years.

When he was about fourteen, he wins the Jefferson Medal for writing a paper on the American Constitution. I saw that in a box there in the closet, not too long ago. He never told me. In the whole city of Chicago, my pa wins that. And then quitting school when he was sixteen.

He hung iron for a while, trying to grab on to any darn thing in the thirties. My pa was a mill hand and a self-educated man. He brought me up to believe in the American system. I believe in the words of Jefferson and Tom Paine: the American Dream that people have a right to say what they wanta say, do what they wanta do, and fashion a world into something that can be great for everyone. Not to have someone fuck you over. To stand up and spell your name, of what the hell origin it is. That's the American Dream: my name is Man. Maybe that's what screwed my head up a little bit. What I was taught in school and what I saw going on in the street were two different things.

When you were in school you were taught to lift yourself up by your bootstraps, develop a strong work ethic, almost Calvinistic. Toil, sweat, and you will succeed. People were looked up to how many things they could acquire. If a guy owned a three-flat building, it made him a smart guy. Most kids of my generation had that kind of jazz drummed into their heads very early.

When you're a kid in school, about twelve and thirteen, the questionnaire would say: What's your name? You'd say: Sadlowski. What does your dad do? You'd put down: steelworker. The counsellor would put you into industrial arts. A fancy name for you know what. That's where me and my pals wound up: making little holes in glass to make chimes, making shoe boxes and junk like that. Little ashtrays you could give your father at Christmastime.

If your name was Rosenheim or had a nice Anglo ring to it—and your father happened to be a doctor or a businessman—they gave you a business administration course or fine arts. All the kids I knew wound up in the steel mills. The son of a gun from U.S. Steel would come at graduation time and recruit guys. They still do that.

I was eighteen when I went to work in the mills. The union meant something to the guys then. It meant a helluva lot more than it does now. A lot of kids in the mills never knew conditions with a nonunion shop. A lot of 'em aren't sons of steelworkers and didn't get it around the breakfast table.

My grandfather, my dad's pa, was a mill hand. Jaja (dziadzia), that's what we called him. I'd ask him: "Where'd you come from, Jaja?" He'd say Poland one day, one day Russia, one day Germany. The biggest gun, that's where I come from, all right? He came from the southeastern part of what is now Poland.

He got off in South Chicago with a tag on his coat. He came to work here at the South Works, U.S. Steel. A bricklayer helper at the furnaces. He got burned up in a big blast-furnace explosion in 1907. He laid in a hospital for a year. He carried the scars to his grave. Then he put in thirty years at the B & O Railroad. He was a roustabout, gandy dancer, track gang laborer. Until the late thirties. He was on pension for some goddamn thirty years. Used to get a hundred eight dollars a month. I used to cash his check at the saloon up here. He's the only guy I know who beat the system. He didn't die until he was ninety.

I loved the guy. We became pals. I was a twenty-year-old kid and he was an eighty-some-year-old man. I used to give him shaves, a couple, three times a week. And slug beer with him. He couldn't tell ya what happened yesterday, but he could tell ya when McKinley was shot, the guy's name, where he was shot, and how many bullets he put in 'im. Here was a man couldn't read or write his own name, but he had a vivid consciousness of what the hell was going on around him.

He was involved in the 1909 steel strike. My jaja would tell me this story in broken English. "We go see Judge Gary in big Chicago." He'd call downtown big Chicago. Gary was the honcho of U. S. Steel, chairman of the board. "Yes, sir, Judge Gary, need 'em, catch 'em more money." Judge Gary would say: "Whatcha need 'em more money for?" Jaja said: "Buy clothes, go church on Sunday." Gary said: "Go church in overalls, good enough." That was his way of saying Judge Gary was a no-good prick. An indisputable fact.

I ran for griever when I was twenty. That pleased my grandpa very much. Here was a guy that's been out of that goddamn mill for forty, fifty years, but he knew all about the union and what made it tick. When I ran for district president, I beat the guy my jaja used to say was a big shot. I beat him two months after my grandpa was dead. He never lived to see it. 1964.

I was twenty-four, twenty-five. I remember guys comin' into the office takin' their caps off, guys who were sixty-five years old. One old guy holds his cap in his hands: Mr. President Sadlowski—all that kinda shit. I'm a punk kid in here, and here's this old guy. It don't lay right with me. I stopped all that. I opened them doors. I took a hammer and chisel, we take the hinge off the door.

My grandpa went to his grave feeling hopeful. He believed in the American Dream. You can make it better. What the hell is it worth fighting for unless you can make it better? I don't think U. S. Steel got me licked. I don't think the bosses of our union got us licked. If I do, what the hell's the sense of this trip?

"I felt low when I lost. Naturally. But, boy, we drew crowds like you never seen before. I met a lot of people. Sudbury, Canada. They mine nickel six thousand feet in the ground, the most destitute spot on the North American continent. You go on to the Mesabi Range in Minnesota—you'll always meet one guy, ten guys, twenty guys in any community—who would have that social consciousness. If you went into the New Mexico and Utah copper fields or the iron mines of Minnesota or Alabama or Oregon or Upstate New York, you'd find a degree of sophistication and awareness that would knock you out. I found more astuteness in the smaller, one-industry towns than in the big cosmopolitan cities.

"The most astute guys were the miners. There's somethin' about 'em. He's rural but worldly-wise. And he sure knows who's fuckin' him. His dream is to get the hell out of there.

"Hell, no, I'm not sorry I ran."

I see guys getting tired of being put down as economic apes, as Archie Bunkers. Even though they didn't have formal education, I've heard some of the greatest stuff come from them. I know a lot of guys that hang iron in South Chicago. Those guys aren't racists. I rarely see a guy walk around with an American flag on a hard hat. Hollywood depicts them that way. You don't become an American by virtue of wearing a damn decal on a hard hat. The workers don't see that either.

Give a guy a chance to see a countryside, and he'll appreciate it. Give him the opportunity to have time to read a book, and he'll read. Give him an opportunity to have time to listen to music, and he'll listen. Human nature is more than punching a time clock and going home. Did you ever watch a guy grow when he's exposed to a new experience? He becomes addicted. He wants more. He starts reading the book, he starts doing this, doing that. Before you know it—boom! —it's like a flower, just opening up one night.

A kid off the street, you show him a tree or a flower, he'll say: "that don't mean nothin'." It *does* mean something. You look at any mill town in the history of this country and you won't find, to this day, flower beds or tree-lined streets. You won't find music halls, unless the guy himself brings a guitar or harmonica. If the boss had his way, you'd never find libraries and books. They're dangerous. Shouldn't there be parks and theaters and libraries in my community?

It's not unique that the people out here felt smoke out of the stack meant bread on the table. I used to think that, too, that the graphite in the sky comes from God, like the snow on the ground. I didn't know U. S. Steel put it in the sky. You start bitchin' about the air, and people say you want to shut the mill town down. They believed U. S. Steel. That's how successful they've been. There's economic blackmail today. When the Environmental Protection Agency gets on their butt about polluting the valleys and streams and air, the head of U. S. Steel says: "We may have to leave." Labor has been buffaloed on this score. Now they're gettin' wise. You can make steel and have clean air and still make a profit.

The unions missed the boat long ago by not taking unionism beyond the gates and into the community. Making it more than just a bread-and-butter thing, pork-chop unionism. I was born and raised across the street from the CIO headquarters. I could look out the bedroom window, and everything was CIO, CIO, CIO. Everybody, even the shopkeepers, were excited. Five million joined, five million working stiffs.

There's no emotion today. Where are the songs being sung? There's an old adage: Once you quit singing, the revolution's over. Right now, out of ninety million working, only one out of five is organized.

The American labor movement could have been the greatest thing the world has ever seen. What happened was the pork choppers wanted to become "part of" rather than "change" the whole political and social system. That catches up with you. You can't play the boss' game. It's tragic when you look back. We develop "labor statesmen," who developed respectability; we develop all those things that are supposedly the American Way.

The American Way, to me, has been one of chasing the dollar. You hear a labor leader say: "What's good for the company is good for us, because if they make a profit, we get more wages." That's bullshit. U. S. Steel is making more profit. We're sure as hell not making more wages. There are two hundred thousand less steelworkers today than there were twenty years ago.

Organized labor is in the hip pocket of the politicians. I sure as hell didn't go down to inaugurate the First National Bank when they laid the cornerstone. I'd seen too many labor leaders go down and lay mortar on City Hall.

Guys think they've arrived because they've been called to a prayer breakfast with the heads of industry. What they should be praying for is to elevate the workingmen's lot rather than sitting down with the bosses, who've done nothing but screw the workingmen.

I don't expect the head of General Motors or U. S. Steel to sit down at the table and by virtue of my having supper with him give me anything I want. I'm going to demand it and take it. The sooner the laboring class—and it *is* a class question—realizes it, the better off they'll be.

"My mother, over the Thanksgiving holidays, was sittin' with my kids. They were playin' hearts, and she was talkin' about the coal mines in southern Illinois. She was tellin' 'em about her father, a big Baptist holy roller. Went to work when he was eleven. All my mother's people worked in the goddamn mines.

"My father met her when the mines petered out. He was still playin' pro ball. Caught a goddamn Illinois Central out of Keokuk. It left him off at El Dorado, along the Kentucky line. You could spit across the goddamn town. Had a little drinking fountain and a town square with a couple of benches. It was a bird town.

"Everybody's lookin' for El Dorado. The city of gold. Bullshit. I could find this city on the map, but I'm never gonna find the city of gold.

"In the twenties, the coal company brought in a bunch of scabs, imported from the Capone gangs in Chicago. The miners marched 'em into the cornfield and shot 'em down. They would get Skid Row bums to act as strike breakers. Goddamn trainload come down, pulled in a siding. The miners were out with their squirrel guns, put 'em back on the train, and sent 'em back.

"I went back there last summer for the first time in twenty-five years. The only things left are just a few graves of my mother's people. Some El Dorado."

A kid today is bewildered, befuddled. He doesn't believe in Calvinism any more, thank God, about working from sunup to sundown. When you go into the shop, it's evident the young worker had destroyed the myth. It's less true than a few years ago, because jobs are tough. But when things get going again, he'd rather spend that fifth day in the park with his girl.

I think that myth about the worker being complacent—he lives in the suburbs, has two cars and a speedboat—that's a lot of bullshit. Did you ever see a working-class suburb? That ain't nothing to write home about.

Buying a piece of land has always been the American Dream. Owning your own home. A kid, starting out today, it's beyond him. The house is sixty, seventy, eighty G's. Twenty-five thousand for openers. A kid can't accumulate that kind of scratch. Send the kid to college? Look at the spiraling costs of that. The dreams his father looked to aren't the same dreams. His expectations *now* are *less* than his old man had. You've got a generation growing up on potato chips and Pepsi-Cola. I don't think the working stiff in this country is holding on to what he has. Frustration is out there. Anxiety is out there. Hope is out there. A want of a better life is out there.

I see changes coming. I hear guys talking of things today you didn't hear fifteen years ago. I hear guys talkin' about inflation and blaming the boss and profits for that crap. I hear guys sayin': "Take the crummy railroads over." I'm not talkin' about radicals. I'm talking about guys who've been doin' their trick for twenty years in the mill. I hear guys saying about how horseshit medicine is in this country and, goddamn it, it's about time we had national health. Call it what you want, call it socialism, damn it, so be it.

A guy asked me: "What's your idea of a good medical program?" I said: "When a guy's sick, you cure him. You don't need green cards with pictures on them and numbers. He's got a stomachache, you cure the guy." He said: "That couldn't be done." Why? If we need another hundred thousand doctors in this country, let's put a priority in making a hundred thousand more doctors and set 'em up in neighborhoods to cure people when they're sick. If we put priorities on things that kill people, why not on things that cure people?

Many of us look back to 1937, '38. The year 2000 is a hell of a lot closer. It's only twenty years away! We've got a society that is burned out, unless . . . unless there's greater distribution of wealth. People are just becoming aware of the conglomerates and how they're chewing us up.

There's a certain instinct that a worker has, much more so than some candy-assed storeowner. He understands who's screwing him, but he doesn't understand how to get unscrewed. The little chamber of commerce storefront man, he never understands he's gettin' screwed. He's part of Main Street, America.

I place my faith in the working stiff, regardless of his hangups. He's still the most reliable guy on the street when push comes to shove.

NEIGHBORHOOD FAMILIAR

RAY KAEPPLINGER

"I been a photographer and had this studio for thirty-two years. I'm the oldest business in the neighborhood. It's a working-class neighborhood: German, Polish, Greeks, Italians. Four churches. I'm getting business through the churches and word-of-mouth. My customers are neighborhood people.

"I do a lot of weddings for a little one-man business. And confirmations, graduations, babies. I love babies. That's what I do best. I can always do good with babies. We give good pictures, and parents like it and they keep comin' back year after year. And then we take their

wedding pictures. I've taken babies of babies that I took twenty years ago."

He's fifty-nine.

I never could take orders. I'm an old-fashioned craftsman. I like to do it my own way. I can't take criticism too much. Even though it's deserved, I can't stand it. (Laughs.) So I borrowed some money and built my own place. Yeah, it's an American Dream. A man that builds from the bottom, builds something up and makes it work. I did make it work. I built this building myself.

My grandparents came from Germany and Luxembourg. My parents were nice middle-class people who worked hard. My dad never wanted to take a dime on relief and worked two jobs all during the depression.

The one thing both of them implanted in all of us was honesty. We never locked our doors. The old-fashioned, honest craftsman, it's been kind of instilled in me, and it's goin' into my own family now. My daughter, she runs a Missy's Très Chic Poodle Salon. We loaned her three hundred dollars to learn how to cut dog hair, and she went to work for the person she'd learned it from. She's good, too. She loves animals.

It's a nice, strong neighborhood. They're not the people that run at the least provocation with the blockbusters. These people have been here for years. For the most part, they're pretty good, but there's a lot of bigotry. They don't want the blacks to move in. As far as I'm concerned, I'd sooner have some blacks come in.

I designed this building myself. I borrowed the money from my father-in-law when I was young, and I paid it off through the years. The year I paid it off, a builder decided to build a huge building next to me. We had no way to fight it. It sure turned out it needed fightin'.

He dug an excavation of fourteen feet deep, right adjoining my studio. This was in the process of three years. We began to be worried our building might get damaged. So close and with rains and nothin' to protect it, the foundation might deteriorate. It was strictly against the building codes. The worst happened. The ice and the snow caved his foundation in and cracked my wall. (He pulls out photographs of the damage.) I talked to the mayor's office and the alderman, but the fix was in.

I tried to get this man to pay for the damage, but he wouldn't pay. I tried to get the building department to do something about it. They wouldn't do anything. The mayor's office wouldn't do anything. So I took him to court. The suit dragged on. There were ten hearings. My lawyer, after the ninth hearing, said: "This is a hot potato." The city corporation counsel warned him if he don't lay down on this case, he'll ruin his law career. It's all on the record.

This builder really had clout. I fired my lawyer and hired another young one. We lost the case in the lower court, but the case my young lawyer built up was so strong, we took it to the appellate court and won the case. The builder took it to the Illinois Supreme Court. And they upheld my victory. We won the injunction closin' down that building.

We decided to have a victory party. I got to sing "The Impossible Dream" at that party (laughs), and I gave a little speech: "Here's How to Beat the City." This was about nine years ago. That was part of the American Dream. I found out our victory was too, too, too quick. It had to go back to the lower courts for the injunction to be implemented. The lower court is completely controlled by the Daley machine. The judge completely ignored the injunction. My dream was shattered, but I wasn't through fightin'.

Now I figured my enemy is not the builder, he's peanuts. My big enemy is City Hall, the clowns down there at the great big den of thieves.

I decided to go to a public-speaking class and learn how to talk. I never had the courage even to second a motion at meetings. The first opportunity I had to use that public speaking was at a budget hearing in City Hall, in the council chambers. Daley was up there presiding. You have to tell 'em ahead of time so you can talk. They had all the speakers there: the police representative asking for more money, the fire department representative asking for more money, the Civic Federation. All these people had their turn. At the end of it all, I was still not called. Mayor Daley said: "Well, that's about all." I got up and I says: "Mayor Daley, my name's up. I want to speak." He knew about this case. The building commissioner, his pal, was directly involved. I says: "Why didn't you call my name?" Then he uses the ploy of mispronouncing names. He named a mishmash of my name. Nobody could understand it. Then I went up and had my say.

I had a speech, notes written down. I said: "This is a budget hearing. This is my tax money. This is what your building commissioner is doin' to the taxpayer." I told the story. I named names. Partway through, Alderman Keane* said: "You could be sued for slander for

---

* A powerful alderman at the time, head of the Finance Committee, who subsequently was sent to prison for malfeasance in office

the things you're sayin'." I said: "I'd welcome a suit for slander. I guarantee it'll be the first step in hell for the Daley machine." After I finished, Daley said: "You mean you want to send me to hell?" I said: "I'll be the first man pushin' you." WBBM-TV got it and they caught the fight, and my daughters were excited. They said: "Man, we're really proud of you." Every year since that, I've been goin' down and speakin', not only about the building department but about the corruption in the police department.

I keep studying through the year. I pick up all articles in newspapers and magazines of how our tax money is wasted. You gotta know what you're talkin' about or they make fun of you.

I also wrote a lot of letters to the editor. I think they're effective. I got into a lot more than city corruption. I wrote about the Vietnam War. 'Cause when you're hurt bad, you can see other people gettin' hurt bad. If our city government can hurt an individual taxpayer like they hurt me, I can also see what our federal government was doin' to other people.

It started me to question authority. It was on a Good Friday. I sat there on this rock. I was hurt bad, I was cryin'. (Laughs.) And that's where the light shone. I said to myself: I'm glad this happened to me. I could see this guy was able to do it with his clout through City Hall and everything fell into place.

Here I am, a dedicated retired army officer, and I saw what authority was doin' over in Vietnam. We're all bein' hurt, the little guys. But it needn't be. We can do somethin'. We don't have to stand by and watch it happen. I've called in to radio shows and sent these letters to the editor. People call in and call me a Communist.

I used to be a real conservative. But now I could see the interwoven thing, that we shouldn't just stand there and look at what our government is doin' and say it's right just because they're an authority.

My wife worked for a company that had City Hall connections, and they got an invitation to Mayor Daley's prayer breakfast in 1974. I looked at the sponsors. Henry Crown, head of General Dynamics. Tom Keane, the crooked floor leader of Mayor Daley's bunch of thieves. Paul Wigoda, another alderman that was in jail, just got released. Howard Miller, this radio commentator who said we should bomb the hell out of those people. These were the sponsors of a prayer breakfast. I said to myself—I didn't tell my wife or anybody—I'm gonna make a protest at this prayer breakfast. I know I'm gonna get in trouble, I'm gonna get arrested, I might get hurt, but I went down anyway. I met my daughter goin' down on the el, and she said: "Are you gonna be on TV again?" (Laughs.) I said: "I think so." But I was really afraid.

I got down there. I paid six dollars. We had these scrambled eggs. They were the worst scrambled eggs I ever had. I tried to make small talk with the people that were sitting at the table there. There were nuns and priests and all kinds of civic people. After the scrambled eggs, Daley gave his talk: Oh, we must support President Nixon. And pray for him. I was polite enough to let him finish. I got up and the TV cameras turned on me and I said: "This is nothing but hypocrisy. You're talkin' about prayer and look at the sponsors: Henry Crown, he's owner of General Dynamics, whose F-lll's, at this very moment, are illegally bombing people in hospitals in Cambodia. Hypocrite! Howard Miller, warhawk, hypocrite! Keane, crooked alderman, hypocrite! Paul Wigoda, hypocrite!" I kept goin' down till Daley's police got to me.

They put the handcuffs on me so tight behind my back, it got so painful when they tried to sit me down in the squad car, I screamed in pain. At the station, the booking officer got a phone call, and I could hear what was coming over because he repeated it. Here's the way it went. Peace Council, subversive. Clergy and Laity Concerned, subversive. Citizens Action Program, subversive. It had to be the Intelligence Division. I knew I was bein' spied upon. Some of the stuff they knew about me, they'd had to have tapped my phone to learn that.

After they made out the papers, they put me in a cell. There's no more sickening feeling to get those heavy gray bars slammed shut. I was nervous. I knew I'd get hell from my wife when I got home. I really felt bad. There was an old black cleanup man moppin' up. He gave me three cigarettes and a book of matches. He was the only human being in that jail.

They told me after three hours that I would not be charged. But they did fingerprint me and mug-shot me. I just smiled, you know (laughs), just to make a nice picture.

When I got home, my older daughter, Missy, the one with the dog shop, she said: "Dad, we saw that, we're proud of you! We're proud you had the guts to do that." I said: "I didn't have the guts. I was shakin' in my knees when I did it." She said: "It was just beautiful."

My wife didn't like it. (Laughs.) I told 'er: "You're takin' care of family affairs now. At this point, let me take care of world affairs." (Laughs.) She's still a pretty conservative-minded person. She's against ERA, which I'm completely for. But she stood by me.

I was always a gentle, peaceful man, and I got hurt. And then the whole world started to open up. Man, there's people that are out there for what they can get, just for greed, and there are people who are tryin' to do things for their fellow man.

I was never a violent man. I couldn't even step on an ant. I went in the service to do my part because I believed America was a great country to work hard for and to fight for and even die for. America's a big mess to me right now. Greed has taken hold too much. The Watergate thing, Nixon, the Plumbers, police-spying surveillance. Look at me, a little guy. There's a hundred pages of police, FBI spying on me.

My neighbors never talk to me about this. They're mostly people that'll keep their heads in the sand. They're people that still canonize guys like Daley and Kissinger and even Nixon. They're only concerned with their plot of land, their little green grass that they have to cut in the summer, their TV, and their can of beer. They'll come down and help me on the building fight because they're directly affected. The whole thing it boils down to is, property is more important than people.

It don't affect my business. I'm gettin' along pretty good now, except I don't like workin' behind that locked door. I was attacked in the studio. It was a date I'll never forget. I had two young men come in, and there were some kids in the studio. The kids like to hang around, they like me. These guys looked bad from the beginning. I sent the kids out right away, I saw I was in trouble. One of the men went into the camera room. You don't do that without bein' invited. The other one locked the front door. I was hit on the back of the head with a heavy object. I went down. The blood was flowin' bad. They hit, continually hitting. They broke open my skull in the front and in the back. (He shows a nasty scar.) This is plastic surgery. It wasn't a robbery attempt, because as soon as I went down they could've scooped up my wallet and ran. But they kept it up. I figured it had to be hired killers. They were hired by people that didn't like me. It was right after I won my legal fees in the building case.

The doctor who took care of me stayed up with me all night in the hospital. He thought I wasn't gonna make it through. He said I must have a strong constitution.

The cops didn't do anything. A young boy came forward with the license number of the getaway car. I gave it to the police. A couple more weeks went by and I called the police. They said: "It's out of the county." So my son and a couple of young friends drove out to the address. We saw the guy working around a pickup truck. I recognized him immediately. As he saw me, he turned his back. We asked the others his name. They said they didn't know, even though they were together. I went to this county's police station, and they said I have to go to the state's attorney. The upshot is, his mother said he was home at the time it happened, an airtight alibi. So I dropped the case. .

Yeah, I bought a gun. It wasn't gonna happen again. I had a buzzer system put on the door. I don't like workin' behind locked doors. It was always a customer would come in and I would trust everybody. Before, we never locked our doors.

It's bad now, but I have a lot of hope for the future. My hope comes from people that care about other people and do somethin' about it. They're not gonna let this world go up in flames. They call me the neighborhood radical, but the young people, they all have a lot of respect for what I do. They never outwardly say so, but you get the feeling. You don't have the public outpouring like in the sixties, but they're honest kids.

I see corruption all over but yet I see hope. All these guys that get away with things, there's got to be retribution, there has to be justice. Too many little people been stepped on, and the people that did it are home free. Somebody's gotta pay! And, by God, even if I have to wait till I die and I get up there—and I really believe there's a heaven —I'm gonna point out these clowns: There they are! Get 'em the hell outa here!

RUTH CURRY, 78

She lives in a large rent-controlled building in Manhattan. "I've lived here thirty-six years. I invite neighbors in for drinks. Life's pretty dull for most of 'em." Her illnesses, several and serious, hardly diminish her ebullience. A niagara of words and associations pour out. "Know how a friend describes me? 'Rapidity of thought and carelessness of execution.' A Jane Austen phrase."

Carelessly lying about are magazines, newspapers, books: a Ring Lardner anthology, Colette, Nabokov, a new biography of Jack London, War and Peace, Crime and Punishment, and the racing form. "I read everything. I have a great knowledge of trivia. I spend sixteen hours a day at it. I always watch the races. There's a big race every Saturday."

In a previous work, a memoir, I had recalled from my childhood a larger-than-life figure: Prince Arthur Quinn, politician, fixer, boozer, half-world hero. She had written me a long, anecdotal letter. "I had a crush on that no-good s.o.b. Mine was a sleeping acquaintance. Vass you dere, Sharlie? I vass dere."

I came from a middle-class family in Indiana. My father was a frustrated doctor who couldn't be second to anyone. He left home when I was little. I understand he had a great wit. I have an anecdote for everything: dirty, good, bad, and funny. It has to be funny. Without humor, you're dead.

I had a hell of a good life. All I wanted was fun. I crammed so much in a little life that I came a cropper like everybody else. I always thought I'd have money, so I was getting broke. I've been broke before.

In 1959, at age fifty-nine—I'm a child of the century, right?—I thought: What the hell am I gonna do now? I never went and looked for a job in my life. I became night receptionist at Lenox Hill Hospital. Twelve to eight. I was security until they finally got security. I loved every minute of it, 'cause I'm a night person. For sixteen years I went every night, up until I got sick in '75. When it came to sixty-five, I was supposed to retire. They didn't know how old I was, so they didn't bother me. My boss said: "Curry, keep doin' what you're doin'." So I did.

Scared? I'm not scared of anything. They forced me to put a special lock on the door here because they had a lot of trouble. I went to work at eleven o'clock every night on the bus in New York, where everything is so terrible. I never felt fear. If it's gonna happen, it's gonna happen. I'm a fatalist. When your turn comes, honey, that's it. There's one thing I'm afraid of: losing my faculties. I don't want to get that way, not being able to enjoy what's here to offer. The body hurts, but if I could just keep the mind. If I die tonight, easy. What is there to it? I want to get me out of sight, burned up and the hell with it, the game's over. I'm not gonna pay 'em to get rid of my carcass.

When I was little, it was a struggling time in America. Most of the people were immigrants, looking for a foothold. It was a feudal time. You either had it or you didn't. There were the robber barons. Of course, somebody had to get this going, and they did. I'd like to castrate the guys, heads of unions. But if capital hadn't sweated labor, the pendulum wouldn't have swung as far as it did. Right now, they've got everybody by the nuts. It's been forced on 'em. If the unions hadn't gotten in where I worked, I'd be makin' fifty dollars a week, not a hundred and fifty. Oh yeah, we're better off than we were. Sure there's hardship, but if a guy really wants to make it, he does. If he's got confidence.

"I would never stick to anything long enough to really make somethin' out of myself. I was always busy getting married, a four-time loser. I musta been a little bitch at heart. At seventeen, I married a boy who was like my brother. Hell of a nice boy. I married him to get out of the nest. I got a kick out of guys bein' crazy about me. I always had guys: New York, Chicago, everywhere.

"There's many guys had more fun with me than goin' to bed with me, 'cause I was a lousy lay. My heart wasn't in it. I was always thinkin' about somethin' else. When I was listenin' to the races, one of my husbands said: 'I'll bet if you were in the throes of an orgasm, you'd say: "Oh my God, I gotta get the scratches."' ' (Laughs.)

"Prince Arthur was a no good but fascinating guy. He introduced me to Johnny Touhy, Bathhouse John, Hinky Dink.* He never had any education, never did a day's work in his life. How'd he make a living? Off anybody he could. He was street smart and cagey.

"I married my second husband out of spite because his mother had no use for me. I think he was a fag. He could make beautiful clothes. It lasted only three months. My third was an Indianapolis fat boy who looked like Jackie Gleason. He was the cutest, flippest guy I've ever known in my life. He was like I was: a natural con man. We wound up in San Francisco. As soon as he trimmed somebody, he'd go out and spend it all. My fourth was Julian Kaufman. He was known as Potatoes. I met him at one of the race tracks."

In 1924, I did work as a photographic hat model. The job was really a snap. I was never pretty, just cute. I always had to be where I shouldn't be. I couldn't stand to go where the little ladies went. I was in a night club every night: Friar's Inn, the Ansonia, the Plantation. I had to be in these joints. That's just the way I was. I knew Al Capone as Al Brown, sure did. I had a tiger by the tail, and I couldn't let go.

I always wanted to be where the action was. In Florida, they set Potatoes and me up for the sting. You've seen the movie, haven't you? Same thing. They set up a store, fixed a guy in Western Union, let us

* The first, a celebrated gangster of the thirties; the other two, turn-of-the-century highly colorful political clouts

win, three, four thousand dollars. When the payoff comes, the guy thinks he's gonna win millions. The horse loses by a nose. I think one of the guys was Count Victor Lustig.* Well, we beat the con men at their own racket.

Did I tell you how we trimmed Arnold Rothstein** for eighty thousand bucks? If I tell you, you'll die laughing. He had a gambling house at the Fairfield Hotel on Seventy-second Street. It was rigged for suckers. We steamed him up about a guy who lost all this money in Chicago and couldn't stop. Tobacco-chewin' Louie. Rothstein was dyin' to get a crack at him. We knew his habit: Lindy's every day of his life. We stalled him four, five nights, and when we knew he was at Lindy's, we had the guy come. For twenty bucks, we bribed the girl, so the line was always busy at Lindy's. They let the guy win. By the time Rothstein came over, we had the guy go. Eighty G's.

You wonder how people can be so goddamn gullible. The way they'd get a sucker. (Laughs.) I had two women approach me two years ago on Second Avenue. I'm gonna tell you, for a moment I almost believed it. This nice pregnant little girl says: "I found this envelope. It has twenty thousand dollars. I'm secretary for a lawyer around the corner. He says it's hot money. They're not gonna go lookin' for it." I saw some bills in the envelope. I knew that old switch. I guess I looked like a real sucker. I knew I was the score. They had it so pat, she and her girlfriend, a colored girl. I almost believed them, knowing it's a sting. Her friend had six thousand dollars coming to her from the Vietnamese thing. Her husband was killed. She'd put it up as good will. They want to know if I'd come up with a couple of G's to prove my good will, and we'll split it three ways, seven thousand apiece.

I said: "Let's go have a drink." I purposely left my purse on the bar with my bankbook open and went to the ladies' room. Naturally, they took a gander at my bankbook. I came back and said: "Let's forget the whole thing, girls." I knew they wanted to blow. They knew I was hip. I thought: What the hell, make it easy for 'em, good-bye. What do I want puttin' somebody in jail for? This girl was no more pregnant than I was. (Laughs.) Did you know that someone in this building was taken for nineteen thousand dollars just two weeks ago?

---

* "My teacher was Count Victor Lustig. He was perhaps the greatest con man the United States has ever known. Lustig's outstanding achievement was getting put in jail and paying a Texas sheriff off with $30,000 counterfeit."—Doc Graham, in *Hard Times* (New York: Pantheon Books, 1970).

** A celebrated gambler who was involved in the Black Sox scandal of 1919

I think the gangsters liked me because I was flippant, funny. I don't think they knew just how to take me. I wasn't a mob's girl. I didn't mix that way.

We went to Florida once with Jack McGurn.* He was an ignoramus. We carried golf clubs with machine guns in 'em. All you had to do was have a banana stand to get killed. Capone had to have a cut in everything. They were looking for Scalese and Anselmi.** At the Jacksonville stop, I sashayed over to the magazine counter, and who the hell do I see but Scalese? He tried to flirt with me. I mean, the guy they're lookin' for is on our train. (Laughs.) Honey, that was the Mafia, and if people tell ya they didn't exist, they don't know what they're talkin' about. All the boys I knew got killed.

When our values became strictly money, you gain, but you also lose. Just take the great men that made money on the stock market. Either they'd rot in jail or commit suicide. Go through the lot of 'em. I knew Jesse Livermore.*** I knew people from all walks of life. I worked with Ruth Etting.****

Wasn't she married to The Gimp?

Oh, that bastard. He and his pimp brother had their mother selling matches out in the street. Lemme tell ya about Potatoes' good friend Max Greenberg, who got killed in a brewery in Newark. It was immediately a battlefront. So I got Potatoes a woman's old gray wig, got him on a boat and out of the country. I picked up the Paris *Tribune* in Germany and saw that the guy who did all the killin' got killed. (Laughs.) So I said to Potatoes: "We can go home now."

I don't think kids today know what havin' a good time is. They're like sheep. They get a great bang out of hurting their parents. I don't mean all kids. The ones who protested the Vietnam War were right. I believe that son-of-a-bitch Kissinger is gonna go down in history as the worst diplomat we ever had.

But I can't understand youth. What burns me up about the young is they conform too much. Long hair, patched jeans. If they really had

---

* Acknowledged as the chief assassin at the St. Valentine's Day massacre, he was dispatched to the undiscovered country from whose bourn no traveler returns, on a subsequent St. Valentine's Day while innocently bowling.

** Scalese and Anselmi were, reputedly, beaten to death by Capone himself during a celebratory dinner.

*** Stock market speculator who committed suicide in the men's room of the Sherry-Netherlands Hotel

**** A popular torch singer of the era

to, were really poor, oh God, they'd be cryin' to high heavens. I've been a rebel all my life. I've always been me. I may be a louse, but I want to be me.

My American Dream? While I live, every day's interesting. I came very close to dying not long ago. I'm not more afraid of death at all. I'm not active any more, I had cancer of the throat. See, I'm chewing gum. I can't go places to eat, but I enjoy living. I'm not talkin' about makin' the world. I just don't want to make it worse. Do you know Abou Ben Adhem? May his tribe increase?

I've been broke, but I've never owed. I'm not mad about anything, I'm not sorry about anything, anybody. I think I had a lotta fun. I just don't like it to end. I like to be profane. I like to say bad things and, 'cause I'm old enough, nobody gives a damn.

CHARLIE DELLAKAMP

Jackson, Mississippi. We're in his office, at the Mississippi Mental Health and Legal Services Project. He's a community worker, concerned with nursing homes.

He is fifty. He has no teeth. They bothered him, so he had them extracted. Now they don't bother him.

My father was a Southern Baptist minister. We moved about quite a bit. Preachers went from church to church. A lot of what we had to eat was what people gave us. They loaded your car down with canned goods, quilt tops, meat they had cured themselves. That kind of thing.

He was hellfire and brimstone, he questioned everything. He was never satisfied with the status quo, but he was not political. My father was prejudiced in his own ways. It wasn't based on race as much as religion. Blacks were welcome in the house but Catholics and Jews were not.

My father was called on many times to preach a service to all-black churches, and he did it very freely. Even back in the thirties. My father was the kind that believed if you wanted to get someone and they were in a beer hall, you went in and sat beside 'em and you drank beer with 'em.

By the time I was twelve, I had already discovered my sexual orientation. As a country boy, I knew nothing about gaiety or homosexuality. I knew what boys did with each other. That went on among farm kids as I guess it did among city kids. On the farm I never heard the word "queer." The word "gay" was not used in those days. Kids would go and spend the night with each other. The excuse was homework. What they actually did was mutual masturbation and playing with each other and things that went on in the barn among country kids.

After I moved to Macomb, I became openly a gay activist. At the same time, my politics were coming out because of the prejudice I had seen toward me. It made me aware of prejudice in other areas: agism, racism and so forth. It turned me to the left.

In 1948, I wrote the Commmmunist party and started a correspondence with quite a few people. I wanted to join. They informed me there was no cell in Mississippi. I was already handing out and selling their newspapers. I sold it to people in the restaurant where I worked and on the streets of Macomb. There was very little adverse reaction. There was more interest in my sexuality than in my politics. At that time, white supremacists didn't feel they were being jeopardized. If it had come along in the late fifties or early sixties, there probably would have been a different reaction.

I remember a young black man who was cutting grass in people's yards. He was having trouble collecting his money, so if he'd go up on their back porches, they'd call the police and accuse him of being a peeping Tom. I tried every way to help on that. There was no ACLU in Mississippi, so I joined the Boston branch. They told me to monitor the court proceedings, which I did.

The Enterprise Journal did a column on the front page about the individual who was putting leaflets and petitions in cars and behind windshield wipers and under doors. He said the individual should be tarred and feathered and run out of town. Everybody knew it was me. When the civil rights movement came along, this editor became a liberal.

I got all sorts of petitions for all sorts of causes, signed by anyone. They didn't even know what it was all about. I would tell them it was for a worthwhile cause, and they would sign.

I really didn't get any harassment over my activities. People were interested in my sexuality. There were a lot of construction workers coming into Mississippi, laying pipelines. They always waited for me after work and wanted to go to bed. They were away from home and didn't care.

The only time my political work was taken seriously was when I persuaded the English teachers to put certain books on the reading list, and they were jerked right off when the authors got in trouble. I was jumped on about that. Members of the Klan came in where I worked to tell me they were going to whip my ass. I was waiting on tables, openly gay, passing out Communist literature. My employer wasn't bothered at all.

I think my mother is the key. She was the kind of person everyone loved, no matter who they were: red, yellow, black, or white. She treated everyone alike, she knew nothing about right and left politics. But her very actions, to me, pointed her out as being socialist, even if she didn't know what the word meant. The very life she lived was an example to me. If she knew what communism or socialism was, she'd be in favor of it. Everything I've said, every radio show, every television show I've ever done, she thought was just great. She always thought I should be a minister.

My father stayed out of it. Only one time did he ever approach me. He had received a threatening letter, dealing with my homosexuality. He said: "What about it?" I said: "All it means is that I'm a homosexual." He said: "I've known that for years." That was the only time it was ever mentioned.

Around 1950, I got my notice to report for the draft. I came to the induction center in Jackson. I told 'em I was a Communist and a homosexual. I told 'em everything I could to keep from being drafted. The only thing they asked was did I have a card to prove it? I told 'em no. They said it didn't make any difference. I was drafted. While I was in basic training in Arkansas, I had a relationship in the barracks with whoever I wanted to. That was no problem.

There were some real shitheads there, pushing for promotions. They accused me of coming in one night drunk and making a pass at the CQ, Charge of Quarters. The next morning, I heard over the loudspeaker I'm to report to the battery commander's office. The first thing he said was: "Do you have a girlfriend?" I said: "Yes, why?" He said: "You've been accused of making a pass." I said: "It's possible. I was drunk last night." They sent me back to my outfit.

I refused to accept a general discharge. So they court-martialed me. That could give me a dishonorable discharge and, I believe, ten years. I was in court two days. I had the support not only of the officers but of all the enlisted men in my barracks. The charge they finally brought against me was indecent assault. The officer I picked as my attorney informed me there was no such thing in the military code of justice as indecent assault against another male. So I was cleared. It was dropped to simple assault, and they gave me three months in the stockade. My battery commander refused to press charges against me, so he took a leave of absence. I guess I was just well liked.

I came to Jackson in 1953. I started working as a banquet waiter at a fancy club. The hatcheck woman came down with cancer and wouldn't let anyone take care of her but me. I had had training in the National Guard in medical work. She put up a cot in her bedroom for me to stay there to give her shots for pain. Her mother and her father, Southern Baptists, decided I had to go, that they couldn't explain it to the church. We had to get out.

We started looking for a nursing home and found only one that had the facilities. It was cold and impersonal. We found a little nursing home that had warmth, just beginning. They hired me in 1955 to take care of my friend, and I became assistant to the administrator. Even after she passed away, I remained. I still moonlighted as a banquet waiter, because at the nursing home, for a long time, I made only 17.50.

My employer was well aware of my sexuality. People called her at home and at work all the time and laid her out for putting up with me. Even her own family tried to get her to fire me. But she defended my rights even though she didn't agree with me.

A lot of movement people all over the country knew of me. They used my house whenever they needed a place to stay here in Jackson. On the street where I live, I was considered a freak. They tried to petition one time to get me out of the neighborhood. It didn't work. When they'd see people coming in and out of my house of all races and beatniks and long-haired guys, they would gather in the morning, around their garbage cans, and watch. If my guests ever parked in front of their houses, they would call me and threaten to have the vehicles towed away. Now they don't pay any attention. There has been a change in the people in the neighborhood. Some couldn't care less who the hell goes in and out of my house.

CLAIRE HELLSTERN, 30

She is director of nursing at the Near North Adult Clinic. It is in the neighborhood of Cabrini-Green, one of Chicago's large public-housing projects. "It was predominantly black when I came there. It's becoming more Spanish.

"I was born in Galena, Illinois. It reminds me of Rome because of

the hills surrounding the city. My grandmother delivered me. She's Irish and had about eight children. She was eighty last January. She sews for the church. She still drives. She lives out in the country by herself. Sees if anyone needs food, if someone has to go to the hospital. She would never have to worry if anyone came to the funeral. When her husband died, there were like nine hundred people at the funeral. People from big cities say: I wonder who's gonna show up. She's in a small town. I think that's how America used to be. My energy stems from her.

"My parents are Irish and German. My name means 'bright star.' My father was a math teacher and cook and Cub Scout leader. He was very strict. My mother is an angel. They were very patriotic. They were proud to be Americans. They were homeowners, they had a victory garden, they kept their property clean, they helped out their neighbors. I'm glad I didn't have a weak father. He said he was responsible to God for the four of us children. But they tried to make us independent. When my brother was gonna be drafted and was thinking of . . . I said: 'Oh no.' They said if he wanted to go to Canada, it was up to him, his decision.

"In high school, I wanted to be a nurse. So I went to the Mayo Clinic in Rochester, Minnesota. At St. Mary's School of Nursing, we had a sister we named Flash Gordon, 'cause she walked around the dormitory with a flashlight. We had room inspections, unannounced. Sisters would walk around with white gloves, going over tops of furniture. I got involved trying to ease up some of the strictness. If we were responsible for people's lives, we should have some control over our own."

Summer of '68, I was a student nurse in Chicago. I had a lotta energy. I wanted to be a volunteer at the Democratic Convention. I knew it was hot and that people would be coming to town. So I went to Mayor Daley's office: "Would you like to set up a first-aid station?" And they said no.

So I went with McCarthy. The McCarthy people were totally unorganized. I called the hospitals and I said: "Could you volunteer a couple of hours?" I got thirty-five doctors.

During the week, we had people that thought they had mono, they had the flu. They were just tired. A couple with measles, chicken pox. Some worried about their blood pressure. And then, Wednesday night. I had some people run off fliers to tell everyone where to come. I didn't expect anything to happen. I thought it was good public relations. Then the march to the Amphitheatre, and something did happen. So we had like seven to ten rooms full of kids. We had one or two policemen. We had reporters, battered, cut. It was such a madhouse.

Some had to be transferred to the county hospital for x-rays and so forth. Everybody was afraid to go along. I went. That was quite an experience. I was with about thirty-five patients. There were people picked up for pickpocketing, mugging. Some were allowed to talk to their lawyers, some were not allowed to make calls. Everything was going on that night.

I saw both sides. It made me feel that just because you have long hair, you're not right. I saw so-called hippies, they didn't care about one another, other people. And just because you're in an officer's uniform, you're not right. I can't stand categorizing people and saying it's totally right or totally wrong. Because I now work in a high-risk area, I think it's unfair to say that the police are totally all wet.

My girlfriend married the deputy mayor two weeks after the convention. I was at their wedding. I didn't want to say anything political, so I talked to Mayor Daley about wakes and funerals. I told him I had introduced the couple. He didn't look well. He had this deepish purple red. I pinched his cheek. I said: "How are you feeling tonight?" He said: "I feel great." I said: "You don't look great. I think you should take care of yourself." I was also seated with the police commissioner. It was very painful not to lash out at them. I felt they should have had more insight.

I'm not impressed by big people. The one person who really impressed me recently, this lady who lives in the row houses at Cabrini-Green. Somebody came into her house, had a knife on her, and she was in her sixties. He was gonna attack her and rape her and rob her. She jumped out of the second-story window, fractured both her legs, and came to see me at the clinic. Then she went to court and testified against him. They lived in the same community. Now that is a person with guts. This is the type of person that impresses me.

There were some greasy-lookin' guys that looked very rough. They witnessed a terrible crime. Some fella was knocked down and run over several times. I talked to the lawyer, and he said they were the last people he'd ever expect to testify in court. They did. Or people that donate anonymously. Or people that volunteer their time. Those are the people who impress me.

I've been going with a guy who says I'm too colorful. He's very politically motivated, a public-relations type. He would be perfect in advertising. I mean, he'd dust everything off before he sat down. He'd have all the linens and the white carpet out. You would never know if you could trust him because he would never reveal his feelings. The polished image. They're uncomfortable when someone else comes along. They'll make it financially, but I don't know if they'll ever really be comfortable with themselves. I don't think they remember who they are, even if they look in the mirror.

Once I went with him to the home of Gary's Mayor Hatcher. I was trying to raise some money for the clinic. There were tops of corporations there. He was uncomfortable. He said: "Claire, you're a little too colorful."

I don't think I lack tact. If you're working with people who are depressed and they have a low income, or you're working with teenagers who are gang members, you have to be flexible. You can't lack tact. Otherwise, you're gonna get knocked when you go out the door. People from the ghetto, I think, are more sensitive. They can tell if you like 'em or if you have an attitude. I'm probably more cautious than I used to be because I've had my purse taken a few times.

I got into Cabrini-Green because I wanted an unusual job. I must have called every clinic. It's rewarding. I do fund raising, teaching students, public relations, writing grant proposals. I function as an ombudsman. One person was upset because her daughter was labeled retarded. I investigated. Scores were missing. So to straighten it out, I made a few phone calls. It's difficult for a nurse to get all that in one job. Either you're in service or doing exit interviews or you're a supervisor. It's narrow. My job is never boring. A lot of people are bored with their job. I love to go to work.

I don't think I'm a do-gooder, it's just my job, my responsibility. I always believed in that. From my grandmother, I guess.

The reason I get a lot of calls is I tell people: "If there's a problem, call me." They all call me Claire. It makes me feel fantastic to have people call my name. There are a lot of secretaries and shopkeepers who are anonymous to the customers. When people up and ask: "Could you help me with this?" it's very pleasant.

They say there's nobody to take children on outings. So I got about ten people to take the kids out. They all came over to my apartment. I used to go down to the projects at night asking the parents—they didn't have a phone—can the kids stay overnight? It's easier to get parents' permission from a lower-income group 'cause there's more children. And they trust me.

Our greatest problem is unemployment. Forty percent around

here. People on welfare lose their self-respect. I've seen it happen. I think everybody on public aid has to work if they're physically able. It's important to develop discipline in getting up on time, reporting, having some self-respect. People don't really want to have a handout. It isn't so great to be on public aid.

I was walking by the dry cleaners on Clark Street, and I saw this little tiny lady, who's four foot eight, with purple house slippers, her knee was bent into touching her other leg. I started talking with her. Her name was Ellie, and she had been in Dixon State Hospital for thirty years. Blond hair, little tiny fingers. My date took the three of us to dinner (laughs), and we went to the state psychiatric hospital to visit her friend.

I became a friend of hers, and she introduced me to Daniel, who was blind and retarded, with a speech problem. And then I met another lady, Mary, who weighed about four hundred pounds. Frequently the four of us, I would do things with them.

Mary lived down in a basement apartment, twelve people, paying a hundred and fifty dollars. Now she's had a bypass and she's down to a hundred and fifty pounds. I got her a job. When she weighed four hundred pounds, she had one pair of slacks. So she still calls me. Then I got Ellie a job, selling things over the phone. For the first time in her life, she's living in her own apartment. If you can imagine, after thirty years in an institution. And Daniel has learned to be a skier. He's blind and has an IQ of about sixty-seven. He's learned to cook. They were like children, they loved to do things. It was a challenge. Plus we had a ball.

If you could imagine what a circus we looked like, sitting in a restaurant. They weren't unattractive, they weren't grotesque. They were unusual, and they knew it. The three of them knew they could get an audience, and they liked it. We got on a bus, and they are singing. One of the people on the bus said it's worth two dollars admission.

I've probably had more experiences than most people my age, and I've probably been in more danger more often. I saw a lady today that had a mastectomy, and she showed up with a black eye and there's ten children, but at least she comes back and talks to me. Maybe I can help her.

I think the way to make America better is if the average person could be the idol. Then being a movie star or a politician would not be the only thing that people would go towards. If they can't achieve that, they feel they're nothing.

I remember being on a bus, it was very crowded. This guy in the back weighed about two hundred and fifty pounds, his shirt was half unbuttoned. He had a beard and longish hair and was probably in his late thirties. He kinda waved me back, so I sat down next to him. I'm very outgoing. When I see some teenaged guys I say: "Hi, how are ya?" I rap with 'em. When you're aggressive, you take 'em off guard. Plus they know you're not stuck up. People call out from the window drapes: "Claire, Claire." I don't remember who they are because I've talked to so many. We have over seven thousand patients. So anyway, this guy, I start talkin' to him. "How you doin'?" And he said terrible. He used to be in trucking, he's collecting unemployment. I said: "Did you ever do any hotel work? Go down to Marriott, they're gonna be three thousand jobs." "First of all," I said, "you better wear a suit, shave your beard, cut your hair. If you have a job already, you could probably walk in with a beard, but when you're really on the line, you have to go overboard." I gave him several other places to look up. And he lights up a cigarette on a crowded bus. First, I said to him: "Do you have a couple of hundred dollars for a fine? You just told me you're out of work." I said: "Please put your cigarette out." He wouldn't do it. I'm thinkin' to myself: What nerve. Here I am helpin' the guy, and he's riskin' everybody on the bus. And I said: "You're gonna be sorry." And I was smilin', too, so I yell: "Help! Help!" on the bus. Everyone starts laughing. Because they heard me talking to him. I didn't talk loud, but I wasn't whispering. See, on a crowded bus, if I'm talking to someone next to me, the people right ahead of us can hear me and to the left, unless I have a telephone or a walkie-talkie. So they started laughing. So he put out the cigarette.

I think you have the right to assert yourself, how you feel. If you're in a car and you're gonna park and someone starts honking, you assert yourself, not honking back or screaming. There's something about cars and screaming. Their nerves. There are ways of doing it through humor.

It takes a strong fella to be able to date me. If they're prejudiced, they're uncomfortable where I work. Maybe he's been ripped off, it has been an element of danger, Or in some areas of the United States, it could be over a job. In Texas, I was told, the Spanish and the blacks were at one another's throat because there are so few jobs. I'd work on changing his attitude gradually. I wouldn't allow certain obnoxious words. I don't like vulgarity. I don't like racial slurs. I expect respect for myself. He would respect where I work or he'd drop out of the picture. After all, I work with beautiful people.

People have really got brains. I had one patient who was ninety-six when he died. He was brilliant. I had a crush on him. He built the University Club. He was a WASP but very modest. He repaired everything himself. His electricity, his plates, his shoes. He was doing all his own work. I think it's good to have heroes.

I've been responsible for myself since I was seventeen. My parents worry all the time. They pray. We go home for the holidays, everybody goes around the table, and we have this prayer. It's a big joke. I started it. Someone prays for a date and they want so and so. Sometimes it's sentimental. My father prays I leave the clinic. In a joking way but serious. He knows I'm not going to.

My friends always invite me because they want to hear all the stories, all the adventures. Humorous. One girl says: "Claire, one of the days of your life is like ten years of my life." I have met the poorest to the richest, the most powerful to the student. I've met the radicals, the conservatives, the bureaucrats. Unfortunately, they don't communicate. We have fighting everywhere. With weapons being sold and talk about the neutron bomb, it would be hard to say you're not worried. But I don't have any doubts about this country. I think we can improve. If I thought it was impossible, I should move elsewhere.

Let's clean up the act and go on.

ALONE

GEORGE MALLEY

A rainy day in June. It's a neighborhood of one- and two-story family dwellings on Chicago's Northwest Side. A blue-collar community. "Call it middle-working-class," he says.

He was living elsewhere when I first met him, about twelve years ago. "I moved from the old neighborhood where I lived for eighteen years. There was a new breed coming in with rehabs. These quite clever people, young professionals. Intellectuals, they were not. (Laughs.) Pseudo-intellectuals, yes.

"We decided to get out. We were no longer happy. We didn't speak the same language. In fact, we didn't exchange the same kind of looks. (Laughs.) But I still haven't found what I'm looking for."

I feel lonely. I am afraid. I don't see hope when I look at people. I used to think the world was such a wonderful place. I used to think that ultimately man would surmount everything. What disillusioned me is man's tremendous capacity to be selfish. He is so unwilling to compromise. He refuses to give, you understand? I do not see a bright American Dream. It is a dream without lustre.

I'm listening to the media. What else do we have access to, outside of our own families and the small circle of friends? They try to deliver a package, but they leave you on the fence. You understand what I mean? I don't accept what I hear. I'm left to my own resources. Then I stop to think: Can I trust myself? My intellect is limited. We're absorbing so much knowledge that there is less and less and less time to understand what the knowledge is all about, see? And time is running out.

Over a long period of time, man has been disappointed. He almost expects disappointment as a way of life. He doesn't expect anything else. I don't think he can conceive of a world run the way it should be run.

I don't talk to my neighbors about it because my neighbors don't want to hear anything. They brush you off. Football, they'll talk to me. Horse racing, they'll talk to me. Their jobs. But don't try to take them outside themselves. You're in trouble if you do.

During the sixties, I used to talk to my boys a lot. At the time, they took issue with me. I thought they were trying to turn the world I knew upside down. Now, strangely enough, I see a hell of a lot of what they had to say come about. I lived to see the change. But now, my boys have taken the opposite stance. Now they're for law and order at any price. They're for hit 'em over the head if there's no other way.

I guess they've become adults. In our society, when you become an adult, you stake your claim. They have property now. They both have homes. They're doing fine. Once my sons called me bigoted, narrow-minded. I said: "Fifteen years from now, you're going to be a different person." I was right. But I am the one that changed most dramatically.

Twelve years ago, I didn't understand things in light of what I see today. I'm surprised at myself. I feel I could live with black people now. Yes, I still worry about violence. But I'm sure the black man has the identical worry, even more so than I have. So we're sharing something in common, see?

I have learned you better not become too attached to anything. You understand what I mean? Don't get so attached to something that you can't let go of it. My boys are now reaching the point where they're accumulating things. The foremost thought in their mind is to protect it. They have to look for someone to protect it from. All right? So God help the first one that gets in their path.

My father was born in Austria. It was the dream of everyone to come to this country. If you didn't better yourself, at least you'd eat. He was an iron worker, one of the most intelligent men I've ever known. He could neither read nor write. His signature was an X. But when he talked, everything that came out of his mouth was original.

When my father talked, that was my father that was speaking, not Aristotle or Plato or Socrates or someone else. That was my father, and I knew it was him, you know? This is a good feeling. These are some of the lessons I tried to teach my boys. I tell 'em: "I recognize so much of what you say as being the source of other intelligences. I'm looking for *you* in all this conversation. I can't find *you*. Where are *you*?"

As a youngster, I was geared to think in terms of dollars and cents. If I do this, what is it worth? If I get an education, what is it worth to me in dollars and cents? Everything was money. I never thought about knowledge for the sake of knowledge, for the sake of truth. I am not blaming my parents, for I don't think they understood it themselves.

For the past dozen years, my most contented moments are when I'm alone. I like to get up at four o'clock in the morning and sit in this chair and just be alone with my thoughts. Oh, the thoughts range from things of the past, religion, science, what lies ahead—oh, just what it is all about. Knowledge has only real value when there is understanding. It's tremendous, it's exhilarating.

I'm not the most clever man in the world, I'm not the most educated. I did get through fifth grade and quit. But I'm not the most stupid person either. I may have only a fraction of the brains a learned man may have, but I'm forced to use every part of it. Sometimes I find I'm using more than the educated man.

We have to redefine what education is. Are we talking about reading, writing, and arithmetic? What should we learn that will enable an individual to go out on his own? What is education? When can I really say I know something? Every goddamn thing we know, we have to relearn every how many years?

The average man equates the accumulation of goods with power, supremacy, intelligence. If I have more than you, I'm better than you are. It's just like the neighborhood drunken bum. Never worked a day in his life. He's walkin' down the street and he kicks a bag, a million dollars in it. Now he's an eccentric millionaire. He's no longer a bum or a drunk. You see what I mean? Power. But has he changed? What's changed is that other men will accept him as superior. The almighty buck.

I wish I lived in a world that didn't know what money was. I wish I lived in a world where I didn't gauge the worth of a life by the color or shade of a man's skin. I wish I could live to see the day where Washington enacted a law that made man, once a month, come to a common meeting place and gave him a lesson that forced him to think, to exercise his brain. Just to get a man used to it and find out how delicious it can be.

My sons tell me I'm too soft for this world any more. And I tell 'em: "Thank God."

STIRRINGS IN THE NEIGHBORHOOD

MARY LOU WOLFF

"I was born and raised on the West Side of Chicago. My father was a wood finisher. His parents came to this country from Sicily around the turn of the century. When he was a young kid, they came to Illinois, where there was work for the men. They worked on the railroads out west. The kids and the women stayed and farmed on small plots of land. There were just two of us, my brother and I. We never discussed anything, ever."

She is forty-five.

We had history in school. I always felt a little uneasy with it. When I was a kid, if I went to the Chicago Historical Society, I felt strange there. I thought that was just for high-class people. I just felt foreign.

I'd see some of the suits Abraham Lincoln wore or something. But I remember just feeling ill at ease. The words "democracy" and "government," they just reminded me of school and the nuns giving lessons. As if what they were talking about was musty and had nothing to do with living on Chicago Avenue. Yet I knew things were happening to me.

I read a lot. But it was the Nancy Drew series type of stuff. There was only one thing to be, I thought. To get married and be a mother of kids. My first inkling that there might be something else came when I was in high school. St. Mary's. I joined a group called the Young Christian Students. We read things like social encyclicals of the church. I began to be aware of things like social policies about labor. I had never heard of such a thing before, even though my father was a workingman.

I was beginning to meet a type of people I never met before. There were people from Europe, from worker movements, who would occasionally stop by. There were students. I liked hanging around there and talking to these people. They seemed to treat me seriously, as if I understood what they were talking about. Often I didn't, but they assumed I did. I liked that.

I went to a Catholic girls' college for a year. It was not upper-middle-class, but I thought it was. During the first week I was there, they had a tea to welcome the incoming freshmen. They told us what we should wear. You should have heels on and a pair of white gloves. That completely threw me because I didn't have a pair of white gloves. I felt completely out of place. So after a year, I decided to quit.

I had romantic ideas. I don't know why I thought to be a worker, to work in a factory, was the best thing of all. Now I think it's crazy. I wish I'd stayed in that college.

I worked at a series of dead-end jobs. I made paper boxes. I soldered radio parts. I was a waitress. I was not successful at any of these things. Suddenly I realized how boring all this is. I was confused. Here was my romantic notion of a worker, and I didn't want to be that either. I once went to a candy company. They looked at my background, the little bit of schooling I had, and they wouldn't hire me. They said: "We think you're a union organizer." I had nothing to do with it. (Laughs.)

After a series of these crazy jobs, I went to work at the headquarters of the Young Christian Students. I edited a magazine for working women. I had a very small salary. Finally, I gave all that up and got married. I was twenty. After I had a few kids, I'd be reading the paper and I'd think about those people from the days before, and I missed them. The way I handled the feeling of vague discontent, I'd say: "That was all kid stuff. Now you have responsibilities. Put those dreams aside. That's over and done with. Those are crazy people."

I had nine children. It was absolutely full-time. Once in a while somebody would remember and say: "Could you come and give a speech?" I'd always say: "No, I'm a mother, I'm too busy." Sometimes I'd spend hours in a rocking chair with a baby, looking at him and wondering what was gong on.

My friends were all very nice. We'd get together and exchange recipes for coffee cake. We'd talk about the drapes we were gonna make. I enjoyed all that. But I'd always come home feeling vaguely discontented. I spent a lot of time reading, though not in any disciplined way. I'd just pick up a book here, sometimes it would be a classic, but I'd find myself wishing there were somebody around I could talk about the book with. There was nobody.

My husband made an effort to try and understand what it was I was talking about. Often, he would throw up his hands and say: "Mary Lou, I don't know what you're talking about. What is it you want to talk about? Do you want to go out and buy a new dress?"

Around the time my last baby was about three, in the sixties, there was a lot of upheaval in the church. We were active Catholics. Vatican II happens. Questions of conscience are being raised. Questions of the war. Edward got to be seventeen or eighteen, and I began to wonder. Nothing political about it. I didn't want my son to go to war.

I didn't even know where Vietnam was. Also at that time, the older kids began to say: "I don't want to go to church." I couldn't comfortably tell them: "You're going to go because that's what we do." I'd find myself havin' a cup of coffee, and I'd be thinking that's a good point they brought up. It happened that circumstances all clicked together. The baby was of an age where I could leave her with the older kids. A new young priest came to our parish. I said to him: "So much of the church is concerned with the education of kids. We adults right now are not certain of so many questions and upheavals and changes. Why don't you have something for us where we could sit and discuss? I'm interested in adult education."

After a few weeks, lo and behold, I don't know where he found these people. They lived in the neighborhood for years, and I never knew any of 'em. We came together in the basement of the rectory. It was a shock to me to find out they were all saying: "Yes, we have felt isolated. We had nobody to discuss any of these things with. We'd sure like to talk about some of the changes."

We decided to start an organization. This was the year there was an incredible number of dead elm trees. There's kids, delinquency, heavy traffic, all kinds of problems. But if we could get those elm trees cut down, that would be a good start. Everybody would see that right off the bat.

Some people said: "Let's ask the alderman." The rest of us instinctively said: "Why should we go to him? He had his chance and did nothing. Let's go right down to the department in charge of this." One woman, Dolores Cruz, toured every street in our neighborhood and made a list of every dead elm tree. A group went down and gave this list to the head of Streets, Sanitation and Forestry. He took the list, put it aside, and forgot about it. Nothing was done. That was a lesson for us.

Dolores came up with a good idea. She made a sign for every dead tree in the whole area: *This is a Dead Tree. It Should Be Cut Down.* It made fun of the officials because they were always cuttin' down trees in front of people's houses, but they were the wrong trees. We had two hundred twenty-five signs up. Within a few days, all those trees were cut down. We learned our first lesson: calling attention, making fun of officials, and going over the head of the alderman.

There was another dramatic issue: a street that was made a speedway when they built the Kennedy Expressway. It was a neighborhood side street that became dangerous. For years we were trying to get stoplights. Nothing happened. There was a motorcycle accident. Two kids were killed. We visited every house, and the response was overwhelming. Three or four hundred people came to our first meeting. We started our organization.

I felt once again: Okay, my duty is done. Now I gotta get back to my house. I went back home and started baking cookies again.

Then another little bunch of women said: "Why don't we have a Great Books discussion class?" We all laughed. No people in this neighborhood would be interested. This is not that kind of a neighborhood. Within a few weeks, we had a Great Books discussion class made up of just the regular working-class people. One of the first ones we read is the Declaration of Independence. We spent three hours discussing the first half of the first sentence. This is the first time I, as an adult, ever discussed with other adults what the Declaration of Independence could possibly mean to me. There were intelligent people thinking about the same kind of things that we were thinking about.

Every once in a while I'd pick up a newspaper and read about CAP, Campaign Against Pollution. Father Dubi was the young priest at the head of it. They broke rules. They carried on a fight against Commonwealth Edison and finally won an antipollution ordinance. They went into other issues and changed their name to Citizens Action Program.

Our neighborhood was right at the cross section where the Crosstown Expressway is going to be built. People are asking us where is the expressway going to be built, so we know what street it's gonna go down. Should we be opposed to it if it's on this street or opposed if it's on that street? Finally somebody said: "Why should we be for it at all?" There was a moment of silence. We all looked. That's right. We don't want it at all! Somebody else said: "That's silly. You don't think there's any way you're gonna stop 'em. That's all set for years." The rest of us said: "No. We're not gonna have it come through."

CAP was organizing against it and asked if we'd be interested in meeting with some other people. We were invited to go on an action, which we'd never heard of. This was a new step in organizing. They were gonna go to the office of the alderman and ask him if he had any financial interests in the expressway.

It was on a Sunday afternoon. A whole new thing happened. We went to the alderman's office. Father Dubi was our spokesman. There wasn't room in the office, Alderman Pucinski said, so he'd come out. Pucinski said: "I'll just stand on top of this car here and talk." He took the microphone away from Father Dubi and climbed on the car. Father Dubi pulled the microphone away from him: "This is our microphone, we're using it." I was stunned. I couldn't believe this. A priest pulling a microphone away from an alderman.

We never saw anything like this before. After it was over, the crowd lingered around. Pucinski came out again and Len said: "Are you sure you don't have any financial holdings?" Pucinski got mad and said: "If you weren't a priest, I'd punch you right in the nose." Father Dubi pulled his collar off and said: "Go ahead and punch, try it."

The people I was with said: "Oh, come on, this is turning into a brawl." They were turned off by this. I thought it was great. It was connected with my impatience about too much talk. I began to realize

I liked direct action. Not only was it more exciting, but it was a glimmering of the idea that you don't get anywhere if you talk too much. At some point, you must act.

Action. The word came into my vocabulary. They'd call up from CAP and say: "We're gonna have an action tomorrow morning at city hall." It would be a confrontation with some official. We were trying to see the plans for Crosstown. The officials wouldn't let us see them. It was as simple as that at first. They'd say: "It's not your business, you wouldn't understand them." Or: "We don't have them ready, we're studying them." We heard that many times. They'd been studying for several years.

Here, suddenly, was a group of people I liked, admired, saying: "You don't have to always be polite." This was a complete shock. That's something you're taught from the time you're a baby. If you want to get anywhere, you have to be polite. Follow the rules. If officials say, "Sit down and wait," you sit down and wait.

These people were saying you can stand up and demand things. At first, I was troubled by this. What does that mean? Do you insult people? I began to realize, no, I don't see anybody insulting anyone. I see people acting nervy. They're not doing anything wrong. They're just not agreeing to follow somebody else's rules.

I began to think there are rules made by some people, and the purpose of those rules is not really order. The purpose is to keep you in your place. It may be your duty to break some of those rules. I liked it, I enjoyed it.

We once went to see George Dunne* when the board of county commissioners was in session. The commissioners sit down in a well, you're like spectators at the Coliseum. You just sit there and look. The commissioners are sitting in beautiful red velvet chairs. We arrived a little bit early. We had been there the week before, and George Dunne warned us he would throw us out if we ever interrupted the meeting. So what we did was come early.

Everybody was standing in the gallery. We said: "Let's not stand up here, let's go down there." How do we get down there? There's no door. There was a wooden railing that separated the spectators from the actors. It's easy. You just climb over the railing. Everybody climbed over, and were in the main section. We said: "While we're here, let's try out these seats. Look at those big seats. Boy, these look great, don't they?" The secretaries were horrified. They said: "You

* President of the board of the Cook County Commission

can't sit there, you people. Get out of there." We said: "Why? We're taxpayers." Everybody sat down in the seats. When Mr. Dunne came out, he was horrified, too, and said: "You people just better get out." We said: "No, we want to meet with you." He refused and went back to his office. So we sat there and had our own meeting in the seats. Now it's not a big thing, this kind of trespasssing is just new to all of us.

Once we wanted to meet the head of a bank. We had a large group of people. The guards came out and said: "Don't step over into this carpeted area. This marks the corporate offices, you people can't step in it." I mean, it's not that important. But it became important for us to say: "Are you kidding? Of course we can step on this. Here, watch our feet. We're going to step on this carpet. Now what are you gonna do about it?" (Laughs.) A lot of people think that's causing trouble. But it isn't that. Often you have to sit down and examine what rules are for. Some rules are good and some rules are just to keep you in your place.

I was always a very quiet, polite person. If I had to speak in front of anybody, my face would flush. I would get embarrassed. But the people from CAP seemed to see something different in me. They began to treat me in a way that I wasn't even treating myself. They expected me to do things I never thought I could do. Maybe I *was* different than I thought I was.

People were saying that I'm an organizer. I didn't know exactly what an organizer did. I thought of them as mysterious people. Later I found there was nothing mysterious about them. It was just the work they did. They gave me serious books to read about corporate America, things about expressways. Normally I would think: Let my husband read them. Housewives don't have time for this. But they'd say: "Read it and let us know what you think." I was flattered. At first I reacted out of flattery. But after a while, I began to realize they actually think I'm intelligent enough to know something serious. I was getting some knowledge of politics, and some deep personal changes were coming about as well.

They were gonna have a meeting at McCormick Place, about five or six hundred people. We need somebody for a keynote speaker, somebody who's gonna turn the crowd on. I was wondering who they were gonna get. Father Dubi said: "I propose we have Mary Lou." I was absolutely stunned. My past reaction would have been to say: "Oh, no, I don't think I can do it." But now I thought: If they think I can do it, though it scares me, I'll try. So I went home and wrote my speech myself. The day came, lo and behold, I got up and I knew it was a good speech 'cause the crowd was reacting.

At the end, I said—it was a little corny—any time there's a gathering like this, of people coming together and deciding they have to fight, if Jefferson or those people are around anywhere, they must be thrilled, they must be saying: This is what we had in mind.

From that moment on, I began to think it was possible, though difficult, to have a democracy. It was an experiment, risky, chancy. But you couldn't say: "Okay, we got a democracy." It's an ongoing process that has to be carried on with each generation. All that occurred to me as I was writing the speech. I've done more reading and thinking about it since. And I know that's right. It was the first time I realized what that was about.

One election day, after our workers covered every precinct, an elderly man with a heavy German accent came up to me and said: "This is the first time I ever voted." I thought he was a new citizen. He said: "No, you don't understand. I voted for years, but this is the first time I ever *really* voted. I knew why I was voting a certain way. This is the first time I ever understood what democracy was about."

I don't like the word "dream." I don't even want to specify it was American. What I'm beginning to understand is there's a human possibility. There are many, many possible things people can do personally. There are many possible things people can do publicly, politically.

Certainly circumstances have to come together. How do you make them come together? That's where all the excitement is. If you can be part of that, then you're aware and alive. That for me is the dream, if you want to call it that. It's not a dream, it's possible. It's everyday stuff.

NANCY JEFFERSON

◇————————————————————◇

She's director of the Midwest Community Council, a grass-roots organization on Chicago's West Side. It is comprised of five hundred block clubs. "Its purpose is to organize people to speak for themselves and make their own decisions for the community. I don't get tired where I work. I work maybe thirty hours a day." (Laughs.)

I'm a farmer's daughter, one of thirteen children from the hills of Tennessee. Paris. My father still lives in Tennessee, a man that can't read and write and gave us so much. His will was that all of us be able to read and write. Dad didn't have a formal education, but he's the most educated man I've ever met.

I say to the folks on the West Side: "It's up to you to educate your child." Most parents think: I can't help my child, I only went to fourth grade. We started an awareness group, and I gave them what happened to me. My father makes an X for his name, but he taught me how to read. I remember all thirteen of us had to sit down in front of the fireplace. Sometimes we had oil in the lamps and sometimes we didn't. If we didn't, Dad had made a big fire, and the glare of the fireplace would give us light. We had to read every night.

I was eleven years old before I knew my father couldn't read or write. We'd get to a word and we'd stumble over it. He'd say: "Read that over again. You're stumblin' over that word." We thought he knew what that word was. He knew it didn't sound right to him. He'd tell us: "Chop it up, like you're choppin' cotton. You know how you get weeds out of cotton. Chop the word up like that an' put it back together again." That was really teaching phonics. (Laughs.)

Now, my brothers and I, we laugh. When we're talkin' about things, I'll say: "Chop it up. Chop it up. Put it back together again." As a result, all of us are great readers.

We were sharecroppers. We were always in debt. He would say to the boys: "Now you go out in that field. There's not gonna be anybody out there but you and that mule. There ain't nobody around to see you. But there are certain things you won't do because it's you. You don't violate yourself."

My mother could read and write, and she did a little poetry stuff. She wrote poems for everybody in the community. She called 'em speeches. She had it all carved out for every one of us. I was going to teach and get people together. She didn't know what social work was or anything like that. "Cecil is gonna be a black president." (Laughs.) She had it all carved out.

The boss, the white man we lived with, didn't want us to go to school. He wanted us to go to the field. We had to get up early in the morning to pick cotton before school time and pick in the afternoon.

I'll never forget the day the boss came down on a horse. He was at the back door. He said to my mother: "I want that gal, the oldest gal, to go to the field today 'cause we gotta get that cotton out." My mother said: "No, she's goin' to school." I would go to school without missin' a day. He says: "What're you tryin' to make out of that gal?" I remember her puttin' her hands on her hips and she said: "She might be a whore, but she's gonna be an educated whore." (Laughs.)

I think that's what it's all about. We have got to invest in ourselves. If the community's gonna change, neighborhood's gonna change, society's gonna change, the world's gonna change, it's by individuals. Not by big bureaucracy, not by the Exxons, not by all that. It's by individuals making that decision: I'm not gonna violate myself and I'm not gonna let you violate me. (Laughs.)

About '59 I was living in a tenement building with small children and was concerned about the dirty streets and the vacant lot that was full of old cars. Having come from the South, I thought I couldn't do anything about that. That's the city, and I'm not part of this city decision. I thought that was just something you live with. While in the South, we were very, very poor, but there was beauty all around you. Green grass and flowers and all that.

One day, the guy was pullin' an abandoned car on that vacant lot. I had this little piece of paper that said I was a community leader. I went right out to this guy and I said: "Who gave you the authority to pull that car on that lot?" The guy says: "I'm drivin' for some company. My boss'll be here." I said: "You better get him, because I want you to pull this car off of this lot." In a few minutes, the boss drove up in a big car. He was white. I walked up to him and says: "I have not given you the authority to put these cars on this lot, an' I want you to get 'em off." You know, he moved those cars. (Laughs.)

If we take the time to educate people, they will have the tools to act with. No person wants to be ignorant. If he has the tools, he understands: This is your street, this is your house, whether you're a tenant or whether you own, this is your community. How do we make people kinship to where they are? Somehow, we lost a part of that humanhood we were taught, that personhood. It's not easy to work person by person, people by people, block by block, precinct by precinct. But I'm optimistic about it.

This mornin' I had a young man. That's why I was late comin' here. He had taken some money from us. I didn't think I'd see him again. I spread the word: "Watch out, he's a bad egg." Today, out of a clear blue sky, he walked into my office. He says: "I want to talk to you." Everybody in the office knew he was in our list to watch out. He says: "I want to pay back my debt at fifty dollars a month. I've gotten a job. I didn't want to see you until I got a job."

I was the happiest person in the world because somethin' brought him back. What you do is not lost. I told him that's what it's all about. It's havin' the courage to repent. You have some courage and somethin' goin' for you inside. He smiled. I don't know what made him come back. Was it the spirit in the community?

In the South, it was the country preacher that held things together. You talked to the preacher about how to get help. With education, it was the teachers. They lived in the community, were part of it. Here, the president of the block keeps the community together.

Remember the policy runner years ago in Chicago? He was around at three or four in the morning, with a truck full of money payin' off. (Laughs.) He never got robbed, illegal as it was. Big Jim Martin was Big Daddy. Everybody went to him for whatever problems there were: for food, for the house that was burned out, for furniture. He used to be there on the corner, and he had time. He delivered the goods and the services to everybody. He was known in the community. He was part of it.

We take in ten blocks. We visualize that as a little town. Each has a president. We have somebody who is over all. He's sort of the mayor of these ten blocks. Everybody begins to get involved in everything: garbage disposal, traffic lights. We're sayin': "Don't disrespect yourself, and don't allow anyone to disrespect you." That brings you into the politics of the city.

The Democratic machine of Chicago has people on the block, precinct captains, who profess to help. They make themselves known to everybody around. Call one Rosemary. Call the other Charlie. What can you do that they can't do?

I know that Charlie. If I'm hungry, I can go to him and say: "Charlie, I'm hungry." Charlie will find me some food. If my son got in jail or whatever, I can go to him. It's that neighborhood concept, it makes the world. But he and Rosemary think of the best interests of the machine. Our Rosemary and our Charlie are our block-club presidents. They think of the best interests of the block.

We just did a job of rehabilitation of a two-block area. It was social rehab as well, everybody gettin' into the act. We employed the young men who were not working to work on the houses in these two blocks. It created a lot of interest: what people can do themselves to organize a community. It's been fantastic.

On the West Side right now, they have become more politically sophisticated than they were in the sixties. I even say to folks: "Don't put your trust in me. Better to trust yourself. I may die tomorrow (laughs), and what're you gonna do? *You've* gotta do it."

We've got a motto. It's all written up: "Your house is part of this block. This block is part of this city. This city is part of this state. This state is part of the United States of America. You're involved all the way."

This summer we did a demonstration on the boulevards of the West Side. People were disturbed that they could never get the boulevard seeded. Every year they'd tell us they ran out of grass. This went on for five years. Now they said: "It will be August before we get to you. We don't have the equipment." We had a meeting. I said: "Let's compute our taxes as to how much we're payin' into the forestry for seeds." We got a couple of accountants.

We had a meetin' with the officials and we said: "We've computed our taxes, and rather than charge you with malfeasance, we will have a press conference tomorrow and say we're going to withhold that part of the money from our tax dollars and buy our own seed. We'll put our folks to work—we've got a lot of unemployed fellows—and we can buy machinery with the money and seed our own lawns. We ain't got no problem."

At nine o'clock the next morning, they came up with hundreds and hundreds of pounds of grass seed, all the workers that we wanted, and we got all our lawns seeded.

Now I said: "You can make decisions about anything you're payin' for. The garbage, the sanitation, the police, the crime, the teachers." We're havin' a lot of fun right now. We have what we call awareness education classes.

The police commander of our district said crime went down, and he laughs and says: "I don't want to say it went down because of what you all are doing, but maybe so." We got seventeen men, they're kinda tough guys. I said to them: "You just stand on the corners." We've got four, five preachers with 'em. It has taken an effect.

It's not the kind of thing that television picks up because it's not sensational. But it is sensational to the people here. My father talked about it. "Don't worry about the papers and all that," he said. "It's peace within you." I'm religious. I believe in the Christian principles. When Christ was here, he must have said: "Let's get it together." (Laughs.)

Down in the country, we used to have to ring the bell if there was trouble or we'd ring it for dinner. You used to pull this rope.

(Laughs.) Sometime, especially if it was cold, you'd keep pullin' and keep pullin' the bell. You'd think you'd never hear a sound. Maybe by the time your hands got raw almost, you'd hear a little tinklin' of the bell. That's just the way I visualize the community. We all keep pullin' at the rope and our hands are gettin' raw, but you do hear a little tinklin'. It does give you some hope that after a while the bell is gonna ring. We gotta do it, we must do it. We have no other choice. As my father said: "If you're the only one doin' it, the only one left in the world to do it, you must do it." We gotta keep pullin'. And I believe the bell will ring.

BOOK TWO

One of the things that makes America such an unusual place is that it is perhaps the only society in history in which a vast number of its members are living their private dream. It is a world that teaches the primacy of the personal, of oneself, which ironically leaves people powerless. This country has always been saved by a new minority, who realize they've been robbed. In the process of righting their private wrongs, they have reanimated our public rights. You who thought of yourself, up to that moment, as simply being a number, suddenly spring to life. You have that intoxicating feeling that you can make your own history, that you really count.

—Nicholas Von Hoffman

DREAMS: PUBLIC AND PRIVATE

V I S I O N S

J O H N   H O W A R D   G R I F F I N

The world has always been saved by an Abrahamic minority. I've seen it in my life from the time of the Nazis. There have always been a few who, in time of great trouble, became keenly aware of the underlying tragedy: the needless destruction of mankind.

This minority overdoes, gives every ounce, to compensate for the lack of awareness in the majority. This minority grows smaller, and when it disappears, it won't be the end of mankind. It will be the end of mankind as we know it.

If we take people as they are, we tend to make them worse. If we take people as they could be, we can get better. The whole emphasis here is on taking people as they are. There is nothing that fills the existential vacuum less than the preoccupation with "me." We're not going to find the way out without some transcendence.

We're in Fort Worth, Texas. He's back home to stay. The conversation is at his bedside. He has been, much of his life, suffering just about all the ills man is heir to: blindness (which he overcame); heart disease; emphysema; diabetes; a damaged kidney (ever since that awful beating by the Klan along some southern dirt road); osteomyelitis, which held him wheelchair-bound for a year.

Novelist (The Devil Rides Outside), anthropologist, theologian, he is best known for his memoir, Black Like Me. It is an account of his transformation from white to black, by means of chemicals; a response to a challenge: to wake up some morning in a black man's skin, to think human rather than white.

When I first ran into him, he was pleading the case of P. D. East, a

*whimsical southern white editor who was risking his large life and
small purse in pursuit of integration, laughter, and sanity.*

My father is a man that I will never understand. He was from Georgia. He was brought up in that fundamentalist religion which said
that anything remotely pleasurable was sin. He set aside Sundays as a
particularly sober time. He was brought up in an incredibly racist
atmosphere. But he never implanted any of these ideas in me. My dad
was a kind of a miracle, a matter of pure grace. He was a wholly
decent, uncorrupted human being.

It was a horrendous sacrifice on his part to send me to a French
lycée at such a young age. In those days, we didn't even have air mail.
It was the belief in the South that France was utterly immoral and
Catholic. They didn't know which was worse.

I had what they used to call a photographic memory. I could memorize a whole school course in one week. I was bored out of my mind,
so they sent me to France, because in French schools you could advance as fast as you could learn. Also, there was a medical scholarship,
and I was utterly impassioned by the sciences.

I missed adolescence in this country and the revolt against my parents. This made me closer to them than most children. When I did
Black Like Me, it was painful for him, though he never said a word.
When the terrible public reaction came and I was constantly threatened, my dad became enormously protective. He sat there and kept
watch with a gun. This is when he began to be radicalized. It was
through the love of his child that his feelings altered.

It isn't my nature to be an activist. Your vocation doesn't necessarily conform to your nature. I was by nature a very quiet person. I
love books, I love research, I love philosophy. But if you get calls, you
can't say no.

It sprang from my horror. I had worked in France smuggling Jewish people out of Germany until France fell. I was twenty, a research
assistant at the Asylum of Tours. When the war came, they con-
scripted all the doctors and medical students into the service. They
couldn't conscript me because I was an American citizen. I was immediately ordered back to the U.S. I refused to go because France had
formed me. How can I flee at this time of need?

I was put in charge of the asylum. Then I got involved with the
French underground, smuggling Jews out of Germany, across France,
into England. We would use asylum ambulances, put our refugees in
straitjackets, and move them that way. They didn't have to speak.

Many of them didn't speak French. They didn't have safe-conduct papers, of course. We didn't know how to steal, we didn't know how to forge. We were infants in this, but we did the best we could.

The Nazis were moving in. I will be haunted to my death by those scenes. We brought the people inside these rooms and kept them hidden. We had to tell the parents who had children under fifteen that we weren't going to make it. Suddenly, I experienced a double reality. The first: a parent said: "It's all over for us. Take our children." We would move anybody under fifteen without papers. You sat there and realized these parents were giving their children away to strangers. The second: I could go downstairs into the streets and find perfectly decent men who went right on rationalizing racism. I feel, unless we can view these things from inside such rooms, we are lost.

In this country, I've been sitting in those rooms for the past thirty years. I was in the same room with Clyde Kennard's mother after he was martyred.* He died of cancer because he was refused treatment when he was in Parchman Prison in Mississippi. Everyone knew it was a frame. They ordered him out of the hospital, back into prison, and into the toughest work gang. I've been sitting in rooms with countless mothers.

There is an awful ethic of consensus which says because this is a popular belief, let's base our ethics on it. Rule by majority is a great idea, but the majority has no right to rule wrong based on prejudice. I can get five people right now—and a whole lot more—and the consensus is that they should lynch me for being a traitor. (Laughs.) But they wouldn't make it right.

I've always been in the alleys of the world. You can't walk down an alley and see people suffering and keep walking. I learned early the horror of living by other people's standards. Maybe one person could simply say: "To hell with success values, live according to a conscience no matter how stupid that conscience is." So I don't know what I'm doing. I just go where I'm asked.

(Laughs.) I don't have a martyr complex. The most distressing thing about this year of helplessness has been the terrible willingness of people to rush me to eternity. (Laughs.) A young theologian wrote me: "After all your trouble, like St. Paul, you long to be dissolved in the arms of Jesus. *Vaya con Díos.* Go with God." I threw it in the wastebasket. (Laughs.) I was furious. I'm not anxious to get rushed on. (Laughs.) I want to live to the last moment.

* A black southern student who had sought admission to a state college

"P.D. East made something funny out of everything. He had the troubles of Job. As he was dying, he said: 'I have terminal Noxema.' When everyone was concerned about my sickness, he would call me up and blast me: 'Damn you, Griffin, your cross is getting bigger than mine. How dare you!' (Laughs.) On the day he died, his wife called me and said his last words before going into a coma were: 'Ask Griffin if he can top this.' " (Laughs.)

When I was blind, I learned all the Brailles. I learned to type and wrote six books. They'd say: "You're extraordinary." I'd say I'm not. It's just that I refuse to let them put me into a cloistered workshop. I resent very deeply the underchallenging of the blind, the young, the blacks. The greatest crime you can commit against the young is to underchallenge them. In the early sixties, when we solicited the same "worthless" students to help us in Mississippi, you had extraordinary heroism.

God knows, nobody is more frustrated than people who reach maturity and are forced into retirement and a life of little significance. What a loss. This is a thing that murders us all. We aren't given a chance to have an early experience with heroism, with ideals. It withers into lovelessness. Every time you love, it's a risk.

That's why we have these words used in a bad way: "sharing," "love." These are words I gag on now, not because they're not magnificent words but because they've lost their significance. They've been trivialized. We take them like we take a dose of medicine.

Life is risk. What a horror if you don't feel these risks. You end up being totally paralyzed. You don't ever do anything.

I have the kind of heart condition where if they catch me in the first nine minutes, they have a chance of saving me. If they can't, why, they don't. It's really fascinating, because I've always lived in danger. I just naturally have a feeling that somehow I'm going to get through it.

Just before he died, J. Bronowski made one of the most electrifying remarks I ever heard: Justice has now become a biological necessity in man. It isn't a matter of choice, but a biological necessity. This is one of my great unfinished themes, because I don't know if I'll ever get to do that book. It absolutely possesses me.

POSTSCRIPT: *A young neighbor, Marc Raines, enters with a pot of soup. "I met Marc once or twice before in my life. He is an enormously sensible young man who is up against the wall with frustra-*

tions. *He needs to do something for somebody. Of course, I have great needs. So he comes. I didn't expect him. He doesn't have to do this.*

"This is one of the privileges of being helpless. It humiliates you to have to depend on others. But it gives them an outlet for which they hunger. This young stranger—I am in no way denied hope. I just wish we didn't have to suffer so much to come to it."

GEORGE PUTNAM

He is a radio commentator, known as "the voice of Orange County." Genial, imbued with the spirit of bonhomie, orotund-voiced, he says: "Oh, gosh, we've got six beautiful counties. I want to be the voice of southern California."

They all come to southern California to look for that great American Dream. They expected to find oranges on trees for the plucking. They expected to lie on the beach and bask in the sun. They expected to go to the mountains and ski. They expected to go out to the desert. Most of all, they wanted a better life than the one they'd had. They didn't want to continue to plow the field of Minnesota and sweat from four in the morning until eight at night, as I used to. Milking cows in the morning and the same sixteen heifers would back up at night.

I was born in Breckenridge, Minnesota, just across from North Dakota. My granddad at twenty-one was the sheriff of Richmond County, North Dakota, a fellow who stood six feet tall, weighed two hundred and forty pounds. He'd lay the sidearms on the table and say to these desperadoes: "You leave or I leave." Grandfather never left.

I dreamed of getting out of Minnesota and wanting to be a lawyer. I used to go to the theater and see these great lawyers on the screen. I'd read the life of Clarence Darrow and dreamed of one day saying to the jury: "Ladies and gentlemen, my client is not guilty of this charge." The depression came along, and I found it necessary to leave school and go to work.

In 1934, I worked at a small Minneapolis station. I would sweep the floors and wash the windows and stand by until somebody got drunk and I'd go on the air. That's how I got started. Since then, I've interviewed nine presidents.

285

In Minnesota, I became involved with the Farmer-Labor party and campaigned for Floyd B. Olson, the governor. He'd be considered about twenty degrees to the left of present-day reactionary Communists. The Farmer-Labor party believed in giving these poor farmers their fair share.

Franklin D. Roosevelt took my fancy, a magnificent man. When I went to New York, I became enamored of Alfred E. Smith and Fiorello La Guardia. They became like fathers to me.

Something happens to every youngster. I wouldn't give a damn for a kid who isn't ultraliberal, if not radical, in his teens. By the time he's into a job and has responsibilities, a wife and a family and making his payments, he's moving into center ground. By the time he's fifty or sixty, it seems to me he should be just right of center. It's the normal growth and development of the human being. One has a sense of responsibility the older he gets.

When I went to the meetings conducted by Norman Thomas, the Socialist party of America, suddenly down the aisle came the great Red flag with the hammer and sickle. The Socialists initially had the Red flag. The Communists stole it from them. When he spoke of nationalizing every phase of our life, this began to irritate me. As they clenched their fists and sang the "Internationale," this, too, bothered me.

At that time, there were elements in NBC concerned with Russian war relief. The people of AFRA* placed me on the board, which was dominated by leftist elements. This frightened me. They were not concerned with the United States and our well-being. They were concerned with the Soviet Union.

I said, "Aha!" when I saw their names appearing in *Red Channels* as being Communist infiltrators. So I said the hell with it. Let's get back to the middle ground where we belong.

Wasn't Red Channels *ultimately discredited?*

I have no respect for the authors of *Red Channels*. I understand it was written by some druggist or wholesale grocer.

John Henry Faulk, one of the persons listed, sued for libel and was awarded three million dollars.

---

* American Federation of Radio Artists; later AFTRA, American Federation of Radio and Television Artists

Oh yes, I've interviewed John on several occasions. A charming person. Walter Winchell heard my voice on the radio and said I've got one of the finer voices. He put it in his column. Overnight, I graduated from a few hundred dollars a month to a couple of hundred thousand a year.

With reason comes change. When you're very young, you're extremely radical. You're looking for new ideas. I've never lost my humanitarian instincts. I've been a member of the NAACP since I was just a kid. I'm a lifelong member of the Urban League. I have a thousand trees planted in my name in Israel. My way of life has nothing to do with politics, only the well-being of people. But if we don't survive as a nation, what are the other things worth?

I believe we need the B-1 bomber. We need the Trident submarine. We need the cruise missile. We must also have the MX missile. We need the neutron bomb, which can neutralize the forty thousand Soviet tanks along the western part of Europe. The next war, if it comes, God forbid, will be conventional. We will resort to nuclear weapons only in emergencies.

I believe there are two things the president could do about unemployment and crime in the streets. We all wring our hands, but few of us come up with the proper solution. I would suggest as follows: Take those roving bands of kids, sixteen and seventeen, who've dropped out of school and put them in something like a Civilian Conservation Corps until they are eighteen years of age. Reinstitute selective service, and then put those kids into an armed stand-by force, learning to be young men until they are twenty. By that time, you will have built some of the future leaders of America. By taking them off the street, you will have eliminated much of the crime. A part of the money they would accrue would be sent home, and you'd be getting some of their parents and associates off welfare. At the same time, you would be building a military machine that would not wage war—I repeat—but prevent war.

The overkill arguments are based on the wrong premises. The Soviets are gauged to strike first. We talk of retaliation. They have a civil defense to protect their people. We do not. If the bell rang, where the hell would you run to? The Soviet Union could risk losing ten million people, but we would lose between 150 and 175 million. No nation could sustain that kind of loss.

My information comes from Admiral Moorer, the former chief of the Joint Chiefs of Staff, Major General George Keegan, the former head of Intelligence for the military of the United States, and from

Jane's *The World's Fighting Ships.* Too many people will not say on the record what they say off the record. The people have a right to know. George Putnam is neither to the right not to the left. He believes in survival and preparedness. We're being encircled throughout the world by the Soviet Union. Eventually, I worry about China and its hordes of people. I see the world in constant turmoil, with its haves and have-nots. They want what we got. They want to take it away, our precious freedom.

I worry about our young people. Do they have the dreams, the guts, the sinews, the red-blooded ability, to preserve our way of life? The thing our grandparents came over here to find. They found a nation founded, if you'll pardon the expression, under God and a divine Constitution. Every youngster should have the dream of becoming president of the United States. Of course, I believe in Horatio Alger, and I love it.

I'm an eternal optimist. A friend of mine once said: "You could be found in a raging torrent, in a canoe upside down, lose your paddle, and still say we're gonna prevail."

ELIZABETH ROSS

◇─────────────────────────────────────◇

"I'm from Arden, Delaware. It was founded in 1900 by Frank Stevens, a follower of Henry George.* So were my parents. They were different from other socialists because they were not Marxists. They believed that capital and labor were friends, that the landlord was the big villain.

"Stevens was mad about Shakespeare. He named Arden after the Forest of Arden."

I moved there in 1911, when I was six. We had lived in a dingy Philadelphia apartment. I was never allowed to go off the porch, and they said: "If strangers offer you candy, don't go with them." (Laughs.) Arden was a paradise for children.

It was just open fields, with grass growing everywhere, clumps of trees, maybe twenty or thirty houses with red tile roofs. It was sur-

---

* Founder of the single-tax movement, he believed that "all surplus value went to the landowner. He called it unearned increment." He ran for mayor of New York City in 1886, and it is generally agreed he was robbed of victory by Tammany Hall.

rounded on two sides by a forest. Woodlands that were untouched. There weren't any row houses. They were scattered around. There wasn't any asphalt. The roads were mud, and they were so wonderful to walk in when you were a kid, in your bare feet after a rain.

My mother was born in Lincoln, Nebraska, the daughter of a barber. They kept moving and moving and moving to escape their debts. My father was born in Kentucky. My grandfathers fought in the Civil War, one on the side of the North and one on the side of the South. (Laughs.) My parents were working people, oh God, oh yes.

Her mother died when she was young, and she was sent to live with Pennsylvania Dutch people; they made her a slavey. An aunt rescued her, brought her to Philadelphia, and sent her to stenography school. She became a crack typist and, oh, felt very independent. Her uncle, a German radical, converted her to Henry George. She met my father at one of those meetings.

My father's father was a nobbler. He shaped steel with long tongs. He earned sixty dollars a week when ordinary workers were earning six. After the Bessemer process came in, he never got another job. His sons had to support him. Life was hard. So their thing was to come east, young man. That's where you get it. My father came to Philadelphia, went to night school, and came under the influence of Henry George. They thought of themselves as ordinary people. They had all the moral values of that era.

At Arden, the community owned the land. You rented it, you got a 99-year lease. The first person that asked for the lease got it, no matter who you were, your financial status, your race, your religion, anything. In those days, you could rent half an acre for fifteen, twenty dollars a year. You know what a half-acre of land is? It's quite a hunk. We had a big garden, an orchard, a lawn.

Stevens, who was an actor and lecturer, made some money in the terra-cotta business. He took that money and, with a Philadelphia architect, bought this 160-acre farm in Delaware. They deeded it to humanity forever.

The first people who came to Arden, the early settlers, were idealists, they were socialists, they were anarchists, they were Georgists. There weren't very many Georgists. (Laughs.) The idea was: If the land was communally owned, no one would have an advantage over the others. Everybody would be equal.

People came and lived in tents until they could build their houses. They became their own carpenters. They were fleeing from the industrial age and the moneygrubbing and all that. They were going back in time. It was almost like a feudal society without the landlord.

Stevens wanted a town of craftsmen who could produce their wares and interchange them. That didn't work at all. This was when America was being flooded with cheap manufactured goods. Frank himself had a blacksmith shop and made wrought iron. His son, a wonderful carpenter, made beautiful carved-oak chairs and tables. We, in Arden, couldn't afford to buy our own work. We had to depend on well-to-do people outside of Arden. We all had to get jobs in Wilmington and Philadelphia. Arden became merely a haven.

It was wonderful being a kid there because the grownups treated us with respect. They treated us like we were one of 'em. I remember, at a barn dance, riding on Scott Nearing's shoulders. His brother, Guy, was a poet and a botanist, a born teacher. He would take us kids down to the woods and teach us all the flowers and mushrooms and take us out at night, teaching us all the constellations in the sky. We had a wonderful rapport with grownups. We didn't have any feeling they were authoritarian.

We didn't have any schools. Most of the people were there only in the summertime. We were one of the few families that stayed all winter. There were maybe eight or ten kids. It wasn't worth their while to put in a school for us. Our parents hired some mother who had been a teacher. She could give us no more than two hours a day. So we ran wild the rest of the time. (Laughs.)

It sticks with me when I think of my grandchildren sitting there all day in these goddamn stuffy schools, cooped up. And the discipline. All they care about is the discipline of these kids. They don't care if they learn anything. They care whether they're kept in order. I feel so grateful we didn't have any of that. We were free. We roamed through those woods. We knew every hillock and every rock.

We did better in high school than the city kids because we came there with an intellectual curiosity. The little kids today don't. Learning to read was easy. I don't remember how we learned, but we learned. I've met people who've grown up since, and they all said: "That town was magic to me."

Stevens built a beautiful little theater, which is still there. Every night in the summer, we gave Shakespearean plays. Everybody who asked for a part got it. There was an old Yorkshireman who wanted to play Brutus. He played Brutus every year. I played Titania from the age of fifteen to thirty. Listen, Titania shouldn't be older than thirty. Then I passed it on. I played Ophelia and Juliet . . . (Her eyes glow.) The whole town was invited. There was never any charge.

When the town was formed, somebody had to legally own it. So there were three trustees. My father was a trustee until his death, and then my mother was a trustee until her death. There was a town meeting. The town collected the rents. At the time we moved there, it was fourteen, twenty dollars a year.

Unfortunately, this part of the country grew tremendously. The big strip from Boston to Washington had become thickly populated, very industrialized, and land values soared. But there were no property taxes in Arden. You just paid rental on your land.

The word got around. Some people, not as idealistic as the early ones, saw this as a good thing. They said: "Look, we can get this land without paying anything for it. We'll claim squatter's rights. We'll throw out the deed of trust." They had a great big suit after I left. By the time the first world war came along, there were enough of them to make a real opposition.

It was the first time we knew there were other values in the world. These new people would talk about Hunkies and Polacks and Kikes and Wops. We never heard things like that before.

When the war broke out, the town was split in two. Stevens was a pacifist. When Teddy Roosevelt went to the Philippines, he said: "I pray that your armies will be defeated. I will not keep my mouth shut. If this be treason, make the most of it." He wrote a similar letter to Woodrow Wilson in 1917. The war was a terrible shock to people like my parents. They believed the world had become civilized and that wars were a thing of the past. America will never get into this war. Wilson was re-elected because he kept us out of war. The most popular song in 1914 was "I Didn't Raise My Son To Be a Soldier." When the war came, my parents were devastated.

We would go to the movies in Wilmington and see these horrible Germans. We'd come back and say: "These Germans are beasts." My father would say: "Don't you go to those damn movies any more." The pacifists of the town had their own flag made of blue and white that said: *Peace on earth, good will to men*. I can still see it: blue on a white background. The patriots, the new people, put out these great big American flags.

Frank was so democratic in his ideas, he thought all residents of the town should vote, not just the leaseholders. Even the children. But at the monthly town meeting, he was outvoted by the new people who said: "Oh, no, we're the leaseholders." Our Arden was no longer our Arden.

Now there were strange arguments at the town meeting. The new people fought the trustees: "What do we need this extra money for? We pay the state and county taxes. We fix the roads. What's this money put aside for?" The Georgists said: "We'll buy more farms, then more people will have the same advantage we've all had." The others couldn't see that. They pressed to keep the land rents down so they could speculate.

My mother finally saw a sign on somebody's land: *Lot for Sale*. She was wild, she was furious. Lot for sale! This land is not owned by anybody. She went to the town meeting that night with blood in her eye and tried to explain the principles of Henry George. She fell dead while she was speaking. We were so proud of her to die with her boots on. That was twenty-three years ago. She was seventy-six.

My father died years before, at seventy. He worked terribly hard all his life. He got a job as an insurance inspector and had to travel a great deal. My mother was left alone for months at a time. A woman's life was hard in those days. For us, it was duck soup. For her, she worked all the time. She had this fierce drive to be respectable, as working-class women do. She had to starch our clothes. She ironed our underwear. She would spend all day at the washboard. And yet she was happy to be in Arden. I lived there until 1940. I've been away from there half my life.

Arden still exists. There have been suits against the town to try to break the deed of trust. They haven't been successful. I don't know why. They pay much higher rents, of course. But no more is it the place where poor people can go live in a tent until they can build a house. There were all open fields around Arden. Now it's all built up. It's like a suburb. Employees of du Pont live there. It's manicured. It's very pretty.

We were caught up in everything of the twenties. It saddened our parents. We were caught up in the jazz age and fast cars. When we were little kids in Arden, we didn't see a car or truck once a week. The mail was delivered by a woman in a horse and buggy. By the time of the twenties, there were cars in Arden. (Laughs.) That was the big fight in town meetings. The people who had cars wanted more money spent on the roads to put macadam on 'em. We kept getting more solid citizens all the time.

Arden couldn't escape the times.

There were things going on under the surface I was not aware of as a child. My parents taught me there were no classes in America. There were rich people, but they weren't very different from us. I had to get out of Arden, which was, in a sense, a classless society—we were pretty much equal—before I realized there were very definite classes in America. God Almighty, you picked up the paper every day and saw that mothers would gas themselves and all their children because they didn't know how to get food for the next day. The depression changed my thinking.

My mother was very disappointed when I became a Marxist. She had her ideas and wouldn't give them up. She stuck to them heroically. I look back at Arden as a lovely dream, being with people who were in advance of their time.

I don't think it's so much an American Dream now as it was then. My parents thought America was exceptional. I don't think it is any more. I think the rest of the world has moved in on America, as the rest of America moved in on Arden. Global pressures are moving in on us. I don't see a distinct American Dream any more. It's a world dream.

Three years ago, on the seventy-fifth anniversary of the founding of Arden, they had a big celebration, and people came from as far away as California. It was very tearful. They gave a performance of *Twelfth Night*. I took my little granddaughter. We sat on the grass. I said: "Oh, if only we could have some punk." When we were kids, you kept mosquitoes away with it. Sure enough, they had a big pile of punk, and everybody lighted it. The players came out of the woods singing a charming song. My little granddaughter sat there and said: "I want to see it a trillion times more."

It was the duke's Forest of Arden, wasn't it? Unreal. The dream of your mother and your father.

It was real to them.

MRS. GEORGE UPHAM BAYLIES

She is president general of the National Society of the Daughters of the American Revolution. Its headquarters: 1776 D Street, Washington, D. C. "Our telephone number is 1776, of course with a prefix. We own the largest block of buildings in Washington ever built by a women's organization."

To be a member, one must trace her lineage directly back to a person who either aided or fought in the War of Independence. "We have a DAR manual for new citizens studying to be Americans. We've given out almost ninety million, gratis."

I can't put my finger on the American Dream. All I can say is: love of country. As the flag goes by in the parade, you just swell up with pride and you're happy to be living in a country that is free. I felt the criticism of the United States in the sixties, during the Vietnam War, was misguided. I don't like to have my country criticized.

I became a member of the Children of the American Revolution when I was five years old. I'm a third-generation DAR. It's become a way of life to me. When my grandmother and my mother would come to the Continental Congress in Washington, my sister and I would always say: "Why are they always going to Washington?" Little did I know I'd be following in their footsteps.

My father was a brigadier general, and he instilled a great deal of patriotism in my two sisters and myself. We'd raise the flag every morning and lower it every evening at sunset. It was a ritual and a great privilege, and always exciting.

Father was very stern and very military, but we all loved him dearly. He went to every parade Boston ever had. He'd always end up as marshall, riding a horse. We'd be taken to a certain club in Boston and hang out the window. At one time, when the French president was there, I was riding beside my father on a horse. He had served overseas in World War One and brought back to us these little French caps.

More and more we're getting younger members these days. About a third of our membership are people from age eighteen to thirty-five. I think more young people are becoming concerned. The Bicentennial was, of course, a spearhead. I think they're beginning to realize they would like to cling to something, part of their heritage, roots. Alex Haley did quite a bit of research in our library.

People have a misconception about the DAR. They think we're wealthy. We're not. Anyone is eligible if they can prove their lineage. If one ancestor took part in the American Revolution—(quickly) War of Independence—they're eligible.

If we weren't cartooned or written about, we'd be dead ducks. Some of our members do get very upset, but I just say I can see the funny side of things. I'm a fun-loving person as well as a serious person. I always wanted to be a ventriloquist so I could put words in other people's mouths and stand back. I think that would be more fun than anything in the world, if I could get away with it.

I don't want to sound like a hundred-year-old woman, but there are many things that I don't like about young people and what they're doing nowadays. Living without marriage and that sort of thing. (Laughs.) It seems to be a way of life now.

We're opposed to the ERA. I cannot see what some of these women are driving at. Sometimes I feel embarrassed that I am a woman because of the way they perform. We have a very fine national defense chairman. Phyllis Schlafly. I'm perfectly happy and satisfied with my way of life. Some of these women make fools of themselves.

It's the Soviet threat that concerns us most. A moment ago, a young officer from the Pentagon showed us a film about it. We are opposed to the SALT Treaty. We were opposed to the Panama Canal Treaty.

What is it about the Panama Canal Treaty that disturbs you?

That's really complex. It would take an hour to talk about it. I wish I had my resolutions with me, but I don't. We like to feel we're Number One. The tops. I have no doubts about America whatsoever, though I think sometimes our elected officials have been misguided. I don't go along with everything the government says. It's only natural that everyone has their own opinion.

I've been a member of the DAR for forty-one years. It's a way of life for me. Much of our work is answering mail from members all over the country. And the constant problem with our buildings, leaks and all.

In the letters you receive, is there one subject . . . ?

Yes, but I'm not going to tell you. (A pause) Oh, I might as well say it. Marian Anderson.* Periodically, there's a story about Marian Anderson. They always say the same thing: The DAR refused the use of Constitution Hall to Marian Anderson because she was black.

* In 1939, the DAR denied the use of Constitution Hall to Marian Anderson, the celebrated black contralto. It was a cause célèbre. Eleanor Roosevelt, a member of the DAR, resigned in protest. The concert subsequently took place at the Lincoln Memorial.

We're accused of being racist, and we're far from it. In fact, we do have black members. Well, I'm thinking of one in particular. Her grandfather was black and her grandmother was white, I believe. Or vice versa, I've forgotten now. There were blacks that fought. If they can prove their lineage and if they're approved by the chapter, they're accepted.

Our members get very upset about the Marian Anderson story. Why don't we tell the whole story? We have told the true story over and over again. Actually, her agent came to us, but we were already booked by the National Symphony Orchestra. We fully expected him to ask for another date, which he did not do. We have documentary proof. They made quite an issue of it. Her manager said we had refused it because she was black.

Many of these young newspaper people who weren't even born at the time go to the files. If there's anything said about Marian Anderson, they will have that story. So it keeps getting repeated. Walter Cronkite once told me that a story becomes a fact if it's repeated often enough. I get very exercised about this.

I feel badly about schools, too. The DAR operates two schools in the Appalachia area. Children who come from broken homes. We teach them love of country and patriotism and all. The way we were brought up years and years ago. The old-fashioned way, they call it now. Do you know there are some schools that don't teach American history? How are the young people going to learn about our heroes and heroines if they don't know anything about their own history?

We also do a great deal of work with the Indians. I forgot about the Indians and I really shouldn't because it's a very popular committee.

A woman interjects: "We have Indian members, too. And an Eskimo or two."

Why do you have to explain why you fly your flag? What's the matter with flying it every day? I can't understand people who say: "Well, what's the flag up for today?" My husband and I have a home in Cape Cod, and we fly the flag every night, overlooking the water. It's flown from a sundeck, and it's perfectly beautiful because we have it spotlighted. The flag code says it can be flown at night if it's spotlighted. Last evening, we flew a tremendous flag and the band played "Stars and Stripes Forever." It's really quite a show.

DR. WHITNEY ADDINGTON

He is chairman of the Division of Pulmonary Medicine, Cook County Hospital, Chicago.

I grew up in Lake Forest, one of the most affluent communities in the country. One of my earliest memories was a trip across the country with my grandfather.* We were sitting in the engineer's cab. It was the Great Northern. We were going through the mountains. The steam engine was a huge one. I remember thinking how big the country was and how powerful the engine. And being with someone as confident and powerful as my grandfather. It may explain why I love Thomas Wolfe so much. It was about 1940. I was seven and optimistic.

"My grandfather was very far to the right. Yet there were a lot of things about him that people forget. It was he who proposed monumental changes in Sears, Roebuck, and people called him a radical. At a time when most people were pulling things in, he was expanding. He recognized that the great growth of the country would be in the Southeast and Southwest. He bought up land and built stores when people thought he was crazy. He often told me, toward the end of his life, his greatest pride was what he had done for the employees of Sears: the profit-sharing program. A lot of businessmen in those days criticized him for it."

As my education went on, I knew that life was unfair. Yet I didn't think too much about it. I was so intent on skipping ahead of my generation. I went to Deerfield Academy in Massachusetts and then Princeton. I graduated in '57. We were the dormant ones. We didn't march, we didn't protest, we didn't even have panty raids. We just studied. I was self-centered, getting into medical school, into internship, and into residency.

I have many patients who are well-to-do. Maybe because I've grown up in such affluence and I see such people on weekends as my friends,

---

* General Robert E. Wood, chairman of the board, Sears, Roebuck and Company, during the years of its greatest growth taking care of them is less important to me than it would be to someone who grew up in a different world. At County, the vast majority are very poor. How can you compare this to a fashionable Michigan Avenue practice?

During my internship, I began to realize things were not quite right. I always thought decisions were made solely on what was best for the patient. Then I saw how a surgeon was occasionally selected. If it was an affluent patient, a personal friend of the referring physician . . . I had grown up thinking medicine was free of such things. It wasn't and it isn't. I was very naïve. I began to understand how important people in medicine became important for reasons other than medicine.

There was a president of the AMA who said: Health care is a privilege, not a right. At that point, I decided not to join the AMA. I'm still not a member. I sobered up to the fact that these dreams I had about medicine were not reality.

I had the vision of doctors as hard-working, bright, committed individuals, not preoccupied with getting ahead. We went into medical school for altruistic reasons, we thought. In the last fifteen years it has become so competitive that getting ahead is what it's all about. They're much brighter than we were, but I don't think they can relate to an ill patient as I and my classmates did and can. They have trouble with the human condition.

They're smarter in science. Maybe it's a response to Sputnik or something. They have a terrible time writing. They can't write an expository sentence. They haven't read very much. Most of them never heard of Thomas Wolfe. But they're smarter in numbers, in math and biological systems. They have difficulty speaking about a patient.

I take care of a large number of young adults with lung disease called cystic fibrosis. It is uniformly fatal. Some are poor, some are not. It's so terribly sad. Yet, these young interns ask: "Should we put the patient on a ventilator?" "What's the rationale for this medicine?" It's entirely hopeless, but they won't talk about how sad it is. There are other reasons why physicians have trouble with the death of patients. It's defeat.

Last week I went in to see a twenty-seven-year-old woman who died later that afternoon. She had been terminal for a week. Her husband was there, her mother and father were there. When I walked into the room, a medical student was there, taking her blood pressure. He came out with me and said: "I want to ask you something about this patient." I said "What?" assuming he'd want to talk about the tragedy. He had been working with her for two weeks. He said: "Why are we using this particular antibiotic rather than another one?"*

My father was a businessman. I always wanted to be a doctor. Maybe I didn't like what I saw around me, even though I didn't really know what I saw. Maybe wanting to be a doctor was my rebellion.

I've had a fantasy for some time. An idea better than national health insurance. Instead of having the poorest people sick and the wealthiest people well, I'd turn it around and have the wealthy ill and the poor well. I'd still see it as fee for service, private enterprise. Because of the profit motive, you'd have a better situation than national health insurance. Being a chest physician, I see tuberculosis as a disease of the poor. Last year there probably was not one new case in Winnetka or Lake Forest. But if we could put tuberculosis in Winnetka or Lake Forest, in five years we'd have no tuberculosis in this poor area. It would be to the system's advantage to cure these people. Now it's to the system's disadvantage. It is more expensive to take care of someone who's sick than someone who's well. Therefore, patients who are well and also more affluent are more cared for. Is that clear to you? Anyway, it's just a fantasy. (Laughs.) That's why we need national health insurance. I think capitalism is a great system if you're selling shoes. You can't use the usual principles of evaluation—namely, profit and loss—in taking care of sick people which you can in selling shoes.

I'm very worried. We have four children. Their eyes are open. They're much more sophisticated than I was. They cannot be intimidated. I was intimidated most of my early life. If I thought something unfair or cruel, I was implicitly told not to discuss it. Our children have a comment on everything.

I'm optimistic about my children. I'm pessimistic about the country. There are things, though, that are hopeful. Maybe I'm a cockeyed optimist: I'm impressed by what I see of some of my patients. Among poor blacks there is, to this day, a family. It lacks a man, usually, and the leader is almost always the mother, who is overwhelmed by problems and responsibilities. And yet, I see this every day—there is a strength that is enduring. Even in the terrible moments at County, one is impressed and moved.

---

* A few years ago, I heard Satyajit Ray, the Indian film director, answer questions following a showing of his deeply moving work *The Music Room*. Not one of the questions the young film buffs asked him concerned the theme, the substance of the film. The queries were all about technique and fundraising.

ERMA "TINY" MOTTON

"My husband has holes in the valves of his heart, so he cannot main-tain heavy work. He's uneducated, the same as I. I'm from Caruthers-ville. It's in the foothill of Missouri, on the border of Arkansas. We're right on the Mississippi River. It's a rural community, cotton and soybean country. There are very few small farmers. The big farmers have just about taken it over.

"Life is very rough. Most of the towns run from seven thousand back down to five hundred. The people's ages range from the very young to the very old. There's very little in between, from I'll say twenty-five to forty. These people leave, go someplace where they feel things are better.

"Your low-income white is just the same, a lot of times even worse. They don't get together. It's really something peculiar. I can't under-stand it. Myself, I'm poor and I've been poor all my life and I'll probably die poor. But something happened to me, I can't say what it was . . ."

When I was a little girl, I was taught I was as good as anybody. I could do anything that the next human being could do. When I got to adulthood, I seen what was happening to my children and me, and how they were deteriorating this feeling in me. All that I was raised to believe in, they were killing it. This is not for me. I said I'm gonna get out of this cluck if it's the last thing I do. So I began to do piece-work and leave my children with my mother and put in bits here and bits there, until I finally worked up to the stage that I could say: "Hey, take your welfare check and stuff it."

I mean piecework in people's houses. I mean washing for people, taking care of other people's children when I shoulda been taking care of my own. Ironing and doing things like that. I got tired of looking at people that had no more understanding about life than I did putting me down, making you believe we're giving you a check. "You're nothing, you're nobody. We're taking care of you. What are you doing? What do you need with kids? You can't take care of them." I came from family life. I don't think there's anything greater than having children and a family. It just blew my mind. Hey, I'm a whole woman and I consider my husband a whole man. I'm constantly being kicked in the teeth: You don't deserve to have children, you don't deserve the fulfillment of life, being a mother. It used to humiliate me when welfare workers would come to my house and ask stupid questions: "Where's your husband? When was he home last? How can you afford to have a TV? How come your house is so clean? How can your children afford to wear those kind of shoes?" I was made to believe that I myself was worth nothing. I was brought up by my mother and my father to love myself.

Something was happening. I think anger. I was feeling: Hey, I've got to get out of this rut. I'm not gonna live in slavery, which my foreparents lived before me. I'm not gonna let my kids come up thinking that they're nobody, that they're on a welfare roll.

I took the step, oh gosh, a big step, about twelve years ago when I got my first job, first what I consider a decent job. From there I started pushing. I started taking college courses, reading books, doing everything I could. I couldn't afford college. We would get extension courses coming in through. I plugged in everything I could plug in while I was working. I worked two jobs. I worked four hours for pay, four hours for non-pay. Five days a week. I was going to school three nights a week. The other nights I would work in somebody's house, doing piecework. I studied in the classroom. I studied people. I took good notes. I would never draw myself from my kids because it had never been done to me.

We would go to a little town three nights a week, about fourteen miles from where I'm living. The instructors would commute from the university to this town to teach us.

I was working with children. I found out that just because I was a mother didn't make me really know a lot about kids. Because I had children didn't make me the best mother. So I wanted to learn all there was about children and people. I started studying child psychology, first thing. I started in English composition, a little writing. Then I went on and took childhood development. I took English Composition II and more psychology.

There's a drive. I think not only men have it. I think everyone have it. I think everyone wants to feel good about themselves. They need very bad to like themselves. When you start doing good things for yourself, then you do good things for other people too. That's the key. I had to do something for me and mine, my husband and my five kids. That pushed me into thinking about other people.

What really happened was I learned myself. For the first time, I could see myself. Here I am, Erma "Tiny" Motton, I got all these financial problems, there's times when we don't have enough food, when my husband and my children, they get sick. And I get sick. But I have to keep going and pretend I'm not sick. Work when I'm sick, work when I'm well. Go to school, keep an immaculate house. I sit up in those classes, and I can't read and study when I get home because I'm too tired. I sit up there beside middle-class-income people that have had everything you could dream of, and I made the same good grades that they made. It proved something to me. I was as good as anybody.

I couldn't go home at night and study and go to the bookstore and get the book that the professor suggested. I had to get it all from him. I had to nit-pick it. I had to take good notes, I had to listen, I had to maneuver him into telling me just exactly what he wanted me to put on tests. I had to be smart. I said: "Hey, you are a pretty neat person. You're living under pressure, you make good grades, you calculate, you maneuver a man with a doctor's degree into pulling out of him what he wants from you to give him. Hey, you're makin' it, you know." It just pushed me on.

I said: For me, it's not enough. I let myself get put in a pocket for seven years. I can't blame society or anybody for that but me. I blame Tiny. By the grace of God or something, me and somebody pulled Tiny. Tiny's a long way of bein' out of the pocket, but just like an ant, I'm wigglin' hard. You know I'm there.

What the dream means to me is for my children to be able to live anywhere they want to, even be able to come back home where they were born and raised, and get a good job, hold their head high. Not given something because they're black and not something taken away from them because they're black. But given something because they're a man and they deserved it. That's my American Dream. I do believe something's stirring.

I want to live a long time. I want to see the world really turn about-face and people get together. 'Cause it doesn't have to be like it is now.

WINNING

LEE KUNZMAN

He is a professional auto racer. He has competed in the Indianapolis 500.

"In Indianapolis alone, during the month of May, there are approximately one million flesh-type people. Racing is the world's largest spectator sport, by far."

The American Dream, to me, is winning the Indianapolis 500. Everything else is a step in that direction. I've won thirty professional races, but those are all just little bitty stepping stones to the big one. It goes back to that day, listening on the radio. It programs my life, it controls it.

One Memorial Day, when I was twelve, my real dream began. I was sitting at the radio. I had the 500 on. My folks wanted to leave the house for a family picnic, but I couldn't tear myself away until the race was over. I kept telling my parents: "Someday I'm gonna race in the 500."

Maybe it was the glamour or the announcer that fascinated me, the way he interpreted the race on the radio. Somehow the competitive idea struck a note in me. I just had to do it. Everything else in life was secondary after that.

Satisfaction is elusive. Once you accomplish something, it seems it wasn't quite that difficult. So you expand the dream a little farther, make it more complicated. I've run in the Indianapolis 500 four times. I finished in the top ten twice. Originally, that was pretty satisfying, being one of the thirty-three elite drivers in the world that make the race. But now that I've done that, winning is where it's at. That's what my dream was all about in the first place.

There are many steps to being eligible for the 500. Your resumé is important. In the last couple of years, though, the cost of racing has escalated so much, people with large portfolios have an advantage over the others. (Laughs.) Having a lot of dollars at their disposal.

Today, it's very difficult for the young man with the dream such as mine. The cost of the car alone is about seventy-five thousand dollars. The engines are forty thousand dollars apiece. It takes several of those to make the race. An attempt would come to a quarter of a million or three hundred thousand dollars. Most often, a driver is supported by a car owner and a sponsor. Most drivers, like myself, are like independent contractors: I will drive your car in this race for x number of dollars.

I don't think you ever become totally satisfied. If a person has a life dream, isn't he ever afraid he might fulfill it? Do you think you can live with real success? Many people, I think, don't accomplish their dreams because they're afraid of what success might bring.

My first dream came about when my grandfather built me a little pedal car. He was a blacksmith in this small Iowa farm community, Volga. I was seven or eight. It was really impressive. After I had pedaled it quite a bit, I realized I couldn't go any faster. So my grandfather came up with a different system of gearing.

Because he was fascinated with this mechanical object, it led me to be fascinated. He thought of an improvement to make the car go faster. Ever since, mechanical objects have fascinated me. Since the automobile has played an important role in our lives, it's natural for all young people to deal in it. Some people deal in it longer than others. The childhood dream stays with this person throughout life. With others, it diminishes more quickly.

Ever since I was a child, I've been trying to improve on things, making them do things they really weren't supposed to do. I'm dedicated to the idea of relating man and machine together. That's really the key to a race driver. The car becomes an extension of me. That tool, that object, that car, becomes the way to satisfy my dream. It's not me alone. It's a combination of the two. When I'm in the car, I feel it's telling me what it wants to do. I might be telling it something I want it to do that it doesn't want to do. We talk back and forth. When I'm in a race, if people could hear my thoughts, they would say I was strange because I actually talk to this piece of equipment. I say: "You shouldn't be doing that, car." And the car is telling me: "Yes, I should."

It is human to me. It doesn't keep a low profile either. I will not let it dominate me. I will dominate it. In my mind, I'm saying: I'm gonna use you to get what I want even though you don't want to—to satisfy my dream.

I feel I'm much more intelligent than this machine and can do more things, that I can outthink the machine and change myself, as a machine, to act differently. I'm saying: I'm computer A, and I'm smarter than computer B. Now, sometimes the machine is smarter than I am. It has built-in inherited characteristics that I don't think of and can't solve.

Doing something that you're just on the edge of disaster, you're pushing the limits, constantly. Pretty soon, you find yourself realizing you can go beyond the limits and still survive. This creates the need to do it just a little more. You're still staying on the conservative side of disaster, on the safe side. So you don't have the disaster.

What attracts me, I suppose, is skirting disaster. I've always enjoyed doing things that are not on the super-conservative side, something a little more liberal. Things that might fudge on disaster. That sort of life has always excited me. Like flying an airplane and doing things that're just not really safe. My personal makeup leans towards the daredevil. I transform from an easygoing, fairly calm guy to a person extremely intent when I sit in an automobile. The adrenaline becomes very high. On a highway, I drive very calm and normal. I drive a compact little car that would have a heck of a time going over sixty. But once I get in a racing car and the switch turns, I become that edgy, competitive person that's gotta go fast.

When I heard that 500 on the radio, there were some crashes. I don't remember if anyone was killed. That wasn't important to me at the time. When I get in a race car, I don't think that I could get hurt doing this. I have been. The only thing that enters my mind is the enjoyment. If a problem develops, that's just part of it. Like jogging in the morning and stepping on a rock, twisting your ankle. It's just a handicap.

In 1970, in Missouri, was my first crash. A mechanical failure caused it. It was running well in the race, but something broke, and I made contact with a concrete wall at a hundred forty miles an hour. The car went up like a Roman candle, a long ways from the track. The safety crew was not able to get to me. I was out in the middle of a parking lot. I had quite a few injuries, my neck, back, left arm, and left leg. The car was burning, and I was trapped in it. It's strange being in a position like that. Your survival attitude is so strong, you don't consider you're going to be maimed or killed. That doesn't seem important. It's not really suicidal, it's survival. It's much stronger here than in most other professions.

I was very close to being killed. I had to hold my breath quite a long time. If I took a breath, I'd be breathing fire and flames. Of course, you'd die of pneumonia. I realized nobody was going to get me. My right arm was caught in the car. I made the judgment that it wasn't broken, but pretty much everything else was. I had to make a decision. Do I try tearing my arm and getting out of the car, or do I stay here and wait for someone to get me? Luckily, I went for separating my arm and getting out. To survive rather than die. It just took off part of my arm, but I got out. For a long period, they were afraid to transport me because of my injuries. Luckily, a friend of mine was a doctor, and he happened to be there. He built a special rack to transport me to the hospital. So between the survival instinct and a doctor on the scene, I was able to survive. I crashed another time, in '73, testing a new car. These burns are from the first. Little tattoos from '70.

The spectators, the people in the stands, are not there to watch people get maimed. They're there because they admire you or they wouldn't be there. I think they're there to see their dreams translated through the driver. They're using him to satisfy their fantasies. They see themselves in that seat. They pick out the driver who is their favorite, and you become a very important individual to them.

I would say a very small group, maybe five percent, go to see wild things—crashes, injuries, deaths. It might be somebody in the stands falling over a pop bottle. A certain amount of people want to see horror, but ninety-five percent go to translate their fantasies through you.

About sixty percent of the people in the stands are over fifteen thousand dollars in income. Sixty percent are between twenty-four and thirty-five thousand. They will probably be affluent in later life. They have money and project their fantasies through something else.

Being excellent in racing is being number one. You program everything in your schedule to be that: personal life, home life, whatever. What counts most is how does that affect my racing? My personal life has been affected, of course. My physical appearance has changed. I've spent at least five percent of my life in the hospital, through racing. But, still, that's not important. Racing is what I want to do more than anything else.

I don't have a family. I've put family life on the back burner. Racing will interfere with family life. I don't feel it's fair to expose somebody else to it just because I want to do it. This may be my excuse. Rather than facing maturity, I keep saying that it wouldn't be fair to the other person.

Racing drivers try to keep their lives nonpersonal, even with their mechanics. You depend on that person for your life. Should you feel he's not holding up his end of the bargain and you want to get rid of him, it's difficult to do it if you've become personal friends. More importantly, if you're running competitively with someone and you're trying to get ahead of him, sometimes you have to take serious advantage of him, a strategy that leaves him in the back row. If you're really good friends, that's difficult to do. So you become somewhat detached.

If I never won the Indianapolis 500, I'm sure I would live. I'd be happier if I could win it. You can never satisfy most dreams totally. It's elusive. Something you will chase forever.

CLAUDE HUMPHREY

A defensive end with the Philadelphia Eagles, a professional football team. As a member of the Atlanta Falcons, he had been chosen as a member of the All-Pro team several times.
In 1978, he talked of quitting football.

I started thinking of being a pro athlete after I got into college. I used to tell the girl who became my wife, when we were in high school, that I wanted to be in the magazine. We'd go downtown in Memphis and get off the bus in front of the newsstand. I'd look through all the sports magazines. I used to always tell her that one of these days I'm going to have my picture in there. When I was in college, I got to be in the magazine.

At Tennessee State, all my dreams were geared to becoming a pro football player. I don't know what I would have done if I hadn't been a pro football player, 'cause that's all I ever thought about.

My college coach's name was Joe Gilliam. He was one of my best friends. His son played quarterback for the Pittsburgh Steelers, the first black quarterback. I played catch with this boy when he was in high school and I was in college. The first time I played against him as a pro, I didn't feel anything. I ain't going to try to hurt him, but I'm going to get him every chance I get, friend or no friend. Scratch, kick, claw, everything I could to get to him.

But one particular Sunday when we played in Tampa and I broke through there on Doug Williams, it wasn't the same. I didn't feel the same way as I'd always felt about getting to other quarterbacks. I had a chance to really unload on him, to really hurt him. I found myself backing off and not hitting him. Here was the first black quarterback who looked like he was really going to make it. They were going to let this guy go and be as good as he could be. And here I'm going to unload on him. I found myself not really . . . not really . . . (He trails off.) I wanted this black guy to do good. You understand what I'm saying? It wouldn't be the same if they had Joe Blow at quarterback.

If there were three black quarterbacks in the league, I might not feel that way. But here was a chance for a black guy to show people that he can do it. The quarterback is just a part of a machine like everybody else. It takes all these people working together. It takes the guy he throws the ball to, the guy he hands the ball to. I wanted people to understand it. Anybody could be a quarterback. He didn't have to be white.

Williams was getting the job done real good. He had already completed one long pass against us and had thrown two other good ones that were dropped. I found myself not really wanting to hurt this guy. What was my thinking? I realized I wanted this black guy to do good. It didn't make no difference that he was doing good against me. I didn't want to be the one to mess him up.

Why did I feel this way? You realize I did not want to hurt Doug Williams when I obviously tried to get Joe Gilliam. That was the thing I couldn't understand. I guess I knew that Gilliam didn't really have much of a chance because there was always Bradshaw.* But here, everybody was looking to Williams to be the man. I wanted him to throw six touchdowns on everybody.

That was when I decided that I needed to sit down and to take a real good look at my football future. 'Cause I couldn't play. The game isn't set up where you can play on the field that way. I was thinking maybe I'm losing my instinct to play the game. Maybe I should quit.

When I go out on the football field, my whole personality changes. It has to change. It's a game of skills, number one. But it's a game of aggression, too. You've got to make yourself angry. If you don't, you don't play well. You have to make up reasons to feel this way. John Williams is the offensive tackle for the Rams. He's a good friend of mine. But when I play against John, I have to tell myself that John is trying to hurt me. He's trying to take food out of my family's mouth. He's trying to embarrass me and make me look bad. By the time that I

* Terry Bradshaw, star quarterback of the Pittsburgh Steelers

get to thinking all these things that John is trying to do to me, I'm mad. When I get mad at him, I don't feel anything for him. I can do anything I want to him. It wouldn't have made any difference if I hurt him. Do you understand what I'm saying? If he gets hurt, he won't be taking bread from a kid's family. I don't have any personal feelings toward him at all. Anything I can do to him is okay 'cause he ain't like a person.

The instant the game is over, he becomes John, my friend. I'm ready to go and have a beer with him and to talk and jive and just be buddy-buddy. But once we got out on the field, he's an enemy.

I don't have any friends out there. Even the guys on my own team, really, are the enemy. If I got to work with this guy and he don't do it right, he's taking bread out of my family's mouth. If he don't do it right, he's affecting me. But that Sunday, that moment, Doug Williams was not my enemy. That was the thing I couldn't get straight.

When I got back home, I thought about it. I just felt like I wasn't doing my job. It was the same feeling I had when I got hurt. I made up my mind there was no sense in my playing any more, 'cause my attitude toward the game was not there. So I decided to quit football and go on the farm.

For now, I'm going to play football a couple of more years. I hope my instinct will be more intense. When I work out, I talk to myself. I'm thinking about getting the quarterback. I'm thinking about how I'm going to grab him. If he slips me, I'm going for his foot. If I've got a good shot at him, I'm going to just take it. I could see me grabbing the guy's arm and just pulling myself by him. I can see me going inside on him. I can see the fans yelling.

I got to win. But I have standards I set up for myself, and when I don't meet 'em, it doesn't make any difference that my team won. I have nothing to be happy about. If we lose a game and I did everything I set out to do, I'm sad that we lost, but I'm happy that I did what I did. You understand what I'm saying? That's more important than winning the game.

I don't want to coach because I don't think I could the way I should. I couldn't explain to a kid that he'd have to go out and do it the way I did. I feel it ain't right. It's not logical. I don't think it's good logic for me to be able to hate a person and then turn around and like him, all in the same day.

I build up the hate during the course of the week, so by the time Sunday gets there, I really am pissed off at the guy. It's not right to be able to hurt people and not feel anything. I believe in feeling—in not unnecessarily hurting someone. It's not right to go out and beat a dog or kick a cow. That isn't the way God intended for it to be. You understand what I'm saying? When I'm through with football, all those kind of feelings will be gone.

GATHERING AND LETTING GO

MILDRED OLMSTEAD

We met accidentally at a railway station. She lives in a small farm town outside Cleveland. She works for a wholesale bookseller. Her husband is a middle manager. They have four children, two in college.

I always wanted to be rich, and I really didn't care how. Just to have a lot of money, because we never had a lot. You always want what you don't have.

The American Dream is good. It's one of the things that keep people going. Anybody can do it, can make it. If you didn't have your dream, you'd just give up. People have always got this great idea that's going to hit. You know they're never going to make it, but the dream keeps them alive.

My husband's younger brother is like that. He's always got a scheme. He doesn't believe in working every day. That's not how you do it. Tomorrow he's going to be a millionaire. If he ever lost that, there would be nothing left.

Everything came easily to him. He always just kind of fell into things. That's the way he lives now. He lives by his wits, he's always out hustling somebody. He's got a car wash he runs. Doesn't have the proper drainage, doesn't pay his water bill. He knows someday he's going to make it, there's no doubt in his mind. I don't think he will. He's too gullible. He falls for the fast talkers. Fast people get taken by someone that's a little faster.

He was the golden-haired boy. He was the one that had everything.

Everybody liked him. He had a way with words and could get most anything out of anybody. Something went wrong.

When something goes wrong, it's always somebody else's fault. Has he been taken? Yeah. He always seems to get around the wrong kinds of people. Just on the edge of being in jail. But with all the little failures along the way, he's still scheming to make it big. He told my husband: "In the chess game of life, I'm two moves away from making it." He picked it up from one of those success magazines. He subscribes to them. He sees them advertised on television: how to become a millionaire in twenty days or something.

I'm afraid that one of these days he's going to become very embittered. My husband thinks he's getting really paranoid about "them." He's very right-wing, very anti-Communist, very anti-government. Very, very anti-black. In the last few years, you can see the hate coming in. We get together and have these big political arguments. It used to be a lot of fun, but in later years, it got to the point where he'd be so far out in left field, you couldn't talk to him. He was almost at the point of grabbing a gun and shooting people down himself. It just got to the point where my husband would tell him: "I don't want to argue any more. All we do is get angry."

He has almost like a small arsenal in his home. (Laughs.) He always wants to show you his guns. He had a M-1 or something, some big gun. He said: "It's ready to go." I said: "What do you want one of these for?" He said: "When they come, I'm gonna be ready." I said: "Who are you talking about? What's gonna happen is, when your kids get a little older and they go out on a date and they come home, you're gonna shoot one of your kids." But he's ready for "them" whenever "they" come.

He tries to be a perfect parent in an odd way. I can't describe it. The kids have turned out to be very unnatural. They're not spontaneous. They're almost programmed. The kids hate blacks, naturally. It's been their way of life. It's church every Sunday, and if you don't go to church, you're in trouble. He knows just what he wants them to do. What's going to happen is that the kids are going to rebel, unless it's too late. His wife is a very good person. She just works around the clock. At the beginning, she used to keep him pretty straight. But she's gotten to the point where she goes along with his thinking, even with the guns. It scares the hell out of me.

If I wanted to make a lot of money, I'd rob a bank—(laughs)—if I thought I could get away with it. You're always rooting for the bad guy, as long as he's not really bad and doesn't hurt anybody. You think: Oh God, let him get away. What the heck, somebody else can pay for whatever he steals. There's a side of people . . .

Corruption is a way of life. The games you have to play sometimes, just to survive. There are things that you do. My husband and I were speeding, we got stopped. The officer took his driver's license. Jack went to him and said: "I know I was speeding, but we were really in a hurry and running late. I'm an alderman." The cop gave him everything back and said: "Better watch it." We didn't get the ticket. I said: "You were wrong and really should be punished." Jack said: "I know, but that's one of the games of life."

(Laughs suddenly.) I just said a double thing. I said that I would rob a bank. And then I said I hate corruption. Hmmm. Jekyll and Hyde. (Laughs.)

I'd like to have a lot of money, but when I see people that are very poor, it's unsettling to me. I just think: If I had a lot of money, I couldn't really enjoy it when all these people are like this. I would like to see a time when nobody—it sounds like a kind of Communist state (laughs)—but where nobody was without. That would be nice to see, you know?

POSTSCRIPT: *She was killed in the American Airlines DC-10 crash at O'Hare International Airport, May 25, 1979.*

STEPHEN CRUZ

He is thirty-nine.

"The family came in stages from Mexico. Your grandparents usually came first, did a little work, found little roots, put together a few bucks, and brought the family in, one at a time. Those were the days when controls at the border didn't exist as they do now."

You just tried very hard to be whatever it is the system wanted of you. I was a good student and, as small as I was, a pretty good athlete. I was well liked, I thought. We were fairly affluent, but we lived down where all the trashy whites were. It was the only housing we could get. As kids, we never understood why. We did everything right. We didn't have those Mexican accents, we were never on welfare. Dad wouldn't be on welfare to save his soul. He woulda died first. He worked during the depression. He carries that pride with him, even today.

Of the five children, I'm the only one who really got into the business world. We learned quickly that you have to look for opportunities and add things up very quickly. I was in liberal arts, but as soon as Sputnik went up, well, golly, hell, we knew where the bucks were. I went right over to the registrar's office and signed up for engineering. I got my degree in '62. If you had a master's in business as well, they were just paying all kinds of bucks. So that's what I did. Sure enough, the market was super. I had fourteen job offers. I could have had a hundred if I wanted to look around.

I never once associated these offers with my being a minority. I was aware of the Civil Rights Act of 1964, but I was still self-confident enough to feel they wanted me because of my abilities. Looking back, the reason I got more offers than the other guys was because of the government edict. And I thought it was because I was so goddamned brilliant. (Laughs.) In 1962, I didn't get as many offers as those who were less qualified. You have a tendency to blame the job market. You just don't want to face the issue of discrimination.

I went to work with Procter & Gamble. After about two years, they told me I was one of the best supervisors they ever had and they were gonna promote me. Okay, I went into personnel. Again, I thought it was because I was such a brilliant guy. Now I started getting wise to the ways of the American Dream. My office was glass-enclosed, while all the other offices were enclosed so you couldn't see into them. I was the visible man.

They made sure I interviewed most of the people that came in. I just didn't really think there was anything wrong until we got a new plant manager, a southerner. I received instructions from him on how I should interview blacks. Just check and see if they smell, okay? That was the beginning of my training program. I started asking: Why weren't we hiring more minorities? I realized I was the only one in a management position.

I guess as a Mexican I was more acceptable because I wasn't really black. I was a good compromise. I was visibly good. I hired a black secretary, which was *verboten*. When I came back from my vacation, she was gone. My boss fired her while I was away. I asked why and never got a good reason.

Until then, I never questioned the American Dream. I was convinced if you worked hard, you could make it. I never considered myself different. That was the trouble. We had been discriminated against a lot, but I never associated it with society. I considered it an individual matter. Bad people, my mother used to say. In '68 I began to question.

I was doing fine. My very first year out of college, I was making twelve thousand dollars. I left Procter & Gamble because I really saw no opportunity. They were content to leave me visible, but my thoughts were not really solicited. I may have overreacted a bit, with the plant manager's attitude, but I felt there's no way a Mexican could get ahead here.

I went to work for Blue Cross. It's 1969. The Great Society is in full swing. Those who never thought of being minorities before are being turned on. Consciousness raising is going on. Black programs are popping up in universities. Cultural identity and all that. But what about the one issue in this country: economics? There were very few management jobs for minorities, especially blacks.

The stereotypes popped up again. If you're Oriental, you're real good in mathematics. If you're Mexican, you're a happy guy to have around, pleasant but emotional. Mexicans are either sleeping or laughing all the time. Life is just one big happy kind of event. *Mañana.* Good to have as part of the management team, as long as you weren't allowed to make decisions.

I was thinking there were two possibilities why minorities were not making it in business. One was deep, ingrained racism. But there was still the possibility that they were simply a bunch of bad managers who just couldn't cut it. You see, until now I believed everything I was taught about the dream: the American businessman is omnipotent and fair. If we could show these turkeys there's money to be made in hiring minorities, these businessmen—good managers, good decision makers—would respond. I naïvely thought American businessmen gave a damn about society, that given a choice they would do the right thing. I had that faith.

I was hungry for learning about decision-making criteria. I was still too far away from top management to see exactly how they were working. I needed to learn more. Hey, just learn more and you'll make it. That part of the dream hadn't left me yet. I was still clinging to the notion of work your ass off, learn more than anybody else, and you'll get in that sphere.

During my fifth year at Blue Cross, I discovered another flaw in the American Dream. Minorities are as bad to other minorities as whites are to minorities. The strongest weapon the white manager had is the old divide and conquer routine. My mistake was thinking we were all at the same level of consciousness.

I had attempted to bring together some blacks with the other minorities. There weren't too many of them anyway. The Orientals never really got involved. The blacks misunderstood what I was presenting, perhaps I said it badly. They were on the cultural kick: a manager should be crucified for saying "Negro" instead of "black." I said as long as the Negro or the black gets the job, it doesn't mean a damn what he's called. We got into a huge hassle. Management, of course, merely smiled. The whole struggle fell flat on its face. It crumpled from divisiveness. So I learned another lesson. People have their own agenda. It doesn't matter what group you're with, there is a tendency to put the other guy down regardless.

The American Dream began to look so damn complicated, I began to think: Hell, if I wanted, I could just back away and reap the harvest myself. By this time, I'm up to twenty-five thousand dollars a year. It's beginning to look good, and a lot of people are beginning to look good. And they're saying: "Hey, the American Dream, you got it. Why don't you lay off?" I wasn't falling in line.

My bosses were telling me I had all the "ingredients" for top management. All that was required was to "get to know our business." This term comes up all the time. If I could just warn all minorities and women whenever you hear "get to know our business," they're really saying "fall in line." Stay within that fence, and glory can be yours. I left Blue Cross disillusioned. They offered me a director's job at thirty thousand dollars before I quit.

All I had to do was behave myself. I had the "ingredients" of being the good Chicano, the equivalent of the good nigger. I was smart. I could articulate well. People didn't know by my speech patterns that I was of Mexican heritage. Some tell me I don't look Mexican, that I have a certain amount of Italian, Lebanese, or who knows. (Laughs.)

One could easily say: "Hey, what's your bitch? The American Dream has treated you beautifully. So just knock it off and quit this crap you're spreading around." It was a real problem. Every time I turned around, America seemed to be treating me very well.

Hell, I even thought of dropping out, the hell with it. Maybe get a job in a factory. But what happened? Offers kept coming in. I just said to myself: God, isn't this silly? You might as well take the bucks and continue looking for the answer. So I did that. But each time I took the money, the conflict in me got more intense, not less.

Wow, I'm up to thirty-five thousand a year. This is a savings and loan business. I have faith in the executive director. He was the kind of guy I was looking for in top management: understanding, humane, also looking for the formula. Until he was up for consideration as executive v.p. of the entire organization. All of a sudden everything changed. It wasn't until I saw this guy flip-flop that I realized how powerful vested interests are. Suddenly he's saying: "Don't rock the boat. Keep a low profile. Get in line." Another disappointment.

Subsequently, I went to work for a consulting firm. I said to myself: Okay, I've got to get close to the executive mind. I need to know how they work. Wow, a consulting firm.

Consulting firms are saving a lot of American businessmen. They're doing it in ways that defy the whole notion of capitalism. They're not allowing these businesses to fail. Lockheed was successful in getting U.S. funding guarantees because of the efforts of consulting firms working on their behalf, helping them look better. In this kind of work, you don't find minorities. You've got to be a proven success in business before you get there.

The American Dream, I see now, is governed not by education, opportunity, and hard work, but by power and fear. The higher up in the organization you go, the more you have to lose. The dream is *not losing*. This is the notion pervading America today: Don't lose.

When I left the consulting business, I was making fifty-five thousand dollars a year. My last performance appraisal was: You can go a long way in this business, you can be a partner, but you gotta know our business. It came up again. At this point, I was incapable of being disillusioned any more. How easy it is to be swallowed up by the same set of values that governs the top guy. I was becoming that way. I was becoming concerned about losing that fifty grand or so a year. So I asked other minorities who had it made. I'd go up and ask 'em: "Look, do you owe anything to others?" The answer was: "We owe nothing to anybody." They drew from the civil rights movement but felt no debt. They've quickly forgotten how it happened. It's like I was when I first got out of college. Hey, it's really me, I'm great. I'm as angry with these guys as I am with the top guys.

Right now, it's confused. I've had fifteen years in the business world as "a success." Many Anglos would be envious of my progress. Fifty thousand dollars a year puts you in the one or two top percent of all Americans. Plus my wife making another thirty thousand. We had lots of money. When I gave it up, my cohorts looked at me not just as strange, but as something of a traitor. "You're screwing it up for all of us. You're part of our union, we're the elite, we should govern. What the hell are you doing?" So now I'm looked at suspiciously by my peer group as well.

I'm teaching at the University of Wisconsin at Platteville. It's nice. My colleagues tell me what's on their minds. I got a farm next-door to Platteville. With farm prices being what they are (laughs), it's a losing proposition. But with university work and what money we've saved, we're gonna be all right.

The American Dream is getting more elusive. The dream is being governed by a few people's notion of what the dream is. Sometimes I feel it's a small group of financiers that gets together once a year and decides all the world's issues.

It's getting so big. The small-business venture is not there any more. Business has become too big to influence. It can't be changed internally. A counterpower is needed.

LINDA CHRISTIANSON

She reflects on life in one of the country's wealthiest communities. It is a suburb of a large northern city.

There is no industry in this town. The shopkeepers and the gas station owners don't live here. They simply maintain the services that keep the town alive. The people who live here work in the big city. The men commute. There's a very rigid schedule as to which train the men take in the morning and which train they come home on in the evening. The men insist on sitting in the very same seat in the same car every day.

Oh (laughs), Heaven forbid you've got to go to the grocery store to get some milk at, oh cripes, what is it? at five-fifteen or five twenty-one or some weird hour. Everything in town stops. It's like watching a Mack Sennett movie. The cars come from everywhere and converge on the train station from all directions. Traffic is blocked. You can't move. It lasts only about ten minutes. All these men with their brief cases come zooming out of the cars of the train, scurrying in all directions. All their wives have a certain place that they wait. The men without even looking make a beeline for the car.

This town has more Mercedes per square inch than any place in the world, I think. Before that it was always the Ford station wagon. Not

Buick. It's that play at modesty. We *can* afford a Cadillac, but they're so gauche. Yet they can be lavish in other matters, like vacations. It was a big thing when you got back from Bangkok or Madagascar or Hong Kong, and you threw a dinner party with the food of that country and invited everyone you knew so you could brag about it.

The little wives in the waiting cars, if you lined them up, they'd look like little penguins in a row. The same topcoat, ubiquitous beige. The same style shoes, the same style skirt, almost the same color hair, a little light brown with a little bit of gold in it. Never blond. Oh, no. Never dark brown or black either. Just shithouse mouse brown.

I am a product of World War Two. The movies I saw as a child, the stories I read in children's novels, were all the same thing. As a woman, I'm going to grow up, have a little white house and a white picket fence, have a husband who's very, very well-to-do in some sort of a profession. We're going to wear pretty, lovely clothes. We're going to still be wearing a gingham apron when he comes home from work and be taking chocolate-chip cookies out of the oven. We're going to live happily ever after. It's the American Dream.

There's this unwritten statement: there's unlimited funds. The man works, but it's somewhere off. He wears a suit, he doesn't wear working clothes. You take vacations to lovely places all over the world. Somehow the children are taken care of. They don't go with you. You and your husband go on this romantic vacation somewhere. Anything is possible. You simply want it, and it is. That's the dream I grew up with.

I lived in Europe for a year and had picked up enough languages to get a job as translator for a manufacturing firm doing foreign business. I left that job quickly because my boss decided to play a little game called chase me around his desk. I got a job in a brokerage firm. I did meet and marry a man, a very, very wealthy man.

His family is one of the richest in the city. It isn't that they're just wealthy in money, they're wealthy in power, political power as well as having friends in universities, where they've established chairs.

I found this family was day and night from mine. I would invite them over for dinner. Say I would have some nice placemats at the table. Immediately my mother-in-law would say: "How much did these cost?" It was: "I got this new car and I paid eight thousand dollars." It wasn't: "I got this new car and I'm thrilled and, boy, I can't wait to drive you around the block." It was just a whole new ballgame.

I myself now have picked it up. Instead of my bragging how much this costs, I've gone the opposite way. I'll brag about such a bargain something is. "I have a couple of little antique things that I've found in junk shops that I think cost two or three dollars." When a guest praises them, I'll say: "Yes, why in 1966, I picked that up for two dollars." As soon as it's out of my mouth, I go: Oooh, don't say that. I've become what I didn't like about them.

At the brokerage house I worked for, everybody lived in this community. The movers and shakers, who are the grandsons and great-grandsons of the founders of the firm, the who's who. A young man was hired and doing quite well. Bright, well-educated, you'd have thought he could easily walk through the door. But he and his wife made one very big mistake. They didn't move from the city to a stepping-stone community. If you want to wiggle in the back door of this community without having had your grandfather or great-grand-father as a founder, and without having been in the social register for centuries, there are ways to do it, but you have to work very slowly. You have to establish yourself. The man has to have proved himself in his corporation, at least at the executive vice-president level. The wife has to establish herself in the right kind of charity work. You do it by steps.

This man and his wife had the registered two children. He decided to build a home in this community and was excited, telling me about it. One day, my boss and another senior partner, without trying to hide their voices, complained of all these people from the city moving in. Who do they think they are? They're not part of *us*. After I left the firm, I ran into this man. He had overheard the conversation and never forgot the hurt. He had thought he was in. I'm talking about a white Anglo-Saxon Protestant well-mannered, well-educated man. I'm not talking about anyone from any weird or ethnic group. Yet he wasn't one of *them*.

Because of my husband's position, I didn't have nearly as difficult a time. Yet, talk about an ordeal! I found out there were no children living close-by where we lived. The homes are large, with lawns as big as a football field. When you talk about houses on the block, you might have to walk a block to get to another house. I had two small children and wanted them to have a place to play. I was told of a private club in town. The best thing about it was their summer camp program for children. You had to join this club in order for your kids to get in. To be accepted in this club, the directors have to approve you. If you get one blackball, you cannot join. So we'll have a cocktail party and the directors will meet you.

The cocktail party was to begin at five-twenty. What a weird time, I thought. Why not five, why not five-thirty? We got there a few minutes early. All of a sudden umpteen station wagons came zooming into the driveway. The ladies, in their little deck-shoe costumes, with their plain little cotton skirt and plain little white blouse with little Peter Pan collars, hopped out of the cars. The men, in their very, very subdued suits, with the brief cases, came hopping out. They all came tromping in.

They quickly went to the bar, each grabbed their drink, and one by one made their way over to us. Very few of them said "Hello" or "How are you?" The first question to me was: What was my sorority? Then: What school did I go to? What was my maiden name? And then they turned on their heels. The men, after doing this with my husband, turned on their heels. Within forty minutes maximum, it was over. I'd never been to a more unusual social affair. It was a tribalistic ritual. I was the meat on the altar, the lamb. Thank God I didn't drop an hors d'oeuvre.

By this time, I had been well instructed by my mother-in-law how to dress. I was wearing a two-year-old suit. I barely had any makeup on. I spoke very softly, a "well-modulated" voice. I passed because I didn't say anything controversial. I didn't have a chance to say anything.

The women had hairstyles, the basic dress, everything that took them back to college days. One girl had a cardigan sweater, didn't have her arms in the sleeves. Roped around her neck and tied. It was a very quiet, eastern girls' school getup. They were living in their past. They had not created any present for themselves.

They went to the right Seven Sisters schools and the men went to the Ivy League schools, but they can't talk about books or music. They can't talk about politics. It's a dry, sterile world. They're concerned about who was invited to whose dinner party and who was wearing what. The men are all on one end of the room, and the women are all on the other end. The ladies talk about Johnny's measles and where they buy their husband's socks. The men are all talking about the stock market and investment banking. They're in no other profession. If they're in law, they're in corporate law. So you get right back to number one.

I was concerned about what kind of education my children were going to get. So I started checking around. I went over to the public school and found that the bond issue had not passed for eight years. Everyone had children already grown up or of high school and college age, or they sent them to private schools. The few people in town who could not afford private school weren't enough of a voting force to pass anything. Art was knocked out, music was knocked out. Not one new piece of science equipment in four years. I'm talking about one of the richest communities in the world.

Over the years, many of the old dowagers had inherited, oh, tremendous portfolios of stocks and of property, and huge mansions. Mansions that had to be maintained by staffs of twenty, thirty, forty servants. These dear little old ladies outlived their husbands by twenty, thirty years, and with increasing costs, one servant after another had to be let go. These ladies were forced out of their homes or they passed on. So these big estates were being broken up. Realtors were coming in and subdividing them into one-acre lots. Other people were coming in. The age of younger affluence. They didn't have social acceptance, but they had the money. Living this American Dream, with flags flying and trumpets blaring. They brought with them school-age children, but there is no public school worth a damn here.

There's a hidden community here: families of retired retainers and servants. And those who are never discussed at parties: old dowagers living above stores. Noblesse oblige? I broke up a hundred dinner parties arguing with guests about the great many people on welfare in this community.

I'm a weaver. One day, I got a phone call from the recreation center. Would I teach a weaving class to senior citizens? So I found all these lovely little old ladies on welfare. They were living in tiny one-room apartments above the shops in town. Most of them didn't have kitchens. They had a little hot plate. Some of them, their husbands were top bankers in the city. The money went. Some of them not on welfare are on Social Security, from rent check to rent check.

The children of a couple of the ladies I know intimately live in beautiful homes in other parts of the country. They send Mother an airplane ticket once a year, and Mother is allowed to come and stay in their home for ten days, visit the grandchildren, and then Mother is packed off and sent away.

I have some Irish linens which were my great-grandmother's that are absolutely delightful. I had one of these ladies from my weaving class over one day for tea. These tiny tea napkins I'm talking about, little bitty things that aren't worth a damn as far as that goes.

(Laughs.) She was very carefully fingering it, she wouldn't let go. She said: "I had service for thirty." Some astronomical number. And just started talking about it. There was just that little glimpse I got into her past. I could just see this magnificent dining room with the table *this* long, and candles and beautiful crystal and silver. I could see her sitting at one end of the table and servants coming in. And here she was, in her little housedress, sitting in my living room, fingering the lace on my family's napkin, remembering.

For me, it was a difficult world to exist in. My divorce was messy. In this kind of community, once a couple is divorced, the woman loses her status. She may have been accepted before, she may have been president of this society or chairman of this benefit, as I was. But she's out. Oh yes, I was written up many times at such and such a ball, wearing a blah blah blah gown. I was dropped like a hot potato. The people who were not in were nice and kind. The people who were in were distantly polite or actually rude.

I lived the American Dream. I was married to a multimillionaire. I had immediate status. I was living in a house worth a million dollars. I took trips all over the world. I had servants. All these things without working for them. But it was so goddamn much work. For every dollar of affluence, you end up getting two dollars' worth of trouble.

I'm getting back to the values I had before. I didn't exactly start out from sour milk, so I'm not that far away from the cream. I don't think I could ever stand being poor. I'm quick enough about my wits that I guess I never would be. I'll get enough, whatever "enough" is. I don't know.

CAROL AND TONY DANLOW

Lockport is on the western outskirts of Chicago: new subdivisions, built-up farmland, unincorporated. She describes her neighbors as "working toward a more comfortable life. Their houses are so expensive, for any young couple it would be almost impossible." Theirs is one of those houses. It is tastefully furnished.

She says: "We came from something much more plush than this. We had a commercial building in Evergreen Park and a ten-room apartment, and it was way larger than what this is. It was gorgeous. We had a built-in whirlpool bathtub and a dumbwaiter and all kinds of beautiful things."

Though they have three married children, they look astonishingly young. "We started early," he laughs. They are forty-seven.

In February 1975, they won the big prize of the Illinois lottery: a million dollars.

CAROL: We always enjoyed a little gambling. We played the lottery right from the start, buying maybe ten, fifteen dollars a week. Never really thinking about the biggie.

TONY: I was a truck driver for A & P for twenty-eight years. Liked my job and everything. Once you win, people take on a different attitude towards you. They don't think you should work any more. You'd go to work and all of a sudden, they'd want to know how come. They figure that you're taking a job that somebody else would really need. Even the heads of the company and the union officials, they don't stand behind you on anything. *They're* working and making a heck of a lot more money than this lottery gives a person. It's all right for them to work, but they think you should give up your life's work that you've been doing for twenty-eight years. What is fifty thousand dollars a year nowadays? It isn't much by the time Uncle Sam gets his cut. There's many people doin' that and a lot better.

CAROL: Fifty thousand dollars a year for twenty years. That's how you get it.

TONY: We had two good jobs. We kept working until it just got intolerable with the abuse that you take. We were fortunate. We knew a little about real estate and we invested. That's where we made a lot of money. This was even before the lottery.

CAROL: We were at the Mill Run, the dinner-theater house, where they had the drawing. It was a big auditorium, and you could bring your own cheering section. Which we did in high hopes. You were given a ball with a number on it. It was based on horse position and post. They put it in a big barrel. When my name was called, instant hysteria! (Laughs.) It was wild. It's got to be one of the most thrilling times that could ever happen. It's just chills, butterflies, everything.

TONY: Our son, he was twenty-three then, he musta leaped over six rows of seats, and he's hollerin' he'll never have to work again. I said: "Like hell you're gonna quit." He's a carpenter in the building trades.

CAROL: People were like happy, but you always find out about a few of the green-eyed monsters. We lost a couple of friends we thought were friends. It really must have been jealousy or something. All of a sudden the friendships cooled

TONY: It was all right the first week at work. After that, since they just expected they would quit working themselves, I should quit too. They were always on our backs. But I really liked my job. I wanted to work. It just didn't mean that much to us because we were preparing to retire at the age of fifty as it was. I was forty-four, forty-five when it happened.

CAROL: I was a checker at the A & P store. People would say: "How come you're still working?" The one boss, in particular, right after we won, passed the remark: "I suppose she'll want a gold-covered counter." Stuff like that. It was just dumb little things. After a while, it can get a little aggravatin'.

TONY: I don't think I would have quit if A & P hadn't fired me. The two bosses got their heads together and fired me for insubordination.

CAROL: People think they have to talk to you a little differently. After I quit my job, I was working as a travel agent. Okay, right after I started this job, there was a big write-up in the *Sun-Times* and a picture and the whole shot. These women saw the paper, and one got on the telephone and called the other: "Did you read your paper yet?" "No." "Well, open it up and see who we're working with." She did and she said: "Well, what do you know?" So she says: "What are we gonna say to her tomorrow?" So they said: "I don't know."

They're super-nice people, we're friendly, but I had a feeling they felt they had to be different to me. I went in to work the next day as usual, and they were kind of coy. All of a sudden, this one lady said: "I saw your picture in the paper yesterday." "Oh really?" She says: "I didn't know what we should say to you." They thought I was a different person now.

TONY: One of the first couples that won, they were elderly and he always used to go to the corner tavern and have his coupla drinks. After he won, every time he'd go in there for a coupla drinks, everyone expected him to buy the whole place a drink. You can't do this. Rockefeller doesn't go into a cocktail lounge and buy everybody a drink. (Laughs.)

CAROL: The American Dream? That's what we're doing right now. (Laughs.) To me, this is living. We can go golfing whenever we want to and do the things we want to while we're still able. Just where but America could this have been accomplished?

We've always got our eyes open for a new investment. Anything that's gonna pay the best or pay the most.

TONY: I read in the paper about people who believe in reincarnation. I hope there is none. Because I wouldn't want to be born again and get a chance to live a lesser life. I'm so happy with the life that we've had. If I had to do it all over again, I would want it the same way.

HELEN AND SCOTT NEARING

Along the coast of Maine, heading toward Harborside, the waves of the ocean slash against the rocks. It is a twisting, turning, dirt road, howling distance from the small New England towns where alien hallmarks are now familiar: McDonald's, Kentucky Fried Chicken, Dunkin' Donuts, Holiday Inn, and assorted car dealers.

He is ninety-five. His leathery, lined face reflects rivers, roads, valleys, storms, and blows from fellow men, over all of which he has prevailed. He has written fifty books.

She is seventy-seven. She moves with the grace and lissomeness of a young girl.

With a heavy axe in hand, he is vigorously chopping away at a huge log of hemlock. She is bustling about in the simply furnished stone house. "Helen built this house and the utility building and the outside toilet. She put every stone in place with her own hands," he says. He has become a folk hero among the back-to-nature young.

SCOTT: An American Dream? You are an unwarranted optimist. You know the story about the man who was flying from New York to Chicago? As they approached the airport, the captain announced: "The safe part of your journey is now completed. You are entering Chicago traffic. Be on your guard." (Laughs.)

We have the forest and we have the cove. The drift from the Atlantic Ocean and Penobscot Bay comes into the cove at high tide, and when the tide is down, there are the logs. We have very simple tools. We cut it into about twelve pieces, and each one keeps us warm in the winter.

HELEN: We're not wholly independent. We don't make our own shoes. We don't have our own sheep and make our own wool. But we're doggone close to independence without inconveniencing our-selves. We're not purists. We don't say: If that comes from the store, we won't buy it. We buy reluctantly from a store. Scott can go into R. H. Macy's in New York for a shoelace, and he'll come out with a shoelace. All the glamour of Macy's doesn't attract him. (Laughs.) I admit that if I go in for a sweater, I may come out with a scarf and pair of stockings too. But not Scott.

You had lived in Vermont for twenty years. You had built your own place. You made and sold maple syrup. You were, after a fashion, established. Why did you pull up stakes?

SCOTT: We lived on the margin of a wilderness. Stratton Mountain. While we were there, they cut the mountain off, they took the timber off. The paper interests turned the mountain over to a ski group. It was right across the road from us. We decided we didn't want to live there. We wanted to live with people who earned their living by ordinary means instead of artificialities. We liked the farmers better.

The value of the land went sky high, from about $2.75 to eight thousand dollars an acre. The closer you get to the ski area, the more the land is worth. Small acre lots with little ski chalets. We had seven hundred fifty acres. We bought these acres for twenty-two hundred dollars. It's now worth about six million dollars. We're opposed to any form of exploitation or unearned income. We had done nothing to justify the increase. What made the increase was the Korean War. It was a war profit. If we had sold our place at the new commercial value, it would have been a war profit. We were as against profiteering as we were against war. So we gave that land to the town of Winhall. Under the laws of Vermont, we established the Winhall Town Forest.

They called a special town meeting. Shall we accept the gift of seven hundred and fifty acres? The vote on the resolution was two to one in favor of acceptance. That's the only thing I've ever heard from Winhall. They never said thank you. They never even wrote me and said: "We have the property."

The Korean War was on at the time. Those opposed to acceptance called us Communists. They thought we were trying to bribe the town in some way. They didn't exactly know how. But why should we give them perfectly good forest land? There must be a catch.

HELEN: They thought we were trying to avoid taxes in a way.

SCOTT: We had gone to all the town meetings and attended all the functions.

HELEN: We were foreigners when we left, though.

SCOTT: We were always thought of as outsiders.

During World War One, a neighbor of ours said: "Wouldn't you like to buy German bonds?" Unthinkingly, I said yes. I paid about eight hundred dollars for those bonds. I put 'em away. Eventually, they were worth tens of thousands of dollars. I put 'em in the fire. I didn't want any war profits.

How did you get this way?

I was born in a coal and lumber camp, Morris Run, Pennsylvania. In the 1880s my grandfather was superintendent of the area. The Morris Run Coal Mining Company owned the timber, the land, the roads, the houses, the schools, the churches. You mention it, the company owned it. Anybody who lived and worked there had to behave. This was wholly a company town. I was in a privileged family.

One day, when I was a little kid of five or six, I was out with my grandfather, standing beside one of the railroad cars on which the logs were carried. One of the log chains was lying on the ground. They were half-inch chains about twenty feet long. A man picked up one of those chains and carried it to the car. I said to myself: Why don't the guy do that faster? Why don't he hurry? I went to pick up another of those chains. When I tried to lift it, I knew why he walked so slow. (Laughs.) That was one of my first lessons. The people who work have to move chains and split wood and do all the other things that require energy, determination, and a whole lot of juice. The other people lie in hammocks.

I didn't go to school till I was fourteen. I had private tutors. When my family moved to Philadelphia, I went to public school. I started to study law and found it undesirable as a profession. I decided then I would teach. I taught at the University of Pennsylvania and began to write books.

HELEN: Who was it said to you: "Why don't you just collect your royalties and button your lip?"

SCOTT: (Laughs.) Another teacher. He said: "You damn fool, why don't you take your promotion, collect the royalties on your books, keep your mouth shut, and go on about your business. Why do you talk about these things?"

At the time I was secretary of the Pennsylvania Child Labor Committee. We tried to get legislation to restrict child labor. Enter: Joseph Grundy, who owned a textile mill and was president of Pennsylvania Manufacturers' Association. He employed child labor, of course. Grundy told the school: "Unless you get rid of Nearing, you get no appropriation this year."

On the fifteenth of June, 1915, after the university had closed, after the faculty had scattered for the summer, after the students had all gone home, the president wrote me a very brief letter. He said: "You will not be re-employed for another year by the university. Edgar F. Smith."

The dean and the faculty were one hundred percent behind me. I was living down at Arden, Delaware, at the time, in a single-tax community. When I read the letter of dismissal, I got right on the B & O train. That night, we had fifteen hundred letters in the mail to people all over the United States. From then on, we had a battle. It's still going on. In 1975, the University of Pennsylvania gave me an honorary degree. About sixty years later. (A gentle hint of a smile).

In 1917, the federal government indicted me for writing a pamphlet. I was describing the economic causes of the war of 1914–18. The government took the position that if anybody were to read it, they would refuse to serve in the armed forces and, therefore, it was a treasonable act. I was tried in the federal court. I was acquitted, but the people who published the book were convicted and charged three thousand dollars. The case went to the Supreme Court, and the decision was upheld. We collected 3000 one-dollar bills and handed them over to the federal authorities in New York.

The early part of the century was an exciting period in the life of the United States. Almost every community had a channel of expression: city clubs, trade unions, central bodies, forums, Cooper Union. There were thousands of these opportunities for people in the community to get together and express their ideas, reach their fellow men. When I was at the University of Toledo, from which I was fired (laughs), the Central Labor Union met once a week. Anybody who was in the hall, who was sober and didn't speak profanity (laughs), could get up and speak as long as the audience would listen. The First Unitarian Church had a public forum. Speakers would go from state to state, town to town, get ten dollars here, fifty dollars there, and travel to New York, to California, on the proceeds. There were thousands who would come to hear Gene Debs, myself, Clarence Darrow, crowds, crowds, filling Madison Square Garden.

I debated Darrow: "Is Life Worth Living?" Clarence said no. I was young. Clarence was thirty years older than I was. Here was an old man saying life isn't worth living, and here was a young man saying it is. (Laughs.) I said it's not only worth living, it *must* be lived.

It was a vocal country. The First World War ended it. During the war, all bets are off as far as speaking out is concerned. By the time of the Second World War, public forums had shut up. During the war, the military mind took over. In 1931, I thought that members of the human race ought to be doing a better job. What I saw around me was poverty, ignorance, folly, wastefulness. Why not do the best you can to lead the good life?

HELEN: We discussed it: Why be poor in the city? Let's see if we couldn't buy a place in the country. I don't think we had more than a thousand dollars between us. Scott went up to Vermont and found a poor, rundown farm for $300 down and an $800 mortgage. He had an old secondhand runabout Ford for which he paid—what?

SCOTT: Three hundred dollars.

HELEN: And up we went to Vermont. The soil was poor, about sixty acres, which wasn't much then. We discovered we were able to take care of ourselves there. We were poor in the country, but it was better than being poor in the city. Instead of eating out of garbage cans, we ate out of our own garden. It was quite novel for me. My family had a garden and a gardener.

We had this poor, old, rundown house, and we wanted a little more room. So Scott said just build, build, back it onto the house. That was our first stone house. After that, we built nine stone houses: a main house, a garage, a workshop, a woodshed, a greenhouse, and on it went. A studio for Scott in the woods. He's working on a new book now.

Most of the young people who come up here are middle- or upper-class. We get very few working-class people or blacks. They've had it all, and they're pretty well used to taking it easy. On the other hand, they have made a break from society. They have left their soft and easy homes, and they have packs on their backs. That's to their credit. Many are just drifters, out to have a good time, a fun time, that's all. But we're surprised how many are serious and starting homesteads of their own. I'm optimistic about that.

SCOTT: I was in Albania. I asked the chauffeur how many cars there were in the country. He replied: "Just enough."

HELEN: We have just enough here. Our poor friends think we're rich, and our rich friends think we're poor. We built a strong, spacious, sturdy, beautiful house because we did it ourselves. It is as we

329

wanted it, and it's just enough. If somebody gave us a million dollars tomorrow, we would stay right here, and we'd be hard put to know what to do with a million dollars. Scott would probably throw it in the fireplace.

SCOTT: The job is to keep your head above water and to do your share in making the dying society as tolerable as possible.

MOTHER & SON

DOROTHY LAWSON McCALL, 90

The first visit: 1975.
It is a week before her eighty-sixth birthday. Her son, Tom McCall, is serving his second term as governor of Oregon. Highly popular, a maverick Republican, he will seek an unprecedented third term. She herself, a celebrated Portland "character," has been considering half-seriously, half-whimsically, her own candidacy. "My platform is to do away with 'you retire from business at sixty-five.' I want to smash that thing. Who ever dreamed up that awful law? People should work as long as they are able."

Despite her Boston Brahmin accent, which has hung on during her more than sixty years as an Oregonian, she is unrestrained in her conversation. Her words tumble out; her thoughts, freely associative. A double Manhattan adds a high color to her cheeks. She still plays the coquette.

"It's all put on. It's an act. I'm full of aches and pains, and I've got every kind of thing known to a human being."

"Have you ever been told that you resemble Sara Delano Roosevelt, FDR's mother?" I asked.

"I knew Franklin Roosevelt better than I know my grandson. He was a junior in Harvard when I knew that golden-haired boy. He looked like a Greek god, the most beautiful man you'd ever seen in your whole life. I had a terrible crush on him when I was a little girl."

She has written two memoirs: The Copper King's Daughter *and* Ranch Under the Rimrock.

Casually, she commands: "Fish out the pink book." The thick scrapbook has accounts of the wedding of the year. December 15, 1910. Dorothy Lawson, the copper king's daughter, and Harold Mc-Call, son of the Massachusetts governor: Boston Sunday Post, Boston Traveler, Boston Transcript, The New York Times, Pittsburgh Sun. *Clearly they were the golden boy and golden girl. "You're looking at what's left of her."*

My father, Tom Lawson, had that one hairline between a genius and a fool. He was the greatest genius that ever lived. Oh, he was powerful, my goodness gracious. (She reads the opening passages of *The Copper King's Daughter*):

"Can you shovel gold?" the man asked the little boy. "Could I shovel gold? I nearly collapsed at the thought. After a few moments, I was shoveling gold. That was forty-three years ago, and I've been shoveling gold ever since." Thus spoke Thomas W. Lawson, the copper king, at the height of his career.

My father was known as the boy wonder, millionaire at thirty, and a thirty-time millionaire by the early 1900s. In 1897, he conceived the idea of buying and selling all the best copper properties in America and Europe. With Henry Rogers, of Standard Oil, and William Rockefeller, he organized the Amalgamated Copper Company. In the later crash, Thomas W. Lawson lost millions and certain insiders made millions.

Father was a gambler. He played hunches. After my mother died, we went to Europe. He and I became very close. I said: "Pa, break the bank at Monte Carlo." He did. He put everything on it and won. Thirty thousand dollars closed the bank at Monte Carlo in those days. He went out and spent that thirty thousand dollars because he said it wasn't honest money.

He won fifty thousand dollars on a horse race in Kentucky, and gave twenty-five thousand dollars to the black children's home and twenty-five thousand dollars to a hospital for white children. "That's not honest money," he said.

He lost his touch when my mother died. She was sensible and wise. He was tempestuous. She salted some money away. He'd have put it all on some big deal: winner take all. The stability and wisdom came from my mother, my restlessness came from him.

She gets up, scurries toward a table, and returns with a plaque. "Read that."

"A man will know when he's chosen by the gods for a life of quest. The restless urge within him is an eagle in his breast. Let him turn from the seeking and the eagle will eat his heart. Rest? There is no rest for the seeker with an eagle in his breast."

You can't help yourself, see? I just can't sit down here and be eighty-six. (Sighs.) The thing I want most is peace of mind. I'd take the eagle out of my breast and throw it out. I have arthritis and all these funny, awful things, and I hobble around. But my brain is all right. I don't know what would happen to me if I should be bedridden.

I could have written a book *From Thirty Million to Thirty Cents*, because in 1929 and '30 we didn't have any. We had five children and a ranch out here with a heavy mortgage on it. Men would work for just three meals a day. My husband said: "Could you cook for them in the bunkhouse? I have no money to pay them . . ." Do you know that I cooked forty-five meals a day for five months? The word is "will." I have no traffic with wishy-washy people. You're here in this world to do something. That's why I'm here. That's why I live and breathe.

I'm not a winner. I always play losers. They need me. Winners don't need me. Georgia-Pacific gets along without me. I'm a loser. But we weren't gonna lose that ranch, not on your life. A man lived and died for it. No more money coming in. No more rich father. A rich friend said: "Why don't you take in boarders?" So we took boarders in, my rich friends' children. I swam with them, I read for them, I cooked for them. My husband had to be out on the ranch and work with his men. We held the ranch because I did do it.

See these two solid gold revolvers? "To Dorothy from Pa, 1913." He gave them to me because we were out here in the homestead country, the frontier. These are the only two in the world. I took those up to the Palace Pool Hall, a tough place. I went up to the man and said: "I want to borrow a hundred dollars on these." High school was opening, and my sons didn't have any nice clothes like the other boys had.

I wasn't shamed. My husband was ashamed of only one thing; being in debt. And we *were* in debt. It was touch and go. All our expensive friends, the eastern people, they bought up all of Central Oregon and everything boomed. When those other days came, they all sold out. We are the only ones that stayed with all the roughnecks. We always had plenty to eat. On a farm or a ranch, you can kill something, even if you kill each other. I cooked everything. I kept boarders till '33, four years. I was so proud of myself.

I used to say when I was terribly depressed, I was gonna take one gold gun in each hand and blow my head off and go out like a millionairess. It would have been spectacular, wouldn't it? *Hedda Gabler*, I know it by heart. I have all the books, all the tragic stories.

Where are all the people who were licking our shoes when I was the copper king's daughter? They tried to foreclose on us. This one got hold of our cattle mortgage, the greatest herd west of the Rockies. He said he's hiring men to load the cattle out. A nice little city man. Most prominent people today. He said it's a kindness to take these things away, and I should go back where I belong. I said: "Look here, those men are waiting for my pancakes. You just get the hell out of my kitchen." I had all those rough men there to fight for me. You bet I had a sense of power. I would never let that ranch be lost to Hal and his children. We're a clan, the McCalls.

I'm a Libra. It says that as a mother I eat my children, from the old Greek fable. About twenty years ago, I realized I was eating my children. I was telling them what to do. Today the children are in revolt. I am living in a wonderful age, if I can only hold on to it.

At the grocery store, this big fat boy slapped me on the back and said: "Hello, honey," This lady said: "Did you hear what that boy called you?" I said: "That's the greatest compliment I've ever heard." I slap people on the back. I don't see any class distinction. There should be no class system, so the bureaucrats wouldn't run the world.

The second visit: 1979.

She is as she was four years before, though a touch of weariness is more in evidence.

At the turn of the century, my father controlled all the copper in the U.S. He was thirty-seven years old. Everything he touched had turned to gold. Then he defied Standard Oil, for whom he'd worked, and fought a battle. He saw how rotten stinking they were and started to write *Frenzied Finance*. The first chapter was in *Everybody's Magazine*. They sent three times for my father in Boston. The first time they offered him I don't know how much money. Then they came to the house on Beacon Street and said: "Mr. Lawson, you have two minor children. Someday you'll pick their two little wet bodies out of that river. You better accept that offer." He was not going to stop writing that book.

My father was born with a yen.

"I remember my three trips to Europe with Maude Howe Elliott as chaperone. Her mother was Julia Ward Howe. She took millionaires' daughters out and presented them to the courts of Europe. Traveling was the first thing we did when we moved from Winchester, Mass., which is a nice Booth Tarkington place. Happy people, but not of great fortunes.

"I was brought up, lying in bed upstairs, born with rheumatism. My beautiful mother would be playing the piano downstairs, and they had the gray and blue books of the Civil War. Those men who had been in the war were singing. No more war. My father lit one cigar after another. Every time I smell cigar smoke, I hear that music playing downstairs. One Hundred Main Street, Winchester—wonderful."

My grandfather, a carpenter, came back from the Civil War and died in Cambridge. He left four children, no money, no anything. The younger daughter died from malnutrition. That's what burned inside Tom Lawson when his father died of his wounds. To get a job on State Street. He had heard about them shoveling gold there. A twelve-year-old boy walked from Cambridge to Boston to get that job that got him going in the big fight against Wall Street. He saw his mother die of malnutrition. One day, the grocer said to his mother: "You won't spank Tommy if I tell you what he's done. He's been stealing eggs." He had to steal eggs at eight years old to keep his mother alive. My father was a maverick. We didn't have that word then. It wasn't in the dictionary. He had a vision.

He built Dreamwold after he'd gone to work for Standard Oil in 1900. That whole great thousand acres in Massachusetts with a white fence around it. On his payroll were three hundred men. He said money was not made to be saved. Money, money, money—it is to be put out to the people and everybody should have it. That was his vision.

You're looking at an antique, but I'm my father's fighting daughter.

TOM McCALL

Our first encounter in 1975 was at the Statehouse in Salem, when he was serving his second term as governor of Oregon. A huge, loose-jointed, awkward man, he lumbered out of his office and, foregoing introduction, went at it. "I liked what you said last night at Corvallis. 'Nobody should be afraid to look foolish and worry about what others think.' Right now, with the cost of living soaring, those poor women on welfare can't make it. We've got to raise their allotment."

Our second encounter: 1979. It is at his old, rambling house. "I love this place, but it's up for sale. I've got to pay off election debts. I'm in a deep hole." In running for a third term, he suffered an unexpected, stunning defeat in the Republican primaries. There is an ironic consensus: had he run in the general elections as an independent, he'd have won handily.

I guess I've always been a maverick. I didn't know any better. I grew too fast, had huge feet, round shoulders. Timid, wouldn't walk into a room with two people in it. I sort of knew how black people felt. There was a kindred feeling. I was the clumsiest guy you ever saw.

I was born in Massachusetts. We were all born in my grandfather's house, all five children. It was one of the most magnificent showplaces in the world. He had a hundred gardeners in the summer. He had something called Locomobiles, which correspond to Cadillacs now. He used to have his chauffeur drive us to this private school. He'd sit in the back and tell us stories. He was a marvelous storyteller.

He was just a genius in the stock market. George Westinghouse's stock was way down. He came to Granddaddy and said: "How much can you shake loose?" Tom Lawson told him: "I only got about seventeen million dollars to move around, but let me try. "By the time he manipulated the stock market, Westinghouse was ahead of General Electric in value.

He was a robber baron himself who turned on them. He wrote this most remarkable exposé, *Frenzied Finance*. It ran in *Everybody's Magazine* in 1907, you bet. He just simply exposed the system. He showed how the insurance companies invested money, how they maneuvered. It caused a federal investigation that redid the whole insurance industry. I think he was simply a man of conscience. He got in a terrible fight with the Rockefellers, and they finally crushed him.

The other grandfather, Sam McCall, was the first three-time governor of Massachusetts. While in Congress for twenty years, he was recognized as its most independent and intellectual member. When he ran for the Senate, he was dry-gulched by the right-wing Republicans. That's why I'm so stupid to let it happen to me. I had the example of my grandfather. There are people called hierarchs. They manipulate, they pull the strings, they set the policy. Same now as then.

The people in this state really are independents at heart. They say the two-party system is the only one that works. I could argue that from experience. I believe in a third force. I don't know if you'd call it populist. I guess he's one who reflects the people's aspirations without wearing anybody's collar. (Sighs.) You bet I was stupid not to run as an independent.

I campaigned for a sales tax in 1969 and got beaten eight to one. I apologized the next day. I said I simply wanted to clear the air. No governor's ever dared do that. The next year, I ran and got elected by a bigger margin than before. You see, I don't believe in polls. I figure they said: "Well, Old Tom can't do any worse. Let's try him again and maybe he'll do better."

Oh, there've been some satisfying moments. There was the confrontation between the people's army jamboree and the American Legion convention, fifty-eight thousand people. The people's army, thirty-five thousand, haters of the Vietnam War, the most emotional ones, were gonna confront the Legion in downtown Portland. It was the damnedest confrontation you'll ever see.

We took a park, twenty miles south of Portland, and turned it into an overnight bivouac and disco party. That's where the kids stopped. I warned both sides. I went on the air and said: "Legionnaires, you're not gonna shoot kids because they're bearded. And kids, you're not gonna tear down these people because they saved the world for democracy. Let's get out perspectives straight." The Legion gave me a medal. The kids cheered.

I was told by the political wise men: "You crucified yourself. You'll never be elected dogcatcher." There was a lot of pot smoking and skinny-dipping, but nobody was killed. They said it would be known far into the future as the Governor's Pot Party. 1970. I was reelected by a bigger margin than before.

The American Dream? Gosh, I wish I could articulate it. We're going right, but we're not going right. You sense a feeling of desperation because issues seem so complex and a know-nothing comes along with an simplistic answer, playing on people's fears.

I'd done some audacious things, and they have cost me terribly. I say to myself: If I had held my tongue once in a while . . . But why should I?

I'm sort of shattered, but I'm still useful. I'm just living day to day, making speeches and challenging the know-nothings and trying to tell people that they're being heard again. And wondering where is the glow of yesteryear? Wondering where the heroes went. Gosh, I don't know how long ago they left.

Heroes are not giant statues framed against a red sky. They are people who say: This is my community, and it's my responsibility to make it better. Interweave all these communities, and you really have an America that is back on its feet, a comfortable nation to live in again. I really think we're gonna have to reassess what constitutes a hero.

THEY ALSO SERVE...

◇————————————————————————————◇

POLITICS

JAMES ABOUREZK

◇————————————————————————————◇

He has been a senator from South Dakota. He has decided not to stand for reelection.

It is Saturday afternoon, two days before Halloween 1977. We're in his office in the Senate Office Building, Washington, D.C. He and Senator Howard Metzenbaum of Ohio have been conducting a thirteen-day filibuster against a bill deregulating the price of oil.

As Sam Rayburn said, if you want to get along, go along. That's the philosophy of most people around here. Very few people here stand for something. They have taken public-opinion polls to heart. There's nothing wrong with polling, but it's something else when you start calculating on every single little issue: How am I gonna be cute on this? How am I gonna gimmick this one up so I can go back home and not get in trouble? There are very few guys around here who are not afraid to get in trouble—on *anything.*

They're afraid to commit themselves because there's a yahoo out there raising all sorts of hell. It's more important for them to be in office than to do something while they're there. Instead of politicians, they've become technocrats, reading poll signs wherever they go.

They're sitting there. Their calculation has become so finely tuned, so technical, that they've forgotten what the public really wants. The public doesn't want this shit. Carter got on national TV and said: We'll have to sacrifice because we're gonna run out of energy one of these days. Hell, everybody knows that. It's a finite resource. Why does it always come that two hundred million people sacrifice and fifty thousand at the top are never called upon to sacrifice? What kind of shit is that? That public doesn't know the details of the energy program. It's too complicated. But they can smell a rat.

The public is not wild and crazy. The public appreciates independence. Everybody who goes to South Dakota says: "How did two people like McGovern and Abourezk get elected in that conservative state?" The fact is, the people know us personally. We stand up and say: "Maybe you don't like it, but that's how our conscience tells us to vote." You know something? They appreciate that.

There's no two-way dialogue between senators and their constituents any more. The guy takes a poll, gets on TV, and runs his media campaign according to the poll. He really doesn't hear from his constituents and the depths of their feelings.

Today, I don't think you can accomplish any more inside than you can out. The only victories you're allowed to win here are marginal ones. It doesn't mean a goddamn thing. People say: "You've got to stay, you're the voice of the anti-oil people." They assume I'm indispensable. Hell, we're all soldiers. If one falls, somebody takes his place. Some around here think we're on the command staff rather than just being front-line soldiers.

The thirteen-day filibuster Howard Metzenbaum and I conducted was, in a sense, a soldiers' small mutiny, a takeover. We lost as all such takeovers do, but the issue attracted the country's attention. That's the purpose of a filibuster. I knew of the pressures on us from our peers, from the outside. The *Washington Post* denounced us. I did it because Pete Stavrianos, my administrative asssistant, challenged me: "When I asked you to run again, you said it didn't matter much whether you were here or not. If you can stop those bastards from deregulating natural gas, you'll have done more than you've done in your entire eight years in Congress." So I said: "Why not?"

I had about a thousand letters, telegrams, and phone calls from around the country. It lost because we got no cooperation from the White House. The vice-president came down on the last day of the filibuster and conspired with the majority leader to break it.

One thing I watched very carefully during the natural gas debate—the heavy concentration of advertising on television by Exxon. Do you know where it was concentrated? In Washington, D. C. Heavier than around the country. Senators are sitting there thinking: My God, my constituents are watching this stuff. It started seeping into these guys voting on the floor here every day. And they didn't know it. They were taken by the commercials.

My father came from Lebanon. He landed in South Dakota in 1898. He was a pack peddler. My dad was very grateful to America.

He was a very, very poor farmer in Lebanon. That's the reason he left. It's a beautiful country, except that they were dirt poor.

In 1910, after he'd saved enough money to buy a buggy and a horse, he bought a store. In 1920, he opened another one. He went bankrupt two or three times during the depresssion. He always gave credit to the people who lived there, Indians and non-Indians alike. The Indians were the only ones who paid him back. The whites didn't. (Laughs.) He always said: "Make sure nobody goes hungry."

As a kid, who had dreams? I was eating. Three meals a day. I wanted to be a storekeeper like my dad had been. My parents were uneducated. They couldn't read or write English, but they could read and write Arabic. My father became reasonably successful for a small-town merchant. He wound up owning a couple of stores and a small ranch. It was on an Indian reservation, Rosebud. You're somewhat blinded, being so close to people. I suppose I was somewhat of a racist when I grew up. I patronized the Indians, spoke down to them. I grew up with Indian kids and went to school with them, but I always thought Indians are inferior to us with lighter skins. I only found out in later years, when I went to college, what I was like.

We were always told there was an American Dream, where people have a right to be treated equal. I know that just doesn't happen. According to the advertising campaign, as long as you let the people who are running this country run it, you can experience the American Dream. You're gonna stay out of jail, you're not gonna get in trouble with The Man if you just let him do what he wants. I don't think the dream exists. The privileged can always manage to get a law passed to legalize whatever it is they want. They've found ways not to go to jail when they take property or rights away from somebody else. City or farm, it doesn't matter.

I understand precisely what the oil companies wanted in deregulation of gas. They wanted to plunder the public purse. If I were an oil company president, I would probably be doing the same thing. What I didn't understand was that people who were here, ostensibly representing the public, my fellow senators, would go along with it. We have a government that is ostensibly run by the people, for the people. It's not true. We have a government run by the establishment, for the establishment. If there are some droppings left over for the people, well and good. No more than droppings.

One of these days, those resources are gonna run out. There will no longer be an abundance. You will see the United States, fifty years from now, in the same condition as underdeveloped countries, fighting over fewer and fewer scraps. You'll see the economic, social, and political system changing. The system we now have operates solely on the basis of greed. It works fairly well when there's enough, so that even the greedy are satiated. But when we run out, there's gonna be a catastrophe. There'll be a violent political upheaval. There'll be a change in our system, probably toward socialism. Those people who abhor the word, the idea, if their foresight were not foreclosed by greed, could change the system, could avoid socialism or whatever may come down the road, by some means where rights were balanced more evenly than they are today. It could be fascism too.

I'm pessimistic as to my vision of the American Dream. It can't be fulfilled as long as the few have the power to overwhelm the many.

The ones who run this country are the multinationals, the banks, the Fortune 500. It all comes together at a point. There's a commonality of interest. They don't need a conspiracy. How many banks need to sit down and discuss how much they have to charge for interest rates? How many oil companies need to sit down and discuss how to distribute oil and how much to charge? No need.

If the American people really knew the facts, they could make a fair judgment. You gotta trust 'em. But newspapers and the radio present issues superficially at best. On television, you hardly get a story longer than two or three minutes. How the hell can you present an issue in that time?

The buzzer sounds. He must go to the floor in fifteen minutes. He sighs.

I'd like to see an America where so much power was not in the hands of the few. Where everybody'd get a fair shake. The establishment wants uneven odds. It's marking the cards. Even though you're a better poker player than somebody else, you mark the cards to make damn sure you don't lose.

Maybe the Indians knew it all along. They smelled it way back. Know what they say? Custer had it coming. (Laughs.)

JESSE HELMS

He is a senator from North Carolina. Political cartoons of him, not all flattering, are on the walls of his Senate office. There is a huge Bible on the table.

All of us are inclined to look back to our childhood as the good old days. They weren't all that good. We just remember 'em that way. I think of my parents and the simplicity of their lives. I'm sure their lives were not that simple, but I just thought they were.

I doubt that my father earned more than seven thousand dollars. He was a policeman, later became police chief. At one time, he was both police chief and fire chief of our little town. My home was Monroe, North Carolina, down on the South Carolina line. We used to say it's on the right-hand side of Highway Seventy-four. Money didn't matter to him, his family did. I never heard him envy anybody who had more. None of us realized we were below the poverty level. Other things were more important. I would like to see a restoration of those values. Personal responsibility is no longer number one as it was back then. Or as I remember it.

Oh, I can remember the high school principal. He had as much impact on me as my own father. One morning, right before graduation, he called some of us into his office. It was depression time. He said: "I want you fellows to know that you can be anything you want to be if you're willing to work hard enough for it. I can envision every one of you will own your own home, that you'll have at least one car, maybe two." We laughed, because nobody had two cars then. And scarcely anybody owned his own home. I don't think I'd have gone to college if he didn't give me that little nudge.

"If you get out there and work and do the best you can, you'll make it. If you don't make it, you didn't try. Don't come back cryin' to me." Out of that class of forty-three, we produced a skipper of the *Forrestal*, he's over here in the Pentagon right now, a president of the Chicago Board of Trade, an administrative assistant to the president of the United States, a president of Rexall Drug Company, doctors, surgeons, oral surgeons, a preacher or two. All that out of this little old tiny group. It's got to be something more than accident. During World War Two, he wrote to every one of the boys, once a month.

I dug potholes for the REA the summer before I went off to college. It was twenty-five cents an hour, and my pay for the week was ten dollars. They took ten cents out for Social Security. So I got nine ninety.

REA? Rural Electrification—didn't that come out of the New Deal?

Mm-hmm. Well, I think there's scarcely an American alive today who wouldn't swap what we have today for the days of Franklin Roosevelt.

Philosophically, a lot of people found fault with it at the time. I think Mr. Roosevelt himself never had any idea it would go as far as it has in terms of government, the size of government, the cost of government, the controls of government, and so forth. "During those hard times of the thirties, the government's WPA provided millions of jobs for the jobless. There are millions of jobless today . . . (His voice trails off.)

I am called a conservative or ultraconservative or archconservative or reactionary. I don't know what all those labels mean. It's misleading. If I were to call somebody an ultraliberal, which I do not, it would be just as bad. I think we ought to back off and start basing it on issues. It's so easy to label somebody. Jim Abourezk—if there is an "ultraliberal," I guess it would be Jim. I like Jim as much as almost any man I've ever met. He's just a delightful chap. Maybe Jim and I don't agree on a lot of things. It's not in what we want but in how to get to the same goal.

I have an abiding faith in the free enterprise system. From many sources I made the judgment that this country of ours was really a unique experiment in the history of mankind. If we believe in the free enterprise system, we ought to let it work. That's why Jim and I come down on opposite sides on the question of deregulation. That has nothing to do with my personal affection for Jim.

I don't quite know how to say this without sounding preachy. The Founding Fathers were unique in their reliance upon God. For my own part, when times get toughest I know where to turn. It's helped me.

I've been in forty-three states in the last five years. I see a growing emphasis on personal faith that was there when I was a boy. I know how devout my mother and father were. We had our prayers at home and so forth. Now you have this all over the country, young men and young women. We have a prayer breakfast here every Wednesday morning. When I first came to Washington, there were seven senators. Now we have twenty-five or thirty.

This is becoming a more spiritual, more concerned nation than I've ever seen. I have great hope. Every day, four or five groups of young people come in here. I see a character quality in these young people that did not exist ten years ago. All we heard ten years ago was about sleeping in and drinking and rioting and all the rest of it. Now I see these kids yearning for something they can rely on. A deep sense of spiritual awareness. They have an understanding of politics that ten years ago did not exist.

The minimum wage came up at a little meeting in a courthouse in Shelby. A young fellow got up and said: "How do you feel about the minimum wage?" I said: "I wish it were possible to pass a law for everybody to make thirty dollars an hour without affecting inflation, without destroying business." He said: "I agree. Isn't it true that every time you raise the minimum wage, you kick the bottom rung of the ladder away from just thousands of people who need the job the worse?" I thought that was a rather profound thing for him to say.

I think the young understand the balance sheet. They understand the profit motive. At one time, this wasn't discussed much in the academic world. Today, look at student attitudes about profits corporations make. A lot of folks think corporations make fifty to sixty percent profit. They actually make three to four percent. The students are beginning to understand that. They understand the national debt. They understand Social Security is a basket case. It's their practical understanding of what's possible for government to do and what's impossible. They give me great hope.

In North Carolina, I've taken positions that I anticipated would be hooted down by young people. All they say is: "God bless you."

DENNIS KUCINICH

Mayor of Cleveland at the time of this conversation.

He is thirty-two, looks twenty-two.

At his one-family bungalow, his wife, Sandy, makes coffee. A player piano is about the only piece of furniture that might distinguish it from any other simply furnished home in this working-class neighborhood. "Some of my neighbors are within ten years of retirement." A photograph of Jefferson, in the shadows, is on the wall.

When I was young, I never dreamed of living in a house like this. We had a big family, and every time we expanded, we had to move. We needed more space. We were always renters. My parents never really owned their own home. A number of times we moved, it was because we were kicked out. It wasn't for failure to pay rent. It was because our family was big. I remember sometimes, in order to get a place, one of the kids had to be hid in the closet. (Laughs.)

We moved around so much, we never became attached to any one neighborhood. We always lived above some railroad tracks. We could always hear the sounds of industry. Another time we'd wake up to the sounds of tugboats in the morning. Long and sonorous calls. Now I can hear the airplanes goin' over the house.

I'm the oldest of seven. There were a lot of tough times. My father came from a family of thirteen children, my mother from a family of a dozen. Our story is an ethnic *Gone with the Wind*. (Laughs.)

I spent all my time as a youngster comin' to understand the experience of the ghetto. It was growin' up tough and growin' up absurd. I spent a lot of time out on the streets. When I was five years old, I began to just go off on my own. I'd catch hell from my parents. I grabbed a bus and went down to the baseball game. If you walked in with an adult, you'd get in for nothin'. I got in for nothin' lots of times.

I'd be stopped many times, and people would ask me: "Who are you with?" I was on the streets a lot. That's where I got my education. I made friends with all kinds of people, black and white. People who ran the shops in the neighborhood. I'd stop in and talk to them and run errands.

My dad's been a truck driver ever since he got out of the service as a marine. He's gung ho. His dream was to have all his boys in the marines. My brother Frank served four years, two and a half in Vietnam. My brother Gary served five years, most of it in Hawaii. My father never questioned authority. His authority was the guy who ran the trucking company.

I've always been taught to respect authority, although I was somewhat more independent than the other kids my age. I was constantly getting into squabbles with teachers. I was the first person in my family, on both sides, who ever graduated from college. I love literature. My mother taught me to read when I was three.

In the late sixties, I didn't go right from high school to college. I worked for two and a half years. When I was seventeen, I moved out on my own and rented an apartment above the steel mills. In the same neighborhood where *The Deer Hunter* was filmed. (Laughs.) The frame house I lived in overlooked the steel mills. It was an awe-inspiring sight, when you'd see the smokestacks against the starry night.

When I was in grade school, I would scrub floors and help with janitorial duties to pay my tuition. When I got into high school, I worked as a caddy at the country club, from 1959 to '64. I caddied for doctors, lawyers, insurance salesmen, and real estate people. I was carrying two bags. They called it workin' doubles. Goin' forty-five holes a day, six days a week. During the summer, I'd sometimes make over a hundred bucks a week.

I believe in the work ethic. There's tremendous dignity in work, and it doesn't matter what it is. What some consider menial, I found to be just a chance to make a living. I always tried to do the best I could at the time. Work hard, get ahead, that was my American Dream.

I began to learn at an early age that I had more in common with people who lived in my neighborhood than with people who lived in another neighborhood. We lived next-door to black people. It was integrated. There's a lot of poor and working ethnics who have to struggle their way into the system, who can identify with black people's striving. I'm trying to show both that the color of the enemy is green. (Laughs.)

This is a city run by the Mayflower-type aristocracy. It's as if the people here don't even exist. Until recently. We seized the decision-making power through the ballot box. Where the blacks talk about their Uncle Toms, ethnics have their Uncle Tomskis. If the black movement did one thing, it created ethnic pride.

I'd ask myself why it is that with so many people tryin' to improve society, not that much changes. As I looked around, I saw many of the kids I grew up with trapped, not able to get as far as they would have liked. I started to wonder: What the heck is this? No matter how hard they work, they can't get ahead. Seein' all these people workin' their heads off, you find out the system is rigged.

When I first started, I didn't question the institutions. I never really put it together. I think it was the Vietnam War. I'd see that some people were profiting, while tens of thousands of Americans were dying. Friends of mine went over there, and they died. Kids I rode the bus with to school. I started to think: This is a dirty business. I'd better start to find out more about it.

I began to get into city politics. In 1967, I ran for the city council. I was ready to back any candidate who would really represent the neighborhood. I ended up being the only challenger. I was twenty-one.

I went door to door, and I found out about people. Every campaign I've ever run has been door to door. I spent months just talkin' to people. They don't ask for much, but they don't get anything. They can have a problem with a streetlight that's out, with a street that's caved in, with a fire hydrant that's leaking, with flooded basements, with snow that isn't plowed. (Laughs.)

I've visited tens of thousands of homes over the past years. That's how I got my real education. Door to door.

I was elected councilman in '69. I just turned twenty-three. My ward was made up of Polish, Ukrainians, Russians, Greeks, Slovaks, Appalachians, Puerto Ricans, blacks. It was a good cross section not only of Cleveland, but of America. They worked in the mills around here. Some had lived in the neighborhood sixty years. Same homes. The churches are still here. They still say masses in Polish and Slovak and Russian. They helped keep the neighborhood alive. I loved it.

People were wondering how the heck I got elected to the council. No one believed the old councilman could ever be beaten, he was so entrenched. At first, people wondered if the banks sent me there. Or the utilities. Or some big real estate interests. All the traditional contributors who buy their candidates.

I was elected on a shoestring. I financed nearly my whole campaign out of my pocket, my savings, which wasn't much. (Laughs.) I put together a coalition of people who were disaffected and ignored.

The first thing, some of the older guys came up to me and said: "You got it made now, kid. All you have to do is take your seat and shut up. If you just listen to what we tell you, you're gonna be a big man in this town some day." (Laughs.)

When I started steppin' on toes, I didn't know I was steppin' on toes. I was just representin' the people who sent me to the city council. I didn't know I was offending somebody else. I found out very quickly there were a number of special-interest groups who made City Hall their private warren. There are thirty-three councilmen. Thirty-two to one was usually the score.

The newspaper coverage was usually cutesy-poo. Or sometimes I was compared to Mao Zedong or Stalin or McCarthy. (Laughs.) Or Hitler or Jim Jones. Our organization was likened to the Khmer Rouge or the Moonies. We were talking about the central issue of our times: the maldistribution of wealth. People who are well-off don't want to hear about that.

When I got elected mayor, just as I came to the council, I was expected to respect the system. When I started to challenge it, the titans of Cleveland's business community began to get surly and used their clout in the media to disparage the administration. I came to understand that big businesss has a feudal view of the city, and that City Hall was within their fiefdom.

When I was elected Mayor on November 8, 1977, it was discovered that the previous administration had misspent tens of millions of dollars of bond funds. They could not be accounted for. The city was trying to negotiate the renewal of fourteen million dollars' worth of notes held by local banks. One bank balked: the Cleveland Trust Company.

I had a meeting on the day of default at eight o'clock in the morning, with the council president, the chairman of the board of Cleveland Trust, and a local businessman, a friend of mine. The conversation turned immediately to MUNY Light.* The chairman of the board of Cleveland Trust made it very clear that if I sold MUNY Light to the Cleveland Electric Illuminating Company, he would extend credit and save the city from default. CEI's largest shareholder is Cleveland Trust. Four members of Cleveland Trust's board are directors of CEI. If I didn't agree, I could not expect any help from his bank.

MUNY Light has forty-six thousand customers in Cleveland. MUNY Light and CEI compete in most neighborhoods, street by street, house by house. MUNY Light's rates in the recent decade have been from twenty to sixty percent cheaper than CEI's, but MUNY Light's competitive advantage has depreciated over the years because of CEI's interference in MUNY's management.

From the moment Mr. Weir** told me his price, I decided that a fiscal default was better than a moral default. If I had cooperated with them and sold MUNY Light to the private utility, everyone's electric rates would have automatically gone up. It would have set the stage for never-ending increases, much the same way that Fort Wayne, Indiana, is faced with that problem after relinquishing its rights to a municipal electric system.

While Brock Weir and George Forbes*** were talking, I was listening. And praying, hoping I was doing the right thing in holding my ground. I had to tell 'em no. I felt they were trying to sell the city down the river. They were tryin' to blackmail me. If I went along with the deal, they made it clear, things would be easy. Mr. Weir said he'd put together fifty million dollars of new credit for the city. The finan-

---

* The Municipal Electric Light Plant is owned by the city of Cleveland. "It has been in existence over seventy years." It came into being during the administration of Tom "Golden Rule" Johnson, a populist mayor, early in the century.
** Brock Weir, chairman of the board of CEI
*** President of the city council

cial problems would be solved. My term as mayor would be comfortable and the stage set for future cooperation between myself and the business community.

The media picked up the tempo. Why the heck don't you get rid of MUNY Light? I was asked that on a live TV show. I replied that MUNY Light was a false issue. It wasn't losing money. Its troubles could be traced to CEI's interference. I was in office a little over a year and had inherited a mess. The city had a plan to avoid default to which five of the six banks agreed: an income-tax increase, as well as tighter control of the management of the city's money. That's one of the reasons I got elected.

I knew I was risking my whole political career. But you gotta stand for somethin'.

The referendum was to be held on February 27. Both issues were on the ballot: the income-tax increase and the sale of MUNY Light.

We organized our volunteers. People went out door to door, in the freezing rain and the bitter cold, subzero temperatures and big snow. (Laughs.) We laid out the hard facts. We didn't promise new services. We told the people that unless the tax increase was passed, the state would impose a controlling board and eliminate home rule. The other issue, MUNY Light, was more complex. We were facing the attempt of corporations to run the city. We gave the people a choice between a duly elected government and an unduly unelected shadow government.

We were outspent two and a half to one, but we created circumstances where people came to understand that every person can make a difference. We won both issues by about two to one.

It was the first time in Cleveland's history that we succeeded in uniting whites and blacks, poor and middle class, on economic issues. Usually, they've been manipulated against each other. Not this time.

My concept of the American Dream? It's not the America of IBM, IT & T, and Exxon. It's the America of Paine and Jefferson and Samuel Adams. There are increasingly two Americas: the America of multinationals dictating decisions in Washington, and the America of neighborhoods and rural areas, who feel left out. I see, in the future, a cataclysm: popular forces converging on an economic elite, which feels no commitment to the needs of the people. That clash is already shaping up.

The American Revolution never really ended. It's a continuing process. I think we're approaching the revolution of hope. We have the kind of country which makes it possible for people, if they've lost control of their government, to regain it in a peaceful way. Through the ballot box.

Before I got into politics, I didn't really know whether what I was doin' even mattered. Now I know. One person can make a difference. I think it's something every person can learn. The main thing is, you can't be afraid.

POSTSCRIPT: *In November 1979, with just about all of Cleveland's newspapers, television and radio stations—as well as industry— united against him, he was defeated for reelection.*

VITO MARZULLO

He is serving his seventh four-year term as Democratic alderman in Chicago. "I ran for office twenty times and I won. Seven times for legislature, six times for ward committeeman, seven times for alderman, and only had opposition once. In 1967, I defeated my opponent fifteen thousand to one thousand. Nineteen times nobody filed against me, even for public nuisance. (Laughs.) I've been at the beck and call of the people since 1919."

On the wall of his office in City Hall are photographs of his family, a gathering of his fellow aldermen and, of course, the late mayor, Richard J. Daley. "He was a great humanitarian, a great family man, and a great religious man."

On each of his lapels is pinned a miniature American flag in rhinestones. "I'll wear these as long as I live. You bet your life. Not only on my sleeve. I wear it all over, no matter where I go. I'm proud that I was born in Italy, but I came to this country to be an American. If I wanted to be an Italian, I'd stay in Italy. I say to any foreign person: 'If you don't like what we do in this country, why don't you go back where you came from?' "

I am eighty-one years old. I was twelve and a half years old when I landed from Italy right in this neighborhood. I been here ever since. I got as far as fourth grade, then I went to work in the factory for four dollars a week. Meantime, I went to night school for five years to learn the machinist trade.

In 1918, they got me, a little greenhorn, for Democratic precinct captain. I started just for fun. The first election, I got thirty-one

Democratic votes. Three hundred forty-seven Republicans. The committeeman said: That's the best show we ever made in that precinct." The biggest Democratic vote before was eleven. I got married in 1922. The biggest wedding gift was, I carried the precinct Democratic by eighty votes. Ever since then, nobody was able to catch up with me.

The late Mayor Daley said, when he was living, that I was goin' to more affairs than any elected official in Cook County. He says: "How do you do that?" My answer: "I love people." I appreciate what this country did for me, and I'm not an obstructionist. On this, I still give a lecture to my own married children and grandchildren. I got six married children and nineteen grandchildren.

I'm down here five days a week, I'm down at headquarters two nights a week, I go to every social affair, every civic affair. I even went to Harvard University. They want me because they know I speak from the heart. The trouble we have in this country, from the president down, they don't want to tell the people the truth. They're afraid to hurt their feelings. I hurt somebody's feelings, that's just too bad.

America has changed, and it's gonna change much more. I hope they don't make changes just to satisfy these rabble-rousers, these noisemakers. When I came from Italy, every four, five blocks, they had an ethnic group: Jewish, Pole, Bohemian, Italian, Irish, German. We all had to suffer to learn the American way of life. None of us came here and told the American people: Learn the way I live in Italy or the way I live in Germany or Ireland. Now we arrive at the point where we gotta have foreign-language signs. We gotta learn Spanish or Jewish—no, not Jewish, not Italian, not Pole, just Latino. Instead of having the Latino learn the American way of life, they keep on telling the Latino learn how to read and write Spanish. Now you gotta hire so many, whether they're qualified or not. They don't have so many go to school and learn the American language, the American way of life. I don't like that.

I am allergic to the word "demanding." I like the word "request" better. If they come in like ladies and gentlemen, I treat 'em like ladies and gentlemen. But if they come in like animals, I treat 'em like animals. I don't care who they are. I showed my colors time and again. That isn't because I don't like blacks, I don't like Germans, I don't like Latinos. I like all people. But I never walk in any public office, any business, demanding things, and sneering and defying law and order, and destroying life and property. I don't like that. That's why we fought to civilize the country. We made a good job of it. Are we gonna go back to revolutionary days? No, not me. I believe in God, and I believe in a nice way.

They had an Irish priest over there, Precious Blood, in my ward. He come in with a sixteen-year-old Irish girl, with ten black men and ten Mexican men. I took one look at 'em and they were like twenty devils. I could tell the expression on their faces the minute they walked in. The black men, along with the priest, says: "Alderman, we got certain demands to make." And shaking their arms. This black man had a crumpled paper in his hand. I took one look around and says: "Sir, before you go any further, you don't make no goddamn demands to this alderman, you understand?" The Irish priest, he says: "Alderman, is that the way you're talkin' to us?" I look at him and say: "You shut up. You not only disgrace my religion, you disgrace all religion. What're you doin' down here with all these animals? Get outa here and never come again." So the black man say: "You never be alderman again." I lost my temper, and my Dago blood came out. I lost my temper because the priest was there, the small girl was there. I said: "You dirty, filthy son of a bitch, if I hadda be alderman with your help, I don't wanna be. But I'll be alderman and I'll see each of you dead and buried. Get outa here and don't come back again, because if you do, you'll never go out alive."

They wanted a park. Well, the people around here didn't want it. So I didn't want to approve it. So naturally, I didn't give 'em a chance to talk, I chased 'em out.

Let anyone who come to me like ladies and gentlemen, I don't care who they are, I treat 'em with silk gloves. Let some Italian come in like that, I chase some Italians outa here.

In my ward, I only got five percent Italian. Polish, black, Mexican, Lithuanian, and all other. In 1975, I hadn't made up my mind whether I was gonna run for reelection. Word got out. So one night twenty people came over to headquarters. Mixed, black, Mexican, everybody. Jesus Christ, I thought they were gonna raid the place. I said: "What's goin' on, gentlemen? What's the question?" They said: "We're just here to tell you, Alderman, if you don't run for reelection, we're gonna protest in front of your home twenty-four hours a day. We won't let you sleep. We don't want nobody else to be our alderman here."

In 1919, when I became precinct captain, I was still a machinist. In

1921, I took a job in the county treasurer's office because when you're a precinct captain, you just can't work in a factory. You're active politically. You knock on doors, you go to socials. That's why these intellectuals, all these do-gooders, they don't like that. They like to control everything through the news media.

They gotta yap, yap. Nobody can answer 'em. Naturally they win all the time. Let 'em come before me, and I'd sit on their behind in no uncertain language. They call it the Democratic machine. They don't know the difference between a machine that runs by oil, electricity, and a machine that's operated by humans. When I get through with them, they don't call it a machine any more.

A man that lives within five, six hundred votes, three, four square blocks, gets an interest. Make sure that people register. He goes to weddings, he goes to wakes, he goes everyplace. When these people want somethin', they don't go to the president of the United States, not even to the alderman. They go to the local fella, the precinct captain. The intellectual, the know-it-all, the give 'em a ten-dollar bill, they can't even get a dog out of a dog pound.

Now, we passed the fair housing ordinance. It was all over the *Tribune* the next morning. The original ordinance says: No real estate can discriminate, no person can discriminate. Before we passed it, Mayor Daley sent for me. I said I will not vote for it. Take out "any person." Just apply to real estate, they're licensed. But don't include "any person" because that includes you and me. It was amended.

We had this meeting. One big Polish fella got up: "Will you tell us what the open occupancy law you gentlemen passed in the city council would do to us?" I said: "Sir, there is no open occupancy, it's open housing." I read the amendment. He got up: "Oh, thank God we got an alderman who knows what's goin' on." Then I turned to the priests: "My good religious leaders, let me tell you something. If you can't see further than your nose how the undesirable people are destroyin' life and property, churches and cemeteries, it's too bad. We won't have no country left." I thought the place was comin' down. The noise. The first ones that came to shake my hands were the priests.

"Undesirable" is any man that's un-American, any person who destroys life and property, any person who defy law and order. I don't want 'em, I got a lotta good black people that are damn good people. Believe me, I trust 'em with everything I got in my life. I got a Mexican secretary of mine over there, a wonderful family man. I've got Italian that I call undesirable.

I don't try to be a smart guy. When I go talk to these students, I tell 'em: "God knows how much sacrifice your parents made to send you to this institution of learning. You're gonna go home and put that degree to work. If you do this in a country like America, you cannot fail. However, let me warn you. If you go home and say, 'I got my degree, the world owes me a living,' I got news for ya. You'll be a bum. You can wipe your behind with the degree if you don't put it to work." At Harvard, they all stood up and clapped and clapped and cheered. I tell that to my kids.

Can I tell you a little story about this Italian guy? Italian people go back to Italy to visit once in a while, and they spend a buck. One fella says: "How do you do this?" So he says: "Oh, America, everything you touch turns to gold. You make money left and right." So the fella says: "Jesus, I'm gonna go to America, and I'm gonna make money and come back." So he came to this country, stayed here two weeks, one month, two months, and come back. He couldn't make a dime. So he started goin' to church every morning: "Oh, God, help me find it." So a guy tells him to go to the confession box and pray for God to come down. He'll tell you how to go about it. So the priest is hidin' in the box, and when the guy starts prayin', the priest hollers: "Go to work, you bum." The guy says: "Hell, if I wanted to go to work, I'd go to work in Italy. So I have to come to America to go to work?" (Laughs.)

That's the trouble over here. Lotta these people think the world owes 'em a livin', period. They wanna be on welfare. They wanna live on somebody else's sweat and blood. I don't want that.

Look at me. I could never think that I got as far as I got. After the election, 1968, I went to Italy with my wife. I'm registering in the hotel in Rome and the clerk, when he saw my name, says: "How's Mayor Daley?" He pulled out the Italian newspaper with Daley's picture and my picture in it. Can you imagine, twelve-year-old boy come here from Italy?

I'm not an intellectual, I'm not a millionaire, I'm not a big guy. I'm just an ordinary layman as what I was when I came from Italy, no difference in my ways. First the Lord and then the general public is being very nice to me.

COLEMAN YOUNG

The mayor of Detroit.

My father was many things. After World War One, he became a tailor under the GI Bill. He was already a barber and a waiter. The army was strictly Jim Crow at the time. He was a buffalo soldier in World War One, 370th Infantry.

"Following the Civil War, there were four cavalry regiments assigned to the West. The Seventh and Eighth were white. Everyone's heard of the Seventh, Custer's outfit. The Ninth and Tenth were black.

"They had quite a reputation. The Indians named them buffalo soldiers because of their curly, cropped hair. The Tenth Cavalry was with Teddy Roosevelt at San Juan Hill. History does not record that it was the Tenth that saved his ass. In World War Two, I was a member of the buffalo division.

"I got a lot of this information from my father. There is more continuity among blacks, more preservation of their history, than is commonly recognized. I remember, as a boy of six, my grandmother had a big book. It was the history of colored soldiers. I read everything I could about black history. And labor."

Like most blacks in the twenties, my father was a Republican. With the crash of '29, he became an avid supporter of FDR. He read every damn thing he could lay his hands on. My mother was a schoolteacher. He was very militant. She was the stable one. She worried about me because I was like my father. He was constantly in some argument. He wasn't a big man, but I've seen him beat up guys twice his size by pickin' up a bottle or a scissors or anything at hand. He hated white people until he met a guy who treated him as a peer. A Catholic. We all converted to Catholicism.

My mother insisted on neatness and that we use good English. As the oldest of five, I became her lieutenant in looking out for the rest of the kids. I became a sort of disciplinarian, a stool pigeon. (Laughs.) An enforcer for my mother. (Laughs.)

We came to Detroit from Alabama in December of '23. We lived on the Lower East Side, which was the major ghetto at the time. I was a good student and arrogant. At St. Mary's, I became Scout troop leader. We went on an excursion, but I was turned back from the island because I was black. This was the first conscious anger I felt. After that, I became more alert. That's probably part of my history in becoming a radical. I had so many rebuffs along the way.

When I finished St. Mary's, I was among the city's top ten and entitled to a scholarship. Some brother friar comes along, looks at me in puzzlement, and says: "What the hell are you, Japanese or somethin'?" I said: "No, brother, I'm colored." He took my paper and tore it up, right there in my face. I went back to public schools. That was the end of me and the Catholic church.

The year 1928 had a big impact on me, the boom year. I was ten, workin' for a tailor. After school and all day Saturday, I'd sweep the floor, deliver suits. This is a street unlike any you'd find. It was a neighborhood street. Everybody was doin' something wrong on this street. The tailor was very good, but his back room was a crap game. Next-door was the shoeshine parlor, which had the biggest poker game on the East Side. Down the street, there was black jack and Georgia skin. Mr. Latimer, who ran the confectionery store, made moonshine.

I was gettin' three dollars a week plus tips. People were very generous then, and money was plentiful. It cost a dollar and a half to clean a suit. I'd get two bucks: Keep the change, kid. Mr. Latimer, the bootlegger, bought used bottles. I'd go to fifteen, twenty places, pick up the empty bottles, and sell 'em back to him for two cents each. Hell, I musta made nine, ten dollars a week from the bottles. If I was quiet and stayed in the corner, I could watch the crap game. At the tender age of ten, I knew the odds on all the dice. (Laughs.) These guys were doin' so well, they were admired by the blacks coming up from the South, whose only models for respectability and success were the slave masters, with their delicate hands and fancy clothes. These guys were all dressed fancy and had exotic names like Tricky Sam and Fast Black. There are many people today I don't know by their real name. (Laughs.)

So I'm listenin' to all this crap. These guys had contempt for guys who worked. They called 'em Ford mules. Most of the guys worked at Ford. They'd talk about how they'd go around with the guys' wives while they were at work. They had a motto for Ford: You feed 'em, we'll fuck 'em. I learned from them somethin' I later rejected, 'cause across the street from all this was a little barbershop run by a man named Williams, who was somethin' of a Marxist. I was the pet of the barbers until I was twelve or thirteen, because I would speak out. The guys encouraged me. By the time I was fifteen, I was pretty well accepted.

Now I'm goin' to Eastern High, where I was an all-A student. I graduated in 1935, at seventeen. I thought I wanted to be a lawyer. It seemed as a lawyer, I could fight discrimination. It was a personal thing with me. I read a lot of Dickens. And that's when I discovered *The Souls of Black Folk* by Du Bois. I was reading everything I could by and about blacks.

A week before graduation, the principal called me in and said: "We have four scholarships, two to the University of Michigan and two to City College. You got your choice." I said University of Michigan, of course. He says: "Do you have a job? Money for your board?" I said: "No, I thought the job went with the scholarship." He said: "No." I said: "In that case, I'll go to City College." "Too late," he said, "that's been taken." I found out another black kid had been done the same way the year before. I got screwed and resented it very much. Almost subconsciously, I'm beginnin' to take on an adversary role toward society.

This is '35, '36. I got into Ford as an electrical apprentice. You went to school every night to learn about voltage and electricity. It's basically algebra, and I had taken every mathematics course that was in school. I was heavy in math. So I got a flat one hundred on all the damn stuff. There was one job open, and two of us came out at the same time. I was the only black in the apprentice program. The other guy's average was somethin' like sixty-two. His father was a foreman, so he got the job.

I was still goin' to night school with the illusory hope of becomin' a skilled electrician. They didn't have any black electricians at Ford. I was assigned to the motor building, and there I heard talk about the labor union. I'd go around Williams's barbershop, where I got my hair cut, and it turned out to be a hangout for black UAW organizers. And all kinds of philosophy and arguments over who was the greater man, Booker T. Washington or Frederick Douglass or Du Bois.

I was attracted to this exchange of ideas and way of fighitng back at the thing that had been fuckin' me over all my life. It wasn't a sudden thing. I didn't desert my basic hooliganism right away. I still screwed around the poolroom and did a few things. But I was in transition. I was stealin' less and fuckin' less. (Laughs.)

I knew three aspects of black life. I knew the working-class part. I knew the slicker, the gambler. There was also a middle-class part that

I became alienated from. My mother and father were both light-skinned. Blacks in the early days in the South took their values from the whites. The admonition was: Always marry someone lighter than you, so you'll be whiter. That's a way of escape. I rejected this because some of my best friends were very dark. Guys I had known all my life. We were poor, not middle-class, but since I was light, I could have been accepted. There were Negro churches where, if you were darker, you weren't accepted.

Before I went to Ford and started messin' around with all those labor guys and thought I was goin' to college, I was pledged to a black fraternity. It was a society, exclusive-type club, light-skinned. They were the social dictators of the college-age group. I was invited to a dance, a signal honor. I take my friend to the dance with me, a dark guy. The black society people, the elites, we called 'em, took on the mannerisms of whites. They danced stiffly, not naturally. Everybody's dancin' naturally now. (Laughs.) My friend was the best dancer there, havin' a regular ball. The guys resented Frank and were mad at me for bringin' him. He was too dark. We wound up in a fight, and that was the end of me and black society.

If these kind of people were going to college, fuck college. I didn't want to be a gambler and shoot dice all my life. So I got involved in the labor movement and for the first time hearin' a philosophy that made sense to me: unity between black and white.

It was almost a dual life. I'd go into the poolroom and whatever con game I could, I'd make a couple of bucks. The next minute, I'm across the street in the barbershop arguing some Marxist theory. I found them both attractive. But gradually one took over. You can't do both, right?

By '37, I'm a member of the union, very subterranean. At that time, Ford had a goon squad. They called 'em service men. They couldn't be distinguished from the workers. One of the first things we did when we organized the plant, we made 'em put those in uniform so you could tell 'em.

They'd be in greasy old overalls, and they'd count how many minutes you sat in the goddamn can. The work was so rough, guys got old before their time. If you were workin' at forty-five, you were lucky, 'cause when you slowed down the production line, out you went. You'd go to the toilet, not to take a shit, but just to rest. There was no door, no privacy. I've seen guys go in the damn toilet and get five minutes' sleep. The way they did it, they'd take a newspaper and learned how to tap their feet while they were sleepin'. The service guy comes through and sees him with the paper and tappin' his feet and figures he's awake. It's funny what humans can do to survive.

One of the first UAW guys I met was a southern white. He and I got to be very good friends. Southern whites and blacks have so much in common culturally. They talk the same way, they eat the same way, they come from the same region. Once you get past racism, there's a better exchange.

The major stress was between blacks and Poles. The Poles had been the last group to migrate to Detroit, so they were at the bottom of the ladder. The blacks and the Poles were fighting for a hold on the bottom. They were constantly pitted against each other for the dirtiest job.

Even though the black community had been bulldozed out, the Poles haven't moved. Home really means home to them. Hamtramck is still a major Polish city, and all around you find neat painted wooden houses, old as hell but well-kept. It's really a city within the city.

The guys Bennett* recruited were ex-thugs, wrestlers, boxers—the rougher, the better. They put a guy across from me, a big son of a bitch, musta been about two hundred eighty pounds, six foot three. He knew I was union and kept baiting me. There was a conveyer line that ran between my rollin' machine and his. I had a steel pipe that I used to clear the machine when it became jammed. This guy zeroes in on me. If he got his hands on me, there is no way in hell I could have survived. I could see, he starts across the line at me. I picked up that damn steel pipe and laid it across his head. I stretched him out on that damn conveyer, and it carried him and dumped him into a freight car. (Laughs.) It didn't hurt him that much. Five, six stitches and a few lacerations. They ran my ass outa there. (Laughs.) Officially, I was fired for fighting. The real reason was my union activity.

I went to the post office and began to organize a union. There was a six-month probationary period. Son of a bitch let me work five months and twenty-nine days, and then fired me. I was a volunteer organizer for UAW. Worked on the Sojourner Truth housing project. In and out of several jobs, had to eat. I went in the army, February 1942.

"They set up this Jim Crow Air Forces OCS School in Tuskegee. They made the standards so damn high, we actually became an elite

* Harry Bennett had been hired by Henry Ford to establish the service department. Its primary purpose was surveillance of workers who might be "troublemakers."

group. *We were screened and super-screened. We were unquestionably the brightest and most physically fit young blacks in the country. We were super-better because of the irrational laws of Jim Crow. You can't bring that many intelligent young people together and train 'em as fighting men and expect them to supinely roll over when you try to fuck over 'em, right? How does that go? Sowing the seeds of their own destruction. (Laughs.)*

"*I was washed out as a fighter pilot. I'm told it was because of FBI intervention. I had already graduated from officers' school in October of '42, at Fort Benning. They literally pulled guys off the stage, 'cause FBI, Birmingham, was accusin' them of subversion, which may have been attendin' a YMCA meeting in protest against discrimination.*

"*The army was dominated by southern generals, and most of the posts were old, dating back to World War One. Either all white or all black. The air force introduced a new wrinkle. They started from scratch.*

"*I wrote a letter to the inspector general. You become a little bit of a shithouse lawyer and learn all the army regulations for your own protection. Here we officers were barred from the officers' club. The inspector general flew down and made some changes. This was '44 and the real beginnin' of integration in the army.*

"*From there we went to Midland, Texas, the bombardier training school. Five of us had the whole visiting officers' quarters to ourselves. Each of us had two suites, but we still resented the fact that we were not allowed to go to the officers' club. We wrote the inspector general again. The post commander was a Texan but also a soldier. This was after V-E Day. He called every officer on the post together and said in the classic military manner: 'I may not like this and you may not like this, but these are orders. These officers will be treated as officers, they will have full access to all privileges and nobody will fuck with them, is that clear?' (Laughs.) We're now veterans of two successful struggles, but, wait, there's more to come.*

"*We're now, forty-five of us, at Godman Field, attached to Fort Knox. We're boxed in, Jim Crow. The white officers could go to the officers' club as guests of Fort Knox officers. Nobody invited us. I guess I'd become pretty disgusted, so they removed me from my division and put me in RTU, the Reserve Training Unit, where the troublemakers wound up. We began hearing rumors that they were going to make the Godman Officers' Club all white and the black officers would go to the noncom club. To add insult to injury, we had a few thousand bucks in the officers' club. We swore we weren't going to take this. Well, they shipped us out, one squadron at a time, to Freeman Field, near Seymour, Indiana.*

"They were prepared for our arrival, expectin' trouble. MPs were there to keep us out of the club the night we arrived. We decided to go in groups of eight and nine. We were gonna scatter, play pool, get a drink, buy cigarettes. I'm in the first wave. This white captain says: 'You can't go in here.' We just brushed past him and scattered. The commandin' officer was livid and placed us under arrest, at quarters.

"It was my job to convince the other guys that they should go in and get arrested. (Laughs.) After the first nine, it was tough gettin' the next nine. But we broke the ice, and two more groups went in and were placed under arrest. They had to close the son of a bitch down because the whole post would have been under arrest, at quarters. They wanted to put us in the position of disobeying post command.

"The commanding officer read the damn thing and ordered each of us to come up and sign it. If you did that and disobeyed, they could prosecute you. The post commander says: 'Do you recognize that under the sixtieth article of war, in time of war, disobedience to a direct order can be punished by death? Okay, give him an order. I hereby command you to sign this.' He knocked off a bunch of guys. I'm lucky. They called us alphabetically, right? (Laughs.) I got a little breathing spell. I remembered an article of war that roughly is the equivalent of the Fifth Amendment. We devised a strategy. We'd go through all the formalities, salute properly and say, 'Yes, sir.' Where he gives you a direct order, you say: 'I'm sorry, sir, but under the sixty-sixth article of war, I'm afraid this might incriminate me. I refuse to sign.' There were a hundred and one guys who stood up under that one, one by one. We were all placed under arrest.

"The word spread all over. The black enlisted men were pissed. They stopped gassin' the airplanes. It was chaos. They had five or six C-47s to fly us away, we were such a source of unrest. They had the officers' quarters enclosed in barbed wire, with white MPs patrolling it. And spotlights. Here again, the contradictions of racism screwed them. They wanted to isolate us. But they couldn't bring themselves to ignore the military code: officers are "gentlemen" and therefore entitled to valet service, right? You gotta have somebody make your bed and shine your shoes and cook for you. They could not see themselves assignin' white soldiers to perform these tasks for black officers. So they put some black guys in. (Laughs.) As luck would have it, the sergeant commanding the outfit, I used to play pool with him in Detroit. These guys were our keys to the outside world. They were get-

tin' our messages out. We were heroes all over Fort Knox. Chappie James, the general, was among those arrested.

"*They let Chappie go because he flew the C-47, our communications ship. Every day he went to Washington with orders. He also carried press releases from us, letters to Mrs. Roosevelt, to Judge Hastings, to the NAACP. We had a guy in our outfit who typed damn near as quick as I could talk. I'd dictate a press release, give it to the sergeant, who got it to Chappie, who would fly it in. (Laughs.)*

"*They sent in investigators and they were never able to get one out of a hundred and one guys to identify a leader. That, I think, is really something.*

"*It was only a month later that V-J day occurred. We chose that day to invade the white officers' club in Monroe. It's the same damn thing. We were told the next morning that we had an option of signin' up for three more years or gettin' the hell out immediately. Of course, I opted for immediate and got out.*

"*As a result of that incident, they published a war department memorandum, 450-50, which was the beginning of integration in the army. All officers' clubs, service clubs, and recreational facilities are open to all military personnel, regardless of race. Shortly afterward, Truman integrated the army. Oh, I remember 450-50 very clearly. It didn't come easy.*"

Back in Detroit, I became an international rep for the United Public Workers Union, which was eventually run out of the CIO as subversive. It included the garbage men, the hospital workers, all city workers. The same guys I negotiate with today. (Laughs.)

We had one strike, a garbage workers' strike. We were fightin' for a pay increase. The arguments were interminable. So we got about twenty garbage trucks and filled 'em up. These were open trucks, they just had tarps over 'em. It's in the summertime. You never have a garbage strike in the winter, always in the summer, when the garbage stinks. We let this garbage ripen for about four days and then just parked the goddamn trucks around City Hall and threw the fuckin' keys down the sewer. (Laughs.) Needless to say, the strike was settled pretty quickly.

In 1947, I was elected executive vice-president of the Wayne County CIO Council. I was the first black elected. A bunch of young guys, black and white, who'd come back from the army gave us some zip. They knew I wasn't an Uncle Tom, but I'd be a sleeper, acceptable to the white guys. I was under no illusions. I was at the right place at the right time. That's the way history goes.

I became active in the city. Two black families moved into what's now a slum near Tiger Stadium. They were terrorized by guys runnin' around in Ku Klux robes. We sent a group of white and black trade unionists in with shotguns to protect them. Then we had white guys of the building trade, union leaders, paint the buildings, replace the broken glass, repair the fences. When we got through, the house was worth four thousand dollars more than when they moved in. It cooled everything, just the sight of these white union local presidents doin' this work. I was pretty well known in the black community by then.

I came from the East Side, so I knew everybody in Detroit. Detroit was a pretty small place, and then it grew suddenly. Most of the guys who became leaders came from my neighborhood. Another thing made me better known. The Red scare was on, the witch hunt. The House Un-American Activities Committee came to town. These guys would come to a city, terrorize it, put a goddamn stool pigeon on the stand. He rattles off a list of names and that person is fired, hung in effigy, blacklisted.

I was called before the committee. The first thing I found out, the chairman of the damn thing was from Georgia. I said to myself: Why should I take any shit off a son of a bitch from Georgia? How can he question my Americanism? I took the trouble to research. Ninety percent of his district was black, so less than ten percent of the people down there elected this son of a bitch. And he's gonna talk about my un-Americanism!

My lawyer advised me to take the Fifth Amendment. I thought the first should have been enough. But he convinced me to use the fifth also. I told them if they want to talk about un-American activities, I'm prepared to do so. Lynchin', the poll tax. We just got it on. (Laughs.) The damn thing was broadcast, and everybody in the city heard it. It was as big as the World Series. We had the National Negro Council down and Local 600 of the UAW. We were the first group to go on the attack. The next stop was Chicago, where you guys kicked 'em in the ass a little bit more. They just went downhill from there. It was all over the front pages. They were sayin' I was a surly witness. But that single incident endeared me to the hearts of black people. Fightin' back, sayin' what they wanted to say all their lives to a southern white.

I went through about five years, from '55 to '60, during which I was blacklisted. I couldn't get into any shop at all. Drove cabs, found that interesting. I was cleaning and spotting for about three years. I had little money. From drivin' a taxi to luggin' beef to painting and decorating, whatever I could do. Then I decided to take a shot at politics.

I ran for the city council. I knew damn well I couldn't win, but I tested the political waters. I found I had great strength on the East Side, where I was raised. I ran as a delegate for the Constitutional Convention. It was a real heavyweight affair because it was the first time the constitution had been changed in half a century. There were some big issues at stake. That convention produced a whole new crop of political leaders. Comin' from the left, I won the nomination and surprised the Democrats and the labor movement. The Democrats disowned me and ran a sticker candidate against me. I was still looked upon as a dangerous Red. I won the damn election. At the convention, we were successful in getting a number of things done. I wrote the first version of the civil rights commission from the state of Michigan. It's the only state that has a civil rights commisssion as part of the state constitution.

I ran for state rep. Labor was neutral. Three of the black candidates I had beaten decisively before were put back into the race and split the vote. I was defeated by four votes. In '64, I won as state senator and have been elected to office ever since.

I felt the climate was right for a black mayor. I had come to believe we were fast approaching a military state. The pattern was developing with police chiefs being elected mayors of cities. The code words against blacks were "war on crime." I felt deeply that unless blacks were given fair representation within the department, the police would run our cities.

In '73 I was one of five principal candidates for mayor. There were two other black candidates, a liberal white, and the police chief, John Nichols. I entered late and was considered number five. If there's no majority, the two top guys run off. I ran second to Nichols.

We had a series of head-to-head debates, a classic confrontation. Unfortunately, it was the black community against the white, although it was a clean race. Nichols and I agreed not to engage in overt race baiting, and we adhered to it. I've always respected him for that.

One of the major issues was STRESS, an acronym for Stop the Robberies, Enjoy Safe Streets. The use of decoys. It can be effective, but these cowboys in Detroit turned the damn thing into a shoot-out. I've forgotten how many citizens were killed. It was in excess of twenty and at least six or seven cops. The police paper constantly referred to blacks as jungle bunnies.

One of the major issues was residency. I insisted that as mayor, I'd eliminate STRESS and create a police department that would represent Detroit, half black and half white. And mutual respect between police and people. I was gonna see to it that it would be fifty-fifty in all the civil service departments, with many more women. I surprised a lot of people in doing just that. They expected me to go ninety-five percent black and five percent white. That would've been stupid. I retained a white police chief until I had to fire him. I had a black executive deputy chief. Now that I have a black police chief, I have a white executive.

We've established something new in police work: mini-stations. Fifty in high-crime areas where old people are often victims. People of the neighborhood volunteer, man the stations, give out dog licenses and whatever other small things you do, and free the policeman to walk the beat. We have at least two pairs of officers walkin' the beat.

In the old black bottom area, of old people, ADC mothers, and the Brewster housing project, we opened our first mini-station. When I was elected, only fifteen percent of the police were black. So it was warming to see the welcome the white cops received from gals bringin' 'em doughnuts and coffee. You have to extend a hand to the police, and they have to respect you. The white cops were surprised: old black women and kids bringin' 'em coffee. Most of 'em were scared at first. There's a new attitude in the city. The police are no longer looked upon as a foreign army of occupation.

I think the police expected retribution from me. That's the kind of world they lived in: Knock 'em on the head. They expected me to knock 'em on the head. I had no purpose in punishing police. I only insist they be professional and fair.

During my first two months as mayor, I must have attended at least three police funerals. Always in the cold of winter, it seems. Young men. A terribly sad thing. But since '74, not a single Detroit police officer has been killed in the line of duty. This must be an all-time record for the city. It can't be luck. It reflects a new respect between the people and the police.

One incident, I feel, was the turning point. It was the summer of '74. I'd barely been in office six months. A white bar owner killed a young black man. The same incident started riots before. The usual rumors: he was shot in the back. Ugly crowds gathered. I rushed out there. I stood on top of a car and exhorted the young people tryin' to ram in the door of the bar. They wanted to burn the place down and take the guy. The usual provocateurs I've known all my life. I told my police chief I wanted every black officer out on the street. He said: "How can I know who the blacks are?" I said: "You know goddamn well who they are. Get 'em out here." In about an hour, they were all out there. We had a great number of new black commanders to help control the crowd. Most importantly, we already had a relationship with the people. Ministers and block-club leaders joined me. We walked in advance of the police, pushin' people back, dispersin' 'em, urgin' 'em to go home.

What made it even more terrible: an innocent Polish immigrant, a baker on his way home, was passing through the area. His car was stopped. He was dragged out and literally stoned to death. You can imagine what was happenin'. I immediately summoned Bishop Kravchek and other Polish leaders and expressed my sympathy and asked for their cooperation. They and the black ministers came together. I visited his widow, it was a pretty hostile area, and the mother of the young black who'd been killed. I think this turned the situation around, my being there.

The next day, I said the police behaved in a most professional manner under extreme provocation, bricks and what not. Not a single shot was fired. Here were cops in their riot gear, a lot of 'em were women, little bitty women standin' there with those big truncheons. To me, this was a turning point.

The police and I still have big differences. I don't think they deserve the big pay raise they're gettin'. They're the highest-paid police in the nation. They just received an award through an arbitrator that could break the city. There's something wrong with a system whereby an arbitrator, not elected by anybody, can impose taxes on the people of the city.

Hey, Mr. Mayor, you're an old labor guy talkin', remember? (Laughs.)

Yeah, but I would rather let the damn matter go to a strike than have an artificial settlement. Again, it's my faith in the people. If the policemen have a legitimate grievance, the public will back 'em. If they do not, damn it, the public won't back 'em. That's the way I was brought up in the labor movement, right? You take it to the streets. That's where I came from—the streets. And I'm proud of it. I think if you listen, you can get a hell of an education out there.

I got support from only one industrialist: Henry Ford. He gave me three thousand dollars. He also gave Nichols three thousand dollars. I told him: "You ought to put most of your money on the winner, and I'm the winner." He laughed. (Laughs.)

I think they were also a little concerned about Nichols. He was a no nonsense, take-the-gloves-off type of cop who could cause more explosions. They were worried about their investments in the city. In askin' for their cooperation, I was workin' in their self-interest.

In the last four years, they've been convinced that I'm not a wild man. When the budget had to be cut, I cut the damn budget. It was painful. We have a number of laws on the books which gives a tax preference to businesses located in the city, encourages them to stay rather than leave. It's subject to a lot of argument. Some say this is subsidizing business. I say it's the name of the game. As long as we live in a society which pits workers in Mississippi against workers in Michigan, we have to make concessions to keep our plants. We've made more jobs for people.

We've begun to reverse the flight from the city. We've created new communities within Detroit. In some cities, with urban renewal, they've bulldozed whole communities. Movin' the blacks out and movin' middle-class whites into choice locations. As long as I'm mayor, we're not gonna have that. We'll have an integrated occupancy of the central city.

Do you have a funny feeling, a sense of irony, when you're having lunch with Henry Ford?

It *is* ironic. You reflect on how unlikely this was twenty, thirty years ago. Yet, I'm not doing anything differently. I've always felt people act out of self-interest, not for any utopian reasons. If you understand that, you understand coalition: a commonality of interests. You always move from point one.

We've come a long way from Harry Bennett. Of course, reaction rears its ugly head constantly. We're still plagued with racism. But I've always had great faith in the intelligence of people—if you can get to them. I'm not among those who believe you can package bullshit and sell it to people as long as you tie a pretty ribbon around it.

I'm sixty now, and I'd like to produce a cadre of young people, black and white, who can carry on this work. It's not guaranteed. It would be a big mistake for anyone to believe that the great American Dream is apple pie and a happy endin'. It ain't necessarily so. The whole goddamn thing could go up in smoke. Reconstruction teaches you that, right? It's a continuous struggle all the time. The minute you forget that, you wind up on your ass.

I realize the profit motive is what makes things work in America. If Detroit is not to dry up, we must create a situation which allows businessmen to make a profit. That's their self-interest. Ours is jobs. The more they invest in Detroit, the more their interest becomes ours. That is the way the game is played in America today. I don't think there's gonna be a revolution tomorrow. As a young man, I thought it. I think the revolution's for someone else.

(He laughs softly; a sudden remembrance.) Had I stayed in Catholic school, I would probably have become an altar boy. I would like to have been one. St. Mary's is a beautiful, old German church. It's truly an architectural gem. I was fourteen when I was last there. You come back as mayor for the one hundred seventy-fifth anniversary of the Sisters of Holy Name. The altar's much the same. The nuns prepared a chair for me on the altar, a big chair, like a throne. (Laughs.) I'm sitting on it. That's the highlight of my life as mayor. It impressed me more, thinking back to my childhood, than sitting down with Henry Ford or President Carter. (Laughs) My American Dream. (Laughs.)

JOHN AND KARL

JOHN McCLAUGHERY, 40

He is a leader of the Conservative Caucus. It is a coalition of conservative Republicans and Democrats who are dissatisfied with the trend of the two major parties. The caucus feels it should go more to the right.

He lives in Kirby, Vermont, in a log cabin he built himself. At the moment, he is wearing a marine fatigue cap. He moves about restlessly.

I've asked myself when I first became a disciple of Tom Jefferson's. I was always on the side of widely dispersed power, even in high school.

My mother died when I was a month old. I spent my first twelve

years in the care of elderly ladies. My grandmother lived in a neighborhood that had been settled by people her age years ago. I was the
only kid on the block. My great-aunts taught me to read when I was
three. I remember how stunned I was when I got to first grade to find
nobody could read.

I found myself very much a loner. I read like a beaver, I was small
because I was a year younger. I didn't have a peer group. I made a
virtue out of necessity. I had a long time to think, read a lot, and
shape my own values.

One of my grandmothers was Jesus, the other was Jehovah. They
were both pillars of the Presbyterian church, one in Paris, Illinois, the
other in Pontiac, Michigan. My mother's mother was the Jesus figure:
self-effacing, self-sacrificing, idealistic, pious, a real sweetheart, widely
mourned when she died a few years ago. Grandmother McClaughery,
with whom I spent summers in Pontiac, was a stern, righteous hammer of God. Disciplinarian, great emphasis on character, rectitude,
tradition. A strong woman.

I got a curious mixture of the two. Nine months with Jesus and
three months with Jehovah. Since I didn't have a peer group, I had no
respect for peer-group opinions. If it made sense, I agreed with it. If it
didn't, I felt sorry for anybody else.

I accepted the values, not of my generation, but of my parents'. So
I'm really thirty years older in outlook. I'm forty now, but I have a
seventy-year-old outlook.

Colonial Williamsburg has a particular fascination for me because
I'm a child of the eighteenth century. I've seen the movie at the vis-
itors' center five times, and I go bananas every time. If it wasn't for
medical care, I would opt to go back to be Jefferson's contemporary.

I don't know of any rebellion in my family. They were what you'd
call petits bourgeois respectables. Never any upheavals of any kind.
Steady as she goes. I didn't have any kind of rebelliousness about me.
I was considered to be a model child.

I am not a very proper person in my lifestyle. I wear old clothes,
I'm not a social climber, and I don't go to cocktail parties. But there is
propriety. Albert J. Knock used to say: "There are some things a
conservative just would not do." You're not sure what you would do,
but you're always certain some things you would not do.

I've always been aware of the importance of everybody havin' a
chance to develop his capacities without being inhibited by some kind
of lumbering authority, be it religious, governmental, or peer group.
That's the one thing that really lights my fuse. In September of '76, I

disrupted a Republican state convention because they had obviously rigged the nomination of presidential electors. I stormed out of the back row, shouting at the chair and intimidating everybody within earshot. It turned the whole convention around, over the violent objections of the state chairman, who later got sacked. It was one of the most satisfying episodes of my career. (Laughs.)

I worry about large-size industry, sure, but not as much as I worry about government. In industry, you've got a choice. You don't have to buy their stuff, you can buy somebody else's. In government, you're stuck with it. Government has a monopoly on coercion. General Motors does not. That's why I'm a Republican and not a Democrat. They're too much into collectivism and government planning.

I'm opposed to consumer agencies. It implies that somebody's gonna look out for ya. It's a step backward. It dampens the spirit of looking out for oneself. Which is the only way you can maintain a free republic. I shopped in grocery stores for a boarding club I ran in college. I went in with a slide rule. I figured out the best buys.

Are you suggesting slide rules for consumers?

Oh, yeah. Besides, you've got pocket calculators now for those who are too feeble-minded to use a slide rule. Any fourth grader can learn to use a slide rule.

Any individual can buck the big boys without help from others?

Not *any* individual. The ideal to me is where a sufficient number of individuals can control their destinies and say, if necessary: "To hell with it, I'm not gonna do it." I've always been big on community corporations, small businesses, cooperatives, small farmers, independent professionals.

I helped write the platform for the Conservative Caucus. I think it's a fairly reasonable document. The bit about military superiority gives me some problems because it gets to be an excuse for waste in defense spending, for a colossal hardware boom. It's vastly inflated, not that I minimize the danger of the Soviet threat. I have great sympathy for the infantry people but not for the super-carrier and air-force bomber people. I'm a strong supporter of the Poseidon-Triton systems. I'm not a pacifist by any means.

I turned against the war in Vietnam in 1966. The people we were helpin' weren't worth our help. On balance, I would have preferred the regime in Saigon but not enough to send forty thousand Americans to their death. I didn't see the war in moral terms. Any war is immoral. I was really a hawk. After the Tonkin Gulf incident, I foamed at the mouth along with the American Legion. Now I believe LBJ fabricated it.

I have nowhere to go. I continually question my beliefs. I invite controversy and discussion. I look for people who will challenge me. So far, I've rarely felt myself successfully challenged. But I keep looking for people to do it. If you don't do that, you just lapse into this dogmatic mode where you have all the answers.

The last ten years have been the most frustrating of my life. I've rarely had a challenge to which I could apply my best talents. I spent four years in the Vermont legislature, '69 through '72. It was composed of people who were independently wealthy. Of a hundred fifty members, we had a few lawyers there. Two of 'em I wouldn't have engaged to argue a traffic ticket. I thought I could bring some professional competence to the legislature. I found out rapidly I had no one to talk to. The more I did what I excelled at, the more I was isolated. They sat around the card room, playing cribbage and tellin' stories about dogs that chase deer. When the legislature adjourned, I went to the library. The librarian loves me still, 'cause in all her years, I'm the only member that made more than one appearance in the state library. I went back to my room and typed until the middle of the night. The rest of 'em went to the Montpellier Tavern Inn and imbibed.

Nobody knew what the hell to make of me. I didn't have any relatives, nobody could get a fix on me. I had arrived there as if I had plopped down from a flying saucer. I was a mystery to everyone. Yet anyone who understands Jefferson could understand me in an instant. There's not a dime's worth of difference.

I share with the traditional anarchists, the Kropotkins, the Proudhons, the idea of the barriers struck down, the chains unshackled, and the spirit bursting forth. I have a lot of friends on the far left. They are consistent, with a radical outlook of society. The liberal left is just beneath contempt. They have no propriety, no standards. On the right, people will do things because it makes money for them. But I've got more respect for them than the fuzzy-headed liberal bimbos and those ridiculous panaceas that won't work. They are the lowest form of life. The conservatives are not much fun and sort of tight, so I'm still a loner.

I'm one of the foremost crank letter writers of our time. I'm a fast typist, and in three minutes I can have the thing out and gone. I do it partly to sharpen my own ideas. The last ten years of my life have been built around writing crank letters. I really need an opportunity to do what I can do best before I croak, and where that's gonna come, I don't know.

KARL HESS

We're in Martinsburg, West Virginia. It is a house he built himself, with the help of his wife and two sons. "What's more wonderful than to live in a house and remember everything in it, even your mistakes? It is more than a house. It is an adventure."

They have three cats named Molly Maguire, Mother Jones, and Emma Goldman.

He had written speeches for Barry Goldwater and had ghosted his newspaper column. In 1972, he was arrested in Washington for protesting the Vietnam War.

I was brought up in Washington, D. C. My mother married a multi-millionaire, and I issued forth. We went to the Philippines to live. He had about nine million mistresses, and she didn't like that very much. So she left him and came back here. She wouldn't even take alimony. She became a switchboard operator.

That woman used to walk me everyplace. We'd walk and walk and walk and talk. We'd discuss things. I'd ask a question, and we'd walk to the public library. I could ask her what time it was and she'd say: "Let us go to a clock." Then I'd learn to tell the time. I'd be pointing to a person and she'd show me Gray's *Anatomy* and say: "You figure it out." We'd read books and read books. She taught me how to read so she wouldn't have to answer questions. (Laughs.) To this day, I don't know whether she knows the answers. We used to read the dictionary. You want to know what the word meant, you'd have to look it up. It was like having a rabbi for a father.

When I was fifteen, I was really tired of school. She said it was okay if I didn't go to school any more. But how did you do it? She didn't tell me. I figured out a little thing that worked. I registered in all the schools in Washington and then transferred. I got lost in the book-keeping. I've never heard from them since.

When I was fifteen, I went to work for a radio station. I wrote newscasts for Boak Carter and Fulton Lewis, Jr. I worked for one of the first quiz shows, *Double or Nothing.*

Working on a quiz show, you get to read encyclopedias all the time. Working on a news show, you get to read the news ticker. It was okay until I got arrested for driving without a license. The radio station found out I was fifteen and fired me. I was an unauthorized precocity. I went to the *Alexandria Gazette.* From there on it was no contest. I thought I could do and have anything I wanted. I could move from job to job casually 'cause I was really good at it. I was terribly upward mobile.

I wanted to be a Communist when I was a kid. I joined the Socialist party. I couldn't get to be a Communist. Thank goodness, because the socialists were boring enough. So I got to be a Republican instead. I thought it was the next best game in town. They were radical then. A lot of small businessmen, they were against big business. They're isolationists, *i.e.,* anti-imperialists. They never had sense enough to use that phrase. I didn't go to school, and they didn't like schools. We had a lot in common. After not too long, I went to work for the Republican National Committee. Right after Dewey lost in '44.

When people get to be professional at something, the ideology becomes secondary. You become a technocrat. My politics, from that point on, were the kind of politics that would just advance me. You tailor your politics to the demands of your job. If the job demanded being partial to big business, as it very quickly did, I became partial to big business.

I met a lot of rich people. I thought they really were living right. They dressed good and had people waiting on them. I got the feeling, I think, a lot of newspaper people get who cover rich people. I got the feeling that I was really like them.

I sat on a park bench with Barney Baruch. Okay, I'm making seventy-five dollars a week and I'm sittin' with one of the richest men in the world. A man who changes the course of an empire by waving his hand. What am I gonna think after that afternoon? I think Barney and I must've really struck it off. He'll never remember me, but I'll remember him, right? I expect that he remembers me, and I act as though he does. You get this false sense of identification with these people. It bends your life very much.

I would ride down the street and see working people, and I'd begin to think: It's me or them. Those people want everything I have, that I worked for. As a matter of fact, I lucked into it. I glibbed into it. I conned my way into so much of this stuff just being facile. That's something my mother gave me: language. I worked for H. L. Hunt for a time. I wrote for all the big Republicans. I did a couple of platforms for them. You just get the feeling you're really super-special.

It's overpowering. When I worked for the White House on a special assignment under Eisenhower, if you're a little late for your airplane, they hold it. There were whole months when I never got on an airplane through the regular door. And trains. I had a train held for me in New York. A train that is supposed to leave every hour on the hour. I've been out on boats when the Secret Service brings a helicopter to get you. (Laughs.) After a little bit of this, you gotta figure you're . . . (Laughs.)

You ride with motorcycle escorts. You're zoomin' along in a limousine in all the noise, and you look out on the street and all those people are frozen. You're movin' and they're frozen. That's a powerful lesson. I started looking at me as a separate thing. You're sittin' in a limousine and your hand is on the cordovan leather and you look at your hand. What a lovely hand. And your cuffs: What a beautiful cuff. What gorgeous cuff links. And doesn't your suit fit nicely?

And now it's "we." (Laughs.) *We* desire to be taken to the train station. "We" is the cuff links, the silk shirt, the shoes, and all that gang of stuff. You're a symphony. You're no longer a person. You become imperial. I tell you, after you get in that mood, you fight fiercely.

I believed that I deserved everything I had, and that if anybody else wanted it, they could go get it exactly the way I did. And that everybody else *did* want it. (Laughs.) So you get this defensive thing. It's us against them.

I met Therese when I was working for Goldwater. She used to bring up questions like: "What's so good about war?" So help me, I would say: "If you knew what I know, you'd understand why we should have a war." She would keep saying: "Maybe you should tell me." I'd say: "I can't tell you."

Your whole life is special information, special privilege, separation, and, oh, my, so phony. It's absolutely artificial and it's not true. Maybe you think you've got special information. But sixteen people lied to you. Maybe they know the information, but you don't. You may think because you sit in the park with Barney Baruch, you're in his class. That's nonsense. Any one of them would run you over if they saw you on the street.

I worked for Arleigh Burke for a time, the admiral. He'd been

Chief of Naval Operations. I wrote some speeches for him. I worked also in setting up the Georgetown Center for Strategic Studies. We were fairly close. After I got out of politics, I was riding a motorcycle. I was dressed the way you dress when you ride a motorcycle. I was in the alley waiting for somebody. Into the alley came Arleigh Burke. I didn't have a helmet on. I'm there, I'm naked to the world, not hiding. Arleigh Burke went right toward me, looked at me, walked past, and went on. He didn't know who I was. Because I was never a person. I was always a certain set of clothes, a certain rhetoric, and none of that had anything to do with motorcycles, a person standing there in dungarees and a black leather jacket. You kid yourself if you think you're a person in these situations. You're just a performer, playing a role.

After a time, when you become a professional conservative, you also become a professional anti-Communist. It means not only not liking the Soviet Union. You've got to dislike, fear, hunt down, and harass anybody who professes any left-wing ideology. And you don't care really what it is or what they say. I got involved in the big hysteria. I still think a good deal of it was justified. The Soviet Union is, was, and probably will always be our enemy.

After I'd been an editor at *Newsweek*, I worked on the newsletter *Counterattack*. It was started by three ex-FBI agents. Some big corporations helped them start it, so there'd be an independent source of checking on political affiliations as well as economic. These guys, as FBI agents, knew how to keep files. They had access to a lot of raw material. You get a copy of the *Daily Worker* every day, and you go through it and index every name in it. Say there's a petition and five hundred people sign it. It could be for anything, like preserve mother's milk. You then write the newsletter: John Jones, with well-known Communist connnections. Or a fellow traveler. He's always signing Red petitions. Well, I guess it was useful to somebody. I thought it was useful, 'cause anybody who'd sign a petition in the *Daily Worker* should be drummed out of society. I really felt they're the enemy.

The thing that unhinged me was that Berthold Brecht died. I was gonna put together a special issue of the newsletter. I got all the stuff on Brecht. Boy, whew, man, oh, Brecht, a Communist, admitted even! Wow! Just a terrible fella. So we put out all this stuff on Brecht. Within a week, independent stories came out. All the last years of his life, Brecht had been at odds with the East German government. He was not an authoritarian. He may have been a Communist, but he was not an authoritarian. He was against dictatorship. I got this queasy feeling that I had been participating in the persecution of a man who was actually a hero. That's the last stuff I did for *Counterattack*.

I went over to U.S. Plywood Champion Papers as assistant to the president. I wrote his speeches and did a lot of PR stuff. Very big, in about the middle of the 500 list. I thought the company had something to do with the manufacture of paper. It turns out no. It has to do with the management of people. What finally got me was that the managers were simply a bunch of people attempting to keep their jobs. All they did in life was to make it miserable for the people, the engineers.

Everybody else is out there busy doin' stuff. The managers are just up there figurin' out how little they can pay 'em, how to keep costs down, how to move people around from box to box. They'd just spend day after day makin' up organizational charts.

You grow up with a nutty mother who walks you around town and discusses things with you, and you're likely to have a curious mind. You're gonna want to know how these things work. What got me finally was coming in super-early in the morning and understanding that I was going in early in order to impress the boss. I didn't have anything to do. That's a sad thing, to think you're in your middle years and you're still playing these little games.

They keep saying a good manager can manage everything. Doesn't make any difference whether you're managing a plant to incinerate Jews or a plant to make petunia baskets. I saw that as exactly the case. They did not care what was being made.

I went back to Washington and got into politics. In Washington, you never see anybody who works. You don't have any direct association with them. Occasionally, you see furtive people changing the light bulbs. But they're not real. They're the people who make your life easy for you. They permit you not to have to do anything to waste your time, 'cause your time is so incredibly valuable. Whoo! Just imagine if you wasted five minutes in Washington. Western civilization is going to crumble right away. I got back into the feeling that I was something special. By the time the presidential campaign of '60 rolled around, I was convinced I was anointed.

I was the chief writer of the Republican platform in '60. There was the famous compromise with Rockefeller. It didn't amount to anything, just window dressing. There were no real disagreements. Today Jimmy Carter is a Rockefeller Republican.

Between '60 and '64, everything started going out of focus. After the '64 election came my breaking point. I was Goldwater's chief speech writer. After that election, if you wanted to remain a Republican, you pretty much had to denounce him. I didn't want to do that. I don't know exactly why. I'd never done too much on the basis of principles, 'cause I was very respectful of getting ahead. But I liked Goldwater. To me he's an attractive person. So I remained a Goldwater loyalist. I was writing his syndicated column. But I really had to do something else. Everything was unhinged. But I'm optimistic.

I still feel we're a healthy country, a healthy people. The fact that we got a whole bunch of people taking Valium doesn't mean everybody's taking it. People still help each other. The genuine American Dream is the small town. Or the big city with the neighborhood in it. The American Dream is that comfortable, familiar neighborhood. It's the town meeting. The idea that there's nobody in the world to whom I have to defer when it comes to my life. This doesn't mean that you say: I don't care about anybody else. It simply means: I will speak for myself.

The city neighborhoods can be self-reliant. You can have a neighborhood that can get together and rebuild. I think these things exist in the middle of the city or out here. I think the family farm is going to reappear. Big corporate farms are up against natural limits: water, petrochemicals, fertilizers. They're in trouble. The family farm is productive. If you don't even own the land you live on, everything I'm talkin' about is just bullshit. It's not gonna work. We're gonna have to start talking about big changes. Things such as the ownership of mineral resources. I don't know why in the world West Virginia miners should put up with people in Palm Beach owning the stuff they work on. Why? It doesn't make sense. I understand that it's legal (laughs), but legal doesn't necessarily mean right. If the mines were acquired by manipulation, why can't they be reacquired by another kind? Those mines weren't all built by hardy pioneers. They were opened up by managers who never got their hands dirty in their entire lives.

It isn't really socialism. I can understand why the toes of most Americans curl up when they hear that word. All this romantic nonsense about organizing a mass party. I don't think that's going to work here. What they want here is a community. If you want to be romantic, call it communism. I don't think it has to have a label. It's just the way a lot of Americans have worked together, cooperatively. Barn raisings and Lord knows what.

I've joined the IWW. They appeal to even my oldest conservative nature when they point out that workin' for wages is a bad situation. You work for wages, you're always half a slave. To really be free, you gotta be part of the enterprise.

A HOMILY ON DUTY

FRANK WILLIS, 29

He is the security guard who, in making his nightly rounds, discovered the tape on the door at Watergate.

My mother always wanted me to be honest and to have respect. If there was any problems, I had to come to her, to be outspoken. I had a very honest childhood, from my mother. She worked very hard, but she managed quite regally.

My first security work was in Detroit, where I was employed by the Ford Motor Company. I was about twenty-three. In Washington, I was employed by a private company, watching the Watergate property.

That particular day was a regular normal day. Got up that morning, did a couple of chores, went to wash some clothes, put my uniform in the cleaners, get some necessities, buy groceries, get something to snack on for later, probably look at TV, do some reading, get some rest. About twelve o'clock that night, you're ready to put eight hours in.

I relieved another officer at twelve midnight. He would have in his log exactly the security areas he had checked. Being very cautious, I would like to make my own check. Somebody say, well, I checked here, I checked there, and something comes up later on that doesn't look right. Well, I can say I checked it and it won't be a back-flack on me.

This must have happened between one and two o'clock that night, June 17. How could I forget it? My God. That night, I had made a check of the doors and necessities, the locks and so forth, to make sure no one had left the door open or was hiding in the bathroom. In other words, a complete, thorough overhaul. It's a duty almost like a military-type operation.

About two weeks before this incident, the engineer had come into the building to do some overhauling of the heating units. He put a wood block in the door so he could go back and forth. But this particular incident, it didn't seem that he would put tape on the door. You have to be very observant because you may miss something and it could also save your life.

I found that tape stuck two different times. The first piece of tape I took off the door. I thought it might have been a possibility of the engineer putting that tape on. About a half-hour later, I checked the same corridor and I discovered another piece of tape on the door. It was very odd.

It's like a computer where you feed information into it to make sure the situation is really that, to make sure it comes out accurate. When I found this second piece of tape, it was visually wrong to me. You have to know the meaning of security, because you're dedicated to that. The guy that I relieved, maybe he wouldn't have checked it two or three times. Excuse the expression, I had my whole ass into it.

First of all, I had to take pride in myself. It wasn't the best-paying job, but it was meeting my necessities. I enjoyed the people I was surrounded with, and so I was dedicated to this particular job.

I called the Metropolitan Police on the second piece of tape, and that's when they discovered the Watergate Seven or Six. I still had to do my duty, eight hours. I couldn't call my supervisor and say: "I think I possibly caught something tonight. Can I take the night off?" After they carted them down to the station, I continued to stay on, making my rounds.

I didn't know anything about it until some gentlemen from the Justice Department, FBI, approached me about exactly what I had discovered. I had no idea it would involve the president of the U.S. It could have been something worse than that. It could have been someone from another country. It could have been a national security type of situation. Maybe one piece of tape would have saved this whole country.

I expected some type of—not necessarily praise—but some type of appreciation for doing the job that I had been dedicated to. I was surprised that the company was sort of like saying: This was something you shouldn't have did. Not only did they look at me funny, but

I wondered exactly what I did wrong, since I consider myself an honest person, since I had proven myself. I thought the company would have said: Well, Frank—not necessarily that I've been looking for the vice-president position or president of the company or chairman of the board, but some type of respect for doing the job that I did.

It was a very negative approach. It was sort of strange because I don't exactly know where it came from, if it came from some type of high position or point of view. I felt like I wasn't even with the company any more. That type of thing. Something hot to handle. There wasn't much said. Seeking information, approaching the supervisor, seemed there was something further than where I was.

I had a strong type of feeling because, my God, I'm breaking my ass trying to do a good job, and the company wasn't really giving that type of confrontation back to me. I felt that I was in a very strange type of circumstance, like I was just left right out there in the open.

I worked there, I'd say, about three more weeks. I also tried to establish a union for the company. This was before Watergate even took place. We were trying to get better benefits for the other officers. The company didn't really like this.

We were paid eighty-five dollars a week. That was after taxes. I think it was five to eight thousand dollars that the Federal Labor Board, that investigated some records, said that they had to pay back to security officers, because they were cheating the guys on their vacation time. I did this on my own, to have it investigated. For about two weeks they checked the records, and they had about eighty different names. The company had taken half of our vacation salary and invested it in their own account.

I put myself on the line. I resigned because they refused to have any type of union. And they had to pay about eight thousand dollars and it was like I was coming on too strong.

I figured that when Watergate had broken and, my God, Woodward and Bernstein, they were publicizing this so—the presses were burning. The company that I was working for got their names in the papers free and to possibly receive monetary benefits.

They got publicity. I figured since I was an alert guard—scratch guard, because I hate that title—security officer is better—since I was alert, the company would say: Wow, this guy, maybe he can be in some type of training position, to relate this same dedication to others.

They did give me a fifteen- or twenty-cent raise, and I was promoted from corporal to sergeant. They think they did me a favor.

What could I do with that? I really couldn't take my girlfriend out or maybe have a nice dinner out on the town or something on my days off. I just couldn't cash my three stripes in. You understand? I waited possibly for something. They were really glad that I left.

Did other companies make offers to you?

It's very strange. None whatsoever.

Do you think you were blacklisted?

It was never proven. I went to the university in Washington, D. C., to apply for a security officer's position. I was told by the chief of security that if they hired me, that particular university might get their funds cut off. I'm serious. Here I am, a taxpayer, I mean, eighty-five dollars a week after taxes, for someone to say: "Because of what you did, we might be penalized." I couldn't believe it.

It really hasn't been an easy time for me. I'm keeping my wits up that things will change. You have to have some type of belief, some type of positive outlook. I may not be the best person, but I be honest in my dealings with people in general. That was like a disrespect to my honesty completely to have to sort of beg for something, something that I should have got in a humanitarian way. Maybe somebody else might say: "He doesn't deserve anything because that was his duty doing it." Of course it was.

You hear people believe in truth for all and "In God We Trust" and all these other types of quotes that are used, go to church on Sunday. But it really makes you wonder if they really mean what they say. Where are they when you need that type of support? Everybody says: Crime must pay. If they got away with that, we can get away with that.

I don't have any regrets whatsoever. I feel that, hopefully, I've contributed something. Some people may disagree with me. You don't expect everybody to agree with you anyway. You start finding everybody agreeing with you, something's wrong.

But that's something I can't really forget. I'm not necessarily saying that I have a complete negative view of the people, that I hate them that much that I wish something drastic would happen to them. I mean, if I'm caught in a crime, I deserve to be punished for it. But there shouldn't be quotas set that if you got money, you can get by with it. In other words, sort of like buy your truth. My truth wasn't bought. It was given. I'm not really angry at no one 'cause I feel I did my job.

I believe honesty pays. I still have the same belief that I had then. My ideology was to always be honest and to approach the situation with positiveness. I haven't got a hundred thousand dollars or anything of that sort, but who knows?

Some people I know say: "If I was you, I would have kept my mouth closed." In other words, they would have accepted some type of bribe. Just listening, you could see they were really friends to a point, that they really didn't have too many beliefs. They didn't seem to have anything inside. They was in appearance like me, but they wasn't. That's why they was making faces: "If I was you, I would have took a bribe." I could have took some kind of criminal motivation myself, but I didn't.

Some people said: "You should be angry. If I was in your situation, I would leave the country." I say those people don't have any hope, probably never had any hope. I have hope. If I hadn't any hope, I don't think I would be where I am now. I'm still a security guard. I'm not a millionaire by any chance of that sort. I'm a regular type of guy. I try to be an honest person, I'm just normal and don't disrespect anyone. I try to have true beliefs.

Everything my mother taught me from a small age has paid off. I don't think it could have paid off any better. That made her feel, I think, eighty percent better right there. Hopefully, I can pay her back in many ways. I won't be able to pay her back in all ways because if it hadn't been for her, I wouldn't have been there on June 17, 1972.

EDITOR AND PUBLISHER

PAT AND TOM GISH

Whitesburg, Kentucky. He is editor and publisher of The Mountain Eagle. *It is widely read in the eastern part of the state. She is his associate.*

He has won the John Peter Zenger Award "for advancing the cause of freedom of the press," and the Elijah Lovejoy Award "for courage in journalism."

On this November evening, we are driving past "hollers" and shacks. It is coal field country along Virginia's border. "Contrast has always been great in eastern Kentucky. Nine months of the year, it's as pretty as you can find anywhere. In the wintertime, it's like the end of the world. The fog moves in and we never see the sun. The pollution isn't so much from coal mining as it used to be. We have a Los Angeles kind of inversion with automobile pollution."

Coming into this country from the bluegrass of Lexington, along the cool of Mountain Parkway, through Daniel Boone Park, redolent with autumnal smells and colors, is a stunning experience.

Down in the valley, the valley so low, we see vestigial remainders of what was once an inhabited place. "This was Seco, a company town. Southeast Coal Company. I was born and raised here. My parents came here in 1917 from western Kentucky. Muelenberg County. John Prine wrote a song about it.*

"My father progressed from the lowliest miner to the head of the company." He points to an empty frame building. "I was born in that house. My father moved from miner and living there (laughs) to mine foreman and living over there." (Laughs.) He indicates a higher plateau. "When he became mine superintendent, we moved around the hill to the biggest house in town." (Laughs.) He indicates a still higher place.

Incongruously, a flower shop appears in this abandoned precinct. Is it still open for businesss or is it an evocation of a long-ago search for beauty?

TOM: I've spent many happy days in Seco. You knew everybody in town and you were welcome everywhere. We owned the only car and telephone in town. Telephones and cars did not really become common until the early forties, after World War Two.

PAT: The official always had the cars and the telephones.

TOM: My father was very much on the side of the miner, very pro-union, although the union never really knew it. I saw my father weep

---

* Daddy, won't you take me back to Muelenberg County
Down by the Green River where Paradise lay?
Well, I'm sorry, my son, but you're too late in askin'
Mr. Peabody's coal train has hauled it away.
　　　　　　—from "Paradise" by John Prine

a couple of times in my whole lifetime. One of 'em was when the coal company went nonunion. A kind of warfare developed. It was a fore-runner of the breaking up of the United Mine Workers in eastern Kentucky. He had no illusions about coal operators. The minute the union disappeared, you had men working in the coal fields for two, three dollars in the 1960s. And frequently working forty hours a week without any take-home pay.

Law and order prevailed at Seco. If you or a member of a coal miner's family misbehaved, you became a community problem and were removed from the community. (Laughs.) The troublemakers were forced out. A union organizer, who was a Klansman, went around beating up bad women.

During the labor wars, I remember hiding with my father behind an old garage building to dodge bullets. We were sure we were being shot at because he was a company figure. It was a turbulent period during the fifties and sixties, with the busting up of the union, the calling in of the National Guard, and a military takeover of the county.

I didn't want to be a newspaper publisher. It just happened. In 1947, I graduated from the University of Kentucky and worked for the United Press in Frankfort. I stayed there ten years and came back home. Our home is an area more than it is a place. We're the bastard child of the state. It's not so much coal mining as it is the mountains themselves. People stopped here on the westward trek. This was on the Wilderness Road. They were individualists who stayed here. They liked the loneliness. They liked the hunting, the fishing. These people came over from England as indentured servants.

We could have been an establishment paper. We sometimes won-der what would have happened had the establishment, instead of op-posing us, coopted and embraced us. We weren't thinking of becoming a challenge. We were sure we'd be part of the establish-ment. I still have a hard time considering us as not really part of the establishment. (Laughs.)

PAT: The first thing we did was to cover government happenings. People up here didn't know that public meetings were supposed to be open. The first thing the fiscal court did was to vote to meet in pri-vate. (Laughs.)

TOM: We were banned from fiscal court meetings, we were banned from school-board meetings, we were banned from all public functions. (Laughs.) Dammit, I think they sincerely did not recog-nize that government was a public thing.

PAT: These had been company towns until about five years before. So it was a closed society run by a few.

TOM: We spent the first several years trying to reinvent the wheel. We tried to reestablish freedom of the press and our right to exist. The battle still goes on. In that long process we lost most of our advertising.

PAT: The paper also had a job-printing business. The first thing they threatened you with if they didn't like what you said in the paper was to take away the county printing, which was a major account. We almost went bankrupt.

TOM: We were able to survive only because my father was a person of some prominence and resources. He fed us and paid our light bills and on occasion kept us alive.

At first, my father and mother didn't understand us. One of the things that is personally satisfying to me is that, by the time they died, they both understood and supported us. It was rough on them. Their lifelong friends would come to them and say: "Can't you do something about Tommy and keep him out of this?"

One of the first battles was, of all things, over the county library. We had a God-awful collection of some three thousand beat-up books stored in the shed, the sorriest excuse for a library you ever saw. The fiscal court decided to abandon even what we had and leave us without any pretense of a library. The remarks that were made were pretty stupid, really, and we quoted 'em. To say something is one thing, but to see it in print is something else.

PAT: The other thing was the hospital. We ended up getting the business community and the politicians mad at us at one time. The United Mine Workers in 1965 had established their chain of ten hospitals. One of them was here—were there still some company doctors then? The doctors here considered the union hospitals socialized medicine. They challenged it not only locally, but in the legislature and in the Kentucky Medical Society. They were arguing that the UMW setup was not freedom of choice.

Tom went down to Frankfort with some young union doctors and lobbied for the hospitals.

TOM: The local doctors were antiunion. They did everything they could to close 'em down. So they were sore at us.

The miners treated us with great suspicion because I was the son of a well-known coal company official. I think it was justified suspicion. It's been a very slow process of twenty years or so that they've begun to have any faith in me at all. Things were getting tight in this area anyway. The flood of 1957 came that just about wiped out every-thing in eastern Kentucky. The coal industry entered into a state of almost total collapse. The mines that had been working three, four days a week were working one day a week or none at all. Many mines closed. In '61, we had what amounted to mass starvation. Nothing was being done. We were broke ourselves.

People were walking the streets of Whitesburg, begging for food, begging for clothes, begging for money to see a doctor, begging for money to buy medicine. I don't think the rest of the country recog-nized what was happening. The turning point for me came when a woman appeared, stinking, with an awful odor of dead and decaying flesh, with a note from a doctor saying she must have surgery if she was to live. She was diabetic and had to have her legs amputated. She was walking the streets of Whitesburg, begging enough money to get to a hospital.

We realized something had to be done. The rest of the world must know something about what the heck was going on in eastern Ken-tucky. We spent all our spare moments for the next several years showing around visiting reporters, writers, and government officials by the dozen. This in itself was an almost criminal thing to do. The pride of the area has been so enormous that it became a cardinal sin to suggest that anything might be wrong.

PAT: Whoever we hadn't offended before, we offended now. (Laughs.)

TOM: We didn't miss anybody. (Laughs.)

Then, about four years ago, we were burned down. I'm not sure we know why. We know who lit the match. The state troopers told us that they were convinced we were the victims of a townwide con-spiracy. Everybody they talked to in the courthouse and City Hall had known almost from the day of the fire who did it. They kept it a secret and took part in the coverup. There was an investigation that resulted in four arrests and one conviction.

PAT: All during the trial, the mayor of Whitesburg sat with the city policeman who was convicted. (Laughs.)

TOM: We're not at ease with the town. They wish we would just go away. We're still an embarrassment to them. What Pat and I found heartbreaking is that the townspeople did not come around to tell us they were sorry we had been burned out. They didn't offer any help at all. They stood by and watched us go through several months of torment in which we were accused of having set it ourselves. The community knew better. That's awfully hard to forgive.

Of the twelve hundred people in town, three hundred or four hundred families are professionals: doctors, lawyers, engineers. You would have to tell yourself they're not book burners, because of their education. I think they hated us but just didn't quite know what to do. But they wouldn't mind someone else doin' it.

PAT: I was brought up to believe that God was in His heaven and all was right with the world. One of the biggest shocks I ever got was to grow up and find out it wasn't so.

TOM: We're surviving. I think we made Harry Caudill's* survival possible and Harry made our survival possible. It would have been very difficult for either one of us to survive in most any other mountain town.

PAT: The nice thing about this county is that it's small enough that you can kind of grab hold of it. You have some idea what forces are involved.

I come home every once in a while and storm and walk the floor and say: "We can't stay here any longer." Tom will listen to all this stuff. He doesn't talk, I do. Finally, when I shut up, he'll say: "Would you like to go to Fayette County and help somebody get a new sewer system? Or just where else would you like to go?" (Laughs.) Of course, there's nothing else we would like to do, so we're still right here. We haven't considered ourselves crusaders. We've been doing all along what we thought a good newspaper ought to do.

TOM: I think one of the mistakes made by many newspapers has been to underestimate the intelligence of their readership. They end up fillin' it up with a bunch of crap. I just assume that if it interests me, it will interest everybody else. Our son, who's working summers in the mines with a bunch of old-timers, tells me that at least one day a week they argue among themselves about what they read in *The Mountain Eagle*. (Laughs.) We know it's read and debated.

As I'm about to leave, the telephone rings. Tom answers. Harry Caudill is at the other end. It is a brief conversation.

TOM: Harry asked me did I remember when we did a story about two and a half years ago on some houses and trailers that were covered

---

* A Whitesburg lawyer who has represented eastern Kentucky working people against powerful interests. He is author of *Night Comes to the Cumberlands*, a critically acclaimed book that infuriated the townspeople. "Everybody knew that their ancestors didn't come over as indentured servants and criminals," Tom says sardonically. "That just wasn't so."

up by a strip-mine slide? He tells me that there had been a suit filed by some of the families. They had won a fifty-eight thousand dollar judgment, and the State Supreme Court upheld it today. So we do have an impact every now and then. (Laughs.) We know that our story and our photographs helped in that suit. It's small enough and immediate enough that you know it makes a difference.

There's all kinds of measures of things. There are times when walking up Main Street and going to the post office to pick up the mail and having to face everyone up and down that street and seeing all the hatred is really more than I can bear. Then you have this: suits won and small victories that come along. It all balances out.

As I leave Tom and Pat Gish in this "holler," I glance up at the sky. The stars are never so clear as now.

BOB BROWN

A lieutenant colonel in the United States Army Reserves, he is editor and publisher of Soldier of Fortune.

We're in his office in Boulder, Colorado. On the walls are autographed pictures and plaques: from the Republic of Vietnam to a Special Forces group; another in Vietnamese script; a comic poster of Jimmy Carter, with the caption: "The best friend Panama ever had."

On another wall is a rifle. "It's a commercial version of the CAR-15. It's semi-automatic. It's the type of weapon that was used in Vietnam. I just have it around because it's my trade, so to speak."

He tips back his chair, his feet on the desk. He sniffs snuff. Blue-eyed, wiry, he bears a startling resemblance to Fran Tarkenton, the Minnesota Vikings ex-quarterback.

The American Dream to me is to maintain the prestige of the United States in the world. I'm very much a pessimist about that. If I may paraphrase John F. Kennedy: When it comes to national defense, it's first, not if, but, or when. If we have to increase our defense budget to maintain our freedom, then, by God, let's do it.

Democracy is not free. It's something you must pay for, sometimes in blood. There are too many totalitarian regimes that wish to circumvent our power. You have to make sacrifices to maintain democracy.

I think we have the greatest country that's ever existed. Unfortunately, the vast majority of people here have no appreciation of this. When I go overseas, I see how the majority of the people in the world live. The average tourist never gets beyond the Cairo Hilton.

My childhood was a placid one, boring. We moved about. My father was foreman at Inland Steel, a good, solid, plodding, middle American. My mother was a schoolteacher, a hard-charging, middle-class American. She is really a very aggressive lady. If she were thirty years younger, she'd be president of GM. A great lady. We clashed more in the past than we do now.

I worked as an armored car guard, a private investigator. At one time, I was a judo instructor. Now I'm an active journalist who goes where the action is. I like the adventure. I like the pumping of the adrenaline, being on the fine edge, if you will.

Soldier of Fortune is the only real hard-core adventure magazine on the market today. *True* is folded, *Saga* is folded, *Argosy* is folding. We're different. We take strong editorial stands. We're very pro gun ownership, very much opposed to disarming the populace. We characterize the BATF* as America's Gestapo. They have the same type of scum that operate in the narcotics field. They use all kinds of illegal methods to obtain indictments.

We're very pro-military and believe in the image of the warrior. It's fallen into disrepute ever since the Vietnam conflict. The warrior is the individual throughout history who would come to the forefront, be it Alexander the Great or Hannibal or Caesar or Xenophon, the first mercenary the world's ever seen. Patton, MacArthur, Sergeant York: there's the type of individual that rises above the ranks and performs feats of valor in combat. This has been a long American tradition.

We're losing more and more allies through our gutlessness. Iran's down the tube. We're pulling out of Korea. We've cut off Taiwan. And, of course, Southeast Asia. You don't see the knee-jerk liberal press discrediting the domino theory any more. Why? Because the theory proved a valid one. Now Vietnam and Cambodia . . .

I had three positions during the fourteen months I was in Vietnam. First six months I was an intelligence officer. Then I got transferred

* Bureau of Alcohol, Tax and Firearms

to the Green Berets. I ran an A camp. (He points to a picture on the wall: "Myself and two of my men.") I had approximately a thousand people. Mountain tribesmen. We had five hundred seventy-six mercenaries: Montagnards, Cambodians. Excellent troops, paid by the American government.

The nearest friendly forces were twenty-two kilometers away. We were the old western fort and the Indians. I was minister of defense, minister of education and welfare, superintendent of roads, marriage counsellor, you name it. I was responsible for these people's lives. Even though, officially, I was an advisor, I ran things. It was like a little dukedom.

It was exhilarating. Aside from my philosophy, the reason I volunteered is that I wanted to see what would happen when somebody shot at me. When I found out, I shot back.

In interrogation, I did not use brutality. I simply questioned in depth. If somebody is lying to you, unless he is very sophisticated, he will slip up. I broke one case—did you see the interview I had in *Oui* magazine? I got involved in this murder I didn't participate in. A man was murdered in my camp, and I raised a lot of hell about that. How I broke the murderer was by making him go over his story. He said he never carried a gun. A while later, I said: "How did you alert your team when the Americans came near?" He says: "I fired my carbine in the air." As soon as that happened, man, yip, yip, yip, yip, yip. He just started spilling his guts.

I've been accused of recruiting mercenaries to fight in southern Africa. A lot of poppycock. We have a lot of nuts who've made these accusations. They look at the magazine and come to an emotional conclusion that we're working with the CIA. This is utter bullshit. How do you convince somebody like that? You don't. We just disregard it.

We carry ads about high-risk jobs, jobs as mercs or security guards or advisors. We do know that some of these individuals have obtained work. Not necessarily as mercs—that's a slang term, more and more accepted—but for other strange, if you will, "missions."

Certainly a lot of military personnel buy our magazine. Our stories are about heroes. I had the idea for this magazine kickin' around in my head for years. They revolve around single characters rather than the kind the army puts out: this group does this. We talk about *men*, men that have gone and done things.

Believe it or not, I'm one of the original campus activists. Back in

'57 I was goin' to grad school at the CU.* I happened to be in Chicago that year and was drinking my way around the North Side when I came across a little flyer from the College of Complexes.** I went there and met these Cuban exiles. They were anti-Batista but not pro-Castro. I told them I had a friend who had machine guns for sale. I was thinking: guns for exiles equals money for Brown. I didn't sell them anything. They never had any money. They were typical Cuban bullshit artists.

I came back here and started an anti-Batista movement on campus. I don't like dictators, and there are some who were anti-Communist. At this time, Castro was portrayed as a liberal, a democrat. Oh, we hung Batista effigies and had graveyards with all the Latin-American dictators in them. When Arthur Larson, Eisenhower's advisor, came out to the university, I picketed him about stopping arms shipments to Batista.

I got itchy and thought it would be exciting to go down and join Castro. My buddy and myself were in Miami to check things out. We were impatient. We contacted the July 26th Movement. We'd been in the counterintelligence corps as special agents. This was August '58. Castro was taking over. We're in the lobby of this little hotel, here are these two guys in hats and suits in August. They said: "Wait, you guys." It was the FBI. They heard I was recruiting college students to join Fidel. I allowed as how this was a lot of shit. They said: "You better not go down there, you'll get in a lot of trouble." "We're going anyway."

We couldn't make contacts. The revolution was over. I was twenty-six. I thought I'd go down at the end of the semester and write about the transfer of power. I was too much of an idealist.

I ended up down there. Havana became a mecca for revolutionaries from all over Latin America and the Caribbean. The Americans I knew down there were involved in a lot of shit. Plots were being hatched. We're going here, we're going there. Where can we get the money? I was stringing for AP, picking up a buck here and there. That's how I got to meet General Bajillo.

He had come to Havana with his entourage of Spanish exiles. They'd fought against Franco. He was planning to invade Spain. I became intrigued. That's when my interest in guerrilla warfare

* University of Colorado
** An informal lecture-tavern run by an ex-Wobbly, featuring colorful nonestablishment speakers and "characters"

started. This was a fantastic old man. Even though he was a Communist, he was a very interesting person. I wrote the introduction to this book: *150 Questions for a Guerrilla.* I had it translated, raised four hundred dollars, and published it myself.

When I was down there in 1960, it became apparent what Castro's government was, so I started working with the counterrevolutionaries. I was involved in an attempt to—I prefer to describe myself as a peripheral observer—to invade Haiti and overthrow Duvalier. He was a bad dude. This was November 1966. It was a comedy of errors. I oppose tyrants in whatever form.

When I got back from Rhodesia in '74, I called *Saga* and said: "Here's a dynamite story, an American mercenary in Africa, got pictures." They said: "We're trying to get away from the hairy-chest stuff." I said: "Oh, what the fuck, an adventure magazine? What could be more adventurous?" I had a gut feeling there was a market for this type of thing.

When we came out with our first issue, we had forty-four hundred subscribers. July '75. Today we have a paid circulation of about a hundred six thousand.

We do a lot of evaluations on weaponry. We did a piece on a new gun that was horrible. "Throw this goddamn gun away, this is a jam-o-matic . . ." We have a lot of readership because we tell it like it is. Most gun magazines won't do this because they'll lose advertising.

Forty-nine percent of our readers are Vietnam vets. Nobody prints anything about them. They feel maligned by the majority of this society. We have a piece in every issue about Vietnam. A lot of guys believed in what we were doing there. These are the people never heard from, Nixon's Silent Majority. They're bitter.

Twenty-eight percent of our readers are in the military, sixteen percent are law enforcement, and—this may surprise you—twenty-two percent are professionals, doctors and lawyers. Most everybody that buys our magazine is a gun enthusiast. It's sold everywhere.

I'm certain there's the guy who comes from his job on the assembly line, his frowsy wife is yelling at him, his kids are raising hell. He pops a beer and takes a copy of the magazine, and he says: "I'd like to go be a mercenary someplace." He's never going to, but for that short period of time, he's going to escape.

People are too concerned about two cars and enough gas. If it's a matter of continuing to support Israel versus having a car, there would be a tremendous number of people who would say the hell with Israel. I'm very pro-Israel. I admire them as a people. I admire their tenacity, their willingness to fight for their nation under insurmountable odds. I admire their decisions to act quickly. The Entebbe raid was put together in a week. We dinked around with raids for a year. The Israelis did it, bam. I admire the drive, the balls, the courage.

A democracy is not made for a strong, strong man. In a democracy, you have to find an individual that will appeal to widely divergent groups, conflicting interests. We have no leader alive who entrances me. I liked Teddy Roosevelt: Walk softly and carry a big stick.

We're despised overseas because we want to be friends with everybody. People may fear the Russians, but they don't despise them. The Russians, when they see a situation that would benefit them, say: Fuck world public opinion. Look at Hungary, Czechoslovakia. Who thinks of Czechoslovakia now? We want to kiss everybody's ass.

The United States is the only country in history that had complete, undeniable power and never exploited it. We didn't do it.

What should we have done?

Pax Americana. I would certainly have used the atomic bomb against the Chinese in Korea. When the Russians put up the Berlin blockade, I would have said: "Honor your agreements or we'll drop the bomb." I think there's a good possibility of an atomic war.

Will we win it?

Oh, no.

Will they win it?

Oh, no.

If there's a war and nobody survives, what's the purpose?

You can always find a purpose. Whether you and I as rational men consider it valid is one thing, but it's what goes on in the mind of the individual who's got the little red button to press.

When you were a kid, did you always have the macho image?

I was small. I went out for football, weighed a hundred ten pounds. I didn't last very long because I'm near-sighted, have small hands, my reflexes are slow, and I couldn't run very fast. I went out for track and baseball, but never made any of the teams. That's why I went into boxing. You're on your own. First fight I ever had, I was knocked out in the first round. That's why I grooved with *Rocky*. And John Wayne. Oh, yeah. Tarkenton, eh? I like that. I would like to have been a professional quarterback. Or George Patton.

JANN WENNER

The New York offices of Rolling Stone *occupy four floors along Fifth Avenue. Something of a quadruplex. It exudes an atmosphere of informality and easy success. Against the wall in a hallway toward the back are several fashionably slim high-speed bicycles. On the more visible walls are portraits of Woody Allen, Muhammad Ali. Celebrated people are further celebrated. The staff is young, personable, with an air of knowingness. Not too many months ago, the whole enterprise, people and all, moved from San Francisco to the Big Apple.*

When a journalist was asked about the move east, he said: "It sucks. When we started out," he says, "there was a hard news edge on music and culture. The hard edge has dissipated. The culture itself has become more establishment. Jimmy Carter marched into the Democratic convention after winning the nomination, preceded by a song written by Gregg Allman. Is that a victory or defeat?" (Laughs.)

The publisher's office on the twenty-third floor offers an astonishing view of the city's skyline. He appears younger than he is, thirty-two, and seated in a comfortable easy chair, with an intimation of uncertainty.

"Our circulation, six hundred thousand. That means three million people read it. All the celebrated music people read it. The writers and extremely literate people read it and like it, because they also write it. It's one of the few homes in this country left for good journalism. It's become establishment in and of itself. Rock is a major establishment in this country. It's as big, if not bigger, than the movies of Hollywood."

I wonder if the American Dream is as ugly as Hunter Thompson*
says it is. We know of its rapaciousness over the years and the way it
treats poor people. Is it a better place than those of the callous aris-
tocracies who throughout history have run the world for themselves?
It's been pretty good for me and a lot of others. People willing to
work real hard, who have talent enough and are willing to make
certain compromises, get a lot of rewards, a lot of satisfaction. I'd
rather be here in the heart of the American Dream than in the heart
of the British Dream. (Laughs.)

I never had any doubt about making it. Just seemed natural that
I'd be able to do what I wanted to do. I've always gotten what I
wanted. When I was five or six years old, I was putting out a neighborhood paper. After eight months, 1956 or 1955, or 1954 or '53,
whenever it was, we had a fourteen-dollar profit. I've been doing that
for so long now, it's sort of second nature. It's always worked. That's
why I never had too many doubts about myself.

I was raised in Marin County, north of San Francisco, across the
Golden Gate Bridge. The quintessential upper middle class. One of
the beginnings of suburbia, a kind of West Coast Westchester.

I used to sit under covers at night with a flashlight and read books.
By the time I was in fifth grade, I was reading all the books on the
bestseller list. I read *The Invisible Man* when I was nine years old. I
stopped reading books when I started *Rolling Stone*. (Laughs.) I had
the experience of always being the brightest one in class.

In eighth grade, I stopped going to public schools and went away to a
boarding school. All the children of movie stars use to go to this
school. I was impressed for about three weeks, and then it became
routine. It was sort of like going to college very early. At twelve, you're
thrown into an elite kind of training.

I first knew about status because we had a pool. Some people had
pools, some people didn't. I went to Berkeley. I didn't get accepted at
Harvard. I was disappointed for a day. I reflect on it now that I have
some intercourse with Harvard. We have a lot of Boston writers.
When I speak to the Nieman Fellows,** I always think: God, if I'd
gone to Harvard, it would've all turned out so much differently. I
spoke in front of the Harvard Businss School once a couple of years
ago.

I was in journalism and had a job, two summers in a row, with NBC

* The magazine's celebrated journalist
** A fellowship for journalists who are offered a year's sabbatical by their newspapers

News, San Francisco. In the summer of '64, I worked at the Republican Convention for Huntley-Brinkley. I was eighteen. That was a very privileged experience. Assistant to the unit manager. Convention time comes around, you're in the Huntley-Brinkley booth for four days getting their coffee and their Salem cigarettes.

There are some people who are very political about what they're doing, maneuvering and jockeying for position. I could have ended up being one of those people, but I never had to. It was just luck and timing. And being good at what I do. And enjoying it. If I had jockeyed that plus the raw intelligence and drive I have might have been a potent combination or it might have been just a totally fucked one. I was never structured to do double-dealing.

There was real stress I had to face, about 1970, three years into publication of *Rolling Stone*. The company was bankrupt in essence. I'd gotten too ambitious. I had to contemplate: Fuck it. I can throw the whole thing and let it be. I'm only twenty-four.

I remember one day, just driving around and waiting for an accident to happen. It wasn't suicide as such. It was just driving around very sloppily, saying: Fuck it, maybe somebody'll get me in an accident. I was facing failure, real failure. I'd never faced complete failure before. I was really depressed. In retrospect, to go bankrupt with a little newspaper at the age of twenty-four is not the most terrible thing. It was absurd. It didn't last long. You reach a point where your confidence is really shattered. It takes other people to help build up your confidence: Come on now, face the bastards down. You start to build and put it back together.

People don't like failure. It's a real mark, especially in business. But there's enough fools in business that they'll take failures back in. (Sighs.) I'm not a great believer in failure as a sin. A couple of our writers are fuckups. Two of our best were fired from other papers. Fuckups are a way of life, everybody fucks up.

Starting *Rolling Stone* was intuitive. I was all caught up in the rock and roll revolution. And hi-fi. I was an expert at hi-fi. (Laughs.) I was really writing about what interested me. I was writing about my own youth. It never occurred to me to do market research or big reader surveys. We were just gonna write about rock and roll. Ralph* and I. And that's what we did. We didn't think twice about it. We just knew the music was great and that there must be a million people out there.

---

* The late Ralph Gleason was one of the most perceptive of jazz critics and, perhaps, the first to understand the impact of the rock culture upon the young.

Ralph was always trying to get people to learn from history. I'd hear some piece of music and say that's the greatest guitar ever. He'd say: "Aw, come on. Did you ever hear Charlie Christian?" He laid out the concept for *Rolling Stone*, I wrote it. As time went on, I went beyond Ralph's experiences. I was learning about business and so on.

I was always considered bright or spoiled or precocious or bratty. One of the nicknames I had from a high school teacher was "Nox," short for obnoxious. I don't get too worked up about sometimes having to be mean to people. I can be a very cruel person, but I don't like to be cruel. I don't hesitate to be honest with people if it's for their own good. It's hard at a young age to be firing people, playing with people's lives. But if they're not working out, let them go.

You have to exercise your power with a great deal of restraint because our readers are a very suspicious, well-educated lot. They see a lot of naked power grabbing go down. I don't think anybody can get away with what Hearst got away with at that time. Those were much naïver times.

As for becoming known, a minor celebrity, it has no effect on me. It's been ten years since I've been doing this. It's overnight success that makes people impossible and sometimes kills them. In entertainment, you're dealing with people who are far more successful, really celebrated. You develop a thick skin over reading so much about yourself, especially in New York City, where you read all this gossip bullshit. When nasty stuff was written, I really felt these hurts. Now the insults have to be on a higher level.

The paper isn't just about music, it's about politics. I was raised in a very political family. I was watching the Army-McCarthy hearings when I was eight. I knew what was going on because my mother was passionately involved. It was much more easy to get inflamed and impassioned about politics when Nixon was president than it is now. Now it's dull, although the forces at work are just as insidious and just as powerful. And maybe more frightening because they're operating subtly. But it's hard to work up much passion about Jimmy Carter. That's all the more dangerous.

But I don't believe all this shit about young people being disinterested or campuses being quiet or everybody trying to be a dentist. I think that's another of those myths coming out of *Time* magazine and places like that. They're so stupid, they never saw what was going on in the first place, they're not gonna see it now. They think young people are back toward passivity. That's craziness. They won't perceive it until it comes and hits them over the head. The media got all hot about ecology, but they didn't see the other undercurrents.

There are a lot of serious young people out there. And they are ready to move. People are just taking their lives more seriously in a different way. On the other hand, how many people are there thirty years old who are leaders? The sixties was not a time that encouraged leadership 'cause the fashion was anti-leadership.

As for me, my self-confidence is stronger than ever 'cause things are easier to do. You don't have to prove yourself. You just say: "That's how I feel, and that's the way it's going to be." You're dealing with a larger set of problems and bigger amounts of money. You're moving larger and larger forces. And we're right here in the center of the fucking world.

(He indicates the skyline.) Over there, you can see ABC, CBS, and NBC. And you can see RCA and Rockefeller Center. If New York is the capital of the world, financial and communications, and they say Fifty-seventh and Fifth's the center of New York, and we're at Fifty-eighth, that's insane. Beautiful, I mean.

RON McCREA

◇——◇

He is the editor of the Madison Press Connection, *a daily newspaper. It came into being as a result of a strike, still going on, against the* Capitol Times.
He is thirty-five.

The dream is to create something of your own, to have some measure of control over your destiny. The American Dream becomes pernicious when it is imposed on other people. I haven't been thinking of myself as an American very much over the last ten years. I went through a period of estrangement during the sixties.

"I lived with kids from Africa and Asia when I was in graduate school at Harvard.* I started to feel more of an internationalist than an American. The one thing I really felt myself coming back to was being a midwesterner. If I have an Americanism, it's more of a midwestern Americanism.

* The Fletcher School of Law and Diplomacy

"I grew up in Saginaw, Michigan. My father was the son of a news-paperman. My grandfather had come off the farm and started ped-dling papers and wound up being a newspaper editor in Muskegon. Quite a pillar in that community. My father grew up in his shadow. He finally did get into newspapering himself. His one interest was reporting."

One of my earliest memories was being carried in my father's arms into the press room of the *Saginaw News*. I heard some of the old presses roaring. It was a loud clatter. It was a terrifying sound. I started shrieking. I said—ironically, in later times—I should have taken my lesson from that.

My mother was irritated because my father was always out on an assignment. I remember her telling me: "If you ever become a news-paperman, don't get married." I have, and I haven't. (Laughs.) I'm a newspaperman and I'm not married. I guess I'm married to the news-paper much as a priest to the church.

I always remember liking newspaper people. Going up to Dad's office and dredging up old photographs from the wastebaskets and hearing reporters stand around and talk. They seemed to be involved with the real world and also had a great sense of humor. I went through nine years of college and graduate school, and I had to make a choice between being a university teacher and a journalist. What finally cut it was my remembering how much I liked newspaper peo-ple. Their excesses and their conceits somehow were more charming than those of academics.

Saginaw was a medium-sized town. There weren't the terribly col-orful characters you associate with *The Front Page*. But it was a pleasure to go to the little greasy spoon when my father and the others from the city room had lunch. They were always debating foreign policy or about who was crooked at City Hall. A lot of 'em had drink-ing problems, and my father had to do an awful lot of conciliating of families. I'm sure it was not that idyllic, but it seemed so to me.

I remember the kids in my grade school class coming over to watch the Eisenhower inauguration. How happy my mother was that he was elected! He was a hero of hers. I remember Eisenhower coming to Saginaw on a train during one of his whistle stops. A terribly genial, friendly man, waving to the children, who had all been let out of school that day. It was a beautiful, noncontroversial time. I don't remember much of anything in the fifties that disturbed anyone.

One night, my father and mother came home quite disturbed.

Some people had invited them down to see a film in their basement. One of those films about how communism was taking over the world. They were disturbed by what seemed so extreme. My father has since told me it was difficult to be an editorial writer during the McCarthy period. So many people were frightened. I remember listening to the Army-McCarthy hearings, but I really didn't understand what was going on. I was in fourth grade.

It was a time of a lot of piano lessons and everybody had big cars and television was new. Everyone was into it, watching everything, even test patterns. At the time, neither my mother nor my father was questioning a whole lot. They were very much in the mainstream.

At Albion College, I worked very actively for Barry Goldwater. I read *Conscience of a Conservative* during my freshman year. Somehow this guy had a purity of vision I'd never seen in politics before. I got caught up in what I now recognize as libertarianism. His discussion of individual initiative, keeping the state out of people's lives, made a good deal of sense to me. So I got involved in Young Conservative politics.

I remember going on TV as editor of the college paper and coming out for the war. Aggression from the north had to be stopped. I was just mouthing phrases. When I got to Northwestern, the Medill School of Journalism, in '65, it was a great awakening.

In Chicago, I first realized how diverse the world really was. I remember getting on the el in Evanston and riding down to the University of Chicago. It was a core sample of the earth. Ladies with their fur coats and bags getting on in Evanston, Appalachians as you get near north, then Hispanic people and the great mix downtown, and then the black population getting larger and larger. It was a much different society than I had ever imagined. Chicago was the revolution for me. It shook out the marbles in my innocent brain.

I became conscious, first of Vietnam and, secondly, how the conservative philosophy was often used as a means to justify terrific social inequity. Journalism school was tough and demanded a hard look at things. I started reading critically, particularly on Vietnam and racial issues. I wrote my father about it, and it had a terrific impact on him.

He didn't agree with me immediately. He kept his silence. Even though I've always looked upon him as a very bright man, he's always looked down at himself. I very much wanted him to share the excitement I was feeling. The more he read of the stuff I would push toward him, the more he was taking a hard look at Saginaw.

He'd always known we had the third-largest black population in the state. But as far as I was concerned, it could have been Afghanistan. The city was divided by a river. All the blacks were on one side, and all the whites on the other. There was a strange kind of jungle across the river where the black people lived. That's all I ever knew. I don't think the paper ever covered it. My father may have been blind to things for a long time, but now he began to write about civil rights, getting into the city's racism. And also writing against Vietnam. He and I felt a real closeness, closer than we had ever been.

The editor, who had been an ally of my father's, was transferred to another newspaper. The new guy started blue-penciling my father heavily, challenging him on everything he was writing about war or race. My father was pressing all the wrong buttons, and finally they told him he could no longer represent the paper in the editorial columns. He could take a column under his own name off the editorial page. It was a crushing thing for him. He always believed that a newspaper working together with an enlightened citizenry could turn around a social situation. He had faith in democratic institutions, yet he didn't understand the power structure of his city or even of his own newspaper.

He'd always had great pride—as my grandfather had—in speaking for the newspaper. He did take the column and wrote a piece about an open-housing ordinance that was full of loopholes. The next day the editor said: "Our paper does not ridicule public officials. You'll report to the copy desk." That meant he was through writing for that newspaper.

He was fifty-seven. He had been there thirty years. So he refused to report for work. It was like a sit-down strike. He stayed home for a month. Whether he finally resigned, I don't know. He didn't get severance, he didn't get pension, nothing. He finally landed with the *Toledo Blade* as one of several editorial writers. Even there, they disappointed him by endorsing Nixon and becoming conservative. He's out of writing now and a little bitter about the whole experience.

Sure, he could have followed the boss' orders and done a light, easy column. But there was a certain kind of family tradition. There's a strong Scotch Presbyterian minister strain. I think that's why we all liked writing editorials and pontificating. The Methodists don't have pontiffs, but they make good editorial writers. There's also what I'm tempted to call a martyrlike streak in the family.

I'm trying to keep what I feel is worth keeping in that family tradition but to get away from the deadly, martyr stuff. And I never want to be as naïve about power as my father was.

During the summer of '69, I joined the *Capitol Times*. I got into the guild and was elected an officer pretty soon after that. The only talk I'd ever heard about unions in this business is that the news doesn't stop at five o'clock. You don't punch a card. A real professional doesn't think about time.

I worked there from 1970 to 1977. I became news editor in '72 when some of the older people retired. It was an interesting time to be in charge of the front page. We were going through the Nixon years and Watergate. It was always a feisty, scrappy curmudgeon of a paper. It had a distinctive voice. It was the first paper in the country to endorse Gene McCarthy. It was a pleasure to work for it then. Technically, I'm still employed by them. I'm only on strike.

It's still owned by an independent family, but it's the weak sister of a conglomerate. It's really controlled by a corporation in Davenport, Iowa. When they tried to break the unions—printers were fired wholesale, pay was cut—we called a strike.

Our strike paper, the *Madison Press Connection*, is staff-owned and staff-controlled. We believe the best way to run any operation is to let people have some power over their lives. Everyone was saying this paper would die in six weeks. It's been a year, and we're still doing it. I think it's the same kind of stubbornnesss my father and grandfather had. The only times I get afraid is when I start thinking maybe I'm too stubborn, more than the evidence warrants. But I don't care if I'm editor another year, it's been fun going through it. I've learned I've got to be much tougher about power than my father and grandfather were.

What I can't understand are these young people who come to the *Capitol Times* from around the country. The *Washington Post* sent one of their personnel guys over to screen these people—to find out how they stand on labor and whether they'd cross a picket line to go to work.

We confronted these kids as they drove past our picket line in their cars. We were curious about them. What kind of people were they? We sat down and talked. They said: "Well, you seem like a likable, intelligent guy and I'm a likable, intelligent guy. You have your point of view and I have my point of view. Why can't we be friends?" I said: "Even if I were to agree that you're a likable, intelligent guy, you must never forget I want you to lose your job tomorrow. I want you out of that plant. You've altered the power balance, and you've done great damage to lives." They didn't see it. "This is not political. It's only career advancement." I said: "If you were a strikebreaker at a coal mine, what would your impact be on mine safety?" They couldn't see the connection. Well, they're going to see the *Connection* every day. (Laughs.)

They're simply on the make. America's always been a nation of people on the make. I've never really been one of them. I thought, like my father, goodness would be rewarded. These kids don't give a damn. Their job is all that counts. What gets me is: How can they go to a liberal newspaper and present themselves as progressive journalists? How can they see social injustice if they participate in social injustice themselves?

The young people on our strike paper? The ones scabbing are careerists. The ones working for us are adventurers. (Laughs.) They didn't come for the money. We don't have any to offer. They came here to be in touch with some kind of journalism ideal.

We have probably the most educated citizenry in our history. We have the technical capabilities to solve an awful lot of problems, not only our own but the world's. Yet I'm afraid it's almost a proto-fascist time. There are so many people without controversy in their lives, without ideology, without belief. Almost anything can happen. The soft tyranny is real close to us.

My life has been so much with labor battles, I haven't had a chance to live where I'd like to live—with Bach partitas, the piano, the organ, and the harpsichord. I love to play this music. (Sighs.) But there's the world out there . . . I think we're going to see direct action again. I'm not sure who's gonna do it. There may be too much quiescence in the factories, in the plants. People may have been bought off too well. So I don't know, it's a time of uncertainty. I'm still interested in experimenting, and as long as there's a little flame alive somewhere, I'm willing to search it out.

THE YOUNG: SPECTATORS AND GLADIATORS

◇────────────────────────────◇

THE GIRL NEXT-DOOR

LINDA HAAS, 16

◇────────────────────────────◇

She attends a large technical high school in Chicago. Most of its students are of blue-collar families.

"I live in a changing neighborhood. It's Polish, Spanish, and southern.

"My father is from West Virginia, way up in the mountains. He was a farmer, he was in the Coast Guard. He did a lot of jobs. He was very intelligent, but he refused to go to college. My mother is from a real small town in Missouri. She went to eighth grade, but she was straight A's all the way through. Her stepmother wouldn't let her go to high school. She's bitter over this. My mom really has a thirst for knowledge, and this crushed her."

My father is a butcher for the A & P for twenty-six years. Never misses a day. He could be dying and he goes to work. The German heritage in him, you go to work and that's that. I feel sorry for him because he's like a fish out of water. I just feel he would be happier if he could be back in West Virginia.

The company he works for is changed. There was pride. Now it's just falling apart. They're letting people go with no feelings for how long they've worked there, just lay 'em off. It's sad. He should be getting benefits after all these years and all the sacrifices he's made. Now they're almost ready to lay him off without a word.

They send him from store to store. Before, the only people who did that were the young kids, part-time. My pa is fifty-one. Every week he has to wait to see if they're going to send him to another store. It's humiliating for him to be working for them all these years, he's got to call in every so often and find out if they have another store for him. It hurts his feelings. It's just wrong.

He never says it hurts his feelings, he roars. When he's upset, he takes it out by acting angry. He yells about a lotta minor things at home. Like the phone bill or if the light doesn't work, he'll roar about it for two hours. I know he couldn't care less about the phone bill or the lights. All the things he'd like to yell at other people about, he's letting out over a light bulb.

I just feel sorry for people because I know how I feel. A lot of things have hurt my feelings as I've grown up. I try to see behind people when they do things. Most people, if they heard my father yelling about the phone bill, they'd say: "Wow, does he have a temper!" I try to look beyond, because I know what makes people do what they do.

Lane Tech, where I go, is a mixture. It's working-class, and there are a lot of wealthy people. It's too large, and it's not a happy place. The rich kids have their things, their Gucci shoes and their Marshall Field clothes, and they sit in their part and we sit in ours. We're just acquaintances. There's a few black kids, they're welcome. They stay with black kids. They don't want to be with us. We leave each other alone. We're all like separated.

I think for my father and his generation, the dream was to have a home and security and things like that. It was because of the poverty they came from. I don't know what it is now. The kids I go to school with, when they talk about their dreams, they don't talk about a home and having money in the bank. It's more like trying to have personal satisfaction. They don't know what they want. I don't know what I want. I don't know what my dreams are. There's so many things I'd like to do, and then . . .

I would like to go to college and do something, really contribute something. But I look at my neighborhood and my friends and my family and I think: Me going to college and being a writer, that would separate me from them. I would feel like I was breaking away. Like I just couldn't come back and sit on the front porch with my friends. It wouldn't be the same. I'd be the outcast. Every day I wake up: Oh, I'll go to college. The next day: No, I'm not. I'm going to get a job when I graduate. So I don't know.

Other people I know that went on to college come back to the neighborhood in the summer, to visit their friends—we're sitting around talking, the feeling's different. They treat them differently. It's not really resentment. It's like envy. They can't just goof around with them any more. It's like they regard them as some different person they never met before. It's sad to me. I wouldn't want them to act like I wasn't their friend any more.

The few we knew that have been to college, some of 'em do feel superior and look down upon the neighborhood. They're ashamed to tell people where they live. It's a bad neighborhood where I live, but it's where I live. It's my home and I'm not ashamed. I would love to go to college.

She had just written a paper for her English class: impressions of a neighborhood friend of hers. "Just a guy I grew up with, Spanish. He's a nice person, but he has to be in a gang." She offers it from memory.

Everyone thought he was cool and tough, and he acted that way. He had feelings, but they just died somewhere. He's only sixteen, and he feels nothing. He's like a zombie. People die and his friends die, and it doesn't affect him. He never cries and he never cares deeply for anyone. I just think it's a waste because I remember him before.

When he was young, when we were little kids in grade school, he was really sweet and he did care then and he had feelings. It's just sad to watch him over the years, to regress like that and lose his feelings. When people hurt my feelings, I get it over with. I don't turn bitter. He turned bitter and cynical. He just takes everything as a personal offense. It all accumulates and he can't talk about it, so he turns inward.

He's seventeen now and he's in jail. So that's about it. He was my buddy for about four years. But then we went our separate ways. I don't know where he is. I did last year, but there was nothing left to say. It wasn't the same any more. He's a human being, he's intelligent, and now he's a drug addict, sitting in jail. He's wasted.

He was a good little kid, nice and funny. He was everybody's boy, the little boy you'd like to have for your son. That was him. Mr. Nice Little Boy. (Laughs.) He had talent. I think he would have been an artist. He was always drawing and did good work. He had imagination. When he was seven or eight, he would draw purple cows. Everybody would say: "What are you drawing purple cows for?" He'd say: "Purple cows are pretty. When I'm older, I'll be a farmer and I'll breed purple cows." He was really wild that way. He started hanging around with the older gang members—you know, a tough gang member doesn't stand around with a paintbrush, drawing. Not in my neighborhood. So he gave it up.

Now everyone in the neighborhood is afraid of him. If he wasn't in jail, if he was walking down the street, everybody would go in their houses. He wouldn't do anything to them, but that's the way they feel because they've heard of him now. He's created this image for himself, and now he's stuck with it.

In the sixties is when the gangs started getting prominent in my neighborhood. They'd beat you up every day until you finally agreed to join them. He was so young, he didn't know what he was getting into. They were always beating him up, so he figured: Okay, I'll join. The girl members are as mean as the guys. (Laughs.)

They don't mind me. We still get along. We kind of accept each other. I'm about one of five people in the neighborhood that they'll asssociate with that are not in their gangs. They don't try. They think I'm silly for not joining, and I think they're silly. But we get along.

My other friends think they're low-down scum. They can't see how I would even say hello to them on the street. They think it's unusual that I'm able to talk to them yet.

I always aggravate my dad because I'm always trying to see the good in everybody. There's a few I can't tolerate, but most of 'em I get along with.

We're a close family, we do things. I don't need to be feared by people to feel I'm worth something. I have other things in my life. It doesn't matter to me if everybody runs in the house when I walk down the street. They need that. There's nothing at home for them. Somewhere they've got to be important. I have other things.

I was reading in the paper the other day how times were getting worse, how children don't respect their parents, how the crime rate is rising. It went on and on. At the bottom, it said: Written in 1922. I don't think people are worse. I think there are still good people left.

My father is a different person than me. He can't understand them. It's hard to see good in them if you didn't go to school with them. He just can't tolerate them. His whole life, he worked for everything he got. He can't tolerate stealing or fighting. I see his point of view.

My mother's like me. She doesn't want to argue with my dad, so she doesn't say much either way. She loves to learn. She was only eighteen and fresh from the country when she came here. She went to a nursing school she thought was accredited. It wasn't. She started working to survive. Then she got married. Finally, when we were in school, she thought: If I don't do it now, I'm never gonna do it. She went back and got her high school GED.* She went on to college and won all kinds of awards.

They read a lot. That's all my father does. Anything he can get his hands on. I make him read whatever I read. I give books to my parents and I bug 'em to death until they read 'em. I read whatever I pick up, just everything. I don't follow any pattern. I'm reading a book about game shows and a book of poetry at the same time, which is weird. I picked up the habit when I was little, from two of my grade-school teachers.

I'd like to be a writer or do some kind of social work. A house in the suburbs just isn't for me. The PTA and the carpool and the house with the mortgage, that doesn't appeal to me. I don't want to be thirty years old with three kids and my Maytag. I would go crazy. My father's worried that I'd marry some very crazy, unorthodox type of eccentric person like me. He'd like to see me marry some nice Joe Citizen that pays all his parking tickets.

My parents think I stay out too late, because I'm not afraid of being out at night alone. I know everybody in my neighborhood, and it just doesn't bother me. I don't think anything's going to happen to me. Why should I be afraid? I trust people until they give me a reason not to. Usually, I'm not disappointed.

I think everybody has some good in them, if you can find it. I don't think there's anybody that's born bad or born cruel. If you dig deep down enough, there's something in everybody. My dad says I dream too much. But I think there's good in people. I can't say: "Oh, that is a bum." I just can't do that. I'm always looking and hoping there's something there. I can't write 'em off.

I hate to say I'm religious, because I don't go to church. That would be hypocritical. I believe there's a God. I don't know. I *hope* there's a God. I pray when I'm worried and when I pray, I talk. When I'm worried about my friends, I talk. I don't know how I'm supposed to pray. If there's a God, He'll do something. That's about it. I say: "Well, God, here I am in trouble again, talking to you now."

I fear for the world sometimes. I wonder if we're really gonna make it to the year 2000. What is it gonna be like? I worry about the people. What can be done? For myself, I don't worry about much. Whether or not to go to college. (Laughs.) Getting old.

I feel old. To me, every day is a day gone, whether you're five, ten,

* General Equivalency Diploma

or sixteen. My friends are always looking at me: "Is she crazy?" That's sixteen years that are gone now. (Laughs.) I don't worry about getting physically old. That doesn't bother me. Just not accomplishing anything and getting old, that bothers me. What have I done in all these sixteen years? Sixteen years is a long time to be alive and not really doing anything but going to school.

I learned all the whitewash things. I didn't learn about America in school. I learned what they wanted me to learn. What I feel about America, I learned on my own. In school, everything was just great: We never did anything wrong. Everything was justified. Up until I was thirteen, I believed that. After that, I turned myself off, and from then on it was my own opinion.

I like living here. I should appreciate it more. We have so much freedom and stuff. We take a lot for granted. I don't know if it's the greatest place to live, because I've never been anywhere else. So I'm not gonna say it's the greatest until I know. I know it's a good place. At the moment, I wouldn't want to live anywhere else.

THE GRADUATES

SAM LOPEZ, 27

He's the director of the Uptown Center, an adjunct of Northeastern University.

I first met him when he was twelve, a boy in trouble with the authorities and with his family. One of many Chicago West Side Latino kids.

He's the fourth oldest of ten children.

My first year in public school, I was put in an EMH* program for the mentally handicapped. I didn't speak English properly. You had black kids, you had poor white kids, classified as mentally handicapped. I remember the other kids saying: "There's the crazy kids." You felt it. Kids your own age, seven, eight years old, poke fun at you.

* Educational mentally handicapped

When I first got into school, I just couldn't understand a lot of things. I would have considered myself a normal seven-, eight-year-old kid.

Both my parents were illiterate and really didn't understand about school meetings or sitting down and talking to the teacher. I believe my dad went to the eighth grade, but my mother cannot read or write. They both worked in factories. They didn't know how to talk about their kids' problems.

My family was pretty strict. The males were the ones that had the freedom. The females were the ones that had to stay home, cook, clean house. We boys had the luxury of doing nothing. My sisters took the one way out. They got married at early ages. There's one left. She's the baby, she's fifteen. All my sisters got married when they were fifteen years old. It's tragic. They didn't get a chance to experience their life.

My parents weren't home a lot of the time. If they had work, they carried jobs on the night shift, so we were left to do whatever we wanted.

I'm twenty-seven. Some of the things I've experienced, places I've been to . . . When I sit down and talk to them about my experiences, and when I see they have three, four kids and they're twenty, twenty-one, it's kinda sad. I was a regular street kid. At age nine, I was out till eleven at night. I was introduced to drugs when I was about nine, ten. Sniffin' glue.

I think all parents want their kids to have good things. But in my family, school wasn't the number one factor. The males make it through grade school, possibly through the first year of high school, quit and get a job, help support the family. I can preach to my younger brothers about going to school. They've quit. I'm the first one in the family, of all the generations, that went to college.

I'm embarrassed all the time when I go home. I'm put on a pedestal. I just feel funny about it. Everybody says: "Sam's comin'! He's here! He's here!" Everybody sits around the table. Here comes my professor. (Laughs.) What always gets me is just because you're a college graduate, they think you have the answers for everything.

I was always the rebel. I was always called the black sheep. I was the adventurous one. I wasn't afraid to experiment with drugs, to be out late at night. My oldest brother was in a Latino gang. He would bring home downers, drugs. He would be afraid to take 'em. I'd say: "Give 'em to me if you don't want 'em." (Laughs.)

As time went on, I began to hate school. As a little kid, I had curly hair. The others would say: "Look at sheephead." One way to get attention, you cause a ruckus. I was always the one to disrupt the class, because everybody else, the smart ones, were getting attention.

One teacher pushed me down a flight of stairs because I was late. I'll always remember her. She was an enormous woman. She wore bobbysocks with high-heeled boots. She was at the top of the stairs. "Lopez, you're late." Everybody else was Johnny or Jim or Joe. I was always Lopez. (Laughs.) She started poking me in the chest so hard that I fell down a flight. All I can remember was this rage. I ran up the stairs and punched her, and I ran out. Before you know it, a truant officer came. I was suspended twenty-two times in grade school.

One day a cop brought me home about ten-thirty one night. My parents said: "We want nothin' to do with him." My mind went blank. What the hell are they talking about? The police took me to the Audy Home.* That's the first time I was ever there.

"A guy grabbed me by the back of my shirt: 'Sit down, take off your shoes.' There's a whole ritual they make you go through. They frisk you. It's a prison for juveniles. They take kids from under twelve to sixteen, I think. I sat there, and he slapped me on the back of my head. 'Pick up your shoes by the toe and pound them on the floor.' If you have anything, it will fall out. Okay?

"All I can remember is a cold, dingy place. Everything was one-two-three. If you don't follow the rules, you're put in Blackstone. It's like isolation in prisons. The hole.

"Your whole day was sitting in a room, listening to the radio, and watching television. The Dating Game was a big hit because it dealt with women. There was no educational program, no counseling. If you're only gonna be around for two weeks, till your court appearance, you stay in intake. You do absolutely nothing. You just deteriorate. Everybody's lumped in one room, tempers are hot. We sat there from six in the morning until ten at night, except for meals. If you're gonna be there for a month, you go upstairs, where you're assigned to classes and jobs.

"My first night, I was sexually accosted by another kid. All of a sudden, this guy was in the bed with me. His hand was over my mouth. I was terrified. We started tussling about and shoving. The guard came in. The kid told me: 'If you say anything, that's it.' The

* A city home for children in trouble

guard said: 'What's goin' on?' No one said nothing. It was in the
winter. He opened the windows for the whole night, while we slept
freezing.

"Before you go to bed, they tell you to spread-eagle. They look up
your butt hole. They tell you to run your fingers through your hair.
What they're looking for is cigarettes or knives.

"You have kids who have serious problems and kids who are just
runaways from home. They're mixed in one. I was in there, off and
on. The first time, it was for a week."

We went to court, and my parents took me back. I knew I definitely
did not want to be home. And I hated school. As soon as they let me
out, I was back on the street, hanging on corners with guys. I became
one of the leaders in the old neighborhood. Those that have the most
problems and are the most gutsy are looked at as—wow!

Sometimes when I didn't go home, I'd stay with friends. I remember sleeping in a condemned building. It was past a certain hour, and
my dad had threatened me that if I came home late, he'd break my
arms. If I stayed out late, I was gone for two or three days at a time. I
would only come home when I knew he wasn't there. My brothers
and sisters would sneak me in and feed me. Times were hard then.
My dad wasn't working. I remember my brothers and sisters fighting
over the last piece of bread. If there was any meat or whatever, my
dad got it. He was still the honcho of the house. I remember us kids
fighting over what was left. This used to get me so angry. All I could
remember is: I don't want to be like this.

Then, some people came into my life. We'd moved to a neighborhood, mostly Italian. There weren't too many Mexicans. It took me a
long time to get in with the guys. I behaved just like they did. Soon
my name was known all over the community. I was the big guy. If
there was anything coming down in the neighborhood, I was to
blame. That's how Shirley Garzatto heard of me.

She was about twenty-eight, married, and had two kids. I had never
met an artist before, somebody who could paint. I was intrigued. She
introduced me to oil painting, sculpture, writing. We would go to the
Art Institute. Through her and the club at St. Timothy, a lot of us
guys were introduced to the Ice Capades. I'd never been to the Ice
Capades. It was square to go where families went with their kids.
(Laughs.)

That's when I first met Rose. We were in opposing gangs. They
wanted to take over our corner. She was about fifteen. I was thirteen.

Who the hell is this girl? She's controlling all these guys. (Laughs.) As time went on, Shirley and Shirley's husband, Gonz, got us together. Hey, this seems like a real nice home. People cared about one another. They come home, they sit down, they talk. Paintings on the walls.

Shirley and Gonz were determined to keep me in school. I'd go there after school, mad about the day's events, and talk about it. I could never do that at my own house. I began to like it. Someone sitting there helping me. I'd say to myself: Hey, why not stay here? My parents were upset. They confronted Shirley and Gonz. I finally ran away from home. I was gone a couple of weeks, in and out of old buildings, friends' houses. Cops were looking for me. That's when the whole court procedure started.

My parents didn't want Shirley and Gonz to have me, okay? They got their lawyer to have me put away somewhere. Our first time in court, Gonz and Shirley were given the OK to be my foster parents. I was going to school and started to get off the street. My parents were determined to take me out of their house.

We musta been in court now eight times. Every time we'd go to court, I would get very emotional. I couldn't sleep. I'd wake up in the morning with butterflies in my stomach. I felt I was gonna die. You're going before this group of people who really have no idea who you are, what you're about. There were no feelings involved. No one asked: "Sam, how do *you* feel about it?" A guy is sitting high on the top of the bench. The probation officers are standin' around. A person from the state is supposed to be representing me. They were deciding whether or not to send me away. They were talking amongst themselves. I just got angry. I said: "Wait a minute. What about me? Who am I? I'm standing right here in front of you and you're not asking me. I feel like I'm a rubber ball, bouncing all over." I made a little scene in the courtroom. They decided to send me away to South Dakota. I became a ward of the state. I was fourteen.

"I was on this big airplane for the first time in my life. I got sick as a dog. On the plane, I met this black guy, Kelly. I don't remember his first name. We became very good friends. He was about my age. Before you know it, I was landing where all the cowboys were. All I can remember is everybody asking me: Was I an Indian? I remember driving up this long, dirt road in a big station wagon, nothing, no trees, no buildings.

"The place was called Sky Ranch, run by the Franciscan Brothers.

You picture Catholic Charities as preaching humanistic ways. I saw these guys as guards, that's all they were. If you behaved bad, they had a board. It was made of oak. It had twelve holes in it. The wind resistance slows up a flat board. If you put holes in it, the wind whistles through. So it hits harder. That's what you got hit with. I remember one kid, a fat kid, who was about twelve. He was so brutally beaten with this board, his butt looked like a sun eclipse. You were also hit on the head with keys that they put in their hand.

"Kelly and I made it known that we were gonna be the leaders of this place. There were guys older than we were. Everybody was fighting for recognition. You were forced to say the rosary every night before you went to bed. On my third night there, I said no, this isn't for me. I'm not gonna stay here. So I got Kelly up and we took off.

"It's pitch dark on this dirt road. We're walking through prairies and we're scared as hell. This truck comes along and we told 'em we're brothers. (Laughs.) We weren't thinking, right? Our parents' car ran out of gas and we want to go to the nearest town. It was a pickup and we hopped in the back. We're riding about ten minutes and the guys say: "We're here." It was a town, population seventy-five, the gas station was the firehouse, general store, post office. Here we are in an all-white town. Word was already out that we had been gone. We sat in a bar and the guy gave us a Coke. I guess he called the ranch. They came in and took us back.

"They cut our hair real short so we could be marked as kids who did something bad. We got our lashes with the board. All I could remember is I'm not gonna show this guy any emotion whatsoever. I wouldn't give him the satisfaction of crying.

"When I would get letters from Shirley and Gonz, words would be cut out. What the hell, we're not criminals. They said what was cut out was not good for my mentality.

"One other thing stands out in my mind. A lot of us were playing with a cat. One brother, a tall guy, musta been six four, saw us having fun. He put the cat in a cracker box, got out a 12-gauge shotgun, and shot it right there in front of us. Why?

"Some of 'em would punch you for not listening or not doing your chores. The kids did all the work. We were servants to the brothers. You fed 'em breakfast, you cleaned their plates, you made their beds.

"The brothers would buy pop, candy, but they'd never share it with the kids. Kelly and I decided we wanted some pop. We knew where one of the brothers hid it. So we proceeded to drink twenty-four bottles of 7-Up. (Laughs.) We drank all the pop. We filled the

bottles up with water. The next day, at lunch, he asked one of the kids for 7-Up. He proceeds to drink the water and he spits it out. He went and got the whole case and opened every bottle. He tasted every one and said: 'All right, who did it?' No one said nothing. Kelly and I had developed a rapport with the other kids. They looked up to us. So he says: 'Since no one's talkin', I want a line formed, single-file.' It went all the way up the spiral staircase, three flights. Every one was given a whack. He knew it was us, so he proceeded to punch on us.

"I wasn't learning nothing. All I know is I was lonely and wanted to survive to get home. We were let out for Christmas. I went straight to Shirley's house. My parents somehow found out I was home. The courts came into play again. If I wasn't on that plane to go back to Sky Ranch, I'd be in severe trouble.

"I got tired of just hiding out every night, so I showed up. The court decided that I still couldn't stay with Shirley. Since I didn't want to go to my parents, they sent me away again. It was another Catholic Charities school, in Terre Haute, Indiana.

"They sat me down and told me that if they couldn't straighten me out, nobody else could. They also had a board with holes. We'd invent ways to avoid punishment. When they took movie privileges away, we'd put fingernail clippers or a little piece of mirror on our shoes and watch the movie, with our back to it.

"Working kitchen help was the privileged job because that's where the best food was that the brothers ate. Here again, we were servants to the brothers and priests. They had a whole cabinet full of liquor, and they would have parties. I would collect all the drinks in one glass and drink it. So I got into some problems.

"One brother was out to get me. From the day I came in, he said: 'Watch your step. Let down your barriers, I'm gonna catch ya. And when I do . . .' I never did nothing to him, I'm new at the place, at breakfast time, I was supposed to serve. You had those white jackets and bow ties and a napkin around your arm. You were assigned tables and they had a little bell.

"This guy asked for coffee. I put the pot on the stove and heated it. I had potholders holding it, and I sat it on the table. I got out as quickly as possible, knowing he was gonna pick it up and burn himself. He picked up the pot and you heard: 'Awwww!' He yelled: 'Lopez!' He marched me down to the room where they would hit the kids. You stand spread-eagled, with your legs open, and you'd have to hold your ankles. He said: 'Lopez, I finally caught you.' You could just see the glee in his eyes, that he really wanted to lay the wood.

He hit me with the board ten consecutive times. Again, I didn't cry, I didn't flinch, I didn't budge. After the beating, I stood up and said: 'Are you satisfied? Are you pleased?' I was very sarcastic. He said: 'Lopez, get down.' This time, he faked me out. If I'da known he was gonna kick me, I woulda been prepared. He came with the board, lifted it away, and came up with his foot and got me in the crotch, and down I went. I can remember crying. (Laughs.) They took me upstairs to bed.

"They always had psychological counselors asking questions. Telling me to look at a bunch of scrap paper and what I see in it. (Laughs.) I developed good rapport with one brother, the only one who felt for the kids. He said: 'There's no way you're gonna get out unless you do what you're told.' So I finally decided to do my bit and they released me. I was about sixteen."

My parents picked me up at Terre Haute. On the way to Chicago, I told my dad I'm not coming home. You can beat me, put me away, but I won't go. One night I was home. The next day I was gone. I tried going back to high school, but I couldn't deal with it. Shirley got me into the Art Institute. I took sculpture classes, did some oil painting. At one time, because of Shirley, I wanted to be an artist. She gave me books to read. *Down These Mean Streets* and *Manchild in the Promised Land.* When I read those books, I saw myself. I guess she was the person that put it into me to be somebody.

I got a job as head shipping clerk. I was all excited about it. I'm waiting for the other guys to show up. I go to the boss and ask. He says: "What other guys? You're the head shipping clerk." (Laughs.) I did volunteer work, reading for little kids in Uptown and helping on a drug-abuse program.

What I didn't like were these middle-class social workers coming into the community, with a condescending attitude toward the neighborhood people. Just using their theories to solve problems. I remember encounter groups and people crying: "Touch me, feel me." Fortunately, they folded.

I was about twenty. I was attending college and working at the center, helping design its programs. My major at Northeastern was in psychology. I was intrigued. I took classes in human behavior and adolescence. If I learned anything, I learned about myself. I don't think it prepared me for a job, but it prepared me to understand my being.

The students we recruit at Uptown are ex-cons, former drug addicts, dropouts, unemployed. I feel we can't take them on unless we take on the social ills they bring with them. A person can't go to school if he's having a housing problem. He can't study if he's having a health problem. If we're gonna be in the community, we've got to deal with what affects these people outside the walls of the center.

Not long ago, as I was coming down the stairs, I saw Rose, the leader of the rival gang from the old neighborhood. I said: Oh, no— do I say hello? Finally, I said: "Rose!" She looked at me, I looked at her. We really didn't know what to say. She told me she was trying to get into a neighborhood college. I convinced her to come up to the center and talk to me about school. Rose is now running our social welfare program. An official at Northeastern calls up: "Hey, Rose, I have a student on welfare. Can you help?" All kinds of people call: "We heard about the things you've done. Can you help us?" She is absolutely terrific.

I've been pushing Rose. I'd like to have her graduate in three years. We've talked about graduate school. She has tremendous insights about people, people's needs. I think she'd be a great candidate for MSW.*

People have to be educated. Poor people and working people are taught, at least by this society, that they're made to be just shit workers. You run the factories, you make our cars, while we get fat. In educating them, we first have to make them aware that something is wrong. And it's not because they're dumb.

I think that's what makes me sad about my parents. What's made me different from them is that I always had that eagerness to get up and go. When I see people being real passive and not having that insight to want to experience different things and try to change, I get mad.

We don't talk about those days, only sometimes I'll hear my ma say, when one of my brothers is acting up: "I'm gonna do to you like we did to Sam." All my brothers and sisters are pretty passive. My dad and ma have learned nothing.

I don't see my life as something of the American Dream. I didn't make it because of the dream. I don't think America helped me, if by America you mean the White House, the system, the elements. I made it because I was aggressive enough to fight the elements that say: "No, you will never make it." I made it because there were certain people in my life, ordinary people, who helped me.

* Master in Social Work, a degree Sam Lopez received last year

I feel optimistic. I see myself moving on. I don't know where I'll be in two, three years. I might be in Texas, who knows where? But I think I will always be trying to bring about change, whether it's in a human being's life or in a community. I like challenges. There's always something.

I'm very amazed, you know. I'm proud of myself. I still carry a lot of anger in me. But I'm dealing with it. I've really worked my ass off. The only thing that gets me is that I want to do more. (Laughs.)

ROSE RIGSBY, 29

My first encounter with her was thirteen years ago. A black heart was tattooed on her pale arm: "Somebody told me, 'You ain't got no heart,' so I put one on my arm."

She was celebrated among her peers in a lower-middle-class white neighborhood in Chicago as a gang leader.* She had quit high school after three months: "I was involved in some kind of trouble." When she was not "away" in city or state institutions, she lived with her mother, stepfather, and ten brothers and sisters.

She had written a long letter to a fifteen-year-old friend who had been "away" for two years in a state institution: ". . . Don't go on like you do, or you'll end up like me, a big fat zero in the eyes of God."

At fourteen, she had written a poem:

> *I'm not a child of my mother nor of God*
> *but a child of my own.*
> *I live not of the soil or sod.*
> *A child of independence, no one holds my hand,*
> *a child not of this earth nor belonging to this land.*

> *If I am for myself alone,*
> *What am I?*

Right now, I'm in college and I work for the Uptown Center. I do people work. It's working with students that aren't regulars. We have to deal not just with the academics. We have to deal with the whole person.

You can't tell somebody, "I'm only interested in the grades you're

---

* Lily Lowell in *Division Street: America* (New York: Pantheon, 1966).

getting," if they don't have any heat or food. It doesn't make any sense. A student comes in and says: "I can't go to class today, I don't have a babysitter for my kids." "The landlord turned the heat off." "I don't have carfare." So we help 'em.

I have a place here. I feel needed. It's important to feel needed. Thirteen years, I didn't think God and I were traveling the same road. (Laughs.) I did feel a big fat zero in His eyes. I never thought I'd find a place to belong in this world. Now . . .

Most people don't feel needed today. They go to their jobs, they become the suit they wear. Like the lady filling out the forms. She becomes so good at it that she really doesn't hear anything you say. You can sit there and talk to her and say the most outrageous things, and she just keeps on filling out her forms.

She asks my religion, and I said something outrageous. She'll say: "Spell it." She asks what race, and I say Negro. She writes it down because she hasn't even looked at me. She doesn't know I'm sitting there.

Thirteen years ago, my life, and now, it was unbelievable. I was walking down the street, taking my son to the doctor, and a fella walked by and said: "Rose." I turned around, I looked and said: "Sam." I haven't seen Sam Lopez for seven years. Out of the blue. We started to talk, and he told me about the programs Uptown was running. It seemed real. Oooh, this is something I could do. He said: "Come up, look around. If you like it, you got a place." It was that simple. I told him it was destiny. (Laughs.)

I didn't completely finish eighth grade. They kicked me out. I didn't *want* to go. What was I learning? I knew how to read and write and add. What else do you have? There was no challenge. What was I making the grades for? They teach you how to conform, how to pledge allegiance, how to believe in the flag, and how to sing "God Bless America."

I'll never forget my Uncle Chuck decided to tell us what America was. We had a guy named Nicky, who didn't want to go in the army. Oh, man, I thought we were going to have a war in the living room. My uncle starts yelling and screaming about jumping out of airplanes, getting shot. This guy Nicky is sitting in the chair, saying: "I don't want to do that." They told him he was a Communist. They said: "Whatsamatter with you, kid, you're seventeen years old, you're supposed to go to war, it's time to go." Then I saw guys bite the dust. I thought bombs were gonna fall any minute. They'd had a few drinks. We're just lookin' at this guy, waitin' for my dad to hit 'im from one side, my uncle from the other. He's just rockin' in the rockin' chair: "I don't wanna do those things." "You gotta do it. Every kid's gotta do it. You gotta grow up and you gotta be a soldier." Then I find out my Uncle Chuck was in the service, but he never fought. He played guitar all through the war. My father got Purple Hearts. (Laughs.)

They told him he would have to fight for his country to stop communism or else he was a Communist. We're sittin' on the couch, waitin' for him to get bombed. We know they're gonna kill him or else kick him outa the house. They're yelling: "I saw my friends die next to me." He said: "I don't want my friends to die." They said: "What's the matter with ya? Friends gotta die. You gotta go fight this war, ya Communist." He tells 'em: "I don't even know what communism is." They tell 'im: "We know what it is. All you gotta do is get Karl Marx, he'll tell ya what communism is." So they run to get out the encyclopedia. They're gonna find Karl Marx. He's still rockin' in the rockin' chair.

They get Karl Marx, and they're reading passages and saying: "Do you understand this?" He said no, still rockin' in the rocking chair. I'm looking over their shoulders to see what they're reading to him. I looked down at the picture of Karl Marx and, oh, my God, it looks like my Uncle Chuck. "Be quiet, be quiet," Nicky says, "they'll bomb you, too." We had to get that guy out of there. I really thought they were gonna kill him. It was a strange night.

What is America? You tell me. Is it the two-car garage and 2.5 children, trees all the same size?

I figure I'm going back to school at twenty-eight years old, I have a better chance of fighting them off if I don't like their ideas. It's not that I want to get an education to be successful. But I just can't be nothing.

I was kicked out of school, I got to be a problem. If you don't do what somebody tells you, you're a problem. We just stick our problems in this institution or that one, and we don't have to look at them any more. We don't have to deal with them on a day-to-day basis. We've eliminated the problem.

I remember when President Kennedy was killed, it was one of my regular visits to the crazy house. We're maybe a hundred people in a big day room, watching the president's funeral on television. The people were crying, but they didn't realize why they were crying. Some were just wandering around, trying to figure out why the rest of us were crying. We were all alone. All we had was each other. We had our own little America: a hundred crazy people. I think there are a lot of crazy people walking around. They'll tell you they are sane, but they're not.

I saw the craziest judicial system that ever existed. It was called juvenile court. What due process of law means does not exist here. You don't have the right to speak for yourself. They give you a caseworker to speak for you. Nobody asks you anything. They all talk to one another.

Your great crime: you're incorrigible. We put the problem away until it's twenty-one. If the problem is thirteen years old, it's doing eight years time for what? Being a problem. The things we continue to do in the name of justice in a crazy house. We tell them: Stay in your place. When people revolt against that, we call them names. We put labels on 'em.

My family always had enough to eat and a place to stay, but there was never any talk of college. There was never money for that. The main thing was to see you through high school. They never talked about what's going on in the country. I had a big argument with my mother about the Vietnam War. She said: "There's a solution for the whole thing." A problem kid? Put it away. A problem country? Bomb it into the ocean.

I'm a counselor. I don't have a title. I don't want a title. We had a case of this man and wife. They were both going to school. They had two children. They told the father he should go to work, not school. They are on welfare, and the man doesn't have training to be anything. What we try to do is get this guy enough money to live on and feed his children while he goes to school. He has a dream for himself, for his family. You can see it in people's faces. They have been told so long that their dreams aren't worth anything. When you see 'em come back and start up, you wanta keep 'em going. The system says: No, he's able-bodied, let's get him to work.

He has a problem with the English language. He's Spanish-speaking. First you got to get it over, he's not stupid. It's just language. We had a great lawyer, and she did a hell of a job and we fought 'em on their own grounds and beat 'em back. It meant something to this man and his wife and two little kids. We got him what he was entitled to. After eight months. I can't tell you the feeling. It was a natural high. We were all floatin' around.

Thirteen years ago, when I first met you, they'd say: "Hey, that's Rose, that gang leader—she's trouble."

From leader of the problems to dealer of the problems, huh? (Laughs.) That's a long way, huh? I didn't have any hope then. I would stay in the neighborhood and probably marry some guy that would beat me up and drink a lot. I would have a ton of little kids running around, sometimes enough to feed 'em, sometimes not. That would have been it. If I had a husband that worked every day and only beat me up once a month, I should keep my mouth shut.

The day I met Sam Lopez, I had finished my GED* and I'd be eligible to go to the college of my choice. I took the test because I wouldn't have been happy working in that factory. Someday I'd wake up and be fifty years old and I'd say: "Oh, my God, I've made nine thousand candy bars and I'm totally unhappy."

My mother said to me recently that she was proud of me. I waited twenty-nine years to hear her say that. I have much more understanding of her than I had before. I'm not in conflict with her now. She's having conflicts with herself. She always saw her job as raising children. All of a sudden her job's over. There's nothing left. She wakes up, she's fifty-two, fifty-three years old, and says: "Who needs me any more? They're all gone." She and my father cared very much for their children but didn't know what to do. She called me up and wanted to know if I could help her. That was a complete turnabout.

There was a lot of fears she had. I think a lot of things she feared were in herself. They were coming out in her children, and she didn't know how to deal with them. They were coming out in one child, specifically—me. Maybe she saw things in me she wished for herself. Certain strengths, and she was afraid of those things. My mother's not a fighter, she's a quiet, hard-working woman. She was afraid of people that fought back. I think she's questioning for the first time in her life.

We learned a lot of prejudices where we grew up. Blacks on one side of the tracks, Latinos on the other. Our street-corner gangs, their gangs. We learned where our place was supposed to be. I see friends now who learned it too well. I see this girl I went to grade school with, married, divorced, married again, got four little kids. I'll talk to her and tell her: "You can get out of this." She says: "I can't do what you're doing. I'm not good enough. I'm not smart enough." They were told they were no good, they would always be bums. They were told by their parents, by the police, by the school, by the neighbors yelling out of windows: "Hey, get off this corner, you don't belong

* General Equivalency Diploma

here. You're just a bunch of bums." They all grew up believing that. Some of the people I see now, I just want to shake them and tell them: "You don't have to believe that any more."

Remember the last two lines of that poem you wrote when you were fourteen?

Yes. (Softly) "If I am for myself alone,/What am I?" I think we're all connected. I must have found my place. I must have found my connection.

THE GIRL ACROSS
THE TRACKS

SARAH PALMER

She's in the back seat of the car, talking a blue streak. We're leaving her town in northeastern Minnesota—population: around 2500—heading toward the Eveleth Airport and then Duluth.

She is the mother of three: two boys, ten and eight; and a girl, six. She is twenty-seven, unmarried.

"My grandfather came from Ireland, my grandmother's people from Norway. She was sixteen years old when she married him, a lumberjack. They had babies in the prairie. Little twins, and they both died. There was no medical care for miles."

My stepfather's a miner, iron ore. He and my mother had two children. I was between marriages. My two brothers and my next sister were born to her second husband. My two oldest sisters were from her first husband. There are eight of us, and we share four fathers.

We were ostracized because my mother's an alcoholic. Constant harassment and assaults all the time at school. You go play with a kid in her yard, the mother comes out and screams and tell you to get out of there, because you aren't any good, because you're a Palmer kid. For me, it's always been that way.

When I was fourteen, I bummed around with friends and stayed here and there. Then I moved in with my little boy's father, Bill, and his parents. I got pregnant with Joey, and I moved away to my sister's in Minneapolis. I wouldn't marry Bill because it wasn't what I wanted to do. His parents accepted me, totally. I took care of their little kids and they went and drank, so it was fine.

Bill's father worked in a mine in Hibbing and his mother was a bar waitress. My stepfather worked in the mine and my mother was a bar waitress. You know the terrible thing? I'm working in the same bar she worked in.

I skipped school pretty frequently because I'm bright. I was born bright. There's a hereditary thing. My grandmother was teaching school at sixteen. My mother graduated from high school at fifteen. God, she was bright. Or is. Whatever. There's not much left of her now, though.

I stayed at places until people didn't want me there any more. I'd sneak down in their basements until their parents caught us. "Get outa here." I was too small to pass for eighteen, couldn't get work. The summer I was fourteen, I babysat for a woman for three months. 1964. Believe it or not, we didn't know much about pot even then. Our big thing was Pfeiffer's Beer. (Laughs.)

When I was sixteen, with Joey in Minneapolis, I got my first job. I worked in a White Castle as a carhop. I worked as a food waitress, as a cook, as a bartender. I worked in offices and almost went crazy.

All these years, I've wanted to raise my children and teach them. I wanted to give them the security and nurturing we all need, to develop well, so we're not twisted. Our psyches can get so bent out of shape if we're not constantly caressed and reassured. My main goal since I conceived my oldest child was to be a good mother. And have my children grow up the way I'd like to have grown up myself.

Oh, I would have liked to have gotten up in the morning and have clean clothes to wear and have food on the table. Have a mother there with food for me. I would like to have gone to school in my pretty little dress and my nice shoes and my hair maybe in braids or pigtails or curls. And come home from school and have my mother sitting there, waiting with lunch and a kind word or something. That's my American Dream. I thought normal families were like *Leave It to Beaver*.

Beaver gets up in the morning. Mommy's there, Daddy's off to work, and everybody kisses good-bye. Beaver goes to school, comes home at lunch. His mother's sitting there with homemade soup and a glass of milk. In the evening, Daddy's coming home from work, and they all sit down after they've washed up and they have dinner together. And everybody's so interesting and important to one another. I watched *Leave It to Beaver* when I was between eight and twelve years old, I suppose.

I wanted to be a normal mommy, what I thought was normal. So I cleaned my house many times, tried to attach myself to men I really didn't care about but I felt that I should. I wanted to make a "family." (Laughs.) Gradually, I realized that a family doesn't have to be *Leave It to Beaver* to be real. In fact, it's much more real if it's not.

My family, it's hardly *Leave It to Beaver*. Bobby and Jeannie jump on the couch, and if you walk by, they spring on you sometimes. Joey will take his bike apart and television sets and stereos. Sometimes he can't put them together again, but, by golly, he knows how they work. Bobby, they call him Bobby Barbarino at school, 'cause he's cool. From *Welcome Back, Kotter*. John Travolta plays Vinnie Barbarino. So Bobby's now Mr. Cool. (Laughs.)

Jeannie, she's got big brown eyes and long brown hair and just a cupid face, just a darling way of her. And she's aware of every bit of it, really. She's six, she'll be seven. She's a flirtatious woman.

She watches *Charlie's Angels*. She identifies with it. I think she's uncomfortable with the way I am because I'm not terribly feminine. I think Jeannie feels that I am not exactly what she wants to be when she grows up. Her father visits her: "How would you like a nice little dress? When we go to Grandma's house, she'll put your hair up in curls." She plays the flirtation game with her father, too. Little girls always do. She'll roll her eyes up at him, and he'll buy her an ice cream cone. She'll walk across the room and look coyly back over her shoulder, and he'll kiss the earth she walks on. She does take very much advantage of him.

The kids haven't watched *Charlie's Angels* this summer. I won't have 'em playing manipulating games in our house.

Since I've been on my own, I've discovered I'm not responsible for anybody's actions but my own. I'm not responsible for anybody's life but my own. Except for my children, until they're old enough to be responsible for theirs. Therefore, somebody can come up to me and say: "Your mother is an alcoholic." Depending on how they say it, I can say: "You're right, she is." Or I can walk up and pop them in the chops a few times and convince them that it's none of their business.

I've run into a lot of girls like myself, but they haven't made it. I found myself. I've just been finding it out all along. About a year ago, I finally felt I arrived at some kind of peace within myself. Most of my friends have sold out or gone into hiding. Getting married to somebody they don't care for, just to have financial security. Having abortions because they don't want the burden of having a child. Marrying somebody is prostituting yourself. Killing a child because you don't choose to have a child around to mess up your head, it's not a very kind thing at all.

I feel strong about this because I was an unwanted child. There was never room for me. I know if I had another child, there would always be room in my home, in my life. That child would be eagerly awaited and welcome.

We have welfare. We get four hundred twenty-four dollars a month, and that's kinda hard sometimes. They attempt to put me down sometimes: clerks when you use food stamps, sometimes drunks in bars. You go out for an evening after the kids are in bed. Your friend watches them and you go uptown for a drink, and a drunk comes up and says: "You welfare mothers are all alike, getting drunk all the time." I make no secret of being a welfare mother. I don't hide behind anything. I don't need that. I am on welfare because my children need to eat and I need to eat, and that's that. Welfare bum? They've said it, but it's behind my back. They don't come up to my face and say it.

I'm going to get off welfare myself as quickly as I can. I don't feel I owe any gratitude to the welfare system, because they're not doing it out of the kindness of their heart. They're doing it because they're forced to do it. That's the only thing. You go in the office, and they look at you like you're an object or a nonhuman something. They make you sit. You have to sit for as long as they want. They go for a coffee break. When they do come in, they're so impersonal and so patronizing. They're in that huge old building, a mausoleum. You sitting in there and you hear echoes. People walk down the hallway and their shoes echo. It doesn't matter.

I was taught in school—Horatio Alger, okay? Nose to the grindstone. As a girl, I was taught: "Don't get mud on yourself, don't get dirty." By teachers. My mother was there to tell me that. (Laughs.) Little girl this and little girl that. I had no influence as to how to be a woman or a person—or how to be anything. The only thing I knew was how to be me. I had very few neuroses to wipe off. Very few indelible marks on my soul. (Laughs.)

You know my dream since I was five? To be a writer. Isn't that funny? Sometimes I even break down and write poetry. I'd tell stories to my teachers, and they had me read them over the tape player because I enunciated everything so well. I went to eighth grade and then I got my GED. I got a scholarship off that when I was nineteen. I had a year at the University of Minneapolis. I went because—what else do you do with a scholarship? I thought everybody who took the GED gets a scholarship. I didn't know it was because of my high grades.

I'm satisfied with the way I am right now and the way my children are developing. I feel like I've reached a plateau, and I'm ready to start climbing again. Oh, I'm very strong and very intelligent. It's true, I won't deny it.

I'm dependent on welfare, but I'm independent in myself. I don't need a man to depend on. Each of my children have their own father. I don't want to be married, though each has asked me. I don't feel they're people I want to be married to. Joey's father woulda married me, but we were both too young and I didn't like him any more. Bobby's father first tried to get me to have an abortion, and I wouldn't do it. Then he tried to persuade me to go away, have the baby, give it up, come back, and then we'd be married. I said: "No, I'll do it this way. I'll have my baby, and you get out of my life." When I told Jeannie's father I was pregnant, he said: "Oh, no, I don't want to get involved." Far out. He said: "What am I going to do?" I said: "I don't know what you're going to do, but I'm going to have a baby." He tried to get me to go to New York or someplace to have my baby ripped from my womb. I told him to go away. Not quite so gently.

I'm not concerned what they'd say about me, but I'm afraid my children'd get what I got because of my mother. But I know now I was right. If a child has a home to come to, it doesn't much matter what happens to him on the street. 'Cause when he comes home, if his mother's there—"Hey, you want to make a cake tonight?"—they know they've got a home, they've got strength, and they've got a mother who'll say: "Leave my kid *alone*." My main job now is teach my children how to roll with the punches.

My kids are in school all day now, so I'm looking forward to time on my own, time to grow. I haven't finished, of course. Nobody does.

FAMILY PORTRAITS

FRANK MUELLER

He had volunteered to drive me from Frankfort to eastern Kentucky.
"I've been attending the university, off and on, for about ten years.
I take courses I enjoy. I'm not interested in any goal or degree. I let
my curiosity guide me."
On the way back, there is time for reflection.
He is twenty-six.

Before I was seven, in Muncie, Indiana, I remember every day of
my life, at noon, listening to the big red radio in the kitchen. *Paul
Harvey News.* My mother needed it. She thought the things he said
were profound. What she enjoyed most were those little human-
interest things. The voice of conservative America that's kind of
fallen apart. It doesn't have the widespread acceptance it had at one
time.

My father didn't listen, at that time, to anybody. He was suffering
from failure in his life. In the late fifties, he got a shot in the arm with
a new job. He was a phone solicitor. He grabbed a hold of the ball
again and ran with it. He probably would have gained the success he
was always after if it hadn't been for my mother's death. It knocked
the pins out from under him. He had been treating her badly, and I
guess the guilt got him. He was tailspinning again.

He was of German-American stock. Both his parents came over on
the boat. It was right at the turn of the century, and there were aspirations kickin' about. His family instilled in him a desire for monetary
achievement. Several members of his family did achieve.

My father couldn't settle on anything long enough to make that
kind of money. He was bouncing around too much as far as the family
was concerned. The few ventures he got into were shot down by the
depression. It beat him badly. He was a gifted individual. I think
everybody felt that. He had a couple of years of college at a time when

everybody didn't get a couple of years of college. He just couldn't seem to make 'em click. He says himself he's been a flash in the pan all his life. He says it even today. He's in his seventies.

He really believed that if he worked hard enough, he'd achieve the success he wanted. The depression shot holes in these certainties. He talks about it now, forty years later. Hard work won't necessarily bring about success. It embarrasses the other members of my family who feel they might lose status by this man's failure.

After my mother died, my father and I were with each other, off and on. We had several little fallings-out. He had always been a salesman and was always embellishing. He lied about a lot of things, and that began to get on my nerves. I couldn't trust him a lot of the time. I said things a kid shouldn't say to his father. He said things he shouldn't have said to me. I was twelve when I left him.

I stayed with my brother and his wife for a while. Then I stayed with another brother who lives in Lexington. At seventeen, I lived by myself. After my mother died, I found it necessary to be independent. When I was *very* young, I was accused by everybody in the family of being overly independent. It was necessary.

In the last two, three years, he's acquired a level of understanding of what I'm pursuing. But he doesn't approve of my aspirations. He thinks it's downright silly to employ myself in writing poetry. Writing generally is a waste of time in his estimation. He's always played down the written word. He claims his mind gets ahead of his pen. He's a real gifted man with speech. He can sway people just by talking to them. Salesman to the *n*th degree.

I always identified with Willy Loman's son Biff. But my father's not Willy today. He's questioning everything now. He's quite sick and is faced for the first time in his life with the absolute of death. He wishes for it. He's tired of living. It's become a burden to him. He's withdrawn to himself. He was always a gregarious person who needed to be around people all his life. Now he stays in his apartment and refuses to leave it. He lives on Social Security, on crossword puzzles, and on solitaire. He plays it for hours. He hasn't been more than twenty-five feet away from the apartment in three years. That's the fact of the matter.

When he's questioning all the things he did with his life, it really disturbs my older brothers. It knocks the pins out from under their conception of "father."

I have three brothers. The one next to me works in a factory as a machinist. He's the only one who doesn't measure his success in dollar signs. He's incredibly gifted, the student of the family. My father never encouraged scholarly endeavor, inquisitiveness. My other brothers, like my father, chastise him because he doesn't apply himself to making a lot of money. He's content, doing what he wants to do. He loves to hunt and fish and enjoy life.

My oldest brother is molded in the vein of my father, a gregarious, silver-tongued devil. Worked for one company for years as a salesman and went up quite high, then took a good hard shot in the fanny. They canned him. His bullshit caught up with him. He bounced back and got a hell of a fine job by anybody's standards. He's got a $70,000 home and a level family.

My other brother is quiet and methodical, real sharp in math. He works for Rockwell International. Started out hoisting seventy-pound gears all day, decided this shit was not for him, hotfooted it out here, got himself in as foreman, and now he's in acccounting, makes tens of thousands of dollars a year. They're both damn near the success set by our family's standards.

My father's staying with me and my wife. My brothers' wives don't want him around. They come right out and say so. I think he represents the horror of failure. Both my oldest brothers and my father were steeped one hundred percent in the idea of strength and supremacy, machismo and success.

For the last five, six years, I've done a lot of menial work. I really enjoy it. Besides pushing a broom here and there, I've worked in restaurants, I've baked pies and stuff, I've washed dishes. At one time, I used to look down at those jobs. I don't know why. I think it was handed to me via my family. Kurt Vonnegut calls them "truths at your mother's knee." My father's more likely than my mother's.

BETH CAMPBELL

She is an editor on the staff of a midwestern magazine. She is twenty-eight.

"My father wanted me to get a teaching certificate or take secretarial courses so I could cope in the real world. He sees the world as a real hard place . . ."

My father just worked. He brought work home. He worked late into the night. He worked weekends. He lost touch. I don't know who his friends are any more. He talked about retiring in five years. I can't imagine what he'll do. I don't think he even enjoys his job that much. He's very generous and has always sacrificed for his family.

Something happened with his company, the one he worked for. He's self-employed now. He doesn't get all his money. They held back a certain amount he's supposed to get in retirement. All of a sudden the company announced: "We're not gonna give you as much as we told you originally." And they got away with it. After that, he didn't believe any more. It made him question business. He thought they were paternal, they wouldn't do anything to hurt him, he's worked so hard. All of a sudden, they screwed him. I remember he looked so weary and worn out. I worried about him dying. (Laughs.) It was some kind of disillusionment with business, with free enterprise or whatever it was he believed in so much. All of a sudden, I felt: Is everything my father worked for really going down the drain?

All the kids have moved away to other states, no one's close. He sees them once or twice a year. He continues to work real hard, and I'm not sure what for. The big house? We have a summerhouse with boats on a lake that we all loved when we were kids. I won't go there this summer. My younger brother won't go there this summer. My older brother will go with his kid and spend a week there. And that's it. So there are all those empty boats, pulled up on the beach. And old bathing suits hanging on the line. It makes me real sad. I feel this responsibility to go back to New Hampshire summers, to this lake.

Every weekend something would go wrong. The pump would break, and he'd end up crawling under the house with all the spiders. His weekends were spent pretty much maintaining our resort. My mother and her mother spent a whole summer there, and my father still comes up on weekends. She feels guilty as can be. A broken motor-boat is on the beach. There's a sailboat that's pulled up. There's a canoe that's pulled out. There's another that's moored on the dock, floating listlessly. (Laughs.)

My father once talked about selling the house. I'd hate for him to sell it 'cause my best memories are from New Hampshire.

I dream about it all the time, empty boats. (Laughs.) I think of the toolshed, too. It was a place to change bathing suits. When you come back, you see your bathing suits from past years, mildewing, hanging up on little hooks. All the old games are there—tetherball and badminton sets. They're just toys in the attic.

I don't have any sense of the American Dream. It may have been my father's dream, but to me it wasn't a dream at all. I talked about it with him once. He kept defending himself and saying: "I am happy." I was really angry at him. How could you have totally denied all your own wants? You've lost it all, and no one appreciates it. He has to deny it because if he were to accept it, his whole life would seem sad. But he did give me wonderful memories, and all that stays with me.

My own dream has nothing to do with other people. It has to do with a dirt road and picking blueberries, eating outside, hearing waves. I'm very much a city person now. I go to movies all the time. I go to plays. My dream is to leave it all and go back to my childhood. My father's dream, my childhood reality, is now my dream. But I can't go back. It doesn't seem possible.

All the lines in my father's face, it's not just aging. He feels out of touch. When I was young, I saw him as a hero. He seemed handsome, athletic, rich. I remember him giving my mother money for shopping, seeing ten-dollar bills, twenty-dollar bills, coming out of his pocket.

My mother would get mad at me and say: "You kids are spoiled brats. You don't know what it was like to live in the depression." She's weird about money. They go to Europe for vacations. She always took pride in going to Filene's basement and getting bargain clothes. She feels guilty about spending money. He never let us know about money. It almost embarrassed him. If he bought a new car, we'd see him drive in. It would be a surprise.

When I was young, he seemed very competent. When I became an adolescent, I didn't like him any more. He seemed corny. He seemed too proud of me, always wanting to brag about me, show off his daughter. It just embarrasssed me. I think I was real mean to him at that age, real cold. I remember my mother saying: "How can you treat your father that way? It really hurts him." When I was in college, I felt real guilty. He paid for it. I couldn't wait to have a job. I didn't want to owe him anything. I took great satisfaction in being my own provider.

He kept saying I was selling myself short. Apply to Radcliffe, apply to this place, that place. I said: "Dad, I'm not the smartest kid in the class." He'd say: "You can do it." I would end up crying. My parents puzzled about that. They don't understand where their kids' lack of self-confidence comes from. I think it comes from them always pushing us.

None of his kids is real competitive. He always wanted us to go out there and compete. None of us played competitive sports. My mother would say: "People will walk all over you." I'm secretly competitive.

(Laughs.) I'm embarrassed by winning, I'm ashamed of losing, so I avoid a situation where I have to either win or lose.

My father very much believes in capitalism and the free enterprise system. I remember him when I was pretty young having an argument with this kid. My father was really enraged. Without competition, you don't have any free enterprise. He was just furious.

He wouldn't feel any embarrassment about admitting voting for Nixon. My mother was always coy about how she voted. He's opposed to things like welfare. "I worked hard. I didn't have special benefits." He doesn't say all this, but it's his thinking. His father worked real hard, paperboy and stuff, and he doesn't want to see anybody get anything free. My younger brother would argue with him. My older brother has adopted his point of view. I'm totally apolitical.

I have to force myself to read newspapers. I live in more of a fantasy world. I wasn't political in the sixties. It made me uncomfortable. I felt real confused. It was a difficult time for me. I avoided as much as I could. I was pretty ignorant of Vietnam and all that. I feel I should have done things, but it doesn't come naturally to me.

I don't have a sense of this country. It seems so distant and far removed from me. I don't feel like I'm an American, 'cause I don't know what it means to be American. I only know what it is to be Beth. (Laughs.) I am ashamed. I can't be generous with others unless I've taken care of myself.

I'm kind of detached curious. I like to be in control of my own world. I want a certain amount of detachment so I can maintain control. The thing that's made me sad lately is that I am aware that I don't keep old friends. I just burn my bridges behind me. When I left my old job, it was a relief not to have to deal with my friends there any more. Whenever there are chances to get together, I try to get out of it. I'm not comfortable with my past, ever. It's my instinct not to hold on to the past.

POSTSCRIPT: *Her father and mother were killed in an auto crash, May 1979.*

◈──◈

A CERTAIN SMILE

JENNIFER TAYLOR

◈──◈

She is twenty-seven. "Most people look at me and think I'm twenty-one. I think I have inside me a childlike curiosity. When people talk to me, they sense that I am older because of my ideas and thoughts." She smiles, laughs, and appears constantly good-natured.

I am a born-again Christian. I look up to God and His Absolutes. But I hate the idea of being called a religious fanatic. I know people who might consider me one. I don't try to convert people. I speak of faith only if the conversation should lead that way. I'm not going to say: "Hey, you need Jesus." I abhor that. I'm not on drugs. I'm not uptight. I do drink.

My parents are Methodists and went to church every Sunday, but it didn't really mean that much to them. I've seen changes in their lives in the past year. They're now watching Billy Graham on TV and Oral Roberts on TV. They never did that before. I think they've seen a change in their daughter when I accepted the Lord, at a Youth for Christ rally. I was thirteen. They see a girl who is really happy about life, and the morals that I have are what they want me to have.

This last time I left home, my dad said: "We'll be praying for you." That just totally floored me. He has never said anything like that before.

When I was in High School in Ohio, a close friend of mine came from a Christian family, a family that believes in Jesus Christ, who came into this world to unite man to God. That's what brought me to Wheaton, a Christian college. Also, I wanted to get away from Ohio and be near a big city like Chicago.

Billy Graham went to Wheaton. I admire the man, and I respect the man, and I believe everything he is saying is scripturally true and that he has been called by God to be an evangelist. I also know, by a friend of mine who does know him, that he lives out what he believes. He isn't just talking. This thing about finances of the Billy

Graham Foundation and stuff like that, I don't know what is true and what is not, but if he is wrong, he will be the one who has to face God about that.

Do you like Oral Roberts too?

Why did you have to ask me that? (Laughs.) I can't answer it. Oral Roberts is more "Put your hand on the TV set and believe that you will be healed." That doesn't come out of Billy Graham.

You don't believe in faith healing?

Yes, I do. Yeah, I do, 'cause I've seen that happen. A friend of mine, one of her legs was shorter than the other. This was in Sweden, and a faith healer prayed for her, and her leg did grow to the length of the other. People could say it was psychological, but I do believe in the Almighty God, who has the power to heal.

I'm one of those people who believes Christianity is the only way. Eastern religions, as I see them, have no room for the individual to grow, be creative, be your own person. In Hare Krishna, they all dress the same and wear their hair the same. I cannot go along with these religions at all.

I was against the war in Vietnam. I did not like America acting as the savior of the world. I did not like our men being killed, being maimed. I can't recall our discussing the war at home. Being in the air force community, my dad worked on the experimental bomber plane. My mom and dad just don't express what their feelings are. I've never heard them say anything against blacks or foreign people. I know they don't have bad feelings towards them.

In college, I was not concerned about issues. I had been a real diligent student in high school, straight A's, in the library all the time. When I came to Wheaton, all of a sudden: Let's have fun, let's go to a party. I'm probably one person who made it through Wheaton who followed the code. Most people don't follow that. No drinking, no smoking, no social dancing. You could do square dancing but not disco dancing.

My sister put it well: "It sounds like you're going to a convent." It never hindered me as a person at all. My sister is four years older than me. She's very pessimistic. In high school, she did try to commit suicide one time by taking a whole bottle of Bufferins. She's a nurse.

Her view of life is down. My view is that God has given me a life to live, and I want to glorify Him and be of service to Him and grow as a person and learn from my jobs and help others. I remember a line from an Emily Dickinson poem: "If I've just helped one person in this life . . ."

At one time I didn't think America was a great land. Now I do. Since traveling extensively through Europe and Mexico and Guatemala, seeing these other countries, I feel we do have real freedom here. There's one other country I do admire and that is Sweden, even though it is socialistic. Elderly people are really taken care of there. They have free hospital care. Two-thirds of their taxes goes to the government, but they have lots of benefits. It would be impossible in this country. I can see the money going into the wrong hands and not being dealt out. We're too large to work as a socialist government.

Success to me is being the kind of person Christ wants me to be. It is not money. I see people with money who have deteriorated as people. I'm not going to bow down to someone because he's a big shot. A boyfriend, because he has a lot of money, is not going to win me over at all. It's his heart inside that counts.

If I was a man, I would probably be a conscientious objector. I would never want to kill. I've become more radical in the last couple of years, so I might be out marching. I'm not so namby-pamby any more. Because I've come to terms with what I feel is right and wrong. I'm a bit more vocal in my beliefs. I stand up for what I believe. I think Christ was a radical, too. In his day and age, saying he was the Son of God, wow.

This is not a Christian country. I see America going downhill. I see people being hard. I see people lying. I see people doing whatever they can to get ahead. I see families breaking up. I see divorces all around. I see the ghettos getting larger. The only hope for change begins when people know Christ is a person. Christ has made the difference in history. The old prophets said: Repent, repent, repent. To a degree, I see that right now. In the Book of Amos, it says to these fat rich Jews—very wealthy—no offense to Jews, it's just this particular case—you're not concerned about the poor, you're not concerned about the people around you. I think that's true. People are just out for themselves.

I don't see hope in man. I see man as basically evil. I'm not a humanist. He believes man is basically good. I believe in Genesis. No, I don't believe in evolution. I see no change for better on this earth.

My optimism comes from the knowledge that there will be a world in heaven where there will be eternal happiness. In the meantime, I want to help the poor and elderly people. I give at least ten percent of my salary to some missionaries, and where I see a person lacking money, I help. I don't know, maybe people were just the same way back in the early days of this country. Maybe the United States isn't as bad off as I think it is. Man is man and has not really changed that much as far as the insides go.

PANDARIK DAS (HAROLD LEWIS)

"Pandarik Das is my spiritual name. Pandarik means 'lotus.' Das means 'servant of God.' My purpose in life now is to come to grips with the question: Who am I really? Am I an American? Do I belong to this society, this family? Am I finished when I die? Or am I something else?"

He is a member of the Hare Krishna. His family is upper-middle-class. He is twenty-five.

I went to private school, one of the more expensive ones. At one time, I thought I'd be a scientist. I can't remember all the other ideas. As I was entering high school, I began to feel very dissatisfied with everything, very angry. The Vietnam War was becoming more hotly debated. Marijuana, LSD, all that was insinuating itself into school life. I was fifteen during the Democratic Convention of '68.

My thoughts weren't clear. Otherwise, I wouldn't have gone on the path of self-destruction. Many of my companions were doing the same thing. I was looking for some way to become satisfied in life. I can't blame my friends. I was one of the leaders in drug taking, muddying, dirtying our minds.

My family had done their best to take care of me, but I was becoming more of an ingrate, more of a burden. They were spending all this money on a private school, and I was shucking it away, taking dope and being angry at them for no reason at all. It was very fashionable at the time: Hate your parents, your country. Hate this, hate that.

I was resentful even to the point of being suicidal. In 1969, when I was sixteen, my parents had me hospitalized. I was in for ten months. It was private, the best, but the psychiatrists couldn't tell you what you were supposed to become, what this is all for. The psychiatrists weren't able to show that there is some pleasure higher than the material. They say they'll make you normal. But what is their idea of normal? I knew pretty much what they wanted to hear from me. So I told them. I can hardly remember what I said, but I had no intention of doing any of it.

I got out in 1970. I was seventeen. The whole world was going by, governments were changing, the sun was going up and down, and I'm just thinking of smoking a joint, some kind of quick excitement. I made a half-hearted try at college. I don't know how much my folks shelled out on that one. At the end of one quarter, it was F, F, F. Again, we're back in the fog. I decided I'd be better off someplace else. Got a cheap hotel room in the French Quarter of New Orleans, got bored, went to Dallas, and almost got killed by some guy with a knife.

I was on a roof, with a knife at my throat, likely not to be alive in another five minutes. That got me to thinking: Why am I wasting my life if at any moment I'm going to die? This body will be cut up and then where am I? I began to think of body and soul, consciousness and matter. Of course, I believe in immortality and reincarnation.

I was thinking about my family again in Chicago. I wanted to give something to them for a change instead of always taking. Hare Krishna devotees were on the street here, too. I took them up on their invitation to Sunday dinner. It was a gradual thing, not a lightning bolt. In the fall of '72, I moved into the temple.

The first symptom you notice is a lessening of anxieties, of desires. People are always unhappy because they can't fulfill these desires, these material dreams. The human being who adopts the philosophy of hedonism is no different from an animal. The animals run around without any clothes and have sex whenever and wherever they feel like. A dog does it in the street. That's a dog's life, not a human being's. It's the nastiest kind of life I can imagine. You can't be happy thinking me, me, me. We surrender to God, the Supreme Me. In serving God, we serve society.

Understanding karma does not allow you to act in an immoral way. We don't go to the airport and hold people up with .45's.

Our salespeople seem to do rather well at airports without .45's. Most of our funds come from the sale of books. Selling doesn't exactly require a Ph.D. You approach somebody in a friendly way, usually the women pin a flower on somebody. There is such a thing as a salesman being too pushy. But we consider it our duty to be very aggressive.

Look, every man, woman, child, animal, everybody on the surface of the earth is going to get old and die. None of these deaths are going to be pleasant. The material world is arranged by God as a place of catastrophes. We've given man too much credit for inventing.

Man has a little bit of independence, trying to serve God or trying to kill God. When human beings misuse their intelligence trying to become gods, trying to defy God, they become responsible for catastrophes. The fault of modern civilization is teaching man that this 150-pound lump is very important.

If you're going to sincerely boo-hoo-hoo about Vietnam or the Robert Taylor Homes, first check the unnecessary violence we're committing against other living entities, because that cheapens our regard for all life. You're not going to get rid of gratuitous violence against human beings if you continue to wantonly slaughter animals.

I made a lot of highfaultin talk about God, but I don't see God. By our Hare Krishna standards, I'm just a barbarian. I have a great journey ahead of me, and it's very exciting.

You're twenty-five. You have a long life ahead of you.

That's your guess.

TOUCHING THIRTY

BRUCE BENDINGER

He's a freelancer in the world of advertising, highly successful. He has worked for some of the large agencies. He now picks and chooses his jobs; he can write his own ticket.

Casually, he describes his apartment. "It's a bilevel octagon, I'd say. This used to be the backyard of a 75-year-old house." A sculpture "reaches almost to the ceiling. It's called Song Without Words. *It's like livin' in a sculpture, really. You kind of flow from one place to another. The light comes through very nicely in the afternoon, bounces off the big painting over our heads." There is expensive hi-fi equipment.*

He is seated at the piano, playing and singing a song he wrote.

> Everybody's runnin' around alone or in crowds
> Got their feet on the ground, the head in the clouds
> See 'em shufflin' on, watch 'em scuffle and scheme
> Everybody's livin' that everyday American Dream.

"—then we do a little jazzy solo in the middle—"

> Ain't no easy answers any more
> So everybody plays at keepin' score
> Talkin' about peace but they keep on makin' war
> Does anybody here really know what people are for?

Oh yeah, I'm doing okay. I have some gifts, and I've been lucky enough to make a living with doing what I enjoy doing, which is kind of making little creative things happen.

I was always writing little skits in school and doing cartoons. Whitefish Bay, Wisconsin. The most famous person who came from Whitefish Bay was Bernadine Dohrn. She made the FBI's 10 Most Wanted list. It's a little suburb north of Milwaukee, very kind of upper-middle-class.

I was one of the war babies. Kids who were born that period, the baby boom, were all very much their parents' dreams. Born in the middle forties. And when you hit the eighth grade, Sputnik hit, so you got all this educational pressure. You go to high school, and you're always moving into a new science lab and a new math course. Just as I was leaving the university, the war hit. I was kind of at the right place at the right time.

I didn't really become aware of it until my junior/senior year in college. When I was a freshman, it was the Cuban missile crisis, and patriotism ran pretty deep then. It was a pretty clear-cut good guys/bad guys thing. For a while it was a kinda nice adventure. You're gonna be a Green Beret or something. I had a kid and a bad back, I was pretty well out of that. I married right after college. It seemed like a good idea at the time.

I went to the University of Wisconsin, and a week after I graduated, I came down to Michigan Avenue, started at J. Walter

Thompson, and I've been in the business eleven years. That was back in the sixties, when things were pretty exciting. They treated me pretty good. I treated them pretty good. I was the youngest this and the youngest that there. I always knew what I could do. I was pretty sure of myself. I was a quick study. That's important in this business because you're always getting a whole bunch of new data thrown at you and you gotta become an instant expert for somebody. It's a strange business. I was one of the *Wunderkinder* on the street. I'm thirty-three now.

I broke in when I was twenty-one. When I was twenty-eight, I was a vice-president and creative director of the biggest agency in Chicago. Being creative is funny. Back in '72, there was a poll in some magazine of creative people in the advertising business, and I was the youngest one in Chicago to be named. I was one of the hundred most creative people in the United States of America. And they spelled my name right. I didn't subscribe to the magazine afterwards, so they named somebody else the next year. (Laughs.)

The week before I turned thirty, I quit the whole thing. And just kind of went my way, making some music, making ads for friends of mine. And been making a living at it now for about three and a half years. I've had a lot of strange experiences. The most strange was spring of 1976 when I was the creative director for the president of the United States. President Ford.

Shaggy beard, long-haired, blue jeans, and there I was in the Republican primaries. I was in the Oval Office for a couple of tapings and watching the president. You know, it was like those little woodpeckers on the side of the glass, where they nod their heads back and forth? He's being briefed on reality by one of a sequence of bright young aides. Nodding his head. That's the government. There was no sense of vision or purpose, except for maybe some leftover Grand Rapids Chamber of Commerce philosophy. The computers are still deducting everybody's paychecks and everything is still working, but I think it's more inertia than a conscious process.

By the time I landed, the thing was really a mess. I just tried to get things straightened up. In the morning you do a couple of sixty-second radio spots for the local primaries: This is Jimmy Ray Lee Bob, and ah want all mah friends in the second Tennessee Congressional district to vote for your president, President Ford. Afternoon, you write positioning memos and plead with whatever people you get to talk to to try and get the man to act like the president instead of somebody who's worried about hanging on to his congressional seat.

Then you shudder at the day's faux pas. By the time I got there, it was already cast in bronze. We were doin' a five-minute speech, and there was a very drastic typo and the guy—this was the president—just read on blindly right through it. It didn't make any sense at all. Everybody was so freaked out, nobody talked about it. It was the emperor's clothes all over again. What did I do? That was it. Every week I picked up my check and flew back to Chicago to spend the weekend with my friends. I did political work in Chicago for people like Adlai.

I've got a personal political commitment. At that point, the political decision was to help Gerald Ford win the nomination from Ronald Reagan. I signed on to help him out until the end of the Republican primaries. I got a reputation in the business for being a handler. Some dumb problems end up getting dumped on somebody's lap, and I got a reputation for handling those sorts of problems.

When I had just started at a large advertising agency, I was a kind of noblesse oblige civil-rights guy. I had a jazz band in high school and made a point of it being integrated. I said to the agency that there were a lot of jobs black people could handle as well as anybody, and maybe it's a good idea if we made a little extra effort to develop some training program and find a couple of bright kids to get in the business.

I went through the channels and was told very politely, just between us WASPs, the company had done as much as it was gonna do. Well, they shot Martin Luther King in Memphis, and back in Chicago, Madison Street burned out for five miles. All that day on Michigan Avenue, you could see the whites of everybody's eyes. Left work early and took the train through the burning city to their suburban homes. Next month, the whole advertising community was very enthusiastically behind a program just like the one I suggested. I don't know where the moral is. It's a hell of a price to pay.

You learn somethin' in the advertising business. Even if the guy's got a Ph.D., his level of attention and awareness is pretty low. It's the old hit the mule with a two-by-four first to get his attention. You got the guy watching the ten o'clock news, and if you want to sell him something, you got to be pretty simple. I don't watch TV much. When I do, I watch commercials more for the technique than to be sold anything. People got a lot on their minds. You can't be subtle. There's no market for it.

In the early seventies, I was creative director of the American Petroleum Institute, just before the energy crisis hit. We were their agency. You're sitting around, and there's the assistant to the President of Mobil and the director of marketing of Gulf and the director of public relations of Conoco and the executive vice-president of Standard Indiana, et cetera, et cetera. All these guys sitting around and nodding their heads wisely, saying: "This winter there will not be a shortage of liquid fuel." And two months later, I'm standing in line with every other *zhlub*, begging for two dollars' worth of gasoline at the gas station.

There aren't too many dreams left. Used to be when you grew up, all these little Horatio Alger books, you'd form U.S. Steel or some big deal. Now the only dreams left are direct a film or be a rock star. I thought maybe I was gonna be a big advertising hero. I was lucky to find out pretty early on that wasn't really it. I found out that wasn't it 'cause I got it. Most people don't have their dreams come true. I had a couple dreams come true. Now I'm trying to save my life on a little more human scale. I'm lucky enough to get hired for being me. When I'm not working, I sit home and tend the garden or write a song about it.

I've been married twice. I live with company. I have a real nice lady. Right now, it's really working. It worked yesterday, it worked today, and it's probably gonna work tomorrow. She's in the rag biz. She handles some French clothing lines and a New York dress line. My daughter lives with her mother in Connecticut. Her dream is to be Nadia Comaneci.

One of the things that kids carry around is a lot of their parents' expectations. We were the childhood they never had 'cause of the depression. We were the abundance they didn't have. We were the security they didn't have. It seemed like it was all going to really work. Here are all the dreams, all the aspirations (slaps hands together)—dead, gone. People no longer operate under the assumption that tomorrow's gonna be better.

I got a song that starts out "Once upon a time." This is a real nice place to put it in. It's called "1955." (He sits at the piano, plays, and sings.)

> *Remember John Foster Dulles on the brink?*
> *Days when we always knew exactly what to think*
> *And thinking positive with Norman Vincent Peale*
> *Days when we always knew exactly how to feel.*
> *Remember Panmunjon and parallel thirty-eight?*
> *Days when enemies were easier to hate.*

Remember when we had a leader named Ike
In days when presidents were easier to like?
Though ignorance is bliss, it seems all good things must end
And it seems that only dreams are here to stay.
It isn't like it was in 1955, my friend.
No, it isn't even like it is today.

I also have a parable of the Oval Office floor. There's an old wooden floor from when the White House was first built. Back in the fifties, Ike walked all over it in his golf shoes and just tore the shit out of this old wood floor. Today, the Oval Office is covered with plastic. It seems a pretty good parable, as parables go these days.

I don't find my attitudes much different than my contemporaries'. We're all in the media business. I'm a little more idealistic than most of my friends. Most people really gave up on the whole deal, for reasons that I don't necessarily disagree with. There's a feeling that you really can't do anything. So why bother? And let's have another drink.

You're in the business of being a professional smart ass. It all just kinda rolls off the tongue. It seems casual and we can talk about heavy, tragic sorts of circumstances and everybody's kinda callused and numbed. You tune in the box, and there's gonna be a hundred dead in Somalia or some bureaucratic nonsense that has made some poor family homeless. You get real numbed to the whole thing, you really do. And the lifestyles represented on television make people discontent with their own lives, without any ability to do anything about it. You're talked to by all these ultimate experts, and in between you get barraged with all these commercial messages. The net communication is that your life will be better if you buy this object, whether it's some sort of placebo drug or a little jolt of sugar or a little dose of alcohol or a trip to Florida. It's served up to you on three channels every night.

Passion? (Pauses.) I'm taken aback by it a little bit. I love life, I try to get the most out of it every day. But if you're talking about this crazed sparkle in the eye, messianic sort of feeling, I think that sort of stuff's kinda dangerous. I don't trust it. If I see my eyes start to sparkle too much, I'll put on dark glasses.

This whole cowboy-capitalism jaunt that the country's been on for two hundred years is comin' to an end. The transition's gonna be kinda messy, it always is. But once you come out on the other end, people are gonna see that—Wow! I can't do everything. I can't be king. I can't be president. If I keep my wits about me, I can do a pretty good job tending the garden.

JODEAN CULBERT

An actress in Chicago. She is thirty-one.
"I grew up in a very democratic, Wobbly-type of house. The American Dream was very anti-Joe McCarthy. My father was a professor at the University of Illinois, very political. He was the ultimate dove."

I was in Vietnam from '68 into '72, with USO show tours. So Vietnam means something very different to me than it does to most people. I could tell an incoming shell from an outgoing shell, and you knew when to run for the bunker. I remember grabbing props and getting in a helicopter. It so happened it was a body-bag helicopter. That's a very different thing than sitting home and watching it on your television.

When I was in Okinawa, we used to watch the B-52's take off. I shall never forget a Christmas, watching them take off at four o'clock in the evening, with their wings touching the ground, loaded with bombs, and come back about eight o'clock in the evening, the wings flying real high. It was the strangest experience to be right there in the middle of it. It was something almost like a documentary movie they were watching on television. It was very real for me.

I was involved with the whole revolution of the sixties. I believed we could change the world. It's like Joni Mitchell said: "We're stardust, we're golden!" We really believed it. We went into college and were all special. I know everybody's special. We were *special*. You know? We came from parents who had given us everything.

I think there's a backlash to the fifties with people who are coming into their own, let's say twenty-two to twenty-five. There's a generation gap. My parents and I are much closer than people who are twenty-five. The generation gap is about five or six years. Sometimes they really blow me away. They really amaze me.

I went to a gathering the other night. Nobody extended themselves too far. Nobody said anything that was terribly controversial. Everybody talked a lot, but nobody got into big fights. They talked about their jobs, their apartments, who was making a killing where, who was doing better than somebody else, who was gonna make more money, who got a raise (laughs), who got a bigger by-line. I got real bored.

I can't figure out those other people. They're so competent. They're just on top of it. They don't make mistakes in conversations. They're cool, they've got it together. They get much further much faster in their jobs, okay? If somebody's fighting, they find a way to circumvent it. Once I lost a job because I wouldn't give in. They wouldn't think of doing a thing like that because it was foolish, see? You don't make foolish moves. What do you have to gain by making a foolish move? Obviously, they saw us fail, there was nothing to gain.

I don't see any fire. There is just no electricity going! I don't see anyone waving their arms, getting mad, slamming a door or smoking too many cigarettes because they're mad. Or—"Wait a minute, you're gonna listen to me."

I become awkward, defensive. They make me feel foolish. With all my passion and over-ness, wanting to break down and cry, they're going: "Why are you getting so upset?" I go: "Because it's *worth* getting upset." "What's worth getting upset?" "Well, that's the way I am." I can't imagine a life where you don't get upset about . . . Why can't people return the bottles and their cans? I never buy nonreturnable bottles, it's an issue with me. I'm fanatical about it. They laugh at me, and what happens is I shut up. Because I'm a fool.

Daddy was saying: "How did we get to this point? How did we get through the McCarthy era and end up with Nixon publishing his memoirs and—what's he charging? $19.95?" He says: "Sometimes I just wanna quit. It just doesn't mean anything to me any more." He says: "I feel like I've been played for a fool." He fought in World War Two, he believed in this country. He doesn't feel so American with a capital A any more. There's some kind of spunk gone out of him. He's gotten very inner. He fires up and then just shakes his head. He says: "Who's the last politician you heard who really laid himself on the line?" He says: "It's all bullshit." And my father is not a man who swears.

I quit reading the newspapers. Now I've quit watching the news. 'Cause it was so blasé! I would sit there and jump up and down in front of the television set.

Now I'm coming out from under cover. The kids of the sixties have been hiding out, in Colorado, back to the land. I think now they're gonna start coming out of the woodwork. They're getting into their thirties and they're gonna start feeling they were on the right track. Their revolution died. They beat themselves wearing hair shirts, and they became cynical and all those things you do in retreat when you've been wounded. All of a sudden, you go: *"They're* nuts, I'm not nuts. Wait a minute, I was right." Maybe you went about it wrong, but doggone it, the principles were right. Isn't it strange, but ten years later, I still believe them?

I think they'll start talking again, if nothing more than to each other. We're at this point, and I'm not gonna be cool. I'm not gonna shut up, I'm not gonna let you go away and make yourself a drink in the kitchen and be cool.

Or else I suddenly hear myself, my voice being too loud in a room. I still yell too loud. Maybe it's because we all had to yell to be heard over the loudspeakers at those rallies. (Laughs.) They learned how to behave. I mean, who wants to have their picture on television as a has-been Yippie? Who wants to be on the news, yelling and screaming with your hair hanging down in your face? That's not cool.

I don't want to change! I don't want to cool out. I don't care how foolish I sound. I don't want to be like them. I don't want to be just competent. I don't think that's any way to live. I think that's a hell of a way to live and a crummy way to die.

Who wants to die cool? Nobody cool ever changed the world. Nobody cool ever wrote great literature. They're all talking about writing the Great American Novel. How can you write the Great American Novel if you're too cool to get involved with the world?

Maybe there isn't anything to believe in any more. Is that it? I'm not a red-white-and-bluer, but maybe there just isn't anything left. Maybe we're just gonna all eventually get credit cards. And Visa will own all of us and Bank Americard and American Express will own us all and we'll have our little plastic cards and the government will be one big conglomerate. We'll all have our jobs, and as long as you've got your new chrome furniture, your latest album, and your stereo equipment, what else do you need? I think that's real sick, don't you? America's gonna turn into one big fat bore, one big fat nothing. I want America to wake up and get in the running.

My father doesn't talk about politics very much any more. Oh, Lord, before he used to sit on the back porch and talk to our cat about politics if he couldn't get anybody else's attention. (Laughs.) Now he just looks at me and shakes his head and says: "I don't know what's happening, Jo." There's no excitement in it for him any more. He was involved with kids all the time. He says: "They come in, they go to class, there's just nothing." He can't figure out what they're thinking about.

Talk to me about it, don't run away. Ecology-wise, what's wrong? Don't you want to pass a bill? Can't you return your bottles? I don't care if people suddenly stop inviting me to their cocktail parties. I'm beginning to feel they don't have it all in the bag. I feel like I've lost my dream and am getting it back. I feel like I'm at my coming-out party.

TOM BURNS

◇―――――――――――――――――――――――――――――――――◇

Blond, blue-eyed, cool, slim. He rarely smiles, nor does he frown. His occasional laugh comes as a surprise. He's thirty-two.

"I believe in the ideal: excellence of the human being, mind and body. I hope to achieve some happiness or delight or whatever. The United States has got the best platform to achieve that with the input of people and their ideas from all over the world. Everybody's still coming to the United States and looking for the American Dream."

I live in a rooming house, a single room, with old Poles and Mexicans, Puerto Ricans. Everybody in the building knows each other. My landlord is Sicilian. I have a working relationship with him, personal enough to fight and embrace and stuff like that. I've been here so long, I'm part of the family. I'm sort of an unofficial social worker.

I got involved with a Chicano girl. Her father owns a barbershop in the neighborhood, and she sort of led me here. It became the best place for me to live, the best environment for my purpose, at the cheapest cost. I'm a Vietnam veteran, and there are a lot of veterans here. We have a lot of understandings in common.

My father was a drill instructor during World War Two. He settled in Peoria, that's where I was born. I was the only child. He was in management in Hiram Walker's, sort of lower echelon. I mean, he was an inspector. He's retired and just a few days ago, they moved to Fort Lauderdale. That was their dream, and they did it. (Laughs.)

My parents are upset, but they don't feel as bad as they used to. They thought I was the devil or dead. I was their dead son. They've been kinda sheltered and don't know much what I do. We can't communicate, it's too emotional. So I don't see them very often. I never felt close to my parents, so I'm really lonesome. I might go to Florida to see them over the holidays. They sent me two hundred bucks to do it. (Laughs.)

My father wanted me to be a doctor. I don't know what my mother wanted. It's the highest-paying profession and the most prestige and all that. I had friends in high school whose fathers were doctors. They went on to college to become doctors. So I did too. I didn't flunk out of school, but I lost interest. Vietnam. I became interested. Not as a radical. I was very depressed. So I left school and went into the army. Airborne.

I remember going to Riverview* when I was a sophomore in high school, that parachute ride. Nothing like that before—or since. I saw this advertisement for the army: jumping out of an airplane with a parachute. The combination of Vietnam and Riverview . . .

I wanted to be a correspondent. I figured that was the best way to understand Vietnam. The talent scouts came to jump school. I signed a paper and I didn't get what I wanted. I became a doctor in the army. (Laughs.) I was a Green Beret, yeah, a medic.

I wanted to carry a camera instead of a gun. When I got there, I got the gun. I got scared. I got worried about my skin. I was scared the whole time I was there. It was the best experience of my life. That's one of the reasons I'm on skid row now. I haven't found anything to satisfy me as an occupation. That's the story of a lot of guys who live there. They're DPs, foreign and domestic.

An old Polish guy lives here. He was captured at the beginning of World War Two and spent the whole war in prison. They're always harping about the communists. My thing is health, right? What're you gonna do if the Russian tank comes down the street? Are you gonna be like the Hungarian kids who were killing Russian tanks in Budapest? Where did the guts come from? These people are sitting in bars and going down, down, down. What could they do if there was a crisis? Maybe American tanks will come down. (Laughs.)

(Sighs.) It's just easier to live there than anywhere else for me. I can get along with other people or even the room I live in. I got my window right by my bed. I can open it up, I can keep it cold. It's not a sealed-in apartment. No locks on my doors. There you can live the way you want. If I don't want to wash my clothes, I don't have to. If I don't want to keep my room clean, I don't have to. If I want to, it's because of myself, not for anybody else. I like to be left alone.

I don't have an alcoholic or drug problem or things like that. I don't want to have it. I want to have a family and achieve my goals. I want to go ahead and do the best I can. Be excellent. Like the old Greeks say: The source of happiness or delight comes from . . . (he trails off.) Excellence is that little thing that's gonna allow me to feel

* A celebrated amusement park in Chicago. It has since been dismantled and is now a parking lot.

comfortable everyday and have the family and children. That's a big goal. A lot of things I do are just preparing for that.

Some days are better than others. Once in a while, I have one of those excellent days. I just feel real good. It's because I've achieved. I've gotten closer to my potential.

This morning I shoveled some snow. I got a few bucks. I prefer to work outside, with my hands, physical. I just do whatever I can, whatever I can get. I didn't have anything planned for today. I knew this person would probably want their walk shoveled, so I made a phone call. I just came by, and they left their apartment open. I'm pretty trustworthy. I've worked for this person since last summer. She just bought a house, and I've been helping her. She's come in handy for me. I've got a lot of money in the bank now. (Laughs.)

I do odd jobs. I'm not a craftsman. But I'm getting familiar with everything as much as I can. I worked in factories, day labor, off and on. Today, I'm officially working for the same lady. She wants to teach me how to stretch canvas. She's an artist. She's kind of behind on her contracts for art. Monday I'm working for another lady, trying to seal up, insulate her house a little bit. I've done a lot of house painting. That's for me kind of the first step in handiwork. I'm not as good as a professional, but I'm cheap and I'm dependable.

I've already had my home in the suburbs. I came from a nice neighborhood. I had a car from the time I was sixteen. That's another reason I left school. I started reading Dostoevski and Dr. Zhivago, and I started thinking. I'm not happy. Where does your happiness lie? Where do you find it? I feel like I can't rest.

"Ghetto" was just a word to me until I saw it. I worked on the South Side for a doctor. Officially, I was a chauffeur, but I was wearing a white coat and taking blood pressure and sort of doing a consultant thing. I used to walk all through the ghetto by myself all the time, all hours. I'm getting a little bit older, so I do that a little bit less. I don't want to get killed by my curiosity.

I had a number of confrontations. It's something like a skill. Coming out smelling sweet. A lotta times it doesn't start with some guy jumping on ya. They feel you out for what you have to offer or what you have in yourself that they can overcome. It's a power play. It can start with: "Hey, you got a match?" "You got a quarter?" and more and more. I've been robbed a couple of times, but I've never been physically assaulted.

I do the same thing with them. I size them up for the same thing:

power. What's the guy got and what are my chances and how should I
...? I'm in my back alley and I'm wearing a bracelet. I used to wear
bracelets and necklaces and earrings. The guy says: "I want that
bracelet." At the time, I was feeling real confident. I say: "You want
it because I got it. You don't really want it." I wait for him to make
his move. It's like war. You don't want anybody to walk over you. You
present yourself in a way so that they will hesitate, and be prepared to
accept the consequences. Be prepared to die if you want to go to
extremes.

You wouldn't be prepared to die for that bracelet?

I don't know. It's not the bracelet, it's the symbol. That's never happened to me. What're you gonna do in combat? You never know until
it happens.

Would you actually die for a symbol?

It all depends on the situation. In the army, I was a hippie. Outside, I
was a warmonger. When I was at Fort Bragg, about every other weekend I'd go to D.C. I'd go to parties and, of course, they were involved
with antiwar activities, and I would get people coming up and getting
kind of hostile.

I didn't defend the war. I was neither way. That's one of the reasons I went. I wanted to see for myself. That's another reason I'm on
this street. I got into ghettos or factories in Chicago. Every time I hear
a complaint, I know everybody's opinion is biased. I gotta get my own
bias, I don't want somebody else's. I'm a see-for-myself type. That's
why I am where I am today.

I've been out on the road in the middle of snowstorms and hitch-
hiking, the whole bit. Mexico, Canada, Alaska, whatever. With nothing, it seemed to be when I got the most. You become an animal,
become really alive when it really becomes critical. When you're in
trouble, that seems when you're most alive. Even with the war thing,
with these veterans that can't find satisfaction in life.

Adventure, yeah. I might as well do something with my unhappiness. I'm not into suicide, I didn't want to do that. But maybe one
step less. Going to Vietnam, right?

Somebody told me I'm a very accepting person. I accept anybody
no matter who they are or what they should be. It's accepting myself,

that's the problem. I had more excellence before. I'm trying to work myself up again. Junk food has been part of my downfall. I believe in health food. I'm educating myself to neo-health.

I shut off a lot of people more than I did before. I say: "I gotta take care of myself." Now I want money. I'm out for myself now. I gave everything away. Now I want a bank account. I want to get married. I want all that stuff. I've been out of money a lotta times, but the last time really kinda scared me.

My landlord says: "Come on out, let's go to other building and work. Spend some time with me. I'll pay you for the work you did." I'd rather stay here. Pay me what you want. I don't expect anything out there. He's like my godfather. He says he's gonna pay me, but that's words. You know how things work in Chicago. (Laughs.) I was getting a little depressed.

Some people are open, some people are not. I got tired of guessing and wondering if this guy's gonna drink or this guy's gonna approach me for sexual favors. A lot of people come up one way and end up another. I found everything. (Laughs.)

One of the reasons I don't have a job or family is that I'm open to the point of obnoxiousness. It's hard for me to lie. They think I'm too idealistic. I want to be number one over me but not over anybody else. When everybody's number one, we'll all be number one together. See? Rather than who wins. I play basketball, but I lose track over the score. I'm competing with myself. I try to enjoy being good and not worry about being bad.

I've been to see psychiatrists, psychologists, and all that. This one guy said I was crazy but not crazy enough to get state aid. (Laughs.) I think everybody's crazy. (Laughs.)

WILLIAM GOTHARD

◈————————————————————————————————————◈

A casual encounter during a Los Angeles–Chicago flight; an ensuing conversation at O'Hare International Airport while he's between planes.

"I'm a twenty-seven-year-old white American male. I'm a corporate attorney. Spent most of my life in New York, went to high school in Ohio, college in California, and practice in Los Angeles. And I'm overweight." (Laughs.)

I'm a member of the nomadic middle class. My family moved seven times since I was born. Longest I've been in one place was eight years. My father is of the new managerial class, unaffiliated. He never worked for a company. He was a school administrator, an animal unto himself. You go from place to place, like a minister. To a bigger congregation or a bigger school district. I come from a family of Methodist ministers. (Laughs.) Middle-class suburban Methodist rather than the Bible-thumping, Gospel-singing Methodists.

We have no roots. Our heritage is either German, Dutch, or English. The furthest I can trace back is my great-grandfather. I don't know if he was born here. He ministered to the Oneida Indians. We still have an Indian bible. He died around 1907. That's all I know about my heritage.

We would never sit down at the dinner table and talk about what it means to be an American. When I was a child, my parents would take me around America. We would go to Gettysburg. I was a big Civil War buff. I visited forty-six states. I like to live the American experience. It's not one experience, it's many. There's so much here. Very few people have found the American Dream. When you stop searching, you no longer have it.

I admire my father. The reason he ceased being an administrator and became a professor is, it wasn't a joy any more. He was tired of politics, he was tired of the changing attitude among teachers.

He was a school administrator in Levittown, the great American Dream town at the end of the war. On the GI Bill, you could buy a home you could not afford before. Young people could settle down. It was like your Model T's. You could have it in any color, just as long as it's black. It was the beginning of assembly-line homes.

We lived in Garden City, the upper-crusty part. The quality of education there was super. When I was in fifth grade, I was first clarinet in the school band. That was hot tuna in those days. (Laughs.)

Talk about Middle America. My father was an Eagle Scout who went to the National Jamboree in '39. He's in Kiwanis and president of Rotary. My brother was an Eagle Scout with a Bronze Palm and five merit badges past Eagle. When I was young, I was very overweight and struggled on these hikes. I *had* to make Eagle, it was an inner thing. I did, got twenty merit badges past Eagle, was president of the Key Club, and an acolyte in the church. It was no mean trick for me. I lost thirty pounds running around the block. (Laughs.) I felt it was important to my family, that's why I did it. My mother was president of faculty wives.

I've been blessed with a wonderful set of parents. We were never wealthy, but I was sent to some very good schools. When my father was making thirty thousand dollars a year, I was at Stanford and Columbia. I appreciate how much they had to sacrifice for me.

One of my big gripes is the crisis of the middle class today. If you're poor or minority, you get preferential treatment, financial aid to go to school. If you're rich, Iacocca's kid, it doesn't matter. But for the professional middle class, paying for a good education is just out of sight.

I really love America, though—I hate to say it—I have a foreign car. (Laughs.) They're built better. There's pride in craftsmanship. I'd like less dependence upon government to solve our problems. What I want is the same spirit that made this country what it is.

I think we have the best political system, bar none. I see problems. I have never felt discrimination because I am white, middle-class, and male. Now it's the other way around. We're at the bottom of the list.

America became strong because people, out of their own initiative, have succeeded. Sons and daughters of fishmongers and tailors became lawyers, doctors, and corporate presidents. They drove themselves. We live in a socially mobile society where you can succeed if you have the drive. I realize if you were born in Watts or Harlem, the cards are stacked against you. You got a long way to go. Yet Jews have prospered in this country. They have a tradition of education, of upward mobility. The Irish and the Italians have made it too. With Hispanics and blacks, it's harder to melt in as easily. But in certain of these ethnic groups, you don't have this initiative. The primary thing is survival.

I believe if anyone is blessed with enough drive, enough parental guidance, he could become president of the United States. A little far-fetched, perhaps. (Laughs.) He could become a lawyer. (Laughs.)

Los Angeles, where I work, typifies in one city the best and the worst of American life. The home of franchise foods, home of the automobile society, home of Hollywood, your fantasia, your ultimate American Dream. Without roots.

I want to get married, have two kids, two cars, two color TV sets, and live in the suburbs outside Los Angeles. But I want to maintain my individuality. At the firm, I hate to be called just by my last name, Gothard, or just by my proper first name, William. I like Bill. As a professional person, in front of a client, I'd want my secretary to call me Mr. Gothard.

I'm very optimistic about this country. I've never lived through the depression. That might have sobered my outlook. I've never had a silver spoon in my mouth, but I've never known hunger. If I had, I might be less optimistic. I'm like Merrill Lynch. I'm bullish on America. (Laughs.)

SAM LOVEJOY

◇————————————————————————————————◇

He exudes good cheer. His optimism appears incurable. The documentary film Sam's Nuclear War *was based on his activity in Massachusetts.*

He is thirty-three.

I was born in '46. When I was five weeks old, we landed in Japan, 'cause my father was in the occupation forces. The American military was so paranoid that all the high-ranking officers stayed out on the U.S.S. *Missouri* in Tokyo Bay for like a year, year and a half. My family was an experimental one, shipped to Japan, wife and kids, and put on the mainland to find out whether they'd eat us or something. When they found out that the Japanese were people, the officers got on the mainland. We were one of those trial families. We lived in a huge mansion. I just can't believe that we had only fifteen servants. (Laughs.) My father was a lowly captain in the army. He was killed during the Korean War. I was six. We moved back to Massachusetts, where I grew up.

I went to school in Wilbraham, a small town of five thousand people. Everybody knew everybody. Thanksgiving to me was always a wild idea. July Fourth was a great thing. I remember sort of learning about the dream. The colonies and the nitty-gritty.

My father, who grew up here, had made friends with an old farmer. He was Mr. Americana and was very much interested in town meetings. He was conservative in a lot of ways and taught me that Republicans have the courage of their convictions and liberals talk a lot and don't stand for anything. They'll swing with the wind.

There was just this old man and this young boy out in the orchards. He would tell me story after story, and I was just swept away by a sort of participatory democracy. Mrs. Murray fighting Mr. Porter about the dog-leash law. It really intrigued me to watch these two neighbors who were friends yell at each other about things they took very seriously.

I think what had the most sway with me was a good education in a small New England town with a lot of good neighbors and a lot of hard work. I've always respected work. By the time I was nine, I was driving tractors. When I was thirteen, I drove trucks on the highway. I've just always read anything sitting around: books, newspapers, magazines. It was the fifties. Everybody thought the world was ours. Everything was beautiful.

I went to prep school as a day kid, I didn't board there. Very, very rich kids, very smart. It was a comeuppance to find out how disgusting these rich people could be. There I was, working very hard, and here were these young kids wearing shoes that cost five hundred dollars a pair. It would have paid a year's tuition for me.

I have a feeling a person should get what they earn. There's a difference between working hard and making a lot of money, and inheriting it. Money really screws people up. Every rich person I met has been maladapted. (Laughs.)

I graduated valedictorian and all that junk. I became one of these Sputnik quiz kids. There I was in fifth grade, and the Russians beat us. They got to space before we did. So Congress passed a bill that gave hundreds of millions of dollars to schools to make us into scientists. They just slammed math and physics and chemistry and science and all that stuff into us. By the time I was in prep school, I had taken every advanced course in the books. I ended up in Amherst.

At the time, the Vietnam War was going on full tilt, 1966. I started reading up on it. A friend had been drafted, and I had gotten letters from him, saying: "God, this is weird." I convinced myself the war was crazy and got involved with teach-ins.

There was a watershed experience for me. I was sitting in a multivariable quantum mechanics calculus course. The math teacher was a classic cartoon character. He was short, he had thick glasses. He was a brilliant mathematician and social maladapt. Whenever these guys say anything, you have to write it down, every dot, every symbol. I'm sitting there, scribbling it down, and all of a sudden this thing dawns on me. What the hell are you doing here? What the hell does what you're learning here have to do with the real-live bad world out there? I stopped taking notes and walked out of class as soon as the bell rung.

I'm living on a commune in Montague, Massachusetts, sharing my life, my resources, my property, my energy, my thoughts, with a group of people. It's an organic farm. We can live comfortably. Twelve adults and two children on ten thousand dollars a year. We have gardens, cows, pigs. We sell hay, milk, and maple syrup.

Everything was together here, but around the summer of 1973, I was getting nervous. Just about the time I was starting to wonder where to put my energy next, there came an announcement of the Montague Nuclear Power Plant. Initially, I was against it because of an environmental concern. I was worried about the impact of a multibillion-dollar project on the beauty of this little rural town.

I wasn't opposed to nuclear power. I believed all that junk I learned when I was a physicist. You saw nuclear power as salvation. I was just like all those scientists today who have no social consciousness, who believe everything can be solved by technology. Science to them has become a theology. They keep using that word, "faith."

I read everything I could get my hands on. I re-read my physics books. I spent days in libraries. People around the farm were surprised at me for being so dedicated. I convinced myself more and more that it was a horrendous idea. Legally, there was no way I could stop that plant.

No power plant's ever been stopped before by the Atomic Energy Commission. Eisenhower, Kennedy, Johnson, Nixon, and Ford were all totally pro-nuclear. Carter certainly is. You had the utilities coming into town. They compared nuclear components to Indians trying to stop the railroad.

Our town meeting has full say in land-use matters, and the utilities were saying: "Screw you, we're gonna roll over you." Where were all those things I'd been taught in the past? Meanwhile, the corporations have a multimillion-dollar PR budget, and how am I gonna raise five thousand dollars to educate Montague?

They had built this symbol of the nuclear plant in town, at the proposed site. A 500-foot-tall skinny tower. It had a lotta red lights and white blinking lights. The first time I saw the tower, I said: "Oh, oh, someone's gonna knock that thing down." The more I looked at the tower, the more it was the symbol of everything. I decided I would knock it down.

There was a rule that the utilities needed one full year of environmental data before they could get a license. They had built the tower in June of '73. I figured if I knocked it down before June of '74, I'd disrupt the data collection and delay the plant for a year.

I tried to get a movement going in town. It was unsuccessful. There was a feeling that you can't fight a large corporation. A lot of people were turned off because the utilities were bribing the town, offering a ninety-nine percent cut in property taxes. The town officials were extraordinarily pro-nuclear. They had been bought off by this tax plum. They thought I was crazy.

It was George Washington's birthday, 1974. I cannot tell a lie, I did knock down the cherry tree. It did have a lot of red lights. (Laughs.) I went out to the site at two o'clock in the morning, and I knocked down the tower. I undid the turnbuckles, the guy wires that held the tower up, and it came crashing down. It was a simple process, took a couple of hours.

I went down the street to the police station and turned myself in, handed them a four-page statement, and took full responsibility. I'd read up on the law. I used some quotes from the criminal statutes in my statement, which surprised the judge seven months later. I turned myself in and was charged with a five-year felony for malicious destruction of property.

It was the first time the media covered any position other than the pro-nuclear one. The front pages of every newspaper in western Massachusetts had. TOWER TOPPLED, NUCLEAR PROTEST. The shock value was important. People suddenly realized that there was someone out there.

I didn't decide on civil disobedience until a month before. I did some political reading and got into Thoreau. Initially, I thought I'd knock the tower down and send some sort of letter to the media. Then I decided to bring a civil disobedience action to the environmental movement. These were liberal, straight people, not really understanding the need for action other than lobbying Congress. They've always suffered from this white middle-class hocus-pocus.

So I decided turning myself in would neutralize the paranoia about attack on property. It would be interpreted as violent if I didn't turn myself in. And it would give me a second arena. The first was knocking down the tower, the second was going to court.

I was my own lawyer. I put Howard Zinn and Dr. John Goffman on the stand.* Dr. Goffman testified that nuclear power was a human killer. I was acquitted after a nine-day trial under orders from the

---

* Howard Zinn is professor of political science at Boston University. Dr. John Goffman was associate director of the Livermore Radiation Laboratory at Berkeley, a scientist at the Manhattan Project, a founder of the Atomic Energy Commission. In 1968, he warned of low-level radiation as harmful to humans.

judge to the jury. I think the trial convinced the judge to be no-nukes. They polled the jury, and eleven of the twelve said they believed I was not guilty even before the end of the trial.

They were old people, young people, middle-aged people, men and women. It was a perfect cross section of the county. None of 'em had ever heard the facts of nuclear power. I was on the stand for two days, and I answered every question, even the most obnoxious, from the prosecutor. I told 'em everything. I had to show 'em my life-and-thought processes. The potential for education was extraordinary. Nuclear power was being challenged on the front page of the newspapers for two full weeks.

The day the trial ended, the utilities announced a 4½-year delay in the schedule of the Montague plant. Instead of going to prison, I ended up becoming a movement person all over again. (Laughs.) I started traveling all over the country.

I am an optimist. I couldn't be a political organizer if I were a pessimist. I truly believe that human beings have common sense. If someone is told the facts, common sense will prevail. Anybody that sells me an elitist line—"Leave it to me"—I'm not asking anybody to trust me, to believe me. I am asking them to question themselves.

We are told that some issues are too complex for ordinary people, that experts . . .

Bullshit. It's the best argument to delude the people. It's the same thing we heard about the Vietnam War. If we're gonna have democracy in this country, by God, we're gonna have to start telling people the facts. Einstein said it thirty years ago: We must take the facts of nuclear power to the village square, and from the village square must come America's voice. I grew up in a village square, so to speak.

Experts always talk in technical terms, and people have not been able to understand, so they have turned off. It's very simple: Do we need the stuff? How much does it cost? Does the procedure work? Are there any impacts? All a nuclear plant is is a system to boil water to spin a turbine.

The first group to oppose a nuclear plant at Seabrook were the clam diggers. That's how we got our name. Clamshell Alliance. What a great name, getting away from all those politically yicky acronyms. It was catchy, it was fun to hear, it had an environmental vibe.

We made a commitment to nonviolent civil disobedience to stop the plant, to occupy the site. Eighteen were arrested. The majority of the Seabrook people were against the plant. One of the main anti-nuclear voices was the wife of the police chief.

We called a second demonstration. The Seabrook police refused to make any arrests. The state police were called and arrested a hundred eighty people. They thought we were gonna be a bunch of crazies. They found old, young, middle-aged, responsible, disciplined, re-spectful people. They used five busses to carry us away. The bus drivers were state police themselves. The chief ordered them to drive a mile away from the site so the demonstrators wouldn't see them. Two of the five bus drivers disobeyed. They drove up to the rally, parked the busses, and allowed everybody to cheer and wave and express their love. Then they drove away.

The state police locked 'em up for a night in the armory, all in one big room. There was a lot of dialogue between the demonstrators and the police.

On April 30, we brought over two thousand people to the site. The governor distrusted his state police and mobilized the National Guard. Over fourteen hundred people were arrested and locked up in five armories for two weeks. It created more publicity than the Clamshell Alliance had ever anticipated. The arrestees conducted workshops. The National Guard guys were standing around, listening and participating. They're just funky people from local towns, just like you and me. They got called off local jobs and didn't see what the hell they were doing here, guarding a bunch of very nice people.

Know what happened at the end of the two weeks? The people in the armories kicked in money for a kitty to buy kegs of beer for the National Guard troops.

There were well over two hundred people over the age of sixty. Older people tend to have that free time and that ability to reflect more than people busy and hung-up on occupations and the rest of it. There were surprises too. One old woman said: "You should do to the public-service company what we did to the niggers in South Bos-ton." (Laughs.) Know what happened? She's grown to see there is no real difference between her racism and her prejudice against antiwar demonstrators, and what the corporations are doing to us. She's edu-cated herself.

The media is selling us on the notion of apathy and paralysis in the country. Bullshit. The movement did not die. It did the most intelli-gent thing it could do: it went to find a home. It went into the com-munity. It's working, unnoticed, in the neighborhood. They're starting to blossom and make alliances, connections. I've been all over the country, and I have not been into one community where I did not meet people exactly like me.

If there's ever gonna be change in America, it's gonna be because every community in America's ready for it and—boom! There's gonna be a big tidal wave, and it's just gonna crash down on Washington, D. C., and the people are finally gonna be heard.

---◇ ◇---

EPILOGUE

---◇---◇---

THE WOODS

BOB ZIAK

---◇---◇---

We're in logging country: Knappa, Oregon. It is near the mouth of the Columbia River.

He's a chunky, muscular man, built along the lines of Hack Wilson, the old Cubs slugger. He is sixty-two.

Enthusiastically, he talks of "the vast coniferous forest. You're always aware of the scent of trees if you're a logger. It turns you on. You know you've struck a cedar that may have been buried in the ground for a couple of hundred years."

The beauty is going. The old timber that was majestic has been eliminated. In the old days, the Douglas fir was mixed through with Sitka spruce, western hemlock, and the great cedars. All through the woods, you found a beautiful mix of trees. Today, trees are planted in predetermined spaces, predetermined distances apart. It is something to be controlled.

The forest to me is an awesome and beautiful place. You see this little baby elk that we have in the woods here? Isn't it a little beautiful cuddly thing? But watch that elk grow, and eventually he becomes a magnificent bull, with a huge rack of antlers, a deep chest, and proud eyes. He's not cute and cuddly any more. He is awesome. This is the way it is with trees. You see cute little Christmas trees you'll put on the table. They're immature little things. They have not attained the magnificence that nature puts on these trees at five hundred years. They take on character. They're always in a battle. The wind's after them, the lightning's after them ...

The timber companies don't want a single tree standing any more. They don't understand that a tree, a snag, is not only a hotel for birds and bats and bees. They are magnificent works of art created by nature and beyond the ability of man to equal. I don't think they have any feeling for beauty, for something that is old. There's a tree down the road here a few miles that's over ten feet in diameter at the butt. At the very tiptop of it is a magnificent crown of jewels: a nest of bald-headed eagles. Timber companies are indifferent as to your feelings. The only feeling they want is the tons of pulp to come out of there.

Today, when they come to a canyon, they start switchbacking, criss-crossing back and forth with bulldozers, tearing up the ground, silting the creeks, and putting five acres of ground out of production per mile of road. Old-time loggers were not able to reach many of the rough places, so these patches and trees were left. The younger loggers were not here to see what there was before. It you've never known something, it's difficult to appreciate what has been lost.

I was born and lived here in a logging camp. My dad was a logger. He was a big, rawboned, powerful man of a very happy nature. (Softly) I can see him coming home now with his logging clothes on, a rifle in his hand, and a deer on his back. The first sounds I can remember are the voices of loggers and the sounds of locomotives and donkeys. As a kid, it seemed to me more plentiful of everything. The forests were still virgin. There were fish in the sloughs, lots of water-fowl, and it was a very happy time. No one can grow up here and not be aware of the birds and the animals and the river. It gets in your blood, in your thinking, in your way of life.

In the old days, when you approached a lumber camp, you began to feel the tempo, the intensity, the turmoil. It was something like a war zone. You could see loggers everywhere, going somewhere, coming back. There were always locomotives, moving, backing out, switching. You'd hear the sound of the pop-off valves of escaping steam. And the smells of crude oil. There was always excitement there.

They had the old highball days. You really traveled. One tough, old hook tender told a new man: "We don't walk around here. We don't run around here. We fly." There were frequent accidents—broken arms, broken hips, men just killed outright.

The camp was a little company town. They had some fellas that they called Wobblies, organizers. They tarred and feathered them up here at Big Creek and made them walk nude down the tracks. My mother remembers that. She was broken-hearted about what they did to those men.

Who's "they"?

The company men who were afraid of losing their jobs. They had no protection, so they took it out on the Wobblies. Old-timers used to talk about firings. They had three crews: one working, one coming from the labor pool, and one going. Work was tough. The methods weren't safe. They were running the men too hard, driving them, working them too long hours and too many days. If the company didn't like you for one reason or another, they fired you.

My dad was a union man. Today, all of us loggers belong to the union. My sister still has her union book at home. As a young girl, she was a waitress in the cookhouse. It was a large dining room. They rang the gong, and that was time to eat. The food was good, and they ate heartily. You hardly saw a fat logger in those days. They were all rawboned. It was very physical. The machinery has taken over so much of that today.

I can remember yet the fallers that were falling trees. The saw, not a power saw, made a beautiful swish, swish, swish, swish, a rhythm to it. These men had no shirts on, just down to their wool underwear. Each one with a big chew of tobacco in his mouth. One stopped and looked at his partner and said: "Get off and let me ride for a while." Meaning he was doing all the work. (Laugh.)

Each man excelled in his own part. Your value as a faller meant not only how much timber you could put down but how much you could save. Long before the tree ever came down, you would hear them holler: "Timmmberrr!" (He sings it, and his voice fades to a last dying note.) That call would go down the hill and all through the canyons.

The timber is getting so much smaller now. Logging can't be compared to what it was before. Something wild, something beautiful, something free, it's gone. I've been on the hills here and can see so far away, all this logged-off land. It is almost impossible for me to comprehend that mere men destroyed all this timber. Every foot of that ground has been stomped by men. What happened to all that timber? It's one of the few things in the world that boggles my imagination.

Sure, some of the animals are dangerous to you. They're after your life. They've crippled many guys and killed people. They're wild in another way now. They're wild from being pursued by people in four-wheel drives, campers. I don't kill any more. I was very young when I quit. When I'd kill something and watch it die and look at the eyes, I knew I'd taken what attracted me in the first place—a life. What did I have but a carcass? And I wasn't hungry.

I just quit killing because I took the beauty of the animal—the deer or elk or bear. If it was a duck, I'd want to smooth the feathers when it was dead and stiffened up, so that it wouldn't look obscene. The animals aren't wild any more, they're just pursued.

We've just gone through a cow elk season, to thin them out. The forestry department said there were too many, too much damage to young trees. They were killing these elk at a time when it was an absolute disgrace. The vegetation was completely frozen out. The cows, heavy with calves, would bunch up in the timber and lie there very still, conserving the body fat and heat to get through this starving period. Yet the hunters are out there pursuing them.

I have a little sanctuary down here, and I'd see big beautiful honkers coming in, Canadian geese. They're free. I don't pinion them. To pinion a bird is like cutting off the leg of a child to keep it from running around. It turns you off to see them drop, a leg spinning, dangling on a thick piece of skin, shot by hunters. Guys go out there and shoot too many. There's no time to pick 'em up. They're thrown away.

Before I die, I'd like to hear the howl of timber wolves that used to exist here in our woods. We have too damn many hunters and no wolves. We need more cougars, less hunters.

Bears are fair game too. When a bear damages a tree, what he actually does is set that tree to produce more seeds. I've taken ten-foot stumps and found in the very center bear marks that the tree may have received five hundred years ago, just as good as they are today. So bears aren't all that bad. We asked the timber company how many goddamn bears will you allow? I'm a believer that the animals and birds have some inherent right to the land. The man can't say: "I own this. Everything else, off."

We had a ruckus with a pack of houndsmen over the killing of bears. Killing 'em left and right. Hounds are worth thousands of dollars, and the houndsmen are really well organized with a powerful lobby. It was a fist fight. Fortunately, I'm able to take care of myself pretty well.

There was a pickup truck with a bunch of guys in it. As I was walking to my truck, one of the fellows motioned me over. We'd had bad blood many times before. He once knocked on my mother's door and told her: "If any of your sons touches one of my hounds, I'll kill every goddamn one of 'em." I saw him again when he was found guilty of killing bears out of season. Outside the courthouse, we almost came to blows. This time, as I drove up, he punched me right in the face, through the window. I piled out and was able to neutralize the fellow. I had him about one foot apart, my face from his. He spat a mouthful of snoose right in my face. Immediately, I changed the look of his mouth with a good smash in the face. He got back in the truck, and I've had no trouble with him since.

I've been threatened, telephone calls to be killed. It was so tense for a while that I had to carry a pistol. Many times I'm alone in the woods, running a big cat, miles back there. Houndsmen are on these roads. They're all equipped with knives, rifles. It would be the easiest thing in the world to put a bullet through my head over in some canyon.

Sometimes people are hesitant to make a move, even though they know it's right. I was walkin' up this road with a company man. Lo and behold, here were some beautiful big bear tracks. She's in here, an old sow, probably got some cubs. We can't let the houndsmen see her. They have a network: one guy tells another, and down they come with their hounds. This company man—he had about number ten size shoes—was goin' up the road, scuffin' out bear tracks. (Laughs.) He was protectin' the bears when his job said get rid of 'em. Innermost in many men are subconscious desires they don't allow to surface.

I only express my thoughts to people who understand what I'm talking about. Many don't care, don't feel, but there are surprising ones who will help. I got a letter from a man who works for a big lumber company. It says: "You stepped on my toes many times. I'm ready to retire now, and I want you to know I'm for you. I don't care to let you know who I am because they'll send me off to Siberia."

Many people's voices are stilled because of the position they're in. I happen to be a single man, and it'll be pretty hard to starve me. (Laughs.) So I can say what the hell I want. When my father died, I quit the woods and took an early retirement. I log my own place.

The chance to live my life out without being a rich man is probably the greatest gift that any person could ever receive. I have no feeling that I've ever been beaten or I'm a poor man. I'm rich in many things. I feel I have a responsibility while I'm on this earth to preserve some beauty and pass it on to the next generation. Because if I do not pass something on, these children and the children's children will have a barren world.

I believe that only by being in the presence of beauty and the great things in the world around us can man eventually get the goddamn hatred of wanting to kill each other out of his system. We begin to understand that we're only in this world such a short time it's incredible we should spend these few years hating and killing each other.

THE TRAIN

CLARENCE SPENCER

We're on a day coach of the train bound for Washington, D.C. August 25, 1963. It is on the eve of the march, led by Martin Luther King. The hour is late. Most of the passengers are asleep or trying to. He is wide awake. He is seventy.

It's something like a dream, children. I'm just proud to ride this train down there, whether I march or not. I'm so proud just to be *in* it. It means something I wanted ever since I've been big enough to think about things. That's my freedom, making me feel that I'm a man, like all the rest of the men. I've had this feeling ever since I was about ten years old.

I was born and raised in the state of Louisiana. I did all kinds of work. I followed saw mills. I followed the levee camps, railroads, sugar farms, picked cotton. And I all the time wondered *why* in the world is it that some human being thinks he's so much more than the other. I can't never *see* that. I just can't *see* it. I don't *understand* it. I speak to you, you hear me, you understands me. You work like I work, eats like I eats, sleeps like I sleeps. Yet and still, how come? Why is it that they have to take the back seat for everything? So this trip is something like a dream to me.

I would put it thisaway. If you was down and out and you was longing for a thing and somebody would come and punch you out in a way that you could find it, you would feel like a different man, wouldn't you? That's the way I'm feelin'. I feel like I'm headed into something, that I would live to see some of the beneficial out of it. Maybe a day or two days. But I would enjoy those two days or one day better than I have enjoyed the whole seventy years which I've lived. Just to see myself as a man. Never mind the blackness, because that doesn't mean anything. I'm still a man.

When this thing started out, I said to my wife: "This I wants to be *in*. I don't want to see it on the television or hear it on the radio. I want to be *in* it. I crave to get into that light." I sit at home one day, and I read a portion of the Scripture in the Bible. I think it's the third chapter of the Lamentations of Jeremiah. This writer went on to say: He have led me and brought me in the darkness and not to light. I would like to get out of that darkness and into the light. That's what I'm working for.

I have fought it from years past up until now, and I'm still meanin' to be in it. In 1918, when I was in the service, I thought I was playing my part in the war, dignifiably. If I can take that, looks to me now I can take it anywheres else. Wouldn't it be that way to you? So this train can't get me down to Washington fast enough for me. Even if I don't be in the parade, just to stand somewhere and see this great bunch of people who have rosed up and some of the white people who have come with us. Let us live together. We can do so.

A man doesn't have to hunt another'n if he doesn't want to. If you says a thing I doesn't like, I can tell you about it. If he treats me wrong, I'm gonna speak to him like he's a man, not like he's an animal. Let him know he had did me wrong. Not anything he says, I must say yes. Every time you speak, it doesn't have to be right because you're speaking. Maybe you say something that I can see even deeper than you can. And lots of times it's the other way.

I got that letter in 1925 from Ku Kluck Klan for no reason at all, not for what I did to this man. They used to have a little magazine out, they call it *True Story*. He bought one and the guy that wrote the magazine, he had a story about a little colored boy and a crocodile was runnin' him. He was runnin' down the road barefooted and like they used to put the colored people in pictures with the hair all standin' up on the head. Let's make a loblolly out of him, you recall it. This man said to me: "Spencer, you from Dixie? I see where the crocodile run behind the little colored boy in the South." I said: "How come a crocodile will run a colored and won't run a white? A dumb beast doesn't know the difference." Did you know that liked to cause a killin' scrape over nothin'? We got to arguin' and arguin' over that. He threatened to kill me and wrote me that Ku Kluck Klan letter, and he got a rope and hung it to a post and it hung down where they were gonna put it around my neck.

When you don't do a person nothing, just try to straighten them out in their silly own doings and then he wanta talk about hangin', that's pretty bad, isn't it? You got the feelin' and you just can't get over it. That thing will wear you for a long, long time to come.

That's why I'm on this train. This train don't carry no liars, this train. That's a good old song.

This train is bound for glory . . .

. . . this train. That's right. We know it. Our people can compose those old songs. Like in the South, we had old blues songs. Things got tough, you couldn't hardly find a job, like back in the thirties. "I'm gonna leave here walkin', baby, that I may get a ride." Get a ride, someway, somehow. That's the way we are fightin' in this. Someway, some means, somehow, we're gonna win it. We haven't got anything to fight with but what's right. This government have been run a long time with justice for *some* people, *not* all the people.

The thing that hurts so bad, we have built this country. My daddy was a slave, my daddy was. We have worked. We have built the railroads. We have built good roads. We have cut the ditches, we have cleaned up the ground. They tell me we've worked three hundred sixty-five years for nothin', and we have worked hundred two, hundred three years for a damned little bit of anything. You know a fella should be tired now, don't you? He should be really tired and wore out with it. But I'm proud to be in this. I'm kind of overjoyed.